THE ASSASSINATION CHRONICLES

Also by Edward Jay Epstein

THE
ASSASSINATION
CHRONICLES

Inquest, Counterplot, and Legend

Edward Jay Epstein

Carroll & Graf Publishers, Inc.
New York

Text of *Inquest* copyright © 1966 by Edward Jay Epstein
Text of *Counterplot* copyright © 1968, 1969 by Edward Jay Epstein
Text of *Legend* copyright © 1978 by Edward Jay Epstein
Additional material copyright © 1992 by Edward Jay Epstein

This edition of *The Assassination Chronicles* is published by arrangement with
the author.

First Carroll & Graf edition of *The Assassination Chronicles* 1992.

Carroll & Graf Publishers, Inc.
260 Fifth Avenue
New York, NY 10001   # 2675 1242

Library of Congress Cataloging-in-Publication Data is available.

ISBN 0-88184-909-X

Manufactured in the United States of America

To my mother

Contents

Acknowledgments

I am deeply indebted to Andrew Hacker, who supervised my master's thesis at Cornell, and James Q. Wilson and Edward Banfield, who supervised my doctoral dissertation at Harvard. I am also grateful to Professors Alan Altshuler, Lois Hacker, and Allen Bloom for helping me better understand the requisites of academic research.

These books benefited enormously from the editorial help I received from Aaron Asher, Clay Felker, Richard Rovere, Toni Mergantime, William Shawn, Steven Frimmer, Fulton Oursler, Jr., and Bob Asahina.

I am deeply appreciative for the research done for me by Pamela Butler, Lys Chuck, Henry Hurt, Rhoda Leichter, Nancy Lanoue, Ko Shioya, and Cynthia Worswick.

I owe special thanks to Tom Guinzberg for publishing *Inquest* at a time when criticism of the Warren Commission Report was not in fashion; to Edward T. Thompson for affording me free rein to research and write *Legend;* to Jones Harris for his help in the Garrison investigation; and to Kent Carroll, Mark Danner, Mike Endicot, Leon Freidman, Norman Mailer, and Victor Navasky for their suggestions for this revised edition.

Preface
The Assassination Labyrinth (1992)

I entered the assassination labyrinth some twenty-seven years ago, when I wrote a brief letter to seven of the most powerful men in America: Chief Justice Earl Warren; former Central Intelligence director Allen W. Dulles; John J. McCloy, chairman of Chase Manhattan Bank; Richard B. Russell, chairman of the Senate Armed Services Committee; Senator John Sherman Cooper, former Ambassador to India; Hale Boggs, Democratic whip in the House of Representatives; and Gerald R. Ford, the Republican leader in the House. These men constituted the President's Commission on the Assassination of President Kennedy, better known as the Warren Commission. Just four months earlier, on September 24, 1964, they had concluded that President Kennedy was murdered by one man, acting alone: Lee Harvey Oswald.

I explained in the letter that I was a student at Cornell University preparing to write a master's thesis on the problem of how the government goes about searching for such an elusive quarry as the truth. I wanted to know from them how the Warren Commission had performed this task—how it had organized its investigation; narrowed its list of possible suspects to a single assassin; separated true from false allegations in its report; and, most important, insulated its fact-finding process from political pressures. To this end, I asked to interview each of them.

Since the members of the Warren Commission had steadfastly refused to discuss their deliberations with outsiders, and the chief justice had invoked an aura of secrecy by pointing out that remaining elements of the case may not be known "in our lifetime," I frankly did not expect a favorable response to my letter. But to my surprise, I promptly heard from all seven commissioners. Except for the chief justice (who suggested I interview the commission's general counsel, J. Lee Rankin, in his place), they all agreed to be interviewed for my thesis.

I met Dulles at his Georgetown home, McCloy at his office on top of the Chase Manhattan Building in New York, Senator Cooper in the Senate Gallery, and Congressmen Boggs and Ford in their House offices. (Senator Russell was unable to keep his appointment because of illness.) Even though I had never conducted an interview before, they all were generous with their time. Dulles even invited me to stay for a leisurely tea while he reminisced how the commission's inquiry differed from those he had conducted at the CIA, and McCloy suspended his incoming phone calls so as not to interrupt the interview. During these discussions, however, it became painfully clear that the commissioners had little specific knowledge of the actual investigation. The four congressional members, busy with their legislative duties, had not attended most of the hearings. At best, the commissioners had established "general guidelines," as Senator Cooper put it, and left the "nitty-gritty" work of analyzing evidence, deposing witnesses, pursuing clues, resolving technical conflicts in testimony, and drafting chapters to its staff.

The staff worked under the supervision of General Counsel Rankin, the soft-spoken former solicitor general of the United States. Rankin saw me in New York and patiently sketched out for me on a yellow pad the organization of the investigation. He drew six neat boxes connected by arrows to a circle labeled "The Commission"; a box representing a key area in the case (e.g., Box I was "The identity of the assassin"). He wrote in each box the name of the junior and senior lawyer assigned to that particular mystery—and suggested I see them. He explained that while he—and the chief justice—theoretically approved each of these separate investigations, in practice these lawyers had organized much of their own investigation. They had selected the witnesses to be called, the leads to be pursued, and the issues to be given priority.

So after Rankin opened the door for me, I next proceeded to interview the staff lawyers. By now, all had returned to private practice or law schools from which they had been recruited, and most of them were exceedingly cooperative. One young lawyer, Professor Wesley J. Liebeler, even turned over to me his working files, which contained his chronological record of the investigation; his draft chapters; memoranda from other lawyers; and, most important, the original FBI summary reports—which showed what had been established about the assassination by the FBI before the Warren Commission began its inquiry. Other lawyers told me in great detail of the problems that still haunted them—failures of federal agencies to cooperate with them, gaps in FBI records, missing witnesses, perjured testimony they were not permitted to challenge, and conflicts they did not have the resources to resolve. They complained of arbitrariness, deadlines, administrative chaos, bureaucratic infighting, and constant pressure from the commission "to close doors rather than open them" because of the time pressure to complete the report before the coming presidential election. Consider what happened to Arlen Specter (now a senator from Pennsylvania), then a fledgling prosecutor. To begin with, the senior lawyer assigned to his area, "the basic facts of the assassination," failed to show up, leaving him virtually the entire burden of establishing the sequence of which shots hit which person in the assassination. Then the Dallas part of his investigation was delayed for almost two months, until mid-March, because of the chief justice's decision not to begin until the completion of the trial of Oswald's killer. By this time, Specter established that there was a critical contradiction between the FBI summary report, which concluded that a single rifle accounted for three separate hits—the first wounding Kennedy in the back, the second wounding Governor John Connally in the wrist, and the third hitting Kennedy's head—and the photographic evidence, which showed there was not enough time for the rifle in question to have fired the first two of these shots. Either the FBI was wrong, or there had been a second gunman. Despite this critical inconsistency, the commission set a June deadline for wrapping up the investigation, giving Specter only ten weeks to reinterrogate the doctors and other witnesses. It was insufficient time to resolve the issue.

I concluded in my thesis that the Warren Commission, instead of conducting the exhaustive, no-stone-left-unturned investigation that had been represented to the public, had presided over a hasty, limited investigation that had not always been able to insulate itself from political and national security considerations. The result was that it had failed to answer the primary question of whether Oswald had acted alone or in concert with others.

In April 1966, after the thesis was accepted at Cornell, it was published as a book, *Inquest: The Warren Commission and the Establishment of Truth*. With the disclosure of the FBI reports and staff files, it radically changed the terms of debate over the assassination.

Up until this point, most of the writing fell into one of two categories: blind faith or demonology. The blind-faithers reasoned that because the members of the Warren Commission were men of unquestionable integrity, they would not conceal evidence of a conspiracy. Therefore, there was no conspiracy. The demonologists, on the other hand, believed because evidence of a conspiracy did exist, the Warren Commission must have been part of the cover-up. The assumption common to both groups was that the Warren Commission had discovered the relevant facts. By demonstrating that this assumption was unwarranted, *Inquest* opened up the possibility that the members of the Warren Commission, though honest, had not dug deeply enough to find the evidence of a conspiracy.

As this view became the conventional wisdom, the floodgates opened to conspiracy theories. I cataloged in *Esquire* magazine, in an article titled "Who's Afraid of the Warren Commission?," thirty different theories about the assassination, ranging from the commission's one-man-alone theory to the *cui bono* theories, which deduced the conspirators from the theorists' view of who benefited most from the death of Kennedy. The logic of this new nihilism proclaimed that the Warren Commission report is dead; anything goes.

In December 1966, Jim Garrison, the district attorney of New Orleans, had begun his own investigation of the assassination. He based it on two local leads. First, Oswald reportedly had associated with an intriguing soldier of fortune in Orleans Parish named David Ferrie. Second, Oswald allegedly had been in contact with an elusive homosexual figure in the French Quarter of the city known by the pseudonym "Clay Bertrand." Before Garrison could determine if Oswald had actually known either man—Ferrie or "Clay Bertrand"—or if the latter even existed, David Ferrie mysteriously died. Less than one week later, on March 1, 1967, Garrison arrested Clay Shaw, a prominent New Orleans businessman, for "participating in a conspiracy to murder President Kennedy." That sensational charge caught the attention of the world.

Even though I was at the time fully occupied studying for my Ph.D. exams at Harvard, Garrison's announcement rekindled my interest in the case. If he had indeed uncovered solid evidence of a conspiracy, it would dramatically confirm my thesis that the commission's investigation had been flawed. In reading through the files of the staff lawyers, I realized that they had left unanswered intriguing questions about Oswald's activities in New Orleans in the summer of 1963. I was attracted by the idea that a local district attorney, not constrained by bureaucratic pressures and national security considerations of the kind the Warren Commission had to cope with, could now find the answers.

At this point, William Shawn, the editor of *The New Yorker*, asked me to write a profile of Garrison, and in April 1967 I went to New Orleans to conduct what was to become my second investigation of an investigation.

After interviewing Garrison and his staff, he suggested I look through the material he had seized from Clay Shaw's home. In Shaw's address book was a Dallas post office box number that partially—but only partially—matched a phone number in Oswald's address book. When apprised of this coincidence, Garrison immediately announced to the press that now he had unambiguous evidence that linked Shaw to Oswald. He explained that not only did both men have the exact same "encoded" number in their address book but also he had decoded it, and it was Jack Ruby's unlisted phone number. But that stunning announcement turned out to be nonsense: The Dallas post office in Shaw's book not only existed, but also it had been assigned to the person who had left it with Shaw one year after both Oswald and Ruby were dead. What concerned me more than that Garrison had made a mistake was that, after learning that his accusation could not possibly be true, he nevertheless continued to repeat it in his press interviews.

If Garrison was willing to concoct and knowingly repeat false "encoded" phone numbers to advance his case in the court of public opinion, it seemed a distinct possibility to me that he had shaped, if not wholly fabricated, evidence to justify his arrest of Clay Shaw after his only real suspect, David Ferrie, had died. His use of hypnosis, drugs, and voodoo practitioners to elicit testimony did not allay my concern that, as with the bogus code, Garrison was faking evidence against an innocent man to maintain the attention of the world media.

At this point I realized that the means by which Garrison was attempting to establish his version of the truth were drastically different from those employed by the Warren Commission. The commission, an ad hoc body outside the judicial system, had attempted to build its one-man-alone case through a meticulously legal-bound process, involving testimony and corroboration in accordance with the customary rules of evidence, whereas Garrison, an elected legal authority, was attempting to build his conspiracy case through unconventional means.

Whereas my first investigation was of a flawed but serious fact-finding process through which a one-man alone theory had been advanced, my second investigation was of a fact-distorting process aimed at foisting a conspiracy theory. The manner in which Garrison used the powers of his office, and his access to the media, to play on the public's fear of government secrecy demonstrated to me the vulnerability of facts to a determined demagogue.

After the profile of Garrison was published in *The New Yorker*, I expanded it into a book, *Counterplot*. By the time it was published in 1969, the acquittal of Clay Shaw in 1969 had all but ended interest in the case.

I had assumed after the Garrison debacle that the still outstanding questions about the assassination would never be satisfactorily answered, and I went on to other subjects. For the next six years I taught political science and wrote about politics and news media *(News from Nowhere, Between Fact and Fiction,* and *Agency of Fear)*. Then, in 1976, two editors of *Reader's Digest* approached me with an offer to write a book about Oswald's relationship with the intelligence services.

The possibility of investigating the deceptive techniques of intelligence fascinated me. I had assumed that the bullet that killed President Kennedy also must have exploded in the inner sanctums of at least five intelligence services that had had files on Oswald prior to the assassination. These were the Soviet Union's KGB, Cuba's Dirección Generale de Inteligencia (DGI), and America's CIA, Office of Naval Intelligence, and FBI.

The KGB's involvement traced back to 1959, when Oswald defected to the Soviet Union and offered to supply military secrets he had acquired during his service in the U.S. Marines. Less than eight weeks before the assassination, Oswald had spoken to a KGB officer in Mexico.

Cuba's DGI had dealings with Oswald in September 1963, when he applied for a Cuban visa in Mexico City. At that time he furnished them with a dossier of his activities on behalf of Cuba. On October 15, 1963, the Cuban Foreign Ministry cabled permission for its embassy in Mexico to issue Oswald the visa.

The CIA had a file on Oswald that dated back to 1959. Its surveillance equipment had recorded Oswald's contacts with both the Cuban and Soviet embassies in Mexico City. In October 1963, after it was determined from these electronic bugs that Oswald had contacted a KGB officer, the CIA urgently requested the Office of Naval Intelligence provide it with Oswald's photograph.

The Office of Naval Intelligence had investigated Oswald as early as 1959, when it was warned by the naval attaché stationed in Moscow that Oswald might have compromised radar secrets. Not only were his fellow Marines interrogated, but also the codes Oswald had access to were changed. In October 1963 it was in the process of responding to CIA flashes on Oswald.

The FBI security case on Oswald dated back to 1962, when he returned from the Soviet Union. On November 18, 1963—just four days before the assassination—it intercepted a letter Oswald had written to someone at the Soviet embassy in Washington, D.C. In it, Oswald stated that he had traveled to Mexico under an alias to complete "business" he had with the Soviet embassy there. Meanwhile, the FBI field office in Dallas was desperately trying to locate Oswald.

How had these intelligence services reacted when they learned that Oswald had been arrested for the assassination? Did they shred their files on him, or archive them?

The problem, as I explained to the *Reader's Digest* editors, was that, as intriguing as the subject might be to speculate about, writing a book about it without new evidence would be a pointless undertaking. The commission's documents had already been picked through, and intelligence officers could hardly be expected to be forthcoming about such a sensitive matter.

At this point the editors explained that there was new evidence that could be made available to me. They had a working arrangement with the KGB officer who had supervised Oswald's case in Moscow and, ten weeks after the assassination, had defected to the United States. His name, as I already knew, was Yuri Nosenko. They would make him available for this project so I could fill in the Soviet part of the jigsaw puzzle. In addition, they suggested they would make available to me the CIA tapes of Oswald in the Soviet and Cuban embassies in Mexico as well as the CIA "traces" on Oswald's Soviet activities.

It was an offer I could not refuse. Oswald's two and a half years in the Soviet Union had presented a void even to the Warren Commission. John J. McCloy explained that despite all its efforts, the commission had been unable to obtain statements on anyone Oswald had been associated with other than his wife, Marina. Nosenko could conceivably fill in part of the blanks. According to the *Reader's Digest* editor, not only had Nosenko dealt with Oswald for Soviet counterespionage since 1959, but also he had meticulously reviewed the entire KGB file on Oswald in early December 1963—and had almost a photographic memory.

What I had not been told when I began my interviews with Nosenko in January 1976 was that he was probably the most controversial defector in the history of U.S. intelligence. But after six hours of questioning him, I was disappointed and confused. His answers were not only imprecise and evasive when it came to Oswald's relationship with the KGB but also at odds with the established facts.

When I discussed these blatant inconsistencies with Jamie Jameson, the CIA officer who had arranged the interview and who was in the process of ghostwriting Nosenko's book, Jameson reassured me that the CIA had completely checked out Nosenko's "utter reliability" and his "full access" to the KGB Oswald file. Then a Soviet diplomat in Washington, presumed to be a KGB officer, also recommended Nosenko to me when I attempted to get permission to interview Oswald's Soviet associates. "Just between us," he confided, "there is no need for you to go to Russia. The best source on Oswald's visit there is in America: Yuri Nosenko." I found it curious that the KGB would suggest that I see a Soviet traitor—indeed, the same traitor the CIA had recommended to me the day before.

Gradually I learned I was to enter a maze within a maze with Nosenko. When I went to see a former director of the CIA, Richard Helms, in Iran in 1975, where he was ambassador, he said the CIA "had no business giving you Nosenko in this way"; it would reopen "old wounds." He explained that "Nosenko's reliability was key to determining what the KGB had to do with Oswald"—but it had never been resolved. "Nosenko hung over the CIA like an incubus," he added with anguish in his voice. An incubus in folklore is an evil spirit that rapes a woman in her sleep—without her fully realizing it. Was he suggesting at some level that the CIA had been similarly seduced by Nosenko? "All I am saying is that the case was a nightmare—a nightmare that still won't go away."

I found myself investigating yet another investigation: the CIA's effort to establish the truth about Oswald's putative KGB case officer. Helms had provided me with the names of what he called the "inquisitors" in the case. From them I learned that Nosenko had been central to a bitter battle within the CIA about the role of Soviet deception; that battle by now had been buried, along with a half dozen executives' careers, but not settled. Nosenko himself, rather than being considered "utterly reliable," had been deemed by the CIA's first set of inquisitors to be a disinformation agent who was only pretending to defect so he could deliver his KGB message to the CIA. Consequently, both Chief Justice Warren and Attorney General Robert Kennedy had been warned against listening to his story about Oswald, and Nosenko himself had been locked away in a specially built vaultlike prison for three years. In 1967 he was released from his vault and rehabilitated after a new set of inquisitors cast doubt on the original findings, but because the CIA was not able to settle the issue definitively, information derived from his debriefings still carried the ominous label "from a source whose *bona fides* has not been established."

My attempt to unravel the Nosenko affair brought me in contact with one of the most extraordinary—and convoluted—executives of the CIA, James Jesus Angleton. Angleton, until when he was dramatically fired in 1975, had been its celebrated chief of counterintelligence and its supersecret specialist on geopolitical deception (and, in this capacity, vetoed Nosenko's *bona fides*). He, and his elite counterintelligence staff, had also served as the CIA liaison with the FBI; the National Security Agency; and, during the Kennedy inquest, the Warren Commission.

In this latter role, Angleton had a great deal of both positive and negative information about the various investigations into the hidden connections of Oswald. From the interrogatives the Warren Commission sent to his office, he knew which leads it was actively pursuing—and which ones it was bypassing. From his liaisons with other intelligence services on these questions, he could deduce what subjects were so sensitive that they were assiduously avoided. From the official records about Oswald that the Soviet government submitted to the Warren Commission, and what he knew was missing from this dossier, he could figure out the "spin"—the elements that government wishes to emphasize and to obscure. And from overlaying the Nosenko debriefing on top of the CIA's own picture of how Oswald was handled by Soviet intelligence, he could draw some conclusions about what had happened during Oswald's missing year in the Soviet Union.

Initially Angleton talked to me evasively about orchids and, ignoring my obvious disinterest in the subject, took me on a tour of a steamy greenhouse in Maryland and elaborately described the various modes of deception that different tribes of orchids use to trick insects into carrying their pollen. "They can play on greed, lust, or fear," he said, pointing to different arrays of curious flowers. By this time it became clear to me that he was not talking just about tricky orchids or duped insects. They were metaphors for a world in which deception was a norm rather than an aberration; a world in which intelligence services could be lured, blinded, and tricked by their inability to discriminate between real and simulated information. Eventually—he could never be rushed into a subject—he fitted Oswald into this perverse world.

He suggested that I obtain through the Freedom of Information Act the correspondence of Oswald's that had been intercepted by the CIA three years prior to the assassination in the agency's illegal "mail cover" program (an operation that Angleton himself had superintended). He was convinced that those letters, when taken "in context" with Oswald's Marine Corps service, showed that Oswald's defection to the Soviet Union was not a spur-of-the-moment decision but a well-prepared and well-orchestrated act that required help. If so, Oswald's preparations might be key to solving this mystery.

What happened during Oswald's two years of active duty in the Marines that led him to defect to the Soviet Union with U.S. military secrets? And who, if anyone, assisted in him in planning this enterprise? Finding the answers to these questions required reconstructing from Marine Corps personnel records the units Oswald had served in before defecting. With the assistance of one of Oswald's commanding officers and six researchers, I located seventy-three Marines who had been acquainted with Oswald (only three of whom had testified before the Warren Commission). Among the snapshots they took, I even found one of Oswald in the same picture as John Wayne, who had been on an entertainment tour of the Pacific bases. While their stories filled in many parts of the puzzle, I ran into the problem that belated witnesses, now anxious to become part of history, tended on occasion to tell an author not merely what they actually recalled but also what they thought they wanted the author wanted to put in his book. For example, no fewer than six Marines at different bases told me stories about Oswald sniping with a gun at another Marine in their presence; all six stories turned out to be false. This problem would only become worse in the future as witnesses became increasingly exposed to the growing body of assassination literature.

Piecing together Oswald's connections in Dallas after he returned to the United States in June 1962 presented a different sort of problem. During this period, Oswald became associated with a small circle of intellectuals who saw themselves isolated by the alien orthodoxy of Dallas conservatism. They wanted to hear about Oswald's experiences in the Soviet Union and his ideas on pacifism, socialism, and civil rights. In the ensuing dialogue on political activism, Oswald showed little inhibitions in proposing violent solutions to problems—such as shooting at a right-wing general. After it turned out that Oswald was the accused assassin of the president, many in this circle panicked —and left Dallas. They showed great reluctance in discussing Oswald, even after thirteen years had passed and passions had cooled down.

By far the most intriguing member of this circle I found—and lost—was George De Mohrenschildt, a dashing, socially prominent geologist in Dallas who, years earlier, had known Jackie Kennedy. De Mohrenschildt also had been the subject of an extensive FBI investigation, and in April 1963 the CIA had initiated an investigation of his activities at a time when he had become close to Oswald—so close that Oswald had showed him his rifle with its telescopic sight.

In March 1977 I arranged a four-day interview with De Mohrenschildt in Palm Beach, Florida. On the second day of the interviews, after suggesting to me that he had been debriefing Oswald with the sanction of the CIA man in Dallas, he was found shot to death. His apparent suicide left a gaping hole in my book, especially since, at the time, his claimed linkage to the CIA appeared to be unverifiable. My book, titled *Legend: The Secret World of Lee Harvey Oswald*, was published in 1978.

In July 1979, the Select Committee on Assassination of the House of Representatives issued its own report about the assassination. Unlike the limited effort by the Warren Commission, this three-year investigation, occasioned by congressional concern over the Watergate revelations of government cover-ups, had delved into some of the deepest recesses of the CIA, FBI, and other government agencies in its search for evidence. Moreover, the committee appointed panels of independent experts, using state-of-the-art technology, to answer unresolved questions about the autopsy results, ballistics matches, firearms tests, and photographic evidence. In doing so it directly addressed and cleared up many of the issues raised by critics of the Warren Commission report (including myself). Yet, all of its laudable work was overshadowed by its headline-making conclusion, "President Kennedy was probably assassinated as a result of a conspiracy."

This conclusion had been based on a single piece of new evidence: the analysis by three acoustics experts of an eight-minute Dictaphone belt recorded at Dallas Police headquarters on November 22, 1963. These experts, assuming that the sounds on this tape came from an open police two-way radio at the scene of the assassination, asserted that, when enhanced, they were "95 percent certain" they could detect four distinct shots. Because two of these blasts were spaced too closely together for Oswald's rifle to have fired them, there must have been two riflemen.

The committee, in light of this analysis, hastily revised its conclusion. As late as 6:00 P.M. on December 13, 1978, based on ballistic evidence that indicated all the shots had come from Oswald's rifle, the committee had concluded: "There is insufficient evidence to find that there was a conspiracy to assassinate President Kennedy." After the committee's executive session was dramatically interrupted by this last-minute acoustical evidence, its general counsel, Robert Blakey, who himself had been a strong advocate of a Mafia conspiracy theory, suggested that the only conclusion consistent with this analysis was that a second rifleman had fired but missed. By the time the committee had released its main findings to the press on December 30, its conclusion had become that a "probable conspiracy" had killed Kennedy.

Unfortunately, after the committee rushed to this conclusion, Dallas motorcycle policeman H. B. McClain, whose radio had been assumed to have been the source for the putative shots, stated that his radio could not possibly have made that recording. Since he had raced along with the president's limousine to the hospital, sirens shrieking full blast, his microphone could not have accounted for the eight-minute recording, which came from one spot. He was also certain his radio had been tuned to the channel for the procession, since he was listening to it attentively, whereas the tape had been made on another channel. The committee now realized, after changing its conclusions, that the very provenance of the tape was in question: No one was sure what was recorded. It could have come from any other locale in Dallas in which a police radio was opened, or have been made at a different time.

After issuing its report, the committee belatedly recommended that the problematic tape be reexamined by a panel of experts selected by the National Academy of Sciences. This panel, chaired by Professor Norman S. Ramsey of Harvard, restudied the tape and was able to prove unambiguously that, wherever the tape came from, it was made one minute after the assassination and therefore had no relevance whatsoever to the sequence of shots (or anything else). The committee's experts, it turned out, had simply analyzed the wrong tape, and the committee's revised "conspiracy" conclusion, incredibly enough, proceeded from this error. But by the time the error was revealed, in October 1982, the committee had been long dissolved, and its erroneous conspiracy conclusion had become part of popular mythology—the beginning of a trend.

The House Select Committee on Assassination, with its alternate conclusions, left the public thoroughly confused. According to a Gallup poll, over 80 percent of Americans doubted that the truth had come out about who killed Kennedy. So like its two predecessors—the Warren Commission, which pressured its investigators to meet a political deadline, and District Attorney Garrison, who disoriented his own investigators by making a premature and unwarranted arrest to hold the attention of the media—this investigation failed because it overreached the evidence.

Even though the conspiracy conclusion of the Select Committee on Assassination proved to be erroneous, its investigation, unlike that of Garrison, produced relevant new evidence and resolved much of the dispute over what happened in Dallas that infamous day. Consequently, I have written new epilogues for *Inquest, Counterplot,* and *Legend,* to take account of these findings, and an afterword on the current state of the evidence. To my surprise, its investigation also contained missing pieces in the life of George De Mohrenschildt that tended to confirm what he had told me just before he died and that led me in 1981 to reinvestigate the circumstances leading to his death. The previously unpublished results are included in the chronicle.

For a decade after the House Select Committee on Assassination released its report, little if any new evidence emerged. By this time, indefatigable assassination researchers had combed through tens of thousands of pages of previously classified documents from the Warren Commission's files that had been released under the Freedom of Information Act but without finding anything other than investigative sloppiness or malfeasance. Aside from the predictable "confessions" from former residents of mental hospitals, some of which became the basis of books, few new witnesses came forth; and those who did after all this elapsed time had uncorroboratory stories. Like unstable metals, oral knowledge had a definite half-life, after which it rapidly deteriorated.

Then, in September 1991, from the crumbling Soviet Union, came a real possibility for uncovering documentary evidence that could cast new light on the assassination. A Soviet official in Moscow offered to make available the entire KGB archive on Oswald to ABC News for its program "Nightline." Up until this point, except for some suspect documents provided by the Soviet Foreign Ministry to the Warren Commission in 1964, Oswald's two-year residence in Moscow and Minsk had remained almost a total blank. When the producers of this program told me about this project, I was, of course, eager to cooperate. Since I had already obtained for *Legend* the CIA "traces" on some two dozen people with whom Oswald had been in contact in the Soviet Union—which involved little more than a superficial matching of names in Oswald's address book against the CIA's computerized Soviet phone books and Soviet diplomatic directories—I now wanted to trace these names in Oswald's KGB files to see if they revealed any heretofore unknown activities, such as being trained for an espionage mission. Who did Oswald connect to in this last remaining *terra incognita?*

Unfortunately, this coup did not take place. The "archive," which was apparently no more than a surveillance file, would not actually be turned over to ABC. A KGB official would himself read the file, brief an ABC correspondent on it, and allow him to read a few selected (and sanitized) documents. Obviously, under these conditions it would be impossible to know what incriminating or embarrassing documents had been excluded. The KGB had simply found a channel for repeating the story—which may or may not have been true—that the Soviet government had presented to the Warren Commission in 1964. Its presentation on the twenty-eighth anniversary of the Kennedy assassination had no value other than to create the illusion that the KGB had opened its file.

Like the ineluctable fall of an imperfect hero in a Greek tragedy, it was inevitable that the flawed investigations of the Kennedy assassination ultimately would be transmogrified into a myth—one that reflects the fantasy and paranoia of the times. So it is not surprising that a Hollywood movie that depicted an assassination conspiracy so pervasive that it accounted for the war in Vietnam as well as a continuing coup d'état in America captured the imagination of the American public (and was nominated for an Academy Award in 1992). Oliver Stone's film *JFK*, which employed a half dozen assassination researchers for technical advisers, and had a budget of some $40 million, represents itself as another investigation into the Kennedy assassination. Since this film demonstrates yet again how fragile is the matrix of facts we call reality and how easily destroyed it is by even well-meaning fictionalizers, I have added a chapter examining it.

Finally, despite the damage to the truth done by the tragedy of errors that have overtaken some of the investigations, the physical evidence tells a powerful story that has been largely neglected by assassination researchers in their relentless quest for the smoking gun (despite the invention of smokeless gunpowder) of a conspiracy. I thus conclude this twenty-seven-year assassination chronicle with an afterword summing up the evidence of the state and the state of the evidence.

May 1992
New York City

BOOK ONE

INQUEST

*THE WARREN COMMISSION AND THE
ESTABLISHMENT OF TRUTH
(1966)*

1

Overview:
THE TEN-MONTH INVESTIGATION

November

On November 22, 1963, President John F. Kennedy was assassinated in Dallas, Texas. The burst of shots came at 12:30 p.m. as the Presidential motorcade slowly passed through downtown Dallas. The President was shot twice and fatally wounded. Governor John B. Connally of Texas, seated directly in front of the President, was also wounded. The President was immediately rushed to Parkland Hospital where, despite desperate efforts to prolong his life, he died at 1 p.m.

Less than one hour later Lee Harvey Oswald was arrested in connection with the murder of Dallas policeman J. D. Tippit. Oswald, a twenty-four-year-old ex-Marine who had once defected to the Soviet Union and who worked in the building from which the shots were believed to have come, was immediately suspected of being the assassin. Early the next morning he was formally charged with having assassinated the President. For almost two days, through more than twelve hours of interrogation, Oswald maintained that he was completely innocent. Then, on the morning of November 24, he himself was fatally shot in the basement of the Dallas city jail by Jack Ruby, a Dallas nightclub-owner.

On November 25, after "a conference with the White House," Texas Attorney General Waggoner Carr announced that a court of inquiry would be held by the State of Texas "to develop fully and disclose openly" the facts of the assassination. This investigation was intended to be part of a broader inquiry in which the FBI would first conduct a full investigation and report its findings to the President; then the Texas court of inquiry would examine witnesses of the assassination in public hearings; and finally a Presidential Commission would evaluate all the facts that were established and report its conclusions to the President. Waggoner Carr named two prominent Texas lawyers, Leon Jaworski and Dean Robert G. Storey, as special counsel for the investigation.[1]

On November 26 Senator Everett M. Dirksen proposed that the Senate Judiciary Committee conduct a full investigation into the assassination. This suggestion received considerable support from both Democrats and Republicans on the floor of the Senate. The next day Congressman Charles E. Goodell proposed in the House of Representatives that a Joint Committee, composed of seven Senators and seven Representatives, conduct an inquiry into the assassination.

On November 29, "to avoid parallel investigations and to concentrate fact-finding in a body having the broadest national mandate,"[2] President Lyndon B. Johnson appointed a commission "to ascertain, evaluate, and report on" the facts of the assassination.[3] Earl Warren, the Chief Justice of the United States, was chosen as chairman, and from its inception the commission was generally known as the "Warren Commission."

To complete the Commission, President Johnson chose six men who had distinguished themselves in public life and who represented important and diverse elements in the political spectrum. Two were senior Senators: Richard B. Russell, Democrat of Georgia, who had held his seat in the Senate for thirty uninterrupted years; and John Sherman Cooper, Republican of Kentucky, who had formerly served as Ambassador to India and who was generally regarded as a leading member of the liberal wing of the Republican Party. Two were leaders of the House of Representatives: Hale Boggs, Democrat of Louisiana, Majority Whip of the House; and Gerald R. Ford, Republican of Michigan, chairman of the House Republican Conference. Two members were international lawyers: Allen W. Dulles, the former director of the Central Intelligence Agency; and John J. McCloy, former United States High Commissioner for Germany and former President of the World Bank.

The Commission was empowered to prescribe its own procedures and to employ such assistance as it deemed necessary. All government agencies were ordered to cooperate. There were few, if any, precedents in American history for such a Commission.

December

The First Meeting. On December 5, 1963, just thirteen days after the assassination of President Kennedy, the Warren Commission held its first meeting.[4] The Chief Justice presided. Allen Dulles later said, "Although we faced a difficult and perhaps unprecedented task, each of us had had a lifetime's experience in dealing with extraordinary problems, and we knew what had to be done."[5] Viewing the executive order which had created the Commission as an "unequivocal Presidential mandate" to conduct an independent investigation, the Commission decided that "the public interest in insuring that the truth was ascertained could not be met by merely accepting the reports or the analyses of Federal or State agencies."[6] All the members agreed that the Commission would hold its own investigation.

The next order of business was the selection of a general counsel. The first person suggested for this position was rejected because he was "too controversial."[7] Warren then proposed J. Lee Rankin, a former Solicitor General of the United States, and the Commission "immediately and unanimously" agreed upon him.[8]

Finally the Commission decided to ask Waggoner Carr to postpone the Texas court of inquiry until the Commission had completed its investigation.[9] After the meeting Chief Justice Warren wrote to Carr on behalf of the Commission, stating:

We are most anxious, as I am sure you are, to take no steps
which could impede investigation or which could lead the
public to mistaken conclusions based upon partial factual
information.[10]

Warren further suggested that public hearings might prejudice the trial of Jack Ruby, and said that for these reasons the
Commission felt that "a public inquiry in Texas at this time
might be more harmful than helpful. . . ."[11] Warren then invited Carr and his special counsel to "participate in the Commission's work, and counsel with it."[12] Carr accepted the offer,
and he (or his special counsel) attended most of the Commission
hearings.

The General Counsel. On December 8 Warren called J. Lee
Rankin in New York City and asked him to be general counsel
for the Commission. It was understood that Rankin would organize the investigation for the Commission and be its "executive
director" as well as its counsel.[13] Rankin left for Washington the
next day and devoted the next ten months to Commission work.

Neither Rankin nor the Commission realized at the time how
demanding the job would be.[14] Rankin not only superintended
the investigation and the writing of the Report, but also examined most of the important witnesses who appeared before
the Commission; he adjudicated the disputes that constantly
arose among the staff lawyers; and he acted as liaison between
the Commission and other government agencies.[15] Rankin
found that he was "the man in the middle"; all the investigators'
problems were passed through him up to the Commission; all
the Commission's directives were passed through him down to
the staff.[16] A member of the staff described it as "an extraordinary arrangement. Rankin was the only person the Commission
would talk to; everything had to be funneled through him."[17]

Although they generally agreed that Rankin was a competent
administrator, his soft-spoken and permissive manner led some
of the staff lawyers to feel that he might "tone down" their arguments when presenting them before the Commission.[18] It was
also felt that Rankin at times was "too responsive" to Warren
and that he refused to "stand up" to the Commission.[19] These
criticisms, however, failed to take into account the very basic
fact that Rankin worked for the Commission.

On December 9 the FBI submitted a Summary Report of its investigation to the Commissioners. This four-volume report, which summarized the entire FBI investigation to date, was considered "of principal importance" in the formulation of the investigation.[20]

On December 13 Congress, in a Joint Resolution, empowered the Commission to subpoena witnesses and to compel their testimony by granting them immunity if they pleaded the Fifth Amendment. This latter power, however, was never used by the Commission.

The Second Meeting. The Commission met again on December 16. J. Lee Rankin was sworn in as General Counsel; henceforth he would sit in on all Commission meetings. The main purpose of this meeting was to determine the scope of the investigation.[21] First the FBI Summary Report was considered. This report paralleled, McCloy said "perhaps too closely," the Commission's mission of ascertaining the facts of the assassination, and thus the Commission decided to reserve judgment on the conclusion of the FBI Summary Report until all its premises were critically reappraised.[22] There was also some question as to whether the FBI report should be made public.[23] The Commission decided as policy that no evidence should be released before publication of the Commission's Report, because "piecemeal releases" might only serve to confuse the public and add to the irresponsible rumors.[24]

Although the investigation was to be "independent," the Commission decided to rely on federal agencies to conduct its basic investigation. Rankin explained that it would have been impractical for the Commission to attempt to recruit its own investigative force.[25] Dulles added that independent investigators would cause needless friction in dealing with government agencies and would complicate the security problem.[26] Furthermore, since the Commission had been promised the full cooperation of federal investigative agencies, it was deemed unnecessary "to employ investigators other than the legal staff."[27]

Finally the Commission decided to review thoroughly the investigative material on which the FBI had based its Summary Report.[28] Because this imposing task required assistance, Rankin was authorized to organize a staff of independent lawyers to help in analyzing these thousands of investigative reports and sorting out the issues that required verification or further investigation.[29] The Commission then planned to hold hearings to examine the more important witnesses and evidence.[30]

The Staff. The FBI investigative reports began arriving at the Commission's offices on December 20.[31] With the reports came Howard P. Willens, a young and energetic Department of Justice lawyer who was to play an important role in shaping the investigation. The then Deputy Attorney General, Nicholas deB. Katzenbach, had asked Willens to act as a liaison between the Commission and the Department of Justice. Willens said that his was supposed to have been a part-time job, but, upon seeing the amount of work that confronted the Commission, he returned to his office, "packed up" his desk, and moved into the Commission's offices.[32] Willens took charge of the administrative function; he divided up the work among the staff, made schedules, requested assistance from other agencies, and "kept the investigation moving."[33] Some considered him "hard-driving" and "aggressive"; others considered him "the hero of the investigation."[34]

Rankin chose Norman Redlich, a New York University law professor and an editor of *The Tax Law Review*, as his special assistant. Rankin said that Redlich had deep understanding of the law and was more than simply a lawyer or editor.[35] In addition, Redlich had the asset of tremendous energy; when necessary, he could work from 8 a.m. to 3 a.m., seven days a week.[36] Redlich, however, tended to be a "perfectionist," and this quality engendered some friction among the lawyers. Some felt that Redlich was "unyielding on points of law," but most agreed that he made an important contribution to the Commission.

Both Redlich and Willens considered themselves to be Rankin's deputies, and, at first this caused some confusion. However, as the investigation progressed, Redlich became occupied with special projects—for example, preparing the examination of Marina Oswald—and Willens became occupied with day-to-day administrative problems.[37] Rankin, Willens, and Redlich, each in his own way, were indispensable to the work of the Commission, and each influenced the outcome of the investigation.

In late December, Rankin selected the "senior counsel" for the staff. He said that above all the Commission wanted a "balanced" staff drawn from all parts of the country—lawyers whose reputations would add weight to the Report.[38] Rankin thus chose lawyers who were held in high esteem by their regional Bar Associations:

From New York City, Francis W. H. Adams, a former police commissioner and a leader in the Democratic Reform movement; from California, Joseph A. Ball, a well-known trial lawyer and a member of the United States Judiciary Conference Advisory Committee; from Philadelphia, William T. Coleman, Jr., a former special counsel for the City of Philadelphia, a consultant with the United States Arms Control and Disarmament Agency, and one of the best-known Negro lawyers in America; from New Orleans, Leon D. Hubert, Jr., a former United States attorney and professor at Tulane University; from Chicago, Albert E. Jenner, Jr., a former assistant attorney general for Illinois and vice-chairman of the National Joint Committee for the Effective Administration of Justice.

The criterion of professional eminence led not only to the selection of lawyers with outstanding reputations, but also to the selection of extremely busy lawyers. When Norman Redlich was asked how such men could have given up nine months of their practice, he answered, "Very simple. They didn't."[39] The lawyers were employed on a consulting basis, receiving $100 a day and expenses. Some of the senior counsel worked for the Commission for only a few days and lent their reputations but not their time.[40]

The bulk of the work devolved on the "junior counsel"—lawyers in their early thirties who had had distinguished law-school records and private practices.[41] Willens, who selected most of the junior counsel, said, "We wanted independent lawyers, not government men, who had been at the top of their class and who could work 16 hours a day."[42]

Melvin A. Eisenberg, a twenty-nine-year-old New York corporation lawyer who had been first in his class at Harvard, was chosen by Redlich as his assistant. Arlen Specter, a former assistant district attorney of Philadelphia and former co-editor of

the *Yale Law Journal* (with Howard Willens), was the next lawyer selected. Samuel A. Stern, a Washington lawyer and a former law clerk to Chief Justice Earl Warren, and Burt W. Griffin,
a former assistant United States attorney for the Northern District of Ohio, were also selected by Willens. David W. Belin, an
Iowa trial lawyer, and W. David Slawson, a Denver lawyer,
were both recommended to the Commission. Finally, Wesley J.
Liebeler, a former Wall Street lawyer who considered himself
"definitely not establishment" and who sometimes played the
role of devil's advocate on the staff, was recommended to Willens by the dean of the University of Chicago Law School.[43]

The "junior counsel" also worked as consultants, receiving
$75 a day and expenses. Rankin noted that, "unlike the senior
lawyers who were losing money every day they worked, many of
the junior lawyers were making more than they made in private
practice."[44] In any event, the junior lawyers spent considerably
more time on the case than did the senior lawyers.[45]

The Commission approved the lawyers on the basis of short
one-paragraph biographical statements that were submitted by
Rankin. Commissioner Ford said, "We gave Rankin a free hand
in selecting the staff. I trusted his judgment."[46]

The Organization. The three weeks from December 21 to January 10 were critical in the formulation of the investigation.[47]
On December 28 Howard Willens drew up a memorandum
which set forth the *modus operandi*.[48] This memorandum proposed that the investigation be divided into five separate areas.
A senior and junior lawyer would be assigned to each area and
would resolve the minor problems and inconsistencies in that
area. Under this arrangement, only the major problems would
be passed on to the Commission. After ascertaining the facts in
its area, each team would prepare a draft chapter on its findings, and this would correspond to a chapter in the Report. The
areas were arranged on a descending scale of generality. The
first area was to be concerned with the basic facts of the assassination itself; the second area would narrow down its focus to
the identity of the assassin. The third area would deal with Oswald's background and motives, while the fourth area would be
concerned with possible conspiratorial relationships Oswald
had. The fifth area would deal with the death of Oswald. A sixth

area, Presidential protection, was later added at the request of the Commission.[49]

This plan, it should be noted, did not provide for a separate investigation into the murder of Dallas Policeman J. D. Tippit. Instead, the Tippit investigation was considered to be part of the Area II investigation of the identity of the President's assassin.[50]

Finally, the memorandum suggested that Marina Oswald, the alleged assassin's widow, be called as the first witness in the Commission hearing. This would give the lawyers additional time to recommend witnesses in their areas for the Commission hearings.[51]

Toward the end of December, Willens and Rankin arranged for the appointment of liaisons between the Commission and other government agencies cooperating in the investigation. Appointed were Inspector James J. Malley from the FBI, Inspector Thomas Kelley from the Secret Service, R. G. Rocca from the CIA, and Abram Chayes from the Department of State.[52]

January

The Sorting Process. As the lawyers arrived in Washington during the first three weeks of January, they were assigned to areas by Willens and Rankin. Francis W. H. Adams and Arlen Specter, both of whom had considerable investigative experience, were assigned to Area I, "the basic facts of the assassination." Their principal job was to establish the source of the shots.[53]

Joseph Ball and David Belin, both experienced criminal trial lawyers, were assigned to Area II, "the identity of the assassin." Their task was to develop evidence which identified the assassin.[54] Albert Jenner and Wesley Liebeler were assigned to Area III, Oswald's background. Their job was to explore Oswald's life and to delineate factors which might have caused him to assassinate the President.[55]

William Coleman, who had considerable experience in dealing with government agencies, and W. David Slawson were assigned to Area IV, "possible conspiratorial relationships." Their main concern was Oswald's movements outside the country, and their task was to ascertain whether any other person or group influenced Oswald in the assassination.[56]

Two former United States attorneys, Leon Hubert and Burt Griffin, were assigned to Area V, "Oswald's death." They had two problems: to ascertain, first, whether Ruby had had any assistance in murdering Oswald, and, second, whether Ruby had had any prior connection with Oswald.[57]

Samuel Stern was assigned to Area VI, "Presidential protection." His task was to scrutinize the precautions taken by the Secret Service and FBI. J. Lee Rankin was nominally the senior counsel in this politically sensitive area.[58]

Each team of lawyers was assigned a secretary and an office in the Commission's headquarters at 200 Maryland Avenue N.E., conveniently located between the Supreme Court and Capitol Hill. Willens brought in two lawyers from the Department of Justice—Charles N. Shaffer, Jr., and Stuart R. Pollak—to assist with the clerical and administrative duties. (Francis Adams, apprehensive over the division of labor, privately warned Warren of a "burgeoning bureaucracy.") In the basement of the building the FBI installed a scale model of the assassination site, as well as film projectors and other necessary equipment.[59]

After the lawyers were organized into teams, the initial phase of the investigation, the sorting-out process, began. Willens divided the more than twenty thousand pages of investigative reports furnished by the FBI and Secret Service into areas and then parceled them out to the teams of lawyers concerned with each area. The teams then read, analyzed, and collated the relevant material in the reports, sorting out possible inconsistencies, unresolved questions, and matters that required further investigation.[60]

In the process of reducing the mass of investigative material to manageable proportions, there was the possibility that some pertinent information would be lost. Wesley Liebeler took the position that a lawyer in one area might not perceive the relevance of information to another area. Liebeler therefore suggested that one lawyer read all the reports.[61] Rankin replied that it was important to get the material into the hands of the lawyers charged with investigating it, and that later, "if time permitted," a member of the staff could read all the reports.[62]

The First Staff Meeting. At the first formal staff meeting, held in late January, Rankin told the lawyers. "Truth is your only client." He instructed them to gather the facts without forming conclusions and not to accept the FBI Summary Report as final.[63] The lawyers then were introduced to the Chief Justice, who cautioned them that their investigation might involve national security problems and asked them not to discuss their work outside the Commission.[64]

The Third Commission Meeting. The Commission met on January 21, mainly to discuss procedural questions. Hearings were to be held in February, and the immediate problem was to decide the form they would take. Would they be open or closed to the public?[65]

The Commission gave several reasons for its decision to hold closed hearings. One reason offered was that hearings open to the public "might interfere with Ruby's rights to a fair and impartial trial."[66] It is doubtful, however, if this was the decisive reason. Only a few witnesses (none of whose testimony pertained to Ruby) were called before the Ruby trial was completed.[67] If Ruby's trial had been the only consideration, the Commission could have held closed hearings until Ruby's trial was completed, and then held open hearings.

The Commission also expressed concern that open hearings "might prejudice innocent parties" if hearsay testimony were made public out of context.[68] It is not clear in this respect why the Commission hearings raised problems that Congressional hearings do not raise. The fact that the Commission *did* permit the most damaging type of hearsay evidence and allegations to be published eventually indicates that this was not a major reason.

The most substantial reason that the Commission gave was that, since testimony could not always be taken in logical sequence, it "was impractical and could be misleading" to hold public hearings.[69] This was also the main reason why Warren requested Waggoner Carr to postpone the Texas court of inquiry. Evidently the Commission was greatly concerned that the public might reach mistaken conclusions if testimony were released unevaluated and out of context.

Another problem faced at the third Commission meeting

arose from a telegram sent by Mark Lane, a New York lawyer who claimed to represent the interests of Lee Harvey Oswald. Lane requested that he be appointed "defense counsel" for Oswald and be permitted to cross-examine the witnesses.[70] This request was rejected because the Commission considered itself to be an "impartial fact-finding agency," not a court, and thus there was no need for a "defense counsel."[71]

In addition, at this meeting the Commission approved a resolution "governing questioning of the witnesses by the members of the Commission staff."[72] And it was decided that Marina Oswald would be the Commission's first witness.[73]

The Problems. On the next day, January 22, Rankin was informed by Waggoner Carr, the Attorney General of Texas, of an allegation that Lee Harvey Oswald had been a paid FBI informer. Henry Wade, the Dallas District Attorney, had also heard this allegation.[74] Rankin immediately told Warren of this development, and an emergency meeting of the Commission was called for that afternoon.[75] The members began arriving at about 5:30 p.m. for what Representative Ford described as "the most tense and hushed meeting" he remembered.[76] The Commission decided to ask both Carr and Wade to come to Washington immediately.[77]

On January 24 Carr and Wade flew to Washington and met with Warren and Rankin. Neither of the Texas officials knew the source of the story, or if it was true, but they gave such details as Oswald's alleged informant number, his salary, and the time he was supposedly employed by the FBI.[78]

The Commission met again on January 27 to discuss the problem further. The decision was to inform the FBI of the allegation and at the same time to conduct an exhaustive investigation of Oswald's relations with government agencies.[79]

While the Commission was considering the problem of Oswald's alleged association with the FBI, the staff was faced with an equally serious problem stemming from the movie film of the assassination. This film was taken by Abraham Zapruder, an amateur photographer, and graphically shows virtually the entire assassination. In ten seconds of color film, the President is shown waving and smiling, then suddenly reaching for his throat and slowly slumping over. About a second later Governor

Connally is apparently hit. About three seconds after that the fatal shot visibly strikes the President's head.[80] The film was first viewed by staff members on January 27, 1964; FBI experts and Secret Service agents attended the session.[81]

It became apparent, from a frame-by-frame analysis of the film, that the shots were not evenly spaced apart in time, as had been assumed. In fact, the first two shots seemed to hit Kennedy and Connally within a period of one and a half seconds. The proximity of these two shots raised doubts as to whether an assassin could possibly fire a bolt-action rifle two times in one and a half seconds.[82] This problem grew more complex as the investigation proceeded.

The Delay. At the end of January, Rankin told the staff that the field investigation would be postponed until the completion of the Ruby trial.[83] Rankin later explained that the Commission did not want to interfere with Ruby's rights, and that he felt more time was needed to prepare for the investigation.[84] Rankin instructed the staff to continue reading the investigative reports and to draw up preliminary plans for the field investigation by March 1.[85]

February

The Hearings. The Commission hearings began on February 3 with the testimony of Marina Oswald. For the first four days of the Commission's hearings J. Lee Rankin respectfully and patiently questioned Mrs. Oswald about all aspects of Oswald's life.[86] Her answers did not completely satisfy the staff.

At the next staff meeting, on about February 6, some of the lawyers requested that Marina Oswald be questioned further. Rankin, however, announced that the Commission had decided that they believed her and that there would be no further questioning of her. The announcement precipitated a heated argument in which one prominent lawyer threatened to resign unless Mrs. Oswald was cross-examined. Rankin reportedly "lost control" of the meeting, and there were few formal staff meetings held after this one.[87]

Staff Meetings. Rankin said the staff meetings generated "more heat than light."[88] And Howard Willens explained that the reason only four or five staff meetings were held after February was that they were not really necessary. He went on to say that the Commission believed that this type of investigation could best be coordinated from the top and that there was no reason, from an administrative point of view, for "all the lawyers to discuss all aspects of every problem."[89]

Another staff dispute arose over the question of whether or not witnesses should be "prepared." Trial lawyers usually "prepare" a witness by discussing his story with him before he testifies, in order to reduce inconsistencies and irrelevancies. Norman Redlich pointed out that in the British system of commission inquiry witnesses testify without advance preparation, and he took the position that the Commission's witnesses should *not* be "prepared."[90] Most of the lawyers on the staff with trial experience thought that Redlich's position was impractical.[91] They maintained that if witnesses testified completely spontaneously the record would be confused with irrelevancies, and pertinent points might be obscured. Rankin appointed Redlich, Belin, and Liebeler to study this problem as a committee. A compromise was then worked out, in which lawyers were to submit memoranda containing their off-the-record conversations with witnesses.[92] When the investigation finally began, however, there was simply no time for preparing memoranda, and thus Rankin told the lawyers to use their own discretion in preparing witnesses.[93]

Goldberg and Craig. In late February, Alfred Goldberg, a senior United States Air Force historian, joined the staff. Warren apparently wanted the Report to have a historic as well as a legal perspective.[94] Goldberg, who worked directly under Rankin, was to play a major role in writing the report. He was also assigned the task of preparing a "Speculation and Rumor" appendix.[95]

On February 25 the Commission asked Walter E. Craig, President of the American Bar Association, to advise the Commission whether "the proceedings conformed to the basic principles of American justice."[96] Apparently the position taken at the January 21 meeting, that the Commission was a fact-finding agency and not a court, was reconsidered. The record indicates, however, that Craig's assignment was no more than a formality.

The Commission heard only four witnesses during February: Oswald's widow and her business manager, James H. Martin; Oswald's mother; and Oswald's brother. Waiting for the Ruby trial to end and the staff's field investigation to begin, the Commission heard no substantive evidence concerning the assassination itself.

March

The Investigation. During the first two weeks in March the lawyers continued preparing the material in their areas. Each team prepared a list of witnesses to be called during its field investigation, and these lists were submitted to Rankin for his *pro forma* approval.[97] The teams sent questions that required further investigation to Willens, who forwarded them to the FBI, the Secret Service, or the CIA. When questions arose as to the operations of government agencies, the teams prepared questionnaires for the agencies concerned.[98] The lawyers also outlined the major problems in their areas and drew up preliminary plans of attack. These plans did not necessarily have to be submitted to Rankin, who explained that he wanted lawyers "to be independent and have a free hand" in their own areas.[99] One lawyer commented that the preparations were so hectic that there wasn't time for formal agendas and the lawyers were thus forced "to play it by ear."[100]

On March 14 the Ruby trial ended and the investigation proper began. On March 18 Willens, Ball, and Belin flew to Dallas and laid the groundwork for the field investigation.[101] Willens arranged facilities for the staff in the United States Attorney's offices in the Post Office building. Barefoot Sanders, Jr., the United States Attorney for Dallas, acted as liaison between the Commission and the Texas authorities.[102]

Meanwhile, Ball and Belin informally interviewed police officials and the key witnesses to the assassination, and Ball arranged for some of the eyewitnesses to appear before the Commission in Washington the following week.[103]

On March 20 Ball and Belin conducted an off-the-record reconstruction of Oswald's assumed movements at the scene of the assassination. Most of the eyewitnesses who were to appear before the Commission participated in this re-enactment.[104]

By March 23 most of the lawyers had arrived in Dallas to conduct their field investigations. These investigations consisted mainly of taking depositions from witnesses whom the lawyers had selected after reading the investigative reports. In the depositions, each witness was sworn in and then examined by a lawyer.

The Hearings. While the staff was conducting its field investigation in Dallas, the "more important" eyewitnesses to the assassination testified at the Commission hearings. The Commission held a total of fourteen days of hearings in March; the most unusual hearing took place on March 4, when Mark Lane testified. Lane asked to be heard in an open hearing, and the Commission granted his request.[105] Ironically, this hearing took place on the day that the Ruby trial opened, and the Commission permitted Lane to give hearsay testimony concerning an alleged meeting that took place in Ruby's nightclub.[106]

Staff Changes. As the investigation progressed, it was necessary to alter the staff organization. Francis W. H. Adams, the senior lawyer in Area I, was unable to participate in the investigation, and the junior lawyer, Arlen Specter, had to manage this broad area singlehanded.[107] William Coleman also was unable to work full time for the Commission, and Stuart R. Pollak, a young Justice Department lawyer, was assigned to Coleman's area.[108] Because Ball and Belin were fully occupied with their investigation in Dallas, Eisenberg, who had been Redlich's assistant, was given the job of examining expert witnesses at Commission hearings.[109] John Hart Ely, a Supreme Court law clerk, was appointed to the staff and assigned to help Jenner and Liebeler develop Oswald's biography.[110]

The Staff's Image of the Commission. By the end of March it became apparent to the lawyers that there were actually two separate investigations, the Commission hearings and the staff investigation.[111] Opinions differ as to what the Commission actually did. Joseph Ball commented that the Commission "had no idea of what was happening, we did all the investigating, lined up the witnesses, solved the problems and wrote the Report."[112] Wesley Liebeler, when asked what the Commission did, replied, "In one word, 'Nothing.' "[113] Melvin Eisenberg compared the Commission to a corporation's board of directors, with Rankin as president and the staff members as the officers.[114] Howard Willens reflected the consensus of the staff when he said, "The commissioners were not in touch with the investigation at all times."[115] J. Lee Rankin, on the other hand, said that some of the younger lawyers "simply didn't understand how a government inquiry worked" and that the Commission, through its experience and collective wisdom, gave the investigation its direction and focus.[116]

In any case, there was little direct contact between the Commissioners and the staff lawyers, and to most of the lawyers "Warren was the Commission."[117]

April

The investigation continued in Dallas during the first two weeks of April. Almost one-half of all the depositions taken by the staff were taken in this period. During this time Ball, assisted by Goldberg, Belin, Stern, and Ely, tried to establish Oswald's movements from the time of the assassination until his arrest.[118] Hubert and Griffin investigated Oswald's death; and Liebeler and Jenner, by interviewing Oswald's acquaintances and relatives, tried to cast light on Oswald's motive.[119]

In Washington, Specter and Redlich were concerned with the problem emanating from the film of the assassination. Rifle tests had established that the murder weapon could not fire two bullets within the time period during which the film showed that both Kennedy and Connally were hit. Specter then advanced the hypothesis that both men were hit by the same bullet. To test this hypothesis, he arranged wound ballistics experiments and further analyses of the film.[120]

Hearings. The Commission held only seven days of hearings in April. Probably the most important witness to testify was Governor Connally. Connally testified, as will be more fully discussed later, that it was "inconceivable" that he was hit by the bullet that hit Kennedy. His testimony, and other evidence, cast considerable doubt on the single-bullet hypothesis.

May

The Deadline. At a staff meeting in early May, Rankin told the lawyers to "wrap up" their investigations and to submit their chapters by June 1.[121] The deadline for releasing the Report was June 30.[122]

Some teams, however, had not yet resolved important problems in their areas, and others had turned up new evidence that required further investigation. In addition, the FBI had not yet answered a number of questions that the staff had submitted.[123] In short, the investigation was nowhere near completion.

On May 24 Rankin, Redlich, and Specter went to Dallas to supervise an elaborate re-enactment of the assassination. A limousine with stand-ins for the President and Governor Connally took part in the simulation of the event. The main purpose of this reconstruction was to test the theory that both men were hit by a single bullet.[124]

The Commission held only four days of hearings in May. These meetings were mainly concerned with governmental processes.

Publishing. In late May, Warren announced that the supporting volumes of testimony and evidence would not be published.[125] The reason given was that it would be too expensive in view of the Commission's limited financing.[126] A number of lawyers believed, however, that the Commission was obliged to publish this material, and they protested the decision to Rankin. Rankin then called Senator Russell, who apparently did not know of Warren's decision.[127] The Congressional members of the Commission reportedly considered the expense justified, and the Commission agreed to publish what was to become twenty-six volumes of hearings and exhibits.[128]

June

Despite the June 1 deadline, only two lawyers had completed their draft chapters by the middle of June. Specter had submitted his chapter on the source of the shots by June 1, and Ball had turned in his chapter on the identification of the assassin the following week. Redlich, who had editorial responsibility for the chapters concerning the assassination, found Ball's chapter to be "inadequate," and over Ball's protests he undertook to rewrite it himself.[129]

The Commission reportedly was not apprised of the situation, and, as the date approached for releasing the Report, Willens and Redlich went over Rankin's head and told Warren that some of the lawyers still had not completed their investigations and that it was impossible for the Report to be completed by June 30. Warren then reportedly lost his temper and demanded that Willens close down the investigation immediately.[130] The deadline was, however, extended to July 15.[131]

Hearings. On June 5 Mrs. John F. Kennedy testified before the Chief Justice at her home. She was the last witness to testify on the assassination itself.

On June 7 the Chief Justice and Commissioner Ford went to Dallas to hear the testimony of Jack Ruby. Afterward Warren and Ford spent about two hours at the scene of the assassination.[132]

On June 17 the Commission announced that it had completed its hearings.[133] Ten days later it was announced that the Report would not be released until after the Republican National Convention, which was to begin on July 13.[134]

July

As the summer dragged on, most of the lawyers left Washington and continued working for the Commission only on a very limited part-time basis. All five senior lawyers—Adams, Coleman, Ball, Hubert, and Jenner, in that order—had returned to their private practices and made virtually no contribution to the writing of the final Report.[135] Of the junior lawyers, only

Liebeler, Griffin, and Slawson continued working for the Commission on a full-time basis.[136]

The major responsibility for writing the Report devolved on two men, Norman Redlich and Alfred Goldberg. Redlich, who worked up to eighteen hours a day, seven days a week, said on reflection, "It was very depressing; it seemed as if it would go on forever."[137] Goldberg told Warren that it was "impossible" to finish the Report by the July 15 deadline, and the deadline was extended to August 1.[138]

The Colloquium. Because there was strong disagreement among the staff on the use of psychological terminology to describe Oswald's actions, Rankin arranged for three psychiatrists to meet with staff and Commission members to discuss the problem. After a colloquium that lasted an entire day, the lawyers concluded that there was insufficient basis for drawing psychological conclusions about Oswald.[139]

On July 20 Liebeler submitted his chapter on Oswald's motives. Redlich and Rankin thought that it was "too psychological," and Goldberg was given the task of rewriting it.[140]

August

Throughout the month of August, Goldberg and Redlich continued writing and rewriting chapters. These were submitted first to Rankin and then to the individual Commissioners, after which they were sent back to the staff for additional rewriting. Some chapters were rewritten as many as twenty times by nearly as many hands. The problem of getting consensus seemed almost impossible, and bit by bit the August deadline was extended into September.[141]

Meanwhile, the pressures to publish the Report increased. Rankin reportedly received frequent calls from McGeorge Bundy of the White House staff,[142] and most of the Commissioners considered it was absolutely necessary for the Report to be released well before the Presidential election, lest the assassination become a political issue.[143]

September

On September 4 the galley proofs of the final draft were circulated among the Commission and staff for final comments. Two days later Wesley Liebeler submitted a twenty-six-page memorandum attacking the key chapter involving the identity of the assassin. The chapter had to be revised.[144]

The Final Hearing. On September 7 Commissioners Russell, Cooper, and Boggs went to Dallas to re-examine Marina Oswald. Under Senator Russell's rigorous questioning, she changed major aspects of her story and altered her previous testimony. More rewriting was thus necessitated.[145]

Finally, on September 24, the Report was submitted to President Johnson.[146]

At a farewell dinner the next day, the Chief Justice told the staff that its relationship to the government was analogous to "a lawyer-client relationship," thus suggesting that the lawyers' knowledge of the Commission and investigation was privileged information.[147]

On September 28, 1964, ten months after the Commission was created, the Warren Report was made public. Having completed its task, the Commission dissolved itself.[148]

PART ONE

_____

Political Truth

2

The Dominant Purpose

The purpose of the Commission was never fully stated in its Report. The executive order which created the Commission listed the "purposes" as examining evidence, conducting further investigations, evaluating the facts and circumstances, and reporting the findings to the President.[1] This order told what things the Commission was to do, but not *why* it was to do them. There is, however, an important distinction to be made between the function of the Commission, which was to ascertain the facts, and its ultimate purpose, which influenced the Commission's approach to its work, either consciously or unconsciously.

Chief Justice Warren gave only the formal purpose of the Commission when he stated, "The purpose of this Commission is, of course, eventually to make known to the President, and to the American public everything that has transpired before this Commission."[2] However, ascertaining the facts is not usually in itself a legitimate purpose for a government investigation. Warren himself had stated in the Supreme Court decision of *Watkins* v. *United States:* "No inquiry is an end in itself," and concluded that a Congressional investigation cannot "expose for the sake of exposure."[3] The Warren Commission was no doubt an extraordinary commission created in an extraordinary situation. The paramount purpose may well have been simply to make the truth known, but the question remains: Why?

The circumstances surrounding the Chief Justice's appointment to the Commission suggest the underlying purpose. Anthony Lewis, then *The New York Times* Supreme Court correspondent, reported that when Warren was first asked to serve on the Commission "he flatly said no." President Johnson then called Warren to the White House and spoke to him "about patriotism, about the new President's urgent need to settle the assassination rumors, about the special trust people in foreign lands would have in an investigation over which he presided." Warren thereupon agreed to serve on the Commission.[4] J. Lee Rankin confirmed this account and said that "Warren accepted, only with the greatest reluctance, because the President had made it plain to him that the nation's prestige was at stake."[5] These accounts clearly imply that one purpose of the Commission was to protect the national interest by settling "assassination rumors" and restoring American prestige abroad.

Other members of the Commission also conceived of the Commission's purpose in terms of the national interest. Allen Dulles said that an atmosphere of rumors and suspicion interferes with the functioning of the government, especially abroad, and one of the main tasks of the Commission was to dispel rumors.[6] John J. McCloy said that it was of paramount importance to "show the world that America is not a banana republic, where a government can be changed by conspiracy."[7] Senator John Sherman Cooper said that one of the Commission's most important purposes was "to lift the cloud of doubts that had been cast over American institutions."[8] Congressman Gerald Ford said that dispelling damaging rumors was a major concern of the Commission,[9] and most members of the Commission agreed.

There was thus a dualism in purpose. If the explicit purpose of the Commission was to ascertain and expose the facts, the implicit purpose was to protect the national interest by dispelling rumors.

These two purposes were compatible so long as the damaging

rumors were untrue. But what if a rumor damaging to the national interest proved to be true? The Commission's explicit purpose would dictate that the information be exposed regardless of the consequences, while the Commission's implicit purpose would dictate that the rumor be dispelled regardless of the fact that it was true. In a conflict of this sort, one of the Commission's purposes would emerge as dominant.

The Dilemma

The Commission was, in fact, faced with just such a conflict at its meeting on January 27. The subject of this meeting was the allegation that Oswald had been a paid informer of the FBI.[10]

Three days earlier Chief Justice Warren and J. Lee Rankin had met secretly with Texas Attorney General Waggoner Carr and Dallas District Attorney Henry Wade.[11] The Texas officials related a story alleging that Oswald had been working for the FBI as an informant since September 1962; that Oswald was on the FBI payroll at $200 a month on the day he was arrested; and that Oswald had been assigned an informant number, 179.[12] The source of the story seemed to be Alonzo Hudkins, a Houston newspaper reporter.[13]

Neither Carr nor Wade knew whether the story had any basis in fact, but Wade, a former FBI agent, had some reason to believe that there might have been a connection between Oswald and the FBI. Wade had apparently heard that Oswald's address book contained the telephone number and license-plate number of Dallas FBI agent James Hosty.[14] The Commission had received the list of names in Oswald's address book in a December 21, 1963, FBI report, but Agent Hosty's name had been omitted from that list by the FBI.[15] Wade also had heard that a government voucher for $200 was found in Oswald's possession.[16] In addition, a Western Union employee had claimed that Oswald was periodically telegraphed small sums of money. Also, Wade thought that Oswald's practice of setting up postalbox "covers" each time he moved—a practice Wade himself had used as an FBI agent—was an "ideal way" to handle undercover transactions.[17]

The Commission heard the full allegation at its January 27

meeting. Commissioner Ford observed: "The Commission itself had not grounds at the moment for rejecting or accepting [the rumor]. Members simply knew that the whole business was a most delicate and sensitive matter involving the nation's faith in its own institutions and one of the most respected federal agencies."[18]

J. Lee Rankin presented the problem to the Commission in no uncertain terms, stating:

> We do have a dirty rumor that is very bad for the Commission, the problem, and it is very damaging to the agencies that are involved in it and it must be wiped out insofar as it is possible to do so by this Commission.[19]

Quite clearly, the problem was the "dirty rumor." It was considered "dirty" not because it was known to be untrue but because it was known to be "damaging" to the government. The solution proposed was to "wipe out" the rumor. This would satisfy the implicit purpose of the Commission.

In this particular case, if the rumor was true, making the truth known might very well result in irreparable damage to the FBI and might heighten suspicions and speculations about the assassination itself. On the other hand, dispelling the rumor, even if it was true, would protect the national interest. Ford stated aptly that "the dilemma of the Commission" was how to approach this problem.[20]

Allen Dulles observed that the allegation was "a terribly hard thing to disprove," because written records were not always kept on undercover agents.[21] "If this be true," Hale Boggs responded, "[it] make[s] our problem utterly impossible, because you say this rumor can't be dissipated under any circumstances."[22] Again, the problem was seen as one of dispelling rumors.

Two Approaches

The Commission's approach to the problem had to be consistent with the national interest. Ford wrote that the Commission "would not be justified in plunging into the matter in some irresponsible manner that might jeopardize the effectiveness of an important agency's future operations."[23] This precept suggests a limiting case for the Commission's explicit purpose of making the truth known; would the Commission be justified in exposing information that would most certainly damage the future operations of an agency as important as the FBI?

J Lee Rankin proposed that the Commission permit the FBI to investigate the matter and "clear its own skirts" *before* the Commission investigated it. He suggested that he personally should speak to J. Edgar Hoover and

> tell him this problem and that he should have as much interest as the Commission in trying to put an end to any such speculations, not only by his statement . . . but also if it were possible to demonstrate by whatever records and materials they have that it just couldn't be true.[24]

Rankin said that he would also tell Hoover that the Commission would reserve the right to investigate the matter further "if it found it necessary, in order to satisfy the American people that this question of an undercover agent was out of the picture."[25]

Although apparently there was considerable support for this course of action, two Commissioners were not entirely satisfied by it. Senator John Sherman Cooper suggested an alternate approach in which the Commission would apprise Hoover of the facts but at the same time pursue its own independent investigation into the rumor. Cooper said that the Commission was "under a duty to see what Hudkins [the immediate source of the rumor] says about it, where he got that information."[26] Senator Richard Russell agreed, saying:

> Of course, we can get an affidavit from Mr. Hoover and put it in this record and go on and act on that, but if we didn't go any further than that, and we don't pursue it down to Hudkins or whoever it is, there still would be thousands of doubting Thomases who would believe this man was an FBI agent. . . .[27]

Thus two approaches were proposed. Rankin had suggested that Hoover be given the opportunity to disprove the rumor *be-*

fore the Commission investigated it; Senators Cooper and Russell had suggested that the Commission fully investigate the rumor while informing Hoover of its course of action.

The Chief Justice then concluded: "We must go into this thing from both ends, from the end of the rumor-mongers and from the end of the FBI, and if we come into a *cul de sac*—well, there we are, but we can report on it."[28]

Warren's concern for "security" was possibly reflected in a statement he made to newspaper reporters less than a week after the meeting. On February 4 a reporter asked him if the full report was to be made public; Warren replied: "Yes, there will come a time. But it might not be in your lifetime. I am not referring to anything especially but there may be some things that would involve security."[29]

Although the Commissioners' discussion of this problem gives some insight into the Commission's dominant purpose, conclusions cannot be based on what are, in fact, selected and possibly out-of-context statements. Certainly the purpose of dispelling rumors was evident in the dialogue, but great concern was also shown by Senators Russell and Cooper for investigating the matter fully. The dominant purpose becomes clear not so much from the dialogue as from the Commission's subsequent course of action.

The day following the Commission meeting, Rankin discussed the allegation with J. Edgar Hoover. Hoover immediately assured Rankin that "any and every informant" was known to FBI headquarters and that "Oswald had never been an informant of the FBI."[30]

On February 6 Hoover submitted an affidavit to the Commission, stating that a search of FBI records disclosed that Oswald "was never an informant of the FBI, was never assigned a symbol number in that capacity, and was never paid any amount of money in any regard."[31] A week later Hoover sent the Commission the affidavits of ten FBI agents who had had contact with the Oswald case; each denied that Oswald was ever developed or used as an informant.[32] On February 27 Special Agent Robert Gemberling submitted an affidavit explaining why the FBI, in its December 23 report,[33] had deleted the name of FBI agent James P. Hosty from the list of names in Oswald's address book. According to Hoover, this was done because "the circumstances under which Hosty's name, et cetera, appeared in Oswald's notebook were fully known to the FBI."[34]

On May 6 Alan H. Belmont, assistant director of the FBI, appeared before the Commission and offered to leave Oswald's file with the Commission. Rankin advised the Commission to retain the file, although the staff would *not* be permitted to examine it. This was ordered so that "the Commission could say in its report, 'We have seen everything that they [the FBI] have.' "[35] Warren, however, refused to accept the file, saying:

Well, the same people who would demand that we see everything of this kind would also demand that they be entitled to see it, and if it is a security matter we can't let them see it.[36]

The file thus was returned to the FBI, and, according to Samuel Stern, the lawyer in charge of the area, no independent check was ever made of it.[37]

Finally, on May 14, J. Edgar Hoover testified before the Commission and again categorically stated that Oswald had no connection with the FBI.[38]

Although this latter approach produced very authoritative denials of the allegation, it amounted to no more than taking the FBI's word that Oswald did not work for them. Certainly, if the rumor was true, it was possible that the FBI would have admitted it. But, since such an admission might severely shake "the nation's faith in its own institutions" and jeopardize the future effectiveness of the FBI, it was in the national interest, as well as the FBI's interest, to deny this allegation in any case. As Rankin pointed out to the Commission, the FBI had an interest in ending the rumor.

Despite the fact that the Commission had agreed to approach the allegation from "both ends" and to hear Alonzo Hudkins, the source of the story, Hudkins was never called as a witness or questioned by the staff. Instead, Leon Jaworski, Special Counsel for the State of Texas, was asked to speak informally to Hudkins about the rumor.[39] According to Rankin, Jaworski reported back to the Commission that "there was absolutely nothing to the story" and that it was "sheer speculation based on nothing but Hudkins' imagination."[40] It was thus decided it was unnecessary to call Hudkins as a witness or to pursue the matter further from that end.[41]

There was, however, other evidence that suggested that Hudkins *did* have an actual source for his information. On January 24, three days prior to the Commission meeting, the Secret Service submitted about thirty investigative reports to the Commission.[42] One of these reports, carrying the control number 767, contained a Secret Service interview with Hudkins. Hudkins told the Secret Service agents that his information came from Allan Sweatt, the chief of the criminal division of the Dallas sheriff's office.[43] According to Hudkins, Sweatt stated:

> Oswald was being paid two hundred dollars per month by the FBI in connection with their subversive investigation [and] that Oswald had informant number S-172.[44]

Allan Sweatt was never questioned by the Commission or its staff. The Commission apparently never attempted to ascertain Sweatt's source for the information or whether he had direct knowledge of the FBI's subversive investigation in Dallas.[45] In addition, no effort was made to clarify the nature of the FBI's subversive investigation or to determine whether there was any relationship between the Cuban exile groups which Oswald had been trying to infiltrate and the groups which interested the FBI.[46] Also, no check was made of the FBI files to see if number S-172 (or 179) possibly could have been assigned to Oswald.[47]

In short, no efforts were made by the Commission or its staff to investigate the rumor itself.

The Commission thus did exactly what it agreed *not* to do in its meeting; it relied entirely on the FBI to disprove the rumor.

The important question is not whether or not Oswald was employed by the FBI. Even if he had been an FBI informant—and no evidence developed to substantiate this possibility—this fact might not be particularly relevant to the assassination itself, although it might have explained Oswald's movements prior to the assassination. However, the important question is: How did the Commission choose to deal with a potentially damaging rumor?

Two courses of action were open to the Commission. It could have investigated the rumor itself and called as witnesses the persons known to be the immediate sources of the rumor. This approach quite probably would have exhausted the rumor, but it *might* have revealed information damaging to the national interest.

On the other hand, the Commission could have turned the whole matter over to the FBI.

This approach would not only have served to dispel the rumor, but would also have ensured that no damaging information would be revealed in the process unless the agency concerned itself chose to reveal it.

In the end, the Commission took the second approach. The entire matter was turned over to the FBI, to affirm or deny, and the Commission relied solely on the FBI's word in concluding that "there was absolutely no type of informant or undercover relationship" between Oswald and the FBI.

The way the Commission dealt with this problem cannot be explained simply in terms of its explicit purpose of making known to the President and the American public everything that went on before it. Nowhere, not even in the "Speculations and Rumors" appendix, does the Report mention the allegation that had so preoccupied the Commission. Nor does the information Carr and Wade furnished on January 24 appear anywhere in the Commission proceedings.[48] Furthermore, the Secret Service interview with Hudkins has been withheld even from the National Archives.[49] And details of the problem were kept secret even from some staff lawyers for a time.[50] Quite clearly, the Commission handled the problem in such a way that it would *not* be made known.

The Commission's treatment of this problem was, however, consistent with the purpose of dispelling damaging rumors. If the Commission had called Hudkins and Sweatt as witnesses and fully investigated the allegation, the result very well might have heightened doubts and suspicions. If the Commission had disclosed the information furnished by Wade, Carr, and the Secret Service reports, the disclosure most probably would have led to new rumors and speculations. The surest and safest way to dispel the rumor was *not* to investigate it, but to keep secret the allegations and publish only the affidavits of denial. The Commission's course of action in this case can thus be explained only in terms of the purpose of dispelling damaging rumors. The fact that the Commission chose this approach, despite its earlier rejection of it, indicates the pervasiveness of this purpose.

Furthermore, the extent to which the purpose of dispelling rumors dominated the investigation is of critical importance to an understanding of the Commission's workings and decisions.

3

The Vulnerability of Facts

By early February 1964 it became evident that it was possible for a lone gunman to have accomplished the assassination if and only if President Kennedy and Governor Connally were hit by the same bullet. "To say that they were hit by separate bullets," a Commission lawyer stated bluntly, "is synonymous with saying that there were two assassins."[1] This conclusion stemmed from an analysis of the movie film of the assassination.

A frame-by-frame analysis of the Zapruder film shows three distinct moments of reaction: frame no. 225 (President Kennedy raises his hands to his throat); frame no. 235 (Governor Connally slumps forward); and frame no. 313 (bullet strikes the President's head). By this analysis, only ten frames, or about one-half second (at the camera speed established by laboratory tests as 18.3 frames per second), elapsed between the time both men were first apparently wounded.

It is possible that both men had delayed reactions to the shots, but even in this case the maximum time between the first two shots could still be fixed. Since an oak tree's foliage obstructed the line of fire between film frames 166 and 207 (see map on

Texas School Book Depository

ASSASSIN'S POSITION

ROUTE OF MOTORCADE

OAK TREE

ELM STREET

166   FOLIAGE OF OAK TREE BLOCKS
ASSASSIN'S LINE OF SIGHT BETWEEN
FRAMES 166 AND 207

Elm Street map,
with Zapruder
film frame numbers

207   EARLIEST POINT PRESIDENT
COULD HAVE BEEN HIT

240   LAST POINT CONNALLY
COULD HAVE BEEN HIT

313   FATAL SHOT

ZAPRUDER'S POSITION ●

facing page), and other evidence shows that the President could not have been shot before film frame 166, the Commission concluded that the earliest point that the President could have been first hit was film frame 207.[2] Medical experts, including Connally's doctors, established with certainty, and the Commission agreed, that Connally was not in a position to be hit after film frame 240.[3] Thus the maximum time that could have elapsed between the times both men were first shot was 33 film frames or about 1.8 seconds.

However, it was also established that the minimum time in which the assassination weapon could be fired twice was 2.3 seconds (or 42 film frames).[4] This minimum figure was based on the length of time required to open and close the bolt of the rifle (and did not include the aiming time).[5]

Thus, according to the established facts, it was physically impossible for the assassination rifle to have been fired twice during the time period when the President and Governor Connally were first wounded. Either both men were hit by the same bullet, or there were two assassins.

The Autopsy Report

The answer to the crucial question of whether it was *possible* for both men to have been hit by the same bullet depended on the findings of the autopsy, conducted on the night of the assassination at the Bethesda Naval Hospital in Maryland. Quite simply, if the autopsy had found that the bullet which struck the President in the back had exited from the front of his body, then it was possible that the bullet continued on to hit Connally, who was seated in front of Kennedy. If, however, the autopsy revealed that the bullet had *not* exited from the front of the President's body, it was obviously impossible for both men to have been hit by the same bullet.

Although "certain preliminary draft notes" relating to the autopsy were subsequently destroyed,[6] the Commission published what purported to be the original "Autopsy Report" as an appendix to the Warren Report.[7] This autopsy report says:

The missile contused the strap muscle of the right side of the neck, damaged the trachea [windpipe] and made its exit through the anterior surface of the neck.[8]

The Commission's autopsy report clearly states that the bullet exited from the front of the President's neck, and thus it was possible for the same bullet to have hit Governor Connally. (The Warren Report explained that a previous theory that the bullet lodged in the President's strap muscles and later fell out onto his stretcher was disproved and rejected "during the autopsy").[9]

The Commission's autopsy report, however, differs substantially from earlier reports of the autopsy findings. On December 18, 1963, more than three weeks after the autopsy, the *Washington Post* reported that the autopsy had found that the bullet did *not* exit from the President's neck, and that the throat wound was caused by a fragment from a third shot which had hit the President's head.[10] Similar versions of the autopsy findings appeared in most of the major newspapers and medical journals.[11] *The New York Times*, citing a source familiar with the autopsy report, stated:

The first bullet made what was described as a small, neat wound in the back and penetrated two or three inches. . . .
The pathologists at Bethesda, the source said, concluded that the throat wound was caused by the emergence of a metal fragment or piece of bone resulting from the fatal shot in the head.[12]

If this version was in error, it was not immediately corrected. As late as January 26, 1964, *The New York Times* reported that investigators were satisfied that the first bullet hit the President in the back and that "that bullet lodged in his shoulder."[13]

Newspaper accounts are often inaccurate; the fact that this story was widely circulated does not necessarily mean that the original source was accurate. These newspaper accounts therefore cannot be accepted as evidence, but they do raise a question as to whether the autopsy report published in the Warren Report was in fact the *original* one.

The FBI Summary Report and the FBI Supplemental Report

There is one document, however, which casts considerably more light on this question: the FBI Summary Report. Immediately after the assassination, President Johnson ordered the FBI to conduct a complete investigation and report its findings to him.[14] In early December, J. Edgar Hoover submitted to President Johnson through the Attorney General a four-volume report summarizing the FBI's investigation.[15] On December 9 these volumes were submitted to the Commission; a fifth volume, subtitled "Supplemental Report," was sent to the Commission on January 13, 1964. Considered "of principal importance" by the Commission, the FBI Summary Report (with the supplement) was an authoritative and official summary of the facts as of January 13, 1964, before the Commission began its work.

With regard to the autopsy, the December 9 FBI Summary Report states:

> Medical examination of the President's body revealed that one of the bullets had entered just below his shoulder to the right of the spinal column at an angle of 45 to 60 degrees downward, that there was no point of exit, and that the bullet was not in the body.[16]

The FBI Summary Report thus says unequivocally that the bullet in question had not exited from the front of the President's body; it implies that the bullet had fallen out onto the President's stretcher while he was in the hospital in Dallas.[17]

The Warren Report thus directly contradicts the FBI Summary Report on the autopsy findings. The possibility of a clerical error or misinterpretation in the December 9 FBI Summary Report is diminished by the FBI Supplemental Report, dated January 13, which states:

> Medical examination of the President's body had revealed that the bullet which entered his back had penetrated to a distance of less than a finger length.[18]

"Medical examination of the President's body" can have referred only to the Bethesda autopsy of November 22; *before* the autopsy, the bullet hole was not discovered; and after the autopsy, there was no further medical examination.[19] The FBI Summary Report and the Supplemental Report thus say, in short, that the autopsy revealed that the bullet did *not* exit from the President's neck, and that it penetrated the President's back to the depth of only a few inches. How can such a contradiction on such an essential point be explained?

There can be no doubt that the autopsy findings were known to the FBI when it prepared the Summary Report. Two FBI agents were present at the autopsy.[20] The autopsy report was forwarded to the FBI.[21] Moreover, at the time the autopsy was performed, the FBI was the only agency charged with ascertaining all the facts of the assassination.

Arlen Specter, the Commission staff lawyer who developed the autopsy evidence, explained that the doctors were unable at first to find the bullet's path through the President's body. At this point, he said, both FBI agents "rushed out of the room" and telephoned the result to their Maryland field office. Meanwhile, according to Specter, the doctors found the path, but by the time the agents submitted their reports the FBI Summary Report had "gone to press."[22]

There are, however, a number of problems inherent in this explanation. First of all, there exists Secret Service testimony that one FBI agent remained in the room at all times.[23] Second, two Secret Service agents, who were also in the room throughout the autopsy, indicated in their testimony that no path was found through the body.[24] Third, the December 9 FBI Summary Report could not possibly have gone to press until at least eleven days after the autopsy of November 22.[25] Finally, Specter's story in no way explains why the FBI Supplemental Report (dated January 13) also states that the autopsy revealed that the bullet penetrated to a depth of less than a finger length.

The Dilemma

Clearly, the FBI Summary and Supplemental Reports and the Warren Report give diametrically opposed findings regarding the President's autopsy. This presents a dilemma. On one hand, if the FBI reports distorted such a basic fact of the assassination, doubt is cast on the accuracy of the FBI's *entire* investigation; indeed the Commission's investigation and conclusions were, in the final analysis, predicated on the accuracy of the FBI reports.

The second horn of the dilemma is even more painful, for, if the FBI's statements on the autopsy are accurate, then the autopsy findings must have been changed after January 13. This would mean that the document in the Warren Report which purports to be the original autopsy report is not.

This dilemma cannot be resolved in terms of what one considers to be "inconceivable." To some it would be "inconceivable" that the FBI would make a repeated error of this magnitude and import in its final report to the President; to others it would be inconceivable that the Warren Commission would substantially alter the basic facts. The answer may, however, be found in the evidence surrounding the autopsy.

The Evidence

Consistency with the evidence does not necessarily prove validity, but inconsistency *does* prove invalidity. The FBI Summary and Supplemental Reports and the Warren Report give diametrically opposed versions of the autopsy; both versions can be measured against the evidence to determine which is invalid.

The FBI Summary and Supplemental Reports claim that the autopsy revealed that: (1) the first bullet entered "just below [the President's] shoulder," (2) it penetrated "less than a finger length," and (3) "there was no point of exit." The Warren Report claims that the autopsy revealed that the first bullet: (1) entered the "rear of the neck," (2) passed completely through the neck, and (3) exited through the throat.[26] Each of these three points can be tested against the evidence.

1. Entrance. The decisive question here is: Was the entrance wound in the back above or below the "exit" wound in the throat? The Commission established that the bullet was travel-

ing downward and was undeflected.[27] The entrance wound therefore had to be *above* the exit wound, i.e., at or above "throat" level. But the FBI Summary Report states that the bullet entered "just below his shoulder . . . at an angle of 45 to 60 degrees downward."[28] If this were the case, this bullet could not have exited from the throat.

The Warren Report states that the bullet entered the "rear of the neck," a position which would permit the bullet to exit through the throat wound.[29] Commander James J. Humes, the Navy pathologist who had conducted the autopsy and signed the Commission's autopsy report, testified that the conclusion that the bullet had exited was based mainly on the fact that "the wound in the anterior portion of the neck [was] physically lower than the point of entrance posteriorly."[30] Humes supported his assertion with two schematic drawings of the President—profile and back—which show the purported point of entry in the back of the neck (Commission Exhibit 385, on page 72, is one of these drawings). Although the artist who made these drawings was not familiar with the autopsy itself or photographs of it—he had made the drawings solely on the basis of the verbal instructions of Commander Humes[31]—these schematic drawings were offered as evidence in lieu of the photographs and X-rays of the autopsy, which were "unavailable."[32]

Other evidence, however, indicated that the entrance wound was well below the point shown in the schematic drawings and, in fact, was *lower* than the throat wound. The face sheet of the autopsy report (from Commission Exhibit 397, see page 73; the letters A and B and the lines leading from them to the wounds have been added by me.—E.J.E.), which is not part of the official autopsy report itself, was prepared by Commander Humes *during* the autopsy.[33] The face sheet shows front and back diagrams of the President's body. On the front diagram (left) the throat wound (A) is just below the collar line; on the back diagram (right) the entrance wound (B) is much farther below the collar line. Thus, although Commander Humes testified in March that the entrance wound was above the throat wound, during the autopsy he marked the entrance wound below the throat wound.

It is possible that during the autopsy Commander Humes inaccurately marked the relative positions of the entrance

wound and the throat wound on the face sheet, but there is
further evidence that the entrance wound was well below the
collar line. Secret Service Agent Clinton Hill, who was called
into the autopsy examination for the express purpose of observing the position of the wounds, testified that he "saw an opening
in the back, about six inches below the neckline. . . ."[34] Secret
Service Agent Glen A. Bennett, who was in the car immediately
behind the Presidential limousine, stated that he saw a "shot hit
the President about four inches down from the right shoulder."[35] Two other Secret Service agents who were present at the
autopsy repeatedly described the wound as a "shoulder"
wound.[36]

Although this testimony is consistent with the FBI Summary
Report's description of an entrance wound "just below his
shoulder," and inconsistent with the Warren Report's description of a wound in the "rear of the neck," it is by no means
conclusive. Human observations are often inaccurate, and it is
possible that a coincidence of errors occurred.

However, there is more substantial evidence which fixes the
position of the entrance wound. The FBI Supplemental Report
includes photographs of the President's jacket and shirt which
graphically show the entrance holes (FBI Exhibits 59 and 60,
pages 76 and 77). These photographs, which were omitted from
the Warren Report and the twenty-six volumes of supporting
evidence,[37] show that the bullet hole in the jacket is 5 and 3/8
inches below the collar and that the bullet hole in the shirt is 5
and 3/4 inches below the collar.[38] This position virtually coin-
cides with the position shown in the face sheet of the autopsy
report and with the FBI's description of the wound. It is, however, obviously inconsistent with the position of the entrance
wound in the Commission's schematic drawings and with the
wound described in the Commission's autopsy report.

It is possible that President Kennedy's jacket was in some
manner raised more than six inches, so that the hole in it coincided with the purported entrance wound in the "back of the
neck." (The Zapruder film, however, gives no indication of this.)
It was, however, virtually impossible for the hole in the shirt
(Exhibit 60) to have coincided with an entrance wound in the
"back of the neck" (see Commission Exhibit 385, page 72). This
could only have happened under either of the following two

COMMISSION EXHIBIT 385

conditions: (1) the entire shirt, collar included, was raised six inches; or (2) a portion of the shirt was raised over the collar line (and thus doubled over). Obviously a *closed* shirt collar could not have been raised six inches on the neck, and therefore, for the shirt hole to have coincided with the purported entrance wound (which was above the collar line), the shirt would have to have been doubled-up over the collar. Since only one bullet hole was found in the back of the shirt, this could not have been the case.[39] Thus, according to the FBI photograph of the President's shirt, the bullet entrance hole in the President's back was *lower* than the throat wound. This is clearly inconsistent with the statement in the Commission's autopsy report.

2. Path. Did the bullet pass completely through the President's neck? The FBI Summary Report says that the autopsy revealed that it did *not*; the Warren Report claimed that the autopsy revealed that it did. It is a *sine qua non* law of forensic pathology that if a bullet passes through a body it must leave a discernible path.[40] Dr. Milton Helpern, Chief Medical Examiner of New York City and one of the foremost experts on forensic pathology, explained that "there is no such thing as a rifle bullet's passing through a neck without leaving a path."[41] Dr. Helpern estimated that a 6.5-mm. bullet passing through the President's neck would leave a track approximately 1/4 inch in diameter.[42] Evidence indicates that no such track was found.

Two Secret Service agents were present at President Kennedy's autopsy. Agent Roy Kellerman testified:

> There were three gentlemen who performed this autopsy. A Colonel Finck—during the examination of the President, from the hole that was in his shoulder, and with a probe, and we were standing right alongside of him, he is probing inside the shoulder with his instrument and I said "Colonel, where did it go?" He said, "There are no lanes for an outlet of this entry in this man's shoulder."[43]

Lieutenant Colonel Pierre A. Finck is a nationally known expert on forensic pathology and wound ballistics. It is extremely unlikely that he would make such a definite statement if there could possibly have been a "lane for an outlet."[44]

Agent William Greer also testified that the autopsy doctors could not find a path for the bullet. One doctor told Greer that the bullet could very well have fallen out through the entrance wound if heart massage had been applied by the Dallas doctors.[45] When asked if "anything [was] said about any channel being present in the body for the bullet to have gone on through . . ." Greer replied:

No, sir; I hadn't heard anything like that, any trace of it going on through.[46]

Commander Humes testified that the autopsy doctors were unable "to take probes and have them satisfactorily fall through any path at this point."[47] Humes testified that he had not discerned a path for the bullet but had *deduced* its path from the entrance and the assumed exit wound, and from a slight bruise on the right lung.[48] Thus the autopsy surgeons were unable to find a path for the bullet.

Although the failure to find a path is consistent with the FBI Supplemental Report's statement that the bullet "penetrated to a distance of less than a finger length," it is inconsistent with the Warren Report's statement that the bullet passed through the President's body.

3. Exit Wound. The FBI Supplemental Report states that the autopsy revealed that the bullet did not exit from the President's body; and it implies that the throat wound was caused by a "projectile" from a third bullet that had hit the President's head.[49] The Warren Report states that the autopsy revealed that the bullet exited through the throat wound.

The throat wound, to be sure, was not seen by the autopsy surgeons because a tracheostomy operation, performed in Dallas immediately after the shooting, had obliterated the outlines of the wound. Only a few Dallas doctors actually observed the wound.[50] Dr. Malcolm Perry, who performed the tracheostomy, described the wound as a small puncture wound approximately 5 millimeters in diameter.[51] The bullet, however, was 6.55 millimeters in diameter; and the relatively small size of the wound suggested that it was caused by a fragment rather than a whole bullet.[52]

VIEW OF THE BACK OF PRESIDENT KENNEDY'S
SUIT COAT SHOWING BULLET ENTRANCE HOLE.

EXHIBIT
59

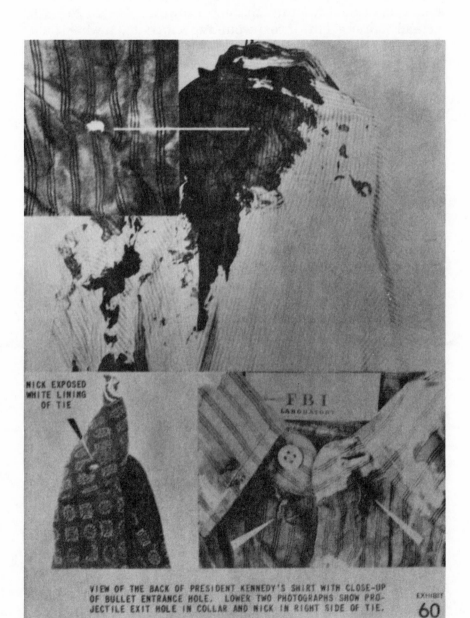

NICK EXPOSED WHITE LINING OF TIE

FBI LABORATORY

VIEW OF THE BACK OF PRESIDENT KENNEDY'S SHIRT WITH CLOSE-UP OF BULLET ENTRANCE HOLE. LOWER TWO PHOTOGRAPHS SHOW PROJECTILE EXIT HOLE IN COLLAR AND NICK IN RIGHT SIDE OF TIE.

EXHIBIT
60

The Commission's version of the autopsy held that a *whole* bullet had exited from the throat.[53] However, the doctors who actually observed the throat wound specified that a whole bullet could have exited through the throat wound only under certain conditions. Dr. Ronald Jones testified that he thought that such a small throat wound could have been caused by a whole bullet only if it was traveling at an extremely low velocity, "to the point that you might think that this bullet barely made it through the soft tissues. . . ."[54] This would present a problem: a nearly spent bullet most probably could not have continued on to cause all Governor Connally's three wounds, and therefore it could not have been found on Connally's stretcher. Nor, if the bullet exited from President Kennedy's throat, was it probable that it was found on his stretcher. Yet a nearly whole bullet was found on one of the two stretchers in the Dallas hospital. It is possible that the bullet found on the stretcher came from the second shot, but this would necessarily mean that, if the first bullet to strike the President exited from his throat, it escaped the limousine and was never found. Thus, although it is possible that the throat wound was an exit wound for a whole bullet, the probability of this is severely diminished by other circumstances.

Furthermore, if accurate, the testimony of Secret Service Agent Roy Kellerman makes it extremely doubtful that the throat wound was caused by the first bullet to strike the President. Kellerman, who was in the front seat of the President's limousine, testified that he distinctly heard the President say, "My God, I am hit," *after* the first shot.[55] Since the projectile that caused the throat wound also punctured the windpipe, it is medically highly improbable that the President could speak *after* he received the throat wound.[56] This fact would be consistent with the FBI's version of the autopsy, which implies that the throat wound was caused by a fragment from a later bullet, but inconsistent with the Commission's version of the autopsy, which holds that the first bullet to hit the President exited from his throat.

Conclusion. The Warren Report and the FBI Summary and Supplemental Reports give diametrically opposed versions of the autopsy findings on the crucial question of whether or not the first bullet to hit the President exited from his throat. The Commission published an autopsy report that said it did; the FBI said that the autopsy revealed that the bullet "penetrated to a distance of less than a finger length" and did *not* exit from the front of the body. One of these documents changed a central fact of the assassination.

At the very least, the Commission failed to resolve an important contradiction. Although the Commission sent a questionnaire to the FBI which asked the FBI to explain other points in the FBI Summary and Supplemental Reports, no questions were asked about the FBI's version of the autopsy.[57] If the FBI Summary and Supplemental Reports were inaccurate, it was incumbent upon the Commission to explain how an error of this magnitude could have occurred.

The evidence, however, indicates that the FBI reports are not erroneous. The photograph of the President's shirt is in itself cogent evidence that the bullet entered the President's body below the collar line, which is consistent with the FBI Summary Report's description of a wound "just below his shoulder." It is inconsistent, however, with the Commission's description of a wound in "the rear of the neck." If a bullet fired from above the President entered six inches *below* the collar line and was undeflected, it is inconceivable that it exited through the throat. The fact that the autopsy surgeons were not able to find a path for the bullet is further evidence that the bullet did not pass completely through the President's body. And the evidence surrounding the exit wound, although not conclusive, strongly indicates that it was caused by a fragment from a subsequent bullet. If the FBI reports are accurate, as all the evidence indicates they are, then a central aspect of the autopsy was changed more than two months after the autopsy examination, and the autopsy report published in the Warren Report is not the original one. If this is in fact the case, the significance of this alteration of facts goes far beyond merely indicating that it was not physically possible for a lone assassin to have accomplished the assassination. It indicates that the conclusions of the Warren Report must be viewed as expressions of political truth.

PART TWO

The Investigation

4

The Limits of the Investigation

The Problem

The critical problem in government investigations is inherent in the evaluation, not the accumulation, of data. The fact that the government can amass a virtually unlimited amount of information on any given subject only intensifies the problem. Each increment of data requires a proportionate increment of man-hours of reasoned judgment for evaluation. However, reasoned judgment is a limited commodity. This tends to be especially true in a government inquiry, because those men with sufficient authority to sit in judgment are almost invariably men occupied by other important responsibilities. The more important the inquiry, the more responsible the judges must be, and thus the more limited their available time. In a high-level inquiry the inevitable gap between the almost unlimited data and the extremely limited amount of evaluation time can be bridged only by a staff. The staff's function is to organize the data, sorting out the important from the unimportant facts, so that the data can be evaluated by the judges in the limited time available.

The Warren Commission probably represents an extreme example of this problem. The seven members of the Commission were all busy as well as eminent men whose time was severely limited by other pressing responsibilities. For example, Chief Justice Earl Warren had agreed to serve on the Commission only on the condition that it would not interfere with his work on the Court.[1] And the Supreme Court is one of the most time-consuming jobs in government; every brief must be read by each justice, and none of this work can be delegated. Thus, Warren could devote to Commission work only the time left after he had attended to his court duties. The other members, possibly to a lesser degree, had the same problem.

The amount of data the Commission received was truly prodigious; twenty-eight government agencies furnished more than three hundred cubic feet of paper. The FBI alone sent the Commission twenty-five thousand reports, which were mostly unindexed, unsummarized, and uncollated.[2] Quite obviously this mass of data had to be reduced to manageable proportions before the Commission could evaluate it.

The task of organizing and structuring the data was delegated to the legal staff. The Report stated:

As these investigative reports were received, the staff began analyzing and summarizing them. The members of the legal staff, divided into teams, proceeded to organize the facts revealed by these investigations, determine the issues, sort out the unresolved problems, and recommend additional investigation by the Commission.[3]

The staff not only organized the data for the Commission, it also was given the job of verifying the material and filling in the gaps. J. Lee Rankin, the General Counsel, said, "The lawyers *were* the independent investigators."[4] The lawyers took testimony from 418 witnesses, staged reconstructions, developed expert testimony, made inquiries to federal agencies about inconsistencies in their reports, and, in short, conducted the basic investigation and critical reassessment of the evidence for the Commission.

The Threshold Question

The threshold question for the Commission was: Was there more than one assassin? If Oswald acted alone, the investigation had no more to do than substantiate the case against him and explore his life history for possible motives. If, however, more than one person was involved in the assassination, the nature and scope of the investigation would have to be radically changed; new evidence and new hypotheses would have to be sought, new suspects found, new indictments rendered. Once across the threshold, the investigation would enter a new dimension of uncertainty; no one could know where it would lead, when it would end, or what would be its ramifications.

Was the investigation exhaustive not only in exploring Oswald's life history but also in searching for evidence of a second assassin? This question takes on crucial importance in light of the Zapruder film of the assassination and the FBI Summary and Supplemental Reports. It will be recalled that the film showed that President Kennedy and Governor Connally were hit almost simultaneously, and it was later established that the murder weapon could not be fired twice within this time period. The FBI reports precluded the possibility that both men were hit by the same bullet. There was thus a *prima facie* case of two assassins.

If there had been other evidence that precluded the possibility of a second assassin—for example, if all the bullets had been ballistically matched to the murder weapon—the Commission could reasonably have assumed that somehow the analysis of the film was fallacious. However, although the evidence identified Oswald as one assassin, it did not rule out the possibility of a second assassin. One bullet, which possibly was the fatal bullet, was too fragmented to be matched to Oswald's rifle by means of ballistics.[5] Thus the possibility of a second rifle existed. One identifiable but unidentified palm print was found on the "sniper's nest,"[6] and thus the possibility of an accomplice remained open. The fact that Oswald was able to escape from the murder scene suggested that a second assassin could also have escaped undetected.[7]

Recognizing the difficulty of proving a negative statement to a certainty, the Commission reasoned that if a conspiracy had existed some evidence of it doubtless would have come to the attention of the federal investigative agencies.[8] Since no such evidence had come to light, the Commission concluded explicitly "on the basis of evidence before the Commission" that "Oswald acted alone."[9]

This argument is compelling only if all pertinent evidence found by the federal agencies was, in fact, brought before the Commission. This, however, was not the case. For example, there was eyewitness evidence of a possible second assassin— evidence that never reached the Commission, despite the fact that it was submitted by the FBI.

The Neglected Eyewitness

On December 4, 1963, less than two weeks after the assassination, two FBI agents interviewed Mrs. Eric Walther, an eyewitness. She told them that she was standing across the street from the Texas Book Depository immediately before the assassination and that she saw a man with a rifle in an upper-story window of the building. She stated:

> In his hands, this man was holding a rifle with the barrel pointed downward, and the man was looking south on Houston Street. The man was wearing a white shirt and had blond or light hair.

The FBI report continued:

> The rifle had a short barrel and seemed large around the stock or end of the rifle. Her impression was that the gun was a machine gun. She noticed nothing like a telescopic sight on the rifle or a leather strap or a sling on the rifle. She said she knows nothing about rifles or guns of any type, but she thought the rifle was different from any she had ever seen. This man was standing in or about the middle of the window. In the same window, to the left of this man, she could see a portion of another man standing by the side of this man with a rifle. The other man was standing erect and his head was above the open portion of the window. As

the window was very dirty, she could not see the head of the second man. She is positive that the window is not as high as the sixth floor. This second man was apparently wearing a brown suit coat, and the only thing she could see was the right side of the man, from about the waist to the shoulders. Almost immediately after noticing this man with the rifle and the other man standing beside him, someone in the crowd said "Here they come. . . ."[10]

Seconds later the Presidential motorcade passed Mrs. Walther, and she heard shots.[11]

What happened to Mrs. Walther's account? On December 5 FBI Report DL 89-43, containing Mrs. Walther's statement, was filed in Dallas.[12] It was submitted to the Commission on December 10 and became part of "Commission Document No. 7."[13] It was, however, never brought to the attention of the Commission. Mrs. Walther was not called as a witness. She was never questioned by the staff lawyers, and no requests were made for further FBI investigation of her statement.[14] In short, Mrs. Walther's account was never evaluated.

In view of the mass of investigative reports confronting the staff, it would be reasonable to expect that accounts containing major contradictions might be disregarded without further investigation. Mrs. Walther's account, however, contained no such contradictions. The fact that Mrs. Walther thought that the rifleman was on the fifth rather than on the sixth floor was a common mistake among witnesses.[15] The mistake stemmed from the fact that there were no windows on the ground floor of the book depository, and thus witnesses counting upward tended to mistake the sixth-floor window for the fifth-floor window.[16] Mrs. Walther's description of other details, such as the window and the rifleman's clothes, hair, and position, was consistent with the descriptions given by all other witnesses who saw a rifleman prior to the assassination.[17]

There was another witness who partially corroborated Mrs. Walther's statement—Arnold Rowland. Rowland, the only witness to identify the rifle correctly (as a rifle equipped with a telescopic sight) *before* it was found, testified that he had seen a rifleman in a sixth-floor window and that he had also seen a second person on the same floor.[18] The Commission rejected the latter part of Rowland's testimony partly because of "the lack of probative corroboration."[19]

If the staff had questioned Mrs. Walther it might have found that her statement was inaccurately transcribed by the FBI agents, that her eyesight was poor, or that she had an overactive imagination. On the other hand, it might have found that she knew further details to corroborate her story. The point is that, without having questioned Mrs. Walther, the Commission had no basis whatsoever for evaluating her eyewitness statement that a second man was standing next to the assassin. Yet, since the Commission stated categorically that none of the witnesses "testified to seeing more than one person in the window,"[20] quite obviously it failed to take Mrs. Walther's statement into account. A key question to understanding the workings of the Commission is: Why?

A Thorough and Massive Examination

Many critics of the Commission contend that the Commission controlled the investigation for its own purposes, that it carefully and purposefully selected witnesses who supported its preconceived findings and called no witnesses whose testimony might damage its case.

Such a view has the appeal of simplicity, but there is no evidence that the Commission, or even J. Lee Rankin, exerted detailed control over the investigation. The working papers of the staff show that they were free to call any witnesses they chose, and approval from Rankin was merely a formality.[21] Of the more than four hundred requests for witnesses whom the lawyers wished to interview, not one request was vetoed or denied.[22] All the lawyers interviewed emphatically agreed that the Commission played no part in the selection of their witnesses. Witnesses were selected from more than thirty thousand separate investigative reports, and there is no reason to believe that the Commission had the time or inclination to attempt to control this process. Thus there is no basis in fact for a conspiracy theory as to why certain witnesses were called and others were not.

The reason Mrs. Walther was never questioned by the Commission or staff, though less diabolical, is more revealing of the true nature of the investigation. She was not called, not because the Commission feared or suppressed her statement, but most probably because the staff overlooked it. If it is difficult to accept this explanation, that is only because of the common misconception that the Warren Commission's investigation was the most massive and thorough in history, and that no stone was left unturned in the quest for truth. This picture, painted so effusively by the mass media immediately following the release of the Warren Report,[23] was based not on analysis of the investigation but on faith in the individual members of the Commission.[24] It prevailed most probably because people wanted to believe that the investigation was exhaustive and thus that the doubts and uncertainties had been settled once and for all.

Rather than being "exhaustive," however, the Commission's investigation was actually an extremely superficial investigation limited in terms of both time and manpower, and consequently limited to the more prominent evidence. The limitations of the investigation can best be understood through an examination of its mechanics.

The Mechanics of the Investigation

It will be recalled that the legal staff was divided into six panels of lawyers; each panel consisted of a "senior" and "junior" lawyer; and each panel was assigned a specific area to investigate.

Only the first two panels, however, were directly concerned with the assassination itself. Panel I was assigned the task of establishing the basic facts of the assassination; its senior lawyer was Francis W. H. Adams, a former New York City police commissioner, and its junior lawyer was Arlen Specter, a young assistant district attorney from Philadelphia. Panel II was assigned the task of identifying the assassin; both its senior lawyer, Joseph Ball, and its junior lawyer, David Belin, had had extensive trial experience.

The four other panels were concerned with peripheral areas. Panel III interviewed Oswald's relatives and acquaintances, from his birth to his death, and attempted to reconstruct his life history. Panel IV investigated Oswald's movements outside the United States, and possible previous conspiratorial relationships involving Oswald. Panel V was concerned with Oswald's death and the actions of Jack Ruby. And Panel VI was assigned the area of "Presidential protection."

None of these peripheral panels would necessarily touch on the threshold question of a second assassin. Interviews with Oswald's acquaintances would cast light on the assassination itself only if those interviewed had known of the assassination in advance and were willing to admit it. As can be expected, however, none of the witnesses admitted any prior knowledge of the assassination. Thus, if the threshold question was to be answered, it would have to be answered by the first two panels.

The first limitation on the investigation was time. There was a June 1, 1964, deadline for the lawyers to make their investigation, interview witnesses, and submit their draft chapters.[25] The start of the investigation, however, was delayed until March 14 by the Ruby trial.[26] Thus only ten weeks actually remained for the investigation to be held.

The second limitation was manpower. Francis Adams, the senior lawyer assigned the task of ascertaining the basic facts, came to Washington only "a few days" during the entire investigation.[27] Rankin seriously considered asking for Adams' formal resignation, but as such an action might be misinterpreted as a sign of dissension among the staff, he decided to "leave Adams' name on the report."[28] Adams said that although he had a different concept of the investigation—he thought the FBI Summary and Supplemental Reports should have been verified immediately, so that the basic facts of the assassination could have been made public as soon as possible—the reason he left the Commission was that his law firm needed his services.[29] Whatever the reasons for Adams' *de facto* resignation, the full work load of Panel I devolved on Arlen Specter.

The fact that the lawyers were working as part-time consultants further complicated the problem. Joseph Ball, the senior lawyer on Panel II, was also a senior partner in a large California law firm, and he found it necessary to "commute" back and forth from California almost weekly.[30] Administrative assistant Howard Willens said, "The lawyers would fly back to Los Angeles or Des Moines between every assignment. That was no way to run an investigation. What we needed was forty law drones, fresh out of law school, not a handful of high-priced consultants."[31]

Area I: The Basic Facts

Instead of being handled by forty full-time lawyers, the entire task of ascertaining the basic facts of the assassination fell upon one lawyer—Arlen Specter. Specter had the responsibility for determining the source of the shots, the number of assassins, the exact manner in which the President and Governor Connally were shot, and the sequence of events[32]—in short, all the facts of the assassination.

Ascertaining facts is a time-consuming and arduous process. It is doubtful whether any one lawyer—or even any ten lawyers —could have established with precision in a ten-week period every fact involved in the assassination. Quite obviously, Specter had to be selective. He himself recognized this, commenting that he had to allocate most of his time to a limited number of major problems.[33]

Whereas a positive premise can be proved by establishing only the major facts, a negative premise can be proved only be establishing *all* the relevant facts, even the insignificant ones, and testing all the possibilities. Specter was faced with just such a negative premise: to prove that Oswald had had no assistance. The way in which he handled this problem indicates the extent to which the threshold question was approached.

Specter began his field investigation on March 16, 1964, with a specific assignment from the Chief Justice. Warren told Specter that it was of the utmost importance "to clear up the confusion" over Kennedy's throat wound.[34] One troublesome rumor was that the doctors in Dallas had identified the throat wound as an *entry* wound, and this suggested that Kennedy had been shot from the front. Specter asked when he should leave for Dallas, and Warren replied, "I'd hoped you could catch the evening plane tonight."[35]

Specter departed for Dallas that evening, and during the next eight days he interviewed, both "off-" and "on-the-record," twenty-eight doctors and other medical personnel at Parkland

Hospital.[36] With one minor exception, these interviews comprised Specter's entire field investigation of "the basic facts of the assassination."[37]

Specter resolved the problem of the throat wound. All the doctors who saw the wound agreed that it could have been either an entry or an exit wound. Specter traced the rumor that it was an entrance wound to an answer Dr. Malcolm Perry had made to a hypothetical question. Dr. Perry admitted to Specter that he had no basis for telling whether it was an entrance or exit wound, and he testified that he had only said that it *could* have been an entrance wound.[38] Specter thus accomplished his mission and returned to Washington.

Quite obviously, if a lawyer was required to spend about two-thirds of his entire field investigation on a single problem, as Specter had to do, other problems had to be investigated with less thoroughness. Specter apparently preferred to allocate his limited time to problems that could be resolved instead of to problems that seemed unresolvable. This meant that a number of the more difficult problems were treated superficially. For example, the very important problem of where "bullet 399" was found was never resolved.

The Stretcher Bullet. Bullet 399 is a nearly intact bullet that ballistically was matched to the murder weapon. It was found on a stretcher at Parkland Hospital and turned over to the Secret Service. Although the question of whether it was found on President Kennedy's or Governor Connally's stretcher may have seemed insignificant at the time, it later assumed vital importance. If the bullet had come from Kennedy's stretcher it could not have passed through his body, and therefore Connally could only have been struck by a separate bullet; thus the inescapable possibility of a second assassin was raised. On the other hand, if the bullet had come from Connally's stretcher, it would be consistent with the theory that both men were hit by the same bullet.

The question of where bullet 399 was found first arose at the March 16 Commission hearing, while Specter was questioning Commander James Humes, the autopsy surgeon. Allen Dulles was apparently under the impression that the bullet had been found on Kennedy's stretcher—a reasonable assumption in the light of the FBI Summary Report and Secret Service testimony.[39] Dulles asked if there had been further evidence on this question, and Specter replied:

There has been other evidence, Mr. Dulles. If I may say at this point, we shall produce later, subject to sequential proof, evidence that the stretcher on which the bullet was found was the stretcher of Governor Connally.[40]

Specter, however, was being less than exact in his statement to Dulles. At this time Specter had not yet gone to Dallas, and all the FBI and Secret Service reports indicated that the bullet had *not* been found on Connally's stretcher.[41] Specter's assertion was apparently based not on the evidence, but on his expectation of what the evidence would show. Dulles then asked what happened to the first bullet that had hit Kennedy, and Specter replied, "That is the subject of some theories I am about to get into."[42]

Specter then developed the hypothesis that both men were wounded with the same bullet (bullet 399) and that therefore the bullet had been found on Connally's stretcher.[43]

Four days *after* Specter told the Commission that "the evidence will show that it was from Governor Connally's stretcher that the bullet was found," he went to Dallas and questioned the witness who had actually found the bullet, Darrell Tomlinson.[44] Tomlinson, an engineer who was employed by the hospital, said that he thought that the bullet had *not* come from the stretcher identified as Connally's.[45] Despite a number of confusing questions put to him by Specter,[46] Tomlinson maintained that, although he was not "positively sure," he believed that the bullet had come from the stretcher parked in front of Connally's in the emergency room.[47] Thus Tomlinson provided evidence that contradicted the hypothesis Specter was committed to proving.

Specter said that he had "deductively proved" that the bullet had come from Connally's stretcher by precluding the possibility that the other stretcher was Kennedy's.[48] Two reasons were given for eliminating Kennedy's stretcher as the source of the bullet. First, Kennedy's stretcher was wheeled into "trauma room number 2" immediately after the body was removed from it. Second, two nurses said that the sheets were removed from

Kennedy's stretcher; whereas Tomlinson claimed that there was a sheet on the foot of the stretcher from which the bullet had fallen.[49] Both these reasons were, however, extremely tenuous grounds for precluding Kennedy's stretcher.

The fact that Kennedy's stretcher was moved into trauma room number 2, which connected with the corridor in which the bullet was found, in no way precluded the possibility that the stretcher was later wheeled into this corridor. Since all stretchers were eventually returned to this area to be remade, the key question was: Was Kennedy's stretcher returned before or after the bullet was found? This question was never answered.[50]

The fact that two nurses recollected, four months after the event, that all the sheets were removed from Kennedy's stretcher hardly eliminated the stretcher as the source of the bullet. Also, Tomlinson's memory of a sheet on the foot of the stretcher could be inaccurate, or it was possible that, since the stretcher was parked near the linen hamper, a sheet could have been subsequently dropped on the stretcher.[51] Thus there was no credible reason for precluding the possibility that bullet 399 had come from Kennedy's stretcher.

There was, however, very definite evidence that precluded the possibility that bullet 399 had come from Connally's stretcher. Lieutenant Colonel Pierre A. Finck, the expert on forensic medicine, was asked if bullet 399 could have caused Connally's wrist wound. He replied flatly, "No, for the reason that there are too many fragments described in the wrist."[52] Since the Commission had established that all Connally's wrist and chest wounds had been caused by a single bullet, Colonel Finck's testimony excluded the possibility that bullet 399 had wounded Connally.[53] Therefore bullet 399 could not have passed through Connally and been found on his stretcher.

Colonel Finck's testimony on this point, which was fully supported by the other doctors,[54] cannot be dismissed merely because it collided with the hypothesis that bullet 399 was found on Connally's stretcher. Since Finck's categorical statement that this bullet could not have caused Connally's wrist wound was never challenged, disputed, or corrected, it can only be concluded from the evidence that bullet 399 did not come from Connally's stretcher.

The investigation of the stretcher bullet was by no means exhaustive. Two major witnesses were never questioned. After Tomlinson noticed the bullet, he called over the hospital's security director, O. P. Wright, who then picked up the bullet and turned it over to a Secret Service agent.[55] Wright very well might have been able to corroborate Tomlinson's story or to identify the stretcher that the bullet had come from, but he was never asked. Another witness who was never questioned was David Sanders, the orderly who wheeled Kennedy's stretcher out of the trauma room.[56] Sanders possibly could have answered the question of when Kennedy's stretcher arrived in the area in which the bullet was found.

An investigation in which expert testimony was ignored, two out of the three major witnesses were never questioned, and the working hypothesis was maintained despite the development of contradictory evidence can only be considered superficial. The case of the stretcher bullet illustrates the limits of the investigation; in ten days, or even in ten weeks, a single lawyer could not exhaust all the facts and possibilities in such a broad area as the "basic facts of the assassination." Arlen Specter spent only about ten days on his investigation in Dallas; quite obviously, he had to concentrate on the major problems and neglect some of the more minor ones.[57]

Specter said that he planned his investigation so that he could submit his chapter by the June 1 deadline, and he was, in fact, the only lawyer to meet this deadline.[58] As new evidence continued to develop after June 1, the premature termination of the investigation created a problem.

The Fourth Shot? At the time of the assassination a bystander, James Tague, was wounded by a minute fragment.[59] Although it is possible that this fragment came from one of the three established shots, it is also possible, especially in view of the distance involved, that the fragment came from a fourth shot. A fourth shot would not in itself indicate that a second assassin was at work—Oswald had sufficient time to fire a fourth shot after the fatal one—but it would cast new light on such problems as Connally's wrist wound, the dent in the chrome of the Presidential car, and the sequence of events. It would also raise a question as to why only three cartridge cases were found in the Texas Book

Depository. In any case, the fourth hit on the curb was a basic fact of the assassination, and the way in which it was treated further illustrates the nature of the investigation.

Immediately after the assassination a number of witnesses reported that a bullet had struck the pavement and a bystander had been slightly wounded by the ricochet.[60] On January 11 these reports were submitted to the Commission by the Texas Attorney General and, in the parceling out of the investigative reports, these reports were sent to Specter's panel.[61]

In February, Specter apparently asked the Secret Service field office in Dallas to investigate the matter. The special agent in charge, Forrest Sorrels, reported that no bullet mark could be found on the pavement, and he added, "I did not see how it could have been possible for any fragment of any of the three bullets that were fired to have hit this concrete slab."[62] No further effort was made at the time to find the person who was hit by a fragment or to locate the bullet mark.

There was, however, a photograph of the bullet mark which failed to reach Specter's attention because of the "division of labor." Tom Dillard, a Dallas newspaper reporter, reported to the FBI that he had taken a photograph of the bullet mark. The FBI report of the Dillard interview was passed on to Ball's panel because it dealt primarily with the identification of the assassin.[63] Although Ball questioned Dillard, he apparently didn't realize the relevance of the Dillard photograph, and thus the information did not reach Specter's panel until after Specter had finished his investigation.[64]

In July the Dillard photograph finally was forwarded to the Commission.[65] Rankin immediately requested the FBI to locate the bullet mark, and he sent Wesley Liebeler, the junior lawyer on Panel III, to Dallas to interview James Tague, the bystander.[66] Tague told Liebeler that he had received a minor cut on his face after the second or third shot, and immediately afterward he and a deputy sheriff had located the bullet mark.[67] Liebeler then interviewed the deputy sheriff, who corroborated Tague's account.[68]

In August the FBI established through spectrographic analysis that a bullet fragment had definitely struck the curb about 260 feet from the President's car at the time of the third shot.[69] Thus, while the final draft of the Report was being written, the

FBI laboratory confirmed that the mark on the curb had been caused by a bullet fragment.[70]

However, the chapter on the basic facts of the assassination had already been written, and at this late date there was apparently no interest in reopening the investigation.[71] Instead, a paragraph was inserted in the report, stating:

> . . . the mark on the south curb of Main Street cannot be identified conclusively with any of the three shots fired. Under the circumstances it might have come from the bullet which hit the President's head, or it might have been the product of the fragmentation of the missed shot upon hitting some other object in the area.[72]

The report failed to admit that the mark also might have come from a fourth shot.

An exhaustive investigation would have tested each of these three possibilities against the known facts. Was it ballistically possible for fragments from the head shot to travel 260 feet and strike the curb with sufficient kinetic energy then to strike Tague? Ballistics experts could have been called to testify on the probability of this happening. Did a shot, in fact, miss? The Commission did not reach a conclusion on this point; thus further testimony might have been called for. If these two possibilities were precluded, then a fourth shot must have been fired.

The reason why the problem of the fourth hit was not dealt with by the investigation was, quite simply, that mention of this hit was lost in the shuffle of investigative reports, and it did not come to light until after Specter had completed his investigation. This occurrence suggests that possibly other facts came to light after the June 1 deadline or were "lost in the shuffle."[73]

Thus the investigation in Area I, the "basic facts of the assassination," tended to be limited to the more prominent problems. There was neither time nor manpower to explore problems of a more nebulous nature. Consequently, while known facts were substantiated, unknown facts were left unknown.

Area II

The investigation of Area I was, to some degree, supplemented by the investigation of Area II, "the identity of the assassin." There was, however, an important conceptual difference between the two investigations: whereas the first investigation was charged with ascertaining *all* the basic facts of the assassination and therefore had to be exhaustive in scope, the second investigation was charged with establishing a single positive fact, the identity of the assassin.

Joseph Ball, the most experienced trial lawyer on the staff, said that his investigation of Area II required basically the same process that a lawyer uses in "building a case"; a chain of evidence had to be forged which indisputably linked Oswald to the assassination and also showed that Oswald had the opportunity to commit the act.[74] Ball thus had a very definite, and limited, objective.

First Ball and his junior lawyer, David Belin, reviewed the investigative reports and isolated the "chain of evidence." Ball then prepared a "Harvard outline" of his case, in which each major element of evidence was supported by the minor and circumstantial evidence. From this outline Ball determined the facts that required further investigation and the evidence that required substantiation.[75]

After the Ruby trial ended, Ball and Belin began their field investigation in Dallas. Most of the key witnesses were interviewed informally, and on March 20 Ball held an "off-the-record" reconstruction of the assassin's movements. The purpose of this reconstruction was to prove that Oswald had had the opportunity to commit the assassination and then escape.[76]

The first question dealt with was how Oswald had descended from the sixth to the second floor undetected. Three witnesses on the fifth floor had indicated to the FBI that they had had a view of the stairs after the assassination and that no one had gone down them.[77] This at first led to the theory that Oswald had used the elevator, but this proved impossible because both elevators were found on the fifth floor with their doors open immediately after the assassination.[78] In the re-enactment Ball determined that the three witnesses, in fact, could not have seen the staircase at all times, and thus it was possible for Oswald to have descended the stairs undetected.[79]

Since a policeman had encountered Oswald on the second floor shortly after the last shot was fired, there was also a question of time. Could Oswald have descended from the sixth to the second floor in the time it took the policeman to rush up to the second floor? In the reconstruction, Ball clocked both the assassin's and the policeman's movements with a stopwatch and thereby showed that it was possible for Oswald to have been the assassin.[80]

To prove that Oswald was the assassin, Ball relied mainly on scientific evidence. This "hard" evidence was judiciously and methodically developed by Melvin Eisenberg before the Commission itself. The chain of evidence was indeed compelling.

Bullet fragments found in the President's car were definitely matched by ballistics experts to the rifle found in the Texas Book Depository. The rifle was traced to Oswald, and handwriting experts helped confirm that Oswald had ordered and paid for the gun. In addition, fingerprint experts identified as Oswald's a palm print taken from the rifle, and thus it was established that Oswald had had possession of the rifle. In short, the chain of evidence indisputably showed that Oswald's rifle was used in the assassination.[81]

The fact that Oswald had the opportunity to be the assassin and the fact that his rifle was used in the assassination in themselves made a *prima facie* case for Oswald's involvement in the assassination. Although the possibility that Oswald was unwittingly involved (that is, "framed") was apparently not explored, other circumstances—such as the shooting of police officer J. D. Tippit—severely diminished the credibility of this possibility.

Although the Area II investigation fulfilled, with reasonable thoroughness, its mission of identifying Oswald as the assassin, it tended to disregard possible evidence of accomplices. For example, Ball cited Oswald's palm prints on the book cartons used by the assassin as evidence that Oswald was at the scene of the assassination.[82] However, other unidentified palm prints were found on these cartons, which could have indicated the presence of an accomplice.[83] Ball and Belin did not try to have these prints identified, and it was only at the insistence of Wesley

Liebeler, in August, that the FBI identified most, but not all, of the other identifiable prints.[84] Quite possibly Ball felt that the question of accomplices fell outside his investigation's purview of identifying the assassin. In any case, the Area II investigation focused on the positive evidence that identified Oswald as the assassin; it did not deal with the threshold question of a second assassin.

The Grassy Knoll

There were also problems that fell between Area I and Area II, and were not dealt with by either investigation. A case in point is "the grassy knoll." In March, Ball was asked by Warren to clear up a rumor that the shots had come from the railroad bridge over the triple underpass the President's car was approaching.[85] Ball, assisted by other lawyers, questioned witnesses who were standing on the railroad overpass at the time of the assassination, and the rumor proved baseless. However, six out of seven of these witnesses who gave an opinion as to the source of the shots indicated that the shots had come from a "grassy knoll" located between the overpass and the Texas Book Depository.[86] Echoes often cause misleading impressions as to the source of shots, but five of the witnesses on the overpass said that they had also seen smoke rise from the knoll area.[87] For example, one witness testified, "I definitely saw the puff of smoke and heard the report from under these trees [on the knoll]."[88]

The grassy knoll, however, did not fall within the bounds of Area II, and Ball and Belin did not question the witnesses who were standing on the knoll. And Specter apparently did not have time to attack this problem. Yet, according to the investigative reports, of the ten witnesses who were standing between the knoll and the President's car, and who had expressed an opinion as to the source of the shots, nine thought the shots had come from the knoll directly behind them, and the tenth thought the shots had come from the area between the knoll and the Book Depository.[89] Only one of these witnesses, Abraham Zapruder, was questioned by the staff, and he was called to determine not the source of the shots, but the terms under which he had sold his film of the assassination to *Life* magazine.[90]

Eight witnesses were standing across the street from the knoll; all eight said they thought the shots had come from the knoll.[91] Only three of these witnesses were questioned. Jean Hill was questioned by Specter after Mark Lane had described her account in his testimony before the Commission.[92] James Altgens was questioned by Liebeler primarily about a photograph that he had taken showing a person resembling Oswald in the doorway of the Texas Book Depository. And James Tague was questioned by Liebeler about the "fourth hit."[93]

Despite the fact that almost all the witnesses on the knoll, or with a view of the knoll, who expressed an opinion as to the source of the shots said that the shots had come from the knoll, no thorough investigation was made of this area. Very few of the witnesses who thought the shots had come from the knoll were questioned, and no full examination was made of photographs of the knoll area for indications of a second assassin.

If there was no evidence of more than one assassin, there was also no evidence that precluded the possibility. The conclusion that "Oswald acted alone" was predicated on two assumptions: first, that all the pertinent evidence was brought *before* the Commission for its evaluation; and second, that the staff's investigation had tested all possibilities after making an exhaustive analysis of all evidence and reports that might possibly have indicated the presence of a second assassin.

However, all the pertinent evidence was *not* brought before the Commission or even evaluated by the staff—as was the case with Mrs. Walther's statement. Nor did the staff conduct an exhaustive investigation into the basic facts of the assassination. In fact, only the more prominent problems were investigated, and many of the crucial, albeit less salient, problems were left unresolved—as was the case with the stretcher bullet. Furthermore, problems that developed after the deadline, such as the fourth hit, were never completely investigated. And although the investigation clearly delineated the chain of evidence linking Oswald to the assassination, it disregarded possible evidence of an accomplice in its handling of testimony involving the grassy knoll.

The investigation of the threshold question was thus a limited and relatively superficial one which never pursued answers to many important problems.

5

The Limits of the Investigators

The Commission conducted an independent investigation without independent investigators. The Commission found it unnecessary "to employ investigators other than the members of the Commission's legal staff," because it felt that it could rely on the facilities and investigative reports of the FBI and other federal agencies.[1] Although the Commission in fact relied mainly on the FBI, the investigation in theory was independent, because the legal staff "critically reassessed" the reports and work of the FBI and conducted further investigations where necessary.[2] J. Lee Rankin said, "Our lawyers were the only independent investigators that we needed."[3]

The legal staff thus had a dual role; it was the Commission's "independent investigator" as well as its counsel. In its investigative role, the staff was expected to analyze all the FBI reports for inconsistencies and gaps, and then to investigate and resolve these problems. In its legal role, the staff was expected to develop testimony and to examine witnesses before the Commission. In performing this dual function, however, the "independent investigators" were confronted with three problems that tended to limit the effectiveness of their investigation.

Communications with the FBI

Although the Commission borrowed lawyers from the Department of Justice, accountants from the Internal Revenue Service, and historians from the Department of Defense, it did not include FBI or other investigative agents on its staff.[4] One staff member wrote that this "initial organizational weakness" was probably due to "an early sensitivity to public opinion in view of rumors that Lee Harvey Oswald had a prior connection with the FBI."[5] In any case, the staff was effectively separated from the agents on whom it depended for its information.

Instead of having direct access to the FBI agents, the lawyers had to make each separate request for information and assistance through "channels." For example, Joseph Ball said that on his first trip to Dallas he called the FBI field office for assistance in a problem. He was told that the request must come from FBI headquarters in Washington. It was thus necessary for Ball to telephone Howard Willens in Washington, who then prepared a formal request which was, in turn, signed by J. Lee Rankin and forwarded to J. Edgar Hoover. Three days later Ball was notified by the Dallas field office that his request had been approved, but by this time Ball had resolved the problem and was ready to return to Washington. Ball added that the FBI was "exasperatingly bureaucratic."[6]

Rankin said that although there were some "communication problems" between the staff and the FBI, there was a liaison officer, Inspector James R. Malley, on whom he could call at "any time of the day or night" to expedite important problems.[7] Melvin Eisenberg said that although relations gradually improved, and eventually became good, FBI agents were initially resentful of "amateurs" doing what they considered to be their job.[8]

Other lawyers, however, were less satisfied with FBI cooperation. Joseph Ball said that FBI agents cooperated only on "express orders" from Hoover.[9] Wesley Liebeler said that, although the FBI was extremely efficient in answering questions submitted in writing, the agents would not develop any information that was not specifically requested of them.[10]

The practice of adhering to specific questions is probably the only way for an organization which conducts hundreds of thousands of interviews a year to function efficiently, but in the case of the Commission this method also had the effect of restricting the investigation to the more protrusive facts. For example, one witness, Arnold L. Rowland, testified before the Commission that he had told the FBI agents who interviewed him of a second person on the same floor as the rifleman a few minutes prior to the assassination. Rowland indicated that the FBI agents lacked interest in this second person.[11] He stated:

> . . . the agents were trying to find out if I could positively identify the man that I saw. They were concerned mainly with this, and I brought up to them about the Negro man [the second person] after I had signed the statement, and at the time they just told me that they were trying to find out about or if anyone could identify the man who was up there. They just didn't seem interested at all [in the other person]. They didn't pursue the point. They didn't take it down in notation as such.[12]

Rowland's account never appeared in any FBI report to the Commission.[13] Since Rowland had told deputy sheriff Roger Craig of a second person on the same floor with the assassin immediately after the assassination,[14] it seems probable that he would repeat the same story to FBI agents who interviewed him (as he claimed to have done), even if the story were not accurate. If Rowland did tell this story to the FBI, then FBI agents disregarded a very significant statement because it was not immediately relevant to their specific question. This possibility suggests that the FBI interviewing system was more effective in clarifying and verifying known information than it was in discovering and reporting new information.

Because of the enormous quantity of FBI reports the staff initially assumed that the FBI had carried out exhaustive research in the areas of its main investigation. Liebeler, however, later found that "the most disquieting thing about the FBI investigation was that it was less thorough than it appeared to be."[15] For example, although Marina Oswald had been repeatedly questioned and continually investigated over a nine-month period by the FBI, Liebeler found in August that she still possessed evidence, which had an important bearing on Oswald's trip to Mexico, that had never been brought to the attention of the Commission.[16]

Liebeler thus wrote a memorandum to Howard Willens, stating:

> . . . it reflects badly [on the thoroughness of the investigation] that Marina Oswald still had material on August 26 [1964] not known to the FBI.[17]

Thus the quantity of the FBI's investigative material did not guarantee that all the important facts were reported. In fact, the plethora of unevaluated FBI material probably added to the problem of critical reassessment. One staff lawyer estimated that 90 per cent of these reports were not immediately relevant to the assassination.[18]

The high proportion of irrelevant papers was caused in part by the FBI's policy of submitting reports on all the crank letters and "weird allegations" received by FBI field offices. J. Edgar Hoover explained that, even when an allegation could not possibly have a basis in fact, a report on it was submitted to the Commission "for the record."[19] One FBI document, the five-volume Gemberling Report, is over 1200 pages long, and even contains descriptions of dreams that persons had had after the assassination.[20]

Furthermore, the FBI system of investigating all names mentioned (they were capitalized in agents' reports, listed alphabetically by the field office, then circulated for further investigation to other field offices) produced thousands of pages on people who were only remotely connected with Oswald. Somewhat like a chain-letter in effect, this process produced investigations of and reports on acquaintances of acquaintances of acquaintances of Oswald.[21]

No single member of the staff was able to read all the FBI reports, and therefore no one had a synoptic view of the FBI investigation. The quantity of FBI reports thus may have had the unintended effect of obscuring relevant information.

The staff had only very limited assistance from the Central Intelligence Agency. Wesley Liebeler was one of the few staff lawyers who had direct contact with CIA agents; his experience illustrates the general problem "outsiders" (as the lawyers were considered to be) encountered in dealing with a highly secret intelligence organization. Liebeler, in attempting to identify a heavy-set man in a CIA photograph, found that the photograph itself had a curious history. On November 18, 1963, the FBI received it, together with a report on Oswald's September 27, 1963, visit to the Cuban Embassy in Mexico City, and forwarded both to its Dallas field office. Coincidentally, the file arrived in Dallas on November 22, the day of the assassination. The following day FBI agent Bardwell Odum showed the photograph to Oswald's mother, who later alleged that it was a picture of Jack Ruby. To show that Mrs. Oswald was mistaken, the photograph was introduced into the record as "Odum Exhibit 1." Later Liebeler found that three different witnesses' descriptions of an unidentified associate of Oswald's seemed to resemble the man in the photograph.

Liebeler therefore asked the FBI to identify the man. The FBI replied that it was a CIA photograph, taken outside the country, and that they had no further information about it. Liebeler next wrote to the CIA, asking who the person in the photograph was and why it was sent to the FBI less than a week before the assassination. Weeks later the CIA still had not replied, and Liebeler consulted the CIA liasion with the Commission, R. G. Rocca, who told him that the matter was still being investigated. Later a CIA agent called Liebeler and said that the CIA had thought at the time the photograph was sent to the FBI that the person in the photograph was Lee Harvey Oswald. He explained that it was routinely taken on September 27 by a secret camera located across the street from the Cuban Embassy in Mexico City, and that the person was identified by a confidential source in the Embassy as Lee Harvey Oswald. And so the photograph was included with the report on Oswald. When Liebeler pointed out that the person did not resemble Oswald at all, the CIA agent said that he would investigate further and call back. Despite persistent inquiries, Liebeler heard nothing more about the man in the photograph, and he was not even able to get hold of the agent who had called him. Liebeler added that the CIA was so secretive that it was virtually useless to the Commission.[22]

In all, the CIA submitted only about forty-five reports, and these pertained mainly to investigations conducted abroad and to foreign newspaper reports.[23]

The Secret Service provided agents for specific assignments, though it had neither the manpower nor the facilities to conduct a general investigation.[24] In the final analysis, the staff was thus mainly dependent on the FBI for its information.

Although the FBI conducted a massive investigation—over 25,000 interviews and reinterviews—into the assassination and into the backgrounds of the principal persons involved, the communications problem between the staff and the FBI, and the narrow criteria of the interviews, served to restrict the flow of information to the more salient facts.

The Forensic Problem

The Commission required that all its processes be consistent with the "high judicial standards of its members."[25] This requirement led to the fair and judicial treatment of witnesses, but it also had the unintended effect of restricting the depth of the staff's investigation.

Forensic interrogation is the lawyer's only means of extracting concealed information from a witness; it includes such tactics as cross-examination, trap-questioning, and badgering. The Commission felt that, although these tactics might have a place in adversary proceedings where witnesses have interests to protect, they had no place in the proceedings of the Commission.[26] Since most of the witnesses appeared before the Commission voluntarily and without counsel, the Commission believed that they should not be subject to rigorous cross-examination unless it was evident that they were concealing information.[27] The conflict between the staff's interest in interrogating witnesses and the Commission's interest in assuring that the proceedings were "a model of judicial fairness"[28] became evident after the first witness, Marina Oswald, testified.

Most of the lawyers were not satisfied with Mrs. Oswald's testimony. Liebeler said that it contained obvious contradictions and inconsistencies, and it seemed she might very well be "approximating the truth" in order to tell the Commission what she thought it wanted to hear.[29] Joseph Ball said that Marina

Oswald "left too many questions unanswered."[30] William Coleman asked Rankin to permit Mrs. Oswald to undergo a more rigorous examination, and he reportedly offered to prepare a "trappy deposition" for her.[31]

At the next staff meeting Rankin announced that the Commission had decided against further examination of Marina Oswald. He went on to say that the Chief Justice considered himself to be "a judge of human beings" and he and the other Commissioners fully believed her testimony.[32]

The staff strongly and loudly protested this decision. Coleman threatened to resign unless Mrs. Oswald was examined further, and other lawyers came close to walking out of the meeting. Liebeler asked Rankin for the Commission's objection to further examination, and Rankin replied, "The Chief [Justice] doesn't want it." At this point Rankin lost control of the meeting.[33]

In a memorandum which possibly reflects the intensity of feeling on the subject, Norman Redlich alleged that

> Marina Oswald has lied to the Secret Service, the FBI, and this Commission repeatedly on matters which are of vital concern to the people of this country and the world.[34]

Because of the Commission's insistence on "believing Marina," some members of the staff referred to the Commission as "Snow White and the Seven Dwarfs"—Marina Oswald being Snow White.[35]

The Commission finally relented and allowed further examination of Marina Oswald. She was called as the final Commission witness in September, and she changed an important part of her testimony—Oswald's motive. Whereas in February Mrs. Oswald said she had thought that the motive was fame, she said in September that she had always believed that Oswald was aiming at Governor Connally and not at the President.[36] More than one tenth of the time spent in Commission hearings was devoted to the testimony of Marina Oswald; yet the discrepancies in Mrs. Oswald's testimony were never satisfactorily resolved.

This case illustrates the difficulty the staff had in examining witnesses without being permitted to use the tools of forensic interrogation.

Lawyers taking testimony in their field investigations also were restricted in their treatment of witnesses. For example, one staff lawyer, Burt Griffin, was reprimanded for "using too much discretion."[37]

Griffin had been questioning Dallas police sergeant Patrick Dean about Ruby's entry into the basement of the Dallas city jail, and he found Dean's answers to be inconsistent with his earlier statements and with other evidence as well.[38] In an effort to clarify Dean's statements, Griffin went "off-the-record," sent the stenographer out of the room, and spoke to Dean informally for about twenty minutes.[39] According to Dean, Griffin had bluntly told him that he (Dean) was lying and had offered to help him keep his job if he told the truth.[40] When Dean complained of this treatment to the Commission, Chief Justice Warren stated:

> That so far as the jurisdiction of this Commission is concerned and its procedures, no member of our staff has a right to tell any witness that he is lying or that he is testifying falsely. That is not his business. It is the business of this Commission to appraise the testimony of all the witnesses. . . .[41]

Thus the staff was explicitly prohibited from controverting the testimony of witnesses. Although this was done to protect the rights of the witnesses, it had the effect of depriving the staff of a useful forensic tactic. Without the right to challenge witnesses with other evidence, some of the lawyers felt that "they were reduced to deposition-takers."[42]

The Commission's policy, that the staff's methods had to be consistent with the standards of the Commissioners, also limited the use of such quasi-legal devices as polygraph tests. Rankin said that the "Chief Justice could not give his seal of approval to devices that the courts have ruled illegal."[43]

A polygraph is not, as it is sometimes called, a "lie detector." It only measures emotional stress in a witness that *may* indicate deception or that may indicate other emotions such as fear, anxiety, nervousness, etc.[44] The results of a polygraph test depend largely on the subjective interpretation of the witness's responses and are thus of dubious value in determining the truthfulness of a witness.[45] Nevertheless, polygraphs have considerable value as investigative aids in certain circumstances. For example, if a witness believes that the instrument is in fact a "lie detector," it may provide a strong psychological inducement for him to be truthful.

Although the staff fully realized the limits of the polygraph test, some of the lawyers felt it was the only way to resolve certain problems.[46] For example, Liebeler was confronted with the testimony of a Dallas gunsmith, Dial D. Ryder, which, if true, would indicate that an important part of Oswald's life was unknown to the Commission.[47] Ryder claimed that the day after the assassination he had found a repair ticket for a rifle with the name "Oswald" on it. It was evident from the information on the repair ticket that this rifle could not have been the assassination weapon, and Ryder was certain that he had never worked on a rifle similar to the assassination weapon.[48] Since the FBI was unable to locate any other "Oswald" in the area who might have brought the rifle to Ryder, and since Oswald lived in the same neighborhood as the gun-repair shop, it seemed quite possible that Oswald owned a second rifle.

Two other witnesses testified that Oswald had inquired in a furniture store about having his rifle repaired. This occurred at about the same time that Ryder remembered repairing the rifle, and the witnesses also claimed that they had directed Oswald to Ryder's gun shop.[49] When Liebeler confronted the witnesses with Marina Oswald, both positively identified her as the woman who had entered the furniture store with Oswald.[50] There remained, however, the distinct possibility that the repair tag was spurious and that Ryder had invented the story.

In this situation, Liebeler felt that a "lie detector" probably would have induced Ryder to be truthful.[51] Furthermore, if the polygraph showed no emotional stress on Ryder's part, it would strongly suggest that Oswald's life was still a mystery and that further and more coercive questioning of Marina Oswald was called for. Liebeler said that the problem came down to: Was Ryder lying?[52]

In reply to Liebeler's request for an FBI polygraph test of Ryder, Willens wrote that "the FBI is extremely dubious of polygraphs" and that the Commission had therefore denied the request.[53] The problem of Oswald's "second rifle" thus was never resolved.

The staff's role of "independent investigator" was thus, to some degree, hampered by its role of "Commission counsel." Admittedly, as Eisenberg pointed out, this limitation affected only a very minor portion of the investigation.[54] Most of the witnesses came forth of their own accord and testified freely, and there was no need to subject them to rigorous cross-examination and quasi-legal tactics. There were, however, some problems that could not be resolved by merely accepting witnesses' testimony at face value and probing no further. Naturally a witness would be unlikely to reveal information indicating that he had prior knowledge of the assassination. Concealed information of this nature could have been elicited only through forensic interrogation. By denying the lawyers the use of these tactics, the Commission, in effect, limited the depth of the investigation to information that witnesses were willing to reveal openly.[55]

The Time-Pressure Problem

The third major problem that limited the lawyers in their investigation was time pressure. The constant deadlines limited not only the quantity of the investigation but also its quality.

As the investigation progressed into June, and the Commission was forced to extend the June 1 deadline to July 1, the Commissioners became increasingly anxious to terminate the investigation and to "get the report out."[56] John J. McCloy said that he was concerned with the "ugly rumors" that were circulating in Europe, and he feared that a delay in publishing the Report would "cause them to spread like wildfire."[57] The Congressional members of the Commission felt it was necessary to release the Report well before the election.[58]

Whatever the exact reasons, considerable pressure was exerted on the lawyers through Rankin to "close down their investigations and submit their chapters."[59] To do so, lawyers, in some instances, were forced to leave important problems unresolved.

For example, Burt Griffin had the problem of determining

how Ruby gained entrance to the basement of the Dallas city jail a few minutes before he murdered Oswald. The task was complicated by the fact that there were over one hundred witnesses in the basement at the time, and there were at least six different possible entranceways.[60] To scrutinize the statements of all these witnesses and to eliminate as possibilities some of the entranceways required a methodical approach and a great deal of time.

During his field investigation, Griffin found that Ruby's story that he had entered by the Main Street ramp was contradicted by other evidence. The police officer guarding the ramp categorically denied that Ruby could have entered by that ramp, and four police officers, who had driven up the ramp at virtually the only time that Ruby could have descended, testified that they did not see Ruby on the ramp.[61] This contradiction raised questions both about Ruby's truthfulness and about the possibility that he had had assistance in entering the basement.

In June the Commission reportedly felt that Griffin was spending too much time on this problem. Consequently, Griffin was ordered to proceed with other areas of his investigation, despite his protests that the question of Ruby's entrance was of prime importance.[62]

Thus the question was left unanswered, and the Report could only conclude: "Ruby entered the basement, unaided, probably via the Main Street ramp. . . ."[63]

Time pressure also forced the lawyers to attempt to preclude possibilities by means of tenuous deductive reasoning rather than by further investigations. In some cases this method led to premature conclusions.

For example, one witness, Sylvia Odio, gave testimony indicating that Oswald had visited her in the company of two "Cuban underground fighters" the day before he left on his trip to Mexico. Mrs. Odio claimed that the man who was introduced to her as "Leon Oswald" was in fact Lee Harvey Oswald, and her sister corroborated this identification.[64]

If Mrs. Odio's testimony was accurate, it had important implications for the investigation; it meant that Oswald had two associates, not known to the Commission, who were involved in his trip to Mexico not long before the assassination.

By July the staff still had not questioned Sylvia Odio. Meanwhile, W. David Slawson, the lawyer assigned to the problem, tried to preclude the possibility of truth in Mrs. Odio's story by showing that it was not possible for Oswald to have been in Dallas at the time she claimed. Slawson's analysis was based on the fact that Oswald was in New Orleans at 8 a.m. on September 25 and on the bus bound from Houston to Mexico at 6 a.m. on September 26. Slawson assumed that Oswald had traveled from New Orleans to Houston on September 25 and then had caught the 2:35 a.m. bus to Mexico the next morning. This left only a few hours unaccounted for in Houston and "precluded" the possibility that Oswald had visited Mrs. Odio in Dallas on September 25.[65]

Although the Commission decided, on the basis of this analysis, that Mrs. Odio's story was false and required no further investigation, Liebeler found that a number of details in the woman's story coincided with facts she could not possibly have known, and he gave the matter further attention. On investigating the bus schedules, he found that there was no reason to assume that Oswald had caught the bus at 2:35 a.m. in Houston. Actually, Oswald was not seen on that bus until 6 a.m. that day. Thus Liebeler found it possible for Oswald to have traveled from New Orleans to Dallas on September 25, visited Mrs. Odio, and then continued to Alice, Texas, where he could have caught the Houston-to-Mexico bus. Mrs. Odio's story that Oswald had left her home in Dallas in an automobile with two other men thus could not, in fact, be ruled out.[66]

When Liebeler submitted a memorandum to Rankin showing the fallacy in the earlier analysis, Rankin said, "At this stage, we are supposed to be closing doors, not opening them."[67] Once the memorandum had been submitted, however, Rankin did give the matter further consideration, although the issue was never resolved.[68]

In this case a question which had been prematurely foreclosed was reopened through the persistence of a lawyer in another area. Indeed, other questions may have been closed by fallacious analyses and never reopened. The atmosphere of "closing doors" certainly was not conducive to critical reexaminations of the evidence.

The "independent investigators" were thus constrained in their investigation by the communications problem with the

FBI, the forensic problem caused by the Commission's judicial requisites, and the time-pressure problem. Although these three problems limited to some degree the depth of the investigation, the question remains: How decisive were these limitations?

Despite the restricted flow of information from the FBI, the staff had virtually all its questions answered by the FBI. Despite the judicial restraints, most of the witnesses testified freely and only a small number of questions were left unanswered. Despite the time pressure, most of the salient problems were resolved. The only type of information unlikely to emerge in such an investigation would be information that was deliberately concealed.

The answer as to how decisive the limitation was, therefore, depends on whether or not information was concealed—a question which could not be answered by this type of investigation.

6

The Commission Hearings

The staff investigation was supplemented to some degree by the Commission hearings. However, only 94 of the 552 witnesses testified at the Commission hearings (the other witnesses either were questioned by the staff lawyers in the course of their field investigations or submitted affidavits).[1] In all, the Commission held forty-nine days of hearings, beginning on February 3, 1964, and ending on September 6, 1964—an average of about seven hearings per month.[2]

Commission hearings were defined by the presence of "one or more members of the Commission." With one exception, the hearings were closed to the public.[3] The witnesses had the right to be advised by counsel, but few availed themselves of this right. Most of the hearings were held in the Commission's offices in Washington, although on two occasions they were held in Texas.[4] Most of the basic evidence was introduced into the record at such hearings.

Although these hearings served to substantiate and formalize the findings of the investigation, they produced little, if any, new evidence of consequence. As Commissioner Ford wrote, "There were no startling developments, no sudden turns of evidence that opened up truths previously unperceived."[5] Possibly no new evidence or "truths" came to light because all the significant facts were already known. There were, however, other possible reasons why the Commission hearings did not uncover new evidence on the assassination.

First of all, only a minor portion of the hearings was devoted to testimony relating to the assassination itself. By far the greatest portion of the Commission's time was occupied with testimony concerning Lee Harvey Oswald's biography. The hearings began and ended with the testimony of Marina Oswald, and it accounted for more than 12 per cent of the total Commission hearings. Although Marina Oswald might possibly have cast light on Oswald's prior movements and motives, she seemed to have no direct knowledge of the assassination itself.

The testimony of Oswald's mother and brother, neither of whom had seen Oswald for more than a year prior to the assassination, accounted for another 14 per cent of the hearings. Another 13 per cent was spent on the testimony of the people with whom the Lee Harvey Oswalds had resided at one time or another. In all, 43 per cent of the Commission's time was spent hearing testimony concerning Oswald's life history—a fact which suggests that the main focus of the Commission hearings was Oswald, not the assassination itself.

The Commission also spent considerable time—about 12 per cent of the hearings—on testimony concerning the operation of government agencies. The Commission dealt with such questions as: How was Oswald able to return to the United States after defecting to the Soviet Union? Why was Oswald not under closer FBI surveillance? Were the Secret Service's protective measures adequate?

A number of prominent witnesses, such as Secretary of State Dean Rusk, Secretary of the Treasury Douglas Dillon, FBI Director J. Edgar Hoover, and Director of Central Intelligence John McCone, testified on the procedures of their agencies.[6] Although the inclusion of these notable witnesses gave stature and importance to the Commission's investigation, it did not serve to reveal any new facts about the assassination itself.

The Commission also spent considerable time on other peripheral problems such as the methods of the Dallas police, the activities of Jack Ruby, and anti-Kennedy advertisements. The Commission was obliged to explore all these matters, because they might possibly have been connected with the assassination, but these explorations left little time for testimony concerning the assassination itself.

Thus, less than one-third of the Commission hearings—about 81 hours out of a total of 244—dealt with the pertinent facts of the assassination: the source of the shots, the identity of the assassin, and Oswald's movements on the day of the assassination. During these 81 hours of pertinent hearings, 51 witnesses testified. Most of the evidence was presented by expert witnesses, whose testimony concerned such complex subjects as forensic pathology, ballistics, fingerprints, hair and fiber analysis, etc. Quite obviously the Commission had neither the time nor technical knowledge to scrutinize the expert testimony. Although expert testimony also presents a problem in judicial trials, the problem is usually solved by adversary proceedings in which the defense counsel calls expert witnesses to challenge those of the prosecution.

One Commission lawyer, Melvin Eisenberg, did call "outside" expert witnesses to confirm the government expert witnesses, but this was only done in the case of fingerprint and ballistic identification.[7] In other areas, however, expert testimony received only cursory examination. For example, the autopsy surgeon indicated in his testimony that the first bullet that struck Kennedy passed through his body without leaving a discernible "track" or path.[8] This testimony, however, contradicts a basic precept of forensic pathology: a rifle bullet traveling through the body will *always* leave a path.[9] An outside expert witness might very well have clarified this apparent discrepancy, but such a process of critical re-examination would also have required considerably more time than the Commission could allot even to pertinent evidence.

Thus, although the members of the Commission asked many perceptive questions of the witnesses, the depth to which the hearings could probe was limited to some degree by the relatively small amount of time the Commission devoted to hearing evidence on the assassination itself.

A second possible reason why the hearings failed to uncover new information was that virtually all the witnesses had made statements to the federal investigators or to the staff lawyers *before* they testified at the Commission hearings; the only exceptions were the federal agents themselves and Mrs. John F. Kennedy. Thus, at the hearings, not only would witnesses tend to adhere to their prior statements but quite probably they would remember their written statements more clearly than the event itself.

For instance, four months after the assassination, Harold Norman, a witness who was on the fifth floor of the Texas Book Depository at the time of the assassination, testified in great detail as to how he head heard the bolt of a rifle clicking and rifle cartridges falling on the floor with every shot fired.[10] Commissioner Ford said that he considered Norman's testimony important in pinpointing the source of the shots, and that he was especially impressed with Norman's "remarkable clarity and spontaneity."[11] However, less than a week before Norman testified at the Commission hearings he and many of the other eyewitnesses took part in a re-enactment. A Secret Service agent stood on the floor above Norman and worked the bolt of the rifle (without firing it) and dropped cartridges on the floor.[12] Therefore it was quite possible that Norman's "remarkable clarity" and "spontaneity" came from his memory of the re-enactment rather than the assassination. In any case, very few witnesses contradicted their written statements and gave new evidence.

When a witness did give new evidence in the Commission hearings, it became suspect *ipso facto*, because it was not included in a prior statement. For example, Arnold Rowland testified before the Commission that he had seen a second man on the same floor with the assassin. The Commission, however, rejected this portion of Rowland's testimony partly because of "Rowland's failure to report his story despite several interviews until his appearance before the Commission."[13] It will be recalled that Rowland insisted that he *did* mention this fact to FBI agents but that they were interested only in whether or not he could positively identify the assassin.[14] The Commission never called the FBI agents as witnesses on this matter.

By judging the testimony of witnesses by the standard of their prior statements, the Commission virtually precluded the possibility that new evidence would arise to alter significantly the basic suppositions concerning the assassination.

Some of the staff lawyers thought the Commission hearings were "a joke."[15] Liebeler said that most of the Commissioners were absent most of the time, and that they would stop in "for a few minutes," ask a question "which blew the lawyer's entire line of questioning," and then "rushed out to make a quorum or something."[16] Ball said that he spent considerable time "talking to an empty room."[17]

Although the staff no doubt tended to exaggerate the Commissioners' absenteeism, the attendance records of the Commission show that most of the Commissioners were present for only a minor portion of the hearings. Senator Russell, who attended the fewest, heard only about 6 per cent of the testimony; whereas Allen Dulles, who attended the largest number of hearings, heard about 71 per cent. Only three Commissioners heard more than half the testimony, and the average Commissioner heard 45 per cent.

J. Lee Rankin, however, asserted that the Commission members were "extremely dedicated" and that they would attend whenever they could leave their other responsibilities. For example, Rankin noted that even though Warren had to attend the Supreme Court every day it was in session, he arranged for Commission hearings to commence at 9 a.m. so that he could officially open them before he left for the Court at 10 a.m. Rankin said, "I worried about Warren's health because he was trying to do two full-time jobs at once."[18] Yet, regardless of efforts and good intentions, the fact remained that the Commissioners had other responsibilities and they could spend only part of their time at Commission hearings.[19]

Rankin also pointed out that some of the lawyers were so engrossed in their own investigations that they were not always aware of the work of the Commission.[20] Most lawyers agreed that the separation between the staff investigation and the Commission hearings tended to widen as the investigation progressed.

The degree of separation between staff and Commission is illustrated by an incident involving Commissioner McCloy. McCloy said that he found that the administrative assistant, Howard Willens, "had locked information away in his top drawer" and at first refused him access to the material.[21] McCloy then discussed the matter with Warren, and, according to McCloy,

Warren ordered Willens to make all the material available to the individual Commissioners.[22] Rankin explained that this incident was caused by an "unfortunate misunderstanding," and that Willens was withholding the information because he was waiting for other corroborative evidence.[23] In any case, this incident shows that the Commission was somewhat detached from the work of the staff.

Rankin further said that some of the younger lawyers simply didn't understand how a government investigation functions. He explained that it was important "for the sake of public, as well as historic, acceptance of the Report that the main evidence be brought directly before the Commission."[24] The function of the Commission hearings, then, was to record, rather than to investigate, the evidence.

7

The Hypothesis

On December 9, 1963, shortly after the first Commission meeting, the FBI submitted the Summary Report of its investigation to the Commission.[1] This report contained the seven major facts upon which the Commission, nine months later, explicitly predicated its main conclusion—that Oswald had assassinated President Kennedy.[2] If all the major facts were already established, what were the contributions of the independent investigation?

Norman Redlich said that, although the FBI established the basic facts, the independent investigation determined the relationships between these facts.[3] According to Redlich, the single most important contribution of the investigation was the theory that explained how one man, acting alone, committed the assassination.[4] The way in which this theory developed reveals to some extent the basic orientation of the investigation.

The FBI Version

The December 9, 1963, FBI Summary Report gives the following description of the assassination:

As the motorcade was traveling through downtown Dallas on Elm Street about fifty yards west of the intersection with Houston Street . . . , three shots rang out. Two bullets struck President Kennedy, and one wounded Governor Connally.[5]

Although this account appeared to be basically accurate, the Commission's staff felt that for "the sake of the historical record" the sequence of events should be ascertained with greater precision.[6] Thus, through an analysis of the Zapruder film of the assassination and other relevant evidence, the staff attempted to determine the exact position of the car at the time of each shot and the time interval between the shots.[7]

The Film Analysis

On January 27, 1964, Norman Redlich, Melvin Eisenberg, and Arlen Specter of the Commission staff met with FBI photographic expert Lyndal Shaneyfelt, Secret Service Inspector Thomas Kelley, and FBI visual-aids expert Leo Gauthier to conduct a frame-by-frame analysis of the film.[8] The first problem was determining the exact position of the Presidential limousine at the time of the first shot.[9]

The latest point at which the President could have been first hit is film frame 225. On this film frame it is evident that the President has been wounded.[10] The earliest point at which the President could have been hit was fixed by an oak tree. The Secret Service re-enactment of the assassination showed that the assassin's line of sight was blocked by the foliage of the large oak tree between film frame 166 and film frame 207.[11] The film further shows that the President is smiling and waving on film frame 207, and this makes it highly improbable that the President was shot before film frame 166. Moreover, still photographs and virtually all the eyewitnesses place the car past the oak tree at the time of the first shot. It was thus concluded that the first shot could have been fired only after film frame 207. The staff was able through this analysis of the film to fix the position of the car, at the time of the first shot, within eighteen film frames (about sixteen feet).

However, establishing the position of the car at the time of the first shot raised a new and more serious problem. The FBI had established that the murder weapon could not be fired twice in less than 2.3 seconds. This minimum time was based on the time it took to open and close the bolt of the rifle.[12] In terms of the film, 2.3 seconds are equivalent to 42 film frames—at the camera's established speed of 18.3 frames per second. This meant that the shots had to be spaced at least 42 frames apart on the film to be consistent with the minimum firing time of the assassination weapon. Since the first shot could not have been fired before film frame 207, a second shot from the same rifle could not have been fired before film frame 249. Thus it was initially assumed that Connally was hit after film frame 249, even though this was not apparent in the film.[13]

On February 25, 1964, the Commission finally obtained the original copy of the Zapruder film from *Life* magazine. Up to this point the staff had been using a second-generation copy (i.e., a copy of a copy).[14] The original film is considerably more detailed, and it shows that Governor Connally was hit well before film frame 249.[15] Subsequently Connally's doctors testified that Connally was not in a position to have been hit after film frame 240.[16]

Thus there are only 33 frames on the film between the earliest time at which Kennedy could first have been shot and the latest time at which Connally could have been shot. Yet the murder weapon could not be fired twice within this time period. A new working hypothesis thus would have to be found to explain the assassination.

The Single-Bullet Hypothesis

In early March, Arlen Specter discussed the time problem informally with Commanders James J. Humes and J. Thornton Boswell, the United States Navy doctors who had performed the autopsy on President Kennedy. According to Specter, Commander Humes suggested that since both Kennedy and Connally apparently had been hit within a second of each other, it was medically possible that both men had been hit by the same bullet and that Connally had had a delayed reaction.[17] This hypothesis would explain how both men were wounded in less time than that in which the murder weapon could be fired twice, but it raised another problem.

If both men were hit by the first bullet, quite obviously the first bullet must have exited from the front of the President's body. However, it will be recalled that the FBI Summary Report states that the autopsy revealed that the bullet in question did *not* exit from the front of the President's body.[18]

On March 16, 1964, the Commission heard testimony concerning the autopsy. On this day an undated autopsy report was introduced in evidence. Commander Humes testified that this autopsy report was prepared immediately after the autopsy examination and submitted to "higher authority" on November 24, 1963.[19] He also submitted an affidavit to the Commission, purportedly written on November 24, 1963, stating that he "destroyed by burning certain preliminary notes relating to" the autopsy.[20]

The autopsy report contains a conclusion that is diametrically opposed to the FBI's statement on the autopsy. The autopsy report states that the first bullet hit the President in the rear of the neck and *exited* from his throat, whereas the FBI Summary and Supplemental Reports stated that the autopsy found that the bullet in question hit the President below the shoulder and "penetrated to a distance of less than a finger length."[21]

If the FBI's statements are accurate, it would appear that the autopsy findings were revised some time subsequent to January 13, 1964.

Commander Humes testified that, although no bullet path was found through the President's body, it was deductively concluded that the bullet did indeed pass through the body and exit at the throat.[22] Commander Boswell, who assisted Commander Humes in the autopsy examination, testified that the autopsy report's conclusions were based on the autopsy and the "subsequent conference."[23]

When Commander Humes was asked what had happened to

the bullet that had exited from the President's throat, Specter interjected: "That is the subject of some theories I am about to get into. That is an elusive subject, but Doctor Humes has some views on it."[24]

Thereupon Humes explained:

I see that Governor Connally is sitting directly in front of the late President, and suggest the possibility that this missile, having traversed the low neck of the late President, in fact traversed the chest of Governor Connally.[25]

The single-bullet hypothesis was thus advanced to the Commission.

Melvin Eisenberg said that "at first, some lawyers were incredulous of this hypothesis"[26]; but gradually they became persuaded that this was the only reasonable way to explain the fact that both men had been hit within a second or two of each other. Although the single-bullet hypothesis solved the time problem, it raised new problems.

First of all, there was the problem of the nearly whole bullet (bullet 399) found on a stretcher in the Dallas hospital where President Kennedy and Governor Connally were first treated. It was "preliminarily" thought, according to Specter, that this bullet had come from Kennedy's stretcher.[27]

However, *if* both men were both first hit by the same bullet, this nearly whole bullet could *not* have come from Kennedy's stretcher. According to the single-bullet hypothesis, the first bullet went through the President and Connally, the second bullet missed the car completely, and the third bullet hit the President's head and fragmented. Thus, the single-bullet hypothesis could be maintained only if the nearly whole bullet came from Connally's stretcher.

On March 16, the day when the single-bullet hypothesis was first advanced to the Commission, Specter told Dulles that there was evidence which showed that the bullet was found on Connally's, not Kennedy's, stretcher.[28] However, it will be recalled, there was *no* evidence at this time that indicated the bullet came from Connally's stretcher.[29] Subsequently evidence developed which all but precluded the possibility that the bullet had come from Connally's stretcher. Colonel Finck, a qualified expert in both forensic medicine and wound ballistics, testified that the bullet found on the stretcher could not be the bullet that caused Connally's wrist wound, primarily because more fragments were found in the wrist than were missing from the bullet.[30] The other medical witnesses agreed with this conclusion.[31] Yet, since other expert testimony and evidence precluded the possibility that Connally's wrist wound was caused by a fragment from the third bullet, or by a direct hit from another bullet, the Commission concluded that all Connally's wounds were caused by a single bullet.[32] The bullet found on the stretcher thus could not have been the bullet that caused all Connally's wounds. Nevertheless, despite this inconsistency, it was maintained that the bullet came from Connally's stretcher.

A second problem involved the testimony of Governor Connally in April. Connally testified that it was inconceivable to him that he was hit by the first shot because he distinctly remembered hearing the first shot before he had felt the impact of the bullet striking.[33] Since a bullet travels faster than the speed of sound, Connally reasoned that he could have been hit only by the second bullet.[34] The evidence clearly indicated that Kennedy had been hit by the first bullet.[35]

Connally's contention that he was hit by a separate shot was corroborated by his wife, who testified that *after* the first shot she saw "the President as he had both hands at his neck," and a few seconds later "there was the second shot that hit John [Connally]."[36] Of the more than one hundred eyewitnesses to the assassination, not one testified that both men were hit by the same shot.

It is possible, although unlikely,[37] that Connally did not immediately perceive his wound, or that his memory of the event was confused. However, there was other evidence which corroborated Connally's account.

Both of Connally's doctors testified, on the basis of their medical knowledge of the case as well as of a careful study of the film of the assassination, that Connally was hit *after* film frame 231.[38] Yet, it will be recalled, the film showed that the President was definitely hit by frame 225. Thus, according to the medical testimony, there was an absolute minimum of six film frames between the time Kennedy and Connally were hit. This leads one to the conclusion that the two men were hit by two bullets.

In order to maintain the single-bullet hypothesis it was necessary to assume that other evidence was erroneous. First, it had to be assumed that the FBI Summary and Supplemental Reports' statements on the autopsy were inaccurate. Second, it had to be assumed that expert testimony which precluded the possibility that the bullet found on the stretcher was the bullet that wounded Connally was incorrect. Third, it had to be assumed Connally himself was wrong in his impression that he was hit by a separate bullet. Finally, it had to be assumed that Connally's doctors were mistaken in their conclusion that Connally was not in a position to be hit before film frame 231. The fact that this hypothesis was maintained and further tested indicates to some degree the investigation's commitment to an explanation of the assassination based on a "lone assassin" premise.

The Tests

On April 27, 1964, United States Army wound ballistics experts conducted further tests on the murder weapon. Arlen Specter, who supervised these tests, said that their primary purpose was to determine the penetrating power of the bullets, and specifically whether or not the bullets would penetrate a second object after exiting from the initial object.[39] In other words, the wound ballistics tests were meant to "test" the single-bullet hypothesis.

Colonel Finck testified that properly to test the single-bullet hypothesis it would be necessary to pass a bullet through two human cadavers.[40] However, Specter said that it was "too complicated" to fire a bullet through two objects at a time; thus, in the wound ballistics tests, bullets were not fired through more than one object at a time.[41] Three series of tests were held. In the first series, bullets were fired from the murder weapon through an object (gelatin blocks) which simulated the President's neck. By measuring the average entrance and exit speed of the bullets, it was determined that the bullets lost about 82 feet per second from an original velocity of about 2000 feet per second, traveling through the gelatin. In the second series of tests, bullets were fired from the murder weapon through an anesthetized goat, which simulated Governor Connally's chest, and it was determined that the bullets lost about 265 feet per second. In the third series of tests, bullets were fired through the wrist of a cadaver, which simulated Connally's wrist, and it was determined that a direct hit caused far more damage to the wrist than Connally actually had suffered.[42]

Doctor Alfred Olivier, the veterinarian who conducted the wound ballistics tests, testified before the Commission in May on the results of the test. When asked if the tests had indicated that Connally and Kennedy were hit by the same bullet, he replied: "My feeling is that it would be more probable that it [the bullet which struck the wrist] passed through the President first."[43]

Doctor Olivier explained that this conclusion was based on the fact that a direct hit caused considerably more damage to the simulated wrist than Connally's wrist actually had suffered. Therefore it was deduced that the bullet which had hit Connally's wrist had passed through a prior object. In the tests, the bullet had lost 265 feet per second when it passed through the goat that simulated Connally's chest. Because Connally's chest is about half again as wide as the goat, it was assumed that the bullet would have lost 400 feet per second passing through Connally's chest.[44] Doctor Olivier estimated that the bullet that struck the wrist had lost at least 480 feet per second, and therefore he concluded that the bullet must have passed through a third object—the President's neck.[45]

This conclusion was based on the assumption that the conditions of the experiment closely simulated those of the assassination. However, this was not in fact the case. Since the conclusion that Kennedy and Connally were hit by the same bullet is based on a difference of only about 80 feet per second in the bullet's velocity (4 per cent of the bullet's initial velocity), the disparity between the width of Connally and the goat might be a significant one. The attempt to compensate for the disparity simply by adding 50 per cent to the loss of velocity is at best a dubious extrapolation. The deceleration function for a bullet passing through a non-uniform substance, such as a goat, no doubt requires a more complicated computation. In any case, the fact remains that the goat did not even approximately simulate Connally's chest.

Further doubt was cast on the results of the wound ballistics tests by the testimony of Doctor Frederick E. Light, the medical pathologist associated with the tests. Dr. Light was asked whether he agreed with Dr. Olivier's conclusion that both the President and Governor Connally were hit by the same bullet. He replied:

> I am not quite as sure in my mind as I believe he [Olivier] is that the bullet that struck the Governor was almost certainly one which had hit something else first. I believe it could have produced that [wrist] wound even though it hadn't hit the President or any other person or object first.[46]

Specter then asked Dr. Light if the same amount of damage would have been inflicted on Connally's wrist if the bullet had *not* passed through the President first. Dr. Light answered:

> I think that is possible; yes. It won't happen the same way twice in any case, so you have got a fairly wide range of things that can happen if a person is shot in more or less this way.[47]

The wound ballistics tests were thus inconclusive as to whether or not the President and Governor Connally were hit by the same bullet.

The Reconstruction

In May, Specter proposed that the Commission conduct a reconstruction of the assassination based on the film in order to determine whether Connally and Kennedy were hit by the same bullet.[48] Specter said that the Commissioners initially opposed a reconstruction, "because they felt it would look bad at this late date to show that the basic facts were not known."[49] Rankin, however, gave a different reason; he said that the Commission was reluctant to permit a reconstruction for fear that "an over-enthusiastic lawyer" might "make the facts fit the hypothesis."

Thus the Commission agreed to the reconstruction only on the condition that it would be supervised personally by Rankin.[50]

On May 23, 1964, Rankin, Redlich, and Specter went to Dallas to conduct the reconstruction. The next morning the sequence of events of the assassination was meticulously reconstructed. An open limousine, with stand-ins for Kennedy and Connally, simulated the movements of the Presidential limousine on the day of the assassination. The limousine was slowly pushed until its position coincided exactly with the position of the limousine shown in the film of the assassination; at each point a photograph was taken from the "sniper's nest" in the Texas Book Depository through the telescopic sight of the murder rifle. In this manner, each film frame was correlated with the assassin's line of sight, and the trajectory was measured. Through this reconstruction it was possible to determine the assassin's view and the trajectory on each of the three shots.[51]

On June 4, 1964, the federal agents who participated in this reconstruction testified before the Commission. FBI ballistics expert Robert Frazier, who had occupied the position of the assassin during the test, was asked if it was probable that the bullet "which passed through the neck of the President" hit Governor Connally.[52] Frazier replied:

There are a lot of probables in that. First, we have to assume that there is absolutely no deflection in the bullet from the time it left the barrel until the time it exited from the Governor's body.[53]

Frazier said that it was "entirely possible" that both men were hit by the same bullet, but he continued:

I myself don't have any technical evidence which would permit me to say one way or the other, in other words which would support it as far as my rendering an opinion as an expert. I would certainly say it was possible but I don't say that it probably occurred because I don't have the evidence on which to base a statement like that.[54]

Specter then asked what evidence was missing, and Frazier answered:

We are dealing with hypothetical situations here in placing people in cars from photographs which are not absolutely accurate. They are two dimensional. They don't give you the third dimension.

Secondly, we are dealing with the fact that we don't know whether, I don't know technically, whether there was any deviation in the bullet which struck the President in the back and exited from his front. If there was a few degrees deviation then it may affect my opinion as to whether or not it would have struck the Governor.[55]

Frazier was then asked how the bullet could possibly have exited from the President, missed Connally, and also escaped hitting the car. He replied:

I have seen bullets strike small twigs, small objects, and ricochet for no apparent reason except they hit and all the pressure is on one side and it turns the bullet and it goes off at an angle.[56]

Frazier, the only expert witness to testify on the path of the bullet and the probability of its hitting both men, thus refused to support the single-bullet hypothesis.

Like the wound ballistics tests, the reconstruction showed only that it was *possible* that both men were hit by a single bullet; it did not show that it was *probable*.

Specter, however, considered both tests to be "very important corroborative evidence" that both men were hit by the same bullet.[57]

By June 5 Specter had submitted his chapter on the basic facts of the assassination.[58] The facts and premises set forth in the chapter were selected and organized so as to support the single-bullet hypothesis.[59] Even after the chapter was toned down by the Commission, it asserted:

Frazier testified that it [the bullet which first hit Kennedy] probably struck Governor Connally.[60]

And on the basis of this statement the single-bullet hypothesis was advanced.

However, as has been previously shown, Frazier explicitly had refused to testify as to the probability of both men being hit by the same bullet, and he had clearly enumerated his reasons for not doing so.

Frazier thus did *not* testify that the bullet that hit the President "probably struck Governor Connally." This statement apparently referred to an answer that Frazier had made to a hypothetical question.[61] When asked by Commissioner Ford to *assume* (1) that the bullet had passed through Kennedy and continued in an absolutely straight line, and (2) that Governor Connally was seated directly in the path of that bullet; Frazier had replied that "under those conditions," the bullet "had to" have hit Connally.[62] However, he qualified this answer by stating that he had no "technical evidence" on which to base these assumptions.[63]

The statement of probability attributed to Frazier was thus inaccurate and misleading.

In addition, the chapter cited the wound ballistics tests as "further" evidence that both men were hit by the same bullet, explaining:

> Correlation of a test simulating the Governor's chest wound with the neck and wrist experiment indicated that course.[64]

This correlation, as has been shown, was predicated on a very dubious assumption. In any case, the wound ballistics tests were admittedly inconclusive.

The single-bullet hypothesis was thus advanced on the basis of a misinterpretation of Frazier's ballistics testimony, and substantiated by the extremely tenuous findings of the wound ballistics tests. Evidence that was inconsistent with the single-bullet hypothesis, such as Colonel Finck's testimony concerning the bullet found on a stretcher, was omitted from the chapter. The hypothesis thus tended, in a sense, to be a self-fulfilling prophecy.

Norman Redlich said that he considered the single-bullet theory one of the most important contributions of the independent investigation.[65] Indeed, this theory involved the only substantial change from the basic facts that were established in the FBI Summary and Supplemental Reports. Despite the fact that the staff felt that this theory was the only reasonable way to explain the sequence of events in terms of a single assassin, and no alternate hypotheses were considered, in the final analysis the Commission—for reasons to be discussed later—refused to accept the single-bullet theory.[66]

PART THREE

The Report

8

Writing the Report

The Commission had two distinct tasks: the investigation and the writing of the Report. J. Lee Rankin said, "No one realized how long it would take to write the Report; instead of the estimated one month, it took nearly four months to complete."[1] The original plan was for each team of lawyers to write a chapter about its own investigative area and for all teams to submit their chapters to the Commission by June 1.[2]

However, most of the lawyers had not even completed their field investigations by June. Therefore, to expedite the writing of the Report, Rankin appointed Norman Redlich, Alfred Goldberg, Howard Willens, and himself as a "Re-editing Committee." Redlich was assigned editorial responsibility for the first four chapters in the Report; Goldberg, for the next three chapters; and Willens, for the eighth and final chapter.[3] Rankin acted as intermediary between the Commission and the staff in the writing of the Report.[4]

The first four chapters concerned the assassination itself. Chapter I was a brief seventeen-page summary of the event, which Redlich wrote himself.[5]

The second chapter was a more detailed narrative of the assassination, which began with the advance planning for the Dallas trip and ended with the return of the President's body to Washington. Although Arlen Specter and Samuel Stern made some contributions to the writing of this chapter, it was written mainly by Redlich.[6]

The third chapter focused on the basic facts of the assassination: the source of the shots, the sequence of events, medical findings, etc. This chapter was originally written by Specter and submitted by the June deadline. However, a basic premise of the chapter was that the President and Governor Connally were hit by the same bullet. When the Commission refused to accept this premise, the chapter had to be substantially rewritten by Redlich.[7]

The fourth chapter, which Redlich considered to be "the crucial chapter," dealt with the evidence that identified the assassin as Lee Harvey Oswald.[8] The original chapter was written by Joseph Ball and David Belin, who had investigated the evidence, but in late June the Re-editing Committee rejected this chapter as "totally inadequate."[9] Redlich then undertook to rewrite the chapter himself—a task which took over ten weeks and which involved the very difficult problem of selecting evidence, a problem which will be more fully discussed later.[10] Chapter IV, in effect, presented the case against Oswald.

The next three chapters, for which Goldberg had editorial responsibility, concerned peripheral events. Chapter V dealt with the circumstances of Oswald's death and the actions of Jack Ruby. Because the lawyers who were investigating the area, Burt Griffin and Leon Hubert, Jr., had continued their field investigation well into July, Rankin assigned Murray Laulicht, a twenty-four-year-old law clerk, to assist in writing the chapter.[11] In August the chapter was finally written by Griffin and Laulicht, but Goldberg found the style cumbersome, and he completely rewrote the chapter himself.[12]

The sixth chapter concerned possible conspiracies involving Oswald. Stuart Pollak, a Department of Justice lawyer who participated in the investigation, wrote the part of the chapter on Oswald's movements abroad; and W. David Slawson wrote the balance of the chapter. Pollak then rewrote the entire chapter. Goldberg, however, found that the chapter did not satisfactorily deal with the problem of alleged conspiracies, and he therefore rewrote most of the chapter and supplemented it with an appendix dealing with specific "speculations and rumors."[13]

Chapter VII, about Oswald's background and possible motives, was originally written by Wesley Liebeler, the lawyer who investigated this area. Although it was considered the "most brilliant chapter," the Commission found it "too subtle" and "too sympathetic."[14] Goldberg therefore revised the chapter and rewrote portions of it.[15]

The final chapter was on the general problem of Presidential protection. Samuel Stern wrote the draft chapter, but the Commission considered the treatment of the Secret Service "not critical enough," and Howard Willens rewrote a substantial part of the chapter.[16]

Rankin said that he did not send "the first few drafts" of the chapters to the Commission, because they were "too rough."[17] After the Re-editing Committee had "worked out" initial problems in the chapters, they were sent to the individual Commissioners for comments.[18] The Commissioners toned down the adjectives used in the chapters, raised questions about certain points, and wrote comments in the margins.[19] The Commissioners' criticisms and comments were then collated by the Re-editing Committee, and portions of the chapters were returned to the lawyers to be rewritten. Some chapters were rewritten as many as twenty times before all the Commissioners were satisfied. Through this process, the Commissioners' comments and judgments were incorporated into the Report.[20]

Finally, the evidence relied on in the Report had to be cited in the twenty-six volumes of testimony and exhibits.[21] Approximately twenty young lawyers assisted the staff in the process of cite-checking. If a statement in the Report was not fully supported by the evidence, then, at least theoretically, it had to be modified or deleted.[22] By September, however, most of the lawyers were extremely reluctant to make changes in their chapters. One lawyer, concerned about this attitude, wrote:

Eight months' work of the Commission and staff is in serious danger of being nullified because of the present impatience to publish . . . Staff members are becoming increasingly unwilling to discuss change or refinement, which would cause a printing delay.[23]

Time pressure thus affected the writing of the Report as it had affected the investigation.

The final draft of the Report was completed in mid-September. Rankin then assigned Goldberg the task of "polishing it up."[24] Goldberg said that he needed six months to do a competent rewriting job, and he had less than one week.[25]

The Warren Report—a 469-page document, supplemented by eighteen appendices[26]—was finally made public on September 28, 1964. Who wrote the Report? Although more than thirty persons had had a hand in writing it, it was written mainly by two men: Norman Redlich and Alfred Goldberg.

9

THE SELECTION PROCESS

Americans often assume that facts are solid, concrete (and discrete) objects like marbles, but they are very much not. Rather are they subtle essences, full of mystery and metaphysics, that change their color and shape, their meaning, according to the context in which they are presented. They must always be treated with skepticism and the standard of judgment should be not how many facts one can mobilize in support of a position but how skillfully one discriminates between them, how objectively one uses them to arrive at Truth, which is something different from, though not unrelated to, the Facts.

—Dwight Macdonald[1]

The major problem in the writing of the Report was the selection of evidence. From the tens of thousands of pages of evidence, which facts were to be included, and which facts excluded?

In a trial this problem of selecting evidence is pragmatically solved through the adversary system. The prosecutor and the defense counsel each select those facts which support his own case. The two opposing sets of facts are then reduced, through the dialectical process, to provide a basis for judgment.

However, the writers of the Report quite obviously could not simply select the evidence that supported their case, or the Report would have been of no more value than a prosecutor's brief which was not tested or challenged by a defense counsel. Norman Redlich thought the problem could be solved by the "impartial selection of facts,"[2] but Liebeler skeptically told him, "I suggest, Norman, that you start to make an argument the minute you select a fact."[3]

The difficulties encountered in attempting to select evidence impartially can best be seen in Chapter IV, which sets forth the case against Oswald. The way in which the facts were selected for this chapter reveals, to some extent, the criteria and objectives which governed the writing of the Report.

As had been noted, Chapter IV was first written by Joseph Ball and David Belin, the lawyers who investigated the evidence in this area. However, when the Re-editing Committee found the chapter "totally inadequate," Norman Redlich undertook to rewrite it.[4]

Joseph Ball said that the main difference between his version of the chapter and Redlich's was the "style of writing."[5] Ball claimed to have used "a concise, narrative style"; whereas, Redlich, according to Ball, preferred "a turgid, 'Law Review' style."[6] There were, however, other, more substantial differences between the two chapters.

The Three New Witnesses

Ball said that his chapter relied more on "hard, scientific evidence" and less on eyewitness evidence than did Redlich's.[7] For example, Ball had rejected as "utterly unreliable" the testimony of Helen Louise Markham, who was the only witness who claimed to have seen Oswald shoot Dallas policeman J. D. Tippit.[8] Ball found Mrs. Markham's testimony to be "full of mistakes." For example, although Mrs. Markham claimed that Oswald leaned into Tippit's police car, photographs taken immediately after the shooting showed that the car window was closed. Also, although Mrs. Markham claimed to have spoken to Tippit while waiting for the ambulance, medical evidence showed that he died instantaneously. Finally, although Mrs.

Markham claimed she was the only witness at the scene, there were a number of witnesses present.[9] Ball characterized Mrs. Markham as an unconvincing witness, and he said that, in view of other available evidence, her testimony was not needed for the case against Oswald.[10]

However, when the chapter was rewritten, Mrs. Markham's testimony was given considerable weight, and the description of Tippit's murder was based mainly on her account of the event.[11] Wesley Liebeler, the lawyer who had examined Mrs. Markham, told Redlich that the woman's testimony was "contradictory" and "worthless."[12] However, Redlich had replied, "The Commission wants to believe Mrs. Markham and that's all there is to it."[13] In a subsequent memorandum Liebeler warned that accepting Mrs. Markham's testimony "played into [Mark] Lane's hands" and left the Report open to criticism.[14] At last, after a heated exchange with Liebeler, Redlich agreed to qualify Mrs. Markham's testimony, and it was assigned only "probative" value.[15]

Ball was also extremely dubious of the testimony of Howard L. Brennan, the only eyewitness who claimed he could identify the assassin as Oswald.[16] At the time of the assassination Brennan was across the street from the Texas Book Depository, about 120 feet from the sixth-floor window from which the shots came. Later that day Brennan said at a police lineup that he could not identify Oswald as the assassin.[17] In January, when asked by the FBI, Brennan still insisted that he could not identify Oswald as the assassin.[18] However, when Brennan appeared before the Commission in March he said that he *could* identify the assassin as Oswald, and that he had lied at the police lineup to protect himself and his family.[19]

Ball had several reasons to doubt Brennan's testimony. First of all, in staging a "reconstruction" of the assassination on March 20, 1964, Ball found that Brennan had difficulty seeing a figure in the window, and thus it seemed doubtful that Brennan could have positively identified a man in the partially opened sixth-floor window 120 feet away.[20] Second, Brennan's identification was not based on prominent points in the assassin's clothes or dimensions. Third, Brennan's testimony contained a major error. Brennan stated that the assassin was standing while firing the rifle; other evidence, however, conclusively showed that the assassin fired from a kneeling or sitting position.[21] Finally, as far as Ball was concerned, the fact that Brennan had lied at the police lineup reflected on his general credibility.[22]

In rewriting the chapter, Redlich gave a great deal more weight to Brennan's identification than did Ball.[23] The section was subtitled "Eyewitness Identification of the Assassin," even though the Commission had never fully accepted Brennan's identification.[24] Redlich also added that "Brennan was in an excellent position to observe anyone in the window" and that "the record indicates Brennan was an accurate observer"— even though Brennan was *in*accurate in his description of the assassin's clothing and position.[25]

Although Ball found Marina Oswald to be "at best, an unreliable witness," Redlich based part of his version of the chapter on her testimony.[26] Redlich included, as one of the seven major points in the case against Oswald, Oswald's purported attempt to assassinate General Walker—despite the fact that Marina Oswald's testimony was the main evidence for this allegation and despite the fact that Mrs. Oswald had apparently fabricated or imagined Oswald's attempt to assassinate Richard Nixon.[27] Norman Redlich himself had asserted in February: ". . . Marina Oswald has lied to the Secret Service, the FBI, and this Commission on matters of vital concern. . . ."[28] Yet in rewriting the chapter Redlich chose to rely on Marina Oswald's testimony.[29]

Ball said that Helen Louise Markham, Howard Brennan, and Marina Oswald were not only unreliable witnesses but also unnecessary witnesses.[30] Yet Redlich gave added weight to the testimony of these witnesses.

It took nearly three months to rewrite Chapter IV. As Redlich said, "For a while, the job seemed endless."[31] Every fact had to be supported by other facts, every possibility had to be taken into account, every permutation had to be explored. And then, Redlich continued, there was the problem of consensus; every paragraph had to be written so that all seven Commissioners approved of it.[32]

Finally, on September 4, 1964, Chapter IV was completed and sent to the printer.[33]

The Liebeler Memorandum

Wesley Liebeler read the galley proofs of Chapter IV on the weekend of September 5, and he was disconcerted by the quality of the writing. He later said, "It read like a brief for the prosecution."[34]

Over the weekend Liebeler wrote a 26-page single-spaced memorandum which attacked the chapter point by point and warned:

> To put it bluntly, this sort of selection from the record could seriously affect the integrity and credibility of the entire report.[35]

The memorandum, by its detailed analysis of the way facts were selected, provides an insight into the writing of the Report.

First of all, there was the problem of gaps in the case against Oswald. How were these gaps filled? For example, to eliminate the possibility that Oswald's rifle was used by another person, the Report had to show that the rifle was in Oswald's possession on the day of the assassination. The chapter therefore asserted that "evidence showed" that the rifle was in the Paines' home (where Marina Oswald temporarily resided) on the eve of the assassination, that Oswald visited his wife at the Paines' home that evening, that he left on the morning of the assassination with a "long, bulky package," and that after the assassination the rifle was missing from the Paines' home.[36] Yet, although all these "facts" appeared to provide cogent evidence that Oswald took the rifle on the day of the assassination, Liebeler pointed out an important gap in the chain of "evidence": there was no actual evidence that the rifle was in the Paines' home on the eve of the assassination.[37]

Marina Oswald had testified that the rifle was transported from New Orleans to Dallas in a blanket and that the blanket was stored in the Paines' garage.[38] In September, she said, she had looked inside the blanket and had seen part of a rifle, but in the seven weeks preceding the assassination she had not looked inside the blanket or handled it, and thus she had no way of knowing whether the blanket still contained the rifle. This fact was demonstrated immediately after the assassination, when

Marina Oswald looked at the blanket without opening it and assumed the rifle was still inside it, although, as was later revealed, the blanket was empty.[39] No other witness saw the rifle in the blanket. Thus there was no evidence whatsoever that showed that the rifle was in the Paines' home between late September and the assassination, and it was conceivable that the rifle was removed sometime during this seven-week period. Liebeler noted: "Gaps cannot be filled by ignoring them."[40]

Second, there was the problem involving relevant evidence that was not cited. The chapter based its conclusion that Oswald carried the rifle in the "long, bulky package" mainly on the testimony of two witnesses, Linnie Mae Randle, Oswald's neighbor, and Buell Wesley Frazier, who drove Oswald to work on the morning of the assassination. Both witnesses believed that the bag was less than 28 inches long. However, the wooden stock of the rifle was 34.8 inches long, and thus, if the witnesses' testimony was accurate, the bag could not have contained the rifle.[41] Mrs. Randle said that she had had only a glimpse of the bag, and therefore no weight was given to her estimate of length.[42] Frazier based his estimate of two feet "give and take a few inches" on the fact that Oswald held the package under his arm, cupping the bottom of it with his right hand.[43] The chapter stated: "Frazier could easily have been mistaken when he stated that Oswald held the bottom of the bag cupped in his hand with the upper end tucked under his arm pit."[44] There was, however, corroborative evidence for Frazier's description which was neglected at this point, although it was mentioned elsewhere in the chapter: Liebeler pointed out that the location of Oswald's right palm print on the bag—the heel and fingers were on the bottom of the bag exactly as if it had been "cupped"—indicated that Frazier's description *was* accurate.[45]

Third, Liebeler's memorandum noted in the chapter a tendency to "stretch" inconclusive scientific evidence by selecting testimony out of context and thus making it appear conclusive.[46] For example, the chapter stated that fibers found in the paper bag (found in the Depository) matched fibers in the blanket in which it was *assumed* that the rifle was stored; and that this fact further indicated that the bag was used to carry the rifle into the Depository.[47]

However, Liebeler indicated that the fiber evidence was extremely "thin."[48] Paul Stombaugh, the FBI expert who examined the fiber evidence, testified that since the two types of fibers found in the bag were most common types, and since the blanket contained thirty different types of fibers, of which only two matched the fibers found in the bag, there was insufficient evidence to judge whether or not it was probable that the fibers in the bag came from the blanket.[49] Stombaugh said, "All I would say here is that it is possible that these fibers could have come from this blanket."[50] Yet, even though Stombaugh refused to say it was probable that the fibers came from the blanket, the chapter asserted that the fiber evidence indicated that the bag had once contained the rifle.[51]

Another problem with the fiber evidence was omitted from the chapter: the fibers found on the rifle did not match either those found in the bag or those found in the blanket.[52] If the rifle had been stored in the blanket, as was assumed, one would expect some blanket fibers to have been found on the rifle, but none were. Quite obviously, fibers in the bag which matched fibers in the blanket had no value as evidence unless fibers were also found on the rifle—especially since there was no evidence that the rifle had been stored in the blanket immediately before the assassination. The fact that fibers on the rifle did not match fibers in the blanket possibly indicated that the blanket had not contained the rifle. Yet this portion of the fiber evidence was omitted from the Report.

Liebeler also criticized the way in which the chapter interpreted the fingerprint evidence. In reaching the conclusion that Oswald was at the window when the shots were fired, the chapter attached "great weight" to the fact that Oswald's fingerprints and palm prints were on the cardboard cartons found near the window from which the shots came.[53]

However, Liebeler pointed out that these were cartons that Oswald normally handled in the course of his work, and that the fingerprints thus showed only that Oswald had handled the cartons and not that he was at the window at the time of the assassination.[54]

The final part of the memorandum's analysis of the evidence dealt with Oswald's capabilities as a rifleman.

The first problem was to see whether Oswald could have fired three shots in 5.6 seconds. This time was determined from the film of the assassination. Because the assassin's view of the President was blocked by the oak tree until film frame 207, this was assumed to be the earliest point at which the President could have been shot. On film frame 313, the last shot is clearly discernible. Using frame 210 as the earliest point, as the Report does, a maximum of 103 film frames elapsed between the first and last shot, and, since the camera speed was 18.3 frames per second, the maximum time that elapsed was 5.6 seconds. Thus it remained to be seen whether Oswald was capable of accurately firing the rifle three times in 5.6 seconds.[55]

The rifle tests held by the FBI and the Army were an important part of the evidence. The first tests with Oswald's rifle were conducted on November 27, 1963, by the FBI. Each of three rifle experts—Charles Killion, Cortlandt Cunningham, and Robert Frazier—fired three shots at a target fifteen yards away. All the shots were high and to the right of the aiming point: Killion's firing time was 9 seconds; Cunningham's firing time was 8 seconds; Frazier's firing time was 6 seconds.[56] Thus none of the FBI experts equaled Oswald's time, despite the fact that their target was stationary and only fifteen yards away; whereas Oswald's target was moving and more than sixty yards away.

Later the same day Frazier fired two more series of shots "to determine how fast the weapon could be fired primarily."[57] The first series of three shots was fired in 4.8 seconds, and the second one was fired in 4.6 seconds.[58] Frazier testified that firing in 4.6 seconds "is firing this weapon as fast as the bolt can be operated."[59]

The final FBI tests were held at Quantico, Virginia, on March 16, 1964. Frazier fired three series of shots at a target a hundred yards away. His time for the first series of three shots was 5.9 seconds; for the second series, 6.2 seconds; and for the third series, 6.5 seconds.[60] Not only did Frazier fail to equal Oswald's time of 5.6 seconds, but all his shots were about five inches high and about five inches to the right of the aiming point. Frazier explained in his testimony that the inaccuracy was due to an uncorrectable mechanical deficiency in the telescopic sights.[61]

The Commission evidently was not satisfied with the results of the FBI tests, because it arranged for the United States Army Ballistic Research Laboratory to conduct further tests on March 27, 1964.[62] Three rifle experts—Hendrix, Staley, and Miller, all of whom held Master rifle ratings from the National Rifle Association—fired at three silhouette targets located at distances matching the distances of the Presidential limousine from the source of the shots during the assassination.

Hendrix fired his first series of three bullets in 8.25 seconds and missed the second target; he fired his second series in 7.0 seconds and missed the third target. Staley fired his first series in 6.75 seconds and his second series in 6.45 seconds; both times he missed the second target. Miller was the only expert to equal Oswald's time; he fired his first series in 4.6 seconds and his second series in 5.5 seconds, although he missed the second target both times. Miller later fired a third series, using standard sights instead of telescopic sights. In this series he fired three shots in 4.45 seconds, but the third shot went wild and missed the board as well as the silhouette target.[63]

Although the Army tests demonstrated that it was at least possible to fire three shots in 5.6 seconds with the murder weapon, three factors must be taken into account in evaluating these tests.

First, the experts were timed only from the sound of the first shot to the sound of the last shot. This meant that they had *unlimited* time to aim at the first target and pull the trigger before they were timed.[64] The assassin, however, had only 5.6 seconds for all three shots from the moment the car first became visible, and thus his aiming time was included in the total time. This is a significant factor. For example, if it is assumed it took the assassin one second to react, aim, and pull the trigger, then he had only 4.6 seconds (*not* 5.6 seconds) to fire. Thus, in order to make comparisons, this aiming factor must be added to the experts' time.

Second, the experts were firing at a stationary target, whereas the assassin was firing at a moving target. FBI expert Robert Frazier, who supervised the FBI rifle tests, testified that a moving target "would have slowed down the shooting. It would have lengthened the time to the extent of allowing the crosshairs to pass over the moving target."[65] Frazier estimated this sighting time would be "approximately one second,"[66] but it is unclear whether he meant one second for each shot or for all three shots. In any case, this sighting time would also have to be added to the experts' time in order for comparisons to be made.

Finally, when the Army experts found that the sight could not be accurately aimed at a target, they added three "shims" to the sight to correct the inaccuracy.[67] Thus the Army experts fired with accurate sights, whereas, so far as is known, the assassin fired with inaccurate sights.

Despite the fact that only two of the six rifle experts were able to equal the assassin's time of 5.6 seconds, the draft chapter characterized the shots as "easy shots."[68] Statements were selected from four expert witnesses which appeared to support this characterization, but Liebeler pointed out that these selected statements pertained only to the distance and trajectory of the shots, and *not* to the time factor involved in firing.[69] In other words, the fact that the assassin had only 5.6 seconds to fire the three shots was not taken into account.

The manner in which this testimony was developed indicates that premeditation was involved in the selection process. The two witnesses who characterized the shots as "easy shots," Major Eugene Anderson and Sergeant James Zahm, were not called until July 24, 1964.[70] At this late date the investigation had been closed for more than a month, and Redlich was involved in rewriting the chapter. The date these witnesses testified thus suggests that they were called for the express purpose of characterizing the shots as "easy shots," and the type of questions they were asked seems to reflect this possibility.

Each witness was asked a hypothetical question in which the distance of the shot, the trajectory, and even the street downgrade were given, but the time factor was conspicuously omitted.[71] Therefore, in answering the question, neither witness had to take into account the most difficult problem, firing three shots in 5.6 seconds. Thus both witnesses characterized the shots as "not difficult" and "easy."[72]

Liebeler found these assertions to be contrary to the evidence, which showed that the shot was extremely difficult. The memorandum indicated that in 80 per cent of the tests in which accuracy was a primary concern the experts failed to equal Oswald's maximum time. Moreover, only one of the six experts accomplished this feat, and the average time for all the experts was well over six seconds.[73] Liebeler reasoned that if the experts, firing under far more favorable conditions than Oswald did, failed most of the time to fire three shots in 5.6 seconds, the shots could hardly be called "easy shots."[74]

Liebeler stated that it was "simply dishonest" not to mention the problem with the sight in the chapter.[75] The telescopic sight, it will be recalled, was defective; thus, if the assassin had placed the crosshairs of the sight on the target, the bullet would have missed. Despite the difficulties this would present in rapid-fire shooting, the chapter neglected to mention the problem.

The chapter asserted that Oswald had sufficient proficiency with a rifle to have committed the assassination.[76] This conclusion was based mainly on the rifle scores Oswald had achieved in the United States Marine Corps. Oswald had taken only two tests. In his first test he scored 212, which was considered by the Marine Corps a "fairly good shot"; in his second test, in 1959, he scored 191, which was considered a "rather poor shot."[77]

On the basis of these scores, Major Anderson and Sergeant Zahm—neither of whom had any direct knowledge of Oswald's training or rifle proficiency—testified that "Oswald was a good shot."[78] The chapter again relied on the testimony of these two witnesses for the conclusion that Oswald was a good shot.[79]

Liebeler, however, stated that "this was the worst kind of selection" because it omitted other witnesses who had had direct experience with Oswald's marksmanship.[80] One such witness was Nelson Delgado, who had stood next to Oswald when he had fired a rifle in the Marine Corps on a number of occasions.[81] Delgado testified that Oswald was a poor shot and often missed the target completely. In fact, according to Delgado, Oswald's targets were considered "a pretty big joke, because he got a lot of 'Maggies drawers' [complete misses]."[82] Both Oswald's rifle score in 1959 (191) and Delgado's testimony indicate that Oswald was a poor, rather than a good, shot. Yet the chapter omitted Delgado's testimony and thus was able to maintain that the 1959 rifle tests were taken under poor conditions and that Oswald was a good shot.

Furthermore, the chapter implied that, while in the Soviet Union, Oswald had practiced his marksmanship by participating in hunts.[83] Liebeler stated, however, that there was no evidence that Oswald had thereby improved his proficiency.[84] In fact, there was information indicating that "Oswald was an *ex-*

tremely poor shot and it was necessary for persons who accompanied him on hunts to provide him with game."[85] This information came from the Soviet KGB file on Oswald (furnished by Yuri I. Nosenko, a Soviet intelligence staff officer who defected in February 1964).[86] Although this file casts light on Oswald's rifle proficiency in the Soviet Union, it was never published or referred to by the Commission.

After Oswald returned from the Soviet Union in 1962 there was no evidence that he ever fired a rifle again, except for one time when hunting with his brother. There is also the possibility that Oswald attempted to shoot General Walker. However, the sniper missed Walker, a stationary, well-lit target, at relatively close range.

Thus all evidence of Oswald's rifle proficiency, from his 1959 Marine marksmanship test to his alleged attempted assassination of General Walker, indicates that Oswald was a poor shot. Furthermore, the Commission found no evidence that Oswald had ever practiced firing the rifle.

Liebeler said that the chapter glossed over the evidence that Oswald was a poor shot and had accomplished a difficult feat, and created a "fairy tale" that Oswald was a good shot and had accomplished an "easy shot."[87]

On September 6, 1964, Liebeler submitted his twenty-six-page memorandum to Rankin. At first, Rankin refused to accept the memorandum, saying, "No more memorandums! The Report has to be published!"[88] However, Liebeler was insistent, and finally Rankin read the memorandum and then immediately summoned Redlich to Washington.[89]

According to Liebeler, Redlich heatedly objected to all Liebeler's criticisms.[90] He explained that he had written the chapter exactly the way the Commission wanted it written.[91] He said, "The Commission judged it an easy shot, and *I* work for the Commission."[92]

Finally Rankin adjudicated the dispute point by point.[93] Most of Liebeler's criticisms were rejected, but some changes were made in the chapter. The problem with the sights was inserted in the chapter, although it was also suggested that the defective sights were actually an advantage for the sniper.[94] The fiber evidence, which had been used to indicate that Oswald had brought the rifle into the Texas Book Depository, and the fingerprint evidence, which had been used to show Oswald's presence at the window, were both assigned only probative value.[95] And the statement that the rifle was in the Paines' home the night before the assassination was made less definite, although the chapter still implied that this was a known fact.[96]

Although Chapter IV is not a "prosecutor's brief" in the sense that it presents only one side of the case, it certainly is not an impartial presentation of the facts. In the final analysis, Redlich did "work for the Commission." That he is a man of high personal integrity only adds to the poignancy of the situation. In his role as editor, he had to select evidence that supported the Commission's judgments. As contradictory evidence and inconsistent details therefore tended to be omitted, the selection process tended to make the Commission's judgments self-reinforcing.

10

The Commission's Conclusions

As Commissioner Ford put it, "Conclusions were the work of the Commission."[1] The staff conducted the investigation and drafted the report, but in the final analysis the Commission had to reach the conclusions and take the responsibility for them. There were five main conclusions.

First, the Commission concluded that the shots came from the Texas School Book Depository. This conclusion was based on medical evidence which showed that at least two of the shots came from the general direction of the Depository; on the testimony of eyewitnesses who saw a rifle in the sixth-floor window of the Depository; and on the fact that the murder weapon and three cartridge cases were found on the sixth floor of the Depository.[2] Although this evidence in itself did not exclude the possibility that other shots came from a different source, it constituted ample proof that shots had come from the Depository.

The second conclusion concerned the sequence of events and presented a difficult problem. It will be recalled that the film of the assassination showed that the President and Governor Connally were hit less than two seconds apart, and that rifle tests showed that it was physically impossible for the murder weapon to be accurately fired twice within this period of time. Thus, either both men were hit by the same bullet or there had to be two assassins. Norman Redlich, Arlen Specter, and other members of the staff took the position that the Report had to conclude that both men were hit by the same bullet.[3] There was, however, no substantial evidence which supported this contention, and there was evidence that all but precluded the possibility that both men had been hit by the same bullet.[4]

The Commission was thus confronted with a dilemma. If it disregarded the evidence that Connally could not have been hit by the same bullet that hit Kennedy, and if it concluded that both men were hit by the same bullet, the credibility of the entire Report might be jeopardized. If, however, the Commission concluded that both men were hit by separate bullets, the single-assassin theory would be untenable in terms of the established evidence and assumptions.

In the "spectrum of opinion" that existed on this question, Ford said he was closest to the position that both men were hit by the same bullet, and Senator Russell was furthest away.[5] In fact, Russell reportedly said that he would not sign a Report which concluded that both men were hit by the same bullet.[6] Senator Cooper and Representative Boggs tended to agree with Russell's position. Cooper said, "I, too, objected to such a conclusion; there was no evidence to show both men were hit by the same bullet."[7] Boggs said, "I had strong doubts about it [the single-bullet theory]," and he added that he felt the question was never resolved.[8]

Both Dulles and McCloy said that they believed the most reasonable explanation of the assassination was that both men were hit by the same bullet.[9] The Commission was thus more or less evenly split on this question, with Ford, Dulles, and McCloy tending toward the conclusion that both men were hit by the same bullet, and Russell, Cooper, and Boggs tending toward the conclusion that both men were hit by separate bullets.

McCloy said that it was of vital importance to have an unanimous Report. He proposed, as a compromise, stating merely that there was evidence that both men were hit by the same bullet but that, in view of other evidence, the Commission could not decide on the probability of this.[10]

There then followed what was described as "the battle of the adjectives."[11] Ford wanted to state that there was "compelling" evidence that both men were hit by the same bullet, while Russell wanted to state merely that there was only "credible" evidence.[12] McCloy finally suggested that the adjective "persuasive" be used, and this word was agreed upon.[13] The Report states:

> Although it is not necessary to any essential findings of the Commission to determine just which shot hit Governor Connally, there is very persuasive evidence from the experts to indicate that the same bullet which pierced the President's throat also caused Governor Connally's wounds. However, Governor Connally's testimony and certain other factors have given rise to some difference of opinion as to this probability but there is no question in the mind of any member of the Commission that all the shots which caused the President's and Governor Connally's wounds were fired from the sixth floor window of the Texas School Book Depository.[14]

The question was thus left open by the Commission.

Third, the Commission concluded that the assassin was Lee Harvey Oswald. This conclusion was based on seven subconclusions: (1) the murder weapon belonged to Oswald; (2) Oswald carried the weapon into the Depository; (3) at the time of the assassination Oswald was at the window from which the shots were fired; (4) the murder weapon was found in the Depository after the assassination; (5) Oswald possessed enough proficiency with a rifle to have committed the assassination; (6) Oswald lied to the police; and (7) Oswald had attempted to kill General Walker.[15]

The most compelling of these subconclusions was that Oswald's rifle was used in the assassination. This fact, together with evidence that Oswald had had the opportunity to commit the assassination, made for a strong case against Oswald. The only other possibility is that another person used Oswald's rifle, but Oswald's subsequent actions—leaving the scene, shooting a policeman, and resisting arrest—certainly were not the actions of an innocent person.

The other subconclusions, however, were based on less substantial evidence. Subconclusion (2)—that Oswald carried the rifle into the Depository—was no more than a plausible assumption;[16] (3)—Oswald's presence at the window—was supported only by "probative" evidence (e.g., Brennan's identification); (4) —the presence of the rifle in the building—merely reinforced (1); (5)—Oswald's rifle capabilities—was based on extremely dubious evidence;[17] (6)—that Oswald lied to the police—had little value as evidence since, purportedly, no record of Oswald's interrogation statements was kept; and (7)—Oswald's attempt to kill Walker—was based mainly on the testimony of Marina Oswald.

The Commission's fourth conclusion concerned Oswald's motive. Although the Commission "could not make any definitive determination of Oswald's motives," it listed five factors "which might have influenced Oswald's decision to assassinate President Kennedy."[18] These possible motives were: (1) Oswald's resentment of all authority; (2) his inability to enter into meaningful relationships with people; (3) his urge to find a place in history; (4) his capacity for violence; and (5) his commitment to Marxism and communism.[19]

Wesley Liebeler, who originally wrote the chapter on Oswald's motivation, said that each Commissioner had his own "pet theory" to explain Oswald's actions.[20] For example, McCloy persistently suggested the "killer-instinct theory" to Liebeler, although support for this theory was not evident in Oswald's life history. Finally this theory was worked into the conclusions as factor (4).[21] Ford insisted that Oswald's commitment to communism be listed as a factor (5),[22] although it was not clear how this commitment had contributed to Oswald's decision. A number of Commissioners felt that Oswald was motivated by an "urge to find a place in history," but the only evidence for this theory was Marina Oswald's February testimony, and in her September testimony Mrs. Oswald refuted her own earlier testimony on this point.[23] Nor were factors (1) and (2) based on objective evidence.

Joseph Ball commented that the Commission replaced Liebeler's informed and brilliant analysis of Oswald's personality with "clichés that belonged in a television script."[24]

Finally there was the question of whether or not Oswald acted alone. Ford said that the draft of the Conclusion stated categorically that there was no conspiracy, but he had insisted that this wording be changed to read: "The Commission has found no evidence of a conspiracy."[25] McCloy said that the Commission could render a conclusion only on the basis of the evidence brought before it,[26] and thus the following qualification was added:

> Because of the difficulty of proving a negative to a certainty the possibility of others being involved with either Oswald or Ruby cannot be rejected categorically, but if there is any such evidence it has been beyond the reach of all investigative agencies and resources of the United States and has not come to the attention of this Commission.[27]

It is true that the Commission found no evidence that others were involved with Oswald in the assassination, but, as has been shown, the investigation was by no means exhaustive or even thorough.[28] The question thus remains: How far did the Commission go in approaching the threshold question of a second assassin?

The Zapruder film shows that the assassination could have been committed by one man alone only under one condition: that Kennedy and Connally were hit by the same bullet. However, the FBI Summary and Supplemental Reports' statements on the autopsy, if accurate, preclude this condition. (They state, it will be recalled, that the first bullet did not exit from the front of the President's body.)[29] Furthermore, even if the Summary and the Supplemental Reports are inaccurate, other evidence arose which showed that it was not possible that both men were hit by the same bullet.[30] Unless the basic facts and assumption established by the Commission are incorrect, there is a strong case that Oswald could not have acted alone.

Why did the Commission fail to take cognizance in its conclusions of this evidence of a second assassin? Quite clearly, a serious discussion of this problem would in itself have undermined the dominant purpose of the Commission, namely, the settling of doubts and suspicions. Indeed, if the Commission had made it clear that very substantial evidence indicated the presence of a second assassin, it would have opened a Pandora's box of doubts and suspicions. In establishing its version of the truth, the Warren Commission acted to reassure the nation and protect the national interest.

EPILOGUE I

The House Select Committee on Assassination (1992)

Thirteen years after *Inquest* was published, the House of Representatives' Select Committee on Assassination dealt with the vexing question of the contradictory autopsy reports. The issue, it will be recalled, was the conflict between the FBI and the Warren Commission. Whereas the FBI Summary Report (which had not been released by the Warren Commission) stated that President Kennedy's autopsy found that the bullet that hit President Kennedy's shoulder had penetrated into it only a few inches, then popped out—presumably on the stretcher on which a whole bullet had been found—the version in the Warren Commission report held that the same autopsy had found that the same bullet had passed through Kennedy's body and exited through his throat. Had the FBI, which had been given the original autopsy report, made a mistake? Had the autopsy findings been altered after the FBI had been given its copy? What did the autopsy itself reveal about where the bullets of the assassin (or assassins) had come from? Adding to the confusion, it turned out that neither the pathologists performing the autopsy nor the Warren Commission investigators had been permitted to examine the X-ray photographs of the president's body that could have provided the definitive answer.

In 1979, the Select Committee on Assassination finally decided to resolve the issue of the bullets. It empaneled nine leading forensic pathologists, including Dr. Cyril H. Wecht, a well-respected critic of the Warren Commission Report, and authorized them to reexamine all the autopsy evidence. These doctors were given complete access to the X rays and color photographs of the body and free rein to requestion the personnel involved in the examination of the president on November 22, 1963. They began by establishing through scientific testing that the autopsy evidence had not been tampered with in the interim. Then, through a precise reconstruction of the chronology of what happened following the assassination, they explained many of the discrepancies in the original autopsy.

These experts concluded, without any dissent, that President Kennedy was shot twice, from above and behind. The first shot hit him in the back shoulder—two inches lower than where the Warren Commission's diagram placed it. The other hit him in the head and fatally wounded him. All of Governor Connally wounds had also been caused by a bullet fired from above and behind. Moreover, the trajectory extrapolated from all these wounds led to approximately the sixth floor of the Texas Schoolbook Depository, where a rifle had been found that ballistically matched at least one of the bullets that had been fired. The reexamination left no reason anymore to doubt the Warren Commission's conclusion that the shots that hit both men came from a sixth-floor window of the Texas Schoolbook Depository.

But how many assassins had fired these bullets from the Texas Schoolbook Depository?

The House Select Committee on Assassination recognized that establishing the sequence of which shot hit whom was critical to resolving this question. Its analysis of the photographic evidence confirmed what Arlen Specter had told his superiors on the Warren Commission in 1964: It was not physically possible for the bolt on the rifle in question to have been opened and closed fast enough for that rifle to have fired first the bullet that hit President Kennedy and then the bullet that hit Governor Connally. Either the first shot had hit both men simultaneously, or a second rifle—and second rifleman—participated in the assassination.

The panel of nine forensic pathologists methodically reexamined the photographs, X rays, the bullet found on a stretcher in the hospital, and other evidence to determine if it indeed was possible that a single bullet could have hit Kennedy in the back, exited the front of his neck, pierced Governor Connally's body, exited his chest, shattered the radius bone of his wrist, and superficially wounded his thigh, but on this key issue they were not able to reach an unanimous conclusion. Eight of the doctors deemed this single-bullet theory possible, but Cyril Wecht disagreed. He concluded: "The single-bullet theory is unequivocally repudiated by an objective, thorough evaluation and analysis of all the medical, scientific and physical data."

If Wecht is correct, there must have been two riflemen firing from the depository. And the second sniper, like Oswald, left the building before it was sealed by police.

On the other hand, if Wecht is wrong and the other doctors are right, it means that it was physically possible that a single assassin wounded both men with his first shot, missed with a second shot, and killed the president with a third shot. Consequently, he could have acted alone.

That latter scenario could have happened, however, only if the eyewitness testimony of Governor Connally that he "heard the first shot, reacted to the first shot, and was not hit with that bullet" is wrong. But it appears to be wholly substantiated by the Warren Commission's own frame-by-frame analysis of the film of the motorcade, which clearly shows, one and one half seconds after Kennedy has been initially shot (and is clutching his throat), Connally holding his cowboy hat in his right hand— a feat which would not be possible if his right wristbone had been shattered by that first bullet.

So despite the valiant attempt to establish the single-bullet theory, the possibility, if not probability, remains that two riflemen fired on the presidential motorcade.

BOOK TWO

COUNTERPLOT

GARRISON AGAINST THE WORLD
(1968)

Prologue:
Oswald in New Orleans

On September 28, 1964, the President's Commission on the Assassination of President Kennedy, popularly known as the Warren Commission, issued its formal conclusion that Lee Harvey Oswald, acting alone, was responsible for the murder of John F. Kennedy. In the effort to prove that Oswald had no accomplices in the crime, the Commission attempted to reconstruct as precisely as possible the principal events of Oswald's life. However, despite the availability of diaries which he had kept over the years, as well as other personal effects and documents and the testimony of witnesses who claimed to have known him or known of him, charting the alleged assassin's movements was no easy task. For it was clear to the Commission from the outset that Lee Harvey Oswald was an itinerant, elusive, self-occupied individual. The biography of such a subject was bound to be, at best, a sketchy and imperfect record.

Of all the obscure periods in Oswald's life, few seemed to be potentially more significant, and at the same time more puzzling, than the summer of 1963, just before the assassination; it was then that Oswald again took up residence in his native New Orleans. For the Warren Commission, aspects of that summer in New Orleans seemed especially crucial, since it was during those months that Oswald appeared to have engaged in the sort of murky political activity and intrigue which might suggest a possible motive for the assassination. Although Commission lawyers were able to piece together fragments of Oswald's stay in New Orleans, it was evident, when their Report was published, that important gaps remained in the narrative, gaps which the Commission had not succeeded in filling in.

That fragmentary account of the New Orleans interval begins on April 25, 1963, when Oswald stepped off the night bus from Dallas. He carried with him two duffel bags, containing clothes and a few other personal belongings, including a Mannlicher-Carcano rifle which had been purchased a month before from a mail-order house in Chicago. His wife, Marina, testified that the rifle was partly responsible for Oswald's going to New Orleans. "I wanted to get him further removed from Dallas and from [Major General] Walker," she explained to the Warren Commission, "because a rifle for him was a toy that was too enticing."[1] Oswald, however, told a friend that he decided to move because "New Orleans is my home; I like the high ceilings and the trees and the French Quarter, and everything about New Orleans."[2]

From the bus depot, Oswald telephoned Lillian Murret, an aunt whom he hadn't seen since he was a child. Mrs. Murret recalled that she was surprised to hear from her nephew—the last news she had had of him was when he defected to Russia in 1959—and that she invited Oswald to stay with her family while he looked for a job in New Orleans. During the three weeks he lived with them, Mrs. Murret testified, Oswald said very little about his travels or plans for the future. He spent the days job-hunting, and in the evenings seemed concerned about tracing his own past. He went to Lakeview Cemetery to locate the grave of his father, who had died two months before he was born. And he methodically went down the list of Oswalds in the New Orleans telephone directory, calling each of them until he found the only one who was related to him—his uncle's widow, Mrs. Hazel Oswald. She gave him a framed photograph of his father (which he later apparently discarded).[3]

On May 9, he finally managed to find a job. Responding to a newspaper advertisement, Oswald was hired as a greaser and oiler of coffee-processing machinery at the William B. Reily Company. He rented a furnished apartment on Magazine Street, which parallels the industrial canal, for sixty-five dollars a month. He then called Marina, whom he had married in Russia and brought back to America with him from Minsk, and said he was ready for her to come to New Orleans.

Ruth Paine, the Russian-speaking woman with whom Marina was staying in Dallas, recalled how excited Marina was at hearing from Lee: *"Papa nas lubet,"* "Daddy loves us," she repeated over and over to June, their fourteen-month-old daughter. The next day, Mrs. Paine drove Marina and June to New Orleans. Oswald, she told the Commission, was quite proud of the apartment he had chosen: "He was pleased there was room enough. . . . And he pointed out this little courtyard with grass, and fresh strawberries ready to pick, where June could play. . . . And he was pleased with the furniture and how the landlady had said this was early New Orleans style." But Marina was less enthusiastic. "It is dark, and it is not very clean," she said; and she noticed the cockroaches.[4]

Nonetheless, the first few weeks in New Orleans seemed to Marina a pleasant change from Dallas. Oswald took his family for outings to the beaches, parks, and zoo. On weekends they would tour the French Quarter or go to the shores of Lake Pontchartrain where, as Marina put it, "Lee liked to go and hunt crabs." Oswald told his wife that he was doing "photographic work" (although he actually spent his days greasing coffee machines). In the evening he read books—*Portrait of a Revolutionary: Mao Tsetung* by Robert Payne, *Portrait of a President* by William Manchester, *The Huey Long Murder Case* by Hermann B. Deutsch—borrowed from the neighborhood branch of the public library. Or he pursued his losing battle with the roaches —"He was always in the back of the house, spraying," his landlord observed.[5]

But near the end of May, things changed. Marina wrote to her friend Ruth Paine, "I am very hurt that Lee's attitude towards me is such that I feel each minute that I bind him."[6] Lee had told her that he felt "lost" in America and wanted to return to Russia with her and June. Marina wanted to stay, but her husband insisted that she write to the Soviet Embassy in Washington, to request repatriation. As the summer progressed, he seemed increasingly concerned with sending his family to Russia, and in July he had Marina write a second letter asking the Embassy to rush their visas. Without telling her, Oswald added a note to the letter, asking that his application for a visa be considered "separately" from that of his wife and child. He apparently had plans of his own.[7]

Oswald also seemed to be worried about the "undesirable" discharge he had received from the Marine Corps, and consulted a New Orleans lawyer, Dean Adams Andrews, Jr., about the possibility of having it converted to an honorable discharge. Oswald returned to the lawyer's office at least two more times, accompanied by a stocky, well-built Mexican. Andrews also told the Warren Commission that he later assumed Oswald had been sent to his office by one Clay Bertrand—"mostly a voice on a phone," as Andrews described him, who occasionally had called him to obtain bond or parole for "gay kids"—because, he said, it was Bertrand who phoned him after the assassination to suggest that he defend Oswald in Dallas.[8] The Warren Commission, however, was not able to find any trace of Clay Bertrand or of the Mexican.

By mid-July, Oswald had been fired from his job at the Reily coffee company. Although Marina vaguely knew that her husband was engaged in some sort of "pro-Cuban" project, she had little idea of exactly how he spent his last seventy-odd days in New Orleans. Oswald, however, summarized his pro-Castro activities in a brief autobiographical sketch:

On May 29, 1963, I requested permission from the FPCC [Fair Play for Cuba Committee] headquarters at 799 Broadway, New York 3, N.Y., to try to form a local branch in New Orleans. I received a cautious but enthusiastic go-ahead from V. T. Lee, National Director of FPCC. I then made layouts and had printed public literature for the setting up of a local FPCC. I hired persons to distribute literature. I then organized persons who display receptive attitudes towards Cuba to distribute pamphlets.

I sought response from Latin American consuls of which there are many here in New Orleans. I infiltrated the Cuban Student Directorate and then harassed them with information I gained, including having the New Orleans city attorney general call them and put a restraining order pending a hearing on some so-called bonds for an invasion they were selling in the New Orleans area. I caused the formation of a small, active FPCC organization of members and sympathizers where before there was none.

I am experienced in street agitation having done it in New Orleans in connection with the FPCC. On August 9, 1963, I was accosted by three anti-Castro Cubans and was arrested for "causing a disturbance." I was interrogated by intelligence section of New Orleans Police Department and held overnight, being bailed out the next morning by relatives. I subsequently was fined $10; charges against the three Cubans were dropped by the judge.

On August 16 I organized a four-man FPCC demonstration in front of the International Trade Mart in New Orleans. This demonstration was filmed by WDSU-TV and shown on the 6:00 news.

On August 17 I was invited by WDSU-Radio to appear on the August 17 radio program Latin American Focus at 7:30 p.m. The moderator was Bill Stucky, who put questions to me for a half an hour about FPCC attitudes and opinions.

After this program I was invited to take part in a radio debate between John [Edward S.] Butler of INCA, anti-Communist propaganda representative, and Carlos Bringuier, Cuban exile Student Revolutionary Directorate delegate in New Orleans. This debate was broadcast at 6:05 to 6:30 August 21, 1963; after this program I made a three-minute TV newsreel which was shown the next day (August 22).

I received advice, direction and literature from V. T. Lee, National Director of the Fair Play for Cuba Committee, of which I am a member. At my own expense I had printed "Hands Off Cuba" handbills and New Orleans branch membership blanks for the FPCC local.[9]

Although this résumé was documented with newspaper clippings, letters from the Fair Play for Cuba Committee and the Communist Party, subscription receipts from the *Worker* and from Soviet journals, membership cards in the FPCC, etc., it was neither totally accurate nor candid. For one thing, the "FPCC organization" which Oswald said he formed in New Orleans had never been authorized by the FPCC; in fact, it didn't even exist. While it is true that Oswald wrote to the Fair Play for

Cuba Committee in New York, requesting a "charter" for a New Orleans chapter and a "picture of Fidel, suitable for framing," and offered to rent an office at his own expense, the reply he received was hardly encouraging. V. T. Lee, the national director of the FPCC, wrote Oswald that a charter for a New Orleans chapter could not be granted until a requisite number of members had been duly enrolled, and V. T. Lee expressed doubt that Oswald would find sufficient members in the New Orleans area. Moreover, he specifically asked Oswald not to rent an office.

A few days later, Oswald wrote another letter to V. T. Lee. "Against your advice," he told the national director, "I have decided to take an office."[10] Whether or not Oswald actually did rent an office, however, is a moot point. The cachet "FPCC, 544 CAMP ST." appears on some of the pro-Castro literature Oswald possessed, but the building at 544 Camp Street, which was a block from the coffee company where Oswald had worked, housed an *anti*-Castro group known as the Cuban Revolutionary Council. W. Guy Banister, a New Orleans private detective heavily involved in anti-Castro activities, also maintained offices in that building, and one of Banister's investigators, Jack S. Martin, had helped set up the Cuban Revolutionary Council at that address.[11] After the assassination, it was Jack Martin who alleged that David William Ferrie, for a short time also a New Orleans private detective, was to have been Oswald's "getaway pilot," but later he recanted this story.[12]

In his second letter to V. T. Lee, Oswald also enclosed a circular that read: "HANDS OFF CUBA! JOIN THE FAIR PLAY FOR CUBA COMMITTEE, NEW ORLEANS CHARTER MEMBER BRANCH. FREE LITERATURE, LECTURES, EVERYONE WELCOME." And he added, "As you see from the circular I had jumped the gun on the charter business, but I don't think it's too important."[13] (Using the alias Lee Osborne, Oswald had had two thousand such circulars printed.) Finally, Oswald said that he had decided on a "major change of tactics" for his "chapter."

V. T. Lee did not reply to this or to any of the subsequent letters Oswald sent to the FPCC. He testified before the Warren Commission that he had been quite disturbed that Oswald "had gone ahead and acted on his own without any authorization from the organization" and had violated the "rules of the organization" by setting up a "chapter" under the "name of the organization."[14]

Moreover, Oswald's "FPCC chapter" apparently had only one member: Oswald. Marina testified that her husband had forced her to sign the name "A. J. Hidell, Chapter President"* on the FPCC membership card he had had printed (under still another alias), explaining to her that it was necessary to use a fictitious name so that "people will think I have a big organization."[15] Marina recalled that when a Cuban man had come to their apartment to make inquiries about joining Oswald's FPCC chapter, her husband made no effort to enroll him; he subsequently explained to her that the caller was probably "some anti-Castro Cuban or perhaps an FBI agent."[16] Oswald, it turned out, was right: the inquirer, Carlos Quiroga, a prominent anti-Castro exile leader, later told Secret Service investigators that he had been trying to "infiltrate Oswald's organization."[17] Marina was certain that no one ever joined what she called Oswald's "non-existing organization."[18]

Oswald's description of the "demonstrations" was also somewhat hyperbolic. After single-handedly picketing the aircraft carrier U.S.S. *Wasp* (until he was unceremoniously expelled from the pier by a patrolman), he wrote V. T. Lee, "We managed to picket the fleet when it came in and I was surprised at the number of officers who were interested in our literature."[19] While it is true that on August 9, 1963, Oswald did, as he reports, get involved in a fracas with three anti-Castroites, the incident appears to have been planned and provoked by Oswald himself. On August 1, eight days *before* the reported incident took place, Oswald wrote V. T. Lee that a "street demonstration" which he organized was "attacked" by "Cuban-exile gusanos (worms)" and that afterward "we were officially cautioned by the police."[20] This letter was sent on August 4.[21] The next day Oswald visited the Casa Roca, a haberdashery that served as a center for anti-Castro activity. When Oswald entered the store, the manager, Carlos Bringuier, was discussing the sale of ten-dollar Cuban invasion bonds with two teen-agers. Oswald casu-

---

* Oswald also used the alias "Hidell" on three other occasions: on a vaccination certificate, as an employment reference, and on the order blank for the Mannlicher-Carcano rifle.

ally introduced himself to Bringuier, who claimed to be the New Orleans representative of the Cuban Student Directorate, and told him that he had been trained in guerrilla warfare in the Marine Corps and now wanted to "train Cubans to fight against Castro." To prove his mettle, Oswald furnished some on-the-spot suggestions for blowing up the Huey P. Long bridge ("put powder charges at each end of the bridge from the foundation to where the foundation meets the suspension part"); for derailing trains ("put a chain around the railroad track and lock it to the track"); for making zipguns ("tubing and plunger"); and for making gunpowder ("saltpeter and nitrate").[22] Bringuier, however, held Oswald's motives suspect for at least two reasons: after his group had taken part in a shelling of Havana, he had been warned by an FBI agent that the FBI intended to infiltrate his organization; and only a few days before, Bringuier had received word that a pro-Castro agent was attempting to infiltrate the anti-Castro training camps on Lake Pontchartrain. Uncertain as to which side Oswald was really on, Bringuier even refused to accept a cash contribution from him. Oswald returned the next day to leave his Marine training manual with Bringuier.[23]

Then, on August 9, Oswald again appeared in the vicinity of Bringuier's store. This time, he bore a "Viva Fidel" placard and distributed *pro*-Castro propaganda. With a few other Cuban counterrevolutionists, Bringuier rushed out of his store and began shouting at Oswald. "O.K., Carlos," Oswald calmly said, "if you want to hit me, hit me," but Bringuier refused. At this point, the police arrived and arrested both Oswald and Bringuier.[24]

Oswald was, as he said, "interrogated" by the New Orleans police, but he himself volunteered a good deal of information concerning his phantom FPCC chapter. He said he had been associated with the FPCC since 1959; that there were thirty-five members in his FPCC chapter; that they rotated their meetings among various members' homes; and that A. J. Hidell was president of the group.[25] Oswald then *asked* to see an FBI agent. And when an agent, John Lester Quigly, visited Oswald in jail later that day, Oswald tried to convince him that the FPCC was an active, operative group in New Orleans. But the FBI man came away with the impression that Oswald's admissions were false and merely intended as a "self-serving statement."[26] After spending the night in jail, Oswald was released on ten dollars bail.

According to the Warren Commission, Oswald staged his second "demonstration" on August 16. At the Louisiana State Employment office, Oswald hired the sixteen-year-old son of a local deputy sheriff and a second unidentified individual to assist him in distributing "Hands Off Cuba" leaflets in front of the International Trade Mart. (In Oswald's description, it was a "four-man . . . demonstration.") Crews from two local television stations, apparently tipped off in advance, were standing by to capture on TV tape the pro-Castro activities of Lee Harvey Oswald. He wrote V. T. Lee that this demonstration "was given considerable coverage by WDSU-TV channel 6, and also by our channel 4 T.V. station."[27]

A few days after the demonstration, in an interview with reporter William Stuckey on the "Latin Listening Post" radio program, Oswald freely discussed the role of the FPCC in New Orleans—"to attract new members and feel out the public."[28] Next, Stuckey arranged a live radio debate between Oswald, Carlos Bringuier, and Edward S. Butler, the executive vice-president of an organization known as INCA, which specialized "in distributing anti-Communist educational material in Latin America." Oswald was grilled on his pro-Castro activities, and admitted that he was a "Marxist" who had resided in the Soviet Union for three years.[29] After the program, Oswald obligingly made a three-minute TV tape which was broadcast the following day; he carefully mentions these FPCC-related activities in his notes.

William Stuckey, the moderator of the debate, believed that Oswald's public admissions "finished" the FPCC in New Orleans.[30] But Oswald took a more optimistic view. In a letter to V. T. Lee, he reported, "I was flooded with callers and invitations to debate . . . as well as people interested in joining the FPCC New Orleans branch."[31] In a subsequent letter to the Communist Party, to whose top leaders he had already sent "honorary membership cards" in his "chapter," he expressed the fear that he "may have compromised the FPCC," and asked, "Whether in your opinion I should always remain in the background, i.e., underground."[32]

But Oswald seems to have had little intention of going "underground." His autobiographical sketch was prepared for the express purpose of convincing the Cubans that he was a true friend of Castro's revolution. Marina, in fact, viewed all the activities described in the document—the "FPCC chapter," the demonstrations, the publicity—as mere "window dressing" for her husband's real purpose: getting to Cuba.[33] "He wanted to be arrested," she testified, "he wanted to get into the newspapers, so that he would be known" as pro-Cuban. The FPCC operation was, according to Marina, merely "self-advertising."[34]

In September 1963, Oswald began reviewing his Spanish, doing physical exercises, and practicing "dry firing" his rifle almost every night. Marina thought that these preparations were all related to his impending Cuban trip.[35] He also spent considerable time studying world maps and airline schedules; he explained to Marina that he might have to "kidnap an aircraft" and force the pilot to fly him to Cuba.[36]

Oswald eventually adopted another plan. On September 17, he obtained a Tourist Card, under the name "Lee, Harvey Oswald," from the Mexican consulate general in New Orleans; this would permit him to stay in Mexico for fifteen days. Then, on September 24, he sent his wife and daughter back to Dallas with Ruth Paine (after swearing her to silence about the Mexican trip). The next day, he departed.

The Warren Commission was not able to determine exactly how Oswald traveled from New Orleans to Mexico City. One witness, Sylvia Odio, said that Oswald stopped at her house in Dallas on his way to Mexico, and was accompanied by two Latins who identified themselves as members of the anti-Castro underground. The next day, she said, one of the "Latins" called her and said that he wanted to introduce Oswald "to the underground in Cuba, because he is . . . kind of nuts . . . he told us we don't have any guts, you Cubans, because President Kennedy should have been assassinated after the Bay of Pigs."[37] Although the Warren Commission lawyers remained extremely skeptical about Mrs. Odio's story, they were unable to find any real evidence either to confirm or refute it.

In any case, Oswald arrived in Mexico City on September 27, 1963, and checked into the Hotel del Commercio. He went directly to the Cuban Embassy and applied for a visa to Cuba in transit to Russia, representing himself as the "director" of the

New Orleans branch of "Fair Play for Cuba" and submitting as proof of his pro-Castro sympathies the documentation he had so carefully gathered during his summer in New Orleans. Returning that afternoon, Oswald was told that the Cuban Embassy could not grant him an in-transit visa before he had obtained a visa from the Soviet Union. On hearing this, Oswald grew "highly agitated and angry," according to an embassy employee, and then became involved in a heated argument with the Cuban consul, who told Oswald that "in place of aiding the Cuban Revolution, [he] was doing it harm." Slamming the door, Oswald left.[38] Later in the week, he was also turned down by the Soviet Embassy. He attributed his failure to obtain visas to "bureaucracy and red tape."[39]

After returning to Dallas in October, Oswald rented a room in a boarding house under the alias O. H. Lee, and then found a job as a stock boy in the Texas School Book Depository, a seven-story building overlooking Dealey Plaza in downtown Dallas.

On November 22, 1963, President John F. Kennedy was shot and killed in Dallas as his motorcade passed through Dealey Plaza. Less than one hour later, Lee Harvey Oswald was arrested and was subsequently charged with the crime. Two days later, Oswald himself was fatally shot in the basement of the Dallas city jail by Jack Ruby, a Dallas night-club owner. It was ten months later that the Warren Commission, appointed by President Lyndon B. Johnson to ascertain the facts, rendered its final verdict that Oswald, acting alone, had assassinated President Kennedy.

PART ONE

The First Conspiracy

1

THE PROSECUTOR

Arrested this evening in the district attorney's office was Clay Shaw, age 54, of 1313 Dauphine Street, New Orleans, Louisiana. Mr. Shaw will be charged with participating in a conspiracy to murder John F. Kennedy.
 —Jim Garrison, March 1, 1967, press release

A great many Americans must have responded with some measure of bewilderment when they heard the news that Jim Garrison, the District Attorney of Orleans Parish, Louisiana, had arrested a prominent New Orleans citizen and the former director of the International Trade Mart, Clay L. Shaw, for participation in a conspiracy to murder John F. Kennedy. The conclusion of the Warren Commission, published some two and a half years before, had offered the authoritative judgment that Lee Harvey Oswald alone was responsible for the assassination. And although a host of doubts were subsequently raised concerning the adequacy of the Warren Commission's investigation and the reliability of its conclusions, it seemed incredible that the New Orleans District Attorney could declare, as Garrison had, "My staff and I solved the assassination weeks ago. I wouldn't say this if we didn't have the evidence beyond a shadow of a doubt."[1] Indeed, the possibility that a local prosecutor had found the answers to questions that had baffled the investigative resources of the federal government seemed so remote to most journalists that, soon after the initial stir provoked by Shaw's arrest, news of the "assassination plot" was generally relegated to the back pages and treated about as seriously as flying-saucer reports.

I, for one, however, was prepared to believe that District Attorney Garrison's claims might have some substance to them. In the course of writing my book *Inquest*,[2] I had found that the Warren Commission's investigation had been severely constrained both by bureaucratic pressures exerted from within and by limits of time imposed from without. Far from being the rigorous and exhaustive examination that it was taken to be, the Commission's work was, at certain crucial points, reduced to little more than an exercise in the clarification of superficial evidence. When one delved more deeply, some far more difficult problems than any acknowledged by the Commission began to appear. Even members of the Commission's own staff found this to be true. For example, when one staff lawyer suggested, late in the investigation, that it might be worthwhile to look further into the partly corroborated story of Sylvia Odio, the witness who had said that Oswald was introduced to her not long before the assassination by two anti-Castro Cubans whom he was traveling with, his superior curtly told him, "At this stage, we are supposed to be closing doors, not opening them."[3] It later turned out that some of the doors left ajar but unopened led to associates of Oswald's in New Orleans, so it seemed entirely conceivable to me that Garrison just might have stumbled upon some valuable information that the Commission had, for one reason or another, sidestepped.

Consider, for example, a story at the root of Garrison's investigation, which involved a meeting among Oswald and three men—David Ferrie, Carlos Quiroga, and W. Guy Banister—all of whom the Warren Commission had had reason to be interested in. Ferrie, who, according to the testimony of one Commission witness, commanded a unit of the Civil Air Patrol in which Oswald reportedly had been a member briefly, had been arrested in New Orleans shortly after the assassination, on a tip that he was involved with Oswald, and then released.[4] Carlos Quiroga, the exile who had visited Oswald's home several times in New Orleans, had done so for the purpose, he alleged, of appraising Oswald's pro-Castro activities.[5] W. Guy Banister was the private detective known to be associated with anti-Castro activists in New Orleans and had an office in a building whose address appeared on pro-Castro literature Oswald distributed.[6] All this information, it will be recalled, was in the hands of the Commission, yet none of these three men was questioned by the Commission or its staff. It seemed to me that leads such as these, if they had been pursued, could have provided a possible bridge between the known and unknown worlds of Lee Harvey Oswald in New Orleans. And once such a bridge was crossed, a whole new set of clues to why Oswald killed the President might have been found.

Could Garrison have discovered such a bridge? Skeptics tended to dismiss the possibility on the ground that Garrison was a flamboyant and extremely ambitious politician. According to Aaron M. Kohn, the managing director of the Metropolitan Crime Commission of New Orleans, "Garrison never lets the responsibilities of being a prosecutor interfere with being a politician." However, the fact that Garrison was politically motivated did not necessarily—to my mind, at least—preclude the possibility that he might be on to something. Whereas it might not always have been in the interests of the Warren Commission, which was concerned as much with dispelling doubts as with ascertaining facts, to pursue leads that might generate further doubts, or possibly damage the effectiveness of federal agencies,[7] an ambitious politician, it seemed to me, might well pursue leads to their conclusion, especially since solving "the case of the century," as Garrison called it, would certainly enhance his reputation. Convinced that it was possible—indeed, probable—that Garrison could find details of Oswald's affairs that the Commission had missed, I went to New Orleans shortly after Garrison announced that he was getting to the bottom of the "assassination plot" and had arrested Shaw.

Jim Garrison—he legally changed his given name from Earling Carothers to Jim when he first entered politics—claims to be both a "lone-wolf reformer," influenced by Ayn Rand's writings on individualism, and a Southern Populist in the tradition of Huey Long who, Garrison has said, "had all the political answers."[8] (One "political answer" Long found was the conspiracy issue. Louisiana's electorate tends to divide along both ethnic and geographic lines—between French-speaking Catholics in the South and Anglo-Saxon Protestants in the North; Orleaneans and the rural population; and Negroes and whites.[9] By charging that the Standard Oil Company and other "Eastern monopolies" were conspiring with the established politicians and "lying newspapers" to deprive the people of Louisiana of their fair share of the oil revenues produced in the state, Long raised an issue that cut across the traditional cleavages in the electorate, and tended to unite the "have-nots" against the "haves."[10] Whether the "oil conspiracy" was a real or fancied one is even today a hotly debated question in New Orleans.)

Ever since Garrison was first elected District Attorney, in 1961, he has been a controversial figure in New Orleans. He has fought long and hard against prostitutes, homosexuals in the French Quarter, and the more vulnerable purveyors of vice, but, according to his critics on the Metropolitan Crime Commission, he has neglected the problem of organized crime in New Orleans. "People worry about the crime 'syndicate,' " Garrison once said, "but the real danger is the political establishment, power massing against the individual."[11] When the city's eight criminal-court justices exercised their statutory right to oversee the financing of his anti-vice campaign, Garrison charged that their actions "raised interesting questions about racketeer influences." A court subsequently convicted Garrison of criminally libeling the eight judges, but the conviction was reversed by the U.S. Supreme Court, in a decision that held that individuals have the right to criticize public officials even though the charges may turn out to be unfounded.[12]

Garrison is popularly referred to in New Orleans as the Jolly Green Giant—an image conjured up by his imposing physical stature (six feet six inches) and his political glad hand. When I met him, in mid-April 1967, his welcome was gracious, if slightly fulsome; he told me, almost solemnly, that it was his reading of my book that first set him thinking about launching an investigation of his own. (Later, I learned that this was a standard greeting, extended to almost all critics of the Warren Commission.)

Dean Andrews had just been indicted on five counts of perjury, and Garrison seemed flushed with victory. "Personally I like Dean, everyone does," he said, "but I have to show him I mean business." Andrews, who it will be recalled is the lawyer who had told the Warren Commission that a mysterious figure named Clay Bertrand had phoned him after the assassination and suggested that he defend Oswald, had testified on his second appearance before the Orleans Parish Grand Jury that he could not identify Clay Bertrand as Clay Shaw.[13] Garrison said it was "obvious that Andrews was protecting Shaw." He was certain, at any rate, that Andrews would be convicted on at least one count of perjury: when he was an assistant district attorney in neighboring Jefferson Parish, Andrews had, in his private practice, helped a client (a friend of Ferrie's) obtain a parole—illegal under Louisiana law. "We purposely asked Andrews about that in front of the grand jury," Garrison explained, and Andrews denied it (otherwise, he would have had to incriminate himself).

Over a leisurely dinner at Broussard's, Garrison began to tell me about the conspiracy he had uncovered. It was a diffuse narrative, in which it appeared, as noted earlier, that Oswald had only been feigning the role he went to considerable lengths to establish for himself as a pro-Castroite; Garrison said Oswald had in fact been part of an *anti*-Castro assassination team trained by David Ferrie. Ferrie, in turn, was in some important way—Garrison never explained exactly how—personally involved with Clay Shaw. When a plan to shoot Castro was aborted because Oswald could not obtain a visa to Cuba, the assassination team turned its attention to President Kennedy, and, on November 22, 1963, carried out its mission.

How had Garrison discovered this conspiracy? "It's exactly like a chess problem," he explained. "The Warren Commission moved the same pieces back and forth and got nowhere. I made a new move and solved the problem." The move he meant was the arrest of Clay Shaw. He pointed out that after Shaw was arrested, men from the District Attorney's office searched Shaw's home, in the French Quarter, and found in it a cache of new evidence, which he suggested that I should see, because it would give me "a new perspective on the case."

Early the next morning, I went to the District Attorney's office, which is housed, next to the Parish Prison, in the Criminal District Court Building, a massive structure at Tulane Avenue and South Broad. Garrison had not yet arrived, but one of his assistants, James C. Alcock, told me that Garrison had left word that I should "start going through the evidence." I did so with Jones Harris, a New Yorker of independent means who had devoted the better part of the last three years to a private investigation of the assassination. Six cardboard cartons were brought out containing personal belongings of Clay Shaw: letters, photographs, financial records, blueprints for renovating houses in the French Quarter, the manuscripts of plays he had written years ago, calendars, checkbooks, address books. In one box were a black costume, a net mask, and some plastic slippers—all of which Shaw had claimed were part of his 1965 Mardi Gras costume.[14] Alcock said that the District Attorney's staff had yet to examine all this material, and he suggested that Harris and I look through Shaw's address books and financial records in hopes of discovering some information that might interest Garrison. We were left alone with the evidence.

Though none of these materials, as far as I could see after examining them, had anything directly to do with the assassination, the odd way in which Garrison treated them did give me, when I thought about it later, "a new perspective on the case." I recalled that a judge's order had forbidden discussion or disclosure of any evidence in the case.[15] The very fact that Harris and I were allowed to examine objects seized from Shaw's home and designated "evidence" seemed to be a direct violation of that order. Why, I wondered, should the District Attorney risk having his case thrown out of court on a technicality by letting outsiders go freely through the evidence? Moreover, it seemed curious that Clay Shaw's papers had not already been rigorously scrutinized by Garrison or his staff, especially since Garrison had told several people, including me, that one of the main reasons for arresting Clay Shaw on March 1 was to prevent him from destroying his personal papers. Six weeks had passed, and yet from what I saw it appeared that no real investigation of Clay Shaw was going on at all—but only a search for peripheral characters connected with David Ferrie. If Garrison believed that Shaw had openly conspired to kill the President, why was the inquiry into his activities being treated with such apparent nonchalance?

A discovery that Jones Harris made while we were going through the papers provided considerable insight into the nature of Garrison's investigation. What Harris found was a five-digit number that was common to both Shaw's and Oswald's address books. The entry in Shaw's book was "Lee Odom, PO Box 19106, Dallas, Tex." In Oswald's book, the number 19106 was preceded by the Cyrillic letters ДД (which, like other Russian letters on the page, the Warren Commission had assumed were made during Oswald's two-and-a-half-year stay in the Soviet Union). Though the coincidence of numbers proved nothing in itself, it was striking, and Garrison decided that further investigation was merited. Shortly thereafter, Garrison announced to the press that he had found the entry "PO 19106" in both Oswald's and Shaw's address books, and that the number was a "nonexistent or fictional number," which removed "the possibility of coincidence." Moreover, Garrison said that "PO 19106" was a code that, when deciphered, produced Jack Ruby's unlisted telephone number, WH 1-5601, and "no other number on earth."[16] The method by which Garrison "deciphered" the code is worth following. Starting with the "scrambled" number 19106, Garrison "unscrambled" it (by choosing the nearest digit, then the farthest, then the next nearest, etc.) to produce the number 16901. Ruby's number was 15601, so by unscrambling the digits Garrison managed to match the last two digits in the two numbers. The next step was to subtract the arbitrary number 1300 from 16901, and—presto—15601.[17] Finally, Garrison converted the prefix "PO" to "WH" by a system that, according to the prominent cryptographer Irwin Mann, yields at least six different prefixes: Garrison chose Ruby's.[18]

A few days after Garrison announced that he had deciphered the code, it became known that the number 19106 in Shaw's address book was by no means "nonexistent or fictional." PO Box 19106 had been, as Shaw's address book indicated, the address in Dallas of a man named Lee Odom. Odom stated that he had been introduced to Shaw in 1966 by the manager of the

Roosevelt Hotel in New Orleans, and had briefly discussed with Shaw the possibility of bringing bloodless bullfights to New Orleans; he had left his business address—PO Box 19106, Dallas, Texas—with Shaw.[19] In fact, Odom's post-office box could not possibly have been the number in Oswald's book, because the post-office-box number 19106 did not exist in Dallas before it was assigned to Odom, in 1965—long after Oswald's death, in 1963. It was clear that Garrison had done some questionable interpolating of his own in moving from a coincidence to a conspiracy. First, he had told newsmen that the number in Oswald's book was PO 19106, although in fact it was ДД 19106. (When a television interviewer later asked him how he had determined that the prefix was PO, rather than ДД , he answered, with perfect aplomb, "More or less by looking at it.")[20] Then, without first checking with the Dallas post office whether in fact such an address existed, he had announced that the post-office-box number was fictional. And, finally, he had converted the number in Shaw's book into Jack Ruby's phone number by rearranging the digits, subtracting an arbitrary number, and changing the letters "PO" to "WH." Garrison had constructed a piece of evidence against Clay Shaw and had disclosed it to the press. Yet the District Attorney did not seem particularly perturbed when questions were raised about the logic of his deductions. When he was asked on a local television show how the number of a post-office box that didn't exist until 1965 could have been used to represent Jack Ruby's phone number in 1963, he replied, "Well, that's a problem for you to think over, because you obviously missed the point."[21] Indeed, Garrison counterattacked in a press conference, saying, "We are very interested in knowing who introduced Mr. Odom to Mr. Shaw, how many bullfights Mr. Odom has actually produced"—as if this fact were relevant to his investigation—and, "We are particularly interested in clarifying now why there is also coded in Lee Oswald's address book the local phone number of the Central Intelligence Agency." Using an entirely different system of decipherment—multiplying the number by 10, rearranging the digits, subtracting 1700, and remultiplying—Garrison managed to convert the number 1147, which appeared in Oswald's book, to 522-8874, the CIA's phone number. Oswald's codes were "subjective," Garrison said, in that they varied from number to number.[22] There seemed little point in Oswald's having gone through such an elaborate procedure, however, because the CIA number that Garrison referred to was—and is—listed in the New Orleans telephone book.*

What was Garrison's purpose in all this flimflammery? He himself noted, in an extended interview in *Playboy* for October 1967, that pre-trial publicity prejudicial to the defendant "could get our whole case thrown out of court," yet he himself had jeopardized his case by releasing information that was not only prejudicial to Clay Shaw but unfounded. The story about PO Box 19106 evidently was not part of his pending court case; otherwise presumably he would have kept it secret from the defense and carefully investigated it. It did, however, raise some questions about Garrison's investigation.

---

* Garrison subsequently used another telephone number in an attempt to link Oswald and Ruby: "If you look in Oswald's address book, you will see PE 8-1951 . . . Jack Ruby called that number twice. It is a number in Fort Worth. . . . There was indeed a close relation between Lee Oswald and Jack Ruby."[23] What Garrison omitted to say was that PE 8-1951 was—and is—the telephone number of a television station in Fort Worth.

2

THE SUSPECT

There will be arrests, charges and convictions. This is no Mickey Mouse investigation.

—Jim Garrison, February 25, 1967,
Associated Press

It was aboard a jet flight between New Orleans and New York in late November of 1966 that the Garrison investigation started taking shape. Prompted by stories in the national media that called for a new investigation into the assassination, three prominent passengers—Senator Russell B. Long, of Louisiana; Joseph M. Rault, Jr., a wealthy New Orleans oilman; and District Attorney Jim Garrison—began speculating about the events in Dallas three years before. As their conversation was reported in *New Orleans*, the official magazine of the city's Chamber of Commerce, the three agreed that, in Rault's words, ". . . it would be almost preposterous to believe that one man, an individual such as Oswald, could have been the only one involved in this thing." Senator Long cited deficiencies in the Warren Commission's investigation. "I think if I were investigating," he said, "I'd find the hundred best riflemen in the world and find the ones who were in Dallas that day." Garrison recalled that in 1963 his office had been interested in "a very unusual type of person who made a very curious trip at a very curious time about the date of the assassination," and the District Attorney added that he "might want to now go back into some of those events."[1]

The individual whom Garrison had in mind was David Ferrie, and he was, to say the least of it, "a very unusual type of person." Garrison later characterized Ferrie as both an "evil genius" and "a pathetic and tortured creature."[2] To compensate for being completely hairless, Ferrie pasted what looked like clumps of red monkey fur on his head and wore artificial eyebrows. Explanations of how Ferrie lost his hair have become part of the folklore of the assassination. William W. Turner, author of a so-called official history of the Garrison investigation which appeared in *Ramparts* (and a former employee of the FBI), reported one speculation that the loss might have been "a physiological reaction to exposure to the extreme altitudes required for clandestine flights." He went on to say that Chinese Nationalist U-2 pilots have reportedly experienced the same "hair-loss phenomenon."[3] Fred Powledge, after interviewing Garrison, wrote in the *New Republic* that Ferrie's "interest in homosexuality led him to shave off all his body hair."[4] However, the question was decisively answered by Harold Weisberg, a critic of the Warren Commission, whose stepbrother, Dr. Jack Kety, had treated Ferrie for the disease alopecia, which can render its victims hairless.[5]

Rather like Oswald, Ferrie was a failure at virtually everything he tried. He trained for the priesthood, and was dismissed from two seminaries as a result of eccentric personal behavior. Later, he became a "bishop" in a quasi-political underground cult called the Orthodox Old Catholic Church of North America. For a while, Ferrie ran a service station in New Orleans. His greatest ambition, however, seems to have been to become a fighter pilot. In 1950, he wrote to Secretary of Defense Louis A. Johnson, demanding, "When am I going to get the commission, when the Russians are bombing the hell out of Cleveland?" In a letter to the commanding officer of the First Air Force, he wrote, "There is nothing I would enjoy better than blowing the hell out

of every damn Russian, Communist, Red or what-have-you.
. . . Between my friends and I we can cook up a crew that can
really blow them to hell. . . . I want to train killers, however
bad that sounds. It is what we need."[6] Ferrie never received an
Air Force commission, but he did succeed in becoming the
leader of a unit in the Civil Air Patrol (a civilian organization
made up of volunteers), and he also set himself to training
youths in jungle-warfare tactics.[7] Oswald, according to a witness before the Warren Commission named Edward Voebel, belonged to Ferrie's outfit for a brief time in the nineteen-fifties—
and even may have attended a Civil Air Patrol party at Ferrie's
home, when he was a teen-ager.[8] Ferrie was also engaged in a
long-term project to discover a cure for cancer, and it was said
that at one time he housed thousands of white mice in his apartment in New Orleans.[9] For a while, he was employed as a pilot
for Eastern Airlines, but he was suspended, in 1961, as a consequence of an arrest on a morals charge, and later dismissed.
After that, he managed to make a meager living as a free-lance
pilot, an independent psychologist, a hypnotist, and a private
detective.[10]

Ferrie also became quite interested in Cuban affairs. In the
mid-nineteen-fifties, while Fidel Castro was waging a guerrilla
war against the Batista regime in Cuba, Ferrie attempted to
raise funds for Castro. Captain Neville Levy, a New Orleans
businessman, recalled that Ferrie carried a loaded army revolver with him while soliciting contributions for Castro's campaign.[11] After Castro came to power, Ferrie became rabidly
anti-Castro. He approached Sergio Arcacha Smith, the leader of
the Cuban Democratic Revolutionary Front in New Orleans—
an anti-Castro coalition—and volunteered to train recruits for
an invasion of Cuba.[12] He also, according to Diego Gonzales
Tendedera, the Miami correspondent for *El Tiempo,* flew
firebomb raids against Cuba and helped anti-Castro refugees
escape until 1961, when federal agents confiscated the plane he
was using.[13] After the Bay of Pigs invasion in April 1961, Ferrie
said in a speech to the New Orleans chapter of the Military
Orders of World Wars that he had been a pilot in the abortive
invasion, and then went on to criticize President Kennedy for
failing to provide the necessary air support for the anti-Castro
forces.[14] In 1962, perhaps finally realizing his desire to "train

killers," he reportedly drilled anti-Castroites in paramilitary tactics in St. Tammany Parish, across Lake Pontchartrain from New Orleans.[15]

In 1963, Ferrie was employed as a private investigator for the law firm then representing Carlos Marcello, who was reputed to be the head of the New Orleans Mafia. Marcello had been deported in an extralegal manner—he was abducted by Justice Department agents and put on a plane to Guatemala. According to one story, Ferrie clandestinely flew Marcello back into this country.[16] On the day of the assassination, Ferrie claimed, he was in court, listening to a judge declare the Marcello deportation illegal. To celebrate the victory, Ferrie drove to Texas on a "goose-hunting" expedition with two friends. Meanwhile, Garrison's office received the tip from New Orleans private detective Jack Martin (who had worked for W. Guy Banister) to the effect that Ferrie had trained Oswald in marksmanship and was Oswald's "getaway pilot." Martin was said to be a member of the same cult in which Ferrie was a bishop. On his return to New Orleans, Ferrie was arrested and questioned, but, according to FBI reports, Martin admitted that he had made up the whole story, and Ferrie was released.[17]

The FBI may not have thought much of Martin's tip, but it was this tip that enabled Garrison to begin his investigation, in December 1966, with a specific suspect in mind—David Ferrie. Garrison set about his work with the assistance of a small but industrious staff. His chief investigator, a policeman named Louis Ivon, had requisitioned other members of the New Orleans Police Department to do the necessary legwork. William H. Gurvich, a partner in one of the city's largest private-detective agencies, served as one of Garrison's chief aides for six months, handling interrogations and the extraterritorial aspects of the investigation. Thomas Bethell, a young British writer who was living in New Orleans, was put in charge of research. Assistant District Attorneys Alcock, Andrew J. Sciambra, Richard V. Burnes, and Alvin V. Oser questioned the more important witnesses and prepared the legal groundwork. Other tasks were performed by some of Garrison's personal friends—among them Max Gonzales, a law clerk in the criminal court and a pilot, who made a number of flights with Ferrie in order to gain his confidence, and Alberto Fowler, a Cuban exile and the Director of International Relations for the City of New Orleans, who made discreet inquiries about Ferrie's activities among anti-Castro exiles. Later, a self-styled intelligence expert using the pseudonym Bill Boxley joined Garrison's staff.* Although during its early stages the investigation was generally kept secret from the press, two members of *Life* magazine's staff, David L. Chandler, the New Orleans reporter, and Richard N. Billings, an associate editor, participated in what Garrison described as "an information exchange" and were permitted to observe the interrogation of witnesses, polygraph (or lie-detector) tests, and staff meetings.

Garrison began his investigation in December 1966 by compiling a dossier on Ferrie. Cameras were secretly set up across from Ferrie's apartment, he was followed everywhere he went, and his friends were questioned about his activities. Garrison even attempted to plant an "undercover agent" in Ferrie's private coterie. Little came of this surveillance.[18] For further information, Garrison turned back to Martin, whose tip had first linked Oswald and Ferrie. Martin, who told Secret Service agents that he suffers from "telephonitis" when he has taken a drink and that it was on such an occasion that he telephoned the District Attorney's office about Ferrie,[19] continued to narrate a vast number of disconnected yarns about Ferrie and the assassination. According to a typical one of these, Ferrie hypnotized Oswald and then dispatched him on the assassination mission. According to another, Ferrie had a working association with certain anti-Castro activities conducted by the private detective W. Guy Banister. Garrison found this connection especially provocative, because of the offices that Banister, up to the time of his death, in 1964, maintained in a building one of whose addresses was 544 Camp Street, a block from the William B. Reily Company, where Oswald worked. One of the questions the Warren Commission had left unanswered was why the "544 Camp Street" address appeared as Oswald's headquarters on some pro-Castro literature that he possessed. Since Banister's office was, as Garrison put it, "a mare's-nest of anti-Castro

---

* Garrison subsequently identified "Boxley" as William C. Wood, and claimed that he was a former CIA employee.

activity," Garrison postulated that Oswald might be an "agent provocateur" in Banister's employ.[20]

Garrison followed up this lead by systematically questioning Banister's former employees. One of them, a shipping clerk and sometime private investigator named David F. Lewis, Jr., added richly to the developing drama. Lewis claimed that he had been witness to a meeting among Banister, Ferrie, the anti-Castro leader Carlos Quiroga, and a person he called Leon Oswald, who he later thought might be Lee Harvey Oswald. Although Lewis said he was certain that this meeting had occurred in 1962, a time when Oswald was known to be living in Texas,[21] and although Quiroga categorically denied that such a meeting had ever taken place, Garrison intensified his efforts in this direction. He began digging into the activities of anti-Castro Cubans, and discovered the sites of what had been two secret training camps in St. Tammany Parish.[22] (One of them was rumored to have been the site of the Ferrie anti-Castro drills and commando training.) In the hope of identifying the men under Ferrie's command, Garrison hired Bernardo Torres, a private detective from Miami who claimed to have assisted the Secret Service by spotting potentially dangerous Cubans during a visit President Kennedy made to Miami in 1963. In December 1966 and January 1967 the investigation was broadened to include various efforts to track down, with Torres' help, any Cubans in Miami who might have known Ferrie. These efforts turned out to be unproductive but quite expensive—more than half the total expenditures up to that time—and Garrison began to suspect that Torres' activity did not justify the expense. Toward the end of January, the Florida manhunt was called off.[23]

But Garrison had other leads to follow—notably the old clue from New Orleans lawyer Dean Andrews. Andrews' original story, it will be recalled, which he told to the Secret Service shortly after the assassination, was that Oswald had come to his office a few times during the summer of 1963 in the hope of finding some means by which the "undesirable" discharge he had been given by the Marine Corps could be converted into an honorable one. The day after the assassination, Andrews, who was in the hospital under sedation recovering from pneumonia, said he received a phone call from a man he knew as Clay Bertrand, whom he described as "a lawyer without a briefcase" for local homosexuals. According to Andrews, Bertrand asked him to go to Dallas and defend Oswald. When Andrews was questioned by the FBI, he gave several different descriptions of Bertrand, and finally said that the character bearing that name was merely a figment of his imagination. A few months later, he again changed his story, telling the Warren Commission that he had recently seen Bertrand in a bar, and describing him as "a boy" who was "five foot eight inches" and had "sandy hair." He explained that he had finally told the FBI agents who interviewed him, "Write what you want, that I am nuts"—because, as he put it, "They are on you like the plague. They never leave. They are like cancer. Eternal."[24] No other clues to Bertrand's identity turned up, however, and Wesley J. Liebeler, the Commission lawyer who conducted the investigation in this area, said he was convinced that no such person existed.* Garrison nevertheless now decided to pursue the matter further, and gave Assistant District Attorney Sciambra, a former boxer known by the nickname Moo, a task he referred to as "squeezing" the French Quarter. A crackdown on homosexuals that Garrison had carried out in 1962 was generally thought to have produced a number of informers, but Sciambra was unable to find anyone who had ever heard of Clay Bertrand.[25] Garrison reasoned that Dean Andrews was probably protecting a wealthy client with homosexual associates, and came up with the idea that Clay Bertrand was in reality Clay Shaw, the socially prominent retired director of the International Trade Mart in New Orleans.[26] David Chandler, the *Life* reporter who worked closely with Garrison in the early days of the investigation, was present when Garrison first put forward this hypothesis to his staff. According to Chandler, Garrison offered three arguments for it. First, Shaw had the same first name as Bertrand. Second,

* When I interviewed Andrews in June 1967, he told me that he had made up the name " 'Clay Bertrand' out of solid air" to protect a friend. He explained that on the night after the assassination he received a phone call from the friend, who vaguely knew Oswald as an infrequent customer in a "gay bar" that he owned in the French Quarter. It was this friend, Andrews said, who had recommended him to Oswald as an attorney who might help him "fix" his "undesirable" discharge from the Marine Corps, and now he thought Andrews "could pick up some publicity" by appearing in Dallas as Oswald's lawyer. When the FBI became interested, Andrews explained, he invented the name "Clay Bertrand" to divert their attention from the real person who had phoned him. When I asked why he had told a Warren Commission lawyer that he had recently seen Clay Bertrand, he replied, "Aw, I was just putting the guy on a little."

Shaw was rumored to have friends in the homosexual world. And, finally, Shaw spoke fluent Spanish and, although Andrews had never said that Bertrand spoke Spanish, Garrison was looking for a conspirator involved in anti-Castro activities.[27] Garrison brushed over the fact that Shaw—six feet four and a quarter inches tall, fifty-four years old, and white-haired hardly fitted Andrews description of a five-foot-eight-inch boy with sandy hair. He also ignored the question of why Andrews, having given a false description and a false last name to protect his client, would give the client's correct first name.

In any event, Shaw was brought in for questioning in late December, on the pretext that Garrison was attempting to tie up a few loose ends in the Warren Report. According to Chandler, it quickly became apparent that Shaw had no information to offer about Ferrie or his activities, and the matter was dropped. The District Attorney told his staff to "forget Shaw." In January, when asked if he knew the identity of Clay Bertrand by Richard Billings of *Life*, who spent a good deal of time with Garrison during this period, Garrison replied, "His real name is Clay Shaw, but I don't think he's too important." Ferrie was still, at this time, the only suspect.[28]

By February 1967, the investigation seemed to be at a standstill. Ferrie obviously knew that he was under suspicion, and it was highly unlikely that he would do anything to incriminate himself. The Cuban-exile trail had petered out in Miami. The Bertrand matter had been shelved. Garrison's chief witness was still David Lewis, and, of the four participants in the meeting that Lewis described, Oswald and Banister were dead, Quiroga (according to Garrison) could not be found,* and Ferrie unequivocally denied everything.

At this point, Gordon Novel, a specialist in anti-eavesdropping devices, was recommended to Garrison by Willard E. Robertson, a New Orleans automobile dealer who was one of Garrison's political supporters. (Garrison had been so concerned that the FBI might be tapping his telephones that he had made plans a few weeks before to execute a midnight raid on the FBI field

---

* Quiroga claims that he was in New Orleans during this entire period, except for a two-week vacation, and that he was questioned on January 21, 1967, by Garrison's representatives. He completely denied the Lewis story, and apparently the District Attorney preferred to designate him a missing witness.

office in New Orleans, using a water pistol loaded with a charge of red pepper to disarm the officer on duty; he even invited Chandler, the *Life* reporter, to accompany him on the mission, but for some reason the plan was scrapped.)[29] Upon learning that Ferrie was under suspicion, Novel told Garrison that he knew a good deal about Ferrie's activities in 1961. According to Garrison, Novel claimed that Ferrie, Cuban-exile leader Sergio Arcacha Smith, and two unidentified Cubans had been involved in a "pickup" of arms from a bunker in Houma, Louisiana, belonging to the Schlumberger Well Surveying Corporation. Some of the arms were reportedly deposited in the offices of W. Guy Banister. The purpose of the raid was to acquire arms for an anti-Castro militia, and Novel stated that a CIA contact had indulgently provided a key to the bunker.[30] Novel later claimed that one of Garrison's ideas for breaking the stalemate his investigation had apparently reached involved a plot to kidnap Ferrie. According to this story, Ferrie was to be shot with an atropine dart, injected with sodium pentothal, and forced to confess.[31] Novel had said, "Garrison asked me to order him such a dart gun so that it wouldn't appear on his office purchase records" after the District Attorney "had read about the idea in one of the books about the CIA."[32]

The entire investigation might have expired quietly for want of any truly tangible leads if it had not been for some resourceful moves by three reporters for the New Orleans *States-Item*— Rosemary James, Jack Dempsey, and David Snyder. In New Orleans, the financial vouchers of the District Attorney's office are a matter of public record. By piecing together information gleaned from these records and through various leaks from Garrison's office, the reporters were able to come up with a fairly accurate picture of the investigation, even though it was still being kept secret. Mrs. James wrote an article on the subject and showed it to Garrison on February 16, 1967. He simply shrugged and told her, "I will neither confirm nor deny it."[33] The next day, the story broke. Garrison's investigation into the assassination of President Kennedy was now a public issue. Garrison charged that the news story had seriously interfered with his efforts; arrests that were to have been made immediately, he claimed, had now to be deferred for months. Moreover, he announced that he would seek private financing in order not to have to conduct the inquiry in a "fishbowl." Two political allies, Joseph Rault (who had been on the fateful plane trip with Garrison and Senator Long) and Willard Robertson, thereupon organized fifty New Orleans businessmen into a group that called itself Truth or Consequences, Inc.[34] Its function was to supply Garrison with both funds and moral support. Meanwhile, David Ferrie told a newspaperman that Garrison's investigation, in which he was suspected of being Oswald's getaway pilot, was nothing but "a big joke." He denied that he knew Oswald, and, for good measure, added that he was conducting his own inquiry into the assassination.

For two days, shortly after the *States-Item* broke the news of Garrison's investigation, Ferrie was kept under "protective custody," Billings has reported, at the Fontainebleau Motor Hotel in New Orleans.[35] According to a member of Garrison's staff, this was done at Ferrie's request. In any event, he returned to his own apartment on the evening of February 21. The next day, Ferrie was found dead. An autopsy indicated that he had died of a cerebral hemorrhage caused by the rupture of a blood vessel. The coroner, Dr. Nicholas Chetta, ruled out suicide, because a person is rarely aware that an aneurysm, or weak spot, exists in a blood vessel, and it would be virtually impossible to induce a "blowout." He also ruled out murder, on the ground that if the rupture had been caused by an external blow there would necessarily have been tissue damage, and none was found. He concluded that Ferrie had died from natural causes.[36] But the mere fact that a man suspected of having conspired to assassinate the President had died five days after he was publicly implicated in the crime was sensational news, and reporters flocked to New Orleans. Garrison interpreted a somewhat ambiguous letter that Ferrie wrote to a friend shortly before his death as a "suicide note," and, without waiting for the results of the autopsy, proclaimed Ferrie's death a suicide. Garrison called Ferrie "one of history's most important individuals," and claimed that an arrest had been only days away. "Apparently, we waited too long," he said.[37] No mention was made of the fact that Ferrie had already been placed effectively under protective custody for two days.

Ferrie's death brought a windfall of publicity, but Garrison had lost his prime suspect. And the hundreds of newsmen who had come to New Orleans could hardly be expected to continue reporting cryptic comments from Garrison such as "The key to the whole case is through the looking glass. Black is white; white is black." When they asked for hard news, Garrison told them that he had "positively solved the assassination of President John F. Kennedy," and he added that arrests might take as long as "thirty years."[38] At that point, most of the out-of-town reporters left. Headlines are made of arrests and deaths, not long-term promises.

Garrison, though, had promised that arrests would be forthcoming, and a number of possible suspects were hastily considered. Some were drawn from Ferrie's twilight world of adventurers and self-styled secret agents.[39] Others, according to William Gurvich, were prominent citizens of New Orleans—the president of a food-processing company, a hotel magnate, a nationally known physician.[40] At this point, Garrison received a brief letter from Perry Raymond Russo, a twenty-five-year-old Baton Rouge insurance salesman, who claimed to have information about Ferrie "that might or might not be valuable."[41] This very much interested Garrison, and in the next seven days Russo's story became quite "valuable" to the District Attorney.

The Development of Russo's Story: A Chronology

February 24: While Russo was waiting for a reply from Garrison, he approached a number of local reporters with his story, and taped a television interview with James Kemp of WDSU-TV in New Orleans. Asked whether Ferrie had made any threatening remarks about President Kennedy, Russo said, "[Ferrie] talked in general terms, not specifically about Kennedy, about how easy it would be to assassinate a President of the United States because of the fact he was in public view so much and unprotected more or less, and there were so many people and the availability of exit and the fact that he could drive a plane to get out of the country, and he used to posingly, jokingly pose the question that, you know, he and I could do it; you know, just in a joking way, he said it could be done. And that was all of the conversation during the summer." Russo also stated flatly in the interview, "I never heard of Oswald until the television of the assassination."[42]

February 25: The day after Garrison received Russo's letter, Moo Sciambra was sent to Baton Rouge to question Russo. The greater part of the interview was confined to uncovering Russo's relationship with Ferrie. Russo told Sciambra that he had first met Ferrie in 1962, when he attempted to get a young friend of his in Ferrie's Civil Air Patrol unit out from under what he called the commander's "spell." Russo said that at one point, after he had succeeded in breaking Ferrie's hold over his friend, Ferrie had threatened to kill him. Later, however, he and Ferrie became friends, and worked as partners in selling pornographic films imported from Cuba. Ferrie's main interests, Russo continued, were, first, instructing members of his Civil Air Patrol outfit in "the art of fighting jungle warfare" and, second, his medical research; he was developing an aphrodisiac for homosexuals as well as a cure for cancer. But Ferrie had said very little to him on the subject of assassination, except for some vague remarks about how easy it would be to shoot a President and flee by airplane to Cuba or Brazil. Russo indicated that Ferrie probably had in mind either Eisenhower or the President of Mexico. He did remember, however, that Ferrie had said a few times in the summer of 1963 that he would "get" Kennedy. Sciambra then showed Russo some photographs. The first one he identified was of Sergio Arcacha Smith, the Cuban-exile leader. Russo identified him as an actor in one of the pornographic films. "To be perfectly honest," he said, "I looked at the film quite a bit." (Russo was mistaken in his identification. Garrison's investigators later ascertained that the actor in the film was not Arcacha Smith.) The second photograph was of Clay Shaw. Russo said that he thought he had seen this man from a distance twice before but that he never met him. The last photograph showed Lee Harvey Oswald. Russo thought this person might have been a roommate of Ferrie's, who had a beard.[43]

February 26: The next day, back in New Orleans, Sciambra gave Garrison a preliminary oral report on his interview with Russo in the presence of Richard Billings, of *Life*. Garrison then asked Sciambra to arrange a test for Russo using "truth serum," or sodium pentothal.[44]

February 27: The next morning Russo came to Garrison's office, and Sciambra drafted a long memorandum to Garrison concerning his interview on February 25 with Russo in Baton Rouge. Later, sodium pentothal was administered to Russo by the coroner, Dr. Chetta, at Mercy Hospital. While under the influence of the drug, Russo was again questioned by Sciambra, though no transcript was made of the interrogation. But afterward, Sciambra prepared a memorandum on the results of the sodium-pentothal session which states that Russo made a passing reference to a party in Ferrie's apartment during which a plot was discussed—but only after Sciambra had prompted him by asking "if he could remember any of the details about Clay Bertrand being up in Ferrie's apartment." The name Bertrand was first mentioned, the memorandum indicates, by Moo Sciambra. Later that evening, Russo had dinner with Garrison, Sciambra, and Billings, and Sciambra told Russo that after taking truth serum he had identified a tall man with white kinky hair, and that he had also said that he had been introduced to this man as "Bertrand" at Ferrie's apartment. According to Billings, Russo insisted that he did not remember ever having met anyone named Bertrand. Garrison attempted to resolve this embarrassing discrepancy by suggesting to Billings that the truth serum probably jogged Russo's memory.[45] "They asked me a lot of questions," Russo is reported to have recalled later. "I could figure out what they wanted to know."[46]

February 28: The following day, Garrison brought Russo to Shaw's home in the French Quarter for a look at Shaw. Russo rang Shaw's doorbell and introduced himself as a Mutual of Omaha insurance salesman, then returned to the car where Sciambra was waiting for him and, according to Sciambra, identified Clay Shaw as the man he had been introduced to as Bertrand in Ferrie's apartment.[47]

March 1: Garrison summoned Shaw to his office and had him interrogated for two and a half hours. Shaw categorically denied that he knew either Ferrie or Oswald and that he knew anything about the assassination. When the topic of using truth serum came up, Shaw sent for a lawyer, Salvatore Panzeca. Panzeca agreed to let Shaw take a lie-detector test, provided that the defense had the right to approve the wording of the questions, that the results of the test were not disclosed except at a duly authorized court proceeding, and that Shaw had a day's rest before the test. Garrison replied that he did not have to agree to any conditions. A moment later, he declared that Shaw was under arrest, had him handcuffed, and led him before news photographers to be booked.[48] Then he applied for a warrant from Criminal Court Judge Matthew S. Braniff to search Clay Shaw's premises, stating in his application that a "confidential informer" had told of a meeting in which "David W. Ferrie, Lee Harvey Oswald, and Clay Shaw (alias Clay Bertrand) were discussing how they would kill John F. Kennedy." The arrest, Garrison later told me, was "a command decision." He said he was apprehensive that if he released Shaw the suspect might "destroy vital evidence." This explanation made little sense, for Garrison could have obtained a search warrant without arresting Shaw, no more cause was required than that he have a confidential informant, and he had—Perry Russo. Moreover, he had questioned Shaw in December, and if Shaw had had incriminating evidence in his home it would seem likely that he would have disposed of it then. But, whatever Garrison's motives were, on March 1, 1967, a week after the death of Ferrie, Clay Shaw was arrested for conspiring to murder John F. Kennedy.

3

THE WITNESSES

I've taken unusual steps to protect the right of the defendant and assure him a fair trial. Before we introduced the testimony of our witnesses, we made them undergo independent verifying tests, including polygraph examination, truth serum, and hypnosis. We thought this would be hailed as an unprecedented step in jurisprudence. . . .
—Jim Garrison, October 1967, *Playboy*

In Louisiana, after an arrest has been made, the district attorney either presents the case to a grand jury or files a "bill of information," which, under the Louisiana code of criminal procedure, allows a district attorney to bring a case to trial without a grand-jury indictment. In the case of Clay Shaw, however, Garrison decided to do something that was, in his own words, "virtually unheard of."[1] Instead of going before a grand jury meeting in closed session, he requested a preliminary hearing, which takes place before a judge and is public. The purpose of a preliminary hearing under Louisiana law is to determine whether or not the state has sufficient evidence to warrant a trial. Although it is not unusual for the defense to request a preliminary hearing, if only to attempt to compel the state to tip its hand and disclose vital evidence before the actual trial, such a hearing is rarely, if ever, requested by the prosecution. Why, then, should Garrison, the prosecutor, have elected to disclose some of his evidence before the trial—an apparently gratuitous favor to the defense? Garrison has said that he did so in order to "lean over backward and give the defendant every chance."[2] A preliminary hearing, however, has at least one extralegal consequence that a political-minded prosecutor might find advantageous: it provides the prosecution with a dramatic opportunity to reveal publicly far in advance of the trial some of the more sensational aspects of the case, thus helping to stimulate public interest. Whether or not Garrison's extraordinary move did, as he claimed, enhance the defendant's prospects for justice, it unquestionably worked to focus national attention on the case.

With a full complement of reporters in attendance, the hearing began on March 14, before a panel of three judges, with the testimony of Perry Russo, who was Garrison's surprise witness. Russo testified that he had known David Ferrie since 1960 and had an "open-book invitation" to visit Ferrie's apartment whenever he wanted to. On one such visit in September 1963, Russo said, he had encountered a young bearded man with an "old-fashion bolt-action rifle," to whom Ferrie subsequently introduced him as his roommate, "Leon Oswald." A few days later, Russo attended a party at Ferrie's apartment which eventually, Russo continued, "narrowed down to three persons besides myself"—David Ferrie, "Leon Oswald" (whom Russo identified from a photograph as Lee Harvey Oswald), and a man he called Clem Bertrand. Then Garrison asked Russo whether he recognized "Clem Bertrand" in the courtroom. Russo pointed out Clay Shaw; then, at Garrison's request, walked over to Shaw and held his hand over his head.[3]

The witness then went on to testify that the three men planned the assassination of President Kennedy in his presence. "Ferrie took the initiative in the talk, pacing back and forth," Russo said. "He was talking to both Mr. Bertrand and Mr. Oswald, discussing diversionary tactics." He testified that after the three men had talked about such details as the "triangulation of cross fire," the selection of an appropriate "scapegoat," and the "availability of exits," they ended the conversation by bickering over various methods of escape.[4]

Cross-Examination

Under cross-examination the following day, Russo admitted that he had not been able to identify Oswald positively until after an artist in the District Attorney's office had spent six hours drawing different beards on photographs of Oswald.[5] Russo's television statement of February 24—that he had "never heard of Oswald until the television of the assassination"—was also brought out. Asked by F. Irvin Dymond, Shaw's defense counsel, why he had denied, a few days before Garrison interrogated him, having known Oswald, Russo replied: "I knew Leon Oswald, who was slightly whiskered. . . . I did not, myself, honestly, know a Lee Harvey Oswald." Pressing Russo on the apparent contradiction between the statement he made in the television interview and his courtroom testimony, Dymond asked, "Are you testifying now that you knew Oswald, Leon Oswald, here in New Orleans, that you have identified a picture of Lee Harvey Oswald as the same man, and that after seeing the picture of Lee Harvey Oswald, roughly one hundred times, you still did not know it was the same, that it was the man you knew here in New Orleans?" Russo explained that the picture he had in his mind of Lee Harvey Oswald "was not identical" with that of the "Leon Oswald" he knew in New Orleans.[6]

Dymond also questioned the plausibility of Russo's story, asking him to explain why the alleged conspirators allowed him to overhear their plans to assassinate President Kennedy. Russo replied that Oswald and Bertrand were uneasy about his presence at the meeting until Ferrie said, "Forget him, he is all right, he don't know anything, and it don't make any difference with him." No one, Russo said, even cautioned him not to discuss the meeting.[7]

Dymond also inquired why Russo had not told the FBI or the Warren Commission about the assassination plans he had overheard. Russo answered: "At the time, right after the assassination, I had an involvement with school that was more pressing to me. If they wanted [to] ask me anything, they could."[8] He

also said he didn't volunteer information about the conspiratorial meeting because the FBI indicated that Oswald was the
lone assassin and, he added, "I had no reason to disagree with
these people. They are professionals."[9] Moreover, he said,
"Dave Ferrie was never implicated, as far as I knew."[10] Asked if
he had heard of Garrison's investigation, Russo admitted that
he had read about it in the newspapers and also that "David W.
Ferrie was being investigated." "As a matter of fact," the defense counsel asked dramatically, "didn't you wait until Ferrie
was dead so that there wouldn't be a witness to contradict your
statement as to such a meeting as that?" Russo replied that he
had not realized, when he read the story, that David W. Ferrie
was the same person as the Dave Ferrie he knew because he
"never knew his middle name was W."[11]

Russo also admitted under cross-examination that he had
been hypnotized three times before the preliminary hearing—a
method Garrison said he used in order to "objectify" testimony.[12] Moreover, it was learned that Russo had been under
psychiatric treatment for eighteen months, ending in late 1960,
and had last consulted a psychiatrist as recently as 1966.[13]

The Prisoner

The District Attorney found his only other witness, Vernon B.
Bundy, in the Orleans Parish Prison after the hearing had begun. Assistant District Attorney Charles Ray Ward and other
members of Garrison's staff strenuously objected to using
Bundy as a witness, but Garrison put him on the stand anyway.[14] Bundy, a narcotics addict and petty thief, testified that in
the summer of 1963, while he was preparing to inject the contents of two capsules of heroin into his arm, he saw two men
meet on the shore of Lake Pontchartrain, on the outskirts of
New Orleans. One, whom Bundy described as "a junkie or beat-
nik type" with a light growth of beard, he had later recognized
from photographs as Lee Harvey Oswald. The other man Bundy
identified as Clay Shaw. Like Russo, Bundy had never before
told anyone about his encounter with Oswald.[15] The three-judge
panel ruled that there was sufficient evidence for a trial. The
decision was by no means startling; it merely established that

there was evidence that merited judgment. Yet to many people the ruling suggested that Garrison had won some sort of legal victory. A few days later, on March 22, the Orleans Parish Grand Jury, to which Jim Garrison is legal adviser, returned a formal indictment against Clay Shaw based on essentially the same evidence.[16]

The Sciambra Memorandum

As it turned out, the evidence used at the preliminary hearing was even less sound than it may have appeared at the time. About six weeks after the hearing, James R. Phelan reported in the *Saturday Evening Post* that Russo had told two contradictory stories—one in his first interview with Sciambra, the other in court, after being questioned under hypnosis. Phelan discovered the discrepancy when Garrison, with his customary generosity to journalists, supplied him with a memorandum of Russo's first interview.[17] Nowhere in this document, which ran to thirty-five hundred words, was the supposed meeting among Shaw, Ferrie, and Oswald mentioned, either directly or implicitly. Yet two weeks later, in court, Russo stated that it had definitely taken place. In his first interview, moreover, Russo did not state that he had ever met Shaw, and he himself made no mention whatever of a Bertrand—either Clay or Clem. Assistant District Attorney Sciambra, who conducted this first interview and wrote up the memorandum, later said that Russo did tell him of the assassination plot but that he forgot to include it in his report. (Sciambra also stated that he had burned his original notes of the interview.)[18] Yet Sciambra's own words in the memorandum would appear to belie this explanation: "The next picture that he [Russo] identified was that of Clay Shaw. He said that he saw this man twice. The first time was when he pulled into Ferrie's service station to get his car fixed. Shaw was the person sitting in the compact car talking with Ferrie. He remembers seeing him again at the Nashville Street Wharf when he went to see J.F.K. speak."[19] Here Sciambra specifically states that Russo said he saw Shaw twice, and neither occasion involved a rendezvous in Ferrie's apartment during which Shaw, Ferrie, and Oswald planned the assassination. If Russo went on to describe a third encounter, and that was the only one relevant to Garrison's case, it is difficult to understand how Sciambra could have neglected to include it in the memorandum. Moreover, according to Billings, Sciambra did not mention the alleged "third encounter" in an oral report he made to Garrison the day after the interview. Sciambra reported that Russo said he had seen Shaw only twice —once at Ferrie's service station and once at the Nashville Street Wharf. In fact, the first time Billings heard of the third encounter, during which Russo was supposed to have overheard Bertrand, Ferrie, and Oswald planning the assassination in Ferrie's apartment, was on February 27, two days before Shaw was arrested, when Sciambra himself *told* Russo that he had mentioned the name Bertrand and had described the meeting in Ferrie's apartment. This, it will be recalled, was after Russo had taken the "truth serum." And Russo still, at this time, said that he could not remember anyone named Bertrand.[20]

If a witness tells two contradictory stories, external evidence may make it possible to choose between them. In Russo's case, the corroborative evidence available casts doubt on his second story—the one he told in court. He testified that Oswald was Ferrie's roommate in early September 1963, yet there is evidence that at that time Oswald was living with his wife and their baby daughter on Magazine Street in New Orleans.[21] Russo described Oswald as having a beard in early and mid-September, yet generally reliable witnesses reported that Oswald was clean-shaven at that time.[22] Russo claimed that he saw Oswald in Ferrie's apartment in the first week of October, yet Oswald was known to have been in Mexico and Dallas during this period.[23] Russo said that a friend of his, Niles Peterson, was at a party at Ferrie's apartment the night that he saw Oswald and Shaw there, yet Peterson flatly denies that he saw anyone fitting the description of either Shaw or Oswald. (Peterson did, however, recall a bearded man who was six feet tall and otherwise fitted the description of the man who was known to be Ferrie's roommate at the time—James R. Lewallen.[24]) Russo claimed, further, that a young woman, Sandra Moffitt, accompanied him to Ferrie's apartment the night of the meeting, yet she denies this, and says that she did not meet Ferrie until 1964.[25] In sum,

Russo's court testimony appears to be at odds with a great many of the external points of reference he himself provided.

Hypnosis

A transcript of Russo's first hypnosis session, which Garrison also gave to Phelan, reveals that many of the details of Russo's story were developed under hypnosis.[26] Russo was hypnotized on March 2, the day after Clay Shaw was arrested, by a Dr. Esmond Fatter, who told him to imagine a television screen in his mind. "You are in Ferrie's apartment," Dr. Fatter said. "Look at the picture and tell us the story that you see." Russo talked about some of Ferrie's friends but said nothing about an assassination plot or conspiratorial meeting.[27] Dr. Fatter then probed deeper, saying, "Now picture the screen again, Perry, and it is a picture of Ferrie's apartment, and there are several people in there and there is a white-haired man. Tell me about it." Russo described a party at Ferrie's apartment in which "everybody is drinking beer"; but again he did not mention anything about an assassination plot.[28] Then Dr. Fatter instructed Russo to let his "mind go completely blank" and again "notice the picture on the television screen." Dr. Fatter suggested, "There will be Bertrand, Ferrie and Oswald and they are going to discuss a very important matter and there is another man and girl there and they are talking about assassinating somebody. Look at it and describe it to me." The story that Russo then told is similar to the one he told in court about overhearing an assassination plot.[29]

Although Garrison said that hypnosis was part of his "objectifying machinery,"[30] and that he expected it to be "hailed as an unprecedented step in jurisprudence,"[31] Dr. Jay Katz, a professor of both law and clinical psychology at Yale University, expressed some severe reservations about it. After reading the transcripts of Russo's hypnotic sessions, Dr. Katz said that in his opinion "the hypnotist introduced very leading questions." "This was most striking," Dr. Katz continued, "when he directly asked him, or in fact told him, to tell him about the conversation that took place in respect to an assassination plot." Moreover,

Dr. Katz said that under hypnosis many subjects have difficulty differentiating between fact and fantasy.[32]

After the preliminary hearing, Russo began showing doubts about his identification of Shaw. He told James Phelan, who had spent more than forty hours questioning him for his *Saturday Evening Post* article, that he wished he could have an "opportunity to talk to Shaw for a few hours so I can be sure he was the right man."[33] He told Richard Townley, a reporter for WDSU-TV, in New Orleans, that he was unsure of his testimony and, according to Townley, said it was difficult for him now to distinguish "reality and fantasy."[34]

The testimony of Garrison's other witness, Vernon Bundy, also raised a number of questions. One of Bundy's fellow-inmates in the Parish Prison, Miguel Torres, told an NBC interviewer that Bundy had admitted to him that he was testifying for Garrison "because it's the only way that I can get cut loose" —indicating that unless he did testify, his probation would be revoked and he would have to complete a five-year sentence in prison. Bundy was subsequently arrested on a charge of robbery. Another inmate, John (the Baptist) Cancler, said in an interview that Bundy had told him that his account of the events at Lake Pontchartrain was a fabrication.[35] Of course, felons are not known for their probity, and Garrison dismissed the statements of Torres and Cancler "in view of their criminal records." But if no credence is to be placed in the testimony of Bundy's fellow-convicts, what of the testimony of Bundy himself?

Garrison's entire case at the preliminary hearing, then, was based on the allegations of two witnesses who had both waited four years before disclosing uncorroborated stories and who both subsequently cast considerable doubt on their own testimony.

A Case of Perjury

A few months after the hearing, there was another legal skirmish that strengthened the appearance, if not the substance, of Garrison's case: Dean Andrews, the New Orleans lawyer who had claimed that shortly after the assassination a shadowy figure named Clay Bertrand appealed to him to go to Dallas and defend Oswald, became involved in perjury proceedings. Andrews, after telling a number of stories about Bertrand, and at one point, it will be recalled, claiming that Bertrand was a figment of his imagination, was called before the Orleans Parish Grand Jury in March 1967. Asked if Clay Shaw was Clay Bertrand, he replied, under oath, "I can't say that he is and I can't say that he ain't."[36] Three months later, on June 28, Andrews volunteered to appear again before the grand jury. This time, he told of a "deal" he had made with Garrison not to say categorically that Clay Shaw was *not* Clay Bertrand, even though, he testified, he never thought for a moment that Clay Shaw was Clay Bertrand. Bertrand, he admitted, was a fictitious name he had used in order to protect a friend of his, a bartender in the French Quarter. Andrews acknowledged that he had perjured himself previously, and said, "It doesn't make any difference to me if I'm convicted. . . . Clay Shaw is not Clay Bertrand. Indict me if you want to."[37]

When Andrews was subsequently arraigned, tried, and convicted for perjury, Garrison declared that this represented "a major conviction . . . in connection with this case."[38] It was, if anything, a Pyrrhic victory. Assistant District Attorney Alcock charged at the trial that the name Bertrand had been "foisted on the world" by Andrews,[39] but if Bertrand was indeed a fiction, invented by Andrews after the assassination, how could Russo testify that he had met Shaw before the assassination under the pseudonym Bertrand? According to the Sciambra memorandum, Russo had not mentioned the name Bertrand in his initial interview. It was only after Sciambra told Russo that he had identified one of the participants at the meeting in Ferrie's apartment as Bertrand while Russo was under the influence of sodium pentothal—an identification which, according to Billings, Russo did not recall at the time—and after Russo was allowed to ask leading questions about the case so that, in his own words, he "could figure out what they wanted to know," that the name Bertrand found its way into his story.

In what may well turn out to be a self-fulfilling prophecy, Garrison has predicted that the case of Clay Shaw "will never be permitted to come to trial."[40] According to the Louisiana code of criminal procedure, the district attorney is empowered to fix the date of a trial (which then must be approved by the Court), and thus has effective control over the docket, or schedule of cases. Despite Garrison's announcements on several occasions that a date had been set for the trial of Clay Shaw, an examination of the court records shows that—as of October 1968—no date for the trial has ever been actually scheduled by the District Attorney since the arrest of Shaw in March 1967.[41] This is no doubt partly due to the somewhat unusual procedure Garrison followed in arresting Shaw: instead of waiting until he had obtained sufficient evidence for a court trial, Garrison, it will be recalled, arrested Shaw on the basis of an unsubstantiated (and altered) story of a single witness, and then, *after* arresting Shaw, sought evidence that would corroborate the story in court.[42] The trial was further delayed by the defense, which held that the numerous public statements Garrison had made about the case created an atmosphere in New Orleans prejudicial to the defendant, and asked for a change of venue. (Garrison added to this delay by filing a token protest against the Court's decision to hear the defense's motions.)[43] Finally, Shaw's attorneys asked a federal court to intervene on the ground that Garrison had conducted "a reign of terror by the misuse and abuse of the powers of the public office" and thus had denied the defendant the possibility of obtaining a fair trial.[44] Although a three-judge federal court in Louisiana denied this plea, it ordered Garrison not to proceed with the case until the appeal of this motion could be heard by the United States Supreme Court.[45] Both sides expressed doubts at the time that the case would ever come to trial,[46] but in December 1968 the Supreme Court refused to intervene, and said that Louisiana may proceed. Garrison, in turn, announced plans to try the case early in 1969.[47]

4

THE SEARCH

*If it takes me thirty years to nail every one of the assassins, then I will
continue this investigation for thirty years.*
— Jim Garrison in *Playboy*

After the preliminary hearing, there was a second notable shift
in the nature of the investigation. Whereas the first phase had
concentrated on the activities of David Ferrie, and the second
was devoted principally to efforts to substantiate Russo's allegations about Clay Shaw, the third phase had no single specific
objective. It was, in effect, a hunt without a quarry, a search for
any information from any source that might relate to any aspect
of the assassination. For this desultory pursuit, Garrison reinforced his permanent staff with volunteer recruits from the
growing corps of critics of the Warren Commission. A number
of these people who might best be described as peripatetic
demonologists found in New Orleans an unexpected rallying
point; they were attracted to Garrison like the children of
Hamelin to the Pied Piper. At the head of the line stood Mark
Lane, the author of *Rush to Judgment*, who, together with Wil-

liam Turner, the *Ramparts* writer, spent months assiduously combing Garrison's files on the case for new clues and devising ingenious schemes to produce new disclosures. (When one assistant district attorney protested that by making Xerox copies of the evidence Lane might be jeopardizing the case, Garrison replied that Lane and Turner were "writing the official history of the investigation.")[1] Reports on developments in Texas came from Penn Jones, Jr., the crusading editor of the Midlothian, Texas, *Mirror* and the author of a series of booklets called "Forgive My Grief," the most celebrated feature of which was a death count of individuals who were even peripherally connected with the assassination, and from Allan Chapman, a knight-errant in a two-hundred-year-old crusade against the Illuminati (supposedly a worldwide conspiracy of intellectuals who now control the television networks). Harold Weisberg, the author of a numerically consecutive series of books called *Whitewash*, was charged with the task of going through the twenty-six volumes of the Warren Commission's testimony and evidence for new leads relevant to Garrison's investigation. Two specialists in photographic interpretation, Raymond Marcus and Richard Sprague, scanned films of the assassination to detect previously neglected pieces that might fit into what Garrison calls his "jigsaw puzzle." Three trouble-shooters-at-large also assisted—Vincent Salandria, a lawyer from Philadelphia; Richard H. Popkin, a professor of philosophy at the University of California at San Diego and the author of "The Second Oswald," a conjectural essay originally published in the *New York Review of Books* which suggests that the assassination was performed not by Oswald but by his *Doppelgänger;* and the nightclub and television comedian Mort Sahl.[2] Although these amateur sleuths, who sometimes referred to themselves as the Dealey Plaza Irregulars, provided Garrison with the bulk of the new "evidence" that he cited in numerous public appearances —including a coast-to-coast tour of radio and television shows in connection with the *Playboy* interview—they occasionally proved a source of friction for the professional investigators on Garrison's staff.

Thomas Bethell, who worked on the investigation as a member of Garrison's staff since its inception, described the contribution of the amateurs this way: "The trouble with these third-rate students is that the only way they can make a strong impression on Garrison is by coming up with flamboyant nonsense, thus hoping to be hired as someone with original ideas. They therefore represent a serious threat to the sanity of the investigation. One of them has a bad habit of steering Garrison into crackpot directions, such as the 'Storm Drain Theory,' to which Garrison tends to be susceptible."[3] And the more parvenu experts advocated a certain "original idea," the more susceptible Garrison apparently became. When Allan Chapman, the Illuminati specialist, lent his support to the theory that a shot had been fired from a storm drain in Dealey Plaza that day in Dallas,[4] Garrison stated on television that the bullet that killed President Kennedy was "fired by a man standing in a sewer manhole."[5] Thus, Garrison added a sixteenth man to the team that he claims carried out the assassination and a fifth spot from which he has said the shots were fired. Six months before, Garrison had theorized that there were only two assassins— one, Oswald, in the Texas School Book Depository building and one on the so-called grassy knoll, just beyond the building and on the same side of the street.[6] After discussing the case with Weisberg, who believes that there was another rifleman in the nearby Dal-Tex building, Garrison accommodatingly added a third rifleman there, and also exonerated Oswald from having fired any of the shots.[7] Then Marcus came along with a blowup of some trees and shadows on the grassy knoll, claiming that this revealed some figures concealed in the bushes, and Garrison added four more assassins to the band. (Two of them, he has suggested, were there to pick up stray cartridge cases.)[8] Next, the independent investigator Jones Harris showed Garrison a blowup of a truck parked behind a picket fence, and the "commando team" grew by two.[9] By mid-June 1967, Garrison was saying that the assassination was performed by a fourteen-man team of Cuban guerrilla fighters.[10] Finally, after discussing the matter at some length with Professor Popkin, Garrison posited a "second Oswald," who was sent to impersonate the first Oswald at the scene.[11] (This understandably disconcerted some members of his staff, since the presence of a second Oswald would tend to vitiate the legal case against Clay Shaw: did Shaw conspire with Oswald, as he is accused of doing, or with an impersonator?)[12] The assassins were supported, according to Garrison, by Jack Ruby and some members of the Dallas Police Department.[13]

Although the exact number of assassins changed from one public statement to the next, the "forces behind the conspiracy" grew steadily. In the early stages of the investigation, Garrison had told Senator Russell Long that only a few insignificant men were involved.[14] Then, after Ferrie's death, Garrison began to specify the guilty parties, identifying them as a band of perverts and anti-Castro Cubans. With the arrival of the demonologists, however, the conspiracy was rapidly escalated to include Minutemen,[15] CIA agents,[16] oil millionaires,[17] Dallas policemen,[18] munitions exporters,[19] "the Dallas Establishment,"[20] reactionaries,[21] White Russians,[22] and certain elements of "the invisible Nazi substructure."[23]

On what sort of evidence was this extraordinary conspiracy predicated? Garrison's method of deducing the last member of the team is perhaps indicative. The figure of what may be reckoned as the sixteenth assassin was extrapolated from two newspaper photographs taken about ten minutes after the assassination. The first shows a man in a dark suit apparently examining a curb near the spot where President Kennedy was shot, with two policemen shown looking on. Garrison claimed on a television program that he could detect in this photograph a pebble-like object partly concealed by the heavily matted grass, and he stated that this object is a .45-caliber bullet "which killed John Kennedy, which has markings on it that would show [that] the automatic gun from which it came [was a] handgun."[24] The bullet is not readily visible to the naked eye; in fact, according to one member of Garrison's staff, the photograph is so grainy that it is impossible to be certain that the pebble-like object is not in fact a pebble.[25] The other photograph, taken seconds later, shows the man in the dark suit walking away with his hands closed. Flashing this photograph in front of television cameras in Dallas, Garrison declared that the man (from his appearance Garrison somehow surmised him to be a "federal agent") had "got the bullet clutched in his hand, the bullet that killed John Kennedy."[26] Garrison never explained how he could determine from a photograph that a bullet was being held in a man's closed fist—and even discern its calibre. However, this was the "evidence" that Garrison cited in support of the theory that an assassin was in a sewer, and of his own charge on television that "the bullet which killed John Kennedy, which fell in the grass with pieces of the President's head, was in the hands of the federal government ten minutes after the President was dead." And Garrison went even further. "This means that the federal government knowingly participated in framing Lee Oswald," he said. "Lyndon Johnson had to know this."[27] Garrison himself, however, eliminated this assassin in the sewer in his later press statements; for example, in his July 11, 1968, press conference he listed the "shooting points" as the "Dal-Tex building," the "Dallas Book Depository building," and the "grassy knoll."[28]

Although most of the assassins were identified only as projections of connected dots in enlargements of photographs of trees and shrubbery, the man whom Garrison identified in *Playboy* as the seventh member of the assassination team turned out much to the District Attorney's embarrassment, to be a real person. Garrison alleged that this seventh man "created a diversionary action in order to distract people's attention from the snipers," explaining, "This individual screamed, fell to the ground, and simulated an epileptic fit, drawing people away from the vicinity of the knoll just before the President's motorcade reached the ambush point."[29] Garrison further described this man, presumably one of a number of anti-Castro Cuban paramilitarists, as being clad in green combat fatigues.[30] As it happened, however, the person Garrison was talking about was Jerry Boyd Belknap, an employee of the *Dallas News*, who had fainted in Dealey Plaza about twenty minutes before the motorcade arrived. Belknap explained to the FBI that he had had frequent fainting spells since suffering a serious head injury in an automobile accident in 1960, and that he had been receiving daily medication to prevent these spells.[31] When Garrison learned in June 1967 that the man who fainted was not the paramilitarist he had presumed him to be, he told his staff to forget about the matter.[32] Yet in his public statements he continued to say that he had located this seventh member of the commando team.*[33]

A prosecutor who wants to insure that the story of his investigation remains newsworthy must produce new evidence con-

* According to Bethell, Garrison had the FBI report on Belknap before he made the statement in *Playboy* about the "diversionary action."

stantly. Garrison's corps of Irregulars proved helpful not simply in digging out new evidence but, on occasion, in finding opportunities for Garrison to present it. When Mort Sahl appeared on the Johnny Carson television show in January 1968 and complained about the coverage that the various media had given the District Attorney and his case, Carson agreed to have Garrison on his program, provided that he would not merely reiterate old charges but would present new evidence. Garrison telegraphed Carson accepting the impromptu offer. And on the evening of January 31, Carson devoted most of his show to an interview with Garrison. When Carson asked Garrison to reveal the new evidence that he claimed he had, Garrison reached into a black leather portfolio he held in his lap and pulled out some photographs, which, he said, showed suspects being arrested immediately after the assassination. "Here are the pictures of five of them being arrested," he said, "and they've never been shown before." He went on to say, "Several of these men arrested have been connected by our office with the Central Intelligence Agency."[34] The new evidence Garrison presented that night had been found by Allan Chapman some weeks before, in the photographic department of the Dallas *Times Herald*. Robert Hollingsworth, managing editor of the *Times Herald*, has told me that he personally inspected with a magnifying glass the photographs given to Chapman, and that they showed nothing more than some bystanders, two of whom were employed in the building in which Oswald worked, being routinely questioned by policemen. (Police reports included in the Warren Commission's published evidence [Volume XIX, Decker Exhibits] indicate that a number of individuals were also taken into custody in the confusion after the shooting, and possibly some were photographed.) Carson, who was, of course, seeing the pictures for the first time, had no way of knowing who the individuals in the pictures were or whether they were in fact "being arrested," and he had no way of challenging Garrison's claim that they were connected with the CIA. What Garrison presented to the public that night, then, was not actually new evidence—witnesses pictured in his photographs had testified before the Warren Commission—but a new and totally unsubstantiated interpretation of old evidence.

Any sensational murder case attracts its share of crank letters, publicity seekers, and bogus tips, and, whereas most district attorneys regard such offers of help as a nuisance, Garrison found them a rich source of new witnesses, ready to provide allegations and disclosures of the sort required to keep his story current in the press. Although it is extremely doubtful whether any of these volunteer witnesses will ever testify in court, the case of a man named Donald Philetus Norton illustrates the use to which the testimony of such "secret witnesses" can be put in the open arena of public opinion. Norton, a thirty-four-year-old night-club entertainer, got in touch with Garrison in June 1967, claiming that he had been a CIA courier, and that he had delivered fifty thousand dollars to a man who was "a dead ringer for Oswald" in Mexico in 1962 and had received a hundred-and-fifty-thousand-dollar "pickup" from David Ferrie in 1958. He said, further, that he would like to work as an investigator for Garrison. Norton[35] was immediately brought to New Orleans from Vancouver, where he was living at the time, and was interrogated by Garrison's still-pseudonymous intelligence expert Bill Boxley. Though Norton was more than willing to identify Oswald, Ferrie, and even Shaw as CIA agents, his story contained so many contradictions and implausibilities that Boxley and other staff members concluded that he would be totally ineffective as a witness. (It was later revealed that he was a convicted bank embezzler with a prison record.) But even though Norton was turned down in July as a possible court witness, Garrison referred to him as a "secret witness" in the interview that appeared in the October 1967 issue of *Playboy*. "We have evidence that Oswald maintained his CIA contacts . . . and that Ferrie was also employed by the CIA," he announced. "In this regard, we will present in court a witness— formerly a CIA courier—who met both Ferrie and Oswald officially in their CIA connection."[36] This "courier" was later identified by a member of Garrison's staff as Norton.[37]

Another witness found in the mail—this one with Professor Popkin's help—was Richard C. Nagell, then confined in the psychiatric section of the Medical Center for Federal Prisoners in Springfield, Missouri. Nagell had been arrested while attempting to rob a bank in El Paso in September 1963. After the assassination, he claimed that he had purposely got himself arrested in order to provide an alibi because he had had advance knowledge of the assassination conspiracy; his part in it, according to Garrison, had been to kill Oswald, who was the "patsy."[38] Although Nagell was a convicted felon, whose own defense had raised questions about his mental status, Garrison thought his story worth pursuing and sent a former assistant district attorney, William R. Martin, to Missouri to interview him. Nagell insisted he had proof of the conspiracy in the form of tape recordings. When these could not be found, Nagell told Martin, "They've stolen the tapes," and refused to discuss the matter any further. Though Nagell, like Norton, was finally rejected by Garrison as a court witness, the District Attorney continued to use Nagell's story to bolster his case in public. Explaining Oswald's role as a patsy, Garrison stated in *Playboy*, "We have evidence that the plan was to have him [Oswald] shot as a cop killer in the Texas Theater 'while resisting arrest.' " Garrison said he was unable to divulge the evidence at the time, but the whole thing was one of Nagell's tales.[39] (Nagell was later released from prison and claimed that Garrison's investigator, Martin, was himself a CIA agent and distorted his story.)

Another confidential witness with whom Garrison spent a good deal of time is a Dallas ex-convict who has been under suspicion in Texas for attempted murder. According to Thomas Bethell, this witness "drops into the office at fairly frequent intervals and readily identifies almost anyone you show him a photograph of."[40] He proved more co-operative than accurate. Of thirteen new witnesses found through the mail or with the help of the Irregulars assisting Garrison, nearly all have turned out to have criminal records or to have been under psychiatric care.

To facilitate the publication of his *Playboy* interview, Garrison provided the editors of the magazine with "secret evidence" which, he claimed, was to be used in his court case and was "not for publication."[41] Subsequently, however, Gordon Novel, who was mentioned quite prominently in the interview, sued *Playboy* for libel, and in the course of the pretrial litigation the memorandum containing Garrison's "secret evidence" was examined by Elmer Gertz, Novel's attorney, and entered into the court record.[42] Virtually all of the "secret evidence" consists of uncorroborated allegations of volunteer witnesses. For example, one item in the memorandum states, "Garrison has a witness,

Raymond Cummings [a Dallas taxicab driver], who will testify that he saw Oswald, Shaw and Ruby together in Dallas on one occasion and Oswald and Ruby on another." According to Bethell, Shaw was not mentioned in Cummings' story,[43] and furthermore Garrison himself told James D. Squires, a reporter for the *Nashville Tennesseean*, that he was not using Cummings as a witness.[44] Another court witness Garrison cited in the memorandum was Clyde Johnson, who, Garrison claimed, would testify in court that Clay Shaw and Lee Harvey Oswald had visited him in a Baton Rouge hotel room in 1963 and offered him six thousand dollars to denounce Kennedy for his "betrayal" of Cuba. Johnson had in fact given Garrison's office a statement to that effect on March 30, 1967, but when it turned out that Oswald was in Mexico on the day that Johnson had claimed he had visited his hotel room, Johnson said on a local radio program that he would not repeat his testimony in court, even if he had to take the Fifth Amendment.[45] Again, although his witness had been effectively disqualified as a court witness, Garrison still found some use for him as a "secret witness." A third item in the memorandum states that "Garrison has two other witnesses who will testify that Shaw and Oswald met together in several small Louisiana towns in the summer and fall of 1963." The witnesses referred to were two itinerant mural artists, Mr. and Mrs. Cedric Younger Von Rolleston, who appeared in Garrison's office in July 1967 and claimed that they had seen Clay Shaw with Lee Harvey Oswald in the Bentley Hotel in Alexandria, Louisiana, in October 1963.[46] Subsequently, the Von Rollestons went to the offices of Clay Shaw's lawyers, and requested to see Clay Shaw, then, after meeting with Shaw, swore in an affidavit that they had never before met Shaw and that the identification they had made earlier from photographs in Garrison's office was incorrect.[47] Evidence like this was of course far more effective as "secret evidence," which could be presented confidentially to journalists and editors, than as court evidence.

The "mailbag," as all the unsolicited tips and offers to testify were called around the District Attorney's office, also provided Garrison with data for his public statements. For example, after receiving an anonymous letter suggesting that President Kennedy might have been shot with "frangible" (or dumdum) bullets,[48] Garrison asserted in his *Playboy* interview that "some of the gunmen appear to have used frangible bullets."[49] And it also led to one arrest. William Turner (the *Ramparts* staff writer and former FBI employee) ran across a letter alleging that a Californian named Eugene Bradley had once made inflammatory comments on President Kennedy. Investigating the matter, Turner found an Edgar Eugene Bradley, who raised funds for a radio program called "20th Century Reformation Hour," and who happened to have been in Texas on the day of the assassination —though in El Paso, not in Dallas. On the basis of this information, Garrison, who at the time was in Los Angeles raising funds himself, telephoned his office in New Orleans and ordered Assistant District Attorney Alcock to issue a warrant for Bradley's arrest, charging him with conspiracy to kill President Kennedy. Bethell reported concern among the staff members; there was nothing in the files on Bradley except the letter, and no one in the office had even heard of Bradley as a suspect. The warrant was issued anyway, and Bradley was arrested in Los Angeles and then released on his own recognizance. When Garrison returned to New Orleans, he explained to his bewildered staff that he had further investigated Bradley, but saw little prospect of his ever being extradited by Governor Ronald Reagan.[50] This became another one of Garrison's self-fulfilling prophecies. In November 1968, California refused extradition because Garrison had failed to produce any witnesses to substantiate the charges against Bradley.[51] After he had left Garrison's staff, William Gurvich said, "Jim has a philosophy about national headlines. He believes that everyone reads the headlines concerning arrests and charges but few people read denials or correcting statements."[52]

5

THE THOUSAND-POUND CANARY

To read the press accounts of my investigation—my "circus," I should say —I'm a cross between Al Capone and Attila the Hun, ruthlessly hounding innocent men, trampling their legal rights, bribing and threatening witnesses, and in general violating every canon of legal ethics.
—Jim Garrison in *Playboy*

American district attorneys enjoy a pre-eminent control over the administration of justice in their respective bailiwicks. They have the power to initiate or to terminate investigations, to decide which cases finally to prosecute and which to quash, and, in effect, to adjudicate penalties in advance of trial by negotiating with the defense counsel over a defendant's plea. Institutional constraints on such powers are minimal. As Raymond Moley has long since demonstrated in his classic study *Politics and Criminal Prosecution*, a grand jury, which theoretically acts as the primary check on the discretion of a district attorney, tends in fact to become little more than a rubber stamp for his actions; the members of the grand jury are, after all, only laymen, whereas the prosecutor is a trained lawyer, and the decisions which the grand jury renders are almost exclusively structured by the prosecutor's own presentation of evidence and argument.[1] In Orleans Parish, the district attorney has the additional advantage of being able to subpoena witnesses peremptorily without having to consult the grand jury, and he may even bring persons to trial, by-passing the usual process of grand-jury indictment, merely by signing what is known as a "bill of information" against them; moreover, it is part of his official responsibility to serve as legal adviser to the same grand jury which is supposed to check *his* legal powers.

In the objections which the mass media have from time to time raised against Garrison and his methods, however, seldom have they focused on any questionable use of these legitimate powers of the District Attorney's office. Rather, it has become customary to criticize Garrison for resorting to extralegal means of conducting his investigation. Charges of bribery, in particular, have been frequently leveled against Garrison and his staff, and many of these have received prominent coverage in the press and on television. In June 1967, for instance, it was widely reported that Miguel Torres, the former drug addict who was then an inmate at the Louisiana State Prison at Angola, was alleging that Garrison had arranged to have him transferred to the Orleans Parish Prison and had offered him both a parole and a supply of heroin if he would agree to submit to hypnosis and then testify against Clay Shaw—this despite Torres' insistence that he had never known Shaw.[2] At the same time, John Cancler—the Parish Prison inmate who had debunked Vernon Bundy's testimony at the preliminary hearing in March 1967—claimed that a representative of Garrison's staff had offered to drop the burglary charges then pending against him if he would agree to plant a piece of incriminating evidence in Clay Shaw's home.[3] In the NBC critique of Garrison's case, Sandra Moffitt, Perry Russo's acquaintance, appeared to say that she had been offered gifts of "clothing" and certain other "considerations" in return for her co-operation with Garrison's office.[4] On the same broadcast, Fred Lemanns, sometime operator of a New Orleans Turkish bath, alleged that Garrison had offered to help finance a "private club" for him if he would sign a statement to the effect that he had seen Shaw in the company of Lee Harvey Oswald in the bathhouse of his establishment. (Lemanns went on to say that he finally did sign the statement, even though he knew it to be false.)[5] And *Newsweek*, in its critical report, quoted Alvin Beauboeuf, whom David Ferrie had designated in his will as the sole heir to his estate, who stated that one of Garrison's investigators had offered to pay him three thousand dollars if he would supply testimony to support the case against Shaw.[6]

Garrison himself seems to have taken such charges in stride. "Like every police department and district attorney's office across the country," he once explained, "we have sums set aside to pay informers for valuable information—but we would never suborn perjury."[7] And he chided the mass media for making so much of the allegations of attempted subornation made by these various witnesses. "It's rather naïve," he said, "apart from being ethically objectionable, to assume that our investigators travel around the country with bags of money trying to bribe witnesses to lie on the witness stand. We just don't operate that way."[8]

Regardless of whether Garrison's office indeed operated "that way," it is true that his critics appeared unduly preoccupied with the business of exposing such blatantly unscrupulous practices as bribery and subornation of perjury. By concentrating on these sensational charges, reporters generally neglected to reveal the District Attorney's more subtle uses of those substantial powers invested in his office—legitimate powers to be sure, but ones which may be exercised with no less unscrupulous intent. According to Gurvich, it was a "real education" to see how the District Attorney would apply various pressures to individuals whom he identified as "potential witnesses." Gurvich points to the case of Morris Brownlee, the godson of David Ferrie, whom Garrison once had arrested on a narcotics charge. Though that charge had been dropped earlier by Garrison for lack of evidence, when Garrison became interested in Ferrie and his possible involvement in an assassination conspiracy, he had Brownlee arrested again on the same charge, then brought Ferrie in to see his godson in jail and offered once again to quash the charges if Ferrie would "co-operate" with him.[9] Gurvich describes Garrison's typical *modus operandi* this way: first he would befriend "potential witnesses"; then, after obtaining some leading information or incriminating statements, he would proceed to "put the screws on them"; and when the witness had no other alternative open to him, Garrison would offer to make some sort of "deal" for the witness's "co-operation."[10] Garrison's treatment of Dean Andrews, the pre-talking lawyer who first brought the name of Clay Bertrand to his attention and whom he subsequently had convicted of perjury, represents a telling case in point.

Dean Andrews

Some time in the fall of 1966, Jim Garrison invited Dean Andrews, a long-standing acquaintance who was then an assistant district attorney in neighboring Jefferson Parish, to have dinner with him at Broussard's. As Andrews tells it, Garrison seemed especially concerned with the fact that "Oswald was on his turf a few months before he assassinated Number One." Since Oswald had come to Andrews seeking legal advice during his stay in New Orleans, Garrison was interested in knowing something of Andrews' impressions of Oswald. The two men "kicked a few theories about the assassination around," Andrews said, and then "the Green Giant mooched my copy of the Warren Report because he didn't even own a copy then."[11] A few weeks later, Garrison informed Andrews that he was "reopening" the investigation into the assassination of President Kennedy, and he asked Andrews for his assistance. Specifically, he wanted information on three individuals: David Ferrie, whom Garrison called the "getaway pilot"; the unidentified stocky Mexican man who, Andrews had previously told the Warren Commission, had accompanied Oswald to his office; and Clay Bertrand, the individual who Andrews testified had called him shortly after the assassination and had asked him to defend Oswald in Dallas. But Andrews was able to supply Garrison with little more than the old leads he had already furnished the Warren Commission. He told the District Attorney what has been reported earlier: that his only contact with David Ferrie had occurred when he arranged a parole for one of Ferrie's friends, an action which, he acknowledged, "was not a strictly legal move for an assistant D.A. to make." As for the mysterious Mexican and Clay Bertrand, Andrews told Garrison that he knew the former only as

"Oswald's shadow" and the latter as no more than the "voice on the phone."[12]

Shortly before Christmas, Garrison and Andrews had a second dinner meeting. Andrews recalls that Garrison had come up with the theory that "Clay Bertrand" was in fact a pseudonym for Clay Shaw. According to Andrews, he insisted that Garrison was mistaken, that Clay Shaw was not "in any way, shape or form, Clay Bertrand." In subsequent meetings, however, Garrison persisted in theorizing that Clay Shaw and Clay Bertrand were one and the same; and Garrison, in Andrews' words, "attempted to brainwash me" into identifying Shaw as Bertrand. Andrews claims that he was growing increasingly suspicious of Garrison's tactics, especially in view of this obstinate identification of Bertrand as Shaw. As a means of testing Garrison's probity, Andrews says, he dropped "two bum names —'Mannie Garcia Gonzales' and 'Ricardo Davis' "—men whom he identified for the District Attorney as "Cuban guerrilla fighters." Andrews indicates that he had fabricated both names "out of my head on the spur of the moment . . . to see if the Giant's kosher."[13] A few days later Andrews decided his suspicions were justified. Garrison announced that he had identified the "triggerman" in the assassination plot as "Manuel Garcia Gonzales"; he noted that a certain Emanuel Gonzales had been arrested earlier that year on a charge of carrying a concealed weapon, and he cited this fact as further evidence of his being on the right trail. (Gonzales is hardly an uncommon name among Latin Americans, and Garrison neglected to state what specific connection there was between the man who had carried a concealed weapon in New Orleans and the man who pulled the trigger in Dallas.) Andrews went to Garrison and told him that he had "the right ta-ta but the wrong ho-ho"—that is, the wrong Gonzales. The working relationship between Andrews and Garrison was beginning to deteriorate into a condition of mutual mistrust.[14]

Late in February of 1967, a few days before the arrest of Clay Shaw, Garrison asked Andrews to meet him for dinner once again. He told Andrews that he now had further evidence of Shaw's involvement in the assassination conspiracy, and he requested that Andrews remain silent on the Clay Bertrand matter until he had a chance to build the case against Shaw. Should he have failed to co-operate, Andrews claims, Garrison threatened to send him "to the Bastille." Andrews says that they finally worked out a "deal" whereby he would agree to avoid saying that Clay Shaw was definitely *not* Clay Bertrand. Andrews maintains that he yielded to the District Attorney's demands on the point because, if he refused, "the Jolly Green Giant would pounce on me like a thousand-pound canary."[15]

On March 1, 1967, Clay Shaw was arrested. In the application for a search warrant of Shaw's premises, it was stated that a "confidential informant" had heard "Clay Shaw (alias Clay Bertrand) . . . agree to kill John F. Kennedy." As had been the case with "Emanuel Gonzales," another of the names for which Andrews knew himself to be the District Attorney's original source, Garrison had again put his finger on "the wrong ho-ho" —the wrong man. Andrews claims that he found the "key" to just what Garrison was up to when the District Attorney "busted Clay Shaw as Clay Bertrand—and there ain't no such animal."[16]

The next day Andrews was subpoenaed to appear at the District Attorney's office; again he was asked about Clay Bertrand. In accordance with the deal he had previously made with Garrison, Andrews avoided saying directly that Shaw was not Bertrand. On March 9, a few days before Clay Shaw's preliminary hearing was scheduled to start, Andrews was summoned before the Orleans Parish Grand Jury. He was asked only to give his name, address, and occupation. Andrews himself describes this as another of Garrison's "tricks." "Once you go in front of the grand jury," he explains, "you can't open your mouth or tell anybody what happened in there. . . . If you do, you're subject to be penalized for contempt of court and prosecuted." In other words, by means of the grand-jury subpoena, Garrison had effectively silenced Andrews, the only witness who could say for sure that Clay Shaw was *not* Clay Bertrand.[17]

After Shaw's preliminary hearing was completed, and the defendant was ordered to stand trial, Andrews was again called before the Orleans Parish Grand Jury. He was directed to state under oath whether or not Clay Shaw was the person whom he knew as Clay Bertrand. He answered, as he had agreed to, "I can't say that he is and I can't say he ain't."[18] Andrews was also asked whether he had ever arranged a parole for anyone on behalf of David Ferrie during his tenure as assistant district attorney in Jefferson Parish; he answered that he had not. If he had replied in the affirmative, acknowledging the information he had confidentially given Garrison several months before, he would have risked incriminating himself for having got a parole for a private client. Andrews was also questioned about statements he had previously made in the District Attorney's office, and was then indicted on five counts of perjury. Afterward, Andrews commented, "The Jolly Green Giant seeks out and destroys or cripples his enemies. . . . If you think a district attorney's subpoena isn't raw power, and if you think a district attorney's ability to present a matter to a grand jury and recommend, and interpret the law, isn't raw power, then you just don't know what goes on."[19]

As the case against Clay Shaw progressed, it became apparent to Andrews that Shaw was "just a poor unfortunate who was grabbed out of the sky by the Jolly Green Giant, and his wizards and practitioners of voodoo, labeled Clay Bertrand, and bang, he's been tagged 'it' ever since." Andrews saw that his deal with Garrison was being used to "put the hat on" Clay Shaw—that is, to frame him.[20] In what he claims was an effort to undo this wrong, Andrews voluntarily appeared before the grand jury for a third time on June 28. He testified that he had known all along that Clay Shaw was not Clay Bertrand, the fictitious name which he said he had invented in order to protect the identity of his bartender friend. Furthermore, he acknowledged that he had previously told the grand jury that he was unable to say that Shaw was *not* Bertrand only because of the deal he had made with Garrison. For confessing this, and also in consequence of his earlier refusal to incriminate himself when he denied that he had arranged the parole for Ferrie's friend, Andrews was finally convicted of perjury.[21]

Thus, deftly using the legitimate powers of his office, Garrison had managed to discredit the one witness who could have undermined his court case by testifying that Clay Bertrand did not exist. (A convicted perjurer cannot testify in court in Louisiana.) And he succeeded as well in hoodwinking most of the press; few, if any, reporters and commentators seemed to recognize how the fact of Andrews' conviction tended to undermine rather than sustain the case against Clay Shaw. Though it was broadly reported that Garrison was hailing Andrews' conviction as a "major victory," what was not reported was the larger implication of Andrews' perjury: Andrews had in fact been convicted precisely because he admitted that Clay Shaw, the man whom Garrison had arrested as Clay Bertrand, was *not* Bertrand.

Kerry Thornley

Garrison obtained indictments against individuals who, like Andrews, failed to co-operate with him; to recall Gurvich's words, he "put the screws on" these "potential witnesses" largely as a means of garnering publicity, since it became evident that the press seldom questioned the relevance of these peripheral indictments to the main case being prosecuted against Clay Shaw. And every successful indictment (if not conviction) on a charge of perjury at least *appeared* to enhance the image of the District Attorney's success and the validity of his investigation. In fact, Garrison seemed, on occasion, less concerned with indicting key figures in the investigation than with obtaining indictments *per se*—even if this involved turning friendly witnesses into suspects. The case of Kerry Thornley is particularly enlightening in this regard.

In October 1967, while Garrison was visiting Los Angeles to raise funds for his investigation, he met with David Lifton, a man who had spent considerable time doing independent research into the Kennedy assassination. According to Lifton,[22] Garrison solicited his help in obtaining the "co-operation" of Kerry Thornley, a friend of Lifton's who had served with Lee Harvey Oswald in the Marine Corps in 1959 and who, after the assassination, had written a brief book about Oswald. Garrison explained that Thornley was to play an essential role in his plan to indict for perjury one John R. Heindel, who had also served in the Marines with Oswald. Garrison said that he had reason to believe that Heindel was the man Thornley had once overheard speaking Russian with Oswald, and he wanted Thornley to confirm the fact publicly and under oath. The plan was quite simple: Garrison would first call Heindel before the grand jury and ask him to state whether or not he had ever heard Oswald speaking Russian; Heindel would, as he had previously stated, answer that he had not. Then Garrison would call Thornley before the grand jury and ask him to state whether he had ever heard Heindel speaking Russian with Oswald; Thornley would answer that he had, and Heindel would then be indicted for perjury. Although the question of whether or not Oswald had ever spoken Russian in the presence of Heindel was palpably irrelevant—to the investigations of both the Warren Commission and Garrison—the news stories that Heindel's arrest would produce could be, in Garrison's opinion, quite advantageous to his case. As he explained to Lifton, Heindel's nickname in the Marine Corps had been "Hidel," which was nearly the same as the alias, "A. J. Hidell," which Oswald had used several times, most notably to order the rifle he allegedly used in the assassination. Garrison told Lifton that he could already envision the splendid news stories that would develop out of Heindel's arrest: "John R. Heindel, alias 'Hidel,' was today arrested in New Orleans in the conspiracy investigation. . . ." And aside from the publicity the indictment would generate, Garrison indicated that he could use it as a "legal lever" to induce Heindel to give testimony relevant to his court case against Clay Shaw. "This could be the break I've been waiting for," he declared.[23]

Lifton finally agreed to discuss the matter with Thornley. After Garrison returned to New Orleans, however, Lifton did some investigating of his own, determined that Heindel was probably not the person with whom Oswald had reportedly been conversing in Russian, and immediately telegraphed that information to Garrison. Although Heindel could not be arrested without the "co-operation" of Lifton and Thornley, which would not now be forthcoming, Garrison realized that he could still create the sort of conflict of testimony he had originally intended to use in indicting Heindel—simply by using it with reference to a different candidate for perjury: Kerry Thornley.

Several weeks after their first meeting, Lifton and Garrison had another discussion in Los Angeles regarding Thornley. Lifton's account of the meeting runs as follows:

> We sat down in chairs. Garrison then fixed me with this "mystical stare" of his, and said, in a slow, even tone, as if making some type of biblical pronouncement: "Thornley

lied." (He stretched out the word "lied," by pausing on the *i* sound for about a second or two.)

This took me quite by surprise. After all, only three weeks ago Thornley was to be Garrison's star witness-to-be.

Why, I asked, did he say Thornley lied?

Pause.

Again, "Thornley lied." (As if, by repeating it, it gained in validity.)

Then Garrison told me: "Thornley lied when he said he didn't know Oswald in September 1963." Again, I was dumbfounded. I politely offered the thought that I would go wherever the evidence led; what evidence did he have that this was the case?

Then, Garrison told me: "We have so many witnesses who saw them together at that time we have stopped looking for more."

Then, another pontifical pronouncement: "Thornley's with the CIA."

"But why do you say that, Jim?" I asked.

"Thornley worked at a hotel in Arlington, Virginia."

So what, I wanted to know. My "so what?" type of rebuttal was met by his incredulity, as if "What do you mean, 'so what?'; isn't it obvious to you what this means?"[24]

Garrison also told Lifton that although Thornley denied he had seen Oswald in New Orleans in 1963, his office had located another witness who claimed to have seen Oswald and Thornley dining together in a New Orleans restaurant that year. The witness turned out to be Barbara Reed, a French Quarter resident who reputedly practices voodoo and has from time to time assisted Garrison's investigators by "screening witnesses."[25]

Garrison proceeded to subpoena Thornley before the grand jury. His testimony to the effect that he had not seen Oswald in New Orleans in 1963 did in fact conflict with the sworn testimony of Barbara Reed, and Thornley was subsequently indicted for perjury.* Thus, as Lifton notes, Garrison succeeded in doing

* Apparently Garrison had entertained other plans regarding Thornley. At one time, it was thought he might serve as a likely "second Oswald"—that is, the individual who, according to Professor Richard Popkin's theory, impersonated Oswald before the assassination as part of a ruse for foiling the investigators. In what was evidently an effort to

to Thornley precisely what he had originally hoped to do to John Heindel with Thornley's aid.

> What is really outrageous is that Kerry's subpoena to come to New Orleans to testify was not issued by a man who sought to find out facts, or find out truth, but to *do to Kerry exactly and precisely* what Garrison had intended doing to Heindel!
>
> In other words, Garrison had a theory about Heindel, a theory which posited Heindel's involvement in the assassination, at least after the fact. The point is, Garrison thought Heindel "knew something" and was "hiding" it.
>
> The method for "breaking" Heindel was to get Heindel to testify, get Thornley to testify, establishing a conflict of testimony. Then Heindel was to be charged with perjury, with Kerry (and others) presumably being the witnesses against Heindel.
>
> Now, Garrison called Kerry to New Orleans to do the same thing to him.[27]

Thornley's indictment was the twelfth ancillary case arising out of Garrison's main investigation into the conspiracy charges against Clay Shaw. Six of these involved unco-operative witnesses—Kerry Thornley (perjury), Dean Andrews (perjury), Layton Martens, an acquaintance of Ferrie's (perjury), John Cancler (contempt of court), Sergio Arcacha Smith (burglary), and Morris Brownlee (possession of narcotics); three involved newsmen who had been critical of Garrison—David Chandler (perjury), Walter Sheridan of NBC (public bribery), and Richard Townley of WDSU-TV (intimidation of a witness); two involved former members of Garrison's own staff—Gordon Novel (bur-

---

help Garrison realize this plan, Harold Weisberg, whose series of books critical of the Warren Report includes the one entitled *Photographic Whitewash*, sent a letter on the District Attorney's office stationery to Fred Newcomb, a photographer in California, saying, "Enclosed are four sets of pictures of Kerry Thornley printed backwards but otherwise the resemblance to Oswald and his receding hairline, which when his hair is combed the opposite of his normal fashion, is quite emphatic. What I would like you to do with one of each pair is pretend you were a make-up man doing the minimum necessary to make Thornley look as much as possible like Oswald as for example by pruning off or brushing back the forelock, trimming the eyebrows, shadowing the chin, etc. I would like you to keep one pair for your use out there, send one pair to me and the other two to Jim Garrison. . . ."[26]

glary) and William Gurvich (petit larceny); and one involved a man who, at least according to Dean Andrews, doesn't even exist—Manuel Garcia Gonzales (narcotics). Add to this list the several other newsmen, FBI agents, two directors of the CIA (Allen Dulles and Richard Helms), two administrators of the National Archives in Washington, D.C., Cuban exile leaders, and various other persons subpoenaed to appear before the Orleans Parish Grand Jury, and it becomes clear that the District Attorney exercised his considerable powers not simply to harass unco-operative witnesses but to create as well the impression that certain important individuals were somehow involved in the conspiracy under investigation.

PART TWO

The Second Conspiracy

6

THE TANGLED WEB

The very repetition of a charge lends it a certain credibility, since people
have a tendency to believe that where there's smoke there's fire.
                                                    —Jim Garrison in *Playboy* (discussing
                                                              charges against him)

The principal consideration operating to restrain a duly elected
district attorney from making indiscriminate arrests and
charges—aside from normal ethical considerations—is fear of
exposure by the press if supporting proof should not be forthcoming. Yet, despite some cogent evidence of malfeasance on
Garrison's part reported by a number of journalists, public-
opinion polls indicated that there was actually a substantial increase in the number of people, not only in Louisiana but
throughout the country, who shared Garrison's belief in a conspiracy. If in fact his case was based on little more than wild
rumors and the unsubstantiated testimony of unstable witnesses, why was the press so ineffective in checking Garrison?
In his study of the late Senator Joseph R. McCarthy, Richard H.
Rovere demonstrates how a certain kind of demagogue, when

he is assailed by the press, can turn the hostile criticism to his own advantage. Such a demagogue builds his political base on the systematic exploitation of inchoate fears, and sets about organizing a popular flight from reality. To him, even the most vocal censure, however adverse its ostensible effect, represents useful publicity, for the more rigorously he is assaulted by the press, the more prominently he figures in the popular imagination. A false charge has to be repeated if it is to be refuted, and if the charge happens to be more appealing than the truth, it is entirely possible that it, rather than its refutation, will win general credence. This is especially likely to occur if the demagogue's charge offers a more or less plausible explanation of disturbing events, and if its refutation depends on the word of government officials, since the people most apt to accept conspiratorial interpretations of history are those who are most suspicious of both complexity and authority. As Rovere points out with regard to McCarthy, the demagogue soon learns that "the penalties for a really audacious mendacity are not as severe as the average politician fears them to be, that, in fact, there may be no penalties at all, but only profit."[1]

In a sense, the man who exploits popular fears builds his reputation on the prestige of his adversaries. The more impressive the list of detractors he can cite, the more important his charges appear to be. "Why are they trying to destroy me?" the demagogue asks. But the surest benefits he derives from being publicly criticized are the "right to reply"—a right that is greatly enhanced by the demands of day-to-day reporting, which cause the press to focus more directly on the individual under attack than on the general issue at stake—and the results of the ethic of "objective reporting"—which usually in practice means no more than that the individual criticized gets the last word in the news stories. If the demagogue is challenged on radio or television, he can demand equal time to respond. And, of course, his reply need not restrict itself to a defense of his original position. Indeed, to obfuscate the issue further and mitigate the attack on him, the demagogue may strike out in an altogether different direction. For he is, typically, concerned not with substantive issues but with ways of manipulating the emotions of the electorate.

One way Garrison responded to attacks made on his thesis

that there was a conspiracy to kill President Kennedy was by talking about a second conspiracy that grew out of the first one —a conspiracy of secrecy dedicated to concealing the truth about the assassination. As in a speech he gave in December 1967 in New Mexico, entitled "The Rise of the Fourth Reich, or How to Conceal the Truth about an Assassination without Really Trying," Garrison often seemed more deeply preoccupied with exposing an insidious misprison of felony on the part of federal authorities than with establishing the facts of the assassination itself.[2] To be sure, such an obsessional concern with governmental suppression is not a new phenomenon, nor is it limited to the assassination issue. The political-sociologist Edward Shils has pointed to a highly suggestive link between the generalized fear of secrecy and the Populist tradition in America. In his book *The Torment of Secrecy*, he argues that a repugnance toward secrecy is so deeply ingrained in American political life that even in matters involving national security, secrecy is tolerated only as a necessary evil.[3] To exploit this fear of secrecy, a truly Machiavellian politician could be expected to portray himself as engaged in a life-and-death struggle to wrest secrets from some powerful elite that controls the government and the news media, and to interpret all criticism leveled against him as part of a plot to conceal the dark truth from the populace.

Attack and Counterattack: The *Saturday Evening Post*

The first full-scale criticism of Garrison came in the last week of April 1967, in the *Saturday Evening Post*, when, in his article entitled "Rush to Judgment in New Orleans," James Phelan revealed that the crucial part of Perry Raymond Russo's testimony —the section incriminating Clay Shaw—was contradicted by a statement Russo had made earlier to Assistant District Attorney Sciambra.[4] The day Phelan's story appeared, a bold headline in the *New Orleans States-Item* announced, "MOUNTING EVIDENCE LINKS CIA TO 'PLOT' PROBE." The article under this head, which implied that the CIA was attempting to block Garrison's efforts, because former agents were involved in the conspiracy, had been prepared by several *States-Item* reporters, including Hoke

May and Ross Yockey, who reportedly had a close working relationship with the Garrison investigation.[5] Whether by design or by accident, the charges against the CIA effectively overshadowed the Phelan story, at least in New Orleans.

Newsweek and the CIA

Two weeks later, in an article written by Hugh Aynesworth, *Newsweek* reported that a friend of David Ferrie's had been offered a three-thousand-dollar bribe to implicate Clay Shaw in the conspiracy. The offer had been secretly tape-recorded by the witness's lawyer. Although the tape left it unclear whether the money was to be in payment for true information or false, it was damaging under any circumstances. (At one point, Garrison's representative said, "We can change the story around.")[6] When Garrison learned of the impending *Newsweek* disclosure, he prepared a memorandum on CIA participation in the assassination; this document promptly found its way into the hands of Yockey and May, who wrote it up in an exclusive story in the *States-Item*.[7] Upon being asked about the *Newsweek* charges, Garrison answered by confirming the *States-Item* report on the CIA. "The federal agents who concealed vital knowledge regarding President Kennedy's assassination, and their superiors who are now engaged in a dedicated effort to discredit and obstruct the gathering of evidence, are guilty of being accessories after the fact to one of the cruelest murders in our history," he declared, and he went on to warn that "the arrogant totalitarian efforts of these federal agencies to obstruct the discovery of truth is a matter which I intend to bring to light."[8] An article in the *New York Times* the following day attested to Garrison's success in blurring these charges with his own: although the *Times* article focused on the *Newsweek* report, the headline read, "GARRISON CHARGES CIA AND FBI CONCEAL EVIDENCE ON OSWALD."[9]

Garrison continued his offensive by issuing a subpoena for Richard Helms, the director of the Central Intelligence Agency, demanding that Helms produce a photograph showing Oswald in the company of a CIA agent in Mexico.[10] Subsequently, it was made plain that Garrison had no reason to believe that a photograph showing Oswald with a CIA agent had ever existed,[11] but

Garrison's subpoena drew national coverage and tended to dilute further the effect of the *Newsweek* story. It is worth noting that before Garrison subpoenaed the director of the CIA he had considered another move—arresting Regis Kennedy, an FBI agent in New Orleans who had taken part in the government's investigation of the assassination. Garrison explained to William Gurvich that although the agent would deny the charge, the denial would only add to the effect of criminally charging an FBI agent. But Garrison had second thoughts about attacking the FBI and, according to Gurvich, chose the CIA because, as Garrison himself put it, "they can't afford to answer."[12]

Later, in May, when his claim that the notation of a Dallas post-office box in Clay Shaw's address book was actually Ruby's encoded telephone number was debunked by Lee Odom, the owner of the box, Garrison, it will be recalled, countered by charging that Oswald's address book contained an encoded version of the local CIA telephone number in New Orleans (though he later had to admit that the code was "subjective"). Then, further obscuring questions arising from his dubious interpretation of the "telephone codes," Garrison stated that both Oswald and Ruby had been CIA agents, and asserted on a local television show a few days later that the CIA knew the identity of the other assassins but, he said, "we can't find out [their names] with the CIA keeping its vaults locked."[13]

NBC and "Thought Control"

On the evening of June 19, 1967, NBC devoted an hour to a critical examination of Garrison's investigation, entitled "The JFK Conspiracy: The Case of Jim Garrison." The first part of the program dealt with Russo's allegation that he had seen Oswald, Shaw, and Ferrie plotting the assassination at a party in Ferrie's apartment in September 1963. The NBC reporters demonstrated that at least one other person present at the party had not seen Shaw or Oswald there, and that Ferrie's bearded roommate, who Russo claimed was Oswald, had been identified by other people at the party as James Lewallen. The program then concentrated on Garrison's investigative methods, and a parade of witnesses was presented to allege that Garrison representatives had attempted to bribe or intimidate them. In addition, NBC revealed that both of Garrison's key witnesses, Russo and Vernon Bundy, had failed lie-detector tests before testifying at the preliminary hearing. Frank McGee, the NBC anchor man, concluded, "The case he has built against Clay Shaw is based on testimony that did not pass a lie-detector test Garrison ordered —and Garrison knew it."[14] The lie-detector evidence that NBC used to cap its case against Garrison was almost certainly the weakest part of that case. Yet the fact that NBC found it necessary to conclude its program with a concise statement of evidence established by the familiar and easily understood lie detector suggests a problem the mass media, and especially television, have in demonstrating a complex truth to their audience. Although the lie detector carries a certain authority in the popular imagination, and appears to give an unambiguous answer—the man is either lying or telling the truth—it is in fact merely a device for measuring the emotional stress that a witness is undergoing while he is being questioned. Such stress may indicate nervousness over deception, or it may indicate any of a number of other emotional responses. Since there is no objective way of differentiating among these responses, FBI director J. Edgar Hoover had advised the Warren Commission in a memorandum that lie-detector tests were unreliable and of dubious value.[15] NBC had assembled a good deal of cogent, if complex, evidence to show that Russo's allegation was untrue. But the effort to resolve, for its mass audience, the difficult issue it had so painstakingly presented by resorting to a simple and readily comprehensible indictment based on evidence drawn from a source as dubious as lie-detector tests left the program's conclusions open to serious criticism.*

Garrison, however, did not bother with serious criticism of the program's content; instead, he launched his counterattack by denouncing NBC as a party to an "Establishment" conspiracy to destroy him. "All of the screaming and hollering now being heard is evidence that we have caught a very large fish," he proclaimed the morning after the NBC show. "It is obvious

---

* NBC was not alone in employing lie detectors. *Newsweek,* the *Chicago Tribune,* and the Hearst Headline Service also used them to demonstrate that Garrison's case was based on untruths.

that there are elements in Washington, D.C., which are desperate because we are in the process of uncovering their hoax."[16] To account for NBC's interest in his investigation, he told an interviewer that the network "is owned by Radio Corporation of America, one of the top ten defense contractors in the country." (It is actually twenty-seventh, according to the Department of Defense.) Garrison added, "All of these ladies of the evening are very much alike—the preferred customer is the one with the big bankroll and any position he suggests is eagerly assumed." Moreover, Garrison implied that the program had been secretly financed by the CIA.[17]

Garrison wrote to the Federal Communications Commission to demand equal time, and NBC granted him a half hour of prime evening time on July 15, 1967, to reply to the charges. Once on the air, however, he said, "I am not even going to bother to dignify the foolishness which *Newsweek* and NBC and some of the other news agencies have tried to make you believe about my office," and went on to denounce the media for manipulating the news and practicing "thought control." After giving five specific examples of "suppressed news," he presented his familiar argument that the attacks on his case attested to its validity: ". . . if our investigation was as haywire as they would like to have you think, then you would not see such a coordinated barrage coming from the news centers in the East." And he concluded, ". . . as long as I am alive, no one is going to stop me from seeing that you obtain the full truth, and nothing less than the full truth, and no fairy tales."[18] Garrison had an audience of some twenty million, and for that, he said in his *Playboy* interview, he was "singularly grateful to Walter Sheridan," one of those who had prepared the NBC critique of his case.[19]

Garrison's gratitude was less than total. Not long after the NBC program, he issued warrants for the arrest of Sheridan and also Richard Townley, who had assisted in the preparation of the show, charging them with attempted bribery. Specifically, Garrison alleged that they had offered Perry Russo a free trip to California.[20]* But if this offer technically constituted an act of

---

* Both Sheridan and Townley unequivocally denied the charges. Sheridan told me that it was Russo himself who suggested that NBC pay his expenses to California.

bribery, Garrison himself had taken considerable pains to bait the trap. He told me himself that he had directed Russo to speak to the reporters over a monitored phone and inquire what protection they could offer him if he were to change his testimony. The purpose was, as he put it, "to give NBC enough rope to hang itself." In his public statement on the matter, Garrison charged that the NBC program "will probably stand for many years to come as a symbol of the length to which some powerful outside interests are willing to go in order to interfere with state government." The cases are still pending.[21]

CBS and the "Establishment"

Shortly after Garrison's skirmish with NBC, William Gurvich resigned as one of his chief investigators, after telling the late Senator Robert F. Kennedy that there was no basis in fact and no material evidence in Garrison's case.[22] Gurvich then appeared on the CBS-TV "News Inquiry" into the assassination and said he had resigned because "I saw no reason for the investigation. . . . The truth, as I see it, is that Mr. Shaw should never have been arrested."[23] Gurvich's private-detective agency had conducted most of the lie-detector tests that Garrison had ordered, and at the time of his resignation Gurvich had in his possession a master file of the principal evidence in the case. This defection not only made for embarrassing headlines but opened up the possibility that Garrison's fund of confidential information—or his lack of such a fund—would be made public. In a statement to the press, Garrison described Gurvich's resignation as "the latest move from the Eastern headquarters of the Establishment to attempt to discredit our investigation." It was all part of a co-ordinated plot against him.[24] In another press release, he said, "All they are doing is proving two things: first, that we were correct when we uncovered the involvement of the Central Intelligence Agency in the assassination; second, that there is something very wrong today with our government in Washington, D.C., inasmuch as it is willing to use massive economic power to conceal the truth from the people."[25] Later, in his *Playboy* interview, Garrison implied that Gurvich had been a CIA infiltrator from the start.[26] He also charged Gurvich with petty larceny, claiming the file that he had was worth nineteen dollars. And, for good measure, he charged on the ABC "Page One" television show that Senator Robert Kennedy whom Gurvich had earlier been in touch with, was "without any question of a doubt . . . interfering with the investigation of the murder of his brother" and was making "a real effort to stop it."[27]

Pseudo-Attacks: Earl Warren and Lyndon B. Johnson

After it had become quite clear that criticism of Garrison's case could be used to generate a specter of conspiracy, Garrison took the logical next step and started creating pseudo-attacks on himself. When reporters in Tokyo asked Chief Justice Earl Warren his opinion of the Garrison investigation, he replied, "I want to skirt this very carefully, because the case could someday come before the Supreme Court." Pressed as to whether Garrison possessed any evidence that might contradict the findings of the Commission he had headed, the Chief Justice answered, "I've heard that he claims to have such information, but I haven't seen any."[28] Garrison immediately characterized this "new counterattack" as "heavy artillery whistling in from Tokyo," and said in a press release, "It is a little disconcerting to find the Chief Justice of the United States on his hands and knees trying to tie some sticks of dynamite to the case. However, the Chief Justice is a practical man and I expect he knows what he is doing. . . . The last time he was called into action to perform a service was when the President of the United States was assassinated by men who had been connected with the Central Intelligence Agency."[29] Garrison predicted a new broadside from the federal authorities: "Judging from the careful co-ordination which the Establishment showed in its last offensive against the case, it is safe to expect that other elements of the federal government and national press will now follow up with a new effort to discredit the case and the prosecution."[30]

Another example of Garrison's technique involved Gordon Novel, the electronics expert, who had told him about Ferrie's participation in a "pickup" of munitions from the Schlumberger Well Surveying company, in Houma, Louisiana. Novel rapidly advanced from advising Garrison on anti-eavesdropping techniques, the business that had first brought him to Garrison's attention, to become a witness against Ferrie and, at least in Garrison's mind, an "investigator." Then, according to one account, Garrison was told that his investigator had been furnishing information to NBC reporters, and Novel was subpoenaed to appear before a grand jury.[31] Instead of appearing, Novel left the state and went to Ohio. Garrison filed burglary charges against Novel, alleging that he had participated in the conspiracy to steal arms from the Schlumberger company, and he was arrested in Ohio.[32] After some initial reluctance, Ohio Governor James Rhodes finally agreed to extradite Novel to Louisiana if Garrison would complete the papers within sixty days.[33] Garrison, however, did not take the necessary steps. As the deadline approached, Assistant District Attorney Alcock asked if he should return the papers to Ohio, and Garrison told him not to bother.[34] After Garrison failed to reply to phone calls and telegrams from Ohio authorities inquiring about his intentions in the Novel case, and after the sixty-day period had elapsed, Judge William T. Gillie dismissed the extradition case against Novel.[35] And yet in the *Playboy* interview, Garrison insisted, "The reason we were unable to obtain Novel's extradition from Ohio . . . is that there are powerful forces in Washington who find it imperative to conceal from the American public the truth about the assassination."[36] He went on to indicate that Novel was now a material witness in his case and, according to attorneys for Novel, implied that his former "investigator" was somehow connected with the conspiracy. (Novel filed suit against Garrison and *Playboy* for ten million dollars in punitive and compensatory damages.) And in a speech to the Radio and Television News Association of Southern California, in Los Angeles, Garrison cited his failure to obtain Novel's extradition as evidence that President Johnson was putting pressure on local officials to secrete witnesses from him. He went on to accuse President Johnson of preventing "the people in this country from seeing the evidence," and asserted, with the logic of *cui bono*, ". . . the fact that he has profited from the assassination most, more than any other man, makes it imperative that he see that the evidence is released, so that we can know that he is not involved. . . ."[37]

The New Yorker

When part of this book was first published in *The New Yorker* in July 1968, Garrison responded in his customary style. Calling a press conference, the District Attorney announced that an "intelligence agency of a foreign country . . . successfully penetrated the assassination operation," and that the "detailed information" he had received from this unnamed intelligence agency had "corroborated" statements he had previously made that President Kennedy was assassinated "by elements of the Central Intelligence Agency."[38] He frankly admitted, according to *Time*, that the timing of the disclosure of the foreign assassination study was "designed to rebut" the charges in the *New Yorker* article[39] (which he said was part of a "CIA-inspired campaign" to discredit his investigation).[40] The "intelligence study" that Garrison referred to turned out to be nothing more than a pseudonymous manuscript entitled "The Plot" that had been sent to him three months earlier, after the *New York Review of Books* had rejected it. According to Bethell, Garrison deduced that the manuscript "must have been written by a foreign intelligence agency, and probably the KGB" (the Russian counterpart of the CIA) because it contained "inside information" about the assassination. Actually, a good deal of the "inside information" that Garrison referred to had been, I found, previously published in William Manchester's *Death of a President* and in Garrison's own *Playboy* interview. Garrison referred the manuscript to *Ramparts*, whose editor also decided not to publish it, after it was learned that the author was merely a dissident European writer and not a "foreign intelligence agency." Yet Garrison's deployment of this manuscript was at least tactically effective: the headlines of the *New Orleans Times-Picayune* on July 12, the day *The New Yorker* appeared in New Orleans, read: "FOREIGN GROUP HAS FACTS—D.A., CIA ROLE IN JFK DEATH CONFIRMED, HE SAYS."[41]

7

THE CIA

If the director of the CIA and the top officials of the CIA were in the juris-diction of Louisiana, I would charge them without hesitation.
— Jim Garrison, May 21, WWL-TV,
New Orleans

Garrison's technique in expounding the so-called second con-spiracy is typical of what Richard Hofstadter has classified as "the paranoid style in American politics," to which "the feeling of persecution is central," and which is "systematized in grandi-ose theories of conspiracy."[1] Still, the fact that Garrison ex-pressed his ideas in a paranoid style does not of itself rule out the possibility that there is substance to his claims. Is the CIA, for example, really concealing some involvement of its agents in the assassination, as Garrison has claimed? In May 1967, Garri-son declared on the ABC "Issues and Answers" television pro-gram, "Of course the Central Intelligence Agency had no role in the planning or intending the assassination of President Ken-nedy. I think that would be a ridiculous position for anyone to take."[2] He has, however, taken precisely that position on several occasions. His allegations regarding the culpability of the CIA have varied widely. On May 9, 1967, the CIA was accused of merely concealing evidence,[3] by May 18, Oswald and Ruby were themselves identified by Garrison as CIA employees;[4] on May 21, the District Attorney stated that the CIA knew "the name of every man involved and the name of the individuals who pulled the triggers";[5] on May 24, he added that the CIA was presently hiding the killers' whereabouts;[6] on November 14, he decided that "employees—a limited number—of the Central Intelligence Agency of the U.S. government are involved in the assassination";[7] on January 31, 1968, he said on the Johnny Carson show that "the Central Intelligence Agency was deeply involved in the assassination";[8] and in February he said in an interview filmed for Dutch television that "President Kennedy was killed by elements of the Central Intelligence Agency of the United States government," going on to explain, "The Central Intelligence Agency . . . had worked for a long time creating the tableau—the cover scene—beforehand. This is standard for a Central Intelligence Agency assassination. As a matter of fact, the CIA, when it conducts an assassination, describes it as an executive action. This takes the sin out of it. As a matter of fact, to the CIA employees, the sin then becomes failing to do your job properly, in the executive action. Of course, even as I describe it, I'm conscious of the parallels with regard to Germany under Hitler. What I'm talking about is nothing less than Fascism, which has arrived in America. . . ."[9]

Just how solid the basis for these charges is can be deduced from Garrison's twenty-six-page interview in *Playboy*, which is doubtless the fullest and most coherent single presentation of his case to date. When he was pressed by *Playboy's* interviewer, Eric Norden, for the evidence on which his charges of CIA complicity were based, Garrison mentioned eight specific items: (1) a missing CIA photograph that shows Oswald in the company of a CIA agent in Mexico before the assassination, (2) classified files on David Ferrie, which "would indicate the existence of a conspiracy involving former employees of the CIA to kill the President," (3) suppressed autopsy X rays and photographs of President Kennedy's body and "other vital evidence," which also reveal that former CIA agents took part in the murder, (4) CIA files that reveal, it is implied, that Oswald was involved in the CIA's U-2 project, (5) the fact that the CIA destroyed a document that the Warren Commission had requested, (6) the identification of Oswald's CIA "babysitter," (7) the identification of a CIA "courier," and (8) "the consistent refusal of the federal government" to provide Garrison with "any information" about the role of the CIA in the assassination. This last piece of "evidence" Garrison calls "the clincher."[10]

At least half of the "evidence" on which Garrison's repertory of charges against the CIA was based is itself deduced from evidence that Garrison had never seen. He accomplished this trick by simply sketching in on the *tabula rasa* of missing (or nonexistent) evidence facts that appear to incriminate the CIA. If the evidence is missing, a revelation of its contents is not, of course, easily refuted. And the old suspicion of secrecy qua secrecy also plays a part. "If there's nothing to hide," people wonder, "why is the thing missing in the first place?" Consider Item 1, the missing CIA photographs, on which Garrison based his original charge that the CIA was concealing vital evidence.

1. The Missing Photograph

When Garrison subpoenaed Richard Helms, the director of the CIA, he instructed him to produce a photograph that CIA agents had taken in Mexico City about seven weeks before the assassination and that, Garrison claimed, showed Oswald in front of the Cuban Embassy in the company of a CIA agent.[11] The supposed facts conveyed by this missing snapshot were what led Garrison to assert that the CIA knew the identity of Kennedy's assassins and was concealing the truth. But how had this information been deduced from a missing photograph, which Garrison admitted that he had never seen?

Actually, the story of the CIA photograph had its origin in an incident I myself first reported, in my book *Inquest*, as a means of illustrating the problems that the Warren Commission lawyers faced in communicating with the CIA. According to my account, a man in front of the Cuban Embassy in Mexico City had been routinely photographed before the assassination by a hidden CIA camera and identified as Lee Harvey Oswald; the information had subsequently been forwarded to the FBI. However, as it turned out, I continued, the man in the photograph (which was published in Volume XX of the Warren Commission's testimony and evidence) was obviously not Oswald but a heavy-set individual who could not be identified. The staff lawyer Wesley J. Liebeler, who was trying to clarify the incident for the Warren Commission, inquired of the CIA whether a photograph showing Oswald in Mexico City did in fact exist. He never received an answer.[12] Garrison postulated that the CIA had forwarded the picture of a man who was not Oswald and had withheld a photograph that *did* show Oswald leaving the Cuban Embassy. Furthermore, he conjectured that the most likely reason for suppressing such a photograph was that it revealed Oswald to be in the company of another man—and since the identity of this man was being concealed, he must have been working for the CIA.[13] It seems unlikely that Garrison had any knowledge of this photograph other than what he gathered from the account of it in my book, because he repeats the details of that account, including a certain erroneous detail. Liebeler, who originally told me the story, pointed out a few weeks after *Inquest* was published that the picture in question had been taken of a man in front of the Soviet Embassy in Mexico City, not the Cuban Embassy. Yet Garrison repeated the erroneous information (my own) to contrive an ominous piece of "evidence" that was not simply "missing" but nonexistent.

2. The Missing Ferrie Files

Garrison relied on a similar device in his second item of "evidence," asserting that files on Ferrie were classified because they "would indicate the existence of a conspiracy involving former employees of the CIA."[14] The files Garrison referred to consist of FBI reports on the activities and private life of David Ferrie. After the assassination, FBI agents interviewed a number of Ferrie's associates and turned these reports over to the Warren Commission, which then consigned them to the National Archives. A good portion of these was made public, while the remainder, about thirty-six pages, was kept classified on the grounds that it contained information that might be damaging to innocent parties.[15] (Wesley Liebeler, who also conducted this part of the investigation, told me that these files mainly concerned Ferrie's circle of homosexual acquaintances.)[16] Exactly how Garrison could specify what would be indicated by FBI reports he had never seen is problematical, but again the *tabula rasa* of missing evidence gives him an opportunity to sketch in unverifiable details of a CIA conspiracy.

3. The Missing X rays, Photos, Film Frames

In his third "proof" of CIA complicity, Garrison states that "the President's autopsy X rays and photos and other vital evidence in this case are classified because they would indicate the existence of a conspiracy, involving former employees of the CIA, to kill the President."[17] And in a subsequent statement, he charged more specifically that "Lyndon Johnson's administration is still keeping it [the autopsy material] secret."[18] While it is true that the X-ray and autopsy photographs were never examined by the Warren Commission—and it is certainly possible, as I pointed out in *Inquest*, that a proper examination of this basic evidence could undermine (or, on the other hand, confirm) the Commission's conclusions about the autopsy—it does not necessarily follow that this material has been classified by the Johnson administration, as Garrison suggests, to protect the CIA. In fact, the material was "classified" not by the government but by the Kennedy family, which came in possession of it after the autopsy examination, and subsequently, in 1966, deposited it in the National Archives on the condition that it not be opened to examination to private citizens for a period of five years and thereafter only to persons professionally qualified to evaluate medical evidence. To be sure, the very fact that it was unavailable provided Garrison with "secret evidence": he could claim in his public statements—without fear of immediate refutation—that the CIA was implicated in the conspiracy.

Every once in a while, the evidence proved to exist, and Garrison was caught in the act. For example, he stated in his *Playboy* interview that four frames of the famous Abraham Zapruder film of the assassination—numbers 208–211—were missing from the frame-by-frame reproduction of the film in the testimony and evidence published by the Warren Commission, and he went on to claim that these frames "reveal signs of stress appearing suddenly on the back of a street sign" and to suggest that "these signs of stress may very well have been caused by the impact of a stray bullet on the sign."[19] But frames 208–211, while missing from the Warren volumes, are not missing from a copy of the film that *Life* holds; and after Garrison's charges in *Playboy* were published, George P. Hunt, the managing editor of *Life*, announced that the magazine was releasing for publication frames 207–212 of the Zapruder film—which included the ones Garrison had alleged were missing—for the purpose of ending "what has become an irrelevant discussion." What Garrison termed "the missing frames" have in fact been published in Josiah Thompson's book *Six Seconds in Dallas*, and they reveal no "signs of stress."[20]

4. The National Archives

In his fourth item, Garrison supposedly reveals the contents of classified CIA documents in the National Archives. These documents were prepared for the Warren Commission by the CIA. And although the title of each of these reports—usually referring to the general topic on which Commission lawyers requested that the CIA provide information or answer queries—is listed in the index of Commission documents, the reports themselves are classified, as are all CIA reports containing the names of operatives, informers, and foreign sources. Garrison customarily rattles off the titles of the "suppressed CIA files," as he calls them, and then sets forth their "contents" in his own terms. For example, in *Playboy* he cited Commission Document No. 931, entitled "Oswald's Access to Information About the U-2," and then ominously suggested that Oswald was involved in the U-2 program.[21] He amplified on this "evidence" in a speech he made after the *Playboy* interview appeared, stating, "The reason you can't see that [Commission Document No. 931] for many years is because you will then realize that Lee Oswald was then working for the United States government, as a CIA employee, and they don't want you to know that."[22] Garrison "used" this classified document, which, of course, he had not seen, to substantiate the charge that Oswald acted as a CIA agent. Yet testimony in the Warren Report indicates that it may well contain information on what Oswald heard when, during his stay in the Soviet Union, he dropped in on the trial of the U-2 pilot Francis Gary Powers. In any event, it seems highly unlikely that if the CIA were indeed as sinister as Garrison alleges, it would *admit* in a report to the Commission that Oswald was a CIA agent, especially since its reports were to be read by lawyers working for the Commission who were not (as my own interviews with them demonstrate) particularly inclined to be secretive.

5. The Secret CIA Memo

Garrison asserted that the Warren Commission was never able to obtain "a secret CIA memo on Oswald's activities in Russia"—a memo attached to a State Department document—because the memorandum had been "destroyed" the day after the assassination. This statement is simply untrue. While it is true that one copy of this memorandum was destroyed while being photocopied, another copy was duly forwarded to the Commission on May 8, 1964, as is evident from Volume XVIII of the Commission's testimony and evidence.[23] When Sylvia Meagher, who has indexed the twenty-six volumes of the Warren Commission testimony and evidence—and has tried earnestly to correct the mistakes of the critics as well as those of the Commission—pointed out to Garrison that his charge was based on a fallacy, he acknowledged the error; even so, he went on using the non-fact to support his charge that the CIA was "incinerating" evidence.[24]

6. The CIA "Babysitter"

The sixth item of evidence, the identity of Oswald's CIA "babysitter," was extrapolated from a purchase order for ten Ford trucks.[25] Oscar Deslatte, the assistant manager of a New Orleans Ford agency, who wrote up the order on January 20, 1961, subsequently reported to the FBI that his customers told him the trucks were to be used by an organization known as

"Friends of Democratic Cuba" and requested a discount. Deslatte listed the purchaser of the trucks as "Oswald" (no first name given) and said that the individual with "Oswald" called himself Joseph Moore. When FBI agents asked Deslatte about the incident, he said that he could "neither describe nor identify either of the men."[26] Garrison believes, however, that the purchase was made for the CIA and that Moore, who has never been located, was in fact Oswald's CIA chaperon.[27] It is possible, of course, that Moore was the CIA "babysitter" of some Oswald, but in 1961, at the time the purchase order was filled out, Lee Harvey Oswald was working at the Byelorussian Radio and Television Factory in Minsk.[28]

7. The CIA "Courier"

The seventh item of evidence, concerning a CIA "courier," refers to Donald Philetus Norton, the convicted bank embezzler and night-club entertainer who, as mentioned earlier, had been thoroughly discredited as a witness and was jettisoned by Garrison himself even before he gave the *Playboy* interview.[29]

8. The "Clincher"

Garrison's "clincher," the assertion that the government had not revealed to him any information of the CIA's complicity in the assassination,[30] is a perfect example of Garrison's own brand of logic, in which the fact that he had not found or been given any evidence of CIA complicity was itself proof that the CIA was withholding evidence of its guilt.

Garrison also charged that the CIA was interfering with his investigation, citing as evidence the monitoring of his telephones and asserting that the CIA had paid for a Washington, D.C., trip for Ferrie's heir, Alvin Beauboeuf, and his lawyer and that "most of the attorneys for the hostile witnesses and defendants were hired by the CIA."[31] This is hardly more substantial than the evidence he used to support his charge of CIA complicity in the assassination. Garrison himself had earlier identified the FBI as the party monitoring his telephones, and was so certain of this that he had planned the midnight raid on the FBI's New Orleans office in order to obtain the tapes of monitored conversations. It was NBC, not the CIA, which paid Beauboeuf's expenses to Washington in conjunction with the program it was preparing on the Garrison investigation.[32] Finally, the statement that defendants' attorneys "were hired by the CIA"—a charge the lawyers heatedly deny—reveals a curious impatience with due process. Implicit in the District Attorney's charge is the notion that the defendant's right to counsel (no matter who pays for it) can be construed as interference.

8

THE MEDIA

The press has now reached the point of subsequent control by the Central Intelligence Agency that we literally can't get the truth out.
—Jim Garrison, February 1968,
on Dutch television

Although Garrison was given the opportunity to present his case on all three national television networks, and appeared on more television and radio programs than perhaps any other practicing district attorney in history, one of his major themes was that the press furtively controlled the news as a means of suppressing known facts about the John Kennedy assassination. "Behind the façade of earnest inquiry into the assassination is a thought-control project in the best tradition of *1984*," he has written. "Because of their role in the Establishment and their failure to conduct an effective inquiry, major news agencies have a vested interest in maintaining public ignorance."[1] Most of what Garrison has had to say on this subject has been vague philippies, but in his half-hour NBC rebuttal he did give five specific examples of news suppression, and they are worth examining in detail. Of "powerful news agencies," Garrison alleged:

[1] They do not tell you that Lee Harvey Oswald's fingerprints were not found on the gun which was supposed to have killed the President.

[2] And they do not tell you that nitrate tests exonerated Lee Oswald from the actual shooting by showing that he had not fired a rifle that day.

[3] And they do not tell you that it was virtually impossible for Oswald to have taken his fingerprints off the gun, hidden the gun and gone down four flights of stairs by the time he was seen on the second floor.

[4] Above all they do not tell you of the overwhelming eyewitness testimony that shots were coming from behind the stone wall on the grassy knoll. . . .

[5] You have not been told that Lee Oswald was in the employ of U.S. intelligence agencies, but this was the case.[2]

It is true that the public had not been told any of these things, except by Garrison, but there is a good reason for that. All five of the charges are either false or captious.

1. Fingerprints

Fingerprints were indeed found on the rifle "which was supposed to have killed the President," but the prints could not be positively identified. This was not particularly surprising. Sebastian F. Latona, a nationally recognized fingerprint expert, testified before the Warren Commission that because of the unpolished finish of the rifle, which allowed it to absorb moisture, it was highly unlikely that an identifiable fingerprint would have been left on the weapon. Contrary to the popular impression regarding fingerprints, Latona noted, they are usually discernible only on highly polished surfaces.[3] What Garrison does not say is that a palmprint was discovered on the underside of the barrel of the rifle in question and that three different experts positively identified it as Oswald's.*

2. The Nitrate Tests

Garrison's assertion that the nitrate tests "exonerated" Oswald is equally questionable. In the tests to which Garrison referred, the Dallas police made paraffin casts of Oswald's hands and right cheek, and these casts were then checked for traces of nitrates. Nitrates were found on the casts of both hands but not on the cast of his cheek. The test, however, in no way proves that Oswald did or did not fire a rifle. The nitrates found need not have come from gunpowder; many other substances—tobacco, matches, urine—will leave such residues. Conversely, the absence of nitrates indicates little, because a rifle (which, unlike a revolver, has no gap between the chamber and the barrel) is not as likely to leave nitrate traces on the cheek. In fact, the rifle in question was experimentally fired three times by an FBI agent, and no traces of nitrates were detected on his hands or cheek.[5] According to one FBI expert, Cortlandt Cunningham, the so-called paraffin test is completely unreliable, and its principal use in police work is simply to intimidate suspects; it produces more apprehension than valid evidence.[6] Garrison's suggestion that such tests could have proved that Oswald "had not fired a rifle that day" plays on the gullibility of the general public regarding the reliability of scientific-sounding data.

3. The Time Factor

As for Garrison's statement that it was "virtually impossible" for Oswald to have been on the second floor of the Book Depository building a few minutes after the assassination, it, too, is specious. A Secret Service agent, simulating Oswald's move-

* Although questions have been raised by critics about the circumstances under which this palmprint was found and removed on tape by Dallas police, laboratory tests conducted by the FBI indicate that the palmprint did indeed come from the rifle—since it bore impressions of the same irregularities that appeared on the barrel of the rifle.[4]

ments, reached the second floor from the sixth in one minute and eighteen seconds.[7] In any case, it is impossible to ascertain exactly what time Oswald was seen on the second floor; it could have been as long as five minutes after the assassination.

4. The Eyewitnesses

Garrison's next assertion—that the press failed to report that there was "overwhelming eyewitness testimony" that the shots came from behind a stone wall—is also sophistical. None of the hundred or so Warren Commission witnesses who testified on the matter or were questioned by the FBI said that they saw a rifle being fired from behind the stone wall. The *ear*witness testimony, which is undependable in determining the source of any shots where there is a possibility of echoes, was divided. More than half the witnesses thought the shots originated in some spot other than the Depository building, but only a few of the earwitnesses thought the shots came from the direction of the stone wall.[8] Moreover, the press *did* report that the majority of the earwitnesses thought the shots came from some place other than the Book Depository. In fact, this was reported by Walter Cronkite on the same CBS "News Inquiry" on which Garrison had himself appeared less than three weeks before he made these blanket charges of "news suppression" on NBC.[9]

5. The CIA Agent

Finally, the assertion that Oswald was a CIA agent, as has already been shown, was based on Garrison's own private interpretation of "missing" or classified documents that he had never seen. Of the five examples of "news suppression" that Garrison cited, then, not one was based on accurate information.

As a practicing district attorney, Garrison surely understood both the limits of so-called scientific evidence and its usefulness in impressing the general public. Nonetheless, he told a national television audience that the complex questions surrounding the assassination had long since been resolved by "scientific evidence" that proved Oswald innocent, but that the nation's press had not reported the existence of this evidence. Yet when it is examined, the "scientific evidence" he cites turns out to be either specious or misinterpreted, and the "news" that he claimed was "suppressed" is no more than a series of untruths.

9

THE FEDERAL ESTABLISHMENT

The federal government is a party with a special interest in this case. Our investigation has shown that the federal investigation was faked and the Warren Commission inquiry was faked to conceal the fact that President Kennedy was killed in a professionally executed ambush.
— Jim Garrison, May 29, 1968, press release

Another of Garrison's sweeping charges about a "second conspiracy" was that the federal government—through its agents Lyndon Johnson, Robert Kennedy, J. Edgar Hoover, Earl Warren, and Attorney General Ramsey Clark—was involved in a sinister plot to quash his investigation.[1] It would have been difficult to gainsay Garrison's imputation of federal obstruction if he had charged merely that the government was hindering his case. Certainly federal agencies were less than co-operative, and important federal officials, including Attorney General Clark, openly (and often harshly) criticized the New Orleans investigation. But Garrison's allegations went far beyond the charge of interference in this sense. He accused the federal government of conspiring to wreck his investigation specifically because it harbored a motive of its own in concealing the truth about the assassination, and he leveled his accusation in no uncertain terms: ". . . the United States government—meaning the present administration, Lyndon Johnson's administration—is obstructing the investigation—any investigation. It has concealed the true facts—to be blunt about it—to protect the individuals involved in the assassination of John Kennedy."[2] In other words, he charged that the government knows the truth and, in concealing it, is itself conspiring to protect the conspirators.

So far, Garrison has offered only two specific items of "evidence" to support this charge. The first item is the previously discussed photograph of the assassination site showing a man with a closed fist—which by Garrison's surmise conceals the bullet that killed the President. From this conjecture he went on to postulate that the man in the photograph is a federal agent, that the bullet has been turned over to the federal government, and that the government consequently knows the assassin's identity.[3] The second item of evidence he mentions is a telegram that was supposedly sent to J. Edgar Hoover before the assassination. Garrison charged at a New Orleans news conference in December 1967 that this telegram, which he has been unable to obtain, proves that Oswald telephoned the Dallas field office of the FBI five days before the assassination and gave details of the plot, which were then forwarded by interbureau telegram to Hoover in Washington. This, Garrison claimed, was proof that President Johnson had "actively concealed evidence about the murder of his predecessor."[4] When a reporter asked him what evidence he had that such a telegram ever existed, he answered, "If you and I were in a closed room, I could prove it. But I'm not going to allow any evidence to get out now."[5] His evidence, he later revealed on the Johnny Carson show, was simply a story that Mark Lane had told him.[6]

Apart from such stories by Garrison and Lane, the charge of federal complicity is based almost solely on the fact that there *is* government secrecy. According to Garrison's logic, the government would not classify information pertinent to the assassination unless it had something to hide. Garrison has persistently exploited popular suspicions about secrecy, accusing those who would, in his estimation, benefit most from the maintenance of such secrecy. For example, after noting that part of the Warren Commission's documents are classified in the National Archives, Garrison claimed on a Texas television show in December 1967, "They destroyed evidence in every possible way. The President of the United States, the man who has the most to gain, the man who gained more than any other human from the assassination, is the man who issued the executive order concealing vital evidence for seventy-five years so that we can't look at it, so that you can't look at it, so that no American can see it for seventy-five years. Now, this was an executive order by Lyndon Johnson, the man who gained the most from the assassination."[7]

No such executive order has ever been issued. Many investigative files are withheld from use by law for seventy-five years— a number arbitrarily selected to exceed the life span of persons likely to be mentioned in the reports—in order to safeguard confidential information (such as tax returns), to protect confidential informers, and to avoid embarrassing innocent persons mentioned incidentally.[8] But in the case of the Warren Commission's documents, McGeorge Bundy, acting on behalf of President Johnson, sent a special request to the Archivist of the United States that the seventy-five year ban be waived wherever possible and that much of the material be opened to the public. Following guidelines approved by Bundy, all the agencies involved in the investigation were to review their files and declassify everything except pages containing the names of confidential informers, information damaging to innocent parties, and information about the agencies' operating procedures. There was to be a periodic review by all the agencies concerned.[9] By the time Garrison had begun his own investigation, virtually all the documents that could be declassified according to these guidelines had been opened to public scrutiny.[10] Garrison's claim in *Playboy* that "any document the CIA wanted classified was shunted into the Archives without examination by the sleeping beauties on the Commission" is simply untrue.[11] *All* the relevant documents relating to the inquiry which are now in the Archives were sent there by the Warren Commission after the Warren Report was published. Most of the CIA reports were prepared to answer specific questions put to the Agency by

Commission lawyers, and there is no reason to assume that they went unread.

Garrison's tactic of claiming that the proof which supports his charges has been ensconced in classified documents is hardly an original one. For example, in 1950, Senator Joseph McCarthy asserted before the Tydings Senate Sub-Committee that his celebrated charge of eighty-one card-carrying Communists working in the State Department was supported by classified evidence in FBI files, and he vehemently demanded to know why the Truman administration was keeping secret vital evidence that would show the extent of the Communist conspiracy in the State Department. Taking unprecedented action, President Truman waived executive privilege and ordered the files made available to the Tydings Committee. When it became abundantly clear that these files were concealing no evidence to support McCarthy's charges, the Senator simply declared that the files had been "raped and rifled" before they were shown to the Committee and continued to demand that the "real files" be released.[12] The government, McCarthy charged, was using its powers of secrecy to conceal a gigantic conspiracy involving Communists and fellow travelers. In his campaign against the forces of secrecy, McCarthy also attacked the CIA as "the worst situation of all," and consistently denounced the news media for abetting the conspiracy by suppressing the "truth" and attacking him.[13]

The distinguishing mark of the paranoid style, Richard Hofstadter writes, is "the curious leap in imagination" between fact and fantasy which is made at some critical point in an argument to cover a gap in reasoning.[14] Consider in this light the following remarks by Garrison, taken from one of the many speeches he delivered during the fall of 1967.

> Is this a Great Society which allows innocence to be butchered as Oswald was, with no concern, no interest? Which allows the guilty, the murderers to walk the streets, knowing without any question who they are, knowing what happened, is this a Great Society? Is it a Great Society which causes blackouts in news centers like New York when there's a development in the case? . . . Is this a Great Society which monitors your phone if it has the slightest bit of

curiosity about you? This is not a Great Society—this is a Dangerous Society, a society which despite the lip service to Populism . . . is so morally threadbare that the futures of your children are in danger.[15]

Here "the curious leap in imagination" is made between the fact that some investigative files are still classified and the fantasy that the government is protecting the assassins by censoring the news, monitoring telephone calls, and threatening the futures of children. (It is worth noting, incidentally, that the image of "innocence . . . butchered as Oswald was" creates complications in the case of Clay Shaw, who was, after all, indicted for a conspiracy that involved Lee Harvey Oswald.)[16] In Garrison's case against the news media, a leap is made between the fact that the media failed to broadcast some *un*truths about the assassination and the fantasy of a conspiracy to suppress the news. In his charges against the CIA, a saltatory advance is made from missing or nonexistent evidence to the fantasy of CIA complicity in the assassination. Central to this tripartite conspiracy is the obsessive fascination with secrecy. For Garrison, the CIA epitomizes all that is feared in governmental secrecy: an invisible government, answerable to no one, with unlimited resources and unlimited power. Since all its acts are veiled in secrecy, it may be postulated to be the "secret force" behind any event. The suppression of news is for Garrison the means by which dark secrets are kept from the public, and the conspiracy maintained. The "clever manipulation of the mass media is," in Garrison's words, thus "creating a concentration camp of the mind."[17] The government, Garrison claims, "*is* the CIA and the Pentagon"—an elite that perpetuates its power by concealing the truth about the assassination.[18]

PART THREE

Public Opinion

10

THE TORMENT OF SECRECY

The people of this country do not have to be protected from the truth. This country was not built on the idea that a handful of nobles, whether located in our federal agencies in Washington, D.C., or in news agencies in New York, should decide what was good for the people to know and what they should not know. This is a totalitarian concept which presumes that the leaders of our federal government and the men in control of the powerful press media constitute a special elite which by virtue of their nobility and their brilliance empower them to think for the people.
—Jim Garrison, July 15, 1967, NBC-TV

As his investigation continued, Garrison appeared to become increasingly obsessed with governmental secrecy, and less directly concerned with the issues of his court case. His concern with secrecy became especially pronounced in his television appearances: he stated on New Orleans television, "The CIA has infinitely more power than the Gestapo and NKVD of Russia combined . . . we are blocked by this glass wall of this totalitarian, powerful agency which is worried about its power."[1] On Dallas television he said, "It did not occur to me that the President would have federal agencies conceal the truth from the people, it didn't occur to me that all these honorable men would conceal the truth from the people, that they would frame a man, Oswald, who had never fired a shot, and that they would knowingly protect the assassins."[2] On European television he asserted, "The President of the United States by executive order has taken all this critical evidence and has ordered that it be kept secret for seventy-five years, which means the lifetime of all living Americans. This has got to be the first time in history that the man who profited most from the murder has announced that evidence is going to be kept secret for seventy-five years. . . . I think that he can't be allowed to make the decision that the American people can't see this evidence, it is just an unbelievable situation and he should not be allowed to get away with it."[3] And on the Johnny Carson show, he said, "An element of the Central Intelligence Agency of our country killed John Kennedy and the present administration is concealing the facts . . ." and then went on to say, "The honor of this country is at stake, and if we don't do something about this fraud, we will not survive, and there is no way to survive if we don't bring out the truth about how our President was killed four years ago."[4] On another television program, Garrison explained that he was "trying to get the word out that something is wrong, that they killed John Kennedy and that the next President of the United States that tries to slow down the warfare machine and tries to bring this country to the brink of peace, will be assassinated too. There is no question about it. They will just do it in a different way, a different town, perhaps it will be an accident the next time or another Communist, but he will be assassinated because this juggernaut is self-sustaining, dedicated to a perpetual cold war and it will not tolerate anybody trying to stop it."[5]

In *The Torment of Secrecy*, a trenchant analysis of the sociological background of the excesses which accompanied the investigations of Senator McCarthy and others in the nineteen-fifties, Edward Shils traces the public's fascination with conspiracy and subversion—which helped sustain the inquisitions for the better part of a decade—to a deeper fear of secrecy that has persisted in American political culture since the Revolution. This fear of secrecy is reflected in the demand that all areas of political life be opened to public scrutiny, and the suspicion that any enclave of government or special-interest group that veils its activities in secrecy is harboring a conspiratorial elite. The concern with secrecy becomes pathological, Professor Shils argues, when secrets in and of themselves are considered to be subversive of society and the legitimate boundaries of privacy are transgressed in pursuit of them. Particularly vulnerable to the fear and fascination of secrecy are the alienated and the extremist; Shils explains:

> The ideological extremists—all extremists are inevitably ideological—because of their isolation from the world, feel menaced by unknown dangers. The paranoic tendencies which are closely associated with their apocalyptic and aggressive outlook make them think that the ordinary world, from which their devotion to the ideal cuts them off, is not normal at all; they think that it is a realm of secret machinations. What goes on in the world of pluralistic politics, in civil society, is a secret to them. It is a secret which they must unmask by vigorous publicity. Their image of the "world" as a realm of evil, against which they must defend themselves, and which they must ultimately conquer, forces them to think of the enemy's knowledge as secret knowledge.[6]

Garrison's appeal runs along very similar lines. Implicit in his charges is the suggestion that a special elite, by concealing from the populace the truth about the assassination, has appropriated to itself political control of a nation. Power is maintained through such secret machinations as "thought control," "blackouts in news centers," the "manipulation of the mass media," and the monitoring of telephone calls. The struggle for the possession of vital secrets about the assassination is depicted in apocalyptic terms. A "military-industrial juggernaut," as he said on Dutch television, which is "committed to a land war in Asia with or without hydrogen bombs" will lead the nation to a disastrous war unless the secret of the assassination can be wrested from this elite. Society is described as being so "morally threadbare that the futures of your children are in danger," a society on the verge of becoming "a concentration camp of the mind."[7] Since the leaders of the political world, including President Johnson, Chief Justice Warren, and Attorney General

Clark, were held to be actively assisting the conspiracy by suppressing the true facts of the case, salvation depended, in this view, not on a political process, but on exposing the secrets by which the elite maintains its power.

Whether Garrison has been exploiter or victim of "the torment of secrecy" is problematic; in either case, his relentless agitation against governmental secrecy apparently succeeded, if the barrage of mail his office received after each of his public appearances was any measure, in stimulating a good deal of public concern. After the District Attorney appeared on Johnny Carson's show, for example, and cited a list of classified CIA documents which he said "are secret until the year 2039," and then charged that an element of the CIA had assassinated President Kennedy "and the present administration is concealing the facts,"[8] his office received an estimated two hundred to three hundred letters a day for more than a week after the television broadcast.[9] Thomas Bethell, who read through the daily correspondence for Garrison's staff, found that the vast majority of the letters sent directly to Garrison's office showed primary concern with the notion that the government and the news media were systematically withholding facts about the assassination, and the question that most seemed to occupy the incensed letter-writers was, according to Bethell, "Why is so much information classified secret if there is nothing to hide?"[10] The same themes of secrecy and suppression ran paramount in the mail that *Playboy* received after the interview with Garrison appeared in the October 1967 issue. The responses, which one editor described as "an exceptionally large number even for *Playboy*," were almost ninety per cent favorable to Garrison, but here again the writers of the letters were, characteristically, concerned less with discussing the facts of the assassination than with denouncing governmental secrecy and news suppression. Typical were such comments as: "It is now up to the American people to force President Johnson to open the National Archives"; "What really amazes me is the fact that such people as Governor Rhodes of Ohio and the President, who could open the files in the National Archives for investigation, choose to sit on this vital information"; "Even the Kennedy assassination fades into insignificance against the more important issues. Whether there was actual or incidental collaboration between

mass media and government agencies, whether dishonesty, cor-
ruption, lying, and secrecy pervade the government as strongly
as Mr. Garrison insists . . . the web [of suppression] has
reached into the sacred depths of our national institutions."[11]
To be sure, such mail is not a representative sample of opinion,
and at best only indicates that the fear of secrecy can be tapped
in those most easily aroused to respond—those who write letters.

Yet, if the public-opinion surveys administered by Louis Harris and Associates are an accurate gauge, a very considerable
portion of the population as a whole appeared to have been
persuaded by Garrison's claims. Early in 1967, before the New
Orleans investigation became public knowledge, a Harris poll
indicated that some forty-four per cent of the American people
thought that the murder of President Kennedy was the result of
a conspiracy.[12] In May 1967, shortly after Garrison had announced the discovery of a plot, had gone on to arrest Clay
Shaw, and had charged the CIA with concealing evidence, a
survey by Harris indicated that sixty-six per cent of the American public now believed that the assassination had been carried
out by a conspiracy.[13] A third Harris survey, taken in September, revealed that despite the fact that Garrison's inquiry had
produced no tangible results, sixty per cent of the people still
believed that Kennedy had been killed by a conspiracy.[14] To be
sure, it is by no means clear that Garrison was chiefly responsible for effecting this remarkable change in public opinion. It
can be argued that a considerable number of people are naturally disposed to make a conspiratorial interpretation of any
event as historically momentous as the assassination of a President. Indeed, earlier Harris surveys showed that at least thirty
per cent of the population believed from the outset that Oswald
had not acted entirely alone, and continued to believe this after
the Warren Commission rendered its verdict.[15] Moreover, Harris concluded from the questionnaires filled out by his respon-
dents immediately after the Warren Report was issued that
eleven per cent of the population may be considered "chronic
doubters who tend to feel that the 'real' story about almost any
important public event is never quite told."[16] The fact that there
was a marked increase—from thirty-one per cent to forty-four,
according to Harris surveys—in the number of people who be-

lieved in a conspiracy when the Warren Commission became the subject of heated controversy, owing to the publication in 1966 of a number of books and articles criticizing the Report, may reflect a certain resistance by the general public against accepting a purported "truth" that is neither clear-cut nor obviously irrefutable. The idea that even a few points in the Warren Report were subject to dispute, or that even a few of its facts could be differently interpreted, probably led many people to reject, or at least doubt, the over-all conclusion that the Commission had put forward so emphatically.

In any event, the change in public opinion seems to have been substantial after Garrison appeared on the scene. Between February and May of 1967, Harris surveys indicated nearly half (sixteen out of thirty-five per cent, to be exact) of the people who had believed that Oswald was the lone assassin were now changing their minds. In other words, once Garrison began issuing his charges some thirty million Americans who had apparently been neither predisposed to believe in a conspiracy nor moved by earlier criticism of the Warren Report started having second thoughts on the question of a lone assassin.

In presenting to the public his own conclusions about the assassination of President Kennedy, Garrison enjoyed some strong advantages over all other critics of the Warren Commission. The first and most obvious is simply the authority of his office. As the district attorney of a major American city, Garrison was able to make news at will, merely by submitting charges, issuing subpoenas, and making arrests. Moreover, to many people it must seem almost inconceivable that an elected prosecutor's carefully worded "factual" statements—for example, that "At 12:45 P.M. on November 22, the Dallas police had broadcast a wanted bulletin for Oswald"—could be demonstrably false.

The District Attorney's claim to being an expert on forensic matters made it somewhat difficult, for those accepting that claim, to reject his authoritative-sounding pronouncements on evidence. When Garrison explained on national television how "scientific tests" had exonerated Oswald, few members of the audience were in a position to know that the "evidence" and the "tests" he described with such positive assurances were, in fact, spurious.[17] This imputed expertness on evidentiary matters also gave Garrison an advantage over those who attempted to dispute his statements. For example, when Johnny Carson attempted on his show to refute Garrison's contention that no identifiable prints were found on the rifle used in the assassination, by pointing out that Oswald's palmprint was in fact found on the rifle, Garrison replied authoritatively, "The palmprint was not confirmed by the federal government either,"[18] despite the fact that the palmprint was positively identified as Oswald's by three fingerprint experts, Sebastian Latona and Ronald G. Wittmus of the FBI, and Arthur Mandella of the New York City Police Department—and then further confirmed by the FBI laboratory as having come from Oswald's rifle.[19]

Still another important benefit that Garrison derived from being a public prosecutor with a case pending was the right to refuse to divulge the evidence on which his charges were based. And Garrison exercised his right on virtually all his radio and television interviews. Pressed for the basis of his allegations, he would reply, as he did on the Johnny Carson show, "I am not allowed, as an attorney, to come up with evidence until the case comes to trial."[20] He also utilized this prerogative to make his evidence against Clay Shaw appear firmer than in fact it was, particularly in the *Playboy* interview. Take, for example, his statement that "we know from incontrovertible evidence in our possession who the real Clay Bertrand is—and we will prove it in court."[21] Since Garrison charged that Clay Shaw used the alias of Clay Bertrand, this is an extremely important claim, but although the question of the identity of Clay Bertrand was a central issue in the perjury trial of Dean Andrews, which took place well after the *Playboy* interview was conducted, Garrison failed to introduce any evidence at that time concerning it. Later, a source in Garrison's office suggested that the evidence to which Garrison had been referring in the *Playboy* interview was a library card taken out under the name Clay Bertrand and bearing Clay Shaw's former business address.[22] This card hardly qualifies as incontrovertible evidence. For one thing, the card turned up well after Shaw was arrested, and, for some reason, bore no date of issuance or expiration. For another, the signature on the card was definitely not in Clay Shaw's hand—a fact that Garrison's own staff confirmed.[23] In other words, it appears that someone other than Clay Shaw filled out a library card under the alias that Garrison claimed Shaw used and put Shaw's former business address on it.*

Garrison also enjoyed the advantage of what might be called strategic plausibility. As Hannah Arendt points out in her essay "Truth and Politics," the liar is usually more persuasive than the truthteller, simply because he can fashion his facts to meet his audience's expectations.[24] Since Garrison is under no compulsion to reveal his evidence, there is nothing to prevent him from contriving his own explanation of the assassination. Whereas neither the Warren Commission nor its critics could offer a definite motive for the murder of the President, Garrison can. He states categorically in *Playboy*, "President Kennedy was killed for one reason: because he was working for a reconciliation with the U.S.S.R. and Castro's Cuba." And he goes on to declare that this is not mere speculation, insisting, ". . . we know enough about the key individuals involved in the conspiracy—Latins and Americans alike—to know that this was their motive for the murder of John Kennedy."[25]

To those who expect a momentous event to have some significant cause, Garrison's explanation naturally sounds more logical than the explanation that a lone assassin acted out of personal disaffection.

---

* The affair is discussed at some length by William Turner in the "official history" of the case in the January 1968 issue of *Ramparts*. Turner, however, does not divulge the fact that the signature on the card is not Shaw's.

11

THE MAKING OF A DEMAGOGUE

If the press has any doubts about me, if they think I'm politically ambitious, if they really think I'd charge somebody for some kind of personal gain, then they should raise the question. That's fine. Because I'll survive. . . .

—Jim Garrison speaking before the Radio and Television News Association of Southern California, November 1967

A demagogue can survive only so long as the mass media take him seriously enough to print his charges and give him exposure. The relation is not, however, entirely one-sided. The demagogue, free of any constraint of veracity, is always in a position to provide journalists with the kinds of exclusive stories and sensational charges which stimulate widespread interest—and circulation. The way in which Garrison's case developed, from the abrupt arrest and pre-trial hearing of Clay Shaw to the constantly changing configuration of assassins and conspirators, is perhaps more closely connected to Garrison's struggle to obtain access to the news media than it is to his evidentiary investigation.

Life

Garrison decided to investigate the assassination of President Kennedy, it will be remembered, in November 1966 after he discussed the matter with Senator Russell Long on a plane flight to New York City. Shortly after he returned to New Orleans, the District Attorney informed David Chandler, *Life*'s man in New Orleans, of his plans. He also suggested that *Life*, which had itself just called for a new inquiry into the assassination in a cover story entitled "A Matter of Reasonable Doubt,"[1] might be interested in "a joint investigation."[2] Chandler relayed the offer to the New York office, and Richard Billings, then an associate editor for special events, was promptly dispatched to New Orleans. On December 7, Garrison met with Billings and Chandler and offered to give *Life* reporters complete and exclusive access to his investigation. All he asked in return was that *Life* assist him in investigating matters outside his jurisdiction.[3] Billings agreed to what he termed "an exchange of information," and for the next ten weeks *Life* photographers and reporters became an integral part of the District Attorney's investigation: interviewing witnesses, photographing interrogation sessions, attending staff conferences, and preparing a major story on Garrison's prime suspect, David Ferrie.[4] However, relations became somewhat troubled after Ferrie's sudden death in late February 1967 and, a week later, Garrison arrested a new suspect, Clay Shaw. Garrison later told me that he had been promised a cover story in *Life* if he made an arrest, and when it failed to materialize he realized that *Life* "had knuckled under to White House pressure."[5] Billings categorically denied that any such commitment was ever made by representatives of *Life*.[6] Chandler said that Garrison assumed from the amount of interest *Life* had manifested that an arrest would lead to a cover story, but no promises were ever made.[7]

There were a number of reasons why *Life* never published the extensive story it had prepared on the Garrison investigation. Immediately after Shaw was arrested, Chandler, who had been present at the "brainstorming sessions" in which Garrison speculated that Clay Shaw might be the elusive Clay Bertrand, informed senior editors at *Life* that he now thought the entire investigation might be a publicity stunt.[8] Billings also had some doubts after the arrest of Shaw: he had been present when Assistant District Attorney Sciambra gave Garrison an oral report of Perry Raymond Russo's story, and, at this time, it contained nothing about a "conspiracy" or about a "Bertrand" who fitted the description of Shaw.[9] The publication of James Phelan's story on Garrison in the *Saturday Evening Post* was probably the final straw. Garrison, apparently disappointed over *Life*'s failure to publish, not only had granted Phelan a long interview in Las Vegas, but had also allowed him to examine the documents. And so Phelan found the memorandum from Sciambra which revealed that Russo's original story was very different from the one he had told in court—and although Garrison and Sciambra publicly denied this, Billings was in a position to know that it was true, and *Life* after this quickly lost interest in the Garrison affair.[10]

Playboy

Garrison next sought exposure in *Playboy*, agreeing to allow the magazine to publish an extensive interview about his investigation *before* the case came to trial. The editor in charge of the project estimated that the interview, which contained allegations ranging from CIA involvement in the assassination to the arrival of Fascism in America, represented "$1,605,000 worth of editorial space," although it is not clear whether he is referring to the publicity which the interview would gain for *Playboy* or for Garrison.[11] There is no reason to assume, however, that the decision to publish the interview was based primarily on mercenary considerations; for, in giving Garrison "the chance to present his side of the case" before the trial took place,[12] *Playboy* was, after all, acting in the well-established tradition of American journalism which holds that every story has two sides —and that what is controversial is news. This concept of news does not necessarily require that an account, so long as it fairly represents one side of a story, be factually accurate. In recommending the interview for publication, one senior editor thus wrote:

> Garrison comes off as sincere, eloquent, even brilliant. *But even if he were a nut*—and I don't think it's possible for anyone to read this and come away with that conclusion—I would still want to run this, just because it is the first complete reconstruction of the assassination events as seen through Garrison's eyes. At worst, if Garrison is totally repudiated (in light of the facts he presents this seems highly unlikely), we have an interview in the Shelton-Rockwell genre. At best, if he is vindicated, then we perform a genuine public service, almost in the Pulitzer prize category.[13] [Italics in the original memorandum.]

A second editor's evaluation ran along similar lines:

> Garrison is revealed as an intelligent, hearty, and ballsy guy —certainly not a kook—with a credible case, even if he turns out wrong. He indicts everyone from the CIA, to Warren's Commission, to N.B.C. (he gets a bit gratuitous there and dissipates his venom), and he probably is somewhat paranoid, but I think anyone would be who was conducting a non-Establishment investigation into the assassination.[14]

In a memorandum to Hugh M. Hefner, the publisher, Murray Fisher, a senior editor, summed up the reasons for publishing the interview:

> Even if he's wrong (which is possible), even if he's insincere (which I doubt), even if the accusations about his impropriety are true (which seems not to be the case), Shaw is still going to go to trial in October [1967] and the interview (coming out two or three weeks before it begins) will be very big news.[15]

Since the interview would be "big news" whether Garrison was right or wrong, there existed little incentive to check out the factual accuracy of the piece before publication. (Almost all of Garrison's references to the testimony in the Warren Commission's volumes, which for the most part could have been checked without a great deal of effort, were either incorrect or misleading. For example, in purporting to quote from a Supplementary Investigation Report which appeared in Volume XIX of the Warren Commission's testimony, Garrison simply altered the words in the text from "I advised him" to "I was advised" to make his point.)[16] Despite the prediction of A. C. Spectorsky, the associate publisher, that the interview would lead to twenty-four libel suits,[17] it was rushed to publication in September to anticipate a trial that did not materialize. And although *Playboy* may not have realized the expected $1,605,000 in free publicity, Garrison did his share by appearing on radio and television shows in New York and California in conjunction with the publication of the interview. In *Playboy*, the New Orleans District Attorney found (as he put it in one of the television appearances) "an opportunity to try and communicate some of the issues in the case" to a national audience.[18]

The Anti-Establishment Press

Moreover, Garrison found allies, eager to proselytize on his behalf, among dissident political writers who consider themselves part of what they call "the anti-Establishment press." His charge that there was a conspiracy between the government and the mass media to conceal the truth from the people accords perfectly, after all, with what such journals see as their *raison d'être*. It is therefore hardly surprising to find his speeches printed verbatim in such papers as the *Los Angeles Free Press*, and to find his portrait on the cover of *Ramparts*, with the words:

Who appointed Ramsey Clark, who has done his best to torpedo the investigation of the case? Who controls the CIA? Who controls the FBI? Who controls the Archives where this evidence is locked up for so long that it is unlikely that there is anybody in this room who will be alive when it is released? This is really your property and the property of the people of this country. Who has the arrogance and the brass to prevent the people from seeing that evidence? Who indeed? The one man who has profited most from the assassination—your friendly President, Lyndon Johnson![19]

Garrison thus finally obtained the cover story that *Life*, despite his efforts, had denied him.

Anti-establishmentarianism tends to make strange bedfellows. Among Garrison's most ardent supporters was the *Councilor*, the bimonthly official journal of the Citizens' Council of Louisiana, which claims a circulation of some two hundred and sixty thousand, and which actively campaigns against Communism, the suppression of news by the mass media (supposedly controlled by Zionist interests), race mongrelization (a plot aided by the CIA and the Rothschilds), and the insidious intrusion of federal authority into the sacred domain of states' rights. That Garrison had been "fought by Sterns, Newhouse papers, and Agnes Meyer" (i.e., the NBC affiliate in New Orleans, WDSU-TV; the *Times-Picayune* and *States-Item;* and the *Washington Post* and *Newsweek)* was for the *Councilor* sufficient reason to lend Garrison its enthusiastic support.[20] The logic of *Ramparts* has not been significantly different. William Turner concluded one of his articles on Garrison in the magazine by saying that the anti-Garrison tactics of NBC, *Newsweek*, and the daily press "smack of desperation—and indicate that there is much to hide."[21] The *Councilor* went along with most of the details of the plot theory outlined in *Ramparts*, differing only in its belief that it was "the left wing of the CIA," not the right wing, and that New York Communists, rather than right-wing extremists, were behind the conspiracy.[22] (Perry Russo told the *Councilor* in an exclusive interview that David Ferrie was really a "Marxist" and follower of Che Guevara.)[23]

The New York Review

Garrison's cause also found champions in more highly respected journals that pride themselves on their intellectual credentials—notably the *New York Review of Books*, which rejected the Warren Commission's conclusions because the Commission's investigation was defective but embraced Garrison's investigation despite its far more glaring defects. Professor Richard Popkin, in a lengthy defense of Garrison's investigation in the *New York Review*, argues that Garrison should be given a "fair hearing" in court, and not have his case "prejudged" by the press. He claims that while Garrison has "studiously avoided any discussion of Shaw and the specific evidence against him," the press has interviewed "potential witnesses," evaluated the evidence, made "charges against the District Attorney and his office . . . in effect, trying the case out of court." The "wave of attacks in the press and TV" against Garrison, Popkin contends, "surely prejudices a fair trial." He concludes that no investigation of Garrison is necessary, for "if the evidence is as contrived and cockeyed as the press and TV allege, they should expect that twelve jurors along with [the judge] will see through it."[24] It is true that the right of a defendant not to be prejudged is a fundamental principle of jurisprudence. And pretrial publicity, by prejudicing public opinion, can certainly deny the defendant his right to a fair hearing. Jim Garrison, however, is *not* the defendant. Clay Shaw is! The rights of the defendant have been established precisely to counterbalance the powers of the state. Popkin's plea that the press suspend scrutiny and criticism of Garrison's methods would, if it were taken to heart, undermine a defendant's legitimate protection against the possibility of a prosecutor's using his power and resources to fabricate evidence and intimidate witnesses. Moreover, Popkin's contention that Garrison "studiously avoided" discussing the evidence seems disingenuous, at best. The fact is that an interview that Popkin had with Perry Russo was arranged by the District Attorney himself.[25] It was Garrison, too, who told reporters that he had found Jack Ruby's coded telephone number in both Shaw's and Oswald's address books, and repeated the allegation on television and to newspaper reporters even after it was shown to be false.[26] It was Garrison who stated in the *National Observer*, "There is no way that Clay Shaw can get an acquittal."[27] It was Garrison who allowed Mark Lane and William Turner to photostat evidence in his files. And it was Garrison who, in his *Playboy* interview and on his subsequent coast-to-coast tour, made numerous references either to evidence in the Shaw case or to Shaw himself (including the demonstrable falsehood that Shaw was with President Kennedy "on an airplane flight in 1963").[28] Indeed, Garrison went on about the case in speeches, radio talk shows, television programs, press conferences, and interviews almost without pause. Of course, most of the evidence Garrison discussed is spurious, but surely that makes it all the more imperative for the press not to waive its responsibility for examining it closely.

Popkin's way of dismissing the charges leveled against Garrison is similarly cavalier. He chides the *New York Times* for accepting at face value, and printing on its front page, the allegations made against Garrison by the convicted burglar John Cancler; Popkin points out that when the grand jury later questioned Cancler about the accusations, he invoked the Fifth Amendment. The fact that Cancler exercised his Constitutional right to protect himself against self-incrimination, Popkin concludes, affects the "credibility" of his charges.[29] Yet, does this necessarily follow? Cancler had charged that his fellow prisoner, Vernon Bundy, confided to him that he was going to give perjured testimony at Clay Shaw's preliminary hearing, testimony that would inculpate Shaw.[30] If this is true, Cancler was an accessory before the fact in the perjury, and might indeed have incriminated himself by admitting this to the grand jury. Besides, the mere fact that Cancler took the Fifth Amendment, though it may have signaled a want of courage on his part, surely cannot be said to affect in itself the man's credibility (although there were those among the followers of the late Senator Joe McCarthy who insisted that it did).

Popkin's notion that there is no need for the press to scrutinize Garrison's techniques for recruiting witnesses and assembling evidence because if the evidence is contrived a judge and jury will see through it and "destroy Garrison at the trial" shows an unusual confidence in the legal process. While it is true that a judge and jury can detect contradictions in testimony and other incongruous evidence, there is no certainty at all that they can uncover perjury that has been systematically arranged for, with one perjurer corroborating another's testimony, or that they can recognize artfully fabricated "facts" purposely designed to fit into the pattern of evidence. Exposure of such systematic fraud would, in fact, depend on an outside investigation of the prosecutor's means and methods. Gene Roberts, of *The New York Times,* and Walter Sheridan, of NBC, have stated that in separate inquiries they discovered at least six witnesses who said that they had been offered bribes, blackmailed, or otherwise coerced by Garrison's representatives.[31] All were, in one way or another, vulnerable people. William Gurvich said that while he was working for Garrison he saw the way the powers of a district attorney's office could be used "to intimidate and coerce witnesses."[32] Popkin intimates that Sheridan and Gurvich may have had some ulterior motive in revealing information about Garrison's mode of operation.[33] One can, as the British philosopher A. J. Ayer points out, always sustain one's beliefs in the face of apparently hostile evidence if one is prepared to make the necessary *ad hoc* assumptions, and in this case supporters of Garrison seem all too ready to assume that everyone who criticizes Garrison's conduct is part of a plot to conceal the truth. But such rationalization explains nothing. During the time I studied Garrison's investigation and had access to his office, the only evidence I saw or heard about that could connect Clay Shaw with the assassination was fraudulent —some devised by Garrison himself and some cynically culled from criminals or the emotionally unstable. To fail to report this information so that Garrison might have a "fair hearing" in court could preclude the possibility of the defendant's ever receiving *his* fair hearing in court.

To see the issue of the assassination as of such overwhelming importance that the juridical rights of the defendant may be neglected, the Constitutional rights of witnesses disdained, the scrutiny and criticism of the press suspended, and the traditional methods of the state's prosecution ignored is to accept a curious sort of situational ethics. It is to say that in a search for facts the means can be disregarded if the ends—the facts—are of enough consequence. Fred Powledge, writing in the *New Republic*, suggests the dilemma: "I had the irrational feeling that he [Garrison] was on to something. I had the equally startling feeling that it did not really matter if Garrison were paranoid, opportunistic, flamboyant, or if his witnesses were not candidates for *The Defenders*. Was he *right?*"[34] But can the process of establishing the truth ever be separated from its end product— the truth? Facts must be selected, interpreted, and arranged in the context provided by other information before they take on meaning. Factual evidence can be established as truth, as Hannah Arendt points out, only "through testimony by eyewitnesses —notoriously unreliable—and by records, documents, and monuments, all of which can be suspected as forgeries."[35] If one has reason to doubt the process by which "facts" have been ascertained or confirmed, how can one ever be certain that they bear any relation to the truth, or even that the "facts" themselves are not outright fabrications? For data can be accepted as factual truth if, and only if, the probity of the investigator is also accepted. A demagogue who demonstrates a willingness to alter elements of a story when it serves his purpose may temporarily excite public opinion, but he can never establish his version of the event as the truth.

In view of the shortcomings of the Warren Commission's investigation, it becomes apparent that there is no easy way to devise a process for ultimately answering such complex and elusive historical questions as those provoked by the assassination of President Kennedy. Indeed, there can be no certainty that such a process is even within our institutional means. But there *can* be certainty that as long as the means by which an investigation has been conducted remain suspect the truth will never be fully established.

EPILOGUE II

The Trial of Clay Shaw (1992)

On January 21, 1969, after nearly two years of concocting and playing out his charges in the national media, Jim Garrison finally tried the accused, Clay Shaw, in a court of law in New Orleans. Even though Garrison had announced on February 24, 1967, that he had "positively solved the assassination of President John F. Kennedy"—and, one week later, arrested Clay Shaw for conspiring to kill the president—it now turned out that he had not yet found any evidence whatsoever of the putative conspiracy that he presented at the trial at the time he made this sensational claim. The conspiracy he laid out in court took place at a single meeting in late September 1963 in the apartment of David Ferrie in which three conspirators, Clay Shaw, David Ferrie, and Lee Harvey Oswald, plotted the "cross fire" and "triangulation of fire" in Dallas through which they planned to assassinate Kennedy, and this conspiracy was witnessed by the only other person in the apartment, Perry Raymond Russo. Since Ferrie and Oswald were dead, and Shaw denied that he had attended such a meeting, Garrison's only possible witness was Russo, whom Garrison had not contacted until February 25.

In the trial, Shaw's defense lawyers introduced into evidence Russo's original interrogation by Garrison's staff, which revealed that Russo had insisted as late as February 27 that he had seen Shaw on only two occasions—both times from afar—and at neither time did he see him in Ferrie's apartment or with anyone resembling Oswald. Russo testified on the stand that he had changed this initial account, which precluded the possibility of his having witnessed the putative conspiratorial meeting, only after he had been injected with sodium pentothal and hypnotized. After that, a New Orleans police lieutenant testified that Russo subsequently admitted to him after Shaw had been arrested that Shaw was "probably not" the man whom he met at Ferrie's apartment in September 1963.

Since there was no corroboration of Russo's erratic story—the woman Russo claimed accompanied him that night to Ferrie's apartment testified that that could not have occurred before 1964—the trial, which Garrison only infrequently appeared at, became a travesty. Instead of presenting any further allegations against the man on trial, Garrison's assistants screened the Zapruder film ten times for the jury, and had a dozen people recount what they had seen and heard in Dallas at the site of the assassination—none of which was related to the New Orleans conspiracy, which by now appeared to be nothing more than a pretext for retrying the assassination case, in New Orleans.

In his twenty-five-minute closing statement, Garrison all but ignored the defendant, mentioning Clay Shaw—whose testimony he had not even bothered to attend—only once. He railed instead against "government secrecy" and "excessive government power."

On March 1, 1969, the jury reached a unanimous verdict on its first ballet. To no one's surprise, after his two-year ordeal (and near-bankrupting legal expenses), Clay Shaw was found not guilty.

After Shaw died in 1973, a CIA report about him was released. It revealed that he had not been a CIA employee but, like other American businessmen who traveled to Eastern Europe in the late 1940s and early 1950s, Shaw had been debriefed by the CIA's Domestic Contact Service about what he had seen and heard during his business trips to East Germany, Czechoslovakia, and other countries of interest to U.S. intelligence. Although these debriefings had ended in 1956, they made Shaw particularly attractive to Garrison as an investigative target, since he could be, no matter how tenuously, connected with "the invisible government."

In the end, except for adding a few biographical details about Oswald's travels to Clinton, Louisiana, in the summer of 1963, Garrison's investigation shed nothing new on the assassination itself. Even assassination buffs were dismayed by the dearth of new evidence it produced (some went so far as to accuse Garrison of staging the Shaw affair as a red herring to divert attention from more salient leads in New Orleans). The press, whom Garrison had tried so hard to win over with promises of exclusive disclosures, now condemned him in no uncertain terms. Even the *New Orleans States-Item*, once a keen supporter of Garrison, concluded, "This travesty of justice is a reproach to the conscience of all good men. . . . Garrison stands revealed for what he is: a man without principle who would pervert the legal process to his own ends."

Nonetheless, Garrison continued his public career. After failing to get reelected district attorney in 1973—but surviving federal charges he took payoffs and graft by local gamblers—he was elected an appeals court judge in New Orleans. He also wrote books on the assassination and played bit parts in two Hollywood films: *The Big Easy* (in which he played a local judge) and *JFK* (in which he played Chief Justice Warren).

BOOK THREE

LEGEND

*THE SECRET WORLD OF
LEE HARVEY OSWALD
(1978)*

Author's note

Lee Harvey Oswald was an erratic speller.
I have, for the convenience of the reader,
corrected the spelling and grammatical errors
in all direct quotations from material
written by Oswald, except as noted.

A Man Called Nosenko

On January 20, 1964, Yuri Ivanovich Nosenko stepped off an Aeroflot jet in Geneva knowing full well that if everything went as planned, he would never again see his home in Moscow—or the wife and two children he had left behind. Such was the nature of his mission. He passed easily through the Swiss passport control with his diplomatic documents. Officially he was a member of the Soviet disarmament delegation. He followed closely behind Semyon K. Tsarapkin, the head of the delegation. Together they entered a waiting limousine.

In minutes they were speeding through fog along the highway connecting the airport and downtown Geneva. To their left was the glass and concrete structure of the Palais des Nations, where the seventeen-nation disarmament conference they were to attend was due to convene the next day. Nosenko knew the building well; he had spent almost four months in and around its meeting rooms during another disarmament conference in June 1962. The limousine stopped in front of the Rex Hotel, where the Soviet delegation was staying.

After seeing Tsarapkin to his room, Nosenko decided to take a short walk. On a side street he stopped at a pay phone and dialed the telegraph service. The coded message he dictated sounded innocuous enough when the operator read it back. A moment later it was sent. He knew there would now be no turning back.

With that message Nosenko had set in motion a series of events that would profoundly affect the Western intelligence community for more than a decade. A division within the CIA had been waiting for his telegram for nineteen months. During the previous disarmament conference in Geneva, Nosenko had contacted the CIA and offered to act as a spy for the United States when he returned to Russia. Since that time he had not been heard from, and because of other information the CIA had received, some suspicions had developed about Nosenko's motivations and the value of his offer.

But no one in the CIA could have predicted the furor that his reappearance would cause. No one could have known that Nosenko was about to present information that would accelerate the deterioration of relationships between the CIA and the FBI, cause deep divisions in both services, alter the careers of high-ranking intelligence officers, and raise ominous questions about American security that have not been resolved to this day.

Somewhere within the seven-story headquarters building of the CIA in Langley, Virginia, an officer keyed the name on the telegram to a seven-letter code name: AE-----. Out came the operational file on Nosenko.

According to this dossier, Nosenko was born on October 30, 1927, in Nikolayev, Russia. His father, Ivan Nosenko, was an alternate member of the all-powerful Central Committee of the Communist Party and served as the Soviet Minister of Shipbuilding in the 1950s. When he died in 1956, the most important leaders of the Soviet Union, including Nikita Khrushchev, Georgi Malenkov, Nikolai Bulganin and Kliment Voroshilov, formed the guard of honor at his funeral bier, and he was then buried in the Kremlin wall.

The dossier, based primarily on Nosenko's 1962 statements, noted that since the age of twenty-two Nosenko had served in Soviet intelligence. In 1949 he joined Soviet naval intelligence (GRU), and in the early fifties he served in the Far East, training

Japanese prisoners of war who were to be sent back to Japan as Soviet agents. In 1953 he resigned from naval intelligence to work for the State Security Agency, known now by the initials KGB.[1] He was immediately assigned to the Second Chief Directorate, which has overall responsibility for surveillance and counterintelligence of potential enemy agents inside the Soviet Union. (The First Chief Directorate has the responsibility for espionage and counterintelligence outside the Soviet Union.)

During his first two years Nosenko worked in the American Department of the KGB. His job entailed monitoring the activities of first American correspondents and then military attachés in Moscow. In 1955 he was transferred to the Tourist Department, which specialized in compromising and recruiting foreign visitors to Moscow. In June 1958 Nosenko's section of the Tourist Department was divided into two new sections: the first concerned with British and American tourists; the second with tourists from any other country. Nosenko, at the age of thirty, was appointed deputy chief of the American-British Section.

A year later he was given a special commendation by the chairman of the KGB for operations which resulted in the compromising of American visitors to Moscow. In January 1960 Nosenko was transferred back to the American Department to work against personnel at the American Embassy. In January 1962 he returned to the Tourist Department as deputy chief. From February to June 1962 he was attached to the Soviet disarmament delegation in Geneva as chief security officer. It was then that he first contacted an American diplomat and asked to be taken to see a CIA officer.

Only hours after Nosenko's message was received, a top-level case officer from the CIA was on a jet plane headed for Geneva. This case officer, a member of the Soviet Russia Division, that part of the CIA responsible for espionage activities concerning the Soviet Union, was chosen for the assignment because he had already met Nosenko—and had opened the operational file on him—in June 1962.

On January 23, in the Palais des Nations, the chief American delegate, William C. Foster, proposed a freeze on the production, development and testing of nuclear weapons. His Soviet counterpart, Tsarapkin, extended his lantern jaw and listened passively to the Russian translation of the proposal. He knew, as did the Americans, that it would be eventually rejected. Sometime during this tedious session Nosenko slipped out of the room and hailed a taxi.

The case officer waited with one other Russian-speaking agent from the CIA in a quiet apartment in a suburb of Geneva. These quarters had been rented and maintained over the years for just such a special visitor.

It was late afternoon when the doorbell finally rang. Heavy footsteps could be heard on the stairs. A moment later the case officer recognized Nosenko sauntering into the room. He was a powerfully built man, about six feet tall, with a massive jaw and brooding eyes set deep in their sockets.

The case officer told Nosenko that he was glad to see him again. What he did not tell the Russian was that, after their earlier meeting nineteen months ago, he had been called in by the CIA's counterintelligence staff and briefed for three days and nights on the full context of the Nosenko case. He now realized that it was far more complicated than he had ever imagined, and there was a possibility that this KGB officer was not all he claimed to be.

Nosenko proceeded to explain why he had sent the telegram. Not only did he have important information he was willing to turn over to the CIA, but he also wanted to defect from the Soviet delegation in Geneva and go to the United States. He had decided, he explained, that he could no longer live in Soviet society.

The case officer was astonished by this offer to defect. At their 1962 meeting Nosenko had stated that he had a wife and children in Moscow and could never consider defecting from Russia. What had happened to cause this complete turnabout? the case officer wondered. Why was he now willing to desert his family, his country and a spectacular career in the KGB, where he had risen in ten years to being deputy department chief and to the rank of lieutenant colonel? Rather than press him about his change of mind, the case officer temporized by asking, "What information have you brought?"

Nosenko discussed one or two Soviet intelligence operations

that had come to his attention and then dropped a completely unexpected bombshell. He said that he had personally superintended the KGB file on Lee Harvey Oswald when he had defected to the Soviet Union in 1959 and could therefore completely describe his relationship with Soviet intelligence.

Less than two months had passed since the Kennedy assassination and the murder of Oswald by Jack Ruby. Rumors about the killings commanded ever-increasing columns of newsprint and commentary on radio and TV broadcasts. This bewildering drumbeat of allegations and reports, which raised questions about left- and right-wing factions, the underworld, the FBI, the CIA and the KGB, had caused President Lyndon B. Johnson to convene a commission of inquiry under Supreme Court Chief Justice Earl Warren.

The death of Oswald had left a wide-open void in the assassination case. The basic 201 file that the CIA had maintained on Oswald prior to the assassination came mainly from FBI and State Department reports. It revealed that he was a twenty-four-year-old Marine, born in New Orleans, who had received an early discharge and a short time later defected to the Soviet Union in September 1959. It noted that he had resided in Minsk for about two and one-half years. After marrying a Soviet citizen named Marina Prusakova, he brought her back with him to the United States in June 1962. The last entry in his CIA file before his arrest in Dallas concerned a report of a telephone call that the CIA station in Mexico had intercepted in which Oswald had called the Soviet Embassy in Mexico City from the adjacent Cuban Embassy.

After the assassination the CIA and other investigators had been unable to fill the gap left by Oswald's more than two years' residence in the Soviet Union. Such key questions as why Oswald defected in the first place, what (if any) relations existed between Oswald and Soviet intelligence and whether any legend, or cover story, was prepared by the KGB for Oswald's return to America were simply beyond the capacity of United States intelligence agencies to answer—until this moment.

Now here was the man who could be best qualified to answer these questions. In a matter-of-fact tone, Nosenko explained that the KGB had not heard of Oswald until he appeared in Moscow and told his Intourist guide that he intended to renounce his American citizenship and seek Soviet citizenship. Only then, he claimed, "the KGB decided to look into Oswald's case to see if there was any operational interest, which part of the KGB might have use for him and what was behind the request [for Soviet citizenship]."

His interrogator listened keenly, not knowing what would come next in the story. There was a pause, and he asked what the KGB had finally decided about Oswald.

"It was decided that Oswald was of no interest whatsoever, so the KGB recommended that he go home to the United States . . ." Nosenko answered.

If the KGB had rejected Oswald and ordered him out of the country, why was he allowed to stay for two and a half years? the interrogator asked.

Nosenko explained that Oswald, on learning of his rejection, "made the dramatic gesture of suicide . . . at his hotel . . . by cutting his wrists. . . . Now worried about the possibility that Oswald would do this again if refused asylum, the Soviets decided to give him a temporary residence permit. . . ."

The interrogator persisted: But then why was Oswald sent from Moscow to Minsk?

Nosenko replied, "Merely by chance. The KGB had not wanted Oswald to stay in Moscow, and Minsk was chosen arbitrarily."

Why had Oswald been allowed to marry a Soviet citizen at a time when he was already planning his redefection to America?

Nosenko shrugged and answered, "She already had anti-Soviet characteristics. She was not too smart anyway and not an educated person. . . . The Soviets were glad to get rid of them both."

Nosenko stated with a great deal of assurance that neither Oswald nor Marina had ever been recruited or even approached by the KGB as possible agents. In fact, he added, Soviet intelligence did not bother to debrief Oswald when he came to Russia because he was deemed "unstable . . . and of little importance."

Nosenko claimed to have heard nothing further about Oswald until October 1963, when Oswald showed up at the Soviet Embassy in Mexico City, seeking a visa to return to Russia, a request routinely passed on to the KGB. Nosenko was asked by a superior if Oswald should be allowed a visa. Nosenko advised that Oswald should not be let back in the Soviet Union.

The interrogating team in Geneva immediately relayed Nosenko's story to Langley. It was an extraordinary development. The President's Commission on the Assassination of President Kennedy, headed by Chief Justice Earl Warren (and popularly known as the Warren Commission), was just about to begin its hearings. The other six members of the commission appointed by President Johnson were Congressmen Hale Boggs and Gerald Ford; Senators Richard Russell and John Sherman Cooper; Allen Dulles, the Director of the CIA until 1962; and John McCloy, former High Commissioner of Germany.

Originally it was thought that the commission would have to do little more than hear the testimony of a few key witnesses and validate the results of the FBI investigation. By January 1964, however, it was decided in executive session by the members of the commission that if its report were to be credible, it would have to conduct its own investigation. A dozen lawyers, hired as consultants, were assigned in pairs to six different areas: the facts surrounding the assassination itself; the identity of the assassin; the background and associates of the assassin; the possibility of foreign connections or conspiracies; the killing of the alleged assassin by Jack Ruby; and the general area of presidential protection.

If Nosenko's account were true, the CIA realized, it could deliver a witness who could answer the vexing questions about Oswald's missing years in Russia. So the Soviet Russia Division immediately began sorting through Nosenko's story. On its face, it coincided closely with the version Oswald himself gave in what purported to be a diary found among his effects: his arrival in Russia, attempted suicide, marriage to Marina and decision to return to the United States. But the diary had already been leaked to the press, and even if it had not, there was always the possibility that it had been prepared in Moscow for Oswald as part of a legend. It thus could not be used, the Soviet Russia Division concluded, to confirm Nosenko's account.

Closer scrutiny of Nosenko's story revealed some troublesome omissions. To begin with, Nosenko had not provided any description of the investigation that the KGB would have routinely undertaken to check out various details in Oswald's story in 1959, when he first applied for Soviet residence. In other such cases, the CIA knew, the KGB conducted extensive investigations to establish the subject's bona fides, including even the clandestine examination of records and files in the United States.

Nosenko had claimed, moreover, that the First Chief Directorate of the KGB, responsible for all foreign operations and espionage, did not even have Oswald's name on file until he contacted the Soviet Embassy in Mexico City in October 1963. Yet the CIA knew from FBI surveillance that on two separate occasions Oswald had contacted the Soviet Embassy in Washington before his trip to Mexico. According to the accounts of other defectors from Soviet intelligence agencies, the First Chief Directorate would have been routinely informed of these contacts (as they were in Mexico). Why had Nosenko failed to mention them?

Finally, Nosenko's claim that Oswald was never even debriefed did not fit in with the CIA's expectation of how a defector would be handled by the KGB (based on earlier cases). And how could Nosenko, who was only deputy chief of the Tourist Department, be so certain that no other section of the KGB (or Soviet military intelligence) had debriefed or recruited Oswald?

In Geneva a few days later Nosenko again slipped away from the Soviet delegation and went to the CIA safe house. There the CIA interrogators returned to the question of Oswald's possible relation with the KGB. They asked Nosenko how he could so definitely rule out such a possibility. Didn't Soviet intelligence at least show some interest in the military secrets he claimed to have acquired in the Marines?

"Absolutely not," Nosenko insisted. He claimed he could be certain of this because any debriefings would have had to go through his department in the Second Chief Directorate, which had opened the file on Oswald.

But how could he be so sure that agents of the First Chief Directorate had not contacted Oswald after he returned to the United States? he was asked.

"No matter how I may hate anyone [in the KGB], I cannot speak against my convictions," Nosenko exclaimed. "And since I know this [Oswald] case, I can unhesitantly sign off to the fact that the Soviet Union cannot be tied into this in any way."

But how could Nosenko "sign off" on this case?

Nosenko explained that not only was he the KGB officer who supervised Oswald's file while he was in the Soviet Union, but, after Kennedy had been assassinated, he was the KGB officer appointed to make a "complete investigation" of the Oswald affair. A warplane was immediately ordered to fly the Oswald file up from Minsk, and then, "not trusting official papers," he sent a squad of his own investigators to Minsk to question officials on the spot. He could therefore testify from his first-hand inspection of the complete files that the KGB had no connection to Oswald.

In fact, he offered to testify before the Warren Commission.

Nosenko's offer to defect troubled Richard M. Helms, who, as Deputy Director of Plans of the CIA, actually managed the entire covert side of that intelligence agency. A tall, elegant man with a quiet voice and piercing eyes, Helms had worked in intelligence for more than a quarter of a century. He began handling agents in Europe in the 1940s for the Office of Strategic Services, and when the OSS was dissolved after World War II he remained in a small intelligence nucleus called the Central Intelligence Group, which, in 1947, became the CIA. Under Allen Dulles, Helms had administered and coordinated most of the secret work of the agency, and when Dulles retired in 1962, Helms was elevated to his present position.

As he reviewed the startling development in Geneva, Helms realized that it presented a potentially explosive situation. If Nosenko's account of Oswald in Russia proved credible, it could solve a very serious problem for the Warren Commission—and for the United States government. Nosenko was a live witness who could testify that he had read the entire KGB file on Oswald and therefore could certify that Oswald had had no connection with Soviet intelligence. On the other hand, if Nosenko turned out to be a Soviet-controlled agent sent over to misinform the CIA and the Warren Commission, as some members of the CIA's counterintelligence staff feared, the sky could fall in on Soviet-American relations. At the very least, it would suggest that the Soviets were going to great lengths to contrive a legend about Oswald's residence in the Soviet Union. At the most . . . but that was a possibility Helms did not want to think about.

Despite these considerations, Helms knew that he had little choice but to authorize the defection of Nosenko. A Soviet intelligence officer who claimed knowledge of a missing area in the Oswald case simply could not be ignored or turned back to the Russians. For the short term, Helms decided that Nosenko should be persuaded to remain a defector in place—that is, to remain in his present position in the KGB but work under CIA control. At a later date, if his information proved out, he would be allowed to defect to the United States. Meanwhile, the FBI and the Warren Commission would be fully apprised of the statements Nosenko had made about Oswald.

Meeting in Washington, D.C., the Warren Commission was hearing on February 3 the testimony of its first witness—Marina Oswald, the twenty-two-year-old wife of the accused assassin. Thin and attractive, she spoke through an interpreter. As the session began, she smiled timidly at the Chief Justice and told him that he reminded her of her own grandfather.

Only a week before, the commission had heard in a secret executive session that Marina had suggested to *Life* magazine (which was negotiating for the rights to her biography) that she was a "Soviet agent." After hearing that, Senator Richard Russell, one of the more conservative members of the commission, commented, "That will blow the lid, if she testifies to that." Now the commission had to assess her testimony carefully. Aside from Nosenko, she was the only witness it had who could cast some light on the murky relations Oswald seemed to have had with Soviet authorities during his stay in Russia.

In Geneva, on the same day, the CIA was still trying to persuade Nosenko to stay in place and continue, for the short term at least, working for the KGB. Nosenko, however, rejected such a course. His case officer asked why.

Nosenko claimed to have just received a recall telegram from his superiors at the KGB center requiring him to be on a plane to Moscow on February 4. In his opinion, such a telegram might mean that he was suspected of dealing with the Americans. If he returned, therefore, he risked being arrested, tortured and even executed. He had no choice, he told his CIA interrogators; his escape had to be arranged on or before February 4.

At Langley, Helms realized that the recall telegram gave him no alternative. The CIA could not afford to lose a potentially valuable witness to Oswald's activities in the Soviet Union. He took the matter to John McCone, the Director of the CIA. McCone immediately authorized Helms to bring Nosenko out of Switzerland.

February 4 was a cloudy day in Geneva. At the Palais des Nations, Tsarapkin complained that the Soviet Union was growing increasingly pessimistic about the hopes of reaching an accord on nuclear delivery vehicles. He demanded that the United States agree to the Soviet proposal for the elimination of all foreign bases in Europe before the USSR would even consider further the American proposal. The conference had reached a deadlock. At lunch the Soviet delegate noticed an empty chair in the dining room. It was the one usually occupied by Yuri Nosenko.

Meanwhile, in a car miles away, headed for Germany, Nosenko sat back, smoked an American cigarette and checked his watch. It was after 1 P.M. He knew that soon Soviet security personnel would begin the search for him. First, the delegates' lounges at the Palais des Nations, then the Rex Hotel, where they would search his hotel room, and within a few hours there would be frantic cables to the KGB center in Moscow advising he was missing.

But in another two hours or so the car would be at the German border. The CIA had very efficiently provided him with the necessary documents for the border crossing. He turned to the agent sitting next to him; his fate was now entirely in the hands of the CIA.

In Washington, Helms called a meeting of the Inter-Agency Defector Committee, which included representatives from the State Department, Defense Intelligence Agency, FBI, Office of

Naval Intelligence, G-2, National Security Agency and CIA. These agencies constituted what was loosely called the intelligence community, and they had to be apprised of defectors.

The Director of Central Intelligence was actually empowered by Congress to bring a limited number of defectors to the United States on his own authority, but consultation with the FBI was the accepted practice. When another KGB officer had defected in 1961, the FBI was not immediately informed. Later, when he found out about this defector, J. Edgar Hoover, the FBI Director, exploded, demanding to know why he hadn't been informed. Relations between the two agencies were becoming increasingly strained. President Kennedy tried to resolve the dispute by asking the CIA to coordinate all debriefings of defectors it conducted within the United States which could conceivably bear on domestic security with Hoover's FBI. Helms acceded.

The moment that Hoover heard that a Soviet defector had knowledge of the Oswald case, he told his subordinates in the FBI that they must "dominate the situation." The FBI, not the CIA, should control all parts of the debriefing pertinent to Oswald or the Kennedy assassination. No questions about Oswald were to be put to Nosenko without prior FBI approval. Any report on Nosenko's revelations to the Warren Commission should be made by the FBI. Even at this stage Hoover saw that if Nosenko suggested any sinister relation between Oswald and the Soviets, it could expose a very destructive skeleton in the FBI's closet: what Hoover's private investigation sixteen days after the assassination, had characterized as the "gross incompetence" of the FBI's investigation of Oswald on his return from Russia.

Immediately after the assassination Hoover had wanted to know why Oswald was not on any of the FBI's security indices which included more than 20,000 names of potentially disloyal individuals in the United States. It was known that Oswald had defected to the Soviet Union, offered military secrets, attempted to renounce his citizenship and, after his return consistently told demonstrable lies to the FBI agents who had interviewed him. He had refused to submit to a lie-detector examination on his relations with Soviet intelligence, and he had maintained contact with the Soviet Embassy.

Hoover had ordered Assistant Director J. H. Gale of the Inspection Division to make a full report of "investigative deficiencies in the Oswald case." On December 10, 1963, less than three weeks after the assassination, Gale reported that "Oswald should have been on the Security Index; his wife should have been interviewed before the assassination, and investigation intensified—not held in abeyance—after Oswald contacted the Soviet Embassy in Mexico [in October 1963]."

The last point was especially telling. When Oswald visited the Soviet Embassy in Mexico in October 1963, less than two months before the assassination, the CIA monitored a telephone call in which Oswald made an appointment to see Valery Vladimirovich Kostikov, a "consular officer." This was reported to the FBI.

The FBI knew through a double agent that Kostikov wasn't merely a consular officer of the embassy; he was a high-level officer of the Thirteenth Department of the KGB, heavily involved in controlling saboteurs in Mexico and the United States.

In entering the embassy to meet Kostikov, Oswald had evaded surveillance cameras.[2] Afterward he wrote the Soviet Embassy in Washington that during his trip he had been traveling under a false name and was unable to complete his business "with Comrade Kostin in the Soviet Embassy in Mexico City," because of a mixup at the Cuban Embassy.

The CIA was unable to determine whether this "Kostin" was another name for Kostikov, as it suspected, or an entirely different Russian, operating out of Mexico City. In any case, this letter, which was intercepted by the FBI, suggested that Oswald had been involved in some undercover dealings with Soviet officials in Mexico, Cuba and Washington.

Hoover responded to this report of FBI negligence on December 10 by secretly censuring five field investigative agents, one field supervisor, three special agents in charge, four headquarters supervisors, two headquarters section chiefs, one inspector and William Sullivan, the assistant director of the FBI. When some of the censured FBI executives protested that Oswald had not met the criteria for the Security Index, Hoover wrote back a note stating: "Certainly no one in full possession of all his faculties can claim that Oswald didn't fall within this criteria."

In reviewing Oswald's life prior to the assassination, Gale also concluded—and Hoover concurred—that tighter surveillance of Oswald had been justified "since we did not know definitely whether or not he had any intelligence assignment at that time [from the Soviets]."

Hoover believed that these findings had to be suppressed, and kept secret, if the FBI were to survive. He was so concerned that at one point he wrote that these delinquencies in the investigation of Oswald "have resulted in forever destroying the Bureau as the top level investigative organization." This meant that questions concerning Oswald's connections with Soviet intelligence, even if totally unrelated to the assassination, could not be raised. He thus did not even report to President Johnson that the FBI had an ongoing and open security case involving Oswald at the time of the assassination.

Hoover's line of reasoning was brutally simple. As long as the public could be convinced that Oswald was a lone crackpot, uninvolved in any espionage or subversive activity, the FBI wouldn't be held accountable for not keeping him under surveillance. After all, the FBI was not responsible for crackpots. If, however, the newly appointed Warren Commission suggested that Oswald had any involvement with Soviet or Cuban intelligence, no matter how irrelevant it was to his killing of the President, then there would be no way to keep the FBI's mishandling of the investigation of Oswald prior to the assassination secret, and FBI incompetence would be blamed for the assassination. By an odd twist of fate, the FBI's interest lay in concealing, rather than revealing, any hint of Soviet involvement.

To this end Hoover ordered the Investigative Division of the FBI to "leak" its conclusions that Oswald was the lone assassin to United Press International before the Warren Commission ever had a chance to meet. (In the event things went wrong, Hoover also took the precaution of transferring all the agents involved in the preassassination security case to other posts where they wouldn't be as readily available in case embarrassing questions were asked.)

Now, with Nosenko in a position to elaborate on relations the KGB had had with Oswald, Hoover again had to make sure that no revelations exploded in the FBI's face. He ordered William Sullivan, the assistant director, to check the bureau's sources to see what could be learned about this defector.

In Germany, Nosenko waited for the plane that was to fly him to America. He had been driven directly from Switzerland to a safe house on the outskirts of Frankfurt. He signed the various papers his CIA case officer thrust in front of him. He was told that these constituted his official request for political asylum. He nodded. It was now clear that his defection had succeeded.

On February 9, at a hastily summoned press conference in Washington, D.C., a State Department press officer officially announced that Yuri I. Nosenko had defected from the Soviet disarmament delegation and was now in the United States, where he had been granted political asylum. Both Soviet and Swiss representatives in Washington would be permitted to speak with the former KGB officer so that they could assure their respective governments that he had come to America of his own free will. After these initial news reports Nosenko disappeared from public view.[3]

The Soviet reaction was far more vehement than had been expected. In Geneva, Tsarapkin, who had only two days earlier reported Nosenko's disappearance to the Swiss authorities, denounced the Americans in scathing terms for having "kidnapped" Nosenko.

Such a public denouncement in a defection case was unprecedented. In Moscow, Soviet Foreign Minister Andrei A. Gromyko called U.S. Ambassador Foy Kohler into the Kremlin and, without issuing a formal protest, accused Western intelligence agents of having lured Nosenko to the United States. A woman, identifying herself as Nosenko's wife, appeared at the U.S. Embassy in Moscow (presumably with the knowledge of Soviet authorities) and appealed to Nosenko to return to his loved ones.[4]

The apparent importance of Nosenko's defection was underlined by the flurry of telegrams recalling Soviet diplomats to Moscow from the capitals of Europe, presumably to discuss the revelations Nosenko might be making. There were reports from Eastern Europe that Premier Khrushchev "blew his top" over the case and personally reprimanded his top security officers for allowing the defection.

In Washington, Nosenko's case officer accompanied him to Raleighs haberdashery and waited while he picked out a wardrobe of American clothes. He still had not made up his mind about this enigmatic defector. When he first made contact with him in Geneva in 1962, he thought he had recruited an extremely valuable agent who would work for the CIA in Moscow. For only $300 in cash and the promise that additional money would be held for him in an account in the West, Nosenko had given elaborate information on several major Soviet operations. More important, he would be the only CIA spy working within the vast Second Chief Directorate of the KGB. It had seemed almost too be to good to be true.

Now, in 1964, circumstances had involved Nosenko in the Oswald case and brought him to America. Oddly enough, the defector showed very little interest in the country he had flown to—at least as far as his case officer could see. Nosenko also showed some reluctance to discuss in detail KGB operations. The case officer noticed that he often seemed to be improvising his answers to questions and had a habit of suddenly changing the subject: "Let's have a drink!" A trip to Hawaii was arranged for him—since he showed some interest in escaping the cold— with the idea that a vacation might make him more amenable to questions. But when Nosenko returned to Virginia, the case officer noted, his manner had not changed.

In Washington Hoover read the reports of the CIA debriefing of Nosenko in Geneva with mounting interest. Nosenko's account supported the FBI's conclusion that Oswald was not involved in any sort of espionage activity. Nosenko indicated that the KGB had determined Oswald was "not normal," which fitted in well with Hoover's hypothesis. In a very real sense, Nosenko's story exonerated not only the KGB, but also the FBI by proving that Oswald was not a Soviet agent. The only remaining question was: could Nosenko's story be accepted at face value?

* * *

The FBI had one source, code named Fedora, who was so secret and sensitive that his identity was not immediately disclosed to the CIA, nor was enough contextual information about him turned over to the CIA for its counterintelligence unit to evaluate his bona fides. (In theory, the FBI was supposed to do this as part of its working relationship with the CIA.) Instead, to show the effectiveness of his bureau's intelligence gathering, Hoover sent reports based on Fedora's information directly to the White House.

Fedora, in fact, was a Soviet intelligence agent working under diplomatic cover in New York at the United Nations; he had contacted FBI officials in March 1962 with information about Soviet espionage operations. In his initial meetings with the FBI, Fedora explained that he was an officer of the First Chief Directorate of the KGB and had the mission of collecting information on science and technology from Soviet espionage networks in the United States.

Fedora claimed, however, to be disaffected with the Soviets, and offered to supply the FBI with secret information on Soviet missile capacity and nuclear development plans. Hoover was so taken with his new source that in one report which identified Fedora as "a source of unknown reliability," he personally struck out the "un" from "unknown."

Fedora told the FBI that when Nosenko defected, the KGB center in Moscow was so concerned with the ramifications that it ordered a termination of all operations in New York. Fedora was also able to confirm two important parts of Nosenko's story.

He told his FBI contact that Nosenko was indeed a lieutenant colonel in the KGB, with access to extraordinarily valuable information, and had indeed received a recall telegram from Moscow ordering him back on February 4. This information was passed along to the CIA.

On February 26, FBI agents Maurice A. Taylor, Donald I. Walter and Alekso Poptanich arrived to question Nosenko about the Kennedy assassination and Oswald. Poptanich, of Ukrainian origin, spoke fluent Russian and translated for Nosenko. Nosenko repeated his story with virtually no elaboration or change. Oswald had been allowed to stay in the Soviet Union against the wishes of the KGB, which had had no contacts with Oswald or interest in him whatsoever. The FBI agents returned to the same line of questioning the next day, but Nosenko would not deviate from his original story. They concluded in their report that he had no further information to provide about Oswald or the Kennedy assassination.

Hoover apparently was decided. On March 1, before the Warren Commission had a chance to hear the testimony of the heads of various U.S. government agencies about Oswald's stay in the Soviet Union, Hoover forwarded to the commission the FBI report of Nosenko's statement. The report raised no questions about the reliability of the information or Nosenko's bona fides.

The FBI report on Nosenko did not satisfy the CIA's Soviet Russia Division. It seemed to accept without question KGB procedures for handling an American defector which seemed highly implausible to the CIA's experts. By March 3 the division had formulated forty-four of its own questions (and subquestions) for Nosenko on the Oswald case.[5] Each of the questions was designed to force Nosenko to broaden his basic statement about the KGB's relation with Oswald.

The interrogatives attempted to establish how Nosenko and the KGB initially became involved with Oswald. They thus asked: "When and how did Oswald first come to KGB attention? Was his visa application in Helsinki processed by the KGB in Helsinki? In Moscow? Describe routine handling procedure of U.S. tourists to the Soviet Union? Was Oswald's trip handled any differently?"

The point of concern here was that Oswald had followed what seemed to be a well-prepared defection plan in getting to the Soviet Embassy in Helsinki. In similar defection cases the KGB had advance knowledge and laid the groundwork. In this case, however, Nosenko asserted that the KGB had not heard of Oswald until *after* he appeared in Moscow in 1959.

The CIA experts preparing the questions wondered why the Helsinki Embassy processing the visa request had not informed the KGB officer in Helsinki, as was then the normal process. It also seemed possible that Oswald had told the Soviets in Helsinki that he planned to defect and turn over military secrets

—he admitted at the American Embassy in Moscow that he had made this offer to the Soviets, though he did not specify if it was before or after he had arrived in Moscow—and in this case KGB awareness of the case in Helsinki would seem almost mandatory.

Another detailed question focused on Oswald's request for Soviet citizenship: ". . . How was Oswald's bona fides established? How was the sincerity of his request tested? How was his operational potential investigated and evaluated? Did the KGB ever think that Oswald might be an agent of American intelligence? If so, how did it go about investigating this possibility? Describe as fully as possible the KGB elements involved, the KGB personnel involved, the progressive steps taken, the time required?"

Behind this question was the assumption that a citizenship request from an American citizen would have to be meticulously assessed by the KGB. For one thing, it would have to be established that Oswald was indeed the ex-Marine he claimed to be—and not a CIA agent. If the KGB followed the procedures used in other cases, an effort would be made to check what record there was of him in the United States.

Next, he would be asked to prove his sincerity by giving statements on areas of his life in America which were of interest to the KGB. And then some evaluation would be made of his use as either an agent, a propagandist-agitator, or a Soviet citizen. These, at least, were the procedures followed in other defection cases. Yet Nosenko had hardly touched on this entire area in his debriefings.

The next question attempted to explore the relation of the Second Chief Directorate, which handled the security aspects of the Oswald case, and the First Chief Directorate, which would expectedly be involved in any decision to use Oswald abroad as a spy.

It asked: "When and by whom was it decided that the KGB had no interest in Oswald? Was this the decision of the Second Chief Directorate alone, or was the First Chief Directorate consulted? Which element of the Second Chief Directorate was responsible for Oswald after the decision had been made to grant him a residence permit?"

Another question pressed for information on the subject of

Oswald's debriefing, which Nosenko had so far denied ever took place. "Did Oswald ever offer to give information on the U.S. Marine Corps or other matters to the Soviets? If the KGB did not try to get such information from him, why not?"

Almost a quarter of the questions dealt with Oswald's wife, Marina, about whom Nosenko had said very little.

For example, one question asked: "How did it happen that there were so few difficulties in the way of Marina's marriage to a foreigner and departure from the country with him? Have not similar situations in the past usually resulted in prolonged and often unsuccessful negotiations with the Soviet government? What level of the government or Party would make the final decision regarding Marina's marriage to Oswald and their departure from the country? What official briefings would Marina have received prior to her departure?"

The questions were hand carried over to the FBI for the approval Hoover required. However, to the dismay of the CIA, Hoover refused the request. The FBI liaison stated flatly that the forty-four questions "would not be asked."

On March 9 the CIA's Soviet Russia Division "protested the decision not to ask our questions." The FBI liaison reiterated that Hoover was adamant "that the FBI should handle the matter and our questions would not be asked." The most he would suggest was that eventually the FBI might cover these areas.

The CIA officer supervising the investigation immediately dictated a memorandum stating, "I indicated that I had no confidence in the FBI's ability to cover the Soviet phase. I indicated that it would *not* be possible to complete our job in the Oswald case if we could not get the pertinent information." (Emphasis in original text.) The furor over Nosenko had begun.

The Warren Commission was unaware of the gaps in Nosenko's story—or of the CIA's attempt to fill them in with its forty-four questions. W. David Slawson, a soft-spoken lawyer from Denver on the commission staff, carefully reviewed the March 1 FBI report on Nosenko and made a number of handwritten notes on a yellow pad. He jotted down that Nosenko had reported "Oswald *unknown* to KGB—October 1959. . . . Virtually all Oswald's contacts at Hotel Berlin and

Metropole were KGB informants. . . . No other Soviet Agency could have made use of Oswald without clearing with KGB. . . . No separate KGB file on Marina."

At this very time the commission's staff was becoming increasingly concerned with problems and contradictions in the testimony of Marina Oswald. She had insisted that she did not know the name of her own father and provided only minimal information about her relatives.

The uncle with whom Marina lived in Minsk prior to her marriage to Oswald was a lieutenant colonel in the Ministry of Internal Affairs (MVD), which had responsibility for internal security in Russia. Yet Marina declared that he had not intervened on her or Oswald's behalf with Soviet authorities to facilitate either her marriage or her exit visa from Russia.

More seriously, it was now clear that she had lied to the FBI during its interrogation of her during a ten-week period following the assassination. She admitted destroying a photograph of Oswald with his weapon the day after the assassination. She had withheld evidence indicating that Oswald had attempted to assassinate Major General Edwin Walker seven months before he killed Kennedy. She had falsely denied that she knew about Oswald's trip to Mexico in 1963.

Norman Redlich, the staff lawyer responsible for the preparation of the questioning of Oswald's widow for the commission, summed up in a memorandum that "Marina Oswald has lied to the Secret Service, the FBI and this commission repeatedly on matters which are of vital concern to the people of this country and the world."[6]

Chief Justice Warren, however, ruled out any attempt to test her story either through the use of a lie detector or through threats of punitive legal actions. Some staff members believed that possibly she had committed a felony when she had lied to the FBI after the assassination or when she had destroyed evidence. But as Warren explained to the staff, it would make little sense for the commission to impugn the credibility of its chief witness on the character of Oswald.

The commission also decided to reject a set of highly specific interrogatives that had been drafted by the CIA for the Soviet government. These questions were designed to elicit from the Soviets, if they chose to reply, key details about the procedures under which Oswald had been processed and controlled during his two and one-half years in the Soviet Union. For example, one question asked for the memoranda and minutes of the meetings concerning Oswald's request for Soviet citizenship.

The State Department, however, strongly resisted this detailed set of questions. A February 24 commission memorandum summed up the objections as follows: "The State Department has commented that in its opinion the CIA draft would have serious adverse diplomatic effects. The State Department feels that the CIA draft carries an inference that we suspect that Oswald might have been an agent for the Soviet Government and that we are asking the Russian Government to document our suspicions."

Specifically, the State Department pointed to the danger that the trap questions might succeed in forcing the Soviets to falsify records, rather than make embarrassing admissions, and this would create a crisis for the American government which it was not prepared to deal with. Could, for example, the Soviet government be accused of lying in the Warren Report?

Instead, the State Department proposed that the commission send "a very short and simple request for whatever information the Russian authorities" had available on Oswald. Chief Justice Warren concurred with this view.

By March it was becoming clear to the commission that Nosenko was the only available witness who could shed any information of value on the KGB's involvement, or noninvolvement, with the President's assassin. At this point, however, what the commission members did not know was that the CIA had serious doubts about Nosenko's authenticity. These doubts actually predated Nosenko's revelations about Oswald. They arose, in fact, from information Nosenko had supplied about other cases since his original contact with the CIA in 1962.

Angleton's Assessment

The man in the CIA who was perhaps most concerned with the implications of Nosenko's defection was James Jesus Angleton. As Chief of Counterintelligence, it was his responsibility to guard against foreign intelligence services attempting to affect the plans of the American government by providing "disinformation" to the CIA. In intelligence terms, disinformation is not merely false information, but a message or set of messages designed to mislead or manipulate a government. One of the most effective means for supplying such information is through a double agent, who pretends to change sides in order to add credibility to his message. For information about Soviet intentions, the CIA is almost wholly dependent on Soviet intelligence agents and military officers who declare they have changed their allegiance, or who have been "doubled." Therefore, it is crucially important for the CIA to ferret out the fake double agents supplying disinformation.

Ghostly thin, with prematurely silver hair and a finely sculptured face, Angleton was a man uniquely suited to this convoluted pursuit. Before joining the intelligence service, he had edited the poetry magazine *Furioso* and had worked closely with such poets as Ezra Pound, T. S. Eliot and e. e. cummings. His avocation was propagating his own hybrid orchids from seed, a process requiring seven years of patient waiting to see the results of his planning.

In evaluating defectors from adversary intelligence services, Angleton believed cases could not be viewed in isolation. They had to be analyzed in relation to the bits and pieces of information coming from the enemy over an extended period of time. He knew that Soviet intelligence had the capacity for mounting highly sophisticated disinformation programs with a whole array of dispatched defectors and double agents feeding information to other intelligence services.[7] For Angleton, unravelling such a deception was an intellectual challenge of the first order.

Ever since Nosenko had first approached the CIA in Geneva in 1962 and volunteered information about Soviet espionage operations, Angleton and his staff had pondered the significance of the offer. Only six months before Nosenko's contact, another Soviet intelligence officer, Anatoli M. Golitsin, had defected to the CIA from Helsinki, Finland. Golitsin, who identified himself as a major in the First Chief Directorate of the KGB working primarily against targets in the NATO alliance, was brought to Washington and given the code name Stone.

The information Stone provided in his debriefing had caused

a sensation. According to Stone, the KGB had already planted an agent within the highest echelons of United States intelligence. This penetration agent would be assisted by "outside" men—other Soviet-controlled agents masking themselves as defectors or double agents—who would supply pieces of disinformation designed to bolster an "inside" man's credibility. The "inside" agent, in turn, would be in a position to help confirm the authenticity of the "outside" agents.

Angleton could not afford to neglect this possibility. He knew that the Soviet Union had successfully penetrated both the British and the West German intelligence services in the years since World War II.[8] The specter of a "mole," or enemy agent, burrowing his way into the heart of an American intelligence service caused such consternation in the CIA and FBI that a personal interview was arranged for Stone to brief Attorney General Robert F. Kennedy.

During his debriefing sessions with Angleton in 1962 Stone had called particular attention to a trip made by V. M. Kovshuk to the United States in 1957 under diplomatic cover, using the alias Komarov. Stone identified Kovshuk as the then-reigning head of the all-important American Embassy Section of the KGB and stressed that only an extremely important mission would account for his leaving his post in Moscow to come to the United States. He suggested that Kovshuk's mission might have involved contacting or activating a high-level Soviet penetration agent working within the CIA who had been recruited years before in Moscow.

Stone had further cautioned that the KGB, realizing that he knew about Kovshuk's mission, would almost certainly attempt to discredit or deflect the CIA from the information he was providing. He warned Angleton that Soviet disinformation agents could be expected to make contact with the CIA for this purpose.

Then, in June of 1962, Nosenko had contacted the CIA. Angleton found that the information Nosenko was providing coincided very curiously with what Stone had revealed. Nosenko, for example, claimed to have been Kovshuk's deputy in the KGB, and therefore, in a unique position to know about his trip to America.

But whereas Stone suggested that Kovshuk had gone to see a

Soviet agent working in the CIA, Nosenko said that Kovshuk's agent, who had been assigned the code name Andrey, was actually recruited from American military personnel attached to the Embassy in Moscow. Now, in 1964, Nosenko provided a further clue that this American had worked in the motor pool at the Embassy in the early 1950s—a clue which made the man's identification inevitable. What concerned Angleton was not the identity of this motor pool mechanic, but rather the possibility that he—Andrey—might be a red herring which Nosenko had deliberately put across the trail of Kovshuk to deflect any investigation from a KGB penetration of the CIA.

These concerns of Angleton were heightened by the unravelling of the Sasha case. In 1962, Stone had told of the Soviet recruitment of an American agent who was assigned the code name Sasha; the clues he provided pointed to a CIA contract employee working in West Germany. Then, considerably later, in 1964, Nosenko also told the CIA officers debriefing him about the agent Sasha. But he identified Sasha as an Army officer. For some time, this bit of information threw the CIA off the track of its contract employee (who was later photographed making contact with the Soviet Embassy). It was, for the CIA, a clear case of deflection.

In two cases, Nosenko's information led to the identification and capture of enemy agents. The first concerned a KGB spy in the British Admiralty. Stone had told about this penetration in 1962, a few months before Nosenko contacted the CIA. An investigation pointed to the traitor as one of four people. Nosenko provided the information which enabled the British to apprehend the spy, John Vassall.

The second case involved a major KGB operation in France by means of which military secrets were being taken from a courier station at Orly Airport outside Paris. U.S. military intelligence had, in 1963, received information which alleged that an Army sergeant, Robert Lee Johnson, was involved in Soviet intelligence. But because of a bureaucratic error, the case had not been pursued. The sergeant, however, had lost his access to military secrets at the courier station, and Soviet intelligence had every reason to believe that he was known to U.S. intelligence. Now, in 1964, Nosenko said that he had heard in Moscow that enormously important NATO secrets were coming from a source near Paris. This further tip immediately led to the arrest of Sergeant Johnson.

As Angleton saw it, Nosenko was providing information that was "dated," meaning information which the Soviets would assume to have already been compromised. He tried to assess whether Nosenko was providing dated information by design, or whether he was disclosing original information which happened to coincide with what Stone and other sources had revealed. Angleton considered it odd that two men from entirely different branches of the KGB would know of so many of the same operations. Such an overlay raised the possibility that Nosenko's revelations in 1962 might have been designed by the Soviets to deflect from the leads Stone had provided.

Angleton, a man who meticulously planned environments so perfectly that he could manipulate the design of his own prize-winning orchids, was not inclined to believe in chance coincidences. Yet, as he received the new CIA reports, he saw that to believe Nosenko's story about Oswald one would have to accept a series of even more remarkable coincidences: the coincidence that Nosenko, the first agent the CIA ever had in the Second Chief Directorate, turned out to be the supervisor of the Oswald file; and the coincidence that Nosenko had been chosen to conduct the post-assassination investigation into the KGB's relation with Oswald—which meant that he was picked to investigate his own handling of a case.

Indeed, Nosenko claimed to be in a position to know of each and every contact the KGB had—and did not have—with Oswald over a four-year period, and from this vantage point he could definitively exonerate the KGB from having any relation with Oswald.

Such coincidences Angleton was not ready to accept at face value.

Through his thick horn-rimmed glasses, Angleton studied the transcript of Nosenko's account of Oswald in the Soviet Union. He was particularly troubled by the claim that Oswald had never been debriefed by any part of the Soviet intelligence apparatus. According to Newton S. Miler, chief of operations of counterintelligence, this assertion was "particularly hard to swallow." He pointed out that in 1959, the KGB was reorganizing its espionage apparatus in an effort to overcome the techno-logical advantage the United States had over the USSR. Radar was a target, and Oswald had identified himself as a radar oper-ator. "Not to debrief him . . . defies logic and known KGB his-tory," the chief of operations subsequently commented.[9] More-over, Stone had previously explained in detail that in the case of a military defector or one even with military experience, the Thirteenth Department of the First Chief Directorate would have the primary responsibility for the debriefing.

When the KGB was created in 1954, the Thirteenth Depart-ment was assigned the function of sabotage and assassinations abroad, and it therefore had a special interest in debriefing mili-tary defectors who might be capable of participating in such operations. Oswald, who had served for nearly three years in the U.S. Marines with an Air Control Squadron in Japan, the Philippines, Taiwan and California—and who had repeatedly stated in Moscow that he was willing to provide the Soviets with American secrets—certainly would qualify as a military defector.

In addition, the Soviets had Oswald in the palms of their hands in Moscow; it was known that he had verbally renounced his citizenship before the American consul, severed his relations with his family in America and left himself penniless and com-pletely at the mercy of the Soviets. Why wouldn't he be de-briefed for all he was worth? Angleton reasoned.

Under the procedures Stone described, the Thirteenth De-partment would have had a hand in the debriefings, and Nosenko, if he were who he claimed to be, would have known of them. Why would Nosenko obscure such a procedure? Of course, in the light of the Kennedy assassination, Angleton had little doubt that if Oswald had had any contact with the Thir-teenth Department, even if it were only a brief interview, the KGB would go to great lengths to conceal it.

When Angleton questioned Stone about Nosenko, Stone con-firmed that Nosenko was an officer of the KGB, but insisted that he could not have held the position he claimed as deputy chief of the Tourist Department, or Stone would have known him. More importantly, Stone asserted that Nosenko could not have been in the American Embassy Department in 1960 and 1961, since Stone paid frequent visits there and would have seen him.

In addition, Nosenko claimed to have been a close friend of General Oleg M. Gribanov, who at that time headed the entire Second Chief Directorate of the KGB. Stone questioned this relationship. In short, according to Stone, Nosenko's career could not have been what he said it was.

Now, with Nosenko in Washington, Angleton carefully considered the situation. Aside from breeding orchids, he was a superbly patient trout fisherman. He played defectors much like trout. He called the process elicitation: All defectors—whether fake or real—should be carefully played out for whatever information they possessed. In the contest between intelligence agencies, discovering the disinformation which the enemy was attempting to plant was in many ways as important as any real information which might be divulged.

The Breaking of a Legend

While Angleton was carefully scrutinizing the Nosenko case in the context of other information he had, the CIA's Soviet Russia Division threw its resources into a direct investigation of the basic points of Nosenko's story. Angleton's staff had already passed on to the division Stone's doubts about Nosenko holding the position he had claimed in the KGB. With these doubts in mind, the division's investigators began to reconstruct Nosenko's putative career in the KGB. He claimed to have risen from the rank of captain to lieutenant colonel in fewer than four years. Yet, when the investigators asked him to name the concrete achievements on his part that had led to such rapid promotion, he was unable to cite any successes which would account for this rise in rank.

At first, Nosenko attributed his successes solely to his friendship with General Gribanov, the head of the Second Chief Directorate. Then, under intensive questioning about his relation with Gribanov, he recanted and said he had had no special relation with the general.

Why then had he been promoted to lieutenant colonel? they pressed.

Finally, Nosenko admitted that he had lied about his rank. He had never been promoted to lieutenant colonel, or even major (as he had claimed in 1962). In fact, he was only a captain. He further admitted that he had never been given any special commendation by the chairman of the KGB, as he had also claimed. He explained that he had lied about his rank to make himself more acceptable as a defector to the CIA.

The Soviet Russia Division's investigators knew that it was not uncommon for defectors to exaggerate their importance—it meant more money and attention and increased the chance they would be given asylum in the United States. The fact that Nosenko had claimed in 1964 that he was a lieutenant colonel was understandable in these terms.

But, in 1962, when he had first contacted the CIA, he had claimed he was a major. Why would he have lied then, when he had said categorically that he would never defect?

Nosenko could not explain the discrepancy.

When Nosenko appeared in Geneva in 1964, he had among his papers a Soviet travel document which had authorized him to be in Gorki in November 1963. Nosenko had already explained that the reason he had been in Gorki was because he had participated in a nationwide "All-Union manhunt" for a traitor named Cherepanov. This man, he said, had been caught, secretly tried and executed.

The name was well known to the CIA. In October 1963, a man named Cherepanov had unexpectedly sent a package of documents, with a tourist, to the American Embassy in Moscow. Cherepanov had never previously been in contact with the CIA. He worked, according to the documents, in the same American Embassy Section of the Second Chief Directorate of the KGB in which Nosenko claimed to have worked. Until Nosenko made contact in 1962, the CIA had never had an agent from the staff of the Second Chief Directorate; now suddenly there were two people volunteering information from the same section.

The Cherepanov papers, which dealt mainly with surveillance techniques, dovetailed perfectly with a story Nosenko had told in his first meeting with the CIA in 1962. This story concerned Peter Semyonovich Popov, a lieutenant colonel in Soviet military intelligence. Popov had been arrested by the KGB in 1959 and was subsequently executed as a spy for the CIA. (Popov's undoing, according to Nosenko, had been a note which had been mailed to him at a false address by an American diplomat who had been followed to the mailbox.) Nosenko claimed that the KGB had developed a method of painting a chemical substance on a subject's shoe which left an invisible trail that could be followed without arousing his suspicion. This new technique enabled the Soviets to follow the American diplomat to a letterbox, which was then watched until Popov picked the letter up. To prove that he had known of the surveillance, Nosenko even named the diplomat who had mailed the fatal letter.[10] Within the Cherepanov papers was a note explaining that Popov had been arrested through surveillance; the explanation completely coincided with that given by Nosenko.

The question of how Popov had been captured by the KGB was of crucial importance to the CIA. Only two possibilities existed: either he had been detected through some Soviet security precaution, or else someone privy to the CIA operation involving Popov had betrayed him. Again, the information provided by Nosenko (and Cherepanov) deflected from the idea of a betrayal within the CIA.

The CIA knew that the Cherepanov papers had been immediately photographed by the embassy staff. Then, because of some bureaucratic failing (or suspicion that a trap was being baited), the American Embassy returned the documents to the Soviet ministry, allowing them to identify Cherepanov from the distribution list on the papers.

Within the CIA there was considerable speculation about whether the Cherepanov papers were authentic or an attempt to manipulate the CIA by planting disinformation. By holding this travel document, Nosenko was, in effect, proving that the Cherepanov papers were authentic—or else why hunt the man down and execute him? In addition, Nosenko established his rank as lieutenant colonel and his position in the KGB, which were typed out on the travel document; and finally, by implication, he confirmed his own story about Popov.[11]

The interrogators now concentrated on this travel document. It had been issued by the KGB. Why would it list his rank incorrectly? Nosenko was asked.

"Some clerk made a mistake," he answered. He suggested the clerk might have been new at his job.

To the experts at the Soviet Russia Division such a mistake seemed almost impossible to accept. Moreover, an expert on

KGB procedures determined that Nosenko's possession of the travel document was in itself extremely suspicious. The mandatory procedure in the KGB was for officers to turn in their travel documents in order to be reimbursed for the expenses involved in their Russian travels. Why had Nosenko retained the travel document?

Nosenko was unable to explain.

Since the document falsely identified Nosenko as a lieutenant colonel, and its provenance was suspect, the possibility that it was fabricated in order to provide evidence of Nosenko's importance had to be considered.

But if the document was spurious, then the reason he gave for possessing it—the national manhunt for the traitor Cherepanov —also had to be questioned.

Nosenko had claimed he had been part of the manhunt for Cherepanov because he had known and worked with him in the American Embassy Section of the KGB in 1960. The CIA checked the operational file on Cherepanov. The only mention of his existence before he handed a package of documents to an American in Moscow in 1963 was a report that he had approached British intelligence in Yugoslavia in the late 1950s. Cherepanov had then offered to act as a double agent. The British, however, had decided that this was a KGB "provocation," and they had cut off contact. From this brief file, it was clear that Cherepanov had then been working for the First Chief Directorate, which handles agents outside the Soviet Union.

The interrogators asked Nosenko: How did Cherepanov get from the First Chief Directorate to the American Embassy Section of the Second Chief Directorate?

Nosenko said he was familiar with the case. He had heard that Cherepanov had a "problem." He was suspected of contacting the British in Yugoslavia for treasonous purposes.

What had happened when the KGB found out about these approaches?

He was "booted out" of the First Chief Directorate, Nosenko answered.

But how did he get into the Second Chief Directorate?

Nosenko shrugged. He said that officials in the Second Chief Directorate felt sorry for Cherepanov and gave him a job.

The explanation made no sense to the interrogators. That a

KGB agent suspected of being a traitor would be dismissed from one department and then given a job in the supersecret (American Embassy) section of another KGB department defied belief.

The second major crack in Nosenko's story appeared when a team of code breakers from the National Security Agency, which specializes in intercepting and decoding the messages of foreign nations, scrutinized the cable traffic between Geneva and Moscow during the period in which Nosenko claimed to have received a recall telegram from Moscow. Through their own devices and an extensive word count, the team was able to establish that no telegram had been sent to the Soviet delegation in Geneva on the day Nosenko claimed it arrived.

Up to that point the recall telegram had provided Nosenko with a plausible motive for demanding that the CIA arrange his escape to America. If the telegram was a fabrication, as the National Security Agency team suggested, then a new motive would have to be found for the timing of his defection.

The interrogators hammered away at the circumstances of the recall telegram. They asked Nosenko to repeat the message word for word and, closing the trap, pinned him down on the exact day, hour and length of the telegram.

At first, Nosenko stuck to his story, repeating confidently how the telegram forced his decision to defect. Then, as the questioning continued to focus on the telegram, he grew more hesitant in reiterating its contents and meaning. Finally, confronted with the fact that the CIA had determined no such telegram had been sent, Nosenko admitted that he had fabricated the whole story about the telegram. He explained that he feared the CIA would insist that he continue as a defector in place.

The Soviet Russia Division had now established that Nosenko had deliberately lied about his rank and motive for defecting. In itself, such dissembling did not prove that he was not an authentic defector simply attempting to enhance his standing (with the false rank) and the urgency of his case (with the false telegram). In this case, however, these untrue elements in Nosenko's story had been "verified" by Fedora, the Soviet intelligence agent in New York who was working as a double agent for the FBI.

The CIA began examining more closely Fedora's claim that the Nosenko defection carried such importance for the KGB that all operations had been suspended in New York. Curiously enough, a KGB operation known to Nosenko (and the CIA) was continuing in February and March in Switzerland. It seemed inconceivable to the CIA interrogators that all Soviet espionage would be suspended in New York, about which Nosenko had virtually no knowledge, while a case in Switzerland, where he had served, continued.

To the CIA investigators, it appeared that Fedora was trying to bolster Nosenko's credentials. This heightened suspicions among the counterintelligence staff about Fedora's own mission. Why, they reasoned, would Fedora attempt to verify false elements of Nosenko's story unless he was a controlled channel being used by the KGB to pass disinformation to the FBI?

Presumably Nosenko would have self-serving reasons for building a legend for himself as a lieutenant colonel pursued by the KGB, but why would the KGB confirm this legend? The only hypothesis the Soviet Russia Division could come up with to explain this strange case was that the KGB was behind Nosenko's story.

Both Angleton and the Soviet Russia Division thus began independently to explore the possibility that the man called Nosenko was actually a Soviet agent dispatched by the KGB to pose as a defector.

Only a few miles from downtown Washington, in a secluded house in the suburban countryside, Nosenko faced a blank wall and answered yes or no to a series of questions that by now had been asked a number of times: his full name, his rank in the KGB, whether he had worked in the Tourist Department, whether he had supervised the file on Lee Harvey Oswald and so on. His left wrist was wrapped in a rubber sleeve. His chest was encircled by a corrugated tube. His right palm was strapped to a metal plate. A sensor in the sleeve measured his blood pressure; the corrugated tube measured his rate of breathing; the metal plate measured his rate of perspiration. Wires ran from each of these instruments to three penlike devices, which charted three continuous lines on a rolling sheet of graph paper. Changes in these three body functions could be seen in relation to each question he answered.

This was the first time that Nosenko had been subjected to a lie detector—or what the CIA called fluttering. The Soviet Union did not use such devices for interrogation. The battery of questions took about an hour; then the CIA operator from the Office of Security disconnected the sensors from Nosenko's body and told him he could go back to his room, which was guarded around the clock by other CIA security men.

At CIA headquarters the results of Nosenko's fluttering were carefully analyzed by experts. On key questions, including those concerned with Oswald, Nosenko had shown the sort of emotional stress usually associated with deception. According to the evaluation by the Office of Security, Nosenko had failed his first lie-detector test. However, as the Office of Security always pointed out, such stress reactions could be measuring other emotions than those caused by lying.

The Soviet Russia Division of the CIA put little value on the results of lie-detector examinations; its investigators believed that only a time-consuming investigation would prove, or disprove, Nosenko's story. This would require virtually every assertion of Nosenko's being tested against whatever evidence could be drawn from previous defectors, spies in place, diplomats and other sources.

Every name Nosenko mentioned would have to be traced through the CIA's computer system. Every revelation would have to be compared to previously known information to determine if it was dated and thus valueless from the Soviets' point of view. And finally, the story Nosenko was telling about Oswald would have to be checked against the information the Warren Commission's investigation was producing.

The first step would be to ask Nosenko to handwrite his autobiography. (Handwriting could also be subjected to stress analysis.) He was told to include every name, no matter how seemingly insignificant, of every individual he had met in his career.

The Soviet Russia Division began probing deeper into the putative career Nosenko outlined in his autobiographical sketch. He claimed that for four years—1953–1955 and 1960–1961—he had worked primarily against employees of the American Embassy in Moscow. During the earlier period he gave as his "primary target" a colonel who was a military attaché at the embassy. Yet he was not able to provide any details about the case; nor was he able to recognize his "target's" photograph.

Nosenko was asked, "What finally happened to the colonel?"

He asserted that nothing eventful happened in this particular case. The colonel finished his tour at the American Embassy and routinely returned to the United States.

His interrogators were stunned. In fact, this particular attaché had been caught by the Soviets in the act of receiving documents from a Soviet citizen in Stalingrad—an offer which the CIA had presumed was a KGB provocation—and expelled from the Soviet Union as *persona non grata*. Since the surveillance (and compromising) of this American could be done only by the American Embassy Section of the KGB, which Nosenko claimed to be in, it seemed difficult, if not impossible, to believe that he would not know about this incident—especially since it involved his primary target.

Gradually, as Nosenko's memory proved faulty on other details of the operation of this KGB unit during this period, the interrogators began to suspect that Nosenko could not have been an officer in the American Embassy Section of the KGB's Second Chief Directorate from 1953 to 1955.

The interrogators next turned to the later period he claimed to have served in this section—from January 1960 to the end of 1961. Among other things Nosenko described in detail how his "boys" staked out a "dubok," or hole, used as a dead drop (or hiding place for secret messages) for American intelligence agents in Moscow. He explained that as deputy chief of the section he received daily reports of the surveillance of this location in the first few months of 1961.

His interrogators checked back into the records of the Soviet Russia Division. The dead drop at the precise location Nosenko described was indeed established by the CIA in Moscow for Colonel Oleg Penkovskiy,[12]—a GRU officer who had spied for the British and Americans between 1960 and 1962 and then was captured and executed by the Soviets. After Popov's death, Penkovskiy had become the CIA's prime source of secret information about the Soviet Union. Of course, the Soviet Russia Division was eager to hear anything that would explain how he had been compromised.

The only problem with Nosenko's account was that it was one

year out of date. The dead drop had been set up at the end of 1961, when Nosenko, by his own career description, was transferred back to the Tourist Department. He was asked: How could he have received daily reports on the dead drop when he was no longer in the American Embassy Section?

"You must be wrong about the dates," Nosenko answered.

"*How* can we be wrong? *It was our operation!* We *know* when it was set up," one interrogator shot back. And another question remained: why had he not mentioned this important matter when he had first approached the CIA in June 1962, when the Penkovskiy case was still active?

Again Nosenko had no explanation. He seemed tired by the repeated questions.

Later in the interrogation Nosenko was asked about the physical layout of the American Embassy. He was asked which of the floors in the embassy were used by the Americans for classified work.

After a long hesitation he answered, "The top two floors."

The interrogators, knowing full well that Nosenko had missed an entire floor in his answer, repeated the question. Certainly, if he was the deputy head of the American Embassy Section, he should know that the top *three* floors were used for secret work.

He again answered incorrectly.

He was then shown blueprints of the embassy and asked to point out the location of the microphones secreted there by the Soviets (who had built the embassy for the Americans). He identified seventeen areas in the old section of the embassy but the existence of these microphones had already been pointed to by Stone and others.

He was asked: What about the new wing?

Nosenko answered that he was certain there were no microphones installed in that part of the embassy. He explained that construction delays had prevented the KGB from ever putting in microphones there.

Subsequently the CIA found that there were no fewer than 134 microphones installed in this section by the Soviets.

Finally, the interrogators from the Soviet Russia Division were driven toward the baffling conclusion that Nosenko had never worked in the American Embassy Section of the Second Chief Directorate. They even began considering the possibility that he might never have been involved in the cases he claimed to have handled, but was merely an empty receptacle into which KGB briefing officers had poured the information and disinformation—which they wanted him to carry to the West.[13]

Angleton called in the FBI liaison, Sam Papich. Papich, a large man with a genial smile, puffed incessantly on his pipe as he listened to James Angleton articulate the elements of doubt the CIA had in the Nosenko case. Papich had been in counterintelligence in the FBI since World War II, and now, as FBI liaison to the CIA, it was his job to listen, then report back to Hoover. He had come to view Angleton as an extraordinarily gifted analyst of intelligence problems, but he also knew that he was a man who naturally tended toward the arcane rather than the simple solution. That was Angleton's job as counterintelligence chief: to suspect everyone and everything of being more devious than they seemed on the surface.

Papich understood Angleton's analysis of Nosenko, but that didn't mean it would persuade his chief, J. Edgar Hoover, that Nosenko was a disinformation agent. The fact that Nosenko had lied about a number of matters, including his rank and recall telegram, might simply mean that he was not someone of high personal integrity. The fact that the information he provided for the most part coincided with the information that Stone had given might simply mean that both men had had access to the same information. The fact that Nosenko interpreted it differently from Stone might simply stem from a different bureaucratic perspective. The fact that he had imperfect knowledge of the Oswald case might have meant he had exaggerated his own importance within the KGB—or had a bad memory. Papich had never believed in making gods out of defectors.

Papich also knew that Hoover was already committed to believing Nosenko. Whatever one said about the integrity or memory of this defector, Hoover would point to a long list of names of college professors, businessmen, journalists and tourists who, Nosenko had told the FBI, were targets of KGB efforts to compromise or recruit. This would provide the FBI with numerous cases to investigate—and possibly a few arrests.

Nosenko had also provided leads to a major Soviet espionage ring stealing NATO documents from Orly Airport in France. Why would he provide such information unless he was authentic? Hoover would argue. (Angleton would retort that this particular Soviet operation had been put on ice one year earlier as insecure and the Soviets were only "burning" useless or former agents, but Papich knew such a secondary line of analysis would not be acceptable to Hoover.)

Most important, however, Nosenko confirmed the FBI investigation of Oswald—both *before* and after the assassination. If Nosenko's story were accepted, the FBI would be less likely to be charged with any sort of dereliction of duty in not keeping Oswald on their security indices before the assassination, since neither Oswald nor his wife had had connections with Soviet intelligence. On the other hand, if Nosenko's story proved false, it would leave open the question of Oswald's relation to the KGB, and by doing so, it would also leave open the question of why Oswald had not been kept under tighter surveillance by the FBI on his return from Russia.

Despite the risk of incurring Hoover's wrath, Papich decided to present forcefully the CIA's doubts about Nosenko. That he had always taken to be his job as liaison. Hoover listened stone-faced, without comment or argument. After hearing Papich out, he thanked him for conveying the information. He then ordered that the FBI report to the Warren Commission which simply summarized Nosenko's version of Oswald in Russia, and mentioned none of the reservations—remain unchanged.

The Warren Commission, meanwhile, was racing to meet June deadline for winding up its investigation. The commission had been appointed by President Lyndon Johnson to dispel rumors of conspiracy. When he persuaded the Chief Justice to head the commission, the President argued that unless an end were quickly put to such speculation, there could be dangerous consequences, including war.[14] Each team of lawyers was given three months to conduct its basic investigation, and, by the spring of 1964 all were being told emphatically that the time had come to close, rather than open, doors.

Questions concerning Oswald's residence in the Soviet Union and possible connections with Soviet intelligence fell into the bailiwick of William Coleman, Jr., a highly respected Philadelphia lawyer (who later served under President Ford as Secretary of Transportation), and W. David Slawson. Their area was "Foreign Conspiracies," and in May they drafted their basic report, entitled "Oswald's Foreign Activities: Summary of Evidence Which Might Be Said to Show That There Was Foreign Involvement in the Assassination of President Kennedy."

In reviewing the problem of whether or not Oswald had had any relations with Soviet intelligence, Coleman and Slawson found "a high proportion of all the evidence on Lee Harvey Oswald which relates to his travels to and life in Russia derived from sources that could have been fabricated or otherwise falsified . . . by the KGB or be the result of its careful 'coaching.' "

The Soviet government, in replying to the commission's request for whatever information it had on the Oswald case failed to send any statements of individuals who had known Oswald in Russia. And in the few documents the Soviets did turn over to the commission, CIA translators found that an extremely high percentage of the signatures of Soviet officials on the documents were either illegible or missing. This, in turn, prevented the CIA from using its normal methods of tracing the officials on their computers to verify if they were indeed in the positions and cities indicated by the documents. According to the CIA liaison to the commission, the Soviet documents could be assumed to be no more than a "sham effort."

Given these evidentiary problems, Coleman and Slawson posed a critical question for the commission in their draft report: "How are we to assess whether or not what we know of Oswald's 'real life' is not just a 'legend' designed by the KGB and lived out by Oswald thereafter?"

The only answer they had was the FBI report on Nosenko. Should he be called as a witness before the commission? Coleman and Slawson noted in their report: "Nosenko, if he is sincere, would provide a conclusive answer."

This represented a far deeper issue in the intelligence community than the lawyers on the Warren Commission were cleared to know about. If Nosenko was *not* sincere, as evidence amassed by the CIA now seemed to indicate, it suggested that the Soviet government was building a legend meant to deceive the Warren Commission about Oswald. But in what way?

Neither Angleton's shop nor the Soviet Russia Division believed that Oswald was acting under the control of Soviet intelligence when he assassinated the President. (In fact, circumstantial evidence seemed to diminish that possibility.) It seemed far more likely to both that the relationship Nosenko was attempting to protect might be a prior connection Oswald had had with the KGB.

Under this hypothesis, Nosenko would have been sent, among other matters, to reinforce the legend about Oswald's "instability"—a legend first constructed for Oswald when he had been in the Soviet Union for other purposes—and categorically to deny that Oswald had been recruited before, during or after his defection to the Soviet Union in 1959. Nosenko would also deny any KGB connections or contacts with Marina. Nosenko would have been chosen to deliver the message because the KGB had already established his credentials with the CIA (in 1962) as a dissident officer of the Tourist Department of the Second Chief Directorate—the division of the KGB that plausibly would have handled the Oswald case in 1959.

The CIA decided that there was a strong possibility that Nosenko might break and might even unravel Oswald's tangled web before the Warren Commission put out its final report. Richard Helms called Nicholas Katzenbach, the deputy attorney general, to discuss the incarceration of Nosenko. For both the CIA and the Department of Justice, it was a totally unprecedented situation. Given more time or other circumstances, Nosenko could be questioned in a different atmosphere. But the Warren Commission, under pressure from President Johnson, wanted to publish its verdict in fewer than 120 days. Attorney General Robert F. Kennedy himself backed this extraordinary procedure, which was intended either to break or to confirm Nosenko's story. The decision was made to put Nosenko under "hostile interrogation."

Nosenko was confined to a single room at a CIA detention center, with only a bed, chair and washbasin. He was given only military fatigues to wear and treated as if he were a captured spy rather than a voluntary defector. He was forced to submit to unrelenting interrogation, and when his answers seemed false or misleading, he was openly challenged—or denounced as a liar. No longer was he allowed to ramble on a tangent or suggest going to a bar for drinks.

At one point his interrogators thought he might break. He had been unable to supply any details about a case he was supposedly monitoring for the KGB. His interrogators suggested finally that perhaps he had not in fact handled that case.

Nosenko sat back silently as the interrogator pointed out the contradiction.

Why not admit he hadn't handled this case? his interrogator asked.

Nosenko answered, after long thought, that if he admitted this, he would have to admit that he was not even the person he claimed to be.

The interrogators paused to see whether Nosenko would make such an admission.

After a tense hesitation Nosenko suddenly pulled himself together. He insisted that despite the contradictions his interrogators had pointed out, he had handled the case in question. He admitted that he "looked bad," even to himself, but had no explanation.

From the clues that Nosenko had provided, the FBI had no problem in locating the agent Nosenko identified as Andrey. However, instead of being the high-level agent that Nosenko had originally suggested, Andrey turned out to be only a retired Army sergeant who had worked in the motor pool at the American Embassy in Moscow in 1953–1954. He did not even have access to classified information.

The man readily admitted to the FBI that he had met the Soviets while in Moscow, though he had no information of value to give them. In 1957 Kovshuk had indeed spoken briefly with him, but it was clear he was not in a position to be of any use.

To the CIA, the discovery of Andrey only heightened the mystery. According to Stone, Kovshuk had made a special trip to Washington to see an agent of unique importance. By the reconstruction of dates the CIA determined that the Army sergeant had not been contacted until many months after Kovshuk had arrived. Pressed on this contradiction, Nosenko explained that Kovshuk had had trouble locating the sergeant. Yet it turned out his name and phone number were in the phone book.

To the Soviet experts in the CIA, it seemed impossible to believe that a man as important as Kovshuk, while still heading the American Embassy Section of the KGB, would travel to

Washington to see an ex-soldier who had no classified clearance. But if this sergeant was not the high-level penetration agent Stone had warned about, then who was?

In analyzing Nosenko's disclosures, the CIA officers became increasingly suspicious that Nosenko was painting "false tracks" away from some high-level agent (or agents) inside the United States government. All the pieces—Kovshuk's trip to Washington in 1957 to contact an important agent, Popov's capture in 1959, Penkovskiy's capture in 1962, the leak to the Soviets of classified U.S. secrets in 1961 and 1962—seemed to fit into the same puzzle.

But what about Oswald?

On June 24, 1964, Helms requested a private audience with Chief Justice Warren. When he arrived at the conference room in the Veterans' Building, where they had agreed to meet, he found the Chief Justice sitting alone at a table surrounded by a few empty chairs. It was agreed that no notes were to be taken, no witnesses were to be present. The subject, Helms suggested, had to remain a secret of state. The Chief Justice nodded his agreement.

Helms explained that there were two schools of thought within the intelligence community about Nosenko. The first held that he was a legitimate defector and could be believed so far as Oswald was concerned. The second held that Nosenko was still a Soviet agent, under instructions from the KGB to misinform the commission about Oswald's activities in the Soviet Union. He explained that the CIA could not say with certainty which view was correct, and might not resolve this question before the Warren Report was published.

Warren looked up, visibly disturbed by this development. Helms had just disqualified the only live witness that the commission had concerning the involvement of Soviet authorities with Oswald. Even more disquieting, he was advancing the serious possibility that the Soviets had attempted to insert false information in the official history of the Kennedy assassination through the use of a fake defector. And if the latter turned out to be true, it would imply that the other information the Soviets had supplied to the commission had also been falsified to support the Nosenko version.

Warren asked about the report the commission had received from Hoover which raised none of these questions.

Helms quietly answered that he could speak only for the CIA and reiterated that he could not say with certainty whether Nosenko was sincere or a KGB plant.

Both men looked at each other in silence for a long moment. Then Warren, apparently tired and frayed by the additional duties imposed on him by the Kennedy assassination, said that he would take what Helms told him under advisement. The interview was ended.

Later that same day, at the Chief Justice's request, the Warren Commission met in executive session to discuss the vexing problem raised by Nosenko. (The minutes of this meeting are still classified as secret.)

It was decided that Nosenko wouldn't testify or be interviewed by any members of the staff. The FBI report on him would remain—but as part of the unpublished record of the commission that would be filed away in the National Archives. (Indeed, this report only surfaced after a Freedom of Information Act petition in 1975.)

For this critical period in Oswald's life, the commission would rely almost entirely on a diary that had been found among Oswald's effects and on official records tendered by the Soviet government. (This was decided despite the fact that if the Soviet government were suspected of going to great lengths to fake a defector, the records it supplied would also have to be suspected of being forgeries.)

In any event, there would be no further investigation by the commission into the Nosenko affair, no testing of his story. There was no time for any new inquiries. President Johnson was demanding that the report be issued in September, well before the presidential election in November, and it was already almost July. Final drafts had to be in within thirty days, Warren ordered.

Faced with an unyielding deadline, the commission's staff was in a quandary over what to do about the Soviet section. It seemed to be an immense void for which there were no witnesses. (Oswald did not meet Marina until after he decided to redefect to the United States in 1961.) Coleman and Slawson, who were responsible for writing this chapter, noted that without being able to use Nosenko's story, "We are . . . forced to fall back on Oswald himself, and ask, from all that we have learned about him—literally from infancy to the day of his death —whether he was the kind of man who could successfully have lived out such a [KGB-devised] legend."

The problem here was that the commission had not amassed sufficient information in its decidedly limited investigation to test Nosenko's story against reference points in Oswald's life.

For example, in investigating the origin of Oswald's defection to Russia, Coleman and Slawson concluded that Oswald probably began to lay his plans while serving with the Marines in the Far East. They noted in their report: "Thus, there is the possibility that Oswald came into contact with Communist agents at that time. Japan, especially because the Communist Party was open and active there, would seem a likely point for such a contact to have been made." If such a contact had been made and Oswald had indeed been induced by an intelligence service to defect, then such information would cast an extremely different light on his movements prior to the assassination. Yet, to determine this, it would be necessary to reconstruct the experiences of Oswald's Marine unit in Japan to ascertain what information of intelligence value Oswald had had access to.

More than 100 men had served in Oswald's unit. Any one of them might have held a piece in the jigsaw mystery of Oswald's sudden defection. With only days left to finish writing the report, however, the commission's staff knew that there would not be time to track down and interview these missing witnesses.

In fact, the commission questioned only one Marine who had been in Oswald's radar unit in Japan—and his tour overlapped with Oswald's by only a few months. Even he was not questioned closely about Oswald's access to classified information or contacts he might have had with foreigners.

Nosenko's story provided a crucial hinge for the commission. If it proved to be authentic, the commission could conclude that Oswald had made no prior contacts or arrangements with Soviet intelligence services before his defection, had received no training during his years in the Soviet Union, and was not subsequently given any mission by the Soviets to perform upon his return to the United States. On the other hand, if the story proved to be a fabrication and Nosenko was discovered to be no more than a messenger from Moscow, then the commission would have to assume that all other information from the Soviet Union had been provided as part of the same legend for Oswald. And in this case, the commission would be left with the question of why Soviet intelligence had gone to such lengths to create a cover story for the assassin.

But time had run out on the commission's investigation. Nosenko was still being questioned and confined on September 28, 1964, when the Warren Commission published its report. In failing to resolve the question of Nosenko, the commission had evaded a very central question about the assassination: Why had Lee Harvey Oswald defected to the Soviet Union?

PART ONE

The Passage East

1

"Race Car"

Atsugi, Japan: 1957. "Race Car to Coffee Mill, Race Car to Coffee Mill," the radio crackled. "Request winds aloft ninety angels."

The men inside the darkened control room listened with bewilderment; some laughed nervously, as if the radio codes were some kind of practical joke, designed to break the boredom of a four-hour watch on a sweltering fall night. They knew from their Marine Corps radar training that no plane could fly at an altitude of 90,000 feet. The world record altitude was still 65,889 feet, and the radar height-find antenna—the MPS-11— read only up to 45,000 feet. Why, then would any plane want to know the wind velocity at 90,000 feet? the men wondered.

"Coffee Mill" was the code name for Marine Air Control Squadron One, known as MACS-1, which controlled air traffic for the units of the 1st Marine Aircraft Wing stationed at the U.S. Naval Air Facility at Atsugi, Japan. But what was "Race Car"?

At daybreak a few days later the men in Squadron One received another surprise. A long, thin silver plane, with a needle nose, was wheeled out by a tractor to the edge of a 5,000-foot runway. It looked like no plane that any of the Marines in "Coffee Mill" had ever seen before. Its wings, which stretched out for 80 feet, were more than twice the length of its cigar-shaped fuselage. The wing tips drooped to the ground and had to be supported by aluminum pods with small wheels under them. A pilot, clad in a heavy rubber suit and mask, arrived in an ambulance and climbed into the cockpit. The ground crew then removed five identifying numbers from the tail of the strange plane. As the engine warmed up, it emitted a high, shrill whine, which rapidly increased as the plane began racing down the runway. "When we would hear that noise, some of us would run out of the hut to watch it take off," recalls Robert Royce Augg, now a policeman in Chillichothe, Ohio. In a few seconds, using no more than 500 feet of the mile-long runway, it shot into the air. Then the wheels under its pods fell off and bounced back down the runway. The plane climbed at least a 45-degree angle. Within a couple of minutes the Marines watching their UPA-25 radarscopes saw that the unidentified plane had vanished from the radar. It had also vanished from sight. They made rapid calculations with their pencils as to its rate of climb, but where had it gone? Moments later "Race Car" called.

The landings of this silver plane were just as spectacular as its takeoffs. It would appear from nowhere, circle slowly over the village, bringing excited Japanese out of their houses for a look, and then sail like a glider above the runway before floating down to the ground, its wing tips often giving off a shower of sparks as they touched the concrete. When the plane had stopped, jeeps covered with canvas would position themselves under the wings to keep them from dragging along the runway. Then the same tractor would tow the plane off the runway to a special hangar, which the Marines quickly observed was guarded by men with submachine guns. "They never even let it cool off," recalled one enlisted man. When the men asked their officers about the "weird aircraft," they were told only that it was a "utility plane."

Inside the semicircular radar room called the bubble, the Marine surveillance team peered for hours on end through their UPA-25 radarscopes. Heavy cables snaked their way through the bubble to connect the electrical equipment outside. Because of the constantly working machinery, the temperature was so hot that the grease pencils the men used to mark intercept paths would sometimes melt on the translucent plotting board. Perspiration would run down the men's faces and into their eyes as they sat there, stripped down to their T-shirts. The humming noise from incessantly grinding machinery was so loud that it was impossible to talk without shouting. Only the dim light from the radar screen illuminated the bubble, leaving it so dark that one could not identify even a friend from across the room. The monotony during these long shifts was broken by the occasional appearance of the strange aircraft.

Gradually the Marine Corps radar operators in "Coffee Mill" learned more about the so-called utility plane. As the requests for winds aloft at 90,000 feet usually came soon after the utility plane disappeared from their radar, they put two and two together and deduced that the plane was in fact "Race Car." They also realized that it flew at altitudes above the strength of their radar—perhaps as high as "ninety angels." In their briefings on classified material they were told that the utility plane (called the U-2 for short) was a highly secret reconnaissance project, which was not to be discussed with anyone outside the radar unit.

One Marine, Richard Cyr, remembers that the radar crew would pass the time by figuring out the U-2's rate of climb from watching its blips on the radar scopes. "You could figure out how fast it could climb by just watching the number of seconds it took to go from ground to 30,000 or 40,000 feet and then dividing."

What they were not told, however, was that the U-2 was used primarily for penetrating the airspace of the Soviet Union and China in order to photograph military and industrial targets. Or that the U-2s, which used Atsugi as one of their two main bases, were providing no less than 90 percent of all hard information on Soviet military, ballistic and nuclear bomb activities. The ultrasecret cameras on the plane were then assessing missile emplacements and submarine keel laying in the Soviet Union.

The men of Squadron One were not briefed on the mission of the U-2, although many guessed that it flew over enemy territory. They had no way of knowing that it was the highest-priority target of Soviet intelligence and that its intelligence service was at that very time attempting to gain information which might make it possible for Soviet rockets to shoot down one of the odd-looking planes.[1]

One Marine inside the bubble seemed to go about his work with a good deal of silent efficiency. He was gaunt, with sparkling eyes and a smile that was often taken for a contemptuous smirk. Like the others, he heard the radio calls from "Race Car" and, according to one officer, showed an extraordinary interest in the path of the ghostly plane. That Marine was Lee Harvey Oswald.[2]

Lee Harvey Oswald was born on October 18, 1939, at the Old French Hospital in New Orleans. His father, Robert E. Lee Oswald, an insurance premium collector named after the Civil War general, had died of a heart attack two months before.[3] His mother, Marguerite Claverie Oswald, an attractive brunette of French and German extraction, managed the best she could under difficult circumstances. She immediately placed her other two sons, Robert Oswald, who was five, and John Pic, Jr. (her child by a previous marriage), who was seven, in the Infant Jesus College Home, a Catholic boarding school in Algiers, Louisiana. With the help of her sister, Lillian Murret, she tried to care for Lee while working in New Orleans.

Marguerite retrieved her two older sons from the orphanage within a year and shortly thereafter purchased a frame house for the family. The house was small, but they had a backyard and space for a "shepherd collie dog" named Sunshine. Marguerite opened Oswald's Notion Shop in the front of the house, but the business did not thrive. In December 1941 she placed Robert and John in the Evangelical Lutheran Bethlehem Orphan's Asylum, where she contributed $20 a month to their maintenance. She tried to place Lee in the home then, but they would not accept children under three.

Marguerite sold the house—at an $800 profit—and again moved with Lee. While she worked as a telephone operator, her sister cared for the child. On December 26, 1942, Lee joined his brothers at the Bethlehem children's home. He was then three years and two months old. It was a relatively happy time. His older brothers would take Lee with them from the orphanage on the outskirts of town into New Orleans, where they would spend the afternoon with their mother. Robert in particular regarded Lee as his "kid brother" and ". . . stayed pretty close to him."

In 1944, when Lee was five, Marguerite finally found a businessman willing and able to support her family: Edwin A. Ekdahl. Ekdahl, trained as an electrical engineer, earned a comfortable living for his family. Marguerite withdrew Lee from the orphanage and moved to Dallas to be with Ekdahl, whom she married in 1945. The two older boys were then enrolled at the Chamberlain-Hunt Military Academy in Mississippi, and Marguerite, Lee and Ekdahl settled in Benbrook, Texas, a comfortable suburb of Fort Worth, where they rented a spacious stone house set on a large plot of land. Lee and his brothers fished and swam in a creek just a few hundred yards from their back door. He attended the Benbrook Common School and during vacations traveled extensively with his mother and stepfather.

This idyllic existence was to be short-lived, however. Although the three boys and Ekdahl got along well, he and Marguerite began fighting soon after their marriage. After a series of separations and reconciliations Marguerite decided to confirm her suspicions of Ekdahl's infidelity. In the summer of 1947 she had fifteen-year-old John Pic and one of his friends drive her to the house where she thought Ekdahl was with his mistress. John's friend posed as a Western Union messenger, and when the door was opened, Marguerite pushed her way in to confront the woman, dressed in a negligee, and Ekdahl. She promptly left her third husband and instituted divorce proceedings. (He died of a heart attack shortly after the divorce.)

John and Robert were forced to leave military school to join their mother and brother in a small house next to the railroad tracks in Fort Worth. John, then fifteen, noted that the family was "back down in the lower class." The divorce was granted in June 1948. With the $1,500 settlement—Marguerite did not obtain support from Ekdahl—Marguerite paid her legal bills and bought a small house in Benbrook. Marguerite urged the older boys to join the military to ease her financial burden. Lee, meanwhile, was transferred from one public school to another in the Dallas-Fort Worth area as his mother adjusted her life to being single again. By the time Lee was ten, and in the fifth grade, he had attended six different public schools.

In August 1952, with both her older sons enlisted in the military, Marguerite drove to New York with Lee. When they arrived in New York City, carrying much luggage and their TV set, Marguerite and Lee moved in with John Pic, then stationed in the Coast Guard on Ellis Island, and his wife and baby. The family lived in a small apartment on East Ninety-second Street.

The visit was pleasant at first. John took a leave to get reacquainted with his youngest brother and introduced him to the Museum of Natural History, the Staten Island ferry and other New York landmarks. Lee was first enrolled in the Trinity Evangelical Lutheran School. When John and his wife began to realize that Marguerite was making no effort to get a job or find an apartment of her own, tensions in the household began to rise. The troubles culminated in an argument between the Pics and Marguerite about Lee's behavior. Shortly after that Marguerite and Lee moved into a one-room apartment in the Bronx and Lee transferred to P.S. 117, where he failed to show up on more than half the school days. Marguerite worked in a Lerner's shop, and that Christmas she spent what must have been a week's salary—$39.95—on a "little replica of a Magnus organ" for Lee's present.

In January 1953 the Oswalds moved to a different apartment in the Bronx, and Lee was transferred to Public School 44, which he refused to attend, perhaps because his classmates made fun of his Southern ways. Instead, he chose to learn his way around New York—he spent whole days exploring the subways. On other days he remained at home, reading and watching television.

In the spring of 1953 Lee had his first brush with the law. He was picked up at the Bronx Zoo for truancy and remanded to the New York City Youth House for a six-week observation period. The probation officer assigned to Lee's case, John Carro, noted in his report that Oswald was a "friendly, likeable boy, who portrays very little emotion . . . much of Lee's difficulties seem to stem from his inability to adapt himself to the change of environment and the change of economic status of his family." The psychiatric report of Dr. Renatus Hartogs describes the thirteen-year-old Oswald as a "tense, withdrawn, and evasive boy, who dislikes intensely talking about himself and his feelings."

Oswald also seemed intelligent. Dr. Hartogs wrote: "Lee is a youngster with superior mental endowments, functioning presently in the bright-normal range of mental efficiency. His abstract thinking capacity and his vocabulary are well-developed. No retardation in school subjects could be found despite truancy." At Youth House, Oswald also took a battery of intelligence tests, which showed that he had an IQ of 118, and he scored above average on all the other tests.

During this observation period Evelyn Strickman, an experienced social worker, tried to penetrate the barriers of silence around Oswald. She found a "rather pleasant, appealing quality about this emotionally starved, affectionless youngster, which grows as one speaks to him. . . ." He seemed to have little interest in anything other than watching television—his favorite program was *I Lived Three Lives for the FBI*—and reading magazines. The only ambition he discussed was joining the Marine Corps, as his brother Robert had done. On May 7 Oswald was released from Youth House with the recommendation that his mother seek the assistance of some community organization, such as the Big Brothers, to help Lee better adjust to school life in New York.

When Robert visited the Oswalds in New York, Lee showed off the results of his months of hooky playing. He had mastered the intricacies of the New York City subway system and served as Robert's tour guide throughout the visit.

During his time in New York Lee had apparently also become interested in politics. He later claimed that his involvement with Marxism had begun with a pamphlet protesting the execution of Julius and Ethel Rosenberg for wartime espionage. This pamphlet, printed by the Communist Party, was handed to him by an old woman on a New York street corner.

Oswald returned to Public School 44 that September and made considerable progress. He was even elected president of his eighth-grade class. However, in October 1953 he was again reported to his probation officer for being "unruly"; apparently, he had refused to salute the American flag.

Unwilling to deal with the New York educational system, which she complained treated normal children like criminals— Lee's mother had never been overly troubled by his truancy— Marguerite took Lee back to New Orleans in early 1954.[4] She wrote her son John, "We are back in New Orleans and happy to be back. Lee is his self again after the ordeal in New York. It was almost a tragedy, but a little love and patience did the trick."

Oswald enrolled at Beauregard Junior High School and attempted to expand his previously private universe. He befriended a classmate, Edward Voebel, with whom he played darts and shot pool in a French Quarter poolroom near Lee and Marguerite's Exchange Street apartment. Lee attended several meetings of the local unit of the Civil Air Patrol with Voebel; he even got a paper route to raise the cost of a uniform. Lee played school sports briefly, but he quit the baseball team and was thrown off the football team for insisting that the coach's rules violated his constitutional rights. He also became a voracious reader of books and found a hero: Karl Marx.

In October 1955 Lee turned sixteen. He signed his mother's name to a note informing his school that the family was moving to San Diego and dropped out of school. He then forged a document which stated that he was seventeen and convinced Marguerite to sign it so that he might enlist in the Marines. The Marines, however, rejected his application and told him to return in a year.

Marguerite, concerned that Lee was spending all his time at home reading "deep books," pressed him to get a job. For a few weeks in 1956 he worked as a messenger at Pfisterer Dental Laboratory, where he met Palmer E. McBride, a fellow messenger, who shared Oswald's interest in classical music. On his visits to McBride's home, however, Lee quickly turned the discussion to politics. McBride recalled:

> Lee Oswald was very serious about the virtues of Communism and discussed these virtues at every opportunity. He would say that the capitalists were exploiting the working class, and his central theme seemed to be that the workers would one day rise up and throw off their chains. He praised Khrushchev's sincerity. . . .

Oswald would also accuse President Dwight D. Eisenhower of "exploiting the working class." When McBride took Oswald with him to the home of William Eugene Wulf, the president of the Amateur Astronomy Association, Oswald enraged his host by "telling him of the glories of the Workers' State and saying that the United States was not telling the truth about Soviet Russia." The vocabulary of class warfare which Oswald bandied about suggested that the periodicals and books he was then reading were not the standard fare taught in New Orleans schools. (One magazine that he wrote to in October 1956 for a subscription was the *Socialist Call*, an organ of the Socialist Party.) Wulf's father, who had emigrated from Germany in the 1920s, found Oswald's Communistic rhetoric especially offensive and ordered the boy out of the house.

On another occasion Oswald tried to persuade McBride to join the Communist Party with him "to take advantage of the social functions." According to what he told William Wulf, Oswald was then apparently seeking a cell of sympathetic Marxists. He also made inquiries about the "Youth League" of the Socialist Party. McBride, who was not personally interested in the idea, never found out how successful Oswald was in seeking out and joining a Marxist cell. Their friendship ended abruptly when the Oswalds moved back to Texas in July 1956.

Oswald enrolled in the tenth grade at Arlington Heights High School in Fort Worth but attended classes only until September 28, when he quit school in anticipation of his seventeenth birthday and his enlistment in the Marines. On October 3 he sent the Socialist Party of America an advertisement coupon he had torn out of a magazine, on which he had checked the box "I want more information about the Socialist Party," and enclosed the following letter:

> Dear Sirs,
> I am sixteen years of age and would like more information about your Youth League, I would like to know if there is a branch in my area, how to join, etc. I am a Marxist and have been studying Socialist principles for well over fifteen months. I am very interested in your YPSL.[5]

On October 24, 1956, with his mother's written consent, Lee enlisted in the Marine Corps in Dallas. At his initial medical examination, Oswald stood five feet eight in his stockinged feet and weighed in at only 135 pounds. He noted a history of ear, nose and throat trouble—he had had a mastoidectomy at the age of six. On his aptitude tests he scored better than average in the verbal section and slightly below average on the mathematical and spatial relations sections. No psychological abnormalities were noted. He was handed a plane ticket and that afternoon he boarded an American Airlines flight for San Diego, where he was to report for basic training.

Oswald, like all other enlisted men in the Marines, went through ten grueling weeks of boot camp. Sherman Cooley, who had rarely been out of rural Beauregard Parish, Louisiana, was assigned to the same platoon in boot camp as Oswald. (Marine Corps policy then was to place recruits from the same geographical areas in the same platoon whenever possible for basic training.)

"I wouldn't call the experience a nightmare," Cooley reminisced twenty years later, "but it was holy hell." The men would be awakened in the middle of the night, told to dress with full packs on their backs and then ordered to run for great distances, holding their M-1 rifles at port arms. They were told that there was "the right way, the wrong way and the Marine way." "For example," recalls Cooley, "a drill sergeant might make a man run one-hundred yards and then tell him to do it again—that he had done it the wrong way. The recruit would run the one-hundred yards again, only to be told he had done it the right way—and that he needed to do it again the 'Marine way.' What I hated most of all was all that wasted motion."

Every morning they had to be up at five, and except for short, regimented meal and letter-writing breaks, they spent most of the day attending classes and doing rigorous physical exercise. In December the company went to the rifle range for training in the use of the M-1.

Cooley recalls that Oswald was known as a "s–bird," who couldn't qualify with his weapon. "It was a disgrace not to qualify," says Cooley, "and we gave him holy hell." Other than one day when Oswald reported sick in December, he seemed to hold up well under the razzing.

On January 20, 1957, after having finally successfully qualified with his rifle and completed basic training, Oswald was sent for combat training to the Infantry Training Regiment at Camp Pendleton, California, which is located about 20 miles north of San Diego. There Oswald practiced techniques of am-

Oswald (center, in profile) with a group of Marines, waiting to board USS *Terrell County*.

John Wayne (center) dining in the Marine mess hall on Corregidor. Oswald is standing in the doorway. (Unretouched photograph.)

George DeMohrenschildt in 1964.

James Jesus Angleton in 1975.

The U-2 as it looked on a reconnaissance flight—what the Russians dubbed "the black lady of espionage."

Birthday party in Oswald's apartment in Minsk. Friends include Rosa Kuznetsova (left, rear), Ella German (right, rear) and Pavel Golovachev.

Pavel Golovachev repairs Oswald's hi-fi in his apartment.

Oswald in his apartment with Rosa Kuznetsova.

Oswald's apartment house in Minsk.

View from Oswald's apartment.

MINSK

Key to map of Minsk:

A. MVD training school

B. KGB training school

C. Belorussian Radio and Television Factory

D. Oswald's apartment

E. Prusakov's apartment

F. Palace of Culture

G. MVD-KGB headquarters

H. Hospital where Marina Oswald worked

I. Home of Alexander Ziger and family

J. Home of Erich Titovets

K. Home of Yuriy Merezhinsky

L. Home of Ella German

/////—Many Cubans lived in this area because of its proximity to the Polytechnical Institute, which many of them attended.

xxxx—This is the location of an apartment complex for middle- and upper-level KGB people.

Oswald with Eleanora Ziger and one of her boyfriends
in a park in Minsk.

Oswald with co-workers at the factory in Minsk.

Oswald on his arrival in Russia, from a photograph taken for Moscow newspapers.

Oswald and Marina on their balcony after their wedding.

Oswald preparing to leave Russia, with Marina (right) and the Zigers.

Oswald distributes Fair Play for Cuba leaflets in New Orleans.

Oswald with his rifle and pistol in a photograph
taken by Marina in Dallas in 1963.

phibious landings, tank-supported assaults, hand-to-hand combat and squad tactics, as all Marines—regardless of their ultimate job assignments—were required to do.

One of the Marines in Oswald's eight-man squad, who also shared a tent with him, was Allen R. Felde, a native of Milwaukee, Wisconsin. Felde remembers that even while Oswald was learning combat techniques, he was attacking American foreign policy. He railed against the American intervention in Korea, which he said resulted in "one million" useless deaths. (He blamed President Eisenhower). He also persisted in depicting himself as champion of the "cause of the workingman." Apparently the Marine Corps had not changed Oswald's views.

On March 18, after a brief leave, during which he visited his mother in Fort Worth, Oswald reported to the Naval Air Technical Training Center at Jacksonville, Florida. As he had requested upon enlisting. Oswald was to be trained as a radar controller, a job the Marines gave only to men of higher-than-average intelligence. The course at Jacksonville was a general introduction to aviation fundamentals. For hours on end the trainees were shown films of various Navy and Marine aircraft landing and taking off and listened to classroom lectures on the flight characteristics of combat aircraft. Oswald was routinely promoted to private first class and granted a final clearance to handle classified material specified to be "Confidential." On May 3 he was graduated from the course.

Oswald next was stationed at Keesler Air Force Base in Mississippi, where he took the aircraft control and warning operator course. The thirty Marines in the course were taught how to use radar to identify whether incoming planes were friends or foes, the techniques for overcoming radar-jamming equipment on Soviet planes and the system for alerting allied planes and, if necessary, "scrambling" them to meet an enemy.

The basic device at the time was called the parrot. When a plane was spotted on the radar, it was asked to "squawk," or signal, on one of three channels; the complex electronic machine, known as the parrot, made it possible for the radar operator to then identify from a series of lines which appeared next to the image of the plane on the radar screen whether the aircraft was "friendly" or an enemy "bogey." The class also learned how to plot the path of a spotted aircraft on a transparent plastic board (writing backward so the officers on the other side of the board could read the plotting), to measure the altitude of planes using radar height-finding antennas and to stay in radio contact with pilots.

During the course, instructors warned the students that they would be dealing with highly secret and sensitive information, and they should not be surprised to find counterintelligence agents planted in their unit to make certain that security was being maintained. Daniel Patrick Powers, a football player from the University of Minnesota, went with Oswald from Jacksonville to Keesler and remembered that because of his meekness, Oswald was nicknamed Ozzie the Rabbit. Although Oswald tended to remain apart from the others in the class, Powers, feeling sorry for him, attempted to be friends with him. But Oswald told him very little about himself, other than that his father was dead and his mother lived alone. Powers remembered Ozzie used almost all his weekend passes to go to New Orleans, which was only about 100 miles from the base, and Powers assumed he was visiting his mother. (At this time, however, Marguerite was in Texas, and Oswald's relatives in New Orleans remember only a single call from him. Presumably he was seeing someone else.)

During the battery of examinations in June Oswald surprised his classmates with his proficiency, finishing seventh in the class. Officially designated an Aviation Electronics Operator, with the Military Occupation Specialty—or MOS—of 6741, he was ordered to join Marine Air Control Squadron One, then stationed in Atsugi, Japan.

On August 21, with Powers and most of his other classmates from Keesler, Oswald boarded the USS *Bexar* in San Diego, which steamed out into the Pacific the next day. The ship made one stop in Hawaii, where Oswald went ashore, bought a Hawaiian shirt and took a picture of the statue of Kamehameha the Great, the eighteenth-century rebel who overthrew the established order and united the Hawaiian Islands under his rule. He also sent his mother a postcard, saying, "Well, only one day here but I have been having lots of fun. 12 more days at sea to Japan. Love, Lee." During the twenty-one-day voyage, in which the Marines had constant "war games" and "drills," Oswald demonstrated his skill at chess. Powers, who played with Oswald almost every day, recalled Oswald's becoming exuberant when he won, jumping up and saying, "Look at that, I won. I beat you!" and then chuckling to himself. Oswald spent the balance of his time reading Walt Whitman's *Leaves of Grass*. On September 12 the ship finally docked in Yokosuka—a naval port near Tokyo.

Located about 35 miles southwest of Tokyo was the air base at Atsugi. The base was dotted with deep caves riddled into the sides of the hills—constructed so that the Japanese could keep their fighter planes off the fields to protect them from strafing missions. Originally built by the Japanese during World War II as the hub of their air defense system and the main training base for their kamikaze pilots, Atsugi was now a base of operations for the First Marine Air Wing.

The main runway ran north-south. Behind it was a barbed-wire fence, which separated the Japanese rice fields from the base. The hangars on the west side of the concrete runways housed the Marine equivalent of F-86 fighters—a contingent of which stood on ready-alert on pads outside the hangars. On the east side were Navy Super-Constellations used for locating enemy radar and antisubmarine operators. One huge hangar at the northwest end of the runway stored the U-2 reconnaissance planes.

On the eastern part of the base, about 400 yards from the Marine hangars, was a complex of about twenty buildings, identified innocuously on several signs as the "Joint Technical Advisory Group." It contained one of the CIA's main operational bases in Asia. For these reasons, Atsugi remained a "closed" base, which meant that personnel on the base had to have cards showing their security clearance.[6]

2

The Queen Bee

To Oswald, who had had a peripatetic life almost from the time he was born, the move to Japan presented new opportunities. For one thing, his position as a radar operator at Atsugi gave him a standing that he had lacked as a truant and a high school dropout. Oswald was assigned to work in the radar bubble located at the northern end of the mile-long runway.

On his watches Oswald, like the other men on the crew, rotated jobs. For four hours at a time they would alternate peering into their "crystal balls"—*i.e.,* their radarscopes—plotting intercepts at the plotting board and monitoring radio communications with pilots. Their sector of responsibility was from 270 to 360 degrees on the azimuth of their radarscopes, which took in the area from the South China Sea to Korea. They were supposed to direct friendly planes toward their destinations through the use of radar and to spot enemy planes and then alert the Tactical Air Control Center at Iwakuni, Japan, which would then dispatch interceptor planes. They also served as communications liaisons with the Japanese air defense forces and monitored the air traffic approaching Tokyo.

When Oswald moved to the plotting board, he prided himself on the meticulous paths he drew and bristled at a young "Tab Hunter-type officer" who tried to second-guess his plotting or to correct him. He also showed a keen interest in the briefings on classified material which were held by the unit's intelligence officer. His supervisor, Captain Francis J. Gajewski, duly noted in Oswald's record six months after he came to Atsugi, "As a matter of fact [Oswald] has done good work for me. I would desire to have him work for me at any time . . . he minds his business and he does his job well."

The other men on the enlisted crew who spent all-night watches with Oswald also found that no matter how they provoked him, he refused to talk much about himself. They continued to pry to find out if he was a "cherry virgin" or if he had found a girlfriend, but he warded away both queries and insults with an odd type of half-smile that some took to be a sneer. Sometimes, during a long stretch in the bubble, he would mimic Bugs Bunny—wiggling his ears, squinting his eyes and extending his teeth over his lower lip—earning him the nickname Bugs. When a blip appeared on his scope, however, he would quickly return to it.

Like most of the other privates and corporals in the 117-man MACS-1 unit, Oswald lived in a wooden two-story barracks near the east gate of the base. His roommate was Corporal Thomas Bagshaw, a career Marine. Bagshaw remembers Oswald when he arrived at Atsugi as "very thin, almost frail, shy and quiet." He also recalls feeling sorry for him when other Marines in the barracks began "picking on him."[1] The rougher Marines in the barracks, who generally preferred spending their liberties carousing in Japanese bars and finding women, considered Oswald (who spent his early liberties in the television room of the barracks alone, watching *American Bandstand* and replays of football games) a natural object of derision. They called him Mrs. Oswald, threw him in the shower fully dressed and hassled him in every other conceivable way. Oswald would not fight back; he would just turn away from a provoker and ignore him.

Not all the Marines in the barracks approved of this razzing of Oswald. Zack Stout, who had interrupted his high school education and joined the Marines with a group of his friends, found Oswald both interesting and likable. He recalls that "Oswald was honest and blunt . . . and that's usually what got him into trouble." He also found Oswald one of the few men in the unit with whom he could hold an intelligent conversation and who read serious books. "Ozzie would read deep stuff like *Mein Kampf* . . . or *The Decline and Fall of the Roman Empire,*" and he tried to interest Stout in some of these histories. He was particularly impressed by the way Oswald articulated issues. "His diction was good . . . he used his hands when he talked . . . and he seemed to think about what he was going to say," Stout recalls. "He was absolutely truthful, the kind of guy I'd trust completely."

When Stout began going on leaves with Oswald, he also found that he was seemingly well informed about politics. As far as the other Marines went, Stout explains, "Ozzie treated people as they treated him . . . and if he couldn't for some reason, he'd ignore them."

Another Marine who befriended Oswald at Atsugi was George Wilkins, a worldly recruit from upstate New York who had traveled much of the Western Hemisphere with his father on business trips. Wilkins recalls, "Ozzie reacted to most of the crap by looking at you with that half-grin on his face." He could sympathize with Oswald in resenting the authority of young officers just out of college. He says, "Hell, we all thought we were smarter and better than any of the officers, and Ozzie was just like the rest of us. We all resented authority." When Oswald showed an interest in photography, Wilkins, himself a photography buff, spent some time teaching him how to use a 35-mm camera. Oswald then bought an Imperial Reflex camera and walked around the sprawling base, taking pictures of the various objects that apparently interested him—such as the radar height-finding antennas.

Gator Daniels, who first got to know Oswald aboard the USS *Bexar* on the way to Japan, had been christened Godfrey Jerome, but his Marine buddies quickly stuck him with a nickname reflective of his reputation as an alligator wrestler. A giant of a man, Daniels had rarely been out of the swamps of Florida, where he had helped his father fish and trap before enlisting at the age of eighteen. Gator took an immediate liking to Oswald.

He recalls: "He was simple folk, just like I was . . . we were a bunch of kids—never been away from home before—but Oswald came right out and admitted that he had never known a woman. . . . It was real unusual that a fellow would admit that. Like me, he was naïve about a lot of things, but he never was ashamed to admit it." Daniels, who was greatly admired by the other Marines in the unit, including at least one officer, took Oswald under his wing and tried to help him when he could. "He was just a good egg," Daniels remembers. "He used to do me favors, like lending me money until payday. . . . He was the sort of friend I could count on if I needed a pint of blood." He also came to admire Oswald's innate intelligence. "He had the sort of intelligence where you could show him how to do something once and he'd know how to do it, even if it was pretty complicated."

Oswald had now found at Atsugi a camaraderie with a group of men that he had never experienced before.[2] They encouraged him to drink with them in the local bars around the base and laughed with him when he would come back drunk, waking up his barracks-mates to shout, "Save your Confederate money, boys; the South will rise again!" They also introduced him to the vast array of cheap bars near the base and the girls who worked in them. From neonrise to neonset the bars served as bargain-basement brothels for enlisted men from the base. And they cheered him on when he finally had his first sexual experience with a Japanese bar girl. They took Oswald to Yokohama with them on their "Cinderella liberties"—so called because they had to be back on base at a prescribed hour in the middle of the night, usually midnight.[3] In Yamato, on the outskirts of the base, they turned the Bluebird Café into a squadron hangout and jeered at sailors or airmen who strayed in. While Oswald did not yet gamble himself—his newfound friends considered him "moralistic" in that respect—he did sit up all night watching them play poker.

There were times, however, when Oswald would disappear to Tokyo on a two-day leave and refuse to discuss these trips with even his closest friends. Years later in Dallas he confided to a close associate that he had become involved with a small circle of Japanese Communists in Tokyo while in the Marines.[4] If this was in fact true, none of the Marines Oswald served with had any inkling of the double life he was living—at least at the time.

Zack Stout knew of only one possible piece in the puzzle of

Oswald's absences: He seemed to have fallen in love, perhaps for the first time in his life, with a Japanese girl. When Stout asked where she worked, Oswald told him that she was a hostess at the Queen Bee in Tokyo.

This in itself was extraordinary. The Queen Bee, known for its more than 100 strikingly beautiful hostesses, was then one of the three most expensive nightclubs in Tokyo. It catered to an elite clientele—field-grade officers, pilots (including U-2 pilots) and a few junior officers with private incomes—not to impoverished Marine privates. To take a hostess out of a nightclub customarily required paying not only the girl, but the nightclub as well for the bar business it lost during her absence. The man also had to pay for the accommodations for the evening. For an evening at the Queen Bee, a date could cost anywhere from $60 to $100.

Yet Oswald, who was earning less than $85 a month take-home pay, went out with this woman from the Queen Bee with surprising regularity, even bringing her back to the base area several times. "He was really crazy about her," observed Stout, who met the woman with Oswald on several occasions in local bars around the base. Other Marines, less friendly to Oswald and who saw him with the woman, were astonished that someone of her "class" would go out with Oswald at all.[5] Stout and other men remember that these clubs were frequented by officers, and one could pick up useful bits of information about where the unit was headed. It seemed to him that "You could always find out where you were going from a bar girl before you would on base."[6] (According to one source, Navy intelligence was also interested in the possibility that hostesses from the Queen Bee were being used at the time to gather intelligence and that Oswald was receiving money from someone at the Queen Bee.)

Just about the time that Oswald celebrated his eighteenth birthday on October 18, plans were made for the entire unit to ship out to the South China Sea and the Philippines. The civil war in Indonesia was heating up, and the United States, which had up to this point only secretly supported the Moslem generals against President Achmed Sukarno (through the CIA), was now considering an overt intervention which would possibly require a Marine landing in Borneo. To provide support,

MACS-1 was scheduled to leave within weeks. Oswald seemed very unhappy at the prospect of leaving Japan. Stout assumed that this was because Oswald was having troubles with his hostess from the Queen Bee, who, he told Stout, was now going out with a "buck sergeant" when he had to report back for duty at the end of his "Cinderella liberties."

On October 27, the moment for departure drew near. At about 8:30 P.M. Oswald grazed his upper left arm with a .22-caliber bullet, which he had fired from a derringer he had somehow obtained in Japan. Wilkins rushed into the barracks at the sound of the explosion and saw Oswald quietly sitting on the lower bunk of his double-decker, still holding the pistol in his right hand. Wilkins could see a trace of blood on Oswald's left arm, but the wound did not look serious. Only a few weeks before, Oswald had shown him the silver-plated two-shot derringer and told him that he had ordered it from a mail-order firm in the United States. Knowing that it was illegal for enlisted men to have private firearms, Wilkins turned and left the barracks as others rushed in.

Robert Royce Augg, whose bed Oswald was sitting on, came in just as a Navy corpsman was tying a tourniquet on Oswald's arm. From the other Marines in the barracks, Augg gathered that Oswald had deliberately shot himself "to get himself transferred" before the unit departed from Japan. All Oswald said at the time, according to several witnesses, was: "I believe I shot myself."

In any case, Oswald was rushed to the U.S. Navy Hospital in nearby Yokosuka, where a Navy surgeon treated the wound. The official medical report of the incident, signed by Dr. R. S. Guthrie, stated initially that Oswald had shot himself by accident when he dropped a .45-caliber automatic pistol and it discharged. This apparently was what Oswald had reported, rather than reveal that he had his own .22-caliber pistol—which was a court-martial offense. Later the missile was examined and found to be a .22-caliber bullet. The incident was duly reported, and he now faced military discipline. For nearly three weeks Oswald recuperated in the hospital.[7]

Despite his apparent desire to remain behind in Japan, Oswald was discharged from medical treatment just in time to rejoin his unit. On November 20, with the rest of the men from "Coffee Mill," he boarded a rickety World War II LST, the USS *Terrell County*, and steamed out of the port of Yokosuka, bound for the northern end of the Philippine archipelago. The maneuver was code-named Operation Strongback.

Hitting the Philippine beaches in their amphibious trucks as if it were an actual invasion, the Marines drove nearly 20 miles inland, where they set up a temporary radar control bubble (which was actually a tent). While waiting for their heavier equipment to arrive, the Marines set about exploring the countryside. Encountering a group of local people feasting on pork and dog meat, they offered to trade them government blankets for their knives. The natives gave them a locally fermented "green beer," and as the Marines made approaches to their women, a brawl nearly broke out. The Marines were forced to retreat back to their camp. James R. "Bud" Persons, a young Mississippian who used to enjoy these foraging expeditions, became acquainted with Oswald during this period. "Oswald was easy to get along with," he recalls. "He was quiet . . . he didn't have a fight in him . . . he was not one of those animal like guys."

Less than a week after it set up its forward camp, "Coffee Mill" was ordered to strike its tents and proceed immediately back to the USS *Terrell County*.[8] Once loaded, the LST headed north toward Japan, and the men assumed they were returning to Atsugi. An unfortunate monkey—taken aboard by one of the Marines—had to be dumped overboard once they were under way because the officers suspected it as a disease carrier. On the second day at sea, however, the ship veered around sharply and headed back to Subic Bay in the Philippines. For a week the ship simply sat in the bay, no hint being given to the Marines as to their future destination.

In early December the *Terrell County* headed out into the South China Sea and rendezvoused with some thirty other ships of the Seventh Fleet. "For thirty or forty days, we never saw land," Persons remembers. The rumor floated around that the Marines were to be sent into Thailand to rescue some American oil executives, but there was no official briefing for the enlisted men. Some Marines found relief from the boredom by trying to sink floating oil drums with rifle fire. There was no relief, however, from the sweltering sun. For hours on end they had nothing to do but speculate on the forthcoming intervention and play chess and poker. Gator Daniels even taught Oswald, who had resisted gambling up to this point, how to play "nickel and dime" poker.

"Some of us were sorry we ever taught Oswald to play penny ante poker," Daniels recalls. "He got real good at it." Then he added, "He did a little growing up in that time . . . he started acting like a man." Finally, after a hot and dreary Christmas at sea near the equator, the LST returned to Subic Bay.

The Marines again went ashore with their equipment. This time they set up a temporary camp on the edges of Cubi Point Air Base. There, "Coffee Mill" celebrated a New Year's Eve that was raucous even by Marine standards—Persons was knocked unconscious, and a radar technician in the unit was hospitalized with a serious concussion. When asked if Oswald attended the party, Zack Stout replied, "Ozzie would have walked a mile to stay away from anything like that."

Boredom was rampant in the Philippines, and some of the men established a booze-making operation. Peter Cassisi recalls that the men stole alcohol from the sick bay and put it in a five-gallon water can, along with a hearty mixture of orange and potato peelings. The concoction was then buried for a week to ferment. After the can was dug up, they strained the mixture through their T-shirts. "The stuff was so awful you actually had to hold your nose when you drank it," recalls Cassisi.[9]

A few weeks after the unit landed, on January 15, 1958, there was a violent incident at Cubi Point. Private Martin Schrand, who had traveled by car with Oswald from the aviation school at Jacksonville, Florida, to the radar school at Biloxi, Mississippi, and then to Atsugi and the Philippines, was shot to death while on guard duty.

Persons was also on guard duty that night, patrolling an empty hangar, which on other occasions housed the blue-black U-2. He distinctly remembers hearing the whistle of the high winds off the South China Sea, which he had come to associate with Cubi Point. The officer of the day, Lieutenant Hugh Cherrie, had just made his routine check of the guard. Suddenly Persons heard an explosion, which he instantly knew was a shotgun blast, and bloodcurdling screams from the area that

Schrand was patrolling. "The screams were like some wild thing. . . . I knew I wasn't supposed to leave my post, no matter what happened, but I just said, 'Hell, the guy's in trouble,' and took off over there," he later recounted.

About 50 yards away he found Schrand in a pool of blood, mortally wounded. His shotgun was about six feet away on the ground behind him.[10] Lieutenant Cherrie arrived a few minutes later, as did a medic. It was determined that Schrand had been shot under the right arm by his own shotgun. Suicide was ruled out because the barrel of the gun was longer than Schrand's arm and no object with which he could have pulled the trigger was found at the scene.

At first, because of the distance of the shotgun from the body, it was assumed that he had been attacked by a Filipino guerrilla and, in the scuffle, shot with his own weapon. But when no other evidence of infiltrators could be found, the death was ruled "accidental," on the assumption that the weapon had accidentally gone off when Schrand dropped it. The enlisted men, continuing to suspect that something more was involved in Schrand's death, grew increasingly nervous about guard duty. (The same day that Schrand was shot, Oswald took and passed an examination that made him eligible for promotion to corporal.[11])

Peter Francis Connor had been on sentry duty just before Schrand, and he was called back to take the post after the shooting. "I was really scared that night," Connor recalls two decades later. "I knew something had happened, but nobody told me exactly. It was real dark, and I remember walking along and coming to the spot where he'd been shot. There was a big puddle of blood on the concrete, and I remember there was a bunch of Christmas candy in the middle of it. . . . I guessed it had been blown out of his shirt pocket. . . . It really got to me when I saw that candy."

A few days after Schrand's death "Coffee Mill" was again ordered to disband its camp. This time the Marines boarded a Philippine LST and headed for the island of Corregidor, 40 miles away. There they again set up their radar bubble and arranged sleeping quarters for themselves in the roofless remains of a hospital bombed out during World War II. Strewn all around the site was the debris of the fierce battles and bombardments of that war.

A week or so after they set up camp, John Wayne, then in the midst of filming *The Barbarian and the Geisha,* flew overhead in a helicopter and asked permission to land. A moment later the six-foot-four film star was engulfed by Marines, who rushed out of the radar hut to greet him. Oswald was on mess duty at the time for the third straight month; and a photograph taken of Wayne dining with the men shows Oswald in the background. (See photograph section.) Wayne departed later that afternoon.

During his ten weeks on Corregidor, Oswald became a proficient cook, scrambling gallon after gallon of eggs each morning. Recalls George Wilkins: "Ozzie really could put on a show with those eggs. He could have three gallons of eggs on the griddle and take a mess tray and slide it under the puddle of eggs and flip them all at once. It was quite a sight."

Despite his continuing mess duty, Oswald seemed to enjoy himself on the island in his spare time, as did his fellow Marines. The men were responsible for little but their own entertainment; Sunday visits to the island by American tourists were virtually the only breaks in their routine of swimming, sunbathing and exploring. In his letters from Corregidor, Persons had little to report except that his suntan was the best he'd ever had. Radar duty was so uneventful that the men practiced scanning for imaginary aircraft to avoid being driven crazy by the monotony.

Zack Stout took long walks with Oswald, exploring the battle-scarred fortifications, and found him especially good company. Oswald knew the history of the island and would explain it to Stout. "We'd see all these unexploded shells . . . and tunnels," Stout recalls. "And we'd go swimming every day . . . the clearest, cleanest water I've ever seen, you could see the bombs still lying at the bottom." Their explorations of the island were temporarily discouraged when a native found and killed a 15-foot python in the jungle near the beach. Oswald spent most of the rest of his free time reading serious books and waiting for letters. When he did receive mail, he would abruptly leave the friends he was with to read it in private.

By March 7 the Indonesia crisis had finally subsided, and the Marines boarded another LST, the USS *Wexford County,* with all their radar gear. It took another eleven days at sea before they reached their home base in Japan. Operation Strongback had lasted one day short of three months.

Back at Atsugi, Oswald was brought up on charges for having had an unregistered weapon—the derringer with which he had shot himself in October. The court-martial found him guilty as charged on April 11, and he was sentenced to twenty days at hard labor, forfeiture of $50 in pay and reduction to the rank of private (thus nullifying his having passed the examination for corporal). His confinement was suspended for six months, with the provision that it would be canceled if he kept out of further trouble. Moreover, even though his officers supported his request to be returned to radar duty, he was inexplicably kept on mess duty.

It was at that point that Oswald put in for a hardship discharge. Apparently he hoped to be discharged in Japan, where he had made friends, but this request also was turned down. Stout remembers that Oswald became increasingly bitter at this turn of events and began to argue that he was being singled out for mistreatment by the Marine Corps.

Oswald finally took his resentment out on the man who had reassigned him to mess duty, Technical Sergeant Miguel Rodriguez. Rodriguez, a well-built Mexican-American from Texas, recalls Oswald swaggering over to him at a squadron party at the Enlisted Men's Club at Atsugi, looking at him with "those small, dreamy eyes" and saying, "You've got guts to come in here." Rodriguez ignored his challenge, suspecting at the time that Oswald was prejudiced against persons of Mexican descent. A few nights later Rodriguez saw Oswald at the Bluebird Café, the local hangout for the Marines in "Coffee Mill." This time Oswald spilled a drink on Rodriguez and attempted to provoke a fight. The military police intervened, and the next day Rodriguez signed a complaint against Oswald.[12]

In June Oswald again faced a summary court-martial. At the hearing Oswald elected to act as his own defense counsel and, by cross-examining Rodriguez, attempted to persuade the court that he had spilled the drink accidentally. Rodriguez insisted— and still insists—that Oswald had not been drunk and that he had deliberately spilled his drink on him. The judge ruled that

Oswald had used "provoking words" and sentenced him to twenty-eight days in the brig and the forfeiture of another $55. Oswald began serving his sentence on July 27, 1958.

Life in the Marine brig was designed to be punishing. Prisoners were not allowed to say a solitary word to one another. Except for sleeping and eating periods, the prisoners were made to stand at rigid attention during every moment they were not performing menial duties. The guards, or turnkeys, were especially brutal: when a prisoner had to use the toilet, he had to toe up to a red line and scream his request over and over again, until the turnkey was satisfied and granted permission.

One fellow Marine who was in the brig at the same time as Oswald described the brig as a horror—"far worse than anything in civilian prisons." From his nine-man cell, he remembers seeing Oswald looking out from a single cell. "He was standing there by the bars in civilian clothes. . . . I laughed when I saw him, but we couldn't say anything." Oswald was released from the brig on August 13.

Joseph D. Macedo, another young radar operator in "Coffee Mill," remembers meeting Oswald soon after he was released from the brig. He found him "a completely changed person from the naïve and innocent boy" who had joined the unit in Japan less than a year earlier. "Oswald was a nondrinker and virgin when he came overseas"; then at the six to seven o'clock "happy hours" in the evenings, Oswald began drinking "mixed drinks with the men and became more extroverted and moderately humorous." Now Macedo found him to be again cold, withdrawn and bitter. "I've seen enough of a democratic society here in MACS-1," Oswald said. "When I get out I'm going to try something else. . . ."

Oswald seemed to associate more than ever with his Japanese friends and less with Marines. He frequently went to Tokyo or otherwise disappeared on his passes. One of Oswald's Marine friends recalls meeting him at a house in Yamato with a woman who was working there as a housekeeper for a naval officer. He was impressed at the time that Oswald had found a girlfriend who was not a bar girl or prostitute. In the house was also a handsome young Japanese man, for whom Oswald had apparently bought a T-shirt from the PX on base. While the girls cooked sukiyaki on a hibachi grill, the men talked, but the

Marine was unable to understand exactly what Oswald's relation was to the group.

In September 1958, a new international crisis arose as the Chinese Communists began shelling and blockading the tiny offshore islands of Quemoy and Matsu, which were occupied by anti-Communist troops loyal to the Nationalist government on Formosa. In anticipation of a possible naval intervention in the straits between Formosa and the Communist-held mainland, "Coffee Mill" was ordered to set up a forward radar base at Pingtung on Formosa. Along with his fellow Marines, Oswald boarded the USS *Skagit*, an attack cargo ship.

The trip from Japan to northern Formosa took more than a week. In Formosa the officers commanding "Coffee Mill" found that its crucial "squawk" or identification friend or foe (IFF) system, had been totally compromised. The Communist Chinese seemed to know all the code signals, which, on one occasion, allowed them to penetrate air defenses and appear on the radar screens as "friends" rather than "foes." Lieutenant Charles R. Rhodes, an air control officer from South Carolina, vividly recalls the Communist Chinese jets "breezing right through the IFF system." Someone with access to the squawk codes in the parrot had apparently passed them along to the enemy. "We never knew how they got their planes through," Rhodes observed, "but they had all the signals . . . we really caught hell about that."

When not on radar duty, the Marines also helped the Nationalist Chinese troops build artillery emplacements. This, to Oswald, was further evidence of American "imperialism." He told an American reporter thirteen months later about his indignation at "helping drag up guns for the Chinese [and] watching American technicians show the Chinese how to use them." He added, "It's one thing to talk against communism and another thing to drag a gun up a mountainside."

Lieutenant Rhodes remembers Oswald from the first time he met him on Corregidor as "somebody who looked real lonesome." Whenever possible, Rhodes explained, he tried to be friendly toward him because "I always figured that boy probably had trouble at home—I was born the baby of six kids in the middle of the Depression, and I knew how it felt to be down. Oswald looked like the kind of kid who got the hand-me-downs, just like I had. I even remember once that Oswald told me, 'Lieutenant Rhodes, you're the only officer who's ever been nice to me.' "

Rhodes seemed to hold Oswald's respect, despite having to reprimand him severely on one occasion. "Oswald did a good job on radar," Rhodes recalls. "He was the type of fellow who liked a little attention and praise. . . . He liked to be told when he was doing a good job, and I always tried to say something nice about his work." Then one evening, while Rhodes was in charge of the radar operations, he left the bubble for a few minutes, leaving Oswald at the plotting board. A superior officer happened to go into the bubble and found Oswald asleep at Rhodes' desk. "He didn't do anything to Oswald, but he sure gave me hell, and I had to give Oswald hell," Rhodes said. Oswald's excuse was that he had been on mess duty and was tired.

One night, soon after they had arrived, Oswald was on guard duty at about midnight when Rhodes, the officer of the guard, suddenly heard "four or five" shots from the position Oswald was guarding. Drawing his .45-caliber pistol, he ran toward the clump of trees from which the gunfire seemingly emanated. There he found Oswald slumped against a tree, holding his M-1 rifle across his lap. "When I got to him, he was shaking and crying," Rhodes later recounted. "He said he had seen men in the woods and that he challenged them and then started shooting. . . ." Rhodes put his arm around Oswald's shoulder and slowly walked him back to his tent. "He kept saying he just couldn't bear being on guard duty."

Rhodes reported the incident to his commanding officer, and almost immediately after that, on October 6, Oswald was returned to Japan on a military plane. Rhodes was not told any reason for this sudden action other than the official explanation that he was being sent to Atsugi for "medical treatment." (He had apparently contracted a mild case of gonorrhea, but this had been under treatment before he had shipped out for Formosa.)[13]

Rhodes believed then, as he does today, that Oswald planned the shooting incident as a ploy to get himself sent back to Japan. "Oswald liked Japan and wanted to stay. . . . I don't know why, but I know he didn't want to go to Formosa, and I think he fired off his gun to get out of there. . . . There was nothing dumb about Oswald."

When Oswald reported to the base hospital in Atsugi, he complained of having injured himself doing "heavy lifting" in Formosa, but the only unambiguous symptoms the doctors were able to find were urethral discharges which had persisted from the gonorrhea. With his unit still overseas, Oswald was reassigned to the Marine squadron at Iwakuni, an air base some 430 miles southwest of Tokyo, which manned the Tactical Air Control Center for the northern Pacific area. In the case of a Communist Chinese, North Korean or Soviet attack, it was the job of the center to coordinate the air defenses. This required that continual information about the availability of allied aircraft throughout the Pacific be constantly fed to the center. At any given moment the center had to be ready and able to scramble interceptors.

On this temporary duty, Oswald again was assigned to the translucent plotting board. Owen Dejanovich, a tall, lanky native of Chicago who went on to play professional football, immediately recognized Oswald in the center as someone he had gone to radar school with at Keesler Air Base and tried to renew the acquaintanceship. He quickly found that Oswald had grown enormously bitter since he had last known him.

"He kept referring to the Marines at the center as 'You Americans,' as if he were some sort of foreigner simply observing what we were doing," says Dejanovich. His tone was definitely accusatory. He spoke in slogans about "American imperialism" and "exploitation" which made Dejanovich think at the time that Oswald—whom he called Bugs—was merely being perverse for the sake of shocking the other Marines at the center.

In the evenings Dejanovich would occasionally see Oswald speaking to an attractive Eurasian woman. "She was much too good-looking for Bugs," he recalls thinking, and he wondered why such an attractive "roundeye," who was obviously not a common bar girl, would waste her time with a Marine private.

Another Marine in the unit, Dan Powers, had got the impression from Oswald that this Eurasian was half-Russian and was teaching Oswald the Russian language. Other Marines speculated that Oswald had simply set up a "ranch," or living arrangement, with the Eurasian at Iwakuni. But whenever Dejanovich would see Oswald with this girl at the Orion bar in Iwakuni, he would just shake his head at what he considered Oswald's perverse nature. "Who but Oswald would come to Japan and find a round-eyed Russian girlfriend?" he would ask himself.

Unknown to his fellow Marines, Oswald was during this period in Japan making careful plans and preparations to defect to the Soviet Union—at least, that is what he told reporters when he arrived in Moscow one year later.

3

The Defector

On November 2, 1958, at the end of his thirteen-month tour of duty in Japan, Lee Harvey Oswald boarded the USS *Barrett* in Yokosuka. Two weeks later, after a quiet and uneventful voyage, the troopship steamed into San Francisco Harbor. Most of the Marines aboard cheered at the sight of the Golden Gate Bridge. For them, it meant they would soon see their families and girl-friends. But for Oswald, it was merely the first step of a much longer journey eastward.

Oswald traveled by bus to Fort Worth to see his family on a thirty-day leave. He stayed at his mother's apartment but spent a good deal of time with his brother Robert, hunting squirrels and rabbits with .22-caliber rifles. Robert remembers telling his brother that he had just missed seeing their half brother, John Pic, who was on his way to Japan with the Air Force. Lee seemed disappointed. On December 21 Oswald boarded still another bus and returned to the Marines.

Just before Christmas he reported to his new unit—Marine Air Control Squadron Nine, or MACS-9—in Santa Ana, California. It operated out of an old Navy blimp base, which had on its grounds two of the largest wooden hangars ever constructed, then used mainly to service helicopters. The Marine jets and other fixed-wing aircraft flew mainly out of El Toro Air Base, located across the road from the blimp base. The radar bubble which MACS-9 was assigned to operate was located on a grassy field near the road separating the two bases; behind it, the radar antennas were enclosed by a square of barbed wire.

Along with Owen Dejanovich and a number of other Marines with whom he had served in Japan, Oswald was assigned to Bravo team in the bubble. In theory, his job was not very different from the one he had performed in Atsugi. He would first scan the radarscope for unidentified planes (or ones in distress) in the area south of Los Angeles; then he would be rotated back to the plotting board, where he would wait for someone else to spot a "bogey" aircraft. But unlike Atsugi, where occasional enemy planes strayed into the allied Air Defense Identification Zone, causing alerts to be sounded and intercept paths plotted on the board, little happened in California to break the tedium for the radar operators in the bubble. "All we did was look at radar screens," Mack Osborne, one of Oswald's crew-mates explained. "It was the sort of work a left-handed monkey could do." He added, "The only thing to do at that base was to play around."

While most of the men in the unit enjoyed the easy life at the California base, Oswald arranged to take a Marine Corps proficiency examination in the Russian language, which he took on February 25, 1959. In reading Russian, he achieved a score of plus four, which meant that he had got four more answers right than wrong. In writing Russian, he scored plus three, and in comprehending spoken Russian, he was weaker, scoring minus five. While his overall score was considered "poor" when compared to the results of those studying Russian at language schools, it showed that he had learned, if not mastered, the rudiments of a very difficult foreign language. Moreover, since it would take more than the three months he had been back in the United States to achieve such a stage in written and spoken Russian, except under extraordinary circumstances, Oswald would have had to have begun his training in Russian while he was still in Japan. None of his barracks-mates in Japan, however, remember Oswald's using a linguaphone or records to learn Russian, which suggests that he had some more private means.

Less than a month after taking his Russian examination, Oswald took and passed tests which gave him the equivalency of a high school diploma and made it possible for him to apply to college. Meanwhile, he worked at improving his Russian. For hours on end he would sit with a textbook and Russian-English dictionary, testing himself on words, then scribbling them down in a notebook he kept. He subscribed to a Russian-language newspaper (and renewed his subscription to the *People's World*, the organ of the Socialist Workers Party).

When astonished clerks in the mailroom reported the fact that Oswald was receiving this "leftist literature" to their operations officer, Captain Robert E. Block, he questioned Oswald about this reading matter. Oswald explained that he was only trying to indoctrinate himself in Russian theory in conformance with Marine Corps policy. Although not entirely convinced by Oswald's answer, Block did not press the matter. The Marines who shared a cubicle with Oswald in one of the quonset huts used for sleeping quarters by MACS-9 and watched—and heard —Oswald incessantly practicing his Russian found it more curious. They nicknamed him Oswaldskovich, and he played along with the Russian allusion by calling them Comrade and answering questions put to him with a *da* or a *nyet*.

Richard Dennis Call, another radar operator in the unit, recalls that whenever he played his classical record *Russian Fireworks*, Oswald would knock at his door, saying, "You called, Comrade?"[1] They would then usually play a game of chess with Oswald taking the red players because, he would explain in his mock Russian accent, "The Red Army is always victorious." He even seemed to enjoy being kidded about being a "Russian spy."

By the summer of 1959 Oswald had become so well known as a Russophile within the unit that one Marine asked him to have dinner with his aunt, Rosaleen Quinn, an extremely attractive airline stewardess from New Orleans, because she was studying Russian in preparation for the State Department's foreign-language examination. She met Oswald in a cafeteria in Santa Ana, and they spoke in Russian for about two hours. Although she had been studying Russian with a Berlitz tutor for more than a year, she found that Oswald had a far more confident command of the language than she did and could string entire sentences together without much hesitation. She asked how he had learned Russian, and he shrugged that he had "taught himself" by listening to Radio Moscow.

He then told her that he had also learned some Japanese while stationed in Japan. In Russian they discussed what "life must be like in the Soviet Union." She was impressed not only by his seriousness about the Russian language, but also by his intellectual curiosity. He would readily admit areas in which he had no knowledge or experience and seemed to be "totally guileless." After dinner he walked her back to the rooming house where she was staying and politely said good-night.

Just before she left Santa Ana, Oswald took her to see the film *South Pacific*, and afterward they had a drink at a neighborhood bar. Again they practiced their Russian and spoke of traveling. This time Oswald told her he had plans to go to Europe, but he did not specify what they were.

That summer Oswald also confided in Corporal Nelson Delgado, who shared a cubicle with him in the quonset hut and worked with Oswald for four-hour shifts, every other day, in the radar bubble. Gradually they became good friends. Delgado, a Puerto Rican, found that Oswald "treated him like an equal," unlike the other Marines in the unit. He also came to admire the incisive way that Oswald employed his intelligence to "cut others, even officers, down to their proper size." During their long and uneventful watches in the radar bubble, Delgado tried to teach Oswald Spanish and found him a willing and able student. Oswald even purchased a Spanish-English dictionary so that he could practice on his own. On one occasion Delgado took Oswald to Tijuana, Mexico, with him for the weekend. After spending a few hours with him in a bar, Oswald left Delgado, presumably to meet "friends," whom he did not further identify.

What really seemed to weld the bond between them, however, was their common interest in Fidel Castro, who had in the beginning of that year won his guerrilla war and assumed power in Cuba. Delgado remembers that when he first voiced some sympathy for Castro's revolution, Oswald's ears "perked up." In the course of their discussions Oswald told him that he wanted desperately to go to Cuba and help train Castro's army.

His hero that August was Major William A. Morgan, a former sergeant in the American Army who had joined Castro in Cuba, had renounced his citizenship, and had been promoted to a field-grade rank personally by Castro. One of Major Morgan's more impressive achievements that summer was to act as a double agent and lure anti-Castro rebels into a trap in Cuba.[2]

At one point, Oswald suggested that Delgado accompany him to Cuba, where they both could emulate Major Morgan. Apparently believing that Delgado had some local means of getting in touch with Cubans, Oswald pressed him for someone to contact. Delgado recalls that while they were on radar duty, he scribbled a note to Oswald saying that he should write "The Cuban Embassy, Washington, D.C."

While Oswald had up to that point received very few letters, Delgado noticed that he now began getting mail several times a week. He also learned while looking through Oswald's locker for a tie to borrow, that at least some of these letters came from the Cuban consulate. "The seal," he recalls, "was unmistakable."[3]

The moment Oswald began receiving his correspondence from the Cubans, he began "putting on a coat and tie" and going with Delgado into Los Angeles, about one and a half hours away by bus. At first Delgado did not know whom Oswald was visiting; then Oswald told him his purpose was "to visit the Cuban Consulate." Late one night, while Delgado was on duty with Oswald, "I got a call from the MP guard shack . . . that Oswald had a visitor at the front gate. This man had to be a civilian; otherwise, they would have let him in. . . . I had to find somebody to relieve Oswald."

About an hour later Delgado happened to pass the main gate and saw Oswald in a heated discussion with a man in a topcoat. It seemed odd to Delgado that anyone would wear a coat on a hot California night. Although Oswald didn't tell Delgado who the stranger was, he formed the impression at the time that he was in some way connected with "the Cuba business."[4]

As Oswald's tour of duty neared completion, Delgado noticed a stack of "spotter" photographs showing front and profile views of a fighter plane among Oswald's papers. He realized that they had probably been used as a visual aid in training classes, and wondered why Oswald had them in his possession.

Oswald stuffed the photographs into a duffel bag with some other possessions and asked Delgado if he would bring the bag to the bus station in Los Angeles, put it in a locker, and bring him back the key. According to Delgado's recollection, Oswald gave him two dollars for doing this.[5]

Shortly afterward he asked Oswald if he was still planning to go to Cuba after his discharge. He recalls that Oswald screwed his face into a squint, as if he had not heard Delgado correctly, and then replied without further elaboration, "When I get out, I'm going to school in Switzerland."

Oswald had planned this stage in his journey with consummate care: Marines normally had a two-year commitment to the inactive reserve even after completing their active duty, and at least technically they needed a valid reason for traveling overseas during this time. Perhaps because of this, Oswald applied in March 1959 for admission to the Spring 1960 term at the Albert Schweitzer College, a new liberal arts college in Churwalden, Switzerland, with fewer than fifty students. On his application Oswald professed fluency in Russian, some knowledge of German, a high school diploma and interest in "ideology," philosophy and psychology. He studiously avoided mentioning his political convictions. Instead, he listed Dr. Norman Vincent Peale as one of his favorite authors and gave such reasons as "to live in a healthy climate and a good moral atmosphere" for his desire to attend Schweitzer College. He added to the application, somewhat gratuitously, that he planned to take a summer course at the University of Turku in Finland.

After his application was accepted by the Albert Schweitzer College,[6] Oswald wrote his brother Robert: "Pretty soon I'll be getting out of the Corps and I know what I want to be and how I'm going to be it. . . ." He did not hint at the real destination he had planned for himself since Japan, nor had he told any of his fellow Marines.

In another maneuver Oswald filed papers with the Red Cross in July intended to help him get an early discharge from the Marine Corps. He explained to his mother in a special-delivery letter that Red Cross representatives would call on her to ascertain that he was needed at home to support her. "Please tell them that I will be able to secure a good job . . . just inform them that I have been your only source of income," he wrote. He wanted an early discharge, he wrote, "in order to help you."[7]

Marguerite Oswald fully cooperated with her son by sending

him her own affidavit and supporting letters from two friends, a doctor and a lawyer. With this impressive documentation, Oswald filed for a dependency discharge on August 17, 1959. His request was approved two weeks later, and on September 3, to the surprise of his crew-mates, he was detached from duty and transferred to the headquarters company at El Toro across the road to be processed out of the Marines.

The very next day Oswald filed for a passport in Santa Ana. He noted that the primary purpose of his trip was "to attend the College of A. Schweitzer, Switzerland, and the University of Turku, Turku, Finland," and cited possible travel to England, France, Switzerland, Germany, Finland, Russia, Cuba and the Dominican Republic. Selection of colleges in Switzerland and Finland provided a plausible cover for his travels east. Within six days he had his passport in hand.

On September 11 Oswald signed a statement pledging "I shall not hereafter in any manner reveal or divulge to any person any information affecting the National Defense, Classified, Top-secret, Secret, or Confidential, or which I gained knowledge during my employment . . . ," as was required of all Marines with access to classified material. He was then officially released from active duty and transferred to the Marine Air Reserve Training Command.

Oswald left Santa Ana that day and traveled by bus to Fort Worth, where he arrived at his mother's house at 2 A.M. on September 14. When he arose the following morning, Marguerite was rudely surprised by her son's announcement that he planned to "board a ship and work in the export-import business"; she had counted on his remaining home to help support her.

After withdrawing $203 from the West Side State Bank, his only known bank account,[8] he went to his brother Robert's house on Davenport Street in Fort Worth, where he spent an entire day. "We didn't do much that day—just sat around the house and talked," Robert Oswald later wrote in his book *Lee*. "He told us he planned to go to New Orleans and work for an export firm. . . . However detailed his plans may have been, he kept them to himself." On this day Robert took a picture of Lee holding Cathy, Robert's daughter.

On the morning of September 16 Oswald showed his mother

his passport—she remembers noticing a page stamped IM-PORT-EXPORT—and left for New Orleans after giving her $100. He had stored most of his belongings, including his Imperial Reflex camera, in his brother's garage.

The next day in New Orleans, Oswald went directly to the offices of Travel Consultants, Inc., where he booked passage on the freighter *Marion Lykes*, due to sail the following day from New Orleans bound for Le Havre, France. On the steamship company's application form, Oswald described himself as a "shipping export agent" going abroad for a two-month holiday. He paid $220.75 for the one-way ticket. He spent that night in the Liberty Hotel, from which he wrote his mother: "I have booked passage on a ship to Europe, I would have had to sooner or later and I think it's best I go now. Just remember above all else that my values are different from Robert's or yours. It is difficult to tell you how I feel. Just remember this is what I must do. I did not tell you about my plans because you could hardly be expected to understand."

The SS *Marion Lykes* left New Orleans on September 20, one day behind schedule. Although the freighter had accommodations for twelve passengers, on this trip it carried only four: George B. Church, Jr., a retired lieutenant colonel in the U.S. Army; his wife; Billy Joe Lord, a seventeen-year-old student who planned to study at the Institute of French Studies in Tours, France; and Oswald, Lord's roommate for the sixteen-day voyage.

On their first day out Lord talked to Oswald while he unpacked his belongings. Oswald preferred not to talk about himself, saying only that he was a former Marine who was on his way to Europe to attend college in "Sweden or Switzerland." He didn't identify the college further. Oswald spoke in a decidedly bitter tone about the injustice of his mother's being reduced to having to work in a drugstore to support herself.

When he noticed that Lord had brought a Bible with him, he turned the discussion to religion. He asked Lord how he could believe in God in light of the findings of modern science. When Lord tried to argue with him, Oswald simply stated that "there was no Supreme Being or God," adding that "anyone with intelligence would recognize that there was only matter." Throughout the conversation Lord found Oswald "mentally alert . . . but extremely cynical in his general attitude." The roommates didn't, as Lord put it, "hit it off very well," and he avoided any further philosophical discussions with Oswald. "Oswald was not outgoing, and neither was I," Lord later explained.

Oswald spent the first few days mainly on deck, pacing to and fro, as if contemplating some plan. Mrs. Church watched him with some interest and tried, on several occasions, to strike up a conversation. "He was so vague," she recalls. "There was nothing you could get from him." When she asked him what school he planned to attend in Europe, he evaded "giving the name of the university," stating only that he wanted to study "philosophy or psychology." When she asked him for his home address, he looked at her suspiciously and asked her why she cared. She explained that she wanted to send him a Christmas card. He gave her his mother's address in Fort Worth, apparently intentionally misspelling his name "Oswalt." Unlike the other passengers, Oswald went to great lengths to avoid being photographed. Mrs. Church observed, "Whenever I got my camera out to take some pictures, he would head in the other direction. He told us he didn't want his picture taken."

In the evening the four passengers ate at a common table, and Oswald sat diagonally across from Colonel Church. Oswald usually ate quickly and silently. The one time Church tried to draw him into conversation, Oswald gave him a historic description of the Depression of the 1930s, which he seemed to see as another failure of capitalism. Again he dwelt on his impoverished family. After a few days at sea, Oswald began to spend most of his time in his cabin and even to miss meals. Church assumed he was seasick.

On October 8, the freighter finally pulled into the harbor at Le Havre, France, where Oswald and the other three passengers disembarked. (The steward remembered Oswald for not leaving the customary tip.) Neither the Churches nor Billy Joe Lord recall seeing Oswald on the boat train to Southampton, England, but according to British passport control records, he arrived there on Friday, October 9, declaring to customs officials that he had $700 with him and intended to spend one week in England before proceeding to college in Switzerland.

These were the last witnesses to identify Oswald before he

appeared in Moscow one week later. The stamps on his passport
show that he left Heathrow Airport in London that same day on
an international flight and landed later that evening in Helsinki,
Finland. Since there was no direct flight from London to Helsinki during the time Oswald was in London, Oswald must have
changed planes at some city in Europe.[9] According to Finnish
hotel records, he checked in midnight on Friday at the Torni
Hotel in downtown Helsinki, then moved on Saturday to the
less expensive Klaus Kurki Hotel, where he remained registered
for five days.

Swedish intelligence has found evidence that Oswald traveled
to Stockholm during this period, apparently to consult the Soviet Embassy there.[10] Sometime that same week Oswald visited
the Soviet Consulate in Helsinki and obtained visa number
403339, valid for a six-day trip to the Soviet Union. He also
bought $300 worth of tourist vouchers for the Soviet Union,
although it is not clear where he got these funds.[11] On the evening of October 15 Oswald left Helsinki by train and crossed the
Finnish-Soviet border at Vainikkala, bound for Moscow.[12]

On Saturday morning, October 31, two weeks after his arrival
in Moscow, Oswald emerged from a taxi in front of the United
States Embassy in Moscow and strode past the Marine guards
into the consular section. Richard E. Snyder, who had joined
the CIA in June 1949 as an intelligence operative, then had
served in Tokyo under State Department cover and was now
acting as senior consular officer in Moscow, recalled that Oswald banged his passport down on Snyder's desk. Snyder could
see the tension in his pallid face: "He was wound up like six
watch springs and highly nervous."

When Snyder asked what he could do for him, Oswald stated
coldly, "I've come to give up my American passport and renounce my citizenship." He then handed the veteran intelligence officer a signed but undated handwritten note saying:

I, Lee Harvey Oswald, do hereby request that my present
citizenship in the United States of America, be revoked.

I have entered the Soviet Union for the express purpose
of applying for citizenship in the Soviet Union, through the
means of naturalization. My request for citizenship is now
pending before the Supreme Soviet of the USSR.

I take these steps for political reasons. My request for the revoking of my American citizenship is made only after the longest and most serious consideration.

I affirm that my allegiance is to the Union of Soviet Socialist Republics.[13]

Snyder could see that Oswald's defection had been carefully prepared. "You could tell he'd been rehearsing this scene for a long time before," Snyder explained subsequently.

Oswald's note showed a firm understanding of the legal subtleties governing the revocation of citizenship, and Snyder assessed Oswald, despite his obvious edginess, as "rather intelligent and quite articulate." Even so, since it was the State Department's policy to discourage Americans from defecting, Snyder tried to stall Oswald by asking him his reasons for applying for Soviet citizenship.

"I am a Marxist," Oswald insisted in a loud, arrogant voice.

"You'll be a lonely man as a Marxist," Snyder shot back. Oswald did not smile or show any sign of comprehending Snyder's implication that the Soviet Union was very far from a Marxist society. He simply replied that he had been forewarned that the consul "would try to talk him out of his decision and that he wanted no lectures" from Snyder on Marxism or any other topic.

Although he now realized that there was little real possibility of discouraging Oswald from defecting, Snyder tried to elicit as much information as he could from Oswald that would be of operational significance to the State Department or CIA. When he asked him when he had first become interested in renouncing his American citizenship, Oswald expounded on the "American imperialism" he had witnessed while serving as a Marine in Japan and other bases in the Far East. Snyder prodded him about what he meant by "imperialism," and Oswald, visibly growing angry, retorted that "his eyes had been opened to the way America oppresses and colonizes foreign people from observing . . . actions in Okinawa."

Snyder noticed that Oswald used "simple Marxist stereotypes without . . . independent formulation" and that he made a point of condemning his own government and lauding the Soviets. Having sufficiently engaged him emotionally, Snyder asked

if he was prepared to serve the Soviet state. Oswald spontane-
ously answered that he had been a radar operator in the Marine
Corps and that he had already agreed to furnish the Soviet
Union "with such knowledge as he had acquired while in the
Marine Corps concerning his specialty." Oswald strongly hinted
that he knew something that would be of "special interest" to
Soviet intelligence.

Across the room, John McVickar, another senior consular officer, remembers being stunned by this part of the conversation.
"Oswald said he was going to turn over classified information
he had from his radar-operating days in the Marine Corps. This
raised hackles. . . ." Something about the way Oswald used
what seemed recently learned phrases about Marxism and legal
renunciation of citizenship without understanding their precise
meaning gave McVickar the impression that Oswald might have
been "tutored" before appearing at the consulate.

"[There] seemed to me," he wrote in a 1963 memorandum,
"to be the possibility that [Oswald] was following a pattern of
behavior in which he had been tutored by person or persons
unknown."

At the time, however, there was little Snyder could do to deter
Oswald from his planned course. He thus asked him to return
the following Monday on the pretext that the consulate could
not process his application on a Saturday.[14]

On Monday, however, Oswald did not return, and Snyder
drafted a telegram to the State Department in Washington, stating, ". . . the Embassy proposes to delay action on Oswald's
request to execute an oath of renunciation to the extent dictated
by developments. . . ."[15] The same day the naval attaché in
Moscow cabled the commander of Naval Operations in Washington that "Lee Harvey Oswald . . . stated he was radar operator in Marine Corps and has offered to furnish Soviets information he possessed on US radar."[16] Copies of the State
Department telex on Oswald were also sent to the CIA, FBI and
Office of Naval Intelligence, and the wheels of the intelligence
agencies slowly began to turn.[17]

Meanwhile, in Moscow, Snyder tipped Robert Korengold, bureau chief of United Press International, that Oswald was about
to defect and that he was staying in Room 233 of the Metropole

Hotel. He suggested that a further interview with Oswald might make an "interesting story" for his wire service.

Korengold, an intrepid reporter, rushed over to the Metropole Hotel and pounded on Oswald's door. Oswald opened the door a few inches and told Korengold that he was not granting any interviews.

The next day in Fort Worth, Texas, a heavyset man stopped Robert Oswald, then working as a milk delivery man, and identified himself as a reporter for the Fort Worth *Star-Telegram*. He showed Oswald a telex he had received from Moscow describing his brother's attempt to renounce his citizenship. "Lee is awfully young, looking for excitement," Robert told the reporter, "[and] I don't believe he knows what he is doing." He realized, nonetheless, "how carefully and patiently Lee had planned his defection." Robert Oswald assumed the application to Albert Schweitzer College in Switzerland was "part of the plan," as was his early discharge from the Marines. He had even put the University of Turku in Finland on his application to provide himself a pretext for his presence in Finland, Robert noted.

After finishing his milk route, Robert Oswald rushed home and telegraphed his brother. "Lee," he implored, "through any possible means contact me. Mistake. Keep your nose clean." (The last sentence was a family expression meant to assure Lee that the telegram had indeed come from his brother.) When the U.S. Embassy called Oswald to relay the contents of the telegram, he refused to pick it up at the embassy as was suggested.

On November 3 Oswald sent the American Embassy a letter strongly protesting the refusal of the consul to accept his renunciation of citizenship. "My application, requesting that I be considered for citizenship in the Soviet Union is now pending before the Supreme Soviet of the USSR," Oswald wrote. "In the event of acceptance, I will request my government to lodge a formal protest regarding this incident." Snyder wrote him again, inviting him to appear in person to "prepare the necessary documents for renunciation of citizenship." Oswald did not accept the invitation.

After refusing all further communications from embassy personnel, Oswald wrote his brother a letter, stating defiantly:

Well, what shall we talk about? the weather, perhaps? Certainly you do not wish me to speak of my decision to remain in the Soviet Union and apply for citizenship here, since I'm afraid you would not be able to comprehend my reasons. You really don't know anything about me. Do you know, for instance, that I have waited to do this for well over a year, do you know that I (Russian words) speak a fair amount of Russian which I have been studying for many months.

I have been told that I will not *have* to leave the Soviet Union if I don't care to. This then is my decision. I will not leave this country, the Soviet Union, under any conditions. I will never return to the United States, which is a country I hate.

I received your telegram and was glad to hear from you, only one word bothered me, the word "mistake." I assume you mean that I have made a mistake. It is not for you to tell me that. You cannot understand my reasons for this very serious action. I will not speak to anyone from the United States over the telephone since it may be taped by the Americans.

The next day the embassy made a final attempt to contact Oswald. John McVickar personally brought a letter to Oswald from his half brother John Pic, then serving with the U.S. Air Force in Japan. Oswald did not answer his door at the Metropole. The maid on the floor explained to McVickar that he was rarely seen at the hotel. McVickar left the note at the desk.

Less than a week later Oswald granted his first interview to Aline Mosby of UPI, who came to his hotel room with a camera. Mosby, herself from Montana, thought Oswald "looked like some Okie from the boondocks," not the hard-line political defector she had expected. In his huge room, furnished with ornate and gilded furniture and overlooking the Bolshoi Theater, Oswald looked "even more completely out of place." He had a "sallow complexion" and "seemed a bit awkward" at first, but he grew more confident, even smug, as he spoke. It resembled a two-hour lecture, rather than an interview.

Oswald doctrinally dated his turn to Marxism to his observation of the "class struggle" in New York City, where "I saw . . .

the luxury of Park Avenue and the worker's lives on the [Lower] East Side." He told Mosby that when he read Marx at the age of fifteen, it was like "a very religious man opening the bible for the first time." When he began to read Marxist theory in New Orleans, "I could see the impoverishment of the masses before my own eyes in my mother, and I could see the capitalists." He told her that he then "continued to indoctrinate myself for five years." He claimed that he had saved $1,600 while in active service in the Marines to finance his defection.

Like McVickar, Mosby felt that Oswald used propaganda phrases, such as "capitalist lackeys" and "imperialist's running dogs," with which he was not entirely comfortable. "It sounded as if it were all being given by rote, as if he had memorized *Pravda*."[18] As was required of all correspondents in Moscow, Mosby handed one copy of her piece to the Soviet censor and a second copy to the telegraph office, which she knew would send her copy to UPI in New York only after it had been read and approved by the KGB staff in the censor's office. The next day the UPI story appeared in Fort Worth under the headline FORT WORTH DEFECTOR CONFIRMS RED BELIEFS.[19]

Only two days after granting the Mosby interview, Oswald was visited by Priscilla Post Johnson, who was something more than an ordinary journalist. Before coming to Moscow, Johnson had worked as an assistant to Senator John F. Kennedy and then had gone on to earn a reputation as a keen analyst of Soviet affairs. Although officially working for the North American Newspaper Alliance syndicate in Moscow as a correspondent— which position paid only $25 or so per story—she was also listed in a State Department document of "government employees" who had seen Oswald during this period. During a previous tour at the U.S. Embassy in Moscow, Priscilla Johnson had worked for the Joint Translating Service. Her report of the interview with Oswald, which was furnished to the U.S. Embassy on November 17, discusses Oswald's motives for defecting in considerably greater depth than Mosby's report or Johnson's own brief journalistic account (which was published on November 26).

When asked about factors contributing to his decision to defect, Oswald volunteered to Johnson: "My decision was unemotional. . . . I had discovered Socialist literature at the age of fifteen. . . . I was looking for something that would give me the key to my environment. My Mother had been a worker all her life. All her life she had to produce profits for capitalists." Johnson then probed deeper into his ideology. "I don't claim to be an intellectual genius," Oswald prefaced his remarks. "[But] I believe sooner or later Communism will replace capitalism. Capitalism is a defensive ideology, whereas Communism is aggressive." She pressed him about who had guided him toward communism, but Oswald refused to name any mentors except "Marx and Engels . . . the standard works."

Oswald made a point of attributing his decision to defect to the Soviet Union to his experiences in Asia with the Marine Corps. "I am not an idealist completely," he told Johnson. "I have had a chance to watch American imperialism in action . . . if you've ever seen the Naval base at Subic Bay in the Philippines you'd know what I mean. Americans look upon all foreign peoples as something to be exploited for profit."

Specifically he noted his part in the invasion force sent to intervene in Indonesia in March 1958. Although the intervention was called off, Oswald explained: "We sat off the coast loaded with ammunition and that was enough for me." If his own recollections are to be taken literally, Oswald's plans to defect began to crystallize at about the time his unit arrived in Japan: "For the past two years I have been waiting to do this one thing. . . . for two years I was waiting to leave the Marine Corps and get enough money to come. . . . I spent two years preparing to come here. These preparations consisted mostly of reading. It took me two years to find out how to do it."

He refused to tell Johnson whether Intourist had had advance notice of his arrival in the Soviet Union. Similarly Oswald rejected any suggestion that the American Communist Party might have played a part in the development of his political thought. "The American socialists are to be shunned by anyone who is interested in progressive ideology," he stated. "It is a dormant, flag-waving organization."

Oswald continued to refer to the Soviet government as "my government" throughout the four-hour interview and seemed remarkably well briefed on the Soviets' handling of his case. At one point he sounded like a spokesman for the Soviet government: "It is not my wish nor even that of Soviet officials, but the overall political atmosphere that will determine whether I can become a [Soviet] citizen." Despite her very determined effort to elicit information about any persons who had had previous contact with him in the United States, he just as determinedly refused to name any names. "I never saw a Communist in my life," he insisted.

Meanwhile, back in the United States, the shock waves from Oswald's defection and his offer to give classified information to the Soviets reverberated through his former radar unit in California. Delgado vividly remembers a group of civilians in dark suits arriving in November with stenographers and literally taking over their headquarters company to question Marines about Oswald. One by one, they were ushered into their captain's office.

When his turn came, Delgado recalls, he was asked his name, rank and serial number. Then one of the civilians shot quick questions at him concerning his job in the radar bubble, his knowledge of Oswald's activities and especially his opinion of the sorts of classified information to which Oswald had had access. A number of other Marines in the unit recalled being asked the same questions as a stenographer typed away at her machine.

Richard Call, who had played "hundreds" of games of chess with Oswald, remembers being asked to write out a statement about Oswald's defection for the team of civilian investigators. None of the Marines was told, however, who the investigators were.[20] At about the same time the FBI opened a file on Oswald, though its records indicate that it did not actually begin questioning anyone who knew Oswald until April 27, 1960.

In Japan the U.S. Air Force Office of Special Investigations, which had responsibility for security at Atsugi Air Base, pursued its own investigation and questioned John Edward Pic about his half brother's defection. As Colonel Thomas Fox, then chief of Clandestine Services for the Defense Intelligence Agency, later explained, "The possibility that a defector like Oswald had been recruited or had prior contact with Soviet intelligence while in Japan would have to be fully explored, even if it meant turning the services upside down. . . . A net damage assessment, indicating the possible access Oswald had to classified information would have to be undertaken. . . ."

Since World War II only two other enlisted men from the military forces had defected to the Soviet Union or its Eastern European allies, and both were suspected of having had contact with Soviet or East German military intelligence. In both cases a net damage assessment had been done after the defections to determine what intelligence might have been compromised (although in neither case was a prior KGB contact unquestionably established).[21]

Through his experiences as a radar controller in Japan, Formosa, the Philippines and California, Oswald could have had access to classified information pertaining to almost all aspects of the Air Defense Identification Zone in the Pacific, including knowledge about the height limitations of American radar, the blind spots caused by ground traffic or atmospheric disturbances in various areas, secret radio frequencies, call signs and authentication codes used for identifying incoming aircraft. He also could have had access to the security procedures for changing codes and frequencies, the modes and angles for intercepting enemy aircraft (from which performance data about different air-to-air missiles could be deduced), and the location and effective range of the American and allied aircraft stationed in the Pacific.

At Atsugi and in the Philippines Oswald could have watched repeated takeoffs of "Race Car," the still-supersecret U-2, and, from visual, radar and radio observation, could have established its rate of climb, performance characteristics and cruising altitude. With the proper guidance, he might have been able to decipher elements of its radar-jamming equipment. The frequencies and codes, now compromised, could be varied; the data Oswald might have amassed on "Race Car" presented a more difficult problem.

From Moscow, on November 26, Oswald wrote his brother a long and particularly well-written letter explaining, "Why I and my fellow workers and communists would like to see the capitalist government of the United States overthrown."

"Do you remember the time you told me about the efforts of your milk company to form a Union?" the letter began. ". . . workers must form unions against their employers in the US

. . . because the government supports an economic system which exploits all the workers, a system based upon credit which gives rise to the never-ending cycle of depression, infla-tion, unlimited speculation (which is the phase America is in now) and war. . . . Look around you, and look at yourself. See the segregation, see the unemployment and what automation is. Remember how you were laid off at Convair?"

Oswald then shifted to a planned intervention by the Marines which had still not been disclosed to the American public. "I remember well the days we stood offshore at Indonesia waiting to suppress yet another population, when they were having a revolution there in March 1958. . . . America is a dying coun-try, I do not wish to be part of it, nor do I ever wish to be used as a tool of its military aggressions."

He continued: "I want you to understand what I say now, I do not say lightly, or unknowingly, since I've been in the military as you know, and I know what war is like. . . . In the event of war I would kill any American who put a uniform on in defense of the American Government—Any American."

This letter appeared in Washington, D.C., among the letters from Moscow routinely turned over to a CIA operations sector working under Angleton in counterintelligence. During this crit-ical period it was evident from the letter that Oswald had put himself firmly under the control of his hosts. He had defected, renounced his citizenship, compromised military secrets and denounced his country and family. His fate now rested entirely with the Soviets, on whom he was dependent for legal status, financial support and protection. He was, as Angleton later put it, "in the palm of their hand—and they could squeeze at any time."

His brother received one brief letter from Oswald a few weeks later, stating that he was moving from the Metropole Hotel. Oswald also sent Marguerite a brief note with which he en-closed a personal check for $20 she had sent him. He asked that she send cash; her check was worthless in the Soviet Union, he pointed out.

He was not heard from again for more than a year.

4

A Missing Year

After writing his brother a short note in 1959, Oswald disappeared from sight for more than a year. During this time he had no contact with anyone outside the Soviet Union, nor are there any available witnesses to his activities within that country.[1] The only account that exists of this period is a packet of biographical notes, including a "Historic Diary" presumably prepared by Oswald—or at least found among his possessions in Dallas in 1963.

The chronicle begins in Moscow in October 1959. Oswald, brimming with enthusiasm about the potential for finding democracy in the Soviet Union, informed his Intourist guide, Rima Shirokova, that he was a "communist" and wanted to stay in the Soviet Union. "She is flabbergasted, but agrees to help," he noted.[2] She introduced him to a "balding, stout official in a black suit" who asked him in fairly good English why he wanted to become a Soviet citizen. "I give vague answers about [the] 'great Soviet Union.' He tells me 'USSR is only great in literature.' . . . Wants me to go back home. I am stunned."

While waiting to hear whether he would be allowed to stay in the Soviet Union, Oswald claimed to have been interviewed by Lev Setyayev, a reporter for Radio Moscow. Oswald later wrote a handwritten set of questions and answers regarding his stay in the Soviet Union. In response to the question "Did you make statements against the U.S. there?" he wrote, "Yes . . . I made a recording for Radio Moscow which was broadcast the following Sunday in which I spoke about the beautiful capital of the Socialist work and all its progress."[3] Setyayev also took a studio photograph of Oswald in which he is meticulously dressed in a dark suit and tie.

That afternoon a "police official" informed him that since his visa was due to expire in two hours, he must immediately leave the country. He recorded his disillusionment in highly dramatic terms, reminiscent in style of a Russian novel:

> I am shocked. . . . I retire to my room. I have waited two years to be accepted. My fondest dreams are shattered because of a petty official, because of bad planning. I planned so much. 7 P.M. I decide to end it. Soak wrists in cold water to numb the pain. Then slash my left wrist. Then plunge wrist into bathtub of hot water. I think when Rima comes at 8 to find me dead it will be a great shock. Somewhere, a violin plays, as I watch my life whirl away. I think to myself "how easy to die" and "a sweet death" (to violins). About 8:00, Rima finds me unconscious (bathtub water a rich red color). She screams. . . . Ambulance comes, am taken to hospital where five stitches are put in my wrist. Poor Rima stays by my side as interpreter (my Russian is still very bad) far into the night. . . . I notice she is pretty.[4]

According to this account, Oswald awakened the next morning to find himself in the "insanity ward" of Botkin Hospital. "This realization disquiets me," he wrote; the next day, after an interview with a doctor, he was transferred to an "ordinary ward." In addition to Rima, who came every day, Oswald was visited by another Intourist guide, Rosa Agafonova, whom he found "very beautiful, excellent English, very merry and kind . . . she makes me very glad to be alive."

A week later, having been released from the hospital, he was taken to the Passport and Registration Office by Rima. There he was interviewed by "four officials": "I give them my discharge papers from the Marine Corps. . . . They say wait for our answer." At this point Oswald decided, without consulting any Soviet official, to take a taxi to the American Embassy and turn in his passport.[5]

Stunned by the flurry of journalistic and diplomatic activity that followed his attempt to renounce his citizenship, Oswald remained in his hotel room for the next two months, studying Russian and speaking to no one except his Intourist guides.

He spent New Year's Eve with Rosa, who gave him a "Boratin clown" for a present, and whom he found "strangely tender and compelling." Finally, on January 4, he was called to the Passport Office and given a residence document, instead of citizenship papers.[6] He noted:

> They are sending me to Minsk. I ask, "Is that in Siberia?" He [the official] only laughs. He also tells me that they have arranged for me to receive some money through the Red Cross to pay my hotel bills and expenses. Later in the afternoon I see Rima. She asks "are you happy."

The very next day he received "the huge sum" of 5,000 rubles from the "Red Cross"[7] and was told he would be paid 700 rubles a month in Minsk. In a set of handwritten notes, Oswald explained his acceptance of this subsidy: "My funds were very limited, so after a certain time, after the Russians had assured themselves that I was really the naïve American who believed in Communism, they arranged for me to receive a certain amount of money each month." He knew at the time, however, that the money came technically through the "Red Cross" as financial help to a political immigrant, but it was arranged by the MVD.[8] "I accepted the money because I was hungry and there was several inches of snow on the ground in Moscow at that time, but what it really was was *payment* for my denunciation of the US in Moscow . . . and a clear promise that as long as I lived in the USSR life would be very good."

According to Oswald's diary, he arrived in Minsk, the capital of Byelorussia, on January 7 and was met by two more Intourist guides[9]—one of whom immediately caught his eye. "We attract each other at once," he wrote. The very next day he was personally greeted by the mayor of Minsk, who promised him a rent-free apartment.

He began working at the Byelorussian radio and television factory[10] as a checker. He described a fairly rigorous work schedule: "At 8:00 sharp, all the workers have arrived and at the sound of a bell sounded by the duty orderly, who is a worker whose duty it is to see to it that the workers do not slip out for too many smokes, they file upstairs." He found: "Everyone is very friendly and kind. I meet many young Russian workers my own age. All wish to know about me [and] even offer to hold a mass meeting so I can [speak]. . . . I refuse politely."[11] Because of his subsidy from the "Red Cross," Oswald found his social life fuller than it had ever been before—"theatre, movies or opera almost every day. I'm living big and am very satisfied."

In the spring of 1960 the diary abruptly switched from a tone of buoyant elation to one of growing disillusionment. The turning point came on May Day, 1960.[12] After watching a military parade, Oswald went to a party at the home of his factory manager, Alexander Ziger.[13] He later noted:

> Ziger advises me to go back to the United States. It's the first voice of opposition I have heard. I respect Ziger, he has seen the world. He says many things and relates many things I do not know about the USSR. I feel inside, it's true!!

Two entries later he expanded on this feeling:

> As my Russian improves I become increasingly conscious of just what sort of society I live in. Mass gymnastics, compulsory after work meeting; usually political information meeting. Compulsory attendance at lectures and the sending of the entire shop collective (except me) to pick potatoes on a Sunday. . . .

Later in this entry Oswald railed against the privileged status of the Communist Party secretary in the factory, whom he describes as "a fat, fortyish . . . no-nonsense party regular."[14]

In a manuscript[15] Oswald prepared in 1961, he mentioned "fifteen meetings a month, fourteen of which are compulsory for Communist Party members and twelve of which are compulsory for all others. These meetings are always held after work or on the lunch hour. They are never held on working time. Absenteeism is by no means allowed." He complained that the constant regimentation "turn[s] to stone all except the hard-faced communists with roving eyes looking for any bonus-making catch of inattentiveness on the part of any worker."

In short order, according to the entries in the diary, Oswald himself turned from being enthusiastically pro-Soviet to a bitterly outspoken critic of that society: "I am starting to reconsider my desire about staying. The work is drab. The money I get has nowhere to be spent. No nightclubs or bowling alleys. No places of recreation except the trade union dances. I have had enough."

The diary effectively shows Oswald's progressive disillusionment over the strict party discipline in the factory and the lack of recreational diversions outside work. As such, it provides a convenient explanation for why an American defector who arrives in the Soviet Union fervently committed to Marxism might subsequently decide to return to the United States.

A microscopic examination of Oswald's handwriting in this diary indicates that the entire manuscript was written in one or two sessions.[16] The misdating of a number of events further shows that the writing took place at least one year after the events described. For example, in the October 31, 1959, entry Oswald discusses his visit to the United States Embassy in Moscow that day and notes in passing that John McVickar had replaced Richard Snyder as "head consul." This change he points to did not occur, however, until August 1961, twenty months later, when Snyder was recalled to Washington.

Another anachronism appears in Oswald's diary entry supposedly written on January 5, 1960; he quotes the salary he is to receive at the Minsk factory in new rubles, although the ruble was not revalued until approximately one year later.

Such anachronisms strongly suggest that the entire diary was prepared after the decision was made to repatriate Oswald to the United States.

But if the diary was fabricated well after the events described, what was the purpose of this effort?

A peculiar feature of the diary is that it omits nearly all events that would be inconsistent with his desire to return to the United States, such as Khrushchev's denunciations of the United States, the Berlin crisis, the constant depiction in the Soviet press of U.S. imperialism in Cuba,[17] and focuses, instead, on providing an unencumbered record of his personal activities in the Soviet Union. This would suggest that the diary was prepared, not for propaganda purposes, but to provide Oswald with a consistent cover story accounting for his decision to leave the USSR. That would also explain how he was able to take this material out of the Soviet Union.

Aside from the autobiographical material, there is scant documentation available for this year. The Soviet government provided the Warren Commission in 1964 with Oswald's passport, job application form at the radio factory, hospital records and a report from his supervisor at the factory. These few pages of documents show only that he arrived in Minsk in January, worked at the factory for more than a year and received a poor rating for his workmanship. The voluminous KGB file on Oswald, who as a foreigner was surely under surveillance in Minsk, was not provided, nor were any records of his contacts with Soviet citizens and institutions.

The only other clues to what Oswald was doing in Minsk that year are the materials found among his effects in 1963: a dog-eared address book, a scrap of paper with Russian writing on it, a few odd documents and letters, a photograph album and the recollections of people with whom he spoke about his experiences in Russia. But even these few fragments of evidence do not mesh satisfactorily with the account in the diary. For instance, during the same period that Oswald complains in the diary about the dearth of recreational opportunities in Minsk, he was accorded the privilege of having a 16-mm shotgun (according to a hunting license found among his possessions) and seems to have spent his weekends shooting small game in the countryside.[18]

Similarly the diary also neglects to mention Oswald's attempt to enroll himself during this period in the Patrice Lumumba Friendship University in Moscow, where reportedly he was friendly with several foreign students, including Mary Louise Patterson, the daughter of William L. Patterson, who was then serving on the executive committee of the Communist Party in the United States, and the wife of Roberto Camacho, one of the Cuban leaders then being trained in Moscow.[19] A few weeks after Oswald decided to return to the United States, he received a letter from the university signed by "Voloshin." (Coincidentally, Pavel T. Voloshin, who was then an administrator at Patrice Lumumba University, had been a KGB officer accompanying a group of Russian dancers to Los Angeles in 1959 at just about the same time Oswald was making weekend trips there to get his passport—and possibly to make other arrangements—for his trip to Moscow, according to the CIA.)

Whatever education, if any, Oswald had in the Soviet Union was never openly discussed by him. He did leave a few intriguing clues among his effects. In a manuscript about life in Minsk he wrote at one point, while describing a demonstration taking place at the Foreign Language Institute, "I was in the Foreign Language Institute." This school, from which Oswald dated a number of women, is located on Ulyanova Street, practically adjacent to a KGB training facility.[20] However, in editing the manuscript, Oswald carefully scratched out the suggestion that he was officially connected to the Foreign Language Institute and changed it to read that he was merely "visiting friends" there at the time of the incident.

Another possible clue to Oswald's educational interests during this period was the Soviet publication *Agitator*—the title means "propagandist" in Russian—which was found among his effects in 1963. This magazine was used in the Soviet Union primarily as a textbook for training foreigners in the techniques of propaganda and agitation. Oswald himself later claimed in a résumé to be fully experienced in "street agitation," and a scrap of paper taken from Oswald by a police officer in New Orleans in 1963 had written on it the phone number of an office in the Institute of Scientific-Technical Information and Propaganda in Minsk.

Other glimpses of Oswald's life in Minsk come from an album of snapshots found in Dallas in 1963. Far from depicting the dull, drab life described in the "diary," these photographs show Oswald living a far richer life, both materially and socially, than he had ever lived in the United States. For the first time in his life he had his own apartment with a separate living room gaily decorated with flowered wallpaper, tiled floors and modern furniture. It also had a magnificent view of the bend of the Svisloch River and two private balconies from which to observe the ships winding up the river through the city of Minsk.

Directly across the river was a treelined plaza bounded by the opera house, museums and other public buildings. In the distance could be seen the twin spires of a seventeenth-century cathedral, Minsk's oldest and most beautiful church. From the photographs, it is apparent that Oswald used this apartment for entertaining close friends, including Pavel Golovachev, the handsome son of Hero of the Soviet Union General P. Y. Golovachev, who reportedly traveled in the highest social circles in Minsk.

Other friends were Rosa Kuznetsova, a buxom blonde who worked as an English translator, and Ella German, whom Oswald described as "a silky, black haired Jewish beauty with fine dark eyes, skin as white as snow, a beautiful smile, and a good but unpredictable nature." In one picture Oswald is posed with these two striking women on his twenty-first birthday and notes that both were competing that night for his affection.

He seems also to have had all the accouterments of a civilized life: a sophisticated phonograph (which in one picture Pavel Golovachev helps assemble), records of operas and classical music, shelves full of books, a 35-mm camera and an elegant wardrobe of European-styled clothes. He also appears to have had a very full social life. One picture, presumably taken in the lush park in front of Oswald's apartment, shows him wearing only his suit trousers, snuggled contentedly on the bare shoulder of Eleanora Ziger, the daughter of his friend Alexander Ziger, who is lying in her bikini on Oswald's suit jacket, apparently sunbathing. On her other shoulder, another boyfriend of hers rests his head.

Another photo shows Oswald walking hand in hand with Anna Ziger, Eleanora's mother, and another girl, Enna, down a boulevard in Minsk. Here he is wearing sunglasses, looking like a celebrity. There are also pictures of Oswald, the Ziger family and other friends having a picnic on the outskirts of Minsk. During this outing Oswald posed arm and arm with a dark young foreigner named Alfred, whom he described in his diary as Hungarian (but who was subsequently identified in a letter to Oswald as a Cuban). At the time there was a group of Cubans being trained in Minsk who lived in the area of the radio factory, and Oswald reportedly befriended a number of them.

He also appears to have had during this period a fairly constant group of Russian friends, some of whom he stayed in contact with through letters for the next few years. At one point he and his friends apparently took turns photographing themselves in front of the Victory Monument in Minsk. Oswald also did not seem to be without female companionship. Indeed, an almost constant parade of women, many of whom were attending the Institute of Foreign Languages in Minsk, seemed to be available to him. By his own count, he had affairs with at least five women in Minsk.[21]

While these faded photographs and scraps of paper found in 1963 provide an occasional apercu into the full social life Oswald was leading in 1960, they cast very little light on such central questions as: Why was Oswald allowed to stay in the Soviet Union when another American defector that year was forcibly expelled; why was he provided with a generous subsidy on the eve of his departure to Minsk; why was he given a luxurious apartment and a monthly subsidy and permitted to own a weapon; why was he not used, as other defectors were, for radio appearances and press interviews; and what, if any, training or indoctrination did he receive? Did he have any assignment or eventual purpose other than to be a checker in a radio factory?

5

Wreck of "Race Car"

On May 1, 1960, Francis Gary Powers, a thirty-year-old pilot from Kentucky, watched with some apprehension from the cockpit of his plane as the sun rose over the Hindu Kush Mountains in Pakistan. He had been waiting at the edge of the runway at Peshawar Air Base for almost an hour, perspiring profusely in his heavy rubber flight suit, waiting for President Dwight D. Eisenhower to give the "go" signal, which was required on all U-2 flights over the Soviet Union.

The mission, originally scheduled for April 28, had already been postponed twice, and Powers hoped it would be canceled. He knew that the plane he was to pilot, No. 360, had previously malfunctioned and crashlanded after taking off from Atsugi base in Japan in September 1959. And since that incident he didn't have great confidence in that particular aircraft. At 6:20 A.M., however, presidential authorization came through, and the control tower cleared him for takeoff.

Revving up the new rocket engine that had been installed in the plane, he heard the familiar high whine which sounded like no other plane he had ever flown. A moment later the plane shot up into the sky. In fewer than six minutes it had climbed almost 14 miles—higher than the official world altitude record—and he turned on the autopilot.

At this altitude the temperature outside was 60 degrees below zero, and he no longer found himself sweltering. After entering the sortie number "4154" and the notation "delayed one-half hour" in the log, he again took over the controls as he approached maximum altitude. He knew that at this cruising altitude the U-2 had a very narrow range of speeds, known to the pilots as the coffin corner, where even the slightest miscalculation could prove disastrous. If the plane went much slower, it would stall, and if it went much faster, it would go into a "Mach buffet" and become uncontrollable. Keeping the plane at its exact cruising speed required a great deal of concentration.

The weather that day was far worse than had been anticipated. As he crossed the mountains that formed the border with the Soviet Union, he could see that the Russian side was obscured for hundreds of miles by a solid cloud cover. He headed northwest, toward the Aral Sea. He knew that Soviet radar would already be tracking his flight, as it had done for most of the previous flights, but he doubted that it could pinpoint his exact height and presumed that the Soviets were still targeting their missiles at a far lower altitude than that at which the U-2 actually flew. He also felt protected by the highly sophisticated radar-baffling equipment which emitted a beam designed to confound and confuse Soviet height-finding radar.

About 30 miles east of the Aral Sea, he turned on the cameras over his first target—the Tyuratam Cosmodrome, which was the main launching site for Soviet ICBMs and space satellites. In addition to lenses which had the power to define clearly an object as small as a golf ball on a putting green from an altitude of 70,000 feet, the U-2 carried infrared and other sensors which could monitor the precise state of rocket technology being employed at the cosmodrome. Powers had been told that such hard intelligence was of critical importance for evaluating the capacity of the Soviet military.

Watching the trails of MIG fighters about 30,000 feet below him, he had no doubt that the Soviets were determined to put an end to the U-2 missions. The commanding officer of his 10-10 detachment had warned him that Soviet intelligence was mounting major efforts against the U-2 at its two main bases, Atsugi, Japan, and Adana, Turkey, and had probably amassed a dossier on him and the twenty or so other pilots. He was not, however, told of the full extent of these intelligence operations.

Almost one year before this flight Richard Helms, then deputy director of plans for the CIA, heard from Richard Bissell, who had developed the U-2 program for the CIA, that one of their key agents planted in Soviet military intelligence, Colonel Peter Semyonovich Popov, had passed information back indicating that the Soviets had definite knowledge of specifics of the U-2 program.

Popov was not only a valuable spy, but, for all practical purposes, the most important American agent in the Soviet Union at that time. He had already managed to deliver to the CIA advance plans of Soviet weaponry, running the gamut from fighter planes to missiles, and had also provided reports of a major reorganization of the Soviet Army.

"It brought me right out of my seat," Helms recalled. "Bissell and I wondered where they could be getting their information from."

The factor that had limited the effectiveness of Soviet antiaircraft missiles was not rocketry—they had already succeeded in orbiting a sputnik satellite at a far higher altitude—but the lack of a guidance system capable of operating in the rarefied stratosphere in which the U-2 flew. Both men knew, of course, that there was a trade-off between intelligence and technology in solving the guidance problem. If the Soviets succeeded in acquiring data about the cruising altitude, speed, load and other flight characteristics of this aircraft, they could design the necessary control system for their high-altitude rockets in much less time than had been anticipated. Then, in September 1959, Colonel Popov was arrested by Soviet counterintelligence; thus, no further information on the nature of the Soviet intelligence he alluded to would be forthcoming.

Before this flight Powers was aware that only one other U-2 overflight had been made over the Soviet Union since October 1959—a flight on April 9, 1960, for which he was the backup pilot—but he did not know why the flights were being limited during this period. He had not been told about the sabotage attempt made against his plane in Pakistan on the eve of its departure, which was foiled by American counterintelligence. Nor did he know that a trained Marine Corps radar operator with access to U-2 and radar-measuring equipment at Atsugi had defected to the Soviet Union and offered, on October 31, 1959, to turn over to the Russians all classified information he possessed which might be of "special interest."

The clouds were now disappearing. Across the snow-capped Ural Mountains, which had traditionally divided the Asian steppes from the European portions of the Soviet Union, he could see green fields and clear weather ahead in Russia. Over Sverdlovsk, an industrial center which had never before been overflown by a U-2, he again switched on his cameras.

Suddenly he felt a "dull thump" push him forward. The cockpit was illuminated by the orange flash of an explosion behind the plane. Pulling back on the wheel, he realized that he had no control over the U-2. It began slowly spinning with the nose pointed toward the sky. He opened the canopy and tried to crawl out as the plane plummeted down. At about 30,000 feet the centrifugal force flung him into the air. A moment later he opened his parachute.

Three days later in Burbank, California, C. L. "Kelly" Johnson learned from Richard Bissell that the plane he had designed for Lockheed had been shot down by a Soviet antiaircraft missile. As chief research engineer for Lockheed for more than twenty years he had designed such planes as the Hudson bomber, Constellation transport, P-38 fighter-bomber, and the double-sonic F-104 starfighter, but none of these creations had intrigued him as much as the U-2, which had revolutionized intelligence gathering.

Instead of intelligence services having to rely on spies in the field, whose information was by its very nature unpredictable, fragmentary and vulnerable to being compromised, the U-2 cameras provided photographic evidence of troop movements, shipbuilding, weapon deployment, nuclear tests and other selected targets. According to Bissell, this small fleet of Lockheed U-2s had provided the United States with "more than ninety percent of all its hard intelligence about the Soviet Union."

Kelly Johnson, who knew each plane inside out, tried to piece together from the few bits of available information how the Soviets could have succeeded in bringing Powers' plane down. If Powers had been flying at his assigned altitude, it meant that the Soviets had achieved the capacity to guide, control and detonate a missile at well over 70,000 feet. It also meant that they had the means to overcome the radar-jamming beam emitted from the plane to confuse enemy radar controllers.

Johnson speculated then—as he still does—that the Soviets were somehow able to isolate the radar-jamming signals and use their beams to guide their antiaircraft missile. This could explain the accuracy they achieved without any apparent technological leaps in their guidance system, but it would also require either a penetration by Soviet intelligence of United States radar countermeasures or, by some other means, the ability to take precise measurements of the U-2's radar signals.

In Moscow, in the KGB offices in Lubyanka Prison, Powers sat through another day of interrogation. Two majors shot questions at him, while a translator patiently interpreted them in English and a stenographer took notes. At various points higher officials, including Alexander N. Shelepin, the chain-smoking head of the KGB, sat in on the sessions. Others monitored them through a one-way window.

At one point his captors injected a dog with the poison needle he had been issued by the CIA before the flight, letting him witness the convulsions it went through before it died. They suggested to him that if he had used the needle on himself, such a convulsive death would support the "legend," or CIA cover story, that the pilot's oxygen mask had malfunctioned, enabling the "weather plane" to stray into Soviet territory.[1]

Powers was repeatedly asked to name the altitude he had been flying at when hit by the rocket. He stuck to the prearranged cover story that the U-2 flew at 68,000 feet—far lower than it actually flew. To shake his story, his interrogators then produced the carefully drawn radar plots of his flight, which showed his own coordinates of his path. But since brackets were drawn at various altitudes, some above and some below 68,000 feet, he decided to maintain his story. At one point a major stated the correct altitude Powers was flying, but assuming that they had no way to ascertain this, he denied it was true.

At another stage in the interrogation, he was closely questioned about Atsugi Air Base in Japan, but Powers insisted that he was never at that base. From their questions, however, he could tell that the Soviets were very knowledgeable about the U-2 flights from Atsugi.[2] (Years later, after his return to the United States, Powers suggested that it might have been Oswald who provided the Soviets with information about his flight.)

Even though Oswald might have been in Moscow at about the time the U-2 was shot down and he could not have avoided reading about the U-2, which dominated the Soviet press for months afterward, his diary entries for that period make no mention of the shooting down of Powers. Yet Oswald at the time was probably the only person in the Soviet Union who had observed the U-2 up close and had had access to its pilots and other personnel. Some six months earlier he had threatened at the American Embassy to turn over radar secrets "of special interest" to the Soviets, and this offer was presumably overheard by Soviet listening devices later discovered to be concealed in the embassy. Moreover, he stated in Minsk that while in the Marines, he had served in an "aviation unit" in Japan.

Once the U-2 had been shot down, the Soviet press had turned the incident into a *cause célèbre* of espionage and banditry. The fact that the United States conducted an espionage flight just two weeks before the scheduled summit between Khrushchev and Eisenhower was taken as evidence that the United States wished to step up the cold war rather than end it. The United States' explanation for the "bandit flight" of the "black vulture"—that it believed in the principle of "open skies"—was likened to a burglar claiming that he was forced to break into a house because the doors were locked. Powers was described as a product of people like "Eisenhower, Nixon, Herter . . . the self-assured rulers of the Pentagon," and exemplified the faults of capitalism. For the right price, Powers would do anything, even perform an act as fundamentally immoral as espionage. In July 1960 the RB-47, another American spy plane shot down over Soviet territory, was described as "a bird of the same feather as the U-2 vulture."

In this atmosphere Oswald had the opportunity of becoming a hero by volunteering the pertinent information he had on the "black lady of espionage," as the plane was characterized. This, of course, would have assured the continuation of the subsidy he was then receiving from the MVD. But the only comment Oswald himself made on the U-2 was in a letter to his brother in February 1962, after Powers had been exchanged for Rudolph Abel. He said then, "Powers seemed to be a nice bright American type fellow when I saw him in Moscow," never explaining the circumstances under which he was able to see him. In his diary, Oswald wrote an entry for May 1 that placed him conveniently at a party in Minsk on the day Powers was shot down. But later he told a co-worker back in the United States that he had been in Moscow for a May Day celebration. Other evidence precludes this being any other year than 1960—when Powers was shot down.[3]

Yuri Nosenko, the KGB official who later claimed to have been responsible for the file of Lee Harvey Oswald, was one of the officials who rushed to the KGB center immediately after Powers was captured. He denied, however, that Oswald's knowledge of the U-2 was used by the Soviets. After he defected in 1964, he stated that Oswald was never asked for any information about the American military by either the KGB or Soviet military intelligence (GRU), and he never volunteered any such information. The American counterintelligence officers debriefing Nosenko found this assertion difficult to accept.

At the time of Nosenko's debriefing in 1964, the CIA interrogation officers were not aware of Oswald's knowledge about the U-2 in Japan. They did not realize, for example, that because of security lapses at the base where he was a radar operator, he could have ascertained the altitude of the U-2 and conceivably even deciphered some characteristics of the ultrasecret equipment for jamming enemy radar by noting the difference between the apparent altitude of the U-2 on radar and its actual altitude.

PART TWO

The Passage West

6

The Double Turncoat

On November 10, 1959, within ten days of learning that Lee Harvey Oswald had defected to the Soviet Union, the FBI took precautions against his attempting to reenter the United States under a false identity. The Domestic Intelligence Division, responsible for counterespionage, placed a "flash" notice on his fingerprint card to assure that it would be alerted in the event that Oswald's fingerprints were detected by the bureau's Identification Division. It also opened up a "301" dossier jacket on his case and placed his name on the watch list used for monitoring overseas telecommunications.

After finding that his mother had sent a $25 money order to him in Moscow, FBI headquarters asked its Forth Worth office to interview members of Oswald's family. On April 27, 1960, Oswald's brother Robert told Special Agent John W. Fain that neither he nor his mother had had any word from Oswald since December 1959, nor had they had any contact with Soviet officials.

His mother, interviewed the next day, told Fain that all her letters had been returned undelivered, and she was worried over the safety of her son. She added that she had recently received a letter from Albert Schweitzer College in Switzerland indicating that Oswald was expected to arrive there on April 20, 1960. Asked whether she had furnished him with "any items of personal identification," she replied that he had taken his birth certificate with him when he left on his voyage east.

After receiving the reports from his Fort Worth field office, J. Edgar Hoover sent a memorandum to the State Department's Office of Security, with a copy to the director of naval intelligence, outlining the concern of his counterespionage section: "Since there is a possibility that an impostor is using Oswald's birth certificate, any current information the Department of State has concerning the subject will be appreciated." He also dispatched an FBI agent stationed in Paris to check the Albert Schweitzer College, but there was no trace of Oswald (or anyone using his identity) there.

Nor could the State Department furnish any "current information" on Oswald's whereabouts. On March 28, 1960, the American Embassy in Moscow reported back that it had "had no contact with Oswald since his departure from the Metropole Hotel in November 1959, and has no clue as to his present whereabouts." The trail had grown decidedly cold.

The State Department replied in an operations memorandum: "Unless and until the Embassy comes into possession of information or evidence upon which to base the preparation of certificate of loss of nationality in the case of Lee Harvey Oswald, there appears to be no further action possible in this case." Safeguarding against the possibility that Oswald or an impostor might apply for a new passport outside the Soviet Union, the department further informed the embassy that a "lookout" card had been placed in Oswald's file. (Actually, such a card was never filed for Oswald.)

Since most of the nonsecret cable traffic between the Department of State and embassy in Moscow was then being intercepted by the KGB, which was responsible for monitoring embassy activities, Soviet intelligence was presumably aware now that Oswald, despite his attempt to expatriate himself, was still considered by the State Department to be a United States citizen.[1]

At about the same time the Marine Corps, fully apprised by

naval intelligence that Oswald had offered to turn over classified information to the Soviets, moved to have him severed from the U.S. Marine Air Reserve. On September 13, 1960, after failing to reach him with three certified letters, the Marine Corps officially rescinded Oswald's honorable discharge and downgraded it to an "undesirable discharge."

Meanwhile, in Texas, Marguerite Oswald decided to take matters into her own hands. After a number of phone calls to her local FBI office and letters to her Congressman failed to prod the government into finding her son, she used all her savings to buy a train ticket to Washington. After sitting in a dusty train for three days and two nights, she arrived in Washington at 8 A.M. on January 26, 1961, and called the White House to speak to President John F. Kennedy, who had just been inaugurated a few days before.

When the White House switchboard told her the President was in conference, she asked to speak to Secretary of State Dean Rusk. When asked by a State Department official what the matter pertained to, she replied, "About a son of mine who is lost in Russia." Two hours later she had an appointment with two officials at the State Department. Since Oswald was still technically a citizen of the United States, they were obliged to act on her request and make official inquiries about her "missing son." Memos thus began moving up and down through channels at the State Department.

On February 1, 1961, less than a week after Marguerite Oswald visited Washington, the State Department sent in the diplomatic pouch to Moscow a "Welfare-Whereabouts" memo on Oswald, requesting the embassy "to inform the [Soviet] Ministry of Foreign Affairs that Mr. Oswald's mother is worried as to his personal safety, and anxious to hear from him." This non-classified communication was routinely sent to the consular section. Consul Snyder did not, however, take any action on the request or try to contact the Soviet ministry. He didn't need to.

On February 13, 1961, less than two weeks after he had received the request from Washington, Snyder found a letter from Oswald on his desk, postmarked Minsk, February 5, 1961. He was completely astonished to read that the young Marine, who had belligerently slammed his passport on the embassy desk fourteen months before and categorically stated that he never wanted to live in the United States again, was now writing in a very matter-of-fact tone: "I desire to return to the United States, that is if we could come to some agreement concerning the dropping of any legal proceedings against me."

Moreover, Oswald wanted his passport back, claiming: "If I could show [the Soviet authorities] my American passport, I am of the opinion they would give me an exit visa." Oswald also pointed out that he had never even been asked to "take Russian citizenship"[2] and therefore at least technically retained his full rights as an American citizen. He apparently had been well schooled in the legal definition of citizenship. He concluded: "I hope that in recalling the responsibility I have to America that you remember yours in doing everything to help me since I am an American citizen."

Snyder could not help being struck by the coincidence of dates. Why would Oswald, after all this time, suddenly write to the embassy days after it had received a request to locate him? Since such nonclassified requests were available to Soviet nationals working for the embassy and discussed in areas vulnerable to Soviet eavesdropping devices, it had to be at least assumed that the KGB had access to the request from Washington. And since all mail to the embassy was monitored by the second Chief Directorate of the KGB, it further had to be assumed that the Soviets were fully aware of Oswald's 180-degree turnabout in now wanting to return to the United States—and at least tacitly approved the letter since it had not been intercepted.[3] Given the close proximity of Oswald's letter to the State Department's communication, it seemed "quite probable" to Snyder that the KGB, alerted to Washington's renewed interest in Oswald, took advantage of the opportunity by having Oswald recontact the embassy and request repatriation.

Under these circumstances Snyder referred the question of whether or not to return Oswald's passport by mail back to the State Department's Soviet Desk, which, with its intelligence components, could consider the matter in its full context. He also queried Washington on whether Oswald was "subject to prosecution on any grounds" and, if so, whether Oswald could be so informed. While waiting for a reply, he temporized by suggesting to Oswald that he come in person to the embassy for an interview.

Even though Oswald professed a firm desire to redefect from the Soviet Union to the United States in his letters to the embassy, he had not markedly changed his politics, according to one witness who accidentally encountered him in Minsk during this period.

In March 1961 the University of Michigan Band stopped for three days in Minsk during its tour of the Soviet Union and was given a reception the evening of March 10 at the Minsk Polytechnical Institute. As the band members departed from the institute for the buses that would take them back to their lodgings, Katherine Mallory, a flutist from Endicott, New York, found herself surrounded by a surging crowd of well-wishers. These Soviet students were anxious to speak with their American counterparts, just as students in other cities the band had visited had been.

Miss Mallory welcomed the opportunity to communicate, but she spoke not a word of Russian. She was struggling to make herself understood when she heard a voice asking in English whether she needed an interpreter. As she turned around, she faced a young man dressed in a stylish camel's hair coat that contrasted with the drab garb she had seen on other Russians. She also noticed his accent, which seemed to switch between "Texas and British." He told her he was from Texas but now lived in Minsk.

For ten to fifteen minutes the American translated for her. Most of the questions dealt with aspects of American lifestyles—cars, families and so on—and required short answers. In the midst of fielding questions for Miss Mallory, the American managed to volunteer that he was "an ex-Marine who despised the United States and hoped to spend the rest of his life in Minsk."

Miss Mallory was more interested in talking with the Soviet students, so she didn't pursue the issue of Oswald's views on America. He, in turn, did not press any further information on her and returned to interpreting.[4] She later recognized his picture as that of Lee Harvey Oswald (and thus became the first non-Soviet person to see Oswald since Priscilla Johnson had interviewed him in Moscow sixteen months before).[5]

Within a day or two of telling Miss Mallory of his hatred for America, he wrote another letter to the embassy to expedite his return to America. Resisting the idea of a personal interview at the embassy, he asserted, "I cannot leave the city of Minsk without permission. . . . I have no intention of abusing my position here, and I am sure you would not want me to."[6] Instead, he proposed that "the preliminary inquiries . . . be put in the form of a questionnaire and sent to me." Such a procedure not only would serve to reveal in advance the essential elements that the embassy staff would attempt to elicit from Oswald, but also would permit him to seek assistance in preparing his answers.

After carefully reviewing the problem in Washington, the State Department instructed its embassy in Moscow on April 13 that because of security reasons, Oswald's "passport may be delivered to him on a personal basis only" at the embassy, so identity could be confirmed. Further, it suggested that when he appeared to collect his passport, "he should be thoroughly questioned regarding the circumstances of his presence in the Soviet Union and his possible commitment of an act or acts of expatriation . . . his statement should be taken under oath." The possibility of mailing Oswald a questionnaire was thus ruled out.

Meanwhile, Snyder countered Oswald's claim that he could not leave Minsk by writing him, "The Soviet Ministry of Foreign Affairs has always assured the embassy that it interposes no objections or obstacles to visits to the Embassy on the part of American citizens . . . a final determination of your present American citizenship status can only be made on the basis of a personal interview."

Fully anticipating that this letter might be intercepted by the KGB, he added forcefully, "You may wish to present this letter to the authorities in Minsk in connection with your application for permission to travel to Moscow." If the Soviets still wanted to facilitate Oswald's return, they would now have to send him to Moscow.

On May 16 Oswald again wrote the embassy. Since he still lacked the assurances he wanted, he reiterated, "I wish to make it clear that I am asking not only for the right to return to the United States, but also for full guarantees that I shall not, under any circumstances, be persecuted [sic] for any act pertaining to this case." He threatened that unless the embassy agreed to this demand, he would ask his relatives "to see about getting something done in Washington."

He then added an entirely new dimension to the problem by informing the embassy, "Since my last letter I have gotten married. . . . My wife is Russian, born in Leningrad, she has no parents living and is quite willing to leave the Soviet Union with me and live in the United States." He omitted mentioning that he had met his wife only after writing his last letter and stated flatly, "I would not leave here without my wife so arrangements would have to be made for her to leave at the same time I do." The gambit was clear enough: If the United States wanted Oswald back, it would have also to take his wife.

7

Marina's Story

During the summer of 1961 agencies of the United States government, including the CIA and State Department, attempted to acquire information on the background of the Russian woman whom Lee Harvey Oswald proposed to bring back to the United States with him as his wife. The available files contained, however, no record or intelligence traces on her. It was not until 1964 in Dallas that she furnished federal investigators with any details of her life in the Soviet Union. The story she told then, and repeated to the Warren Commission, was of a poor, parentless girl falling in love with an American defector.

In this tale Marina Nikolaevna Prusakova was born out of wedlock on July 17, 1941, in the seaside town of Molotovsk in the arctic province of Arkhangelsk.[1] It was a time of chaos and confusion. The German panzer divisions were sweeping into Russia, and the Soviet Army was in full retreat. Marina never knew her father or even his name.[2] Her mother, Klavdia Vasily-evna Prusakova, was unable to care for her in the tumult, and left her as an infant with her elderly parents in the city of Arkhangelsk. Captain Vasily Prusakov, Marina's grandfather, was a naval officer who sailed between Murmansk and Scotland and once, as a young man, had been presented to the czar. He always wore his uniform in the house and died when Marina was four. Marina was brought up by her grandmother, Tatyana Prusakov, until she was seven years old, when she was sent to the town of Zguritsa near the Rumanian border to rejoin the mother whom she had really never known.

In the long interim her mother had married an electrical worker, Alexander Ivanovich Medvedev, and was bringing up his family.[3] In 1952 Medvedev found a job in his hometown of Leningrad, and the whole family moved to this city of fountains and palaces.[4] At first, Marina enrolled in the 374th women's school but then switched to the Pharmacy Teknikum, a school specializing in training pharmacists. In the midst of her training her mother died, and Marina found life unbearable in the home of her stepfather, where she felt like a stranger. She ate most of her meals out and took a part-time job in a school cafeteria and then a drugstore on the Nevsky Prospect to pay for her living expenses. Upon graduation in June 1959, she was assigned a job in a pharmaceutical warehouse, but after one day at work she quit this job.[5] She spent the rest of the summer on vacation in Leningrad.

Now, at eighteen, thin and delicate with thick dark eyelashes, she found herself extremely attractive to men. She frequently went to the Maryinsky Opera House, where she would go backstage in the hope of getting connected with the theatrical company. A student proposed marriage to her, but she felt she was too young.

Toward the end of August Marina found the tensions at home increasing, with her stepfather wanting to remarry, and she decided to move to Minsk, where she was invited to live with her maternal uncle, Colonel Ilya Vasilyevich Prusakov, and his wife, Valentina. Arriving in Minsk after a twenty-four-hour train ride from Leningrad, she immediately moved into Colonel Prusakov's spacious apartment on Kalinina Street. This apartment even had a private telephone, a rarity in the Soviet Union. Prusakov had such privileges as an engineer for the MVD, or Ministry of Internal Affairs, which had responsibility for civil law enforcement; his rank of colonel made him one of the more powerful citizens of Minsk. Like most influential government officials, he was a member of the Communist Party.

By October Marina was assigned a position in the pharmaceutical section of the Third Clinical Hospital, located in the center of the city. Her job consisted of filling prescriptions for hospital patients. She was able to keep most of her salary of 45 rubles for personal spending money.[6]

With her new status, Marina pursued a far more active social life. Through the Prusakovs she met students in the professional schools—medicine, architecture and engineering—who constituted a very elite group in Soviet society. She spent her spare time with her new friends at coffeehouses around Victory Square or at their dachas in the country.[7] She alternated between two main suitors—Anatoly and Sasha—preferring not to "pair up."

After working for a year in Minsk, Marina took a month's vacation in a workers' "rest home" in a forest outside Leningrad. Although the men and women were assigned to separate cabins, there was a good deal of intermingling. It was there that Marina befriended a number of men from Leningrad. In November she returned to her job in Minsk.

Throughout the winter of 1961, Marina continued dating both Sasha and Anatoly, unable to decide between them. Then, in March, she was invited to a dance at the Palace of Culture. For two hours she stood in front of a mirror in her room, debating whether she should chance going to an event where both her boyfriends might be present. There would also be a lecture by the mother of one of her friends on her month-long trip to the United States. Finally, at her Uncle Ilya's urging, she decided to go.

She arrived at the Palace of Culture three hours late, missing the lecture entirely. But as she stepped in out of the bitterly cold night, she felt fresh and buoyant. Her cheeks were rosy, not pale like those of the other women at the dance. When she took off her overcoat, she fully revealed herself in a red Chinese brocade dress. Her hair was done in the Parisian style "à la Brigitte Bardot." "That evening," she remembered years later, "I even liked myself."

Almost immediately a knot of young men formed around her, and she was introduced to one named Alik, who seemed instantly drawn to her. They danced, and when they spoke, she noticed he spoke Russian with a slight accent. At first she thought he was from one of the Baltic parts of the Soviet Union —Estonia, Latvia or Lithuania—but then found to her surprise that he was an American named Lee Harvey Oswald living in Minsk.

Marina found herself intrigued with "Alik," as the American liked to call himself.[8] He was both polite and attentive and seemed very eager to dance every dance with her. Afterward they went with a group of other friends to the home of Yuri Mereshenko, whose mother had given the lecture on the United States, where they listened to American records. She was impressed when her new friend spoke up in defense of America, saying that although it had defects such as unemployment, discrimination and expensive medical treatment, there was "more democracy and every person can say what he wants in the press, the radio, or on TV." She was escorted home that night by both Sasha and Oswald.

The next week spring had come to Minsk, and Marina met Oswald at another dance. This time she invited him in when he took her home, and introduced him to her aunt, who was favorably impressed with his manners and neat appearance. After he left, she asked jokingly whether Marina was planning on adding this American to her collection of boyfriends.

Marina finally agreed to allow Oswald to take her out on a date the following Friday, but he was unable to keep the appointment because of an earache he had developed that week. On March 30, the day before his date with Marina, Oswald was admitted to the Fourth Clinical Hospital for an adenoids operation.

Although patients at the hospital were ordinarily allowed to be visited only on Sundays, Marina saw Oswald almost every day while he was recuperating. No one at the hospital stopped her, in her white pharmacist's uniform, and she could come and go as she liked. On Easter Sunday, the day after his operation, she brought him a hand-painted Easter egg, which seemed to please him greatly. She couldn't help feeling great sympathy for him. He had "a very sickly look about him," which made her feel even more sorry for him. When Oswald asked her to marry him from his hospital bed, she couldn't refuse. Although she "did not yet love Lee," she agreed to be his fiancée.

In April, after being discharged from the hospital, Oswald showed her his apartment. She found it instantly appealing, "a small darling one-room apartment with a balcony, a bathroom, gas kitchen and a separate entrance—quite enough for two, especially if they were young." She had long admired this particular apartment house at the bend of the river and the view it commanded.[9] After some consideration she agreed on April 20 to marry Oswald on May Day, and they planted flowers on the balcony in honor of their forthcoming wedding.

While waiting for their marriage application to be approved—a process that takes ten days—they enjoyed springtime in Minsk, taking long walks in the park, boating on Youth Lake, dining in cafés or going dancing with their friends. In the evenings they spent time listening to music together. Oswald had a large classical record collection, including Tchaikovsky, who was his favorite composer, Grieg, Liszt, Rimsky-Korsakov and Schumann. Finally, on April 30, they received permission to be married.

It was a warm Sunday, and everything she saw seemed bright and beautiful. Oswald bought her a bouquet of narcissus, and with their friends, they walked hand in hand to the town hall for the civil ceremony. Afterward, Colonel Prusakov hosted a reception for twenty of their friends at his apartment, and they spent the evening feasting and drinking. Then they walked back to their apartment, blissfully married.

Oswald himself described the romance much more briefly and prosaically. The entire courtship was recorded in a dozen or so sentences in three entries in his diary. The March 17 entry begins: "Went to trade union dance. Boring but at the last moment I am introduced to a girl with a French hairdo and red dress with white slippers . . . dance with her . . . her name is Marina. We like each other right away. . . ."[10]

The next entry, "March 18–31st," continues: "We walk. I talk a little about myself, she talks a lot about herself. . . ."

Finally, in the "April 1–30th" entry, he notes, "We are going steady and I decide I must have her, she puts me off, so on April 15th I propose, she accepts."

The entire courtship from the time he first saw Marina to the time he proposed marriage thus took place in less than one month. It also took place under very unusual circumstances. According to the hospital records of the ear, nose and throat section of the Fourth Clinical Hospital in Minsk, Oswald was admitted for treatment of an ear disorder on March 30 and was operated on to remove his adenoids on April 1. Up until this point they had not as yet had even one formal date. Most of their "romance," culminating in his proposal of marriage, would have to have taken place while Oswald was confined to a hospital bed under medication and Marina was visiting him illicitly. The marriage of an American defector and the niece of an MVD colonel, which would have been unusual under any circumstances, occurred after only an extraordinary three-week courtship in a hospital on the outskirts of Minsk. Curiously, Marina's aunt and uncle, despite their powerful position in Minsk, did not protest her decision to marry a foreigner who was under KGB surveillance at the time (at least, according to Nosenko). Certainly, a colonel in the MVD could have found out about Oswald's correspondence with the American Embassy regarding his repatriation, since this material would have been kept in the surveillance file.[11]

Soon after the marriage Marina applied to Soviet officials in both Minsk and Moscow for documents that would permit her to leave the Soviet Union for the United States.[12] With this set of documents, she then began filing the necessary applications with the American authorities. On her alien registration form, she was asked specifically if she had: "Any other name or names ever used or been known by." She answered, "None."

The CIA was also concerned about Marina's identity when it was discovered that she planned to return with Oswald to the United States. One staff officer noted that part of the "intelligence interest" he had in the case involved "a pattern of Soviet women marrying foreigners, being permitted to leave the USSR, then divorcing their spouses and settling down abroad without returning home."[13]

Subsequently Soviet specialists at the CIA showed some concern over her middle name. The Russians have a strict system which requires that the middle name identify the person's father; therefore, "Marina Nikolaevna" should have had a father named Nikolai. Yet Marina insisted that she did not know the name of her father.[14]

Moreover, there seemed to be a minor discrepancy in the birth certificate identifying her as "Marina Nikolaevna." It gave the name of the village in which she was born as Severodvinsk, yet at the time of her birth in 1941 that village was named Molotovsk. Its name was not changed until 1957.

Since Marina had been employed in the Soviet Union, moved her residence from one city to another and attended trade school before 1957, she would have needed a birth certificate to obtain the necessary travel and work documents, and this certificate should have listed her birthplace as "Molotovsk," not "Severodvinsk."

Marina's only explanation for the discrepancy was that she had lost her original birth certificate and had had to apply for a new one.

Years later Marina told a very different story to her biographer, Priscilla Johnson McMillan (the same Priscilla Johnson who had interviewed Oswald in Moscow in 1959). She said that the name she used until 1958 was Marina Alexandrovna Medvedeva. Up until then, she assumed she was the daughter of Alexander Medvedev, her mother's husband. However, when she wrote away for her birth certificate, she found out that she had been born illegitimate, been given the name Marina Nikolaevna Prusakova and never been legally adopted by Medvedev. Medvedev then told her that her real father was Nikolai Didenko, a traitor who had been executed by the Soviets.

In 1958 Marina changed her name and all her school records to Prusakova and told her friends to call her Marina Nikolaevna instead of Marina Alexandrovna. (The next year she went to live at the home of Colonel Ilya Prusakov.)

In this version, Marina is not clear when she applied for her new birth certificate. The date of issuance on the copy she gave to United States authorities is July 19, 1961.

Marina would have needed a birth certificate in order to obtain her marriage license in April 1961. This could not have been the certificate, dated July 19, 1961, that she handed into the U.S. Embassy. It thus seemed that new documents—and possibly a new identity—were furnished to Marina after it was decided that she would accompany Oswald to the United States.[15]

8

The Russian Gambit—
Accepted

Oswald boarded a jet plane at Minsk Airport on Saturday morning, July 8, 1961. His proximate destination was the United States Embassy in Moscow. The flight to Moscow took only two hours and twenty minutes, but delayed by heavy traffic in the heart of the city, he arrived at the consular section of the embassy just as it was closing at 3 P.M. Richard Snyder, the official with whom he had dealt in the past, had already gone home for the day. Knowing that Snyder lived in the embassy compound, Oswald phoned him at home.

Snyder wasted no time coming over to the consulate section to see Oswald. If nothing else, he was curious to see what had become of the young American who about twenty months earlier had volunteered to turn classified information over to the Soviets. He recognized Oswald the moment he entered. "The edge was off . . ." Snyder later commented. "Oswald seemed considerably subdued, though not contrite or crawling."

With almost no emotion in his voice, he explained that he had decided to return to the United States and needed to have his passport back—the same passport that he had angrily slammed onto Snyder's desk in 1959. He added that he had come to Moscow without any sort of official permission. If true, Snyder realized that this meant that Oswald was traveling illegally since foreigners with the sort of stateless passport that Oswald had were not allowed to travel freely from city to city in the Soviet Union.[1] Finally, Oswald casually mentioned that he was married to a "dental technician," who wanted to return with him to America.

Snyder coolly listened to his story. Whatever he personally thought of Oswald, he knew it was the policy of the United States government to facilitate the return of all defectors—if only to deprive the Soviets of propaganda points. He thus reassured him that he would do what he could to help and suggested that he return for a formal interview on Monday morning since the embassy was officially closed for business during the weekend.[2]

After leaving the embassy, Oswald placed a long-distance call to Marina in Minsk and told her to catch a plane and join him in Moscow. He then set out to book a hotel room. Even though he did not have the required travel documents, and most hotels were full because of the influx of foreigners who had come to Moscow that week to see a film festival,[3] Oswald managed to get a room at the Hotel Berlin, where he was known from his previous stay in Moscow.[4] Marina arrived the next day, and for the first time they were together in Moscow.

On Monday morning Oswald brought Marina with him to the embassy. There she was interviewed by John McVickar and filled out a "petition to classify status of alien for issuance of immigrant visa." While waiting, Oswald reportedly asked about Robert Edward Webster, another American who had attempted to renounce his citizenship in the fall of 1959, and who had been interviewed by Snyder in a Moscow police station just days before Oswald stormed into the embassy for the first time.[5]

After waiting a few minutes, Oswald was called into Snyder's office for his interview.

After asking Oswald only a few questions, Snyder could see that he seemed fully to understand, or was well briefed on, the technical requisites for maintaining United States citizenship.

Other than by a process of formal renunciation, an American can forfeit his citizenship only by formally joining or taking an oath of allegiance to a foreign government, and Oswald steadfastly denied he had ever done either. He even said he had not joined the trade union at the factory in Minsk where he worked, and he had never been asked to join any official organization in the Soviet Union.

He offered his "stateless passport" as *prima facie* evidence that he had never been granted Soviet citizenship and denied that he had ever applied for Soviet citizenship. Snyder knew, of course, that Oswald had stated in 1959 that he was applying for Soviet citizenship but did not press him on the point. He did, however, query him about his threat to turn over classified secrets to the Soviets.

Oswald replied that he was "never in fact subjected to any questioning or briefing by the Soviet authorities concerning his life or experiences prior to entering the Soviet Union and never provided such information to any Soviet organ." While Snyder was not fully satisfied with Oswald's candor and found it difficult to believe the Soviets would not have debriefed a former Marine Corps radar operator, he realized that there was little he could do to challenge the answers. He then handed Oswald a formal four-page questionnaire, which Oswald quickly filled out, answering no to all questions about joining foreign organizations.

Looking up at Snyder, Oswald laconically suggested that he must take some satisfaction in the fact that he was now sitting in his office as a supplicant, repudiating everything he had formerly said. But Snyder did not reply. Instead, he gave him back his passport (stamped valid only for direct travel to the United States), so that he could obtain the necessary exit visa from the Soviets, and wished him well. Snyder realized, however, that the passport expired in fewer than two months, and he did not intend to renew it until the entire situation was reviewed in Washington.

In a report the next day, which went to the CIA, as well as to State Department agencies, Snyder noted, "Twenty months of the realities of life have clearly had a maturing effect on Oswald. He stated frankly that he had clearly learned a hard lesson the hard way and that he had been completely relieved of his illusions about the Soviet Union at the same time that he acquired a new understanding and appreciation of the United States and meaning of freedom. Much of the arrogance and bravado which characterized him on his first visit to the Embassy appears to have left him." The Soviet Affairs Section of the State Department cautioned Snyder to proceed carefully in the "involved case" and to ascertain beyond a doubt "that the person in communication with the embassy is . . . Lee Harvey Oswald."

Oswald and his wife spent the balance of the week in Moscow. Among other things done in preparation for his repatriation, Oswald filed an application to renew his American passport and a request for an immigration visa for his wife. On Friday, July 14, they both returned to Minsk, where they immediately petitioned the Soviet authorities for their exit visas. Within one week they had filed all the necessary papers with the militia office, including application forms and supporting letters affirming their desire to live in the United States. Now that their decision was made, and Oswald had his passport back, they obviously intended to waste no time in processing out of the Soviet Union.

Oswald also proceeded to construct a story depicting Marina as the victim of unrelenting Soviet harassment, which, if believed by United States authorities, might serve to expedite favorable action in her case. On July 15, only one day after his return to Minsk, he wrote the American Embassy: "There have been some unusual and crude attempts on my wife at her place of work." He went to explain, "While we were still in Moscow, the foremen at her place of work were notified that she and I went into [the American] embassy for the purposes of visas. . . . There followed the usual 'enemy of the people' meeting in which in her absence she was condemned and her friends warned against speaking with her."

He also notes in the "July 15th" entry of his diary: "Marina, at work, is shocked to find out that everyone knows she entered the U.S. Embassy. They . . . give her a strong browbeating. The first of many indoctrinations." In the next entry, "July 15th–Aug 20th," he chronicles five more unpleasant meetings, over the summer, including an hour-and-one-half session before the Young Communist League [of which she had apparently been a member], in which they tried to dissuade Marina from going to the United States. He also wrote a letter to his brother Robert in Texas, which presumably would have been read by the CIA as part of its mail cover, complaining of the Soviet "cross-examination [of] my wife." He added, in an obvious reference to the Soviet authorities, "They know everything because they spy and read the mails. . . ."

After having attempted to establish this campaign of persecution against Marina, in an October 4 letter he asked the American Embassy to institute official inquiries about the matter "since there have been systematic and concerted attempts to intimidate my wife into withdrawing her application for a visa." To add an air of crisis to his request, he asserted, "These incidents have resulted in my wife being hospitalized for a five-day period, on September 22nd, 1961, for nervous exhaustion."

Although Oswald continued to elaborate on the story of Marina's persecution in his letters, it seems to have had little basis in fact. The hospital records do not show that Marina was confined or treated for "nervous exhaustion" during this period, and she herself denied in subsequent testimony that she had ever been hospitalized because of any sort of harassment. (She did visit a hospital in August because she had become pregnant and had a series of blood tests.)

Moreover, it seems implausible that Soviet authorities would need to dissuade her from leaving by means of denunciations and social pressures; if they wished to keep her in the Soviet Union, they could simply delay giving her an exit visa, as had been done in numerous other cases.[6] In any case Marina seemed to have excellent relations with local officials through Colonel Prusakov, and at the very time Oswald was writing the embassy about her sufferings, she was 450 miles away at Kharkov on a vacation that lasted almost the entire month of October. During this time she stayed at the home of her uncle, Yuri Mikhailov, whom she later identified as an "engineer in the building trades program in Kharkov."[7]

During Marina's absence from Minsk, Oswald recorded in his diary: "I am lonely and I . . . go to dances and public places for entertainment. I haven't done this in quite a few months now." On the eighteenth, for his birthday, Marina sent him from

Kharkov an inscribed gold and silver cup, which he wrote about to his mother and brother. "I spend my birthday alone at the opera watching my favorite—Queen of Spades," he wrote in his diary. "I am twenty-two years old." A few days later he wrote Marina in Kharkov: "You will never lose me and that's all." He signed the letter, as he did all his letters during this period, Alik. Another dismal winter was setting in on Minsk.

During this period Oswald also somehow found time to write long and impressively documented sections of a manuscript on life in Minsk. Aside from endless statistics about industrial and agricultural production which he ferreted out of local newspapers to illustrate the difficult economic situation in Russia, he portrayed the regimented social and political life of the people in an ironic style reminiscent of Orwell's *Animal Farm.*

He delighted in pointing out the corrupt practices of Communist Party officials and the way they wielded their bureaucratic power to the detriment of the common workers they were supposed to represent. He also noted such discrepancies in socialist societies as elections, in which the voters have no choice, and the faking of "spontaneous" demonstrations.

The almost prisonlike restrictions on travel and movement are also given lengthy treatment in the manuscript:

Even trips to many cities of the Soviet Union are forbidden, even to those who would like to travel there to see relatives. All cities above Leningrad towards the Finnish border fall into this main category, Brest on the Polish border, Odessa (main seaport). Some cities in the Ukraine and Siberia connected with all cities along the Southern border of the USSR from Moldavia to India are forbidden without a pass. All cars, trucks, and other private vehicles are stopped at police check points to these areas. Train and plane and bus terminals are not allowed to sell tickets to these places without being shown a valid passport whose owner's address is in the forbidden city. Persons already living in these cities may travel freely to and from them; however, they may not bring others in without passes; passes are given out by the local KGB office, and one must apply directly to it.

At the beginning of November Marina returned to Minsk.[8] In his diary Oswald seems ebullient, noting in the "November 2nd" entry, "Marina arrives back, radiant, with several jars of preserves for me from her aunt in Kharkov." Within a few days of her return Marina went to the Ministry of Internal Affairs for an interview with a Colonel Nikolai Aksenov. Oswald described him as: "The Ministry of Internal Affairs, whose boss is tough military Colonel Nikolay Aksenov of the 'people's militia.' He holds the title Minister of Internal Affairs. Around the corner is his subsidiary, the KGB, Committee for Internal Security (Intelligence and secret police)." The purpose of this meeting, according to Marina, was to expedite her documents for traveling to the United States.

Several weeks passed after the meeting with the colonel. Then, on Christmas Day, Marina was called to the passport office in Minsk and told that her exit visa had been approved by the ministry in Moscow. They both would receive all the necessary permissions from the Soviet side in a matter of days. Under the "Xmas Day" entry in his diary, Oswald reacted: "It's great (I think?)."

One week later the Oswalds celebrated their first New Year's Eve together at a midnight dinner party at the home of the Zigers. By now Marina was seven months pregnant, and Oswald, anticipating that the expected child would be a boy, wrote its name out on one of the application forms as "David Lee Oswald." With their Soviet visas in hand, he also expected it would be born in the United States.

However, even as the Oswalds excitedly planned their departure from Russia that winter, the State Department was running into a problem issuing Marina an entrance visa. Although she had been granted immigrant status as the wife of an American citizen and was thus eligible for a visa, Congress had prohibited the State Department from issuing any visas whatsoever in the Soviet Union, unless a prior waiver had been obtained from the Immigration and Naturalization Service, an agency of the Justice Department. In this case the Immigration Service declined to issue such a waiver; this meant that Marina would have to be accepted by a third country before she could be issued her visa.

Robert I. Owens, the desk officer in the Soviet Affairs Section of the State Department who was then handling the Oswald case, foresaw that this refusal could greatly complicate the situation of all the other Soviet citizens waiting for exit visas and allow the Soviet government to argue that it was the United States which was impeding emigration from the Soviet Union by refusing to issue entrance visas. In this broader context, he wrote a memorandum urging the Immigration and Naturalization Service to reconsider its decision since "it is in the interest of the United States to get Lee Harvey Oswald and his family out of the Soviet Union and into the United States as soon as possible." He warned that Oswald was "an unstable character" who might reverse his decision unless prompt action was taken. While the memorandum moved through channels in Washington, the embassy in Moscow was instructed not to inform Oswald of the waiver problem.

While impatiently awaiting word from the embassy, Oswald applied for a loan from the State Department to finance his return trip; this meant more forms had to be filled out, and letters sent to relatives in the United States. Also during January, Oswald wrote two letters to the International Rescue Committee explaining his situation and requesting that it contact the American Embassy in Moscow in order to contribute financial assistance for his trip home. This helped him document the fact that he had sought (but not been successful in getting) funds from charitable organizations. While waiting, Oswald also attempted to redress the undesirable discharge that his honorable discharge had been converted into in August 1960.

On January 30, 1962, he wrote an angry letter to John B. Connally, Jr., who had been Secretary of the Navy in 1961, which betrayed considerable anxiety over the change in status of his discharge.[9] In defending himself, he asserted that he had "always had the full sanction of the U.S. Embassy . . . and hence the U.S. government" during his stay in the Soviet Union. He warned, "I shall employ all means to right this gross mistake or injustice . . ." and asked Connally to "look into this case and take the necessary steps to repair the damage. . . ."

Oswald also wrote a letter to his Senator from Texas, John Tower, attempting to enlist his help in redressing his undesirable discharge. His tone here seems far less angry and more moderate.[10] It remained a matter of great importance to him as he prepared for his return. An undesirable discharge could make it difficult for him to obtain employment in the United States; it could also serve as a prelude to eventual prosecution.

Oswald spent considerable time that spring working on a long legalistic petition to the U.S. Naval Review Board to reverse his discharge. The meticulous citing of the U.S. Naval Code of Justice and the impeccable legal logic of the five-page brief suggest that Oswald had either assistance in preparing the petition or, at the very least, access to an up-to-date legal library in Minsk.[11] He argued that he had not been disloyal to the United States, but instead had been forcibly detained by the Soviets. He explained, "After escaping detention in the city to which the Russian authorities had sent me," that he instantly asked the U.S. Embassy in Moscow for its assistance in returning to America. In now requesting to be reinstated in the U.S. Marine Corps Reserves, he offered "the special knowledge I have accumulated through my experiences *since my release from active duty in the Naval Service.*" By underlining "since my release," Oswald was, in effect, offering to turn over information he had acquired in the Soviet Union to U.S. intelligence agencies. Although he dated the letter April 28, 1962, and gave his residence as "Kalinina Street, Minsk," he did not mail this petition until after he had left the Soviet Union.

While still waiting for her U.S. visa, Marina gave birth on February 15 to a girl, named, in the Russian patronymic style, June Lee Oswald.[12] Oswald, though initially disappointed that it was not the boy he expected, wrote a flurry of excited letters to his mother and brother. He also sent Marina daily notes in the hospital signed "Your husband Alik."

A week later Marina returned home with June and formally quit her job in the hospital. Despite Oswald's continuing calls and letters to the embassy, the visas did not arrive. Discouraged by the seemingly senseless delay, Oswald wrote his brother on April 12: "Only the American side is holding us up now," then added, "I really don't want to leave [now] until the beginning of fall, since spring and summer here are so nice."

In Washington, on May 9, the State Department finally prevailed on the Immigration and Naturalization Service to issue the waiver for Marina. It had already received approval to extend a $500 loan to Oswald for the Moscow to New York trip. A cable was immediately sent to the embassy in Moscow, which in turn notified Oswald in Minsk that all his documents were ready and he could come to pick them up.

Oswald had carefully prepared for his passage west. He laboriously wrote out, in one or two sessions that spring, an entire diary that purported to be a contemporaneous account of his first two and a half years in Russia. His handwriting showed progressively more strain and fatigue as he wrote, or copied, the first twelve pages; then apparently he took a break before completing the diary.[13] In this instance, Oswald uncharacteristically printed out his words possibly so that they would be read by others. (In almost all his other writings he used script.) One of the last entries Oswald wrote in his diary, dated April 15, noted that Oswald had "still not told Erich [Titovets] who is my oldest acquaintance that we are going to the States . . . he is too good a Young Communist League member so I'll wait until the last minute."[14] A moment later he finished his "Historic Diary." It has remained almost the sole account of the period from January 1960, when Oswald left Moscow, until March 1961, when he met Marina.[15]

Just before they left for Moscow, Oswald and Marina met with Colonel Prusakov, who gave them some final words of advice. A series of photographs taken by Oswald and his friends shows them boarding the train with their infant daughter and waving good-bye to the Prusakovs and other friends from Minsk through a half-opened window.[16] To Marina, these last days had all seemed to go by in a "frantic rush"; she was leaving behind, perhaps forever, her relatives, friends and country.

Arriving in Moscow on the morning of May 24, the Oswalds went directly to the American Embassy. After a brief interview with Jack Matlock, the consular officer who dealt with Soviet citizens, Marina was fingerprinted and given the U.S. visa that she had waited almost a year to obtain. She was then taken upstairs to the embassy hospital for a medical examination by Dr. Alex Davison. Finding that she was slightly anxious about going to America, Dr. Davison gave her the phone number of his Russian-speaking mother in Atlanta, Georgia.[17]

Meanwhile, Oswald was questioned by Joseph P. Norbury, Jr., the U.S. consul, to determine if any of his activities in the Soviet Union would preclude renewing his passport. Although these were routine and straightforward questions—such as "Are you a Communist?"—Norbury found Oswald extremely guarded in his responses, choosing his words with considerable care. He seemed not only "apprehensive and suspicious," but also at times hostile to the American consul. After about a half hour Norbury completed the interview and, satisfied with Oswald's answers, renewed his passport for travel directly back to the United States.

During the next few days, the Oswalds went from office to office in Moscow to complete their travel arrangements. At one office Oswald handed in his Soviet "stateless person" passport and then, after it had been duly processed, picked it up at another location. He exchanged currencies, registered his daughter June's birth certificate and visa, obtained the necessary transit visas for passing through Poland, East Germany, West Germany and the Netherlands for himself and his wife, and, partly with money given him by the American Embassy and partly with the balance of his savings, he paid $81.29 for two third-class train tickets to Rotterdam.[18] He also was given a final interview by MVD representatives in Moscow.

The Oswalds again stayed at the Hotel Berlin and had dinner at least one night at the Hotel Leningrad,[19] where they sat at a table with an American couple from New Haven, Connecticut. The man, noticing that Oswald seemed to be pretending to be Russian, made a casual comment to him about the American label on his jacket that gave him away. Oswald replied abruptly, "You don't know, I might be a spy."[20] This effectively ended the conversation.

On the morning of June 1 Oswald went to the embassy and signed a promissory note for the balance of his repatriation loan. In all, it amounted to $435.71. He was then given three tickets for the ship SS *Maasdam*, due to leave Rotterdam for Hoboken, New Jersey, on June 4. The embassy had arranged not only the least expensive route home for Oswald, but also one that would give him the minimum time for stopping over anywhere in Europe before boarding his ship. With little time to spare, the Oswalds caught the Moscow-Berlin express. That night they passed through Minsk for the last time.[21]

The next day, a few miles past the city of Brest-Litovsk, the train stopped briefly at the border for a customs and passport inspection, then proceeded into Poland. Among his personal belongings, Oswald carried out with him a manuscript critical of life in the Soviet Union and his "Historic Diary," which further chronicled his decision to redefect.[22] The rest of the journey was uneventful. From the windows of their compartment, they saw the cities of central Europe flash by—Warsaw, Frankfurt an der Oder, Berlin. Then, about fifty hours after it left Moscow, the train pulled into Amsterdam.

They had almost two days for sightseeing in Holland before their ship left, and rather than stay at the hotel, Oswald rented a small apartment in Amsterdam recommended by an official in the U.S. Embassy in Moscow. "Our landlady was so neat that we were even afraid to lie down on the sheets for fear of getting them dirty," Marina wrote later. She also described that Sunday in Holland: "The bells were ringing in the churches, and people were going to church . . . it seemed that the people here had never known trouble, and everything was like a fairy tale; even the houses in Holland looked like houses in a fairy tale, with lots of glass and light."

The brief vacation in Holland ended on June 4, when the Oswald family boarded the SS *Maasdam* and began their crossing to the United States. Oswald spent most of the nine days at sea in his third-class cabin. While Marina tended to their daughter, he went upstairs to the ship's library and scribbled out his political philosophy on seventeen sheets of the ship's stationery. In these notes he attempted to develop a position for himself that would seem reasonable to Americans.

He began by observing, "The communist, capitalist and even the fascist and anarchist elements in America always profess patriotism towards the land and the people, if not the government; although their movements must lead to the bitter destruction of all and everything." After criticizing both Soviet communism and American capitalism and dismissing other political parties in the spectrum as merely "products of the two systems," he concluded: "I have lived under both systems, I have sought the answers and although it would be easy to dupe myself into believing one system is better than the other, I know [it] is not."

With such philosophical underpinnings, Oswald was fully prepared to represent himself as a utopian Marxist fully disillusioned with the Soviet brand of communism—at least for the present.

Anticipating the questions he might be asked by the American authorities on his reentry to the United States, he laboriously wrote out two sets of answers—the first unguarded and the second an edited version—that would pass at least the initial screening. Both sets of handwritten notes were found among his effects in 1963. A handwriting analysis of the two sets of answers suggests that he was changing the second set of answers under pressure and was possibly irritated by the exercise. Moreover, the way in which he wrote down words phonetically, struck them out and inserted words between lines without interrupting the flow of the writing suggests that the answers were being dictated to him.[23]

For example, the response to the question "Why did you go to the USSR?" in the first version is: "I went as a mark of disgust and protest against American political policies, my personal sign of discontent and horror at the misguided line of reasoning of the U.S. Government."

In answer to the same question in the sanitized version, he wrote: "I went as a citizen of the U.S. (as a tourist) residing in a foreign country which I have a perfect right to do. I went there to see the land, the people and how their system works." In the first version he admits writing letters renouncing his allegiance to the United States, while in the subsequent version he flatly denies ever writing such letters. Similarly, he acknowledges being a Communist in the first version but denies it in the second.

To the question "Why did you remain in the Soviet Union for so long?" he changes his answer from "I did so because I was living quite comfortably. I had plenty of money, apartment rent free, lots of girls, etc. Why should I leave all of that?" to the more acceptable "It took me almost a half year to get a permit to leave the city of Minsk for Moscow. . . . [Then] almost one year was spent in trying to leave the country. That's why I was there so long, not out of desire!"

Finally, asked "What are the outstanding differences between the USA and USSR?" he altered his original answer from "None, except in the U.S. the standard of living is a little higher . . . [but] medical aid and the educational system in the USSR is better" to "Freedom of speech, travel, outspoken opposition

to unpopular policies, freedom to believe in God, newspapers. . . ." In moving from one version to the other, Oswald
seemed to be acting on the principle that expediency, rather
than truth, should be the only consideration for answering questions designed to elicit political information from him.

Both this questionnaire and the handwritten statement on his
political philosophy that he wrote aboard the SS *Maasdam*
show evidence of having been dictated to him. The way that
words are phonetically scribbled down without regard for spelling suggests that he was using words that were unfamiliar to
him and hearing them rather than copying them from a book or
prepared text. In both cases, he seems to be writing under the
discipline of another person.[24] But who could have been tutoring him on the SS *Maasdam* in preparation for his landing in
the United States?

Marina did not speak English well enough at this point to
have dictated a long treatise on political philosophy (and since
she would be with him in the United States, there would seem
little point in her tutoring him on the ship). Nor was he seen
speaking to any of the other passengers onboard.[25]

Years later Marina told her biographer, Priscilla Johnson Mc-
Millan, that there was a Russian-speaking waiter named Pieter
Didenko who spoke to them during the voyage. However, there
is no available ship's record showing a person with such a
name.

9

The Homecoming

On June 13, 1962, the SS *Maasdam* steamed past the Statue of Liberty and docked at the Holland-American Line pier at Hoboken, New Jersey. Immigration officers and other officials came aboard, but for some undisclosed reason the 1,400 passengers were not allowed to begin disembarking. For more than an hour they milled impatiently around under the broiling noonday sun before the inspector in charge began processing their passports. Among the departing passengers was Lee Harvey Oswald. After answering a few brief questions about his destination in America, Oswald and his family were waved through passport control and down the gangplank. He had returned to a country he had not seen since he was nineteen.

As he led his family to the area on the pier where the passengers' luggage was unloaded and stacked alphabetically, he could hear his name being called on the loudspeaker system. And a short, broad-shouldered man was waiting patiently for him by his luggage.

The man asked if he was "Lee Oswald," then introduced himself as Spas T. Raikin. He explained he was a Russian-speaking caseworker with Travelers Aid in New York City, who had been dispatched to help them with their arrangements.

Although it was not unusual for him to be sent by the Welfare Department to meet stranded travelers, this time he had been instructed "to find out as much as he could about the Oswalds" by his supervisor. While they waited for the baggage to be cleared through customs, he casually asked Oswald why he had gone to Russia.

Oswald, who seemed extremely guarded in relaying any information, said only that he was "a Marine . . . attached to the Embassy" in Moscow. When he refused to elaborate any further on the subject, Raikin decided it was best not to "rock the boat" by pressing him. From their hour long talk he gleaned very little about Oswald's activities in Russia, other than that he claimed to have met Marina in Moscow and, after they were married, considered renouncing his citizenship so he could remain with her before finally deciding that they both should return to the United States. After hearing Oswald's story, Raikin escorted him to the bus that would take him to the terminal in New York City.

About an hour later, the Oswalds turned up at the Travelers Aid Society office on East Thirty-ninth Street. There they were met by Cleary F'N Pierre, a Haitian professor, who no longer worked for the society but had simply stopped in to visit and been pressed into service since they were shorthanded. F'N Pierre took Oswald on a fastpaced round of visits to the offices of welfare workers involved in expediting his travel from New York to Fort Worth, Texas. Since Oswald only had $63 left, one caseworker called his brother Robert and asked him to telegraph $200 for plane fare. When Oswald learned that his brother had mortgaged his car to raise the $200, he refused to accept the money, arguing that the State Department should pay for the trip. He went to the caseworker's superior, Janet F. Ruscoll, explaining that he had learned in the Soviet Union always to go to the top person in a bureaucracy.

Despite his demands that she contact the State Department, she made it clear that he had no choice but to accept a loan from his brother if he wanted to proceed to Texas. Finally, he relented and agreed to accept the $200 which Robert had already said he would send. A telegram was then sent to inform

Robert that his brother would be arriving the following evening. A room was reserved for Oswald at the Times Square Hotel for that night by another caseworker. After all the travel arrangements had been made, F'N Pierre took Oswald to Pennsylvania Station so that he could ship his excess baggage by train.[1]

The money for the air tickets arrived the next morning. Marvin Lehrman, a Welfare Department supervisor, escorted the Oswald family to New York International Airport. During the ride Oswald again showed no inclination to discuss his reasons for returning from the Soviet Union and quickly fell silent. At 4:15 P.M. Lehrman watched the Oswalds board Delta Flight 821 for Dallas. As far as he was concerned, the Welfare Department case on the Oswalds was now closed.

That evening Robert Oswald went with his wife, Vada, to Love Field in Dallas to meet the flight from New York. After watching a long line of passengers come off the plane, Vada exclaimed, "There he is!" Robert could see his younger brother walking toward him, looking around anxiously. A few steps behind him was his Russian bride, dressed in a heavy woolen dress and carrying their child.

Robert had last seen his brother in September 1959, a few days after he had been discharged from the Marine Corps. He had then looked remarkably happy and fit, in fine physical condition, with a full head of curly brown hair. Now he appeared far more gaunt and weary. His fair complexion had turned ruddy and sallow. The most marked change, however, was his hair. Not only had it thinned almost to the point of baldness on top, but the texture had changed from soft to kinky. Struck by this loss of hair, Robert couldn't help wondering what happened to his brother during the intervening years in the Soviet Union.[2]

As Oswald approached the passenger gate, Robert and Vada ran toward them. In a moment of quick embraces, the Oswald brothers were reunited. As they made their way out of the airport, Oswald kept looking around as if he were expecting someone else. Finally, he asked, "No reporters?" in a voice that seemed to betray some disappointment.

"I managed to keep it quiet, as you asked in your letter," Robert replied, and the subject was dropped. During the hour-long car trip from Dallas to Fort Worth, Robert tried to point out some of the Texas sights to Marina, but everything he said had to be translated by his brother into Russian. Even though they had been married for more than a year, Marina had apparently learned no English.

Robert had invited the Oswalds to live with his family at 7313 Davenport Street in Fort Worth until Lee found a job for himself. In the two and one-half years that his brother had been in Russia, Robert had risen from being a salesman to being an executive with Acme Brick Company, and now he owned a small but comfortable suburban house with a living room, dining room, kitchen and two bedrooms. He moved Oswald and his wife and daughter into the extra bedroom and his own five-year-old daughter, who had previously occupied the room, into the living room. Marina seemed especially pleased with this living arrangement. After enthusiastically examining the kitchen appliances and the shrubs in the garden, she asked her husband in Russian, "Will we be able to live like this?" Oswald answered, "In time. Just give me time."

Marina's apparent delight over material goods did not carry over to Oswald. Robert recalled receiving a letter from his brother a few weeks after he first arrived in Moscow, asking, "Do you think that . . . I am here for personal material advantage?" going on to explain he cared nothing about material goods. "Happiness is not based on one's self, [it] does not consist of a small home, of taking and getting. . . . Happiness is taking part in a struggle where there is no borderline between one's personal world and the world in general."

Lee and Marina Oswald spent their first weekend in Fort Worth unpacking their scant possessions and preparing for their new life in America. Vada, a beautician by trade, cut Marina's long hair into a shorter American style and gave her her first permanent. They then went shopping at a local supermarket, and Marina, pushing her first shopping cart around the store, marveled at the endless display of food.

When they returned home, Oswald showed his brother the notes he had compiled for a book about living conditions in the Soviet Union. Robert read the first fifteen or so pages of the draft, which was mainly about the radio factory in Minsk where Oswald had worked, and was relieved to find that it was not a screeching polemic.[3] He had sharply disagreed with the anti-

American views his brother had expressed in Moscow and now wanted to avoid any further political discussions with him. He had long ago accepted the fact that he and his brother did not see "eye to eye" in politics.

In the days ahead Oswald wasted no time in attempting to establish credentials for himself as an authority on the Soviet Union. Promptly on Monday morning he went to the office of a public stenographer, Pauline V. Bates, and offered her the job of typing up his manuscript on Russia. He explained that he had lived there for three years and now wanted to publish a book on "My life in Russia," as Oswald called it.

Bates was taken aback by the gaunt young man with pale eyes which looked almost dead. As he stood there in his white T-shirt, dark slacks and zip-up jacket, he looked very young, almost like a high school student. The story he told was far more interesting to her. He described from a first hand point of view how repressive contemporary life in Russia actually was. He gave graphic descriptions of the way the Soviet police monitored every aspect of his life—including even the purchasing of paper and pencils—and the censors read his mail. Because of the surveillance, he explained, he had had to prepare the manuscript under clandestine conditions. When he typed it out at night, he said, his wife had had to muffle the sound of the typewriter and watch out for signs of the secret police or informers.[4]

Bates asked how he had gotten the manuscript out of Russia. Oswald explained that he and his wife had taped it to their undergarments when they crossed the border. If they had been searched, he said, they would both have "been sent to Siberia."

After Bates agreed to do the typing at the rate of one dollar a page, Oswald took out a manila envelope filled with scraps of paper stapled together into two different sequences. The first dealt with the city of Minsk, the second with Kiev. The notes were both handwritten and typed in Russian, suggesting that he (or whoever prepared the manuscript) had had access to a Cyrillic typewriter.

During her typing Oswald insisted on being present to make sure that she didn't retain any copies or even make any notes. As she worked that morning, he paced nervously around the room, his eyes always darting past her. At the end of each session he carefully checked to make sure he had taken all the pages from her. He even took the sheets of carbon paper with him.

Bates found the stories "fascinating," and when she told Oswald this, he explained that a friend of his in Texas was going to help him get the book published. He added that the friend was an engineer of Russian origin who was involved in the oil business.

By Wednesday, Oswald was showing increasing concern about the progress of the typing of his book. Peering over Bates's shoulder, he saw that she was up to the part about Kiev. (In all other accounts Oswald gave of his stay in Russia, he omitted mentioning that he had ever been to Kiev.) Stopping her, he asked how much he owed her to date. She had typed ten single-spaced pages at $1 a page. Collecting his notes, he paid her the $10, which his mother had given him, and told her he could not afford any more typing. By now, however, she had become interested in the material and offered to complete the job without being immediately paid for it. Oswald shook his head, rejecting this proposal, and quickly left. His story about Kiev—a Soviet city for which there is no official record of his ever having visited—was not to be completed.[5]

During his first week in Fort Worth Oswald also sought a job as a translator of Russian. Annie L. Smith, a counselor at the Texas Employment Commission, suggested that as a starting point Oswald should contact Peter Paul Gregory, a petroleum engineer of Russian origin who was then teaching a Russian-language course at the Fort Worth Public Library.[6] After phoning for an appointment, Oswald met Gregory in his office on June 19 and asked if he could certify and recommend him as a Russian translator.

Gregory found Oswald completely fluent in Russian (although he seemed to have a Polish accent). After giving him a Russian text to translate, which Oswald did with great ease, Gregory gave him a letter addressed "To whom it may concern," certifying that Oswald was "capable of being an interpreter and perhaps a translator." Oswald's Russian, the letter noted, was acquired during a three-year residence in the Soviet Union. During their meeting Oswald casually mentioned that he had brought back a Russian wife to Fort Worth and also showed him a copy of the first few pages of his manuscript.

Although slightly put off by Oswald's arrogance, Gregory was impressed by Oswald's skill in the Russian language and, taking his address, promised to get in touch with him if he heard of anyone needing the services of a translator. Oswald had succeeded in making his first contact in the fairly large community of Russian expatriates in the Fort Worth-Dallas area.

On June 18 Oswald finally filed with the Naval Discharge Review Board the five-page petition that he had prepared—apparently in Minsk. He was still concerned with his Marine discharge and with getting the sort of documentation that would allow him to work without any questions being asked in Texas.

Toward the end of the week Oswald's mother, Marguerite, arrived from Crowell, Texas, where she was working as a practical nurse. She was sorry not to have been at the airport to greet him but had been confused about the exact date of his arrival. Even though the State Department had informed her by cable that he was landing in New York on June 13, he had suggested in a letter from Moscow to her that he would first stop in Washington, D.C., before proceeding on to Texas. She thus had not expected him so soon in Fort Worth.

After meeting Marina, she raved about her beauty and lavished affection on her newest granddaughter, June. She was more reserved toward Robert and his family, whom she had not seen in several years, although they lived in the same area. Turning to her younger son, she said, "You know, Lee . . . I am getting ready to write a book on your so-called defection."

Oswald looked up sharply and replied, "Mother, you are not going to write any book."

Unconvinced by his unexpected rebuke, she persisted. "Don't tell me what to do. It has nothing to do with you or Marina. It is my life—"

He interrupted before she could finish, calmly explaining that if she wrote such a book, "They could kill [Marina] and her family." His meaning was painfully clear to his family: The Soviet authorities would hold his wife and family hostage for his actions or even his mother's actions. Comprehending his predicament, she dropped the idea of the book. During the remainder of his mother's brief visit to Fort Worth, Oswald avoided mentioning the critique of Soviet society that he had brought out of the Soviet Union and was now preparing for publication.

His own manuscript did not seem to pose the same danger for Marina and her family.[7]

Meanwhile, in Washington, D.C., Oswald's return to America did not go unnoticed by the FBI, which had been monitoring his activities on and off since his defection in 1959. Assigned the identifying number 327-925D, his file contained interviews with his mother, brother and other relatives, as well as information supplied by the Fort Worth Retailers Association, the Office of Navy Intelligence, CIA and State Department. When it became clear in May 1962 that the Soviet authorities were permitting Oswald to return with a Russian wife to the United States, the FBI's counterespionage section became increasingly concerned with the possibility that the Soviets might have assigned Oswald or his wife some sort of intelligence mission.

This would be neither uncommon nor unexpected. Through debriefing literally thousands of Soviet expatriates who came through Europe after World War II, American military and civilian intelligence agencies found that the Soviets often gave Soviet citizens receiving an exit visa some sort of mission, even if it was only as trivial as reporting their addresses to predesignated Soviet embassies abroad. This presumption was especially strong in the Oswald case since the Soviets had apparently gone to some lengths to facilitate their documentation and had some leverage over Marina through her relatives in the USSR. On May 31 Washington headquarters instructed agents at their Dallas field office to question Oswald upon his arrival there.

After hearing on June 26 that Oswald was settled in Fort Worth, FBI Agent John W. Fain asked Oswald to come into the office. At one o'clock that afternoon he arrived at the Fort Worth FBI office and took a seat opposite Fain and another agent, B. Tom Carter.

During most of the hourlong interview the FBI agents found "Oswald exhibited an impatient and arrogant attitude." When asked why he originally went to the Soviet Union, he barked back in an angry voice that he did not care "to relive the past." He also claimed that newspaper stories from Moscow that characterized his attitude as anti-American were false and distorted. Despite his handwritten letter to the U.S. Embassy in Moscow, he flatly denied that he had ever tried to renounce his American citizenship or seek Soviet citizenship. He even refused to name Marina's relatives in the USSR. By this time it was clear to the interviewing agents that they were dealing with a hostile witness, who was not prepared to volunteer, and would probably deny, any detrimental information about himself. No matter how many pointed questions were put to him about his contacts with Soviet authority, he would discuss little more than his job as a metalworker in a television factory in Minsk and his trip back to the United States.

Finally, the agents asked him point-blank whether he had been recruited by Soviet intelligence while he was in the Soviet Union. He coolly answered no and denied that he was even approached for any information by any Soviet official. When pressed about statements he had made in the U.S. Embassy in Moscow, he scoffed at the idea that he had ever offered to make available any of the data he had learned in the Marine Corps. Had he made any "deals" with the Soviets or accepted any assignments, in return for the Soviets' expediting his or his wife's exit visas? the agents asked. Oswald again answered no. Troubled by his flat denials of almost everything they asked, the agents asked, as suggested by Washington headquarters, if he would be willing to submit to a polygraph examination. Oswald categorically refused to take any such lie-detector test and excused himself from the interview.[8]

In his report to the chief of the Dallas FBI office, Fain "set out a lead" on Oswald, suggesting that his Immigration and Naturalization Service records be checked and that Oswald be reinterviewed.

After dinner Robert returned from work and asked Oswald how the FBI had treated him. "Just fine," he replied, concealing his earlier distress. "They asked me . . . Was I a secret agent?" What did you reply? his brother wanted to know. To which he answered, "Well, don't you know?" He laughed after telling the story as if it were some sort of private joke which his brother did not understand.

Less than a week later Marina wrote a letter to the Soviet Embassy in Washington providing her address in Fort Worth and the number of the residency permit which had been issued to her by the Ministry of Internal Affairs in Moscow. At the Embassy it was routed to the attention of "Comrad Gerasimov."

When monitored by a surveillance program the FBI maintained of mail to the Soviet Embassy, it appeared to be a routine bit of correspondence and might have gone unnoticed had not a second secretary at the Soviet Embassy, Vitaliy A. Gerasimov, then been under intense scrutiny by FBI counterespionage. As a CIA report subsequently noted, "Gerasimov . . . is known to have participated in clandestine meetings in this country and to have made payments for intelligence information of value to the Soviets." Since Gerasimov performed routine consular tasks, along with being an intelligence case officer, it was not clear whether the Oswalds' contact with him was merely a coincidence or whether it portended a more serious relation.

In July Oswald attempted to construct a more independent life for himself in Fort Worth. Leaving his brother's house, which was becoming cramped for two families to share, Oswald temporarily moved into an apartment that his mother had rented about ten blocks away on Seventh Street. She had moved back to Fort Worth, intent on living with him and caring for Marina and June, while he found work. From the beginning, however, this living arrangement strained Oswald's patience. For one thing, his mother, a very determined woman, insisted on speaking English to Marina and assumed that she understood.[9] His protests that she did not comprehend a word of English were to no avail. Marina did not seem to mind and went about the house cheerfully singing and helping with the housework.[10]

Returning to the Texas Employment Commission, Oswald offered to do manual labor at a minimum wage. Mrs. Smith, the counselor who had previously tried to help him find employment as a translator, sent him to the Leslie Welding Company, which had informed the commission it was looking for metalworkers for its louver-door factory in Fort Worth. On Friday, July 13, Oswald filled out the application forms, giving Peter Gregory and his brother as references and claiming that he had two and one-half years' experience working with sheet metals. Immediately hired, he was told to report for work on Monday. It turned out to be a monotonous and grueling job—eight to nine hours a day assembling doors and windows at $1.25 an hour—but it provided him with a paycheck.

At the end of July, after cashing his second paycheck for $56, Oswald rented an apartment for himself at 2703 Mercedes Street. The block was lined with trees, and the apartment—two furnished rooms in a duplex—was bare, but clean and pleasant. It afforded Oswald and his family their first bit of privacy since they had left their river-view apartment in Minsk.

When he arrived in his car to help them move, Robert could hear his mother arguing with his brother. She apparently felt that she had made a great sacrifice in moving to Fort Worth to help Lee, and now he suddenly was moving out, without even telling her where he was going to live. Robert, who had learned long before to avoid such quarrels with his mother, quietly assisted his brother in loading his few suitcases and other possessions into his car. Marina, looking bewildered, got in with June, and they drove to the new apartment—about one-half mile away.

August was extraordinarily hot that year even by Texas standards. Oswald had no choice but to continue working 45 to 50 hours a week at the sweltering factory to pay the rent and expenses and to begin repaying his brother the money he had lent him to fly to Texas. Meanwhile, Marina, who had shed her Russian woolens for short American shorts, took her daughter for strolls in the neighborhood and wrote long letters to the friends she left behind in the Soviet Union. She also promptly informed the Soviet Embassy of her new address since she was still a Soviet citizen.

Now on his own, Oswald made no effort to see members of his family, although occasionally he would speak to his brother on the phone. The only person the Oswalds invited to their apartment was Paul Gregory, the twenty-one-year-old son of Peter Gregory. A Phi Beta Kappa student in economics at the University of Oklahoma, Gregory planned to continue in graduate school in the field of Soviet studies, and his father, though himself still teaching Russian, had recommended Marina as a tutor. It was an equitable arrangement. He paid only a few dollars a session—amounting to no more than $40 during the course of the summer—and could practice his Russian with a girl his age who could not speak English.

Since Paul Gregory had a car at his disposal, he would often take them shopping at the supermarkets on weekends. From this, he learned how austerely this young couple was living. Oswald rarely spent more than $4 for the whole week's groceries for his family. He was not, however, ungracious. When they returned to his apartment, Oswald would usually offer Gregory a glass of Hawaiian Punch. Then they would begin a conversation in Russian which might last an hour or two.

Not only did Oswald delight in criticizing American capitalism, but he also went out of his way to criticize the Soviet Union for diverging from the original ideas of Marx and Lenin. He tore into Communist Party officials for betraying the revolution with their dishonest favoritism. It was as if he wanted to test out the anti-Soviet line he had drafted during his crossing of the Atlantic. Marina usually remained silent while her husband expounded his political philosophy, though she did endorse such positions as the Soviets' supplying material to Cuba.

While not particularly impressed with Oswald's intelligence, Gregory realized that Oswald put enormous effort into appearing to be an intellectual. Whenever Gregory dropped over to their apartment, Oswald was studying the works of Lenin. He also wrote in mid-August to the Socialist Workers Party in New York, a group well known for its position that the Communist Party in Moscow had betrayed the principles of Marxism. He requested from them information "as to the nature of your party, its policies, etc." To further imbue himself in their politics, Oswald ordered a book on the "Teachings of Leon Trotsky," the archrival of Stalin after the Russian Revolution in 1917, who was bludgeoned to death by a professional assassin while in exile in Mexico City in 1940. Up to that point Trotsky had led a movement which tried to separate ideological Marxists from domination by Moscow.[11]

But even as Oswald moved to identify himself as a Trotskyite, he wrote the Soviet Embassy in Washington for copies of *Pravda, Izvestia* and other Moscow newspapers that strictly reflected the official line of the Soviet Communist Party. The latter contacts were intercepted by the FBI.

On August 16 Oswald found two uninvited visitors waiting for him when he returned from work, FBI Agents John Fain and Arnold J. Brown. He accompanied them to their parked car, where they repeated many of the questions Fain had previously put to him. Over and over again they asked him if any "deal" had been struck by either Oswald or his wife with Soviet officials before they left Russia. Again Oswald denied that either he or his wife had ever been even contacted.

When it became clear that they would not elicit any information about such solicitations, even if they had taken place, the agents decided to terminate the interview. A decision had already been made in Washington not to question Marina as part of the ongoing surveillance program of Soviet expatriates. Four days later the security case on Oswald was temporarily closed.[12]

The CIA maintained a more discreet interest in the Oswalds. At one point a CIA analyst who had read the State Department cable traffic on Oswald's redefection, suggested "the laying on of interview[s] through . . . suitable channels."[13]

He noted in a memorandum, "We [are] particularly interested in the information Oswald might provide on the Minsk factory in which he had been employed, on certain sections of the city itself and . . . biographical information that might help develop foreign personality dossiers." He thus cautioned his subordinates in the Oswald case, "Don't push too hard to get the information we need, because this individual looks odd." According to subsequent testimony of CIA officials, Oswald was not interviewed by any CIA officer. Since the interest in debriefing defectors by intelligence agencies remained high, if only to learn the procedures the Soviets used in processing an American who wanted to renounce his citizenship, this lapse was inexplicable.[14]

Through its mail-intercept program which monitored letters sent from the Soviet Union to selected cities in the United States, the CIA received further information about the Oswalds during these summer months. Even return addresses provided clues. For example, a letter sent to Marina from Ella Soboleva in Leningrad was subsequently traced from the return address on the envelope to the home of Igor Pavel Sobolev, whose name corresponded in the CIA computer to that of a suspected agent of the First Chief Directorate of the KGB who had been stationed in Vienna up to 1961. The question of whether this was an innocuous letter from the daughter of Sobolev or some confusion of names could not be determined by the CIA's tracing system. It was simply another piece in the jigsaw puzzle for

James Angleton and his subordinates, who were overseeing the program of mail intercepts.

Throughout the summer Oswald had attempted to contact members of the Russian-speaking community in the Dallas-Fort Worth area, if only for Marina to have some people to talk to in her native language. Except for meeting the Gregory family, he had little success until the last week in August, when Peter Gregory and his wife invited him to a small dinner party at their home. Paul Gregory was sent to pick the Oswalds up that night. When he arrived at their apartment, he saw Marina accidentally stumble with the baby in her arms. In a display of hot temper that Gregory had never witnessed before, Oswald became infuriated with his wife for dropping their child. However, he quickly quieted down as they drove to the Gregory's home.

Arriving late, the Oswalds were introduced by Peter Gregory to their three other guests: Teofil Meller, a distinguished Russian scholar, his gregarious wife, Anna,[15] and George Bouhe, a Russian-born accountant in his late sixties, who for the last two decades in Dallas had tried to help émigrés from Russia settle in the Dallas area.[16] Through his tireless efforts at philanthropy, Bouhe had become the unofficial leader of the local Russian community. Because these were all staunchly anti-Communist White Russians, Oswald discreetly avoided discussing his politics that night, except occasionally to criticize the Soviet Union. Everyone seemed to enjoy the dinner that Mrs. Gregory prepared.

As Marina talked about Russia, Bouhe became more and more nostalgic about Leningrad, the city of his birth. Since Marina had lived there before she moved to Minsk, she could answer all his questions about the status of the palaces, parks and boulevards that he vividly remembered from his childhood. At one point, as they sat together on the floor and meandered through their images of that city, Bouhe felt tears coming to his eyes. By the time the evening was over Marina seemed to have charmed all the guests, and Bouhe in particular, who was now determined to use his considerable influence in the Russian-speaking community to help her.

Later that evening Bouhe tried to engage Oswald in a conversation about the cost of living in the Soviet Union. He was interested in knowing what percentage of a person's salary went for rent, food and clothing and was disappointed to find Oswald "reluctant to talk." After persistent questioning, Bouhe ascertained that Oswald had had a budget of 90 rubles a month, of which half had gone for food. No mention was made of the "Red Cross" subsidy. Gregory remembers Oswald's being critical of the Soviet government's economic policies on the grounds that the best products were always reserved for export. To illustrate his point, Oswald displayed his own Russian-made boots, which he said were "no good."

Anna Meller says the conversation that evening was mostly small talk about how Marina liked the United States and whether Oswald had found a job yet. She too found Oswald difficult to talk to: ". . . you could not speak with him about anything. He's against Soviet Union; he's against United States. He made the impression he didn't know what he likes." Marina was shy and told Meller quietly that she needed some things for the baby and clothes for herself.

The very next day Bouhe invited the Oswalds over to meet Elena Hall, a Russian-speaking dental technician living in Fort Worth.[17] He had noticed that although Marina was naturally an extraordinarily beautiful woman, her appearance was marred by a missing front tooth. Assuming that she could not afford the necessary dental work, he hoped that Mrs. Hall could arrange for it at minimal cost to the Oswalds. And after spending that afternoon with the Oswalds, Mrs. Hall generously agreed to try to arrange appointments for Marina at the free dental clinic at Baylor University.

A major concern of most of these people was the welfare of the Oswald family, whose situation approached dire poverty. They collected sweaters and skirts for Marina and found a baby bed, mattress and toys for her six-month-old daughter. Bouhe, who realized that Marina would need some English to get along in Texas, patiently prepared a series of English lessons for her and tried to persuade Oswald to allow her to attend formal classes, without much success. Oswald insisted that he did not want his wife learning English and even tried to reject Bouhe's efforts to find clothes and furniture for his family.

As Oswald became more involved with the Russian-speaking émigrés who lived in Fort Worth and Dallas, he saw less of his own family. He stopped seeing his brother and asked his mother not to come by his apartment or speak to Marina. Marguerite wondered what was behind his secretive behavior. She remembered asking him when he returned why he had decided to leave Russia; he had answered then, "Not even Marina knows why I have returned to the United States."

PART THREE

The Mission

10

The Handler

On October 1, 1962, Marina Oswald sat in the back of a convertible driven by George De Mohrenschildt. She held her daughter June in her arms and, from time to time, spoke in Russian to De Mohrenschildt, an extraordinarily handsome man in his early fifties, and his wife Jeanne. It was a hot sunny day in Dallas, and they were all headed for the suburb of Farmers Branch, where a friend of the De Mohrenschildts, Admiral Henry C. Bruton, had a large house with a swimming pool. The De Mohrenschildts had made arrangements earlier that morning to bring Marina and her child to the Brutons' home. Jeanne had said that it would do them both good to have a day in the sun.

De Mohrenschildt had met Marina and Lee Oswald earlier that summer under circumstances that he would never fully disclose. De Mohrenschildt later claimed to have met Oswald in the presence of Colonel Lawrence Orlov, an oil speculator in Fort Worth. Orlov, however, insists that the only time he accompanied De Mohrenschildt to Oswald's home, the two were already well acquainted. De Mohrenschildt told another friend of his in the oil business, Jim Savage, that he had met the Oswalds through the Dallas Aid Society, but no such organization existed at that time.[1] Although involved in his own diverse business activities in Haiti and the U.S., De Mohrenschildt devoted a large part of his next seven months to arranging—and re-arranging—each of the Oswalds' lives.

It was only a few months earlier, at the beginning of the summer, that De Mohrenschildt had first appeared as a total stranger at the Brutons' front door. He stood six feet two inches tall, with the physique of a powerfully built athlete and wind-blown dark-blond hair. He spoke with such a cultivated Continental accent that Mrs. Bruton at first thought he might be a grand duke, and wondered what this extraordinary-looking man was doing at the door of her secluded house eight miles from Dallas.

With a debonair flourish of his hand, De Mohrenschildt proceeded to explain that he had been drawn to her house by fond memories of the good times he had had there when it was owned by a friend of his—Colonel Schurger. He told how he had helped build the swimming pool and the brick barbecue. At the time it never occurred to Mrs. Bruton that De Mohrenschildt might be inventing some of his own participation in the design of the house.[2]

De Mohrenschildt spoke so convincingly about the former owner of her house that she invited him in to see the renovations she had made since she and her husband had bought the house almost two years earlier. She called it the octopus, since it had wings that fanned out in every direction, and found the eccentricity of its rambling design a welcome change from the more conventional houses she had lived in during her years as a Navy wife. De Mohrenschildt walked from wing to wing, lavishing praise on the changes she had made. He also confirmed her initial impression of his aristocratic origins by telling her that he was the son of a Russian marshal of the nobility who had been killed by the Communists in the Russian Revolution. He had fled Russia when he was still a child, gone to school in France and then, after emigrating to the United States, entered the oil business. He explained that he was now settled in Dallas. Finally, when they reached the swimming pool, he asked if he could show it to his wife. Jeanne de Mohrenschildt, his fourth wife, was an extraordinarily interesting woman. She had been born in Manchuria, the daughter of one of the Russian directors of the Far Eastern Railroad. After dancing through China in a ballet company, she had emigrated to the United States in 1938 and established herself as a dress designer of some note. Mrs. Bruton invited him to use the swimming pool whenever he liked, and for the rest of the summer the De Mohrenschildts drove to Farmers Branch almost every day to use the pool.

Admiral Bruton accepted these constant visitors with slightly more hesitation than did his wife. He had been a lawyer in Virginia before becoming a submarine commander. Eventually he had risen to be director of naval communications. In this capacity he had undertaken to reorganize the global system which the Navy uses to communicate with and control the movements of all its submarines, surface ships, airplanes and missiles and also to pinpoint the location of enemy vessels. He had supervised this top-secret project until 1960, when he re-tired from the Navy and, as a vice-president, joined Collins Ra-dio in Richardson, Texas, where he continued to work on mod-ernizing and refining the communications system. Like many of De Mohrenschildt's other casual friends in Dallas, Bruton re-garded De Mohrenschildt as a likable and charming playboy who seemed interested in little more than telling jokes and amusing women. Although he professed to be an international entrepreneur, his actual business remained a mystery.

The life of George de Mohrenschildt also remained a mystery to the FBI, CIA, Office of Naval Intelligence and other govern-ment agencies that had investigated his activities since 1941. The FBI investigation went on for more than seven years, but all that was known about him for certain was that he had arrived in the United States in May 1938 on the SS *Manhattan*, carrying a Polish passport issued in Belgium, which identified him as Jerzy Sergius von Mohrenschildt and stated that he had been born in Mozyr, Russia, in 1911. Some three years later, when he was briefly detained for sketching a naval installation in Port Aran-sas, Texas, an examination of his personal papers revealed that he was carrying two different biographical sketches of himself. The first identified him as being "of Swedish origin, born April 17, 1911"; the second portrayed him as a "Greek Catholic," born in 1914. The résumés indicated that he had been educated in Belgium and held either a business or philosophy degree. He also claimed such diverse occupations as insurance salesman, film producer, newspaper correspondent and textile salesman, although the FBI was able to establish that he was not actually earning money from any of these professions. Moreover, British mail intercepts in Bermuda at the start of World War II indicated that he was closely associated with intelligence agents working against the Allies.

Gradually the FBI began to fill in some of the pieces of the jigsaw. Though probably of Russian origin, he had served the Polish government in various capacities since the early 1930s, when he was a lieutenant in the Polish cavalry.

While still in the Polish military, he traveled around Europe, supposedly as a correspondent for the government-owned Polish News Service. His educational and business activities in Belgium were financed by payments from the Polish government. When he arrived in the United States, he immediately began doing propaganda work for the Polish Mission in Washington, D.C. While his allegiance to the Polish government seemed clearly established up until 1939, his status grew murkier when Poland was invaded and divided that year between Nazi Germany and Soviet Russia. Presumably the intelligence agents working abroad were also divided between the occupying powers, and from his pattern of associations it was not clear for whom, if anyone, "Von Mohrenschildt" was working, though he seemed to have large financial resources at his disposal.

On the one hand, he volunteered to work for French counterintelligence in New York, and was put on the books of Schumacher & Company, which was then serving as a cover for French intelligence operations in the United States. Working with Pierre Freyss, who was the head of the Deuxième Bureau (or counterintelligence), he made two extensive trips across the United States to recruit a network of agents to gather intelligence about petroleum exports to Europe. He also made a trip by himself to San Francisco, where he recruited at least one promising agent. However, as he later admitted to his wife, Jeanne, even while working for French counterintelligence, he was "playing a double game."

By 1941 De Mohrenschildt had also joined forces with Baron

Konstantin Von Maydell in a propaganda venture called "Facts and Film." Maydell, who had arrived in New York on an Estonian passport about the same time as De Mohrenschildt, was, by 1941, identified by the FBI as a Nazi agent. In June of that year federal agents intercepted a letter from Maydell suggesting that De Mohrenschildt obtain credentials from Nelson Rockefeller, who was then coordinator of information for Latin America, to distribute films in Latin America. The venture came to an end in September 1942, when Maydell was arrested on a presidential warrant as a "dangerous alien" and interred for four years in North Dakota.[3] The suspicion that De Mohrenschildt was involved with Maydell in an Axis espionage ring was heightened when it was learned that De Mohrenschildt was corresponding with Germany through Saburo Matsukata, the son of a former Prime Minister of Japan, who was alleged at the time to be coordinating German and Japanese intelligence activities in the United States.[4] His name was also found written in the address book of a woman in Washington, D.C., who was under suspicion as a Nazi agent.

In the many-cornered world of intelligence, however, it is not possible to determine under whose control an agent is working simply by identifying other agents with whom he is associating. The fact that De Mohrenschildt was helping French counterintelligence build a network could mean either that he had joined the French side or that he was working for another side attempting to penetrate French intelligence. Similarly his association with Nazi agents could have been part of a double game. (His attorney, Henry J. Doscher, later told the FBI that De Mohrenschildt claimed to be working for "the British Intelligence Corps during World War II.") Under such circumstances all that the FBI could do was closely monitor De Mohrenschildt's activities in the hope of tracing his ultimate control.

In 1941 De Mohrenschildt even attempted to join the Office of Strategic Services, which was then being organized as the primary United States intelligence agency. (It evolved into the CIA after the war.) Because of his suspected ties to Nazi and Polish intelligence, he was "security disapproved" for the position.

By this time De Mohrenschildt had found out that he was under suspicion by the FBI, and he crossed into Mexico, which was then becoming the center of German intelligence in the

Western Hemisphere. With America on the verge of entering the war, countries sympathetic to Germany were attempting to funnel their money into Mexico, which maintained its neutrality.[5] While claiming to be a "film producer," he traveled around Mexico. He also cultivated a wide range of acquaintances in the government. Although he managed to spend most of the war in Mexico, government authorities eventually became suspicious of his activities and ordered him expelled.[6]

On his return to the United States, he changed his name from "Von Mohrenschildt" to "de Mohrenschildt" and registered in 1944 at the University of Texas, where in less than a year he obtained a master's degree in petroleum engineering. While at the University of Texas, he again came under FBI scrutiny—this time for his alleged Communist sympathies. During this period he was also the subject of an investigation by the Office of Naval Intelligence.[7]

With his new credentials as a "petroleum engineer," De Mohrenschildt worked after the war in Cuba and Venezuela for a number of American oil companies. While in Caracas, he had several meetings with the Soviet ambassador. He later claimed that the Soviets offered him the opportunity to return to the Soviet Union as a citizen, but he turned down the offer. The Soviet contacts added, however, a new dimension to his case as far as the FBI was concerned.

In 1946 De Mohrenschildt turned up at the Rangely oilfield in Colorado and applied for a job with the oil companies that were developing that field. This time he gave an entirely different version of his background. He claimed that his father had been a Russian engineer in the Ploesti oilfields in Rumania, who had been captured and executed by the Soviet Army. (One year earlier he had told the FBI that his father had escaped to Nazi Germany, where he had been killed in a bombing raid at the end of the war.) He said that he had been brought up by relatives in Poland, then sent to Paris, where he had attended school and worked as a translator. He claimed that during the war he had risen in the Polish underground to the rank of lieutenant colonel and spent most of his time in London as a liaison officer. He said that toward the end of the war he had married the daughter of an American diplomat and had a daughter by this marriage, which lasted only one year.[8] He claimed to have worked for the Shell Oil Company in Holland before coming to America.[9]

His résumé impressed the managers of the Rangely field, and he was hired to help coordinate production among the various companies that were drilling there. While working in Colorado, he became naturalized as an American citizen and also married his second wife, Phyllis Washington. The marriage ended, as his first marriage had, in less than a year. In 1952 he moved to Dallas and married Winifred Sharples, the daughter of a well-connected oil millionaire.

With part of the Sharples' fortunes at his disposal, he had little problem establishing himself in the oil business as an entrepreneur. His ventures, which ranged from wildcat drilling to aerial surveillance of oil-promising areas, resulted in few financial successes. Up until his divorce from his third wife in 1956, he lived like a millionaire in an impressive mansion.

The CIA became interested in De Mohrenschildt in 1957, when he was recommended as a geologist to be sent to Yugoslavia by the American government. At that time an investigation was made of his background. A later CIA summary of the De Mohrenschildt file states:

De Mohrenschildt appears to be a dubious character. In 1942 he was considered a Nazi sympathizer and possible intelligence agent; he spent a good deal of time in Mexico where he was suspected of possible subversive activities; and at the University of Texas, where he enrolled in 1944, he was said to have Communist tendencies.[10]

Despite these suspicions, the CIA's Office of Security did not object to the government's employing De Mohrenschildt in Yugoslavia as a consulting geologist, although he was denied access to classified material. While in Yugoslavia, he tried twice to approach the private island of Marshal Tito by boat, and both times, was fired upon by security guards. At the time, he claimed he was merely sketching the fortifications (as he had claimed fifteen years earlier in Texas). After spending eight months exploring the coasts and interior of that country, he returned to Dallas, where he was debriefed by J. Walton Moore of the CIA's Domestic Contact Service. The information De

Mohrenschildt provided the CIA became the basis for at least ten reports that were circulated within government agencies.

In 1958 De Mohrenschildt went on an extended trip to Ghana, Togoland and Dahomey under the cover of being a philatelist, while he was actually gathering intelligence on the potential of the area for a Swedish syndicate based in New York. Still working for the same syndicate, he went again to Africa in 1959 and returned via Poland.

He then married Jeanne, and together they traveled extensively in Mexico. (In November 1959 Jeanne went to a Soviet reception, where she spoke briefly to Anastas Mikoyan, who was there on an official visit.[11])

In the summer of 1960 De Mohrenschildt disappeared from sight for almost a year, after telling friends in Dallas that he was going on an 11,000-mile walking trip along Indian trails from Mexico to South America. Jeanne accompanied him to the ranch on the Mexican border of Tito Harper, who flew them both to central Mexico. The De Mohrenschildts reemerged in April 1961 in Guatemala, just as the Cubans trained by the CIA were being marshaled for the Bay of Pigs invasion of Cuba. De Mohrenschildt had been in Guatemala for approximately four months, and his route took him within a few miles of the CIA training bases.[12] From Guatemala, he proceeded through Central America to Panama and then flew to Haiti, where he stayed with an elderly friend from Poland, Michael Brightman. According to Jeanne, Brightman had provided them with detailed instructions for their trip at various points en route. After a two-month stay in Haiti, the De Mohrenschildts returned to Dallas, where they took up residence again and, several months later, contacted Lee Harvey Oswald.

Towards the end of the summer, De Mohrenschildt had told Bruton about a young ex-Marine he knew who had defected to the Soviet Union, become disillusioned with communism and returned to the United States. He hoped that Bruton might become interested in Oswald and help place him in a job in the electronics field. According to De Mohrenschildt's recollection, Bruton abruptly changed the subject, so De Mohrenschildt did not press the idea. It was obvious to him that Bruton would not help.[13] After this rebuff, De Mohrenschildt decided to introduce

Marina to Mrs. Bruton as someone desperately in need of assistance.

Arriving at the Bruton's home, De Mohrenschildt let himself in the rear gate and led Marina and Jeanne to the rectangular swimming pool behind the sprawling one-story house. That October afternoon was the first and only time that the De Mohrenschildts had ever arrived with a guest.

Admiral Bruton was away in Europe on business for Collins Radio, but Mrs. Bruton, a warm and friendly woman who always enjoyed their company, greeted the guests enthusiastically. De Mohrenschildt introduced Marina, and Mrs. Bruton was immediately struck with her beauty; Marina's deep blue eyes and thick dark lashes were very much like those of the film star Elizabeth Taylor. When a friend of Mrs. Bruton's son, Philip Weinert, who had dropped over a short time earlier was introduced to the new arrivals, Mrs. Bruton decided to serve them all a round of drinks.

Now, with Bruton temporarily gone, De Mohrenschildt seized the opportunity to press Marina's case. He explained to Mrs. Bruton that Marina and her baby had been cruelly deserted and left without any means of support. Shaking his head sadly, De Mohrenschildt added that since Marina spoke no English, she would have difficulty finding employment. She had no money, he said, and worst of all, no place for her and her child to live. Temporarily, he and Jeanne were taking care of the poor woman, but they didn't have enough room for Marina to stay with them for any great length of time.

Mrs. Bruton listened to the story of Marina with great interest. She was appalled by the woman's desperate predicament. She assumed that in bringing Marina to her home, De Mohrenschildt was acting with the concern of a true gentleman, behavior she had come to expect from him.

The group was still discussing Marina's situation when suddenly a gaunt young man appeared at the gate. The person now approaching them was Marina's supposedly estranged husband, Lee Oswald. At the sight of the unexpected visitor, De Mohrenschildt stiffened and became silent; his glare made it obvious that Oswald was not supposed to be there. Jeanne took Marina into the house without even a word to Oswald. Mrs. Bruton felt decidedly uncomfortable as Oswald approached them, his eyes darting back and forth at the people still sitting around the pool. She couldn't help noticing that he was a "sleazy person" with his hair combed back and very greasy. He had a sort of half-smile and half-squint on his face as he introduced himself. For a few tense moments he sat there silently. Then Mrs. Bruton offered him a drink, and he became surprisingly more relaxed and even friendly. Weinert, a captain in the Army, broke the ice by asking him about his experiences in Russia, and he found Oswald's responses far more articulate and intelligent than he had expected, given what he had been hearing about Oswald. Rather than resentful and bitter, he seemed quite reasonable. As the poolside conversation progressed into the early evening, Marina rejoined her husband and sat obediently at his side, listening to his descriptions of Russia almost as if she could understand English.

De Mohrenschildt remained uncharacteristically quiet, but there was little he could say under the circumstances. Oswald had apparently found out that they were at the Brutons' home and decided to join them after he had finished work at his job in Fort Worth. But by coming in unexpectedly, he had undermined all the efforts De Mohrenschildt had made to portray Marina as a wife who had been deserted by her husband. Clearly Oswald was not acting like a man who had run away from his wife, and from what he said, he still regarded Marina as his wife. De Mohrenschildt knew that Marina and Oswald were not estranged and, in fact, were living together at their Mercedes Street apartment in Fort Worth up to that morning, when he had picked up Marina to drive her to Farmers Branch. If his plan had been to facilitate their moving to separate quarters with the explanation that Oswald had cruelly abandoned Marina, then Oswald's blundering in had upset it. Certainly, under the circumstances, Mrs. Bruton was not about to take Marina and her baby into her home. In any case, in the month ahead, De Mohrenschildt again told the story of Marina being mistreated and again tried to find another home for her, first with a chemical engineer and then with a consulting geologist.

After a polite pause, De Mohrenschildt signaled that it was time to go, and Jeanne, Marina, June and Oswald drove off with him in his open convertible. Mrs. Bruton never saw Marina or

Oswald again, nor did De Mohrenschildt ever again bring up the subject. When Admiral Bruton heard the story of the curious visit, he just shrugged; De Mohrenschildt had always seemed a bit odd to him.[14]

Shortly after De Mohrenschildt had brought Marina Oswald to the Brutons, he returned home from a weekend trip to Houston to find that someone had apparently made a series of pencil marks on a long report he had written about his expedition through Mexico and Central America. He assumed that such telltale marks were used to focus in a camera and that in his absence someone had broken into his apartment and copied his personal papers and other documents. At the time he also had the manuscript that Lee Harvey Oswald had given him to read about his stay in Minsk, and he realized that this document might also have been photocopied in the search. His primary concern was that the CIA was behind the break-in. If this indeed was the case, he decided the best course would be to confront the CIA and attempt to find out exactly why he was being investigated. He thus called on J. Walton Moore, the CIA agent in Dallas who had debriefed him when he had returned from Yugoslavia.

Moore had dined several times at De Mohrenschildt's home in Dallas since then, and these were all friendly occasions, at which Jeanne would enjoy reminiscing about China with Moore (whose parents had been missionaries in China). This time, however, De Mohrenschildt came directly to the point and asked Moore whether his agency or any other government agency was behind the examination of his personal papers. Moore, taken aback by the accusation, flatly denied that the CIA was in any way involved.

De Mohrenschildt then asked whether he was under any sort of investigation because of Lee Harvey Oswald. According to De Mohrenschildt, Moore again answered no.[15] He then pressed Moore to find out if Oswald was suspected of being dangerous in any way, and according to De Mohrenschildt's recollection, Moore shrugged that Oswald was merely a "harmless lunatic" of no concern to his agency. If Moore had answered differently and suggested that Oswald was under some sort of suspicion, De Mohrenschildt was prepared to "drop Oswald."[16] Even though he was to some degree reassured by Moore's apparent lack of concern with Oswald, he still thought it best to try to preempt any investigation that might be caused by the photographing of papers in his apartment. The following day he wrote a letter to Undersecretary of State George Ball offering to submit to the government travelogues he had prepared on his trip to Latin America. He suggested that unless there was some government objection, he planned to publish parts of these stories in Europe and added that the typescript might be forwarded to the Soviet Union, "Where there is a great demand for travelogues and adventure stories." This might possibly allay suspicions about what he was doing with Oswald's descriptions of Soviet cities in his apartment. In October 1962 De Mohrenschildt's letter was forwarded to the CIA and retained in his file.[17]

In any case, De Mohrenschildt was now ready to assist in situating Oswald in Dallas. This would require considerable effort.

11

The Underground Man

On October 7, 1962, George De Mohrenschildt called his eighteen-year-old daughter, Alexandra, and invited her and her husband to meet a young American who had just returned from Russia. His name was Lee Oswald, and he lived in Fort Worth with his Russian wife and daughter, who was almost the same age as Alexandra's son. De Mohrenschildt said that he was going that afternoon to see the Van Cliburn competition in Fort Worth—in which four Soviet pianists were taking part—and suggested that they all meet afterwards at the Oswalds' apartment on Mercedes Street.

Alexandra agreed. She had not seen very much of her father since she had eloped (two years earlier) with Gary Taylor, a college student with ambitions toward being a filmmaker. She knew that there was considerable tension between her father and husband and thought that this invitation might lead to a friendly relation. In any case she had always been interested in Russia and wanted to hear what this new friend of her father's had to say about life in that country.

When Alexandra and Gary Taylor arrived at the Oswalds'

apartment later that afternoon, they found an odd assortment of people gathered in the living room. There was Oswald, sitting silently in a T-shirt and slacks, looking slightly contemptuously at the others who were discussing his future, and Marina, who was far more beautiful than Alexandra had expected. Marina was talking in Russian to Elena Hall, the dental technician who had arranged dental treatment for her at a clinic in Dallas, and Anna Meller, another member of the Russian community, who was also trying to help her adjust to life in America. Oswald's mother was also in the room, looking uncomfortable in the company of the more elegant Russian émigrés. She seemed to have the impression that De Mohrenschildt had already arranged a job for her son in Dallas, and that was why he had suddenly decided to leave Fort Worth.

Oswald had precipitated the immediate crisis by saying that he had been fired from his job at Leslie Welding in Fort Worth. (In fact, he not only was still employed, but was looked on with favor at Leslie Welding.)

As far as Gary Taylor could see, De Mohrenschildt was clearly the leader in planning Oswald's move to Dallas. He suggested it would not be difficult for Oswald to get a job in Dallas and asked those in the Russian-speaking community to see if they could help. Anna Meller knew someone who worked for the Texas Employment Commission. While Oswald looked for work, Marina could stay with the Taylors in Dallas or the Halls in Fort Worth. And until they found an apartment in Dallas, the Oswalds' furniture could be stored in the Halls' garage.

Gary Taylor was impressed, even then, with the role De Mohrenschildt had taken in organizing all the support that Oswald needed for his new life in Dallas. Not only did he seem to be arranging a job for him and a separate home for Marina, but Taylor also got the distinct impression that De Mohrenschildt was providing for Oswald's immediate living expenses. Even at that time, Taylor wondered why his father-in-law, a man of the world who traveled at the highest levels of Dallas society, would bother with such an unappealing young man.

To Taylor, De Mohrenschildt had always been something of a mystery. He knew De Mohrenschildt had traveled around the world, yet he had no visible means of support except his wife's earnings. Furthermore, De Mohrenschildt had disappeared for nearly a year, after announcing that he intended to take an 11,000-mile walk through Mexico to the tip of South America. Taylor, however, later found out from his wife's relatives that De Mohrenschildt and his wife had actually stayed without telling anyone at a friend's house in Guatemala during the period they were supposed to be on their walking trip. This discrepancy had only heightened Taylor's suspicions. Now De Mohrenschildt had become involved with a man who had defected to Russia, and Taylor found himself with an unexpected houseguest—Marina.

The next evening Oswald left his apartment and made his way to Dallas. No one, not even Marina, was to know his precise whereabouts in Dallas for the next month. He had told some friends that he was staying at the Carleton Boarding House, but as Marina realized at the time, that was a lie meant to conceal his real place of residence. He was now, as he himself later wrote in a letter, "underground."[1]

In Russia, only a few months earlier, he had been living a very different sort of life. His apartment, with its balconies overlooking the park and river, was one of the finest in the city of Minsk. The friends he hung around the cafés with were the young elite: the sons of generals, professors and technocrats. He went to parties at the homes of intellectuals and Communist officials. He knew a number of attractive women at the Foreign Language Institute who had shown an amorous interest in him. With the special subsidy provided him by the MVD, he could buy almost anything he desired: a hi-fi phonograph, a collection of opera records, a camera, radio, plane tickets and Western clothes.

He had given up this sumptuous life at the top—at least, temporarily—to undertake this trip. The risks in coming to America were high. He could be investigated, or even prosecuted for the offer he had made in Moscow to provide classified information to the Soviets. He had lied to the FBI about his activities in the Soviet Union and refused a lie-detector examination. Even though he had changed addresses three times, the FBI might attempt to keep him under surveillance. And finally, Marina had misinformed the immigration authorities about her identity by stating that she had never used any other name or alias. If Immigration found out that she had lived under the name Marina Alexandrovna Medvedeva, she could be deported.

He now had to live a more furtive life. Marina and his daughter would be looked after by acquaintances in the Russian-speaking community in Fort Worth and Dallas. Phone calls would be referred to the number of Gary Taylor. His mail would be forwarded to a post office box in Dallas.

On Tuesday, October 9, Oswald went to the offices of the Texas Employment Commission. He was immaculately dressed in a dark business suit, white shirt and tie. He asked to see Helen Cunningham, a counselor with the commission. Anna Meller's husband had already called Mrs. Cunningham, who was a friend of his, and asked her to help Oswald get a job. (Meller himself had not met Oswald but agreed to help after being told by his wife about Marina's dire financial condition.)[2]

Mrs. Cunningham found Oswald "self-contained, able . . . and entirely presentable as far as grooming and appearance were concerned."

Oswald explained that he had had some photographic experience in the Marine Corps and preferred to find a position where he could use that skill.

Mrs. Cunningham turned him over to Louise Latham, a job placement expert who specialized in the sort of clerical-photographic work in which Oswald seemed most interested.

Latham was also impressed with Oswald. She recalls: "Lee had finesse. He was very mannerly. . . . He was the kind of person who would come around and pull my chair out at the desk, or light a cigarette for someone. . . . He was quiet, a good thinker . . . and beautifully groomed."

She first sent Oswald to an architectural firm that had a job opening for a messenger. When he went for the interview, he failed to get the job because he told them that he wanted something with an opportunity for advancement. The employment commission's records note that Oswald returned to them and was then sent on October 11 for an interview at Jaggars-Chiles-Stovall, a large typesetting firm in Dallas.

When Oswald met John Graef, the director of the company's photographic department, he again made a very effective first impression. He looked clean-cut and eager for the job. When asked about his last job, he explained that he had been a Marine.

"Honorably discharged, of course," Graef said half-jokingly.

"Oh, yes," Oswald replied, mentioning his service in the Far East.

The interview lasted only fifteen minutes. Later that day Oswald learned that he had the job as photo-print trainee.

The next day Oswald reported to work in the "print shop" in downtown Dallas. He filled out an employee identification questionnaire, in which he gave Gary Taylor's address and phone number as his own. The foreman, Leonard Calverley, took Oswald to the phototypesetting department, where he would begin by learning how to use the various cameras and reproduction equipment. It was to be a six-day-a-week job, for which he would be paid $1.35 an hour.

The main business of Jaggars-Chiles-Stovall was preparing printing mattes for newspapers, magazines, catalogues and advertising agencies in the Southwest. This required reducing photographs in size, photosetting typescript and using sophisticated lenses and equipment to arrange advertising displays and charts.

Jaggars-Chiles-Stovall also had a contract from the Army Map Service to set the typescript for its maps. Although the maps themselves were not on the premises, this was nevertheless highly classified work. For one thing, the maps were made from secret aerial photographs presumably taken from spy satellites, U-2 planes and other forms of clandestine reconnaissance. For another, the lists of names of cities and areas in the Soviet Union, China and Cuba which were being set could themselves provide clues to the targets of these reconnaissance missions.

Like all the other employees in the typesetting department, Oswald had complete access to the worktables on which the secret lists of place-names for the Army Map Service were kept. In theory, these were supposed to be "restricted areas" in which only employees with a security clearance from the FBI were allowed to be present. In fact, however, little effort was made to enforce these restrictions. There were no guards or security measures which prevented employees from entering the areas in which the classified work was done. Indeed, the employees in the phototypesetting department had to pass constantly through these areas to use the film-drying machine, darkroom and other facilities. Nor was the foreman under instruction to forbid the workers under him from going into these areas.

Calverley recalls that "the government material was available to anyone in the shop . . . it was just lying around all over the place." It was even possible, according to Calverley, for employees to use the cameras in the plant to reproduce the list of names.[3] In any case, given the layout of the plant, it would be virtually impossible to segregate the employees into different sections.

The employees of Jaggars-Chiles-Stovall set the long lists of geographical names, which came from the Army Map Service, on three-inch strips of paper. Some of the names were written in Cyrillic characters and identified Russian cities; others appeared to be Chinese names. And in the fresh batch of names that arrived almost daily some of the employees began to notice the appearance of odd-sounding Cuban names on the list.

At CIA headquarters in Langley, photo analysts were receiving a similar set of Cuban place-names on the latest batch of U-2 photographs from Cuba. Throughout the first two weeks in October intelligence reports had indicated that the Soviets were constructing concrete bunkers and installing electronic equipment at sites in Cuba under conditions of extraordinary secrecy. Hence the U-2 overflights. Then, on October 14, the U-2 planes focusing on the area around San Cristóbal in eastern Cuba photographed newly built structures which could be unmistakably identified as missile launchers for intermediate range missiles. Every city within the eastern part of the United States would be vulnerable to these missiles, when operational.

On receiving this ominous report, President Kennedy summoned an emergency meeting of the National Security Council. The Cuban Missile Crisis had begun.

At Jaggars-Chiles-Stovall, Oswald was taught how to operate such highly specialized photographic equipment as distortion cameras, phototypesetters and Robertson vertical cameras. He was shown how to reproduce perfectly a pictorial display, then to reduce or distort it with optical lenses so that it fitted perfectly on a standard-size printing mat. Soon he became proficient at such techniques as line modifications, blowups, reverses and miniaturizations, as he himself noted in an autobiographical sketch that he wrote some months later in New Orleans.

Oswald used these skills to forge identification papers for himself at Jaggars-Chiles-Stovall under the alias A. J. Hidell, including a fake Selective Service card and Certificate of Service in the Marines. (He also provided himself with a bogus license under the name of O. H. Lee.)

He found that his knowledge of Russian came in handy in the "print shop." He offered on at least one occasion to translate Cyrillic symbols on a list that was being prepared for the Army Map Service and explained to the foreman of the section working on this classified material that these were Russian place-names. This exchange was observed by one of Oswald's fellow workers, Jack Bowen, who also noticed that Oswald kept an "old red book on Russian" in his desk.[4]

Oswald also couldn't resist impressing Dennis Hyman Ofstein, who had taught him how to use some of the photographic equipment, with his fluent Russian. Ofstein, who was the same age as Oswald, had learned Russian himself when he served in the Army Security Agency (the predecessor to the National Security Agency). He was, however, not nearly as proficient in the language as Oswald and therefore tried to practice it by speaking to him in Russian during working hours.

Oswald was initially closemouthed about himself and volunteered little more than he had been a Marine who had served in Japan. Then he asked Ofstein to help him blow up an odd-looking photograph he had brought into the shop. It showed a river in the foreground and an interesting-looking building in the background. When Ofstein asked whether this was a picture Oswald had taken during his tour in Japan, Oswald answered, "No, it wasn't in Japan." Then he changed the subject, as he generally did when he didn't want to answer a question.

A short while later Oswald told Ofstein that the picture had been taken in Minsk, Russia. The building in the picture was a military headquarters, which was tightly guarded by soldiers who had orders to shoot to kill any trespassers, Oswald said. How had Oswald come to have such a photograph in his possession? Oswald explained that he had spent several years in Minsk.

Ofstein asked what he had been doing in Russia. Oswald refused to elaborate. At this point, given his experience in the Army Security Agency, Ofstein assumed Oswald "was there for the country—or he was there against the country."

Little by little Oswald told Ofstein more about his stay in the Soviet Union. He said that the MVD secret police had one of their headquarter buildings in Minsk. He mentioned that he had traveled within the Soviet Union and spent one May Day in Moscow observing Soviet military equipment on parade. One day when they were talking about the Russian language, Oswald casually revealed to Ofstein that he had married a "White Russian" while he was in Minsk.[5]

As they grew friendlier, Oswald asked Ofstein if he knew what the term "microdot" meant.

Ofstein answered no. He had heard of microfilm and microphotography, but not microdot.

Oswald then explained that it was a technique used in espionage. A mass of documents could be reduced through a special photographic process literally to a dot which could be hidden "under a postage stamp." Spies used such microdots for sending data.

Ofstein had no idea why Oswald was discussing this espionage technique with him. Jaggars-Chiles-Stovall certainly did not have any facilities for doing microdot photography, he knew. He assumed that Oswald "had either read this in a book or had some knowledge of it from somewhere . . ." he later testified.

In his personal address book, next to the entry for Jaggars-Chiles-Stovall, Oswald carefully wrote the word "microdot," connecting the place where he worked with a basic technique of espionage. Some eight months after Oswald left Jaggars-Chiles-Stovall, the FBI conducted an investigation of his employment there. Agents showed his fellow workers a photograph of a leather pouch that they believed Oswald might have used to conceal a miniature camera, but no one recalled seeing Oswald with either the pouch or the camera.[6]

During his first month of work at Jaggars-Chiles-Stovall, Oswald saw very little of Marina. De Mohrenschildt attempted to find a separate home for her. He first arranged for her to stay at his daughter's apartment. Then, after staying one night at De

Mohrenschildt's own house, Marina moved to Elena Hall's house for most of October. (She had the house to herself for a week when Mrs. Hall was hospitalized after an automobile accident.)

Usually on Sundays Oswald would get a ride to the Halls' home in Fort Worth with Gary and Alexandra Taylor.[7] During these trips Oswald often talked about his life in Russia. He was not, however, fully candid with the Taylors. Rather than describe the luxurious apartment on the river that he had had in Minsk, he told them that he and Marina had lived in a small eleven by fourteen-foot room near the factory in which he had worked. He complained that he had had to share the kitchen and lavatory with five other families in the building. He made it all sound very dismal.

On Sunday, October 21, Marina invited Gali and Max Clark over to the Halls' house for a Russian dinner which she cooked herself. Gali Clark, whose family had been Russian aristocrats before the Revolution, had come over almost every day to help Marina shop and look after her baby. (Elena Hall was still in the hospital.) Her husband, Max, was a prominent Fort Worth attorney, who had previously been head of security for the Convair Aircraft Corporation.

Oswald came by himself that Sunday to Fort Worth and stayed for dinner. He made little effort to talk to the Clarks but answered all the questions they put to him about life in Russia. He again portrayed his experiences in Russia as disappointing and bleak. He complained about housing, low pay, poor living conditions and the difficulty of traveling within Russia. He compared it to military life—highly regimented with "bosses up and down the line."

Max Clark was not overly impressed with Oswald. He knew he had defected to the Soviet Union, and he assumed that he had been "tagged" and put under surveillance by the FBI.

Before visiting Marina the next weekend, Oswald stopped over at De Mohrenschildt's home. Only days before, the United States and the Soviet Union had moved to the brink of war over the issue of the deployment of Soviet missiles in Cuba. Another U-2 had been shot down over Cuba. But Khrushchev had finally backed down and agreed to remove the missiles. De Mohrenschildt seemed relieved that war had been averted and spoke for a while to Oswald.[8]

When he arrived in Fort Worth that Sunday, Oswald told Marina that he was making arrangements for her to come to Dallas and live with him. He had already begun looking for an apartment for them.

The next week, after work at Jaggars-Chiles-Stovall, he found an apartment on Elsbeth Street in the Oakcliff section of Dallas. It was on the ground floor of a Tudor brick building and had three small rooms. It also had both a front and a back entrance. The rent was $68 a month.

On November 4 Gary and Alexandra Taylor rented a U-Haul trailer and helped Marina move from Fort Worth to Oswald's new apartment in Dallas. After working late into the night helping Marina unpack and clean, Oswald left, saying only that he had a room elsewhere for which he had already paid.

The next evening the landlady at Elsbeth Street received a telephone call from someone trying urgently to get in touch with Oswald. He spoke with an odd-sounding foreign accent and asked her to have Oswald or his wife call "George." When Oswald got the message, he immediately called George De Mohrenschildt. Both he and his wife spoke to him in Russian. (Oswald then told the landlady, whose phone they had used, that they were speaking Czech and that his wife was from Czechoslovakia.)

At about 10 P.M. that night, Anna Meller received a telephone call from Marina, asking whether she could stay at her apartment that evening. She said that she had just had a fight with Oswald. Mrs. Meller told her to come right over.

Again Marina had separated herself from Oswald. She spent a few nights at the Mellers' small apartment, then moved to the home of Katya and Declan Ford in Dallas. Katya Ford was a Russian-born refugee who had been brought to Germany by the retreating German Army. After the war she had come to Dallas, where she had married Declan Ford, a consulting geologist. The Fords had met the Oswalds earlier at a lunch at Anna Meller's house.

De Mohrenschildt thought that this would be an ideal arrangement for Marina since the Fords had a large house, and he tried to persuade them to keep Marina and her baby there as permanent guests. The arrangement, however, lasted only a week.

De Mohrenschildt told everyone in the Russian-speaking community that the problems between Marina and Oswald were irresolvable and that they were now separated for good. He went into great detail about Oswald's allegedly cruel treatment of Marina to explain the breakup of the marriage. (He had told the story of their breakup, it will be recalled, to the Brutons in October—more than a month before it took place.) Marina also told her Russian friends that she was being harshly and sometimes brutally mistreated by Oswald. Indeed, it became a minor scandal among them.

Despite the stories that freely circulated about a permanent separation, on November 18 Marina suddenly agreed to move back in with Oswald to the apartment on Elsbeth Street.

On Thanksgiving Day, Oswald and Marina took a bus to Fort Worth to have a turkey dinner with his brother Robert and his family. Marina and June had just returned to live with him at his Dallas apartment a few days before, and the occasion was a reunion for everyone. Oswald had not seen his brother since the summer. He also saw at Robert's that afternoon his half brother, John Pic, whom he had not seen since he was a child.

After lunch they posed for a family picture: the three Oswald brothers, their wives and children. It was the last time Oswald was ever to see his family together.

12

Out of Control

George De Mohrenschildt arrived late at Katya Ford's Christmas week party and brought with him two uninvited guests: Marina and Lee Harvey Oswald.

There was a murmur of surprise among the other Russian-speaking guests. They had not seen or heard from Oswald in more than a month. Nor had they seen Marina since the day in late November when Oswald had asked her to come back to him, and she had. He had made a point of not saying exactly where he worked—when asked directly, he would merely say a "print shop"—and no one in the Russian community was surprised or disappointed when he abruptly disappeared from their lives.

Now he was back. Katya Ford had not wanted to invite Oswald to her party. She knew that he had treated the efforts of George Bouhe, Elena Hall, Anna Meller and other Russian émigrés to help him and Marina with undisguised contempt. She also knew from Marina that he had treated her cruelly, and so did most of her other guests that night. Indeed, they all had tried to help Marina leave Oswald. Katya realized that his presence at her party would probably make her other guests feel tense and uncomfortable. But Jeanne De Mohrenschildt had called her that afternoon and said that Marina was sad that she had nowhere to go for the holidays and wanted to see her friends in the Russian colony. What could she do but respond by asking the De Mohrenschildts to bring the Oswalds along with them?

Oswald made no effort to speak to most of the people in the room. Indeed, he hardly seemed to acknowledge their existence. He turned instead to a young and exquisitely beautiful Japanese girl named Yaeko Okui.

Yaeko had come to Dallas that year to do public relations work for Nippon Services, Inc., a chain of Japanese department stores. She was also a certified teacher in ikebana, the Japanese art of flower arrangement, and an accomplished musician. Another musician, Lev Aronson, had brought her to the party, but Oswald showed little interest in talking to him.

For almost three hours Yaeko sat with Oswald at the far end of the living room and talked. She seemed able to speak Russian and English with equal ease.

Marina, even when she was singing Russian songs with the rest of the guests, watched her husband and Yaeko with some concern. A number of her friends, including Jeanne De Mohrenschildt, simply assumed that she was jealous over the attention that Oswald was paying to this Japanese girl. Marina's real concern, however, as she later explained to her biographer Priscilla Johnson McMillan, was that Yaeko might be an American intelligence agent. At one point she took her husband aside and warned him that Yaeko "may be a spy. Don't be too frank with her."

George De Mohrenschildt subsequently testified that he was also impressed with the "extraordinary interest which developed between . . . Yaeko and Oswald. . . ." He knew that Oswald had served in Japan in the Marine Corps before he defected to the Soviet Union. He also knew that Oswald had made some "contacts with Communists in Japan" and that these "contacts" had induced him to go to the Soviet Union. At least this was what Oswald had confided to him. Now, as he watched them talk across the room, he wondered whether she might be trying to find out about this earlier period in Oswald's life. In any case, he didn't trust her.

Yaeko herself never fully divulged the contents of this long conversation with Oswald. She told her friend Lev Aronson, who was showing some signs of impatience over Oswald, that they had talked about "nothing at all." She would later say when questioned by the FBI in 1964 that she and Oswald had discussed "flower arrangements."[1]

At about midnight De Mohrenschildt suggested to Oswald that they leave. He had arranged a baby-sitter for Oswald's daughter, and she had said that she could not work past midnight. Oswald wrote down a number that Yaeko gave him, as Marina observed; then he followed De Mohrenschildt out the door.

In January Oswald began the New Year with a flurry of requests for political literature. From Pioneer Publishers, a publisher connected with the *Militant* (to which he was a subscriber), he ordered three political tracts: *The Coming American Revolution, The End of the Comintern* and the *Manifesto of the Fourth International.* He also asked Pioneer Publishers to supply him with the English words to the song "The Internationale." From the Washington Book Store in Washington, D.C., he asked for subscriptions to a number of Soviet periodicals, including *Ogonek, Sovietskaya Byelorussia, Krokodil* and *Agitator.* From the Dallas library (where he used fellow employee Jack Bowen's name as a reference for a card), he took out books about Marxism, Trotskyism and American imperialism in Latin America, particularly Cuba.[2]

As part of his renewed political activism, he had already written both the Socialist Workers Party and the Communist Party in New York City and offered to do work for their publications. As a sample of his skills, he sent *The Worker* a poster, which he had apparently used the equipment at Jaggars-Chiles-Stovall to print. It read: "Read The Worker If You Want To Know About Peace, Democracy, Unemployment, Economic Trends."

He also enrolled himself in a typing course given at Crozier Technical High School on Monday, Tuesday and Thursday evenings. He explained to Marina that the course was necessary to qualify him for a better job when he eventually left Jaggars-Chiles-Stovall.

Since the school was only a few blocks away from the "print shop," as he called it, he could work late on the evenings he had classes, then go directly to them. His teacher, Gladys Yoakum, noticed that Oswald arrived with exceedingly dirty fingernails, an indication he had just finished work.

In January 1963 Oswald also sent $206 to the State Department, thus completing repayment of the $435 loan that had been made to him in Russia the previous spring.[3] He was now free to seek a new passport and travel outside the United States.

Toward the end of January he committed himself to another expenditure. Under the alias A. J. Hidell he ordered from Seaport Traders in Los Angeles a .38-caliber Smith & Wesson revolver. It cost $29.95.

In early February De Mohrenschildt arranged for Oswald to meet a young friend of his named Volkmar Schmidt. Schmidt had come from Germany to the United States about one and a half years earlier to do geological research for the Magnolia Laboratories in Duncanville, Texas. De Mohrenschildt found Schmidt to be not only a brilliant geologist, who he predicted would win a Nobel Prize for his work on petroleum-bearing rock formations, but also a shrewd analyst of human psychology. He also knew that Schmidt was fascinated with political ideology and assumed that he might be interested in meeting a self-styled revolutionary who had defected to the Soviet Union and then redefected to the United States.

Schmidt remembers arriving at the De Mohrenschildts' apartment at 7 P.M. and found Oswald there already with Marina and their daughter. Jeanne had cooked a Russian dinner, and after they had some wine, she set the dishes out buffet style.

While Marina talked with the De Mohrenschildts in Russian in the living room, Schmidt sat across the kitchen table from Oswald. Their conversation lasted more than three hours.

Almost from the moment Oswald began talking about his experiences in the Soviet Union, Schmidt was impressed by his "burning dedication" to what he considered "political truth." In describing the reasons why he had become a Marxist, Oswald talked openly and candidly about the impoverished conditions under which he had been brought up and educated. In comparing social conditions in the United States and the Soviet Union, Oswald seemed remarkably articulate and objective.

Even when Oswald talked about his own difficulties, he seemed emotionally detached from the experiences he was describing.

When the conversation turned to the subject of the Kennedy administration, Schmidt expected that Oswald would express the usual liberal sentiments about the President's attempting to bring about constructive reforms. Instead, Oswald launched into a violent attack on the President's foreign policy, citing both the Bay of Pigs invasion in April 1961 and the Cuban Missile Crisis of October 1962 as examples of "imperialism" and "interventions." He suggested that Kennedy's actions against Cuba had set the stage for a nuclear holocaust and further, that even after the Soviet missiles had been withdrawn from Cuba, American-sponsored acts of sabotage and "terrorism" against Cuba were continuing.[4]

Schmidt changed the subject. He could see that Oswald had extreme and unyielding positions and realized it would do no good to argue with him. Instead, he tried to win his confidence by appearing to be in sympathy with his political views and making even more extreme statements. It was a technique that he had learned years before in Germany, when he studied and lived with Dr. Wilhelm Kuetemeyer, professor of psychosomatic medicine and religious philosophy at the University of Heidelberg.[5]

In an intentionally melodramatic way Schmidt brought up the subject of General Edwin A. Walker, who had been forced to resign from the Army because of his open support for the John Birch Society and other right-wing extremist causes. He suggested that Walker's hate-mongering activities at the University of Mississippi, which the federal government was then trying to desegregate, were directly responsible for the riots and bloodshed—including the deaths of two reporters—on that campus. He compared Walker with Hitler and said that both should be treated as murderers at large.

Oswald instantly seized on the analogy between Hitler and Walker to argue that America was moving toward fascism. As he spoke, he seemed to grow more and more excited about the subject.

Schmidt could see that he had finally got through to Oswald. As he listened to Oswald define more closely his political ideas, he began to work out his "psychological profile," as he called it.

Oswald seemed to be a "totally alienated individual," obsessed with political ideology and bent on self-destruction. Even then, he reminded Schmidt of a Dostoevskian character impelled by his own reasoning toward a "logical suicide."

When he returned home that night, Schmidt thought that he might be able to help Oswald if he could "get him out of his shell." He thought of arranging a small party for him where he could meet and talk to other people interested in political ideas. He particularly wanted him to meet Michael Paine, an inventor and "creative genius" at Bell Helicopter (whose father, George Lyman Paine, had been one of the leaders of the Trotskyite movement in the United States), and the two men with whom he shared a house in Dallas: Everett Glover and Richard Pierce.

He broached the idea of having some people over to meet Oswald the next day with Glover, who owned the house. Glover had already briefly met Oswald at a party at De Mohrenschildt's but had formed no real impression of him.[6] He had also met Marina at De Mohrenschildt's house on a number of different occasions (and De Mohrenschildt, earlier that fall, had unsuccessfully tried to persuade him to let Marina live in his home on the pretext that Oswald had deserted her).

Glover, a research chemist at Magnolia Laboratories, agreed that it might prove interesting to hear what Oswald had to say about Russia and set about arranging the party. As Schmidt suggested, Glover invited Michael Paine and his estranged wife, Ruth. He also asked Norman Fredricksen, another geologist at Magnolia, since he had been studying Russian with his housemates. (Fredricksen's father had been director of Radio Free Europe, a government-sponsored propaganda station in Germany, which beamed programs into the Soviet Union and Eastern Europe.)

The other member of the household, Richard Pierce, also a geologist at Magnolia, invited his girlfriend, Betty MacDonald, who was working as a librarian at Magnolia.

After helping organize the party and paying the expenses, Schmidt himself had to leave the country on business and did not attend. In fact, he never saw the Oswalds again.

On Friday, February 22, George and Jeanne De Mohrenschildt brought Oswald and Marina to Glover's home. Most of the other guests were already there. Michael Paine had been unable to come that evening, but all the others—Ruth Paine, Norman Fredrickson, his wife, Elke, Betty MacDonald, Richard Pierce and Glover—pulled their chairs up in a circle around Oswald and began asking questions about what life was like in the Soviet Union.

Oswald was now the center of attraction. He gave a graphic description of what it was like to work in a Russian factory and live in a Russian city. He told of the tedium of eating day after day red cabbage in one form or another, of the lack of any decent consumer products and of government censorship of the mails. He explained that he had gone to Russia not in the expectation of finding an easy life or personal amenities, but because he was a Communist, in sympathy with the objectives of a Communist society.

At this point Pierce jumped up and, interrupting Oswald, said that it would be better if he refrained from discussing his political views and stuck to the subject of life in Russia.

Oswald shrugged and agreed. Going around the room, he answered whatever questions were asked of him.

While Oswald was conducting his colloquium in the living room, Ruth Paine spoke to Marina in the kitchen, with George and Jeanne De Mohrenschildt translating for Marina. Mrs. Paine had been brought up as a Quaker, and at college and afterward she had been interested in fostering better relations between Russians and Americans. Working with the East-West Contact Service, she had helped arrange cultural exchanges of Russian and American artists, dancers and writers. Now, as she explained to Marina, she was interested in learning Russian. Taking down Marina's address, she suggested that they get together later in the week to see if some arrangement could be worked out whereby she could practice Russian with Marina.

This brief encounter was to be the beginning of a far more involved relationship between the two women.

Just a few days before the party Marina had advised the Soviet Embassy in Washington, D.C., that she wanted to "return to the homeland in the USSR where I again will feel myself a full-fledged citizen." She later explained that she had written this letter at the behest of Oswald, who "handed me the paper, a pencil, and said 'Write.'" (Like the other correspondence from the Oswalds, this letter was immediately routed to the desk of

Vitaliy A. Gerasimov, the Soviet consular officer in the embassy who was then under suspicion [and surveillance] by the FBI as the paymaster of an espionage network in the United States.)

When Marina next spoke to Ruth Paine a few weeks later, she told her that she might have to return to the Soviet Union, though she preferred to stay in the United States. Oswald, she claimed, had told her that he no longer wanted to live with her, and not speaking English, she could hardly live on her own in America.

It seemed a terrible situation to Mrs. Paine. She suggested the possibility to Marina that she might want to live at her home in Irving, a suburb midway between Dallas and Fort Worth. Since she was separated from Michael, she had some extra room for Marina and her daughter. It would also be helpful to her since she could learn Russian from Marina.

Marina said she would consider the kind offer. What she did would depend on what Oswald finally decided.

In early March Marina and Oswald moved from their apartment on Elsbeth Street to another one two blocks away on West Neely Street. It was their eleventh move in fewer than five months.[7] The Neely Street apartment, a second-floor walk-up in a dilapidated building, had a shabbily furnished living room, a small bedroom, a small closetlike study and a terrace. It seemed to have no advantage over their former apartment, except to obscure their trail further. (About one week after they moved, the FBI, possibly alerted by Marina's letter to the Soviet Embassy, sent Agent James Hosty from the Dallas field office to the Elsbeth Street address, where he found that they had moved without leaving a forwarding address. Reviewing the office file, Hosty recommended that the security case on Oswald be reopened.)

Shortly after the Oswalds moved into their apartment on Neely Street, Gary Taylor, who had recently separated from his wife Alexandra, stopped over to visit. He found only Marina at home. She now seemed to have at least a rudimentary understanding of English, and was able to explain to Taylor that Oswald had a job during the day and was also attending night school.

In looking around the apartment, Taylor caught a glimpse of a rifle. He asked Marina why her husband needed it. She shook her head as if it were a question she could not answer. Suddenly, she became extremely apprehensive, and explained to Taylor that if Oswald returned and found her alone with him he would be very upset. Taylor then left.[8]

Oswald, meanwhile, had involved himself in another project —the stalking of General Walker. On Sunday, March 10, he used his Imperial Reflex camera to photograph the alley behind Walker's house in the wealthy Turtle Creek section of Dallas.[9] He also made careful measurements of the distances to various reference points around the house (with a nine-power hand telescope he had apparently brought back from Russia) and collected the timetables of buses that served the area. According to Marina, he put the photographs and other information into a journal which he kept in his study.

Two days after his reconnaissance of Walker's home, he ordered a Mannlicher-Carcano rifle with a telescopic sight from Klein's Sporting Good Store in Chicago. Again he used the alias "A. Hidell" and his post office box in Dallas to order the rifle. He sent the request airmail and enclosed a money order for $21.45.[10]

On March 25 the rifle arrived in Dallas. Oswald picked it up at the post office and brought it back to his office, where he showed it to one of his fellow employees, Jack Bowen.

Things had not been going well for Oswald at Jaggars-Chiles-Stovall. Whether because of the poor quality of his work or because the FBI had found out that he was working at a firm that did secret work—as he told Marina—he had been put on notice that his job would be ending on April 5. When asked by Dennis Ofstein what he planned to do next, he said, smiling cryptically, "I might go back to Russia."

At the end of March Oswald also finished his typing course. A few days later, De Mohrenschildt, still involved in arranging Oswald's life, made an appointment for him to see Samuel Ballen. Ballen, a forty-year-old financier from New York, had founded in Dallas a company called Electric Log Services, Inc., which monitored oil-drilling activities in the Southwest. He had known George De Mohrenschildt for five years as a gregarious and charming man-about-town, and since De Mohrenschildt had strongly recommended Oswald as a man deserving help, he agreed to see if he could find him a job in his company.[11]

Oswald arrived at Ballen's office in the midafternoon and initially impressed Ballen as a competent and articulate young man. He said that he had gone over to Russia "to see what it was like over there," then had become disillusioned and returned. He claimed to have worked in Russia on a newspaper or house organ and learned printing and reproduction skills. He said that after returning from Russia, he had worked in a "printing shop" in New Orleans and had there acquainted himself with American photographic and reproduction equipment. (He apparently was dissembling here about New Orleans in order to conceal the fact that he was currently employed at Jaggars-Chiles-Stovall—a fact which he never told Ballen.)

Oswald then walked with Ballen to the Republican National Bank, where Ballen had a business meeting. It was a warm day, and neither man wore an overcoat. As they chatted, Ballen got the impression that Oswald was too much of an "individualist" to fit in at his company. He decided not to employ him but thought of possibly having him and his wife over to dinner to meet some of his friends. When he left, Oswald told him that he was temporarily staying at the Y.

On March 31 he had Marina photograph him in their backyard. He was dressed entirely in black, with his revolver strapped in a holster on his hip. In his right hand, he held high his newly acquired rifle. In his other hand, he held two newspapers—*The Worker* and the *Militant*.

He made a number of copies of these photographs. He inscribed one to his daughter, June, and gave it to Marina for safekeeping. On another copy he scribbled, "Ready for Anything," and told Marina he was sending it to the *Militant*.[12] On a third picture, meant for George De Mohrenschildt, he wrote, "For George, Lee Harvey Oswald," and dated it "5-IV-63" (April 5, 1963). On the same copy Marina jotted down in Russian, "The Hunter of Fascism. Ha, Ha, Ha," and apparently forwarded it to De Mohrenschildt.[13]

The following Tuesday the Oswalds went to Irving, Texas, to have dinner with the Paines. It had been arranged the week before so that Oswald could meet Michael Paine, and Marina could discuss her future plans with Ruth.

Paine, who had been educated at Harvard and Swarthmore, had spent a good deal of his life in the company of intellectuals and was quite willing to listen to the ideas of this dour-looking man who had defected to Russia and returned. When asked about his job, Oswald made it clear that he resented the way workers were treated at the "print shop" by the bosses. He spoke of himself as a professional revolutionary and said that his present work was only a means to an end.

After dinner Oswald expounded further on his ideas for political action. He suggested to Paine that violent revolution was necessary in America. How would he know the timing and objectives of this revolution? Oswald explained that he could get revolutionary direction "by reading between the lines of the *Militant.*"

Paine, whose father had been heavily involved in the Trotskyite movement, was skeptical of this claim. He asked Oswald to show him how to interpret the revolutionary messages in the *Militant.* Oswald shook his head and let the subject drop.

Meanwhile, Ruth Paine discussed with Marina the possibility of her coming to live in her home for a while. Her Russian was too poor for her to be sure that Marina fully understood her offer, although she seemed interested.

When they returned home that evening, Oswald gave Marina $60 from his savings. He reckoned that it would be enough to support her for six weeks in case he had to go into hiding.

That Friday evening, April 5, Oswald wrapped his rifle in an old raincoat. Marina asked him where he was going with the weapon. Oswald answered, "Target practice." A moment later she saw him board a bus. He returned two hours later without the rifle.

The following Monday General Walker returned to Dallas from a coast-to-coast speaking tour which he designated "Operation Midnight Ride." When Robert Alan Surrey, a close supporter of Walker's, stopped over at his house that night, he noticed two men peeking in the windows in a very suspicious way. They then got into a Ford sedan and drove away. Surrey tried to follow them to find out why they were reconnoitering the general's house but lost their car in traffic.

On Wednesday, April 10, Oswald left a note telling Marina what to do in case he was apprehended by the police, killed or had to flee. He instructed her in Russian to: "Send the information as to what happened to me to the Embassy and include newspaper clippings (should there be anything about me in the newspapers)." He was clearly referring to the Soviet Embassy, which he suggested "will come quickly to your assistance on learning everything." He also reminded her that "the Red Cross will also help you." (Oswald had previously noted that the "Red Cross" was a cover for the "secret police" agency in the Soviet Union which had provided him with a subsidy for some two years.)[14]

He further stated that he had left his address book and "certain of my documents" at home. He suggested: "You can either throw out or give my clothing, etc. away. Do not keep these. However, I prefer you hold on to my personal papers (military, civil, etc.)."

The note gave other terse orders without any explanation—as if none were necessary.

At about 9 P.M. that evening General Walker was seated at his desk in his study, working on his income tax returns. Suddenly a bullet crashed through the window and whizzed by his head to embed itself in the wall. He was covered by a ghostly-white spray of plaster, but otherwise unhurt.

Kirk Coleman, a fourteen-year-old neighbor of the general, heard the shot and climbed up on a fence to see what was happening. He saw one man putting something in the trunk of a Ford sedan, and a few feet away, a second man getting into another car. Both cars then raced away.

Oswald came back home at about 11:30 P.M. Marina could see that he was breathing hard and was extremely tense. She asked what had happened.

He told her that he had just attempted to shoot General Walker and then turned on the radio to hear if there was any news of the incident. But nothing about the shooting was reported.

Marina wanted to know what Oswald had done with the rifle. She feared the police might trace it to their home.

Oswald explained that he had buried it near the scene of the shooting, and then he had taken a bus home. He said he had spent considerable time preparing this assassination attempt.

Why had he shot at Walker? According to Marina, he had come to the conclusion that Walker was a dangerous fascist, like

Hitler. He reasoned that if Hitler had been assassinated early in his career, fascism would not have come to Germany, and "millions of lives would be saved."

Whatever his reasons, Marina insisted that he destroy the notebook of maps, notes and photographs that he had put together as part of the planning of the assassination attempt. She, however, kept the incriminating note of instructions, and even after the assassination, did not turn it over to the police, Secret Service, or FBI. (Only when Ruth Paine found it in a cookbook and turned it over to authorities, did Marina admit that she had had knowledge of Oswald's attempt on General Walker.)

Oswald methodically ripped out the pages and shredded the text. He kept some of the photographs he had taken of the area around Walker's home; however, in one photograph that showed an automobile parked on the street, he apparently took the precaution of obliterating the license plate number of the car by tearing a hole through this bit of the picture. He never explained the reason for the deletion.

The Dallas police, meanwhile, were confounded by the shooting. They recovered the bullet, but it was too badly mangled to be ballistically identified. The only eyewitness, Coleman, reported that two men fled from the scene, so it appeared to have been a conspiracy. Moreover, it seemed to have been well planned.

On Saturday afternoon Oswald retrieved the rifle from its hiding place. That evening George and Jeanne De Mohrenschildt stopped by the Oswalds' apartment.

The first thing De Mohrenschildt said, according to Marina, was, "Lee, how did you miss General Walker?"[15]

Oswald looked at Marina, stunned. She was equally surprised because he had told her that no one except her knew about the assassination attempt.

For De Mohrenschildt, it was a "logical assumption" that Oswald might be the sniper, as he later explained in his testimony before the Warren Commission. He knew Oswald had a "gun with a telescopic lens."[16] He also knew from the bits of the conversation he had overheard between Volkmar Schmidt and Oswald that Oswald hated Walker. And he could see that Oswald had, in recent weeks, become increasingly obsessed with the idea of political activism.

Looking at Oswald, De Mohrenschildt could now see that his remark had greatly disturbed him. He appeared nervous, tense and uncomfortable and seemed, indeed, hardly able to get a grip on himself. If he *had* taken the shot at Walker, as De Mohrenschildt suspected, he was dangerously out of control.

Shortly after this meeting the De Mohrenschildts and Oswalds parted company, never to see one another again.

On April 19 George and Jeanne De Mohrenschildt drove to New York. A few days later a CIA case officer asked the CIA's Office of Security for an "expedite check of George De Mohrenschildt." On April 29, without ever being told the reason for the request, the Office of Security issued a summary report. On May 1, after returning to Dallas for only two days, the De Mohrenschildts left for Haiti, where De Mohrenschildt had a contract with the Duvalier government to develop various natural resources.

On April 23 Marina moved into the home of Ruth Paine in Irving. The next day Oswald boarded the night bus for New Orleans.

13

Oswald's Game

On April 25, 1963, Oswald arrived in New Orleans with only two duffel bags, which contained some hastily packed clothes, his personal papers and the dismantled Mannlicher-Carcano rifle from which he had fired a bullet fifteen days earlier. He left everything else behind.

His rash attempt to assassinate General Walker had left him almost completely cut off from his past acquaintances. Even Marina had pressed him to leave Dallas, afraid otherwise that he might be found out or would even try again to kill Walker.[1] In New Orleans he would not have George De Mohrenschildt to help him make contacts, nor could he any longer count on others. He would have to arrange his own life in the city which happened to be his birthplace.

From the bus depot, Oswald telephoned Lillian Murret, an aunt whom he hadn't seen since he had joined the Marines. She was surprised to hear from her nephew—the last news she had had of him was when he had defected to the Soviet Union in 1959. She had liked him as a child, and without asking him any embarrassing questions about why he had gone to Russia, or returned, she invited him to stay with her family while he looked for a job and apartment in New Orleans.

For the next three weeks Oswald lived in the Murrets' home on French Street. His uncle, Charles "Dutz" Murret, who had been a fairly well-known prizefighter manager, offered to lend him $200 until he got settled, but he declined the offer.[2] He preferred not to take on any debts.

Oswald got on particularly well with his cousin Marilyn Dorothea Murret, a tall attractive woman with long black hair. A schoolteacher by profession, she was also, like him, a world traveler, who had been to many of the same places, including Japan, where she had taught science, and East Berlin. She remembered Oswald as a quiet boy who "read encyclopedias like somebody else would read a novel," and now that he was back from Russia, she wanted to hear all about his travels. In telling her how he was able to arrange for his wife to accompany him out of Russia, he explained that her father was a "Russian officer" who used his influence to assist them.[3]

During this period Oswald said very little of his plans for the future. He spent most of his days job hunting. The day after he arrived in New Orleans, he went to the employment office of the Louisiana Department of Labor, claiming to be qualified as a commercial photographer, shipping clerk or "darkroom man." The interviewer, John R. Rachal, wrote on his application: "Will travel on limited basis. Will relocate. . . . Neat. Suit. Tie. Polite."[4]

In the evenings and weekends Oswald spent considerable time tracing his own past. On his first Sunday in New Orleans he journeyed to Lakeview Cemetery to locate the grave of his father, who had died two months before he was born. And he methodically went down the list of Oswalds in the New Orleans telephone directory, calling each of them until he found the only one who was related to him—his uncle's widow, Hazel Oswald. When he went to see her, she gave him a framed photograph of his father (which he later discarded). He now knew at least something about his family history.

On May 9, Oswald finally found a job through a newspaper advertisement in the New Orleans *Times-Herald* at the William B. Reily Company. Located on Magazine Street in the heart of the city, the company roasted, processed and sold coffee. On his job application form, he indicated that he had lived in New Orleans almost his entire life—and omitted any mention of Dallas. As references, he listed his cousin John Murret and "Lieut. J. Evans" and "Sgt. Robert Hidell"—both of whom were fictitious.

He was told he would begin working the next day, lubricating and maintaining the coffee-processing machinery. The pay would be $1.50 an hour.

The same day Oswald rented a furnished apartment on Magazine Street, about a mile from the coffee company. It had high ceilings, a screened-in porch and a backyard, with strawberries growing wild. He paid the $65 rent in advance and immediately called Marina. He was now ready for her to come to New Orleans.

The phone call seemed to please Marina greatly. She told Ruth Paine in Russian, *"Papa nas lubet"*—"Papa loves us." It was decided that they would all leave for New Orleans the next day. They bundled Marina's belongings in her station wagon and left the next day.

Marina seemed less enthusiastic about the new apartment than Oswald—at least it appeared that way to Ruth Paine, who stayed for three days in New Orleans with the Oswalds. While Oswald seemed proud of the New Orleans-style architecture, Marina complained about the lack of light and the cockroaches.

Nonetheless, the first few weeks in New Orleans were, for Marina, a pleasant change from Dallas. Oswald took her on outings to nearby beaches, parks and the zoo. They also toured the French Quarter at night, and one weekend they went crabbing in the shallow waters of Lake Pontchartrain with Marilyn Murret. As far as his cousin could see, "They were a real cute couple." She recalls: "They were perfectly happy. He was very devoted to Marina. He seemed to love his child very much . . . they just seemed to be very family conscious."

In the evenings Oswald read books he borrowed from the New Orleans Public Library. Most of them were about politics or political leaders.[5]

Marina had still not had a reply from the Soviet Embassy on her request to return to Russia. She was now almost five months pregnant and realized that Oswald would soon have to make some concrete decisions about where they would live. It was clear to Marina that Oswald was now seeking a new direction. And it seemed to be Cuba.

In his conversations, as well as in his writings, he had become increasingly alienated from Soviet-directed Communists. As far as he was concerned, the Soviets were not revolutionary enough, and Khrushchev had clearly acquiesced to Kennedy's demand for the removal of the missiles from Cuba in October.

The alternative he decided on was Castro's Cuba. Oswald had been a supporter of Castro since 1958, when the Cuban was still a guerrilla leader in the mountains (and after Castro came to power on January 1, 1959, Oswald had contacted the Cuban Consulate in Los Angeles). In Minsk he had befriended a number of Cuban students who were being trained by the Soviets for positions of leadership in Havana. Once he got to Havana, he could no doubt find contacts and connections with the Castro government. He even at one point bragged to Marina that he would become a "minister" in the government. In any case, it became clear to Marina, as she later testified, that "his basic desire was to get to Cuba by any means. . . ."[6]

The problem for Oswald was getting there. Since it was illegal at the time for a United States citizen to travel to Cuba, he would have to obtain his visa at a Cuban Embassy outside the country, and to do that, he would need some credentials to prove that he was a supporter of the Cuban government. His game in New Orleans involved creating just such a record for himself.

On May 26 he wrote a letter to the Fair Play for Cuba Committee, an organization which supported recognition of the Castro regime by the United States, and boldly proposed "renting a small office at my own expense for the purpose of forming a F.P.C.C. branch here in New Orleans." He then requested formal membership for himself, application blanks for others, a charter for his chapter and a "picture of Fidel suitable for framing."[7]

Three days later, without bothering to wait for a reply, Oswald ordered 1,000 copies of a handbill from the Jones Printing Company in downtown New Orleans. It read simply: "Hands Off Cuba! Join the Fair Play for Cuba Committee, New Orleans Charter Member Branch, Free Literature, Lectures, Everyone

Welcome!" For this and other such transactions he used the alias "Lee Osborne."

He also rented a small office in an office building at 544 Camp Street, about one block from where he worked. He did not, however, retain the office for long.[8]

A few days later Oswald received a letter from V. T. Lee, the national director of the Fair Play for Cuba Organization, which spelled out the conditions under which he might organize his chapter.

The letter was not overly encouraging. "I have just gone through our files and find that Louisiana seems somewhat restricted for Fair Play activities," V. T. Lee noted. ". . . The south-east is a very difficult area to work because of our lack of contacts." He warned Oswald that in attempting this venture, he would come "under tremendous pressure."

He suggested that Oswald acquire a post office box, a "good typewriter," access to a "mimeo machine" and "people who will carry out the million and one mechanical functions necessary to make it a going operation." He advised Oswald not to rent an office immediately.

If Oswald could recruit the minimum number of members, the national director agreed to grant him a charter. He pointed out that Oswald would be organizing the only Fair Play chapter in the southeast outside Tampa (which V. T. Lee had personally organized before joining the national office in New York).

Oswald was not, however, prepared fully to accept V. T. Lee's advice. His purpose was not to recruit members and build a functioning Fair Play chapter in New Orleans, but to create a dossier of letters, documents and news clippings which would get him to Cuba. All his other activities that summer, Marina later explained, were merely "window dressing."

In June he methodically set about documenting his record as a Fair Play for Cuba organizer. He ordered the necessary application forms and membership cards from the Mailing Service Company of New Orleans, and when the cards arrived, he had Marina forge the signature "A. J. Hidell" on them. "Hidell" was supposedly the chapter president. He then sent two "honorary" membership cards to Gus Hall and Ben Davis, both of whom were members of the Central Committee of the Communist

Party of the United States. And he took a post office box in order to receive return correspondence.

He wrote back to V. T. Lee, stating that "against your advice, I have decided to take an office from the beginning." He also explained that he "had jumped the gun on the charter business" in claiming on the circulars he had had printed that his "branch" was a "charter member." He asserted that different "tactics" would be necessary in New Orleans from those in other cities. Clearly he was going in his own direction.

In mid-June Oswald staged a one-man demonstration on the Dumaine Street wharf where the USS *Wasp* was anchored. He handed out "Hands Off Cuba" handbills to Navy personnel and visitors until he was unceremoniously evicted from the wharf.[9] He subsequently reported to V. T. Lee that although evicted from its office in New Orleans, his group had managed "to picket the fleet when it came in and I was surprised at the number of officers who were interested in our literature."

Since he could not take his family to Cuba—at least, he deemed it impractical—Oswald had to make other arrangements for them. One possibility was for Marina and June to return to Russia. At the beginning of July he had Marina write another letter to the Soviet Embassy in Washington, D.C. In this letter, she asked permission for both her and Oswald to return immediately to Russia and reside in Leningrad. She explained that "my husband expresses a sincere wish to return together with me to the USSR. I earnestly beg you to help him in this. . . . Make us happy again, help us to return to that which we lost because of our foolishness."

Oswald added a handwritten note to Marina's letter, imploring the embassy to *"rush* the entrance visa for the return of Soviet citizen Marina N. Oswald" and to consider his own request for an entrance visa *"separately."* (Emphasis is in the original letter.) If this worked and the Soviet Embassy granted them separate visas, he could use his to obtain a transit visa to Cuba, while Marina and June returned to Russia.[10]

The other possibility available to Oswald was for Marina to return to Texas and live with Ruth Paine. In exploring this option, Marina had written her friend at the end of May: "Lee's attitude to me is such that I feel every minute I bind him. He insists that I leave America which I don't want to do at all. . . .

What do you think?" Mrs. Paine responded by warmly inviting Marina and her daughter to live in her home and even offered to give her $10 a week pocket money. Throughout the summer Marina continued to refer to this generous offer in her letters to Ruth Paine, without ever mentioning that she had also asked the Soviet Embassy to expedite her return to Russia.

Oswald, meanwhile, arranged the travel documents he might need for his trip. On June 24 he applied for a new passport (which would not include his wife or daughter). He listed England, France, Germany, Holland, Italy, Finland, Poland and Russia as the countries he proposed to visit as a "tourist" and gave his profession as "photographer." The passport was issued to him the next day by the State Department.[11] He had already forged a vaccination certificate for himself which was signed by "Dr. Hideel." Still concerned about his undesirable discharge from the Marine Reserves, he stopped over at the offices of Dean Andrews, a New Orleans lawyer with political connections, to see if there was any legal remedy available to him. After Andrews explained that he would require some money for expenses, Oswald did not return.[12]

Since Oswald knew that he would soon be leaving New Orleans, he showed little interest in his job at the coffee company. He went through the motions of greasing and lubricating the machinery and then quietly slipped out and went next door to the Crescent Street Garage, where he spent hours discussing the relative merits of various rifles with its owner, Adrian Thomas Alba.

A keen gun collector, Alba tried to answer all of Oswald's questions, which he fired at him "machine-gun style." For reasons that Alba didn't quite understand, Oswald wanted to know about the penetration characteristics of different guns. He seemed especially interested in buying from Alba a carbine, which was a far more dependable weapon than his own Mannlicher-Carcano. When Alba refused to sell him this particular weapon, Oswald tried to persuade him to order a similar carbine for him, but Alba never did.

On July 19 Oswald was fired from his job at the coffee company for "inefficiency." Although he told Alba that he was going to apply for a position at the Michoud rocket facility, which manufactured missiles for the National Aeronautics and Space

Administration, he was not hired there.[13] Instead, for the balance of the summer, he lived off his unemployment benefits. This gave him more time to pursue his political activities.

In the last weekend in July Oswald gave a one-hour talk on his experiences in Russia to a group of Jesuit scholars at Spring Hill College in Mobile, Alabama. The positions he took on the Soviets' betrayal of Marxism closely paralleled those he had written out during his ocean crossing thirteen months earlier. The engagement had been arranged for him by his cousin Eugene Murret, who was studying for the priesthood there. Afterward Oswald met informally with a number of the Jesuits.[14]

He also apparently spent some time on the campus of Tulane University, handing out his Fair Play for Cuba leaflets and attempting, without much success, to rouse student support for his chapter.[15]

In August, Oswald switched to a new tactic and decided to infiltrate and spy on anti-Castro Cuban exiles in the New Orleans area. He jotted down a list of addresses of "Cuban exile stores"[16] and then visited one of them, Casa Roca, which was owned by Carlos Bringuier, the New Orleans delegate of the Cuban Student Directorate. That summer the Cuban Student Directorate, which was based in Miami, was organizing raids against Cuba, and Bringuier had been called upon to assist a group of twenty-eight Cuban exiles in the area who had been waiting to undergo training in sabotage and guerrilla warfare.[17]

When Oswald entered the store, Bringuier was discussing the sale of $10 invasion bonds with two teenagers, Vance Blalock and Philip Geraci III. Oswald browsed among the haberdashery for a few minutes, then casually joined in the conversation. Introducing himself as an ex-Marine, Oswald offered to join Bringuier's organization and even contribute money to the anti-Castro cause.

Bringuier, suspicious, because of recent events, that Oswald might be an agent for either the FBI or Cuban intelligence, turned down the offer and told him he should send his contribution to the headquarters of the Cuban Student Directorate in Miami.[18]

Oswald persisted, however. He explained that he had been trained in guerrilla warfare in the Marines and now wanted to "train Cubans to fight against Castro." He even offered to accompany the guerrillas on their sabotage missions into Cuba. To prove his worth, he offered some on-the-spot suggestions on blowing up bridges ("put powder charges at each end of the bridge from the foundation to where the foundation meets the suspension part"), derailing trains ("put a chain around the railroad track and lock it") and for improvising homemade explosives ("saltpeter and nitrate").

For an hour or so Bringuier discussed the Cuban situation with Oswald and gradually became interested in him. His organization needed men who could train exiles, and Oswald, from what he said, seemed schooled in some highly sophisticated techniques of sabotage and qualified for the role.

Oswald returned to the shop the next day and, finding Bringuier away, left his Marine training manual with Rolando Palaez, who was tending the shop. He had mentioned that it had a section in it on guerrilla warfare (although, in fact, it discussed none of the techniques he had mentioned).

A day or so later Oswald reverted to his pro-Castro activities. This time he openly handed out his Fair Play for Cuba leaflets, with one or two helpers, in the heart of the French Quarter—only a few blocks from Bringuier's store. A student at Louisiana State University, Brian Ampolsk, asked him on this occasion what he was protesting, and Oswald complained bitterly about the United States' "blockade of Cuba" in October 1962.

On Friday, August 9, Oswald staged another demonstration on Canal Street. Hearing about it from a friend, Bringuier rushed over to Canal Street to see who was involved in this pro-Castro effort. When he arrived there, he was "shocked" to see that it was Lee Harvey Oswald, who had just four days earlier offered his services to the anti-Castro movement.[19] Oswald was now wearing a "Viva Fidel" placard and handing out pro-Castro literature.

Bringuier, infuriated by this turnabout, began cursing and shouting at Oswald. Oswald's reaction, he recalls, was "absolutely cold-blooded." He just "smiled and offered his hand, expecting a handshake." When Bringuier approached, threatening to hit him, Oswald simply said, putting his arms down in a sign of nonresistance, "O.K., Carlos, if you want to hit me, hit me."

At that point the New Orleans police arrived and arrested both Oswald and Bringuier for disturbing the peace. While taking Oswald to the police station to be booked, Patrolman Frank Hayward noticed that he seemed "almost enthusiastic about going to jail." It would be one more bit of documentation for the dossier he was preparing on his pro-Castro activities.

In the station house Oswald and the Cubans were questioned together in a small room. Then the Cubans were released on bail, and Oswald was put in jail overnight. The following morning Oswald was turned over to Lieutenant Francis L. Martello, who had been deputy commander of the Intelligence Division of the New Orleans police, for more detailed questioning on the activities of the Fair Play for Cuba Committee.

In discussing his past, Oswald said that before he had moved to New Orleans that spring, he had lived in Fort Worth, Texas, since 1959. He made no mention of the two and one-half years he had spent in Russia or the seven months he had spent in Dallas. (He also misidentified his wife as Marina Prossa.)

Asked how he had first become involved with the Fair Play organization, Oswald said that he had first got involved with its activities in Los Angeles in 1958, while he was in the Marines, and recounted how he got into trouble for bringing some of the pro-Castro literature back to the barracks.[20]

When pressed about the membership of his chapter, he refused to give more than one first name, "John," who he said was a student at Tulane.

It quickly became clear to Martello that Oswald was "not receptive," and he concluded the interview. Before Oswald was returned to his cell block, he asked to see an FBI agent.

Later that Saturday morning John Lester Quigley, an agent from the New Orleans office of the FBI, was ushered in to see Oswald. He listened while the prisoner made what he considered a completely "self-serving statement."

Oswald claimed that he had had a note from Hidell two days before, asking him to distribute some pamphlets furnished by the "national committee" in New York.[21] When questioned about Hidell, he said that he had never personally met him but had spoken to him on the phone.

What was Hidell's phone number? the FBI agent asked.

It was "disconnected," Oswald replied.

Who were the other members?

Oswald shrugged and said he was introduced to them only by first name.

After an hour and a half of unproductive interrogation, Quigley left.[22] He would promptly check on Oswald with the Office of Naval Intelligence in Algiers, Louisiana, as well as FBI headquarters in Washington, D.C.

Meanwhile, Lieutenant Martello found out from Joyce O'Brien, Oswald's cousin, that Oswald had spent several years in Russia. Before releasing him, he decided to have another talk with him.

Confronted again by Martello, Oswald readily admitted that he was a Marxist and had gone to Russia out of idealism, although he found when he got there, that "it stunk." He added, somewhat incongruously, that he was in America only temporarily and planned to return to Russia.

A little while later bail was arranged by a friend of the Murret family, and Oswald was released.

That evening, Dutz Murret stopped over at Oswald's apartment to make sure his nephew would show up for the trial which was scheduled for Monday. Seeing a picture of Fidel Castro on the mantelpiece, he asked Oswald whether he was mixed up with Communists. Oswald answered no.

At one o'clock on Monday, August 12, Oswald showed up at the Second Municipal Court, which was conspicuously segregated, having separate seating sections for whites and blacks. Oswald chose to sit on the black side of the room (while Bringuier sat on the white side). The judge dismissed the charges against Bringuier and fined Oswald $10, which he promptly paid. On the way out of the courtroom Oswald was filmed by a local television crew, and that night he appeared on WDSU-TV.

According to Marina, this was all part of Oswald's "self-advertising." "He wanted to be arrested," she later testified. "He wanted to get into the newspapers, so that he would be known" as pro-Cuban.

Four days later Oswald organized another demonstration in support of Castro in front of the International Trade Mart. This time he was assisted in handing out leaflets by two young men, and the news media had been tipped off in advance about the stunt.[23] Again Oswald was in front of television cameras.

Hearing about this renewed activity, Bringuier asked a supporter of his, Carlos Quiroga, to go to Oswald's home and attempt to find out more about his Fair Play chapter. Quiroga was to pose as a Castro sympathizer and offer to join the chapter, if necessary.

Later that afternoon Quiroga went to the address rubber-stamped on the pamphlets, "4907 Magazine Street," and knocked on the door. Oswald came out and invited him to sit on the porch and talk about his organization.

Oswald seemed adamant in his support of Cuba; he was even willing to accept some "repression" of the Cuban people, he said, so as to advance the revolution. He stated that if the United States should ever invade Cuba, he would "fight on the side of the Castro Government." He then offered to let Quiroga join his chapter for $1.[24]

Quiroga said he would think about it and left. He later mentioned to Lieutenant Martello that he would consider infiltrating Oswald's chapter if he had the "backing" of either the FBI or local police. Since such support was not forthcoming, Quiroga did not see Oswald again.

At 8 A.M. the next morning Oswald had another visitor: a thin, bearded man who identified himself as William Kirk Stuckey. With Oswald standing on the porch in military fatigue pants and no shirt, Stuckey explained that he had a radio program called *Latin Listening Post* on WDSU for which he interviewed controversial people, and he had been looking for someone to put forth the Fair Play for Cuba position.[25] He immediately sized Oswald up as someone who was determined in his views and polite in his presentation of them and invited him to come to the studio at 5 P.M. to do an interview. Oswald accepted the offer, suggesting that the publicity would be valuable to his organization.

On August 17, Oswald appeared on time and gave Stuckey a thirty-seven-minute interview. It was an articulate and well-argued case in support of Castro. The news director, John Corporon, however, believed the tape was too one-sided and ordered Stuckey to cut it. When it was finally aired, the interview was only four and a half minutes long.

A few days later the local FBI office read Stuckey the file on Oswald. On learning that the Fair Play for Cuba organizer had defected to Russia a few years earlier, Stuckey decided to arrange a radio debate in which Oswald could be confronted with his own record. Aside from Oswald, he invited Bringuier and Edward Scannell Butler, a professional propagandist for anti-Communist organizations.

August 21 was an especially hot and muggy August afternoon, and Oswald arrived at the studio in a heavy gray flannel suit, shirt and tie. Bringuier walked over to him and said softly, "Listen, Mr. Oswald, I would like to explain to you that other than the troubles between you and me, and our ideological differences, I don't have anything against you as a person. . . . Communism is trying to destroy Western civilization and principally the United States. Maybe you are mistaken in good faith. . . ."

Oswald heard him out, smiled and replied, "I am sure that I am on the right side and you are on the wrong one." Then he saw his Marine guidebook in Bringuier's hand and laughingly warned him not to use the book to organize any "expeditions against Cuba" since it was out of date.

The actual debate, called "Conversation Carte Blanche," began a few minutes later. Oswald found himself attacked by both Bringuier and Butler for having defected to the Soviet Union. Their object was to show that the Fair Play Committee was connected to the Soviets.

Even as they hammered away at him, Oswald kept his composure and control. Accused of being a "Communist," Oswald replied that he was a "Marxist."

"What's the difference?" Butler interrupted.

". . . A very great difference," Oswald said, blunting the question. "Many countries are based on Marxism. Many countries such as Great Britain display very socialistic aspects. . . . I might point to the socialized medicine of Britain."

Butler, considering himself a professional propagandist, was very impressed with the way Oswald managed to deflect attention away from the unanswerable charges to points that he wanted to make. He said Oswald seemed to have the attributes, if not the training, of a highly competent agitator.

Bringuier tried a more emotional approach and demanded to know whether Oswald agreed with Castro's recent denunciation of President Kennedy as a "ruffian and thief."

"I would not agree with the particular wording," Oswald responded, slipping away from the damaging characterization. "However, I and the Fair Play Committee think that the U.S. government, through certain agencies, mainly the State Department and the CIA, has made monumental mistakes in its relations with Cuba. Mistakes which are pushing Cuba into the sphere of . . . very dogmatic Communist countries such as China." Without too much effort, Oswald had turned the argument around so it appeared that his position was to prevent Cuba from inadvertently being forced further into the Communist camp.

Stuckey, impressed with Oswald's performance, took him to Comeaux's, his favorite bar in the French Quarter, and discussed with him life in Russia until the early hours of the morning.[26] Why had he left Russia? Oswald explained that it had "gone soft" on communism; Cuba was the only revolutionary country left.

Oswald was now ready to apply for his Cuban visa. He had established in a few short months an impressive record for himself as one of the leading supporters of Castro in the southeastern part of the country. He had appeared on four radio and television programs on behalf of Cuba—and that could be verified. He had been arrested and jailed for his activities—and had a record to prove it. He had formed the only Fair Play for Cuba Committee in Louisiana—and that was documented in letters he had from V. T. Lee and the Communist Party officials to whom he had given honorary memberships. He had spent his own money on propaganda material—and had a file of receipts.[27]

In a résumé he prepared for the Cuban Embassy late that summer, he told how he had "caused the formation of a small, active FPCC organization of members and sympathizers where before there was none" and then had "infiltrated the Cuban Student Directorate and harassed them with information I gained. . . ." He also described the demonstrations he had organized, his "street agitation" and arrest and the subsequent publicity he managed to get to present "FPCC attitudes and opinions." And he gave a fairly detailed autobiographical sketch of his experiences in the Marines, in Russia and in Dallas. As an appendix to this ten-page document, he attached newspaper clippings about himself defecting to Russia, correspondence with the Fair Play for Cuba Committee and Communist Party, subscription receipts from Soviet propaganda magazines, his membership card in the Fair Play Committee and even some tax returns he had surreptitiously removed from the offices of Jaggars-Chiles-Stovall.

In September the FBI intercepted a letter from Oswald to *The Worker* in New York. He stated that he and his family would be "relocating in your area . . . in a few weeks." He sent a similar message to the *Militant,* which was also under close FBI surveillance. By writing these letters, Oswald had effectively ghosted a false trail for himself.[28]

Actually Oswald was headed in the opposite direction—Mexico. There he intended to brief the Cuban Embassy on his political activities and obtain the necessary documentation to get to Cuba. After Marina made the necessary arrangements for Ruth Paine to pick up her and June in New Orleans and take them back with her to Texas, Oswald went to the Mexican Consulate in the Whitney Building and applied for a tourist card to visit Mexico.

He told Marina that she might never see him again—at least not in America.

14

The Cuban Connection

That same September, in a safe house in São Paulo, Brazil, CIA case officers met with Dr. Rolando Cubella, a minister without portfolio in the Cuban government. Some two years earlier Cubella had said he was disillusioned with Castro and offered to defect to the United States. A former *comandante* of Castro's army, a hero of the revolution and a close personal friend of Castro himself, Cubella was in a unique position to provide intelligence about the intentions of the Castro government. The CIA thus persuaded him to stay in place in Cuba in the hope that it would have in him a source within Castro's inner council.

Now, for the first since the meeting in 1961, Cubella, given the cryptonym Amlash, had made contact with the CIA. The case officers went to the meeting with the expectation that he might have some hard intelligence for them. They were hardly prepared for what he actually offered.

Cubella came right to the point. He was interested in seeing the overthrow of the whole regime in Cuba, and the first step, as far as he was concerned, had, of necessity, to be the assassination of Fidel Castro.[1] He said that he would be willing to undertake this "inside job" if he could be sure he would have the support of the United States government in undertaking it.

This extraordinary offer was relayed to CIA headquarters on Saturday, September 7. It was channeled directly to the Special Affairs Staff. The SAS, as it was known, was the division within the CIA with responsibility for all covert activities against Cuba. Headed by Desmond Fitzgerald, a personal friend of Robert F. Kennedy, this division had agents scattered around the world and its own station in Miami—the "Jmwave station"—which alone employed 300 staff officers and thousands of Cuban operatives. Its mission was to overthrow the Castro government.

On the same day, in Havana, Fidel Castro went to the Brazilian Embassy for a reception, called aside a reporter for the Associated Press, Daniel Harker, and granted him a private interview. Castro emphatically warned against United States leaders "aiding terrorist plans to eliminate Cuban leaders." He suggested that Cuba was "prepared to answer in kind." And so that there would be no doubt about the nature of his threat, he added, "United States leaders should think that if they are aiding terrorist plans to eliminate Cuban leaders, they themselves will not be safe." He specifically pointed to the CIA as being involved in the plans.

The story went out over the wires that evening and appeared in newspapers across the United States (and it was printed in the New Orleans *Times-Picayune* on September 9, while Oswald was still there).[2]

The CIA counterintelligence staff was struck by the coincidence of Castro's choosing the Brazilian Embassy as the place to issue his warning at the very time that the CIA officers in Brazil were discussing eliminating Cuban leaders with Cubella. Indeed, it raised the distinct possibility that Cubella was a double agent sent over to test the intentions of the Kennedy administration toward Castro. Even if Cubella was not under the control of Cuban intelligence, Castro's remarks, which implied that he was aware of a specific action attributable to the U.S. government, suggested that Cubella was "insecure" in the sense that Cuban intelligence knew about his discussions with the CIA. The SAS had its own counterintelligence section, and its chief warned Fitzgerald that Cubella's bona fides were "subject to question." He therefore disapproved of the entire operation. "My disapproval of it was very strong," he later testified. "Des Fitzgerald knew it . . . and preferred not to discuss it any more with me."

The threat of reprisals against American leaders had to be considered and evaluated by the Kennedy administration. The CIA's covert activities against Cuba were then under the direct supervision of a Special Group in the National Security Council, augmented by Attorney General Robert Kennedy and General Maxwell Taylor, a special adviser to President Kennedy.[3] This Special Group designated a special committee comprised of Desmond Fitzgerald and a representative of both the Attorney General and the Secretary of State to weigh the risks involved in proceeding with covert actions against Cuba.

The committee met at 2:30 P.M. at the Department of State on September 12 for a "brainstorming" session, as it was described in the memorandum of the meeting, and concluded that although "there was a strong likelihood that Castro would retaliate in some way . . ." it would probably be at "a low level." The specific possibility of "attacks against U.S. officials" was assumed to be "unlikely."[4]

Shortly after this review Desmond Fitzgerald ordered the SAS case officers, who were directly reporting to him, to tell Cubella that his proposal for eliminating Castro was under consideration at the "highest levels."

On the night of September 25, in Dallas, three men came to the home of Sylvia Odio, a young and exceedingly beautiful Cuban refugee. Her father had been involved in a plot to kill Castro the year before—a plot in which Rolando Cubella had also been involved. Unlike Cubella, however, her father had been captured and was still imprisoned in Cuba.[5] Now, the men at her door claimed to be associates of her father in the anti-Castro underground.

She could see that two of the men were dark-skinned Latins, one looking more Mexican than Cuban, and the third was a gaunt American in his early twenties. From their "greasy" and "lower-class" appearance, it seemed at first unlikely to her that these men could be part of her father's movement. But they provided "so many details about where they saw [her] father and what activities he was in" that she decided to hear them out.

One of the Latins introduced himself as "Leopoldo," then said in Spanish, "We wanted you to meet this American. His name is Leon Oswald." He explained that Oswald was an ex-Marine and expert shot, and he wanted her to introduce him to her contacts in the "underground."[6]

Oswald, apparently not understanding Spanish, just stood there with an odd-looking, half-grin on his face.

Still suspicious of the trio, Odio asked for some time to think about it (and to check on their credentials). As the men were leaving, Leopoldo indicated that they were on their way to Mexico.

Leopoldo called on the telephone the next day to see what her reaction had been to "Leon," as he called the American.

"I didn't think anything," Odio responded noncommittally.

Leopoldo then suggested that "Leon" was slightly "loco" and could be induced to kill Castro if he could be smuggled into Cuba and put in touch with underground leaders there. He repeated that he was an "expert shot."

Again feeling that he was trying to elicit information from her about her father's followers—and activities—Odio ended the conversation by saying she knew of no one who could help this American get into Cuba.

The same day Oswald crossed the border into Mexico at Nuevo Laredo, Texas, on a Continental Trailways bus.[7] Striking up a conversation with one of his fellow passengers, John Bryan McFarland, a doctor from Liverpool, England, Oswald explained that he was "en route to Cuba" and had to go by way of Mexico since it was illegal to travel there from the United States. He mentioned that he had been "Secretary of the New Orleans branch of the Fair Play for Cuba Committee." In the course of the bus trip the doctor inquired about why Oswald wanted to go to Cuba. He replied, "To see Castro, if I could."

The bus finally arrived in Mexico City at 10 A.M. on September 27. Oswald said good-bye to two Australian girls he had met during the two-day trip and walked off alone, lugging two suitcases.[8]

Four blocks from the bus station Oswald registered at the Hotel Comercio under the alias O. H. Lee and was given a room on the third floor. The hotel, rarely frequented by Americans, cost only $1.28 a night.

Oswald then went to the Soviet and Cuban embassies which were located about two miles away. Since the compounds in which both are located are practically adjacent, only a block apart, he could easily go back and forth between the embassies in arranging his transit visa to Cuba.

First, he went to the Soviet Embassy to see if it could facilitate the paperwork, as he later explained to Marina. Then he walked over to the Cuban Embassy, where he was interviewed by Silvia Tirado de Duran, who had been employed three months earlier in the consular section.

Oswald explained that he wanted to stop in Cuba on his way to the Soviet Union, where he planned to resettle permanently in Odessa with his wife. He was, he insisted, "a friend of the Cuban revolution" and presented the documentary evidence he had prepared to show his pro-Castro activities. This sheaf of papers included the record of his arrest, contacts with the Communist and Socialist parties, and even the records he had taken from Jaggars-Chiles-Stovall.

Señora Duran, who herself strongly supported Castro, though a Mexican citizen, was impressed with Oswald's credentials. On his visa application she commented: "The applicant states that he is a member of the American Communist Party and Secretary in New Orleans of the Fair Play for Cuba Committee. . . . He displayed documents in proof of his membership in the two aforementioned organizations. . . ." Taking down his address and phone number, she asked him to return with the necessary photographs for the visa.

After again going to the Soviet Embassy, Oswald returned in the afternoon to the Cuban Embassy with the photographs. His visa still could not be processed, Señora Duran explained, without his first having an entry visa to the Soviet Union. After calling the Soviet Embassy, she informed him that the Russian visa might take months and would require authority from Moscow.

Oswald, apparently frustrated by this turn of events, demanded to see a higher-ranking Cuban official, and met briefly with the consul, Eusebio Azque. After a heated exchange of words, Azque refused to expedite Oswald's visa so that he could leave immediately for Havana. Evidently, his efforts on behalf of the Fair Play for Cuba Committee were not deemed sufficiently important to the Cuban revolution to gain him the special treatment he demanded.

Rebuffed, Oswald stormed out of the embassy.

He returned the next day, even though it was Saturday and the embassy was officially closed. After a brief session with officials there he went back to the Soviet Embassy and suggested that the Soviet Embassy in Washington might be able to resolve the impasse.

After Oswald left, the embassy cabled the KGB center in Moscow, requesting guidance on whether or not he should be granted an immediate visa.[9]

For the next three days Oswald waited in Mexico City for the reply. He ate some of his meals at a small restaurant near the hotel, but aside from a waitress at the restaurant, there are no witnesses to his activities during this hiatus.[10]

On Tuesday Oswald returned to the Cuban Embassy for a final attempt to get his transit visa. At his request Señora Duran again called the Soviet Embassy and handed the receiver to Oswald. He spoke in rapid Russian to a Soviet guard, Ivan Obyedkov. He wanted to know if a telegram had arrived from the Soviet Embassy about his visa.

The guard, apparently unacquainted with the case, asked to whom Oswald had spoken at the embassy.

Oswald explained that he had seen "Comrade Kostikov" on September 28.

The guard suggested that he again speak in person to Kostikov. "I'll be right over," Oswald said, and hung up.

The same day Pedro Gutierrez, a credit investigator for a Mexican department store, saw an American leaving the Cuban Embassy in the company of a tall Cuban, and both got into a car. He later identified the American as Lee Harvey Oswald.[11]

That night he was seen in the hotel with two dark-skinned Cubans.

Early the next morning Oswald checked out of the hotel and hailed a taxi. At 8:30 A.M. he caught the Transporte del Norte bus for Texas, which he had booked the day before.

Even as Oswald was leaving Mexico, the CIA's interest in his contacts there intensified. Its station in Mexico City had been electronically intercepting the phone traffic between the Cuban and Soviet embassies and had therefore monitored, and taped, the telephone calls concerning Oswald's case.

Until October 1 it seemed little more than a routine case of an American citizen attempting to obtain a transit visa to go to Cuba. The name "Oswald" was not even mentioned. But then in his conversation with Obyedkov, Oswald identified himself by name and said that his case was being handled by Kostikov.

Valery Vladimirovich Kostikov, although listed merely as "attache, consular office" on the embassy roster, had been identified for some time as an intelligence officer for the KGB, who specialized in handling Soviet agents operating under deep cover within the United States. The FBI had recently followed another Soviet agent from the United States into Mexico and observed his contact with Kostikov. (He was also suspected of being part of the Thirteenth Department of the KGB, which was involved with planning sabotage and other violent acts.)[12]

Checking through its files, the CIA identified Oswald as "Lee Henry [sic] Oswald, born on 18 October 1939 in New Orleans. . . . A former U.S. Marine, who defected to the Soviet Union in October 1959 and later made arrangements with the U.S. Embassy in Moscow to return. . . ."[13] CIA officers in Mexico next went through the pictures that their secret cameras with telescopic lenses had taken of all individuals entering and leaving the Soviet Embassy. The only individual resembling an American who left (or entered) the embassy at a time coinciding with Oswald's movements was a heavyset man, about thirty-five years old, with an athletic build and receding hairline.

On October 10 CIA headquarters in Washington notified the FBI, the Department of State and the Navy about Oswald's contact with the Soviet Embassy. Also, on orders from Washington, D.C., Winston Scott, the station chief in Mexico City for the CIA, informed the FBI office in Mexico City, the Immigration and Naturalization Service and the U.S. Embassy of the development. Since the CIA is not supposed to investigate U.S. citizens abroad without a "special request," it "did nothing further on the case," according to its own files on Oswald, except to request on October 23 a photograph of Oswald from the Navy to check against its files.[14]

According to a not yet fully declassified FBI report, based on statements attributed to Fidel Castro, Oswald made wild claims at the Cuban Embassy about what he might do for the Cuban revolution, including even possible assassinations of American leaders. According to the same report, the consul assumed at the time that Oswald was being deliberately provocative.[15]

In Havana the Foreign Ministry received Oswald's request for a visa to come to Cuba. Cuban intelligence also apparently received a report on Oswald's contact with the Cuban Embassy in Mexico. According to Fidel Castro, who was interviewed on the subject in July 1967, when Oswald paid his first visit to the Cuban Embassy, he said "he wanted to work for us. He was asked to explain, but he wouldn't." Oswald then returned and told the Cubans in Mexico he wanted "to free Cuba from American imperialism." Then, it was reported to Castro, Oswald said, "Someone ought to shoot that President Kennedy. . . . Maybe I'll try to do it."

On October 15 Oswald's visa was processed in Havana, and three days later the Cuban Embassy in Mexico was notified that it could issue Oswald his Cuban visa contingent on his showing proof that he had obtained a Soviet entry visa. By this time Oswald was back in Dallas.

In a letter to the Soviet Embassy from Dallas, which was intercepted by the FBI, Oswald provided his own version of what happened during his trip to Mexico. "I was unable to remain in Mexico indefinitely because of my Mexican visa restriction," he explained. "I could not take a chance on requesting a new visa unless I used my real name, so I returned to the United States." He blamed the Cuban consul for delaying his visa and added, "I am glad he has since been replaced." He then pointed out, "Had I been able to reach the Soviet Embassy in Havana as planned, the embassy there would have had time to complete our business." He did not elaborate on exactly what sort of "business" he had planned to engage in with the Soviets in Havana or why he was traveling under a false name.

Back in Dallas, Oswald spent a night in the YMCA, moved to a rooming house on North Marsalis Street in the Oak Cliff Section and, one week later, changed his residence again—this time to a rooming house at North Beckley Street. He registered here under the alias "O. H. Lee" and forbade Marina, who was still living with Ruth Paine in Irving, to tell anyone where he was living. After several futile attempts to find a job, he heard through Mrs. Paine of a job opening at the Texas Book Depository. After a brief interview he was hired to fill orders for textbooks at $1.25 an hour.

He had just come back from visiting his wife and daughter at Ruth Paine's house in Irving. Mrs. Paine seemed happy to see him. She wrote her mother on October 14: "Lee Oswald . . . arrived a week and a half ago . . . He spent the last weekend and the one before with us here and was a happy addition to our expanded family. He played with Chris [Paine], watched football on TV, planed down the door that wouldn't close, and generally added a masculine flavor."

On Sunday, October 20, Marina gave birth at Parkland Hospital in Dallas to her second daughter—Audrey Marina Rachel Oswald. Oswald seemed elated. After visiting Marina in the hospital, he resumed his covert political activities.[16]

Toward the end of October Cubella made an extraordinary demand of the CIA. Before he would go ahead with the plan to eliminate Castro (which he had himself proposed in Brazil), he wanted some sort of personal assurance or "signal" from Attorney General Kennedy that the Kennedy administration would actively support him in this endeavor.

Overruling objections by his own SAS counterintelligence chief, Desmond Fitzgerald decided to meet with Cubella himself, as a "personal representative" of Kennedy's. The risk of possibly compromising the President was apparently outweighed in his opinion by the gains in advancing the coup d'état. Although he would not use his real name, Fitzgerald was a well-known figure in Washington and readily identifiable to Cuban intelligence, if the operation was "insecure."

The meeting took place on October 29, 1963. Fitzgerald assured Cubella that once the coup had succeeded and Castro had been removed from power, the Kennedy administration would be fully prepared to aid and support the new government.

Cubella asked for the delivery of specific weapons—a rifle with telescopic sights and a means of delivering a poison injection without detection—but Fitzgerald refused to discuss such specifics.

About two weeks later Fitzgerald arranged a further "signal" for Cubella and his followers in Cuba. He wrote a section of the speech President Kennedy was to deliver in Miami on November 18. It described the Castro government as a "small band of conspirators" that, "once removed," would ensure United States assistance to the Cuban nation.

The day after Kennedy delivered this "signal," Fitzgerald ordered the case officer to arrange another meeting with Cubella —a meeting in which the specifics would be discussed.

Cubella agreed to postpone his scheduled return to Cuba if the meeting could be held that week in Paris. The date agreed on was November 22.

15

Day of the Assassin

Oswald arose early on the morning of November 22, 1963. The evening before, he had hitched a ride to Irving, Texas, with Buell Wesley Frazier, a fellow worker at the book depository who was a neighbor of Ruth Paine's. Now, to be back in Dallas in time for work, he had to meet Frazier shortly after 7 A.M. He slipped off his wedding ring and left it, along with $170 of his savings, for Marina in a dresser drawer. A moment later, he walked down the block, carrying with him an oblong package wrapped in coarse brown paper.

When Frazier had asked Oswald the day before why he wanted a ride to Irving, since he had never before visited his wife in the middle of the week, Oswald explained that he needed to pick up some "curtain rods" for his room in Dallas. When Frazier now saw Oswald approaching with a package, he assumed it contained these same curtain rods.

Oswald was never particularly talkative with Frazier, but as they drove to Dallas that morning, he seemed especially quiet. Just before 8 A.M., they arrived at the book depository. Without waiting for Frazier, Oswald walked quickly into the building, his package tucked under one arm.

Air Force One landed at Love Field in Dallas that morning at 11:40 A.M. and taxied to a green and red terminal building usually used for international arrivals. President Kennedy stepped out onto the top step of the ramp, and the crowd waiting below cheered.

The President then helped Mrs. Kennedy into their waiting Lincoln limousine. Governor John Connally and his wife maneuvered their way into the jump seats in front of the President and his wife. It was a clear November day, and the President decided against using the transparent bubble top for the motorcade through Dallas. At 11:50 A.M. the fifteen-car procession left Love Field.

In Paris at about noon that day the CIA case officer kept his appointment with Cubella.[1] As he had been instructed by Fitzgerald, he referred him to the lines in the speech President Kennedy had made four days earlier which "signaled" American support of a progressive government in Cuba once Castro was "removed" from power. He then took out the poison pen which the CIA laboratory had fashioned only days before and demonstrated how an almost invisible needle shot out from the otherwise innocent-looking ball-point pen. He recommended that Cubella use Black Leaf-40 poison, which was both lethal and commercially available. Before ending the meeting, he also assured Cubella that the high-powered rifle he wanted fitted with telescopic sights would be provided to him.

Meanwhile, in Dallas, employees of the book depository were breaking for lunch. The presidential motorcade was scheduled to pass through the grassy plaza directly in front of the book depository in the next half hour, and many of the workers waited on the front steps of the building for a glimpse of the young President.

Oswald did not join them. He remained on the sixth floor, alone. Moving a few cartons of boxes forward, he erected a waist-high barrier in front of the easternmost window. From this vantage point, he could see the three main streets of Dallas —Elm, Main and Commerce—converge in the plaza below before they reached the elevated expressways that carried traffic out of town.

At 12:30 P.M. the President's car passed the book depository, moving slowly down Main Street. A moment later a rifle shot echoed through the grassy plaza. The President clutched at his throat with both hands.

Then there was another shattering sound. Governor Connally, seated directly in front of the President, felt a sudden thud in his back. He saw his lap soaked with blood and slumped toward his wife.

The limousine came to an almost complete halt. A third shot exploded the President's head.

Leaping off his motorcycle, Dallas Police Officer Marrion L. Baker ran into the Texas Book Depository, where he thought the shots might have come from. He raced up the stairs, preceded by Roy Truly, the manager of the depository. On the second-floor landing he encountered Oswald standing near the soft drink machine. Gun drawn, he asked Truly if Oswald worked in the building.

"Yes," Truly answered, and Baker continued up the stairs.

After getting a soda from the machine, Oswald coolly made his way out of the building. Minutes later it was sealed off by the Dallas police.

After walking seven blocks up Elm Street, Oswald caught a bus going in the exact opposite direction. He stayed on it for only two blocks, then, after walking another few blocks, hailed a taxi. He told the driver to take him to Neely Street in Oak Cliff, only a block from his rooming house on North Beckley Street. It was a few minutes before 1 P.M.

After dashing into his room, Oswald put on his gray zippered jacket and took from the closet his snub-nosed Smith & Wesson revolver.

While he was changing, Earlene Roberts, the housekeeper at the rooming house, heard a car horn and, looking out the window, saw a police car stopped in front of the house. Then it slowly drove away. A moment later Oswald strode out without saying a word to Mrs. Roberts.

At exactly 1 P.M. John F. Kennedy was pronounced dead at Parkland Hospital.

Sixteen minutes later, in Oak Cliff, Dallas police officer J. D. Tippit was found bleeding to death by his radio car. Witnesses at the scene said he had been shot repeatedly by a man in a gray jacket to whom he had been speaking only minutes before.

Meanwhile, about two miles away at the Texas Book Depository, police officers found on the sixth floor three empty cartridge cases and a Mannlicher-Carcano rifle. Checking through the roster of employees, Roy Truly quickly identified Lee Harvey Oswald as "a man missing."

At 1:50 P.M., in Oak Cliff, sixteen police officers moved into the darkened Texas Theater, where a suspect in the Tippit shooting had been reported hiding. Oswald was seated alone in the second row and didn't seem to notice the policemen coming up behind him. Then suddenly, in a last-ditch effort to resist arrest, he flailed out at the police with his fist and drew his snub-nosed revolver. It took only a minute to overpower him.

Dragged out of the movie in handcuffs, the suspect shouted, "Police brutality," to the crowd of onlookers that had gathered. Then he was shoved in the back of a patrol car.

As they drove to Dallas police headquarters, police officers asked the suspect his name. He refused to answer. Then they went through his wallet and found two selective service cards. One identified him as Aleck James Hidell, the other as Lee Harvey Oswald.

At FBI headquarters in Dallas, James Hosty heard from his superior, Gordon Shanklin, that the prime suspect in the Kennedy assassination was Lee Harvey Oswald. The name stunned him. For more than two months he had personally superintended the Oswald file. Only three weeks before, he had spoken to Oswald's wife and Ruth Paine in Irving and had learned that Oswald was working at the Texas Book Depository. Then Oswald had come to the FBI offices and, according to the receptionists who read it, left a threatening note which began: "Let this be a warning."[2] Hosty had recently received word that the FBI had intercepted a letter which Oswald had written to the Soviet Embassy suggesting that he had business with the Soviets in Havana and had been traveling in Mexico under a false name. And finally, Hosty knew from a CIA report that Oswald had had contact with the Soviet agent Kostikov.

Hosty rushed down to police headquarters to participate in the interrogation. In the basement parking lot he ran into Lieutenant Jack Revill, a friend of his who was in the Intelligence Squad of the Dallas police. "Jack," he said breathlessly, "a Communist killed the President."

Revill, dumbfounded, asked, "What do you mean?"

Hosty quickly explained that the FBI had an open security file on Oswald and added ominously, "We had information that he was capable of this. . . ."

By "this," Revill clearly understood him to mean the Kennedy assassination. Even though he had been friends with the FBI agent for nearly four years, he now blew up at him. He wanted to know why the Dallas police had not been given the information before the assassination.

Hosty didn't answer.[3] He was headed for the Homicide Division.

Captain John Will Fritz, a short, stocky man with thick glasses, had a reputation as one of the shrewdest homicide detectives in the Southwest. He had just started questioning Oswald when Hosty and James Bookhout, another FBI agent, burst into his small nine- by fourteen-foot office. He invited them to sit in on the session.

In his forty-one years of police work, Captain Fritz had acquired almost limitless patience in dealing with homicide suspects. He began slowly, asking routine questions about Oswald's education. Then he asked him about his job at the book depository and where he was at the time of the assassination.[4]

Oswald readily admitted that he, like all the other employees, had access to all the floors where books were stored but insisted that when the President was killed, he was having lunch on the first floor.

Why did he leave after the shooting? Fritz inquired.

"I didn't think there would be any work done that afternoon. . . . I just left," he explained. He said he went home, changed his clothes, got his gun and went to the movies.

Fritz asked why he needed to take his gun to a movie.

"Well, you know about a pistol . . . I just carried it."

It was an important admission. If Oswald's pistol matched the shells found at the scene of the Tippit murder, he could not reasonably claim that someone had framed him by using his own gun since he had now acknowledged that he himself had taken it from his room before the killing and kept it in his possession until he was arrested. Fritz asked if he had killed Tippit.

Oswald strenuously denied having killed either Tippit or Kennedy. "The only law I violated . . ." he said, was "I hit the officer in the show; he hit me in the eye, and I guess I deserved it."

Fritz pressed him about whether he owned a rifle.

Oswald categorically denied owning a rifle since he had gone to Russia in 1959.

It was clear to Fritz that his adversary in this interrogation was not a "nut." He seemed to know when to answer questions and when to lie or be evasive. From his answers, Fritz suspected that Oswald might have been trained to resist interrogation. In any case, it was clear that he was not about to break.

In the twelve hours of interrogation that followed, Oswald lost his temper only once. Hosty had asked him if he had been to Mexico, and he had answered no. Then, suddenly, he recognized Hosty's name.

"I know you," Oswald shouted out, banging his fist on the table. "You accosted my wife on two occasions." He went on to accuse Hosty of trying to coerce his wife by threatening to send her back to Russia. Then he quieted down.

Asked by Fritz if he wanted to be represented by an attorney, Oswald asked for John Abt. Abt had recently defended the leaders of the American Communist Party against federal conspiracy charges. (Several months earlier, Oswald had sent two of the defendants, Gus Hall and Benjamin Davis, honorary membership cards in his Fair Play for Cuba chapter.) He tried to telephone the lawyer in his New York office but couldn't reach him.

Fritz returned again to the subject of the rifle. He showed Oswald a picture of himself holding a rifle—the same photograph that Marina had taken of him before the attempted assassination of General Walker. Fritz explained that it had been found among Oswald's possessions in the Paines' garage.

Oswald looked at the photograph for a long moment. Then he concluded it was a "composite." His head had been pasted onto some unknown man's body. He even suggested that photographs taken of him by the police might have been used in putting together this photograph. He was not about to admit that he had ever had this rifle in his possession.

They broke the session for a police lineup; then the questioning resumed again.

Even as the cat-and-mouse game went on between Fritz and

Oswald, the evidence against Oswald was developing. Telltale hammer markers on the cartridge cases found around Tippit's body were traced back to the revolver Oswald had had in his hand when he had been arrested. A number of witnesses had identified him as the man standing over Tippit's body after firing the bullets into him.[5] In the President's assassination, two witnesses who had seen the sniper firing from the window at the Texas Book Depository had been found. A box found near that window had Oswald's palm print on it, as did the rifle. The three bullet shells found just below the windowsill could be proved through microscopic analysis to have been ejected from that same rifle, and a bullet and fragments fired in the assassination ballistically matched the rifle. Fritz knew from long experience that any piece of evidence could be questioned and controverted—that was the very nature of evidence—but taken as a whole fabric, the case against Oswald looked increasingly powerful.

At 1:35 A.M. Oswald was taken from his cell and escorted into a small room lined with file cabinets. Justice of the Peace David Johnston stood there somberly with a piece of paper in his hands.

"Is this the trial?" Oswald asked facetiously.

"No," Judge Johnston answered. "I have to arraign you . . . for the murder with malice of John F. Kennedy." He read the charge in a dry monotone.

"Oh, this is the deal, is it?" replied Oswald. He had been arraigned five hours earlier for murdering officer J. D. Tippit. Demanding to know whether he still had constitutional rights, Oswald again requested a lawyer. It was nearly ten hours since he had first asked for the services of John Abt.

The judge wrote on the bottom of the arraignment form, "No Bond—Capital offense" and ordered Oswald remanded to the custody of the sheriff of Dallas County to await trial.

At a motel in Irving about fifteen miles away Marina and Marguerite Oswald sought refuge from the hundreds of reporters assigned to the story. There Marina shredded to pieces the photograph she had taken of Oswald with his rifle and pistol seven months earlier. Since this particular copy was signed by Oswald and inscribed in his handwriting to their daughter June, it could provide damning evidence connecting her husband inexorably to both murder weapons. (She knew that George De Mohrenschildt had another signed copy, but he was in Haiti and not likely to produce it.) She put the torn pieces in an ashtray and lit a match.

Marguerite Oswald watched Marina try to destroy the evidence. But it didn't burn completely. She herself then flushed the burned remains of the picture down the toilet. She knew her son's life might be at stake. Unfortunately, she knew almost nothing about his recent movements. She had not seen him—or Marina—for more than a year. (However, that night, when questioned by the FBI, she suggested that he might be a "government agent.")

Marina had earlier refused to discuss her husband's activities with the FBI. When agents came to the door, she told them they already had her and her husband under surveillance and knew all there was to know about them. The agents left quietly.

In the weeks ahead she continued to conceal potentially important elements of the case from the FBI, Secret Service and other government investigators. She denied that she had ever seen her husband with a rifle (though she changed her story when confronted with copies of the photograph). She claimed to know nothing about Oswald's aliases (even though she herself had called him at the rooming house where he was living under an alias and had signed the name "Hidell" on Oswald's Fair Play membership card). She avoided mentioning anything about Oswald's prior assassination attempts (until after a note to her in Russian from Oswald was found which suggested what she should do in the event he was captured or killed in the attempt on General Walker's life). And she stated for nearly two months that she had not been informed of Oswald's trip to Mexico in September (when, in fact, as she later admitted, he had described in detail his dealings there with the Cuban and Soviet embassies).[6]

In Mexico City, meanwhile, CIA officers carefully sorted through their file of individuals photographed entering or leaving the Soviet and Cuban embassies during the week Oswald had been in Mexico. Each was compared with a head and shoulder shot of Oswald that the FBI had only delivered hours before. Clearly, the photograph of a heavyset man given to the FBI in October with the report on Oswald did not resemble Lee Harvey Oswald.[7] In fact, none of the photographs taken by the secret cameras were of Oswald. Somehow, despite CIA surveillance, Oswald had managed to enter and leave the Soviet Embassy on a number of occasions without being seen.[8] For all the CIA knew, his visits with Kostikov could have taken place under clandestine circumstances which evaded surveillance.

The CIA counterintelligence staff in Washington also began that morning to consider the implications of Oswald's contact with the embassies in Mexico. Reviewing Oswald's activities there in a memorandum—especially his contact with Kostikov, who was reported to have planned in advance to depart Mexico City on November 22—Angleton's staff suggested that the connection might not be totally innocent.[9]

At 10:30 A.M. the FBI was informed through its liaison with the CIA, Sam Papich, of these possibly "sinister implications." Although J. Edgar Hoover sent President Lyndon Baines Johnson that very day a "background" report on Oswald, he omitted any mention that the FBI had had an open security case pending on Oswald at the time of the assassination.

At 5:15 that afternoon, CIA headquarters received a telegram from its Mexico station that Mexican security police were about to arrest Silvia Duran and hold her "incommunicado until she gives all details of Oswald known to her" about Oswald's dealings with the Cuban Embassy. On the express orders of Thomas Karamessines, the assistant director of clandestine services for the CIA, the CIA station in Mexico was told to stop the Mexican police from arresting her. Karamessines apparently feared, as he later testified, that Duran might reveal during the interrogation that the Cubans were behind the assassination. If that were to happen, the United States would need time to decide on a course of action.

When he was informed that it was too late to abort the arrest, he sent a flash cable to the CIA station in Mexico, stating, "Arrest of Silvia Duran is extremely serious matter which could prejudice U.S. freedom of action on entire question of Cuban responsibility. . . . Request you ensure that her arrest is kept absolutely secret, that no information from her is published or leaked, that all such info is cabled to us, and that the fact of her arrest and her statements are not spread to leftist or disloyal circles in the Mexican Government."

To assist Mexican security officers in their investigation, the CIA provided background information on Oswald and eleven still-unanswered questions about his visit to Mexico, including such provocative queries as: "Was the assassination of President Kennedy planned by Fidel Castro . . . and were the final details worked out inside the Cuban Embassy in Mexico?"; "Were Oswald and his wife paid well and promised a 'plush life' in Odessa, USSR, for the killing of President Kennedy?"; "Who were Oswald's contacts during the period 26 September 1963 to 3 October 1963?"; and ". . . if Castro planned that Oswald assassinate President Kennedy, did the Soviets have any knowledge of these plans? Or, were the Soviets merely being asked to give Oswald a visa?"[10] The apprehension that ran paramount through these questions was that the Cubans might have incited Oswald, either directly by promising him some rewards or indirectly by calling his attention to some public statement made by Castro.

Although Mexican officers proceeded with their interrogation, it soon became clear to American officials, in particular to Ambassador Thomas Mann, that the Mexican government did not want it to develop that Oswald had been conspiring or even influenced by the Cubans on Mexican soil. Relations between Mexico and Cuba were an extraordinarily sensitive political issue.[11]

Under intense questioning, Duran stuck to her story that her only contact with Oswald had been in processing his visa request. She claimed that when told there would be a delay, Oswald shouted angrily at Consul Azque, who retorted that "a person like him, in place of aiding the Cuban revolution, was doing it harm." She acknowledged that she had exceeded her authority in placing a call to the Soviet Embassy on Oswald's behalf and admitted having written her name and phone number for him on a piece of paper at the consulate.[12]

By the morning of November 24 Captain Fritz had completed his questioning of Oswald. He had not obtained the admission of guilt he sought. The prisoner had lied methodically about every piece of incriminating evidence: his ownership, or even knowledge of, the rifle, the provenance of the pistol, the use of the aliases O. H. Lee and Aleck James Hidell, his whereabouts in the book depository at the time of the assassination and his previous trip to Mexico.

At about 11 A.M. Fritz began making the preparations to transfer Oswald from police headquarters to the county jail. A bundle of his clothes was brought in, and he was asked what he preferred to wear.

"Just give me one of those sweaters," Oswald replied, and then slipped into a black sweater with jagged holes in the shoulder. He was ready to go.

Just before he left, Inspector Thomas J. Kelley of the Secret Service spoke to him quietly out of earshot of the others. He explained that the Secret Service was responsible for the protection of the President. And if Oswald were not guilty, as he claimed, then Kelley would be "very anxious to talk with him to make sure the correct story was developing as it related to the assassination."

Oswald said he would be glad to discuss that proposition "with his attorney" but, for the moment, had "nothing more to say."

Kelley watched as Oswald, still handcuffed, was escorted out of the small office by a phalanx of Dallas detectives. He knew that the plan called for him to be taken to the basement, where he would be put into an unmarked police car. An armored car would serve as a "decoy" to distract attention during the transfer.

"Here he comes," someone shouted as the prisoner emerged from the elevator and was led toward the ramp. Additional spotlights were turned on, and television cameras focused on the gaunt man in a black sweater. The swarm of newsmen and other onlookers surged forward.

The car began backing toward the ramp. But Oswald never reached it.

A short man with beady eyes stepped out of the crowd and quickly fired a single bullet into Oswald's abdomen.

Inspector Kelley ran down the stairs, but by the time he reached Oswald he was unconscious. Captain Fritz, who had been walking a few steps in front of Oswald, identified the assailant as Jack Ruby, a Dallas bar owner, who was well known to the police.

Oswald died at Parkland Hospital at 1:07 P.M. without regaining consciousness or speaking another word. All that remained was the burial.

Two hours later Agent Hosty was summoned to FBI headquarters in Dallas. According to Hosty's sworn testimony, his superior, Gorden Shanklin, thereupon ordered him to destroy both the note Oswald had delivered to the FBI shortly before the assassination and the memorandum that Hosty had prepared about the incident.[13] After returning to his office, he followed his orders and destroyed this evidence, flushing the remains down the toilet.

On the morning of November 25th, in Washington, a guard of honor took the casket of President Kennedy from its catafalque in the Capitol rotunda, and carried it down the 36 marble steps to the plaza below. They then gently slid it onto the metal bed of the waiting horse-drawn caisson. Behind the caisson was assembled the long funeral cortege: the limousines that would carry the members of the Kennedy family, the bands of four military services, and a riderless horse, Black Jack, with a pair of empty boots turned backwards in the stirrups and a sheathed silver sword fastened to his saddle. At 10:59 A.M., while the bands played "Our Fallen Heroes," the procession moved off, slowly following the caisson down the route President Kennedy had taken less than three years earlier for his inauguration.

Shortly after 11 A.M., strains of music wafted toward the offices of the Director of the FBI in the Department of Justice annex. J. Edgar Hoover had moved very quickly after Oswald's death to contain speculation about the alleged assassin. Within hours, he had let President Johnson know through his chief aide, William D. Moyers, that both he and his immediate superior, Deputy Attorney General Nicholas Katzenbach, wanted to "have something issued so we can convince the public that Oswald is the real assassin." And in a memorandum to the White House that followed this conversation, Katzenbach proposed specifically that "Speculation about Oswald's motivation ought to be cut off."

At CIA headquarters that morning a list of names of "all known contacts" of Valery Vladimirovich Kostikov, the Soviet Embassy officer who had dealt with Oswald in Mexico, was being traced through the CIA's voluminous files by members of Angleton's counterintelligence staff to determine what information existed on these individuals. Each division of the CIA was asked to cooperate in the "trace," as the procedure is called, by supplying whatever relevant information was in its files. One name on the list caused considerable consternation in the SAS division—that was Rolando Cubella.

When the case officers in the SAS division were notified that Angleton's staff had put out a trace on Cubella only days after Kennedy was killed, there was immediate alarm: they knew that only a few weeks before the assassination Cubella had received a signal from their chief, Desmond Fitzgerald, that Kennedy would back a plot to eliminate Castro. Now, counterintelligence wanted to know about this man. Should they provide the operational file on Cubella which listed his contacts with the CIA and his involvement in the plan to remove Castro from power (as well as the allegation that he might be "insecure," or even a double agent)? Such operational files were always kept separately by the division handling the agent.[14]

After some consideration, Fitzgerald decided against providing the operational file on Cubella to Angleton or his staff. (The "201" dossier, which contained only overt biographical data on Cubella, was all that was available to Angleton—without the operational file.) In addition, Fitzgerald ordered the case officer who had met with Cubella on November 22 to omit from his report any mention of the poison pen. (Subsequently, Fitzgerald's own division would determine that the Cubella operation had been "insecure," and his own counterintelligence chief for the SAS division would write in an undated memo: "Fidel reportedly knew that this group was plotting against him and we cannot rule out the possibility of provocation.")[15] Since this was not turned over to Angleton's staff, which was to serve as the liaison between the CIA and the Warren Commission, none of this would be known to the investigators of the Kennedy assassination.

Meanwhile, at 2 Dzerzhinsky Square in Moscow, a man already known to the CIA as Yuri Ivanovich Nosenko arrived at KGB headquarters. He proceeded to a room where a number of other KGB officers, under the command of General Oleg Mikhailovich Gribanov, were discussing the Kennedy assassination. Looking over Gribanov's shoulder, he quickly read through the Oswald file. Some seven weeks later, he would arrange to meet his CIA contacts in Geneva.

That same Monday afternoon, while intelligence services in far off places were pondering the problems that an unrestrained investigation into the assassination might cause for them, a mole-skinned covered coffin arrived at Rose Hill Cemetery in Fort Worth. Grave-diggers had been told earlier that day that the site they were preparing so hurriedly was for one "William Bobo." They soon learned, however, from the scores of newsmen that thronged around the grave that it was actually for Lee Harvey Oswald. When no pallbearers could be found, seven reporters took off their jackets and carried the coffin to the open grave.

EPILOGUE

Inside Out

By 1967 pressures were building within the CIA to resolve, in one way or another, the fate of Yuri Nosenko.

For nearly three years this extraordinary defector had been imprisoned in a windowless room, with heavy padding on the walls (to prevent Nosenko from injuring himself), in a house that the CIA had converted to a "detention center" just a few miles from downtown Washington. The CIA had no precedent for incarcerating a person inside the United States, but in this case the suspect could not be turned over to the Department of Justice for prosecution without precipitating an international crisis. For if he were brought to trial by the United States government, he would be accused of having been sent over by the Soviet government to misinform the Warren Commission about Oswald's relationship with Soviet intelligence agencies.

When Nosenko was first imprisoned in the spring of 1964, officials in both the CIA and the Justice Department had hoped that he might admit to being a messenger from Moscow before the Warren Report was published. Even as the report was going to press, Attorney General Robert F. Kennedy made frequent phone calls to ascertain whether or not Nosenko had broken. Each time the answer was: "Not yet."

As the weeks dragged on, the CIA interrogators realized that Nosenko was not a man who would easily crack. They experimented with various disorientation techniques, such as gradually setting watches back and manipulating lighting conditions, to convince him it was day when it was really night, thereby confusing his biological clock and sense of time. None of these efforts worked: Nosenko simply repeated his basic story over and over again.

The interrogators made Nosenko describe the procedures and routines used by the KGB for processing cases. When these conflicted with an actual case he had described in earlier debriefings, he was asked to explain the contradiction.

"You misunderstood me," Nosenko would usually answer, showing little interest in this sort of detailed interrogation.

When asked for names, dates and locations which might tend to substantiate his story, he often replied that he had no "memory" for detail. Even in describing his own career in the KGB, he claimed that he could not recall the specific spying operations he took part in or superintended which had earned him promotions.

Moreover, he made little effort to help his interrogators "source" his information by providing the names and positions of the other KGB officers from whom he had allegedly obtained it. For example, when asked how he had found out about the theft of NATO documents from a vault at Orly Airport in France, he replied merely that he had heard it from the "boys" in the KGB unit that opened and resealed documents but claimed that he could not recall the name of his informant or the date that he had acquired the information in 1963 (even though this was only a short time before his defection, when he was supposedly working for the CIA).

Throughout these tense sessions Nosenko stuck steadfastly to his story that Oswald was not connected with the KGB, even when it meant revising some of his earlier assertions. In October 1966, for instance, he was confronted with the fact that through its own surveillance in 1963 the CIA knew that Oswald had contacted a known KGB officer in Mexico City. In the light of such evidence, how could he still maintain that Oswald was not seen by anyone from the KGB?

Nosenko paused for a long moment. Then he explained that K. N. Dubas, the head of the Tourist Department in the KGB, had received a telegraphic report of Oswald's visits to the Soviet Embassy just after Oswald had left. It stated that Oswald had seen "only" personnel from the Foreign Ministry, not from the KGB. On the basis of this telegram Nosenko concluded at the time that if Oswald had seen any consular officers, it was in their diplomatic rather than intelligence roles.

Why had he not mentioned this telegram in his original debriefings or in the intervening years? his interrogators asked.

Up to this point he had forgotten the telegram, Nosenko said with a shrug. Now he recalled the exact wording.

The interrogators knew the dates of Oswald's visits to the Soviet Embassy; they were between September 27 and October 3, 1963. How had he known about the telegram? his interrogators asked.

Nosenko explained that he just happened to have been in Dubas' office when the telegram arrived. Dubas then read it aloud.

On this point it seemed to his interrogators that Nosenko was merely improvising this chance meeting. The more they pressed him about Oswald's relations with KGB personnel, the more adamantly he denied even the possibility of such contacts.

When he discussed the telegram that had come from Mexico to the KGB in October 1963, Nosenko insisted that was the first contact Oswald had had, even indirectly, with the First Chief Directorate of the KGB, which is responsible for foreign intelligence. Yet the CIA interrogators had definitely ascertained through Soviet consular records that Oswald had contacted the Soviet Embassy in Washington, D.C., as early February 1963; this meant, according to procedures which Nosenko himself had described, that the First Chief Directorate would have heard of Oswald before he ever got to Mexico. They further established that these contacts with the Washington Embassy would certainly be in the KGB file on Oswald that Nosenko claimed to have personally reviewed in Moscow only two months before his defection. Unable to resolve this discrepancy, the interrogators noted: "Nosenko's apparent ignorance of Oswald's communications with the Soviet Embassy in Washington discredits his claim to complete knowledge of all aspects of the KGB relationship with Oswald."

Gradually, from the transcripts of these interrogation sessions and from other sources it had, the Soviet Russia Division compiled its final report on Nosenko. This document, which ran to more than 900 closely typed pages, evaluated all the informtion Nosenko had provided the CIA since his first contact in 1962. Point by point, it analyzed the contradictions and omissions in the story. After reviewing all the material, the report concluded that only one explanation fitted the established facts: Nosenko was a Soviet intelligence agent dispatched by the KGB expressly for the purpose of delivering disinformation to the CIA, FBI and Warren Commission.

It recommended that the FBI undertake a full-scale investigation of Nosenko and his accomplices in the deception. If this effort confirmed the fact that he was still a Soviet agent, then some more drastic form of "administrative action" might be called for. This could lead to forcibly deporting Nosenko from the United States to some Soviet-controlled territory (such as East Berlin).

The division's report was forwarded to Angleton's counterintelligence staff for further evaluation.

Angleton had never entirely agreed with the decision to subject Nosenko to hostile interrogation. As a trout fisherman he preferred to play his game patiently, according to their own strength. With defectors, he believed in eliciting whatever information they chose to divulge and then gradually assessing how their story fitted in with other known Soviet operations. For him, deception fostered by Soviet intellligence was not the product of a single agent or act, but rather a dovetailing continuity. By confronting Nosenko with the contradictions in his story, the Soviet Russia Division had, in a sense, given the game away and allowed him to concoct *ad hoc* explanations, albeit feeble ones.

From the division's long report, Angleton could see that there was a plethora of evidence to indicate that Nosenko had lied and attempted to deceive the CIA. But the question that concerned him was: What was this deception designed to achieve? If Nosenko were deported, the answer to this long-term question would be forever lost.

Angleton turned the report over to his staff for full assessment. The chief of research based his analysis solely on the content of the report itself. As far as its substance was concerned, he essentially agreed that Nosenko was probably a fake sent by the KGB to confound the CIA. Indeed, he assigned an 85 percent probability to that conclusion. However, he was unsatisfied with the presentation of the division's report. It seemed to him unnecessarily long and convoluted, with inconclusive and essentially irrelevant sections on the defector Anatoli Golitsin, whose code name was Stone. He recommended that the report be re-edited by the Soviet Russia Division to omit peripheral material on Stone, and to sharpen the focus on evidence that bore directly on the issue of Nosenko's credibility.

To supplement this analysis, Angleton ordered his chief of operations, Newton S. Miler, to fully reinvestigate the Nosenko case. This entailed not only evaluating the division's report, but systematically comparing all the information that Nosenko had furnished during the past five years with that provided by other defectors and agents. To assist him, the chief of operations asked two senior researchers in his department, neither of whom had any acquaintance with the case, to independently review the evidence without consulting with him or each other.

As far as he was concerned, the case for or against Nosenko depended on an assessment of whether or not he had provided information of great value. From his preliminary review, it became abundantly clear that most of Nosenko's revelations involved either worthless information or data about agents who had already been compromised by themselves or others. Aside from a few low-level "throwaway" cases involving American tourists who had been approached by Soviets in Moscow, the only seemingly valuable lead that Nosenko had provided concerned the theft of secret documents from the courier center at Orly Airport by an American sergeant, Robert Lee Johnson.

FBI defenders of Nosenko had long argued that the Soviets would never have given away an agent as important as Sergeant Johnson just to establish Nosenko as a disinformation agent. To test this premise, Miler instituted a full investigation into the case of Sergeant Johnson. He found that, years before Nosenko provided the information that identified Johnson as the leak at the Orly center, Johnson had been arrested by military authorities for selling pornographic films, at which time microfilm of classified secrets was found in his possession. Moreover, on several occasions, his wife had told military authorities of his espionage activities on behalf of the Soviets.

From this and other evidence produced by the CIA, Miler concluded that the Soviets had every reason to assume that Sergeant Johnson had been compromised and known to military counterintelligence well before Nosenko provided his information on the case. The Soviets, in other words, might have been merely discarding an agent who they assumed could no longer be of use to them. (Sergeant Johnson had lost his access to the vault by the time Nosenko discussed the "leak" in 1964.)

After completing his investigation of all the other overlapping cases, the chief of operations reached the conclusion that Nosenko was a Soviet disinformation agent. He assumed that Nosenko had been ordered by the KGB to contact the CIA in Geneva in 1962 for the express purpose of deflecting American intelligence from the information which was being provided by Stone. Nosenko, according to this theory, was then ordered to "defect" in 1964, most probably to provide a covering legend for Oswald's activities in the Soviet Union prior to the assassination. Consulting his two senior researchers, Miler found that both independently came to the same conclusion.

While there was little difference between the Soviet Russia Division and counterintelligence on the question of whether or not Nosenko was a fake, there was considerable disagreement on how his case should be disposed of. Angleton and his staff feared that any rash action, such as an attempt to deport Nosenko physically, could result in unanticipated consequences.

At FBI headquarters J. Edgar Hoover was apprised by his liaison with the CIA of that agency's evaluation of Nosenko as a Soviet disinformation officer. He realized that unless this verdict was immediately reversed, it could have very serious ramifications for his bureau.

For one thing, it would completely destroy the credibility of the FBI's agent in place in the KGB, code-named Fedora. For more than six years Fedora, officially a Soviet diplomat with the UN in New York, had been supplying the FBI with information about Soviet espionage activities. Indeed, a large part of the bureau's counterespionage effort had been built on Fedora's tips. The information Fedora provided was so prized by Hoover that on many occasions he forwarded it directly to the White House. (Later, in 1971, Fedora told the FBI that the secret Pentagon Papers that Daniel Ellsberg had made copies of had been provided to Soviet intelligence agents and forwarded to Moscow. When Hoover gave this information—or disinformation— to the White House, it provoked President Nixon into a series of rash and unnecessary actions, such as the formation of his own investigative unit.)

To enable Fedora to convince his superiors in the KGB that he was an effective spy so he would be allowed to return to New York, the FBI provided him with a large number of United States secrets. All the classified documents which were used to "feed" Fedora had to be cleared by the Department of Defense, CIA, Air Force, Army, National Security Agency, and other concerned agencies, and elaborate records had to be kept of the information provided to Moscow. Not only was this an enormously time-consuming process, but it also allowed Fedora to gauge which information he requested was too secret and sensitive to be provided. This was all part of the game of maintaining a double agent.

Fedora, however, had gone out of his way to back up Nosenko's story when he had defected in 1964. If Nosenko was now ruled a fraud, then Fedora would seem to be part of the same Soviet deception. And if Fedora were really under Soviet control, it could bring down the entire FBI counterespionage structure like a house of cards.

The collapse of Nosenko's story could, moreover, force a reopening of the investigation into Oswald's relations with Soviet intelligence prior to the assassination. Hoover knew that the FBI was vulnerable to criticism for not having fully investigated Oswald when he returned from Russia, especially since, as Assistant Director J. H. Gale of the Inspection Division put it, "we did not know definitely whether or not he had any intelligence assignments at that time." Yet Oswald had been allowed to work in a typesetting firm that did highly classified work for the Army Map Service, obtain a second passport and travel freely to Mexico.

Hoover himself had written in a memorandum to senior FBI officials: "There is no question in my mind but that we failed in carrying through some of the most salient aspects of the Oswald investigation." Now, if the CIA pressed for a reinvestigation, all the FBI's omissions and failures in the original security case involving Oswald would be dredged up again. And this would all come at a time when Jim Garrison, the district attorney in New Orleans, was charging in a carnival-like atmosphere of press releases that agencies of the United States government were involved in the conspiracy to assassinate President Kennedy.

Within the CIA there was also bitter opposition to officially labeling Nosenko's story a KGB fabrication. Ever since Stone in 1962 had provided information about Kovshuk's mysterious trip to Washington presumably to contact an important KGB agent in the CIA, Angleton and his counterintelligence staff had sought to find this "mole," or Soviet penetration agent who was suspected of having burrowed his way into the highest levels of United States intelligence. For five years this search for an enemy agent had gone on.

Nosenko, however, had provided an answer to the puzzle of Kovshuk's visit. He had claimed Kovshuk was his immediate superior in the KGB, and therefore, he knew that he had come over to recruit a former army motor mechanic to work for the KGB. According to Nosenko, that was all: there was no mole. If this explanation were accepted, it would serve to end the suspicion of a high-level penetration of the CIA and allow the Soviet Russia Division once again to concentrate its efforts on gathering data about the Soviets. That, at least, was a rationale given for accepting Nosenko.

There was also disagreement within the Soviet Russia Division on how the Nosenko case should be handled. Leonard McCoy, an officer in the Reports Section, protested through unofficial channels the confinement and mistreatment of Nosenko and the suppression of the information he had provided.

At about the same time there began circulating within the CIA an ugly rumor. An officer in the Soviet Russia Division went to the FBI liaison and told him that he suspected the head of the Soviet Russia Division, who had signed the report indicting Nosenko, of himself being a Soviet agent. An investigation quickly revealed this to be a canard without basis, but the fact that it was spread indicated the tensions and suspicions aroused by the Nosenko case.[1]

Helms, who had become Director of Central Intelligence in June 1966, could see that the Nosenko affair could be "explosive." It had to be settled before it got out of hand. Late that summer he ordered his new deputy director, Admiral Rufus Taylor, to take personal charge of the case. "It's all yours," he recalls telling Taylor.

Admiral Taylor, though in the CIA less than a year, knew from his naval experience how to deal with an issue that had the potential for wreaking "enormous damage" on the intelligence services and further rupturing the relationship between the CIA and the FBI. He moved to defuse it before it could explode.

In the months that followed, a series of sudden decisions turned the Nosenko case inside out. The insiders who had developed the indictment against Nosenko were turned out; the outsiders came in. It all happened without warning or explanation.

The reversal began in September 1967, when Nosenko was abruptly transferred from the custody of the CIA's Soviet Russia Division to that of its Office of Security. Since the latter normally handled routine security precautions—such as administering polygraph examinations of CIA employees, searching for electronic eavesdropping devices and policing CIA facilities—but not counterintelligence investigations, the decision to give it control of the Nosenko case was itself extraordinary.

Under the jurisdiction of the Office of Security, Nosenko was no longer to be kept imprisoned or subjected to "hostile interrogation." His new handler, Bruce Solie, a taciturn but supremely patient security officer, already knew Nosenko. He had sat in on a number of the division's interrogation sessions as a representative of the Office of Security (and had never objected to the division's harsh line of questioning). Solie now adopted a considerably friendlier mode of interrogation. Rather than confront Nosenko with contradictions, he reviewed with him the main points of his story that had been controverted and allowed him to work out in retrospect explanations and revisions. In this review he was assisted by FBI agents assigned to the case by J. Edgar Hoover.

In theory, this was supposed to be a tripartite reinvestigation, conducted jointly by the FBI and the CIA's Office of Security and counterintelligence. In fact, however, Bruce Solie of the Office of Security and the FBI agents "spoon-fed" Nosenko plausible answers that neatly fitted all the gaps in his story. At least this was the view of Miler and some others in counterintelligence, who found it impossible to determine what information Nosenko had volunteered and what had been fed to him by the interrogators. At one point, the counterintelligence staff had Stone prepare a long list of questions for Nosenko, but the Office of Security never allowed Nosenko to answer them.

One of the first steps taken by Solie was to impeach the polygraph examination that had, three years earlier, indicated there had been major deceptions in Nosenko's story. This test had originally been administered by his own Office of Security, and there was almost no precedence for the results of such a "fluttering" to be reversed or disqualified after such an extensive length of time. In this case, however, the Office of Security undercut its own test.

While this revision was taking place, the decision was made to transfer some of the CIA officers responsible for the indictment of Nosenko out of Washington to overseas assignments. The head of the Soviet Russia Division, a Russian specialist for more than a decade, and the division's deputy chief, an expert in Soviet counterespionage who had had a major role in interrogating Nosenko and preparing the final report, were reassigned to Europe. Then, for reasons which may or may not have been related to the case, other Soviet specialists—known within the CIA as Slavs—who had helped prepare the case against Nosenko were dispatched to new positions outside the Soviet Russia Division. (Their replacements, for the most part drawn from the Far Eastern and Middle Eastern Division, were not Soviet specialists or even Russian speakers.) It was, as one counterintelligence staff officer put it, "the great purge of the Slavs."

Finally, to settle what issues remained on the case, Admiral Taylor appointed Gordon Stewart as "adjudicator." Stewart, a highly respected officer on the CIA's Board of National Estimates, knew little about the outstanding issues when he began his review in the fall of 1967. (He had met Nosenko once in 1964 in Frankfurt, Germany, when he was in the process of defecting to the United States.) Taylor provided Stewart with a small office adjacent to his own office, though not with a staff or secretary, and suggested he concentrate on the problem of Nosenko's future, rather than his past.

Reading through the division's 900-page report, Stewart found its organization like a prosecuter's brief—"long and tendentious." It seemed to assume right from the beginning that Nosenko was unquestionably a Soviet agent planted on the CIA in Geneva and then interpreted every discrepancy in his story as further evidence of this thesis.

As far as Stewart was concerned, the evidence itself did not ineluctably compel such a categorical conclusion. While recognizing that the Soviet Russia Division had undoubtedly proved through impressive research and cross-checking that many of Nosenko's assertions were blatantly false, Stewart saw no reason to jump to the conclusion that he was an agent dispatched by the Soviets. He reasoned that it was possible for Nosenko to have lied about a whole range of subjects—including his actual position in the KGB and his motive for defecting—and nevertheless be a legitimate defector who simply wanted to escape from Russia. And the omission of details in his story might be accounted for by a faulty memory. The fact that a Soviet agent had confirmed some of the false elements in his story—such as his rank of colonel and his claim to have received a recall telegram—might be no more than a curious coincidence. Stewart then reviewed some of the transcripts of Nosenko's interrogation and decided that they were conducted in an "atmosphere of excitement" that could conceivably have accounted for Nosenko's misunderstanding some of the questions he was asked. In short, Stewart found that the evidence lent itself to more than one interpretation.

In early 1968 Stewart recommended to Admiral Taylor that the CIA proceed to "distance" itself from the Nosenko case. He argued that the Soviet Russia Division had not proved its case against Nosenko, and the fact that Nosenko had not confessed during three years of "hostile interrogation" meant that there probably would never be ironclad proof that he was a Soviet agent. And even if his defection had been arranged by Soviet intelligence, he was now a "burnt-out case"—useless to Moscow. The only viable alternative for the CIA was to provide Nosenko with a new identity and life in the United States and retain him on the CIA's payroll to assure that he would not freely reveal his story.

Meanwhile, the Office of Security, which by now had assumed full charge of the case, received an abridged version of the division's report. Through heavy editing it had been cut by about 500 pages. With assistance from the FBI, Solie wrote his own report, rebutting what was left of the original indictment and completely exonerating Nosenko.

The Solie Report, as it was called, did not even attempt to explain numerous instances in which Nosenko contradicted himself or omitted key facts. Instead, it argued that the substance of the information he provided allowed the FBI to develop important cases against Soviet agents and end espionage operations such as the one at Orly Airport. The report went on to list all the espionage cases that the FBI had developed from Nosenko's revelations.[2] This the Solie Report took as proof of Nosenko's bona fides. It acknowledged that Nosenko had admitted to lies and mistakes but concluded that these proceeded from a personality problem.

Although the report later earned Solie the CIA's intelligence medal, it did not convince those who had originally investigated the case of Nosenko's innocence. The research section of Angleton's counterintelligence staff found it totally lacking in logic. As the head of research subsequently explained, "it glossed over all the real counterintelligence problems, and fallaciously assumed that just because something could have happened, it did happen." Miler put it even more bluntly. He found the Solie Report "nothing more than a whitewash."

The former deputy chief of the Soviet Russia Division also was shown a copy of the Solie Report. He was astonished to find that it did not address the most damning pieces of evidence in his division's report, such as the bogus recall telegram and other demonstrable lies. It also ignored the findings of the division that most of the "substance" Nosenko had given was, from the point of view of Soviet intelligence, either dated information already provided by other defectors or data rendered useless because the agents in question had lost their access to it. Although he submitted a point-by-point rebuttal of the Solie Report, it fell on deaf ears. In fact, it was never even evaluated.

There were now only a few more details to be taken care of in the renaissance of Nosenko. Gordon Stewart, who was promoted to the rank of inspector general of the CIA, flew to Paris and confronted the former head of the Soviet Russia Division with the CIA's new conclusion on Nosenko. Would he agree that the division had mishandled the Nosenko case?

The former head immediately saw the handwriting on the wall. The CIA was closing the Nosenko case. He acquiesced and admitted that in this case he had failed to supervise his subordinates properly. They had been mainly responsible for the interrogation and the indictment.

The responsibility for the case now clearly devolved on the former deputy chief, who had prepared the indictment of Nosenko. The inspector general told him that the division's report suffered from "poor scholarship" and deficiencies in its "methodology." He asked him if he would be willing, in light of the CIA's review, to change his verdict on Nosenko.

The former deputy chief realized that his career in the CIA was probably at stake, but he still found the evidence completely persuasive that Nosenko had fabricated his original position in the KGB, as well as his motive for defecting, and that Soviet intelligence had attempted to verify this fabrication through channels it controlled into United States intelligence. It all still added up to only one conclusion: Nosenko had been sent by the KGB to the United States as a disinformation agent. Remaining adamant, the officer explained that he could not in good conscience acquiesce to any other conclusion, unless shown new evidence. (He left the CIA several years later immediately upon becoming eligible for early retirement.)

Finally, in October 1968, the inspector general held a roundtable meeting of all the elements still involved in the Nosenko case. Included were Richard Helms, Admiral Taylor, Bruce Solie and others from the Office of Security, the new head of the Soviet Russia Division and Angleton's counterintelligence staff. (Angleton himself was in the hospital that day.) The inspector general set forth his finding that the case against Nosenko had not been proved and indeed may have been seriously mishandled. He then proposed that Nosenko be released, resettled somewhere in the United States and treated like any other defector who had chosen the United States over Russia.

Admiral Taylor instantly agreed with this recommendation. It would cost the CIA very little and enabled the agency to avoid the possibility of a very destructive flap. All the others seated around the table nodded their assent—except for the members of the counterintelligence staff. They explained that they were still fully convinced that Nosenko was a disinformation agent. And while they agreed that there was no alternative but to release him, they insisted that all the information received from him in the past, as well as in the future, be labeled "from a source that allegedly had access but whose bona fides are not established."

Although the inspector general appeared visibly angry over the unwillingness of Angleton's staff to award Nosenko his bona fides, he managed to get agreement on how Nosenko was to be "distanced" from the CIA in the immediate future.

Shortly thereafter the Office of Security made arrangements to buy Nosenko a house in North Carolina. He would also receive from the CIA an allowance of about $30,000 a year, employment would be found for him and he would be granted United States citizenship. In return, he would agree not to talk to any unauthorized persons about his experiences with the CIA. His three years of confinement, his indictment for being a messenger from Moscow and the subsequent reversal all were to be a closely held secret.

In the winter of 1969 Yuri Nosenko, under a new name, took up a new life for himself. Sometime later he was married (Solie was the best man at his wedding).

The years passed, but Angleton continued to be intrigued by one aspect of the Nosenko case. In his ongoing interviews with the FBI Nosenko brought up certain cases that he had not mentioned previously. One concerned a KGB officer who had tried to defect to the Americans in the summer of 1959 but failed. In the position that Nosenko claimed to have had in the KGB, he should have been intimately familiar with the details of this particular case, yet he had avoided mentioning it during his initial debriefings. What made this omission seem to Angleton both significant and sinister was that the blank had been filled in by

Nosenko only in 1967 after the Russians had reason to believe that the CIA would have learned about this incident from another source. This suggested the possibility that some Soviet-controlled source was still supplying Nosenko with the answers he was supposed to have to keep his story current. Angleton knew that if such a source existed, it had to be someone in the FBI or CIA or possibly an agent on the outside.[3]

In December 1974 the long tenure of James Jesus Angleton in counterintelligence came to an abrupt end. The proximate cause of his resignation was a front-page story in the New York *Times* by Seymour Hersh which exposed illicit domestic activities of the CIA in the 1960s and named Angleton, whose name had never before appeared in connection with the CIA, as one of those deeply involved.

On December 20, 1974, William Colby, the new Director of Central Intelligence, asked Seymour Hersh to come to his office. Hersh had been concerned, up to that point, with dossiers the CIA had been preparing on Americans as part of "Operation Chaos." Colby assured Hersh that there was nothing illegal in this program, which was done at the explicit request of the President. However, he directed Hersh's attention to the CIA's program of opening mail from the Soviet Union, which he admitted was illegal and which had been supervised by Angleton. Hersh now had an explosive peg for his story.

Colby had opposed the role of the counterintelligence staff for some years. His dispute with Angleton had come into the open when Colby headed the CIA mission to Vietnam in the late 1960s and decided to terminate all counterintelligence activities in that country.[4] This meant, in effect, that the CIA could not question or evaluate the sources of its information in Vietnam. By routinely questioning the validity of information supplied to the CIA by double agents and continually suspecting that the data might be disinformation, Angleton had tended to inhibit the collection of information from the Soviet Union and Eastern Europe. It made the CIA's task of measuring the intentions of the Soviet Union that much more difficult.

After Hersh left his office, Colby called in Angleton and his chief assistants, including Miler, and told them that the New York *Times* would be exposing their mail-opening program. He asked for Angleton's resignation and made it clear to the assistants that they would not be promoted within the CIA. All accommodated him by resigning.

Among those "purged," as Angleton put it, were the authors of the counterintelligence reviews and evaluations of the Nosenko case. And Leonard McCoy, the reports officer who had become one of Nosenko's champions, was appointed the new research head of counterintelligence. Nosenko himself was then appointed a consultant to this newly constituted counterintelligence staff; he also served as a consultant to the FBI (which was still receiving information from Fedora).

A year later John L. Hart, a retired CIA officer, was given the task of writing another report on the Nosenko case. In July 1976 he called on the former deputy chief of the Soviet Russia Division, who had left the CIA four years earlier. Hart casually asked his former colleague if he could give him any cogent reason for not at this time considering that Nosenko's bona fides as a legitimate defector were now fully established.

The former deputy chief, who had devoted a large part of his career to this case, asked Hart if in his reexamination he had read the division's 900-page report.

"No," Hart answered. He had not had the time to return to the original documents.

"How much time will you be spending on the investigation?" he then inquired.

"They want the report in six weeks," Hart answered.

The former deputy chief did not believe that it was possible for anyone to review tapes of years of interrogation sessions with Nosenko and thousands of pages of analysis in only six weeks. Nevertheless, he explained that he would be willing to change his opinion on Nosenko if there were some new evidence confirming his story, such as a more recent defector.

"Were there any such developments?" he asked.

Hart answered that there had been no new evidence.

Then what was his reinvestigation based on? his former colleague asked.

The "prevailing wisdom" was still the Solie Report, Hart replied.

At this point the former deputy chief realized that this was merely another attempt to seal the case shut once and for all. Hart, who had not even read the 900-page indictment against

Nosenko, now wanted an impromptu statement from him on the case. "Why do you have to speak to me?" he shot back. "You already know what you are going to write in your report—Nosenko is innocent. Do what you have to do, but don't count on me to help."

Hart returned to the United States and wrote his report. It concluded that Nosenko had been a genuine defector and that, therefore, the information he had provided about Lee Harvey Oswald's not being involved with Soviet intelligence was valid. In the winter of 1976, twelve years after his defection, Nosenko's bona fides were thus assumed to be established.

In 1977 I spoke to Miler, who had just heard that his handwritten notes on Fedora and Nosenko had been destroyed after he left his office. Although retired, he still evidenced deep concern over the acceptance of Nosenko as a legitimate defector. He explained: "The net result . . . is a travesty. It is an indictment of the CIA and, if the FBI subscribes to it, that Bureau. The ramifications for the U.S. Intelligence community, and specifically and particularly the CIA, are tragic. Acceptance of Nosenko's information as accurate and of him as a reliable and knowledgeable consultant about Soviet intelligence and general affairs will surely cause innumerable problems for incumbent and future estimators, intelligence collectors, and especially, any remaining counterintelligence officers. Acceptance of his information inevitably will cause the acceptance of other suspect sources whose information has dovetailed and supported even Nosenko's proven lies and misinformation. Acceptance of Nosenko throws the entire perspective about Soviet intelligence out of focus."

Finally, I discussed Miler's assessment with the CIA officer who had originally developed the case against Nosenko. He found it "grotesque" that a man who had been judged a Soviet disinformation agent in 1967 would now be a consultant for the CIA. With Nosenko accredited and the counterintelligence staff purged, the CIA had truly been turned inside out.

EPILOGUE III

The Nosenko Incubus (1992)

Two years after the publication of *Legend*, the FBI's reassessment of its star source, Fedora, was leaked to the *Washington Post*. The year-long investigation concluded now that Fedora, rather than having been a genuine agent, had been a dispatched agent, or "dangle," controlled by the KGB, and that the information he had supplied the FBI over a sixteen-year period, including the data that help support Nosenko's story, had been disinformation furnished by the KGB to mislead and confuse American intelligence. If so, it raised the ominous question of why the KGB wanted to make Nosenko—and presumably his account of Oswald—more acceptable to the CIA and the Warren Commission.

This FBI bombshell was part of the blistering internecine war of leaks and counterleaks that had raged on the surface since the Nosenko case had become a public battlefield. At a deeper level, the dispute cut to the very core of the CIA's Cabala of secret knowledge about the Soviet Union and its allies. The lines were intractably drawn. On one side was Angleton and his supporters in counterintelligence. They believed that the KGB was capable of fabricating secrets that so closely mirrored real ones that the fakes could not be separated from the real without an elaborate analysis of the historic context of both the information and the source.

On the other side of the issue were many of the senior CIA and FBI officers who had recruited Soviet spies and had analyzed the secret documents they had passed on. They believed that Soviet intelligence did not have the capacity to deceive them on any sustained basis; and, with rare exceptions, they could winnow out fake sources from real sources. They therefore dismissed the obsessive hunt for false defectors and disinformation as both unnecessary and counterproductive.

The disputation over whether Nosenko was telling the truth or lying about Oswald's activities in the Soviet Union was no more than the outcropping of a subterranean iceberg. Both sides were using it as a means to destroy each other's position.

After simmering in the deep recesses of intelligence agencies for more than a decade, the Nosenko case was reopened in 1977 by the Select Committee on Assassination. By this time the CIA participants had become exceedingly venomous toward one another. In his testimony, John Hart, the latest CIA inquisitor into the affair, accused his predecessors of unprofessionally—and cruelly—mishandling Nosenko. He accused, for example, Tennent Peter Bagley, the former deputy chief of the CIA's Soviet Russia Division (and the main source about Nosenko for my book) of proposing disposing of Nosenko by drugging him and then dumping him in an insane asylum. Bagley, in denying these accusations, accused Hart of systematically falsifying the record of Nosenko.

Even though the committee members were aghast at the CIA's brutal treatment of Nosenko, they still found it difficult to believe his testimony when he appeared before them (now rehabilitated as a consultant to the CIA). After questioning Nosenko in detail about Oswald, they found—as I had two years before—glaring inconsistencies in his basic story. They noted, for example, "Nosenko told the committee that the KGB had Oswald under extensive surveillance, including mail interception, wiretap and physical observation. Yet, in 1964, he told the CIA and FBI there had been no such surveillance." The committee unanimously concluded "it was certain that Nosenko had lied about Oswald."

That Nosenko had been a false witness about Oswald did not necessarily also mean that he had been planted by the KGB to tell the CIA, the FBI, and the Warren Commission that Oswald had no connections to Soviet intelligence. It was still possible that Nosenko had decided to defect to the United States on his own and then fabricated his story about Oswald to enhance his value as a defector.

Whereas initially the case made by the CIA's Soviet Russia Division that Nosenko's defection had been staged by the KGB seemed persuasive to me—especially since it turned out that the KGB had used agents like Fedora to support Nosenko's story—the passage of fifteen years has changed my view of Nosenko. If the KGB had mounted such a complicated operation as a false defection, it seems unlikely that it could be kept so hermetically sealed that no clue to it would leak out with other defectors. Yet, since Nosenko defected in 1964, there have been twenty-one other KGB defectors, and none of them has provided any substantiation to the CIA's original theory that Nosenko's defection was staged. Nor, after twenty-eight years, has Nosenko made any move toward returning to Russia, which might be expected if he had only feigned disloyalty to the KGB.

I now believe that Nosenko was under KGB control only on his first approach to the CIA, in Geneva, in 1962—when, it will be recalled, he delivered to Bagley what turned out to be misleading information about KGB counterintelligence operations. In that brief 1962 encounter, the CIA offered Nosenko an enormous amount of money—over a hundred thousand dollars—for future cooperation, and I believe this CIA offer, not KGB direction, provided Nosenko with the motivation for his 1964 defection. He reasoned, when he returned to dreary office in Moscow, Why not? But when he defected in 1964, on his own account, he was still wedded to the bits of KGB misinformation about his career and operations that he had given to the CIA, and, to override them, and make himself a more important defector, he fabricated the Oswald story. What he had not counted on was that he would become a living test for the theories being debated in the CIA over Soviet deception.

EPILOGUE IV

The Man Who Really Knew Too Much
(1992)

George De Mohrenschildt died from a gunshot wound to his head at 3:45 P.M. on March 29, 1977, in the otherwise empty oceanfront mansion in Palm Beach, Florida, belonging to his friend Nancy Tilton. The precise time of his death was established by a tape recorder left running that afternoon to record the soap operas for the absent Mrs. Tilton, and that recorded the single set of footfalls in the room and the blast of the shotgun found on the Persian carpet next to him. No suicide note or other clue was found.

I may have been the last person to have seen De Mohrenschildt alive. I had been interviewing him at my hotel about his relationship with Lee Harvey Oswald until about one-thirty that afternoon, when he went to the Tilton mansion for lunch. I was expecting him to return at 4:00 P.M. as scheduled—especially since he had asked me to get a photograph for him that he said would prove important. Instead of De Mohrenschildt, a sheriff's deputy arrived, told me what had happened, and drove me and my researcher, Nancy Lanoue, siren screeching, to the office of State Attorney David Bludworth.

Bludworth proved to be a savvy, charming, but relentless interrogator. Repeatedly he asked whether I had in my possession De Mohrenschildt's small black address book. When I replied in the negative, he politely rephrased the question to cover different possibilities. Oddly enough, De Mohrenschildt had accidently left it on the couch when he left for lunch that day but, some ten minutes later, he returned to reclaim it. Had De Mohrenschildt, before retrieving his book, told someone it was missing? And did this now account for the posthumous interest in it?

Gradually the questioning became more relaxed. When I went for a drink with Bludworth, he explained that De Mohrenschildt's sudden death had caused "havoc" in Washington. The House Select Committee on Assassination believed that De Mohrenschildt was a "crucial witness" and, for the past week, had the FBI search for him in three countries. Just that day, after locating him in Palm Beach, the committee had dispatched one of its investigators to subpoena him. Bludworth knew this, he continued, because that investigator's card had been found at the Tilton mansion. Bludworth's theory was that De Mohrenschildt returned from his interview with me, saw the card, realized he was going to have to testify on this subject, and, not being able to face that ordeal, killed himself with the shotgun.

Two FBI agents arrived shortly thereafter at my hotel. They explained that they were piecing together the chronology that had led to the Palm Beach shooting. Just two weeks before he had turned up in Florida, De Mohrenschildt had literally "vanished" from the Hôtel Metropole in Brussels, leaving his luggage, raincoat, and pipe behind in his room—just minutes before he had been scheduled to meet with a Soviet diplomat. After he was reported missing in Belgium, he had reportedly flown from London to New York.

Both FBI men were polite and precise in their questions. They asked me how I had located De Mohrenschildt in Florida.

I explained that, after many futile attempts to interview him for my book, De Mohrenschildt called me in New York earlier that month and proposed that I pay him four thousand dollars for a four-day interview. When I agreed to this "honorarium," he suggested we meet in Palm Beach, and, in the first two meetings we had, I had given him checks totaling two thousand dollars; the balance was to have been paid him on completion of the interviews. After I satisfied them that De Mohrenschildt had not given me any of his personal papers, they left.

They were thus closing the last chapter in the investigation of De Mohrenschildt that had by now spanned almost four decades. Since 1941, when he was expelled from Mexico for subversive activities, the FBI had scrutinized his alleged connections with German, French, British, and Soviet intelligence agencies without yet coming to any final determination of his status. The CIA file—at least the parts of it made available to the Warren Commission—was no more definitive. It noted that De Mohrenschildt had been "security disapproved" for work in U.S. intelligence in 1941 because of his associations with German espionage agents; on April 29, 1963, the agency's security arm had done an otherwise unexplained "expedite check" on his activities.

But what had brought De Mohrenschildt to the screaming attention of the Warren Commission was not his intelligence intrigues but Marina Oswald's testimony that De Mohrenschildt had rushed up the stairs of Oswald's house in April 1963 shouting "Lee, how did you miss General Walker?" just two nights after Oswald had indeed tried to kill General Edwin Walker. She believed then that Oswald had admitted the shooting to no one but her. How did De Mohrenschildt know their dark secret? When questioned about this remark by the commission, De Mohrenschildt shrugged it off as nothing more than an unfortunate coincidence: a "joke" he had made, based on no knowledge whatsoever, on a day that the Walker shooting was headline news in Dallas.

But in Palm Beach, in what was to be his last interview, De Mohrenschildt had told me a much different version of what led to this incident; one that, if believed, would drastically change the picture of his relationship with Oswald and the CIA.

De Mohrenschildt had claimed that morning that he had been dealing with the CIA since the early 1950s. Although he had never been a paid employee of the CIA, he said that he had "on occasion done favors" for government officials who were connected to it. In turn, these same officials had helped in his business contacts overseas. For example, he pointed to a contract awarded to him in 1957 for a survey of the Yugoslav coast. He assumed his "connections" had arranged it for him, and he provided them with reports on the Yugoslav officials in whom they had expressed interest. Such connections were, as he put it, "at the crux" of oil exploration in underdeveloped countries.

In late 1961—De Mohrenschildt could not pinpoint the date— he had a lunchtime meeting in downtown Dallas with one of these connections, J. Walton Moore. After briefly discussing the trip De Mohrenschildt had just returned from in Central America, Moore purposefully steered the conversation in a new direction, the city of Minsk, where, as Moore seemed to know even before he told him, De Mohrenschildt had spent his childhood. Moore then told him about an ex-American Marine who had worked in an electronics factory in Minsk for the past year and in whom there was "interest," since he was returning to the Dallas area. Although no specific requests were made by Moore, De Mohrenschildt gathered that he would be appreciative to learn more about this unusual ex-Marine's activities in Minsk.

In the summer of 1962, De Mohrenschildt heard more about this defector. One of Moore's associates handed him the address of Lee Harvey Oswald in nearby Fort Worth and then suggested that De Mohrenschildt might like to meet him. He added, as if it was an inducement, that this ex-Marine had returned from Minsk with a pretty Soviet wife.

Before finding some pretext to visit this couple, De Mohrenschildt called Moore again and satisfied himself that Oswald was still of interest to the American government. At this time he was extremely busy trying to arrange for "Papa Doc" Duvalier, the Haitian dictator, to approve his oil exploration deal in that country. Some help from the U.S. embassy in Haiti would be greatly appreciated by him, he suggested to Moore. Although he recognized that there was no quid pro quo, he hoped that he might receive the same sort of tacit assistance he had previously received in Yugoslavia. "I would never have contacted Oswald in a million years if Moore had not sanctioned it," he explained to me. "Too much was at stake."

After receiving what he assumed to be the go-ahead, De Mohrenschildt used his own initiative in befriending the Oswalds and conducting an unwitting debriefing—as the procedure is called when the subject does not realize he or she is being debriefed. Since he had been informed that Oswald's wife spoke no English, he choose a time when Oswald was not at home to introduce himself to Marina and converse with her in Russian about his hometown of Minsk. By the time Oswald returned, he had already charmed her, and offered to introduce them both to the Russian community in the Dallas area. Since the Oswalds did not have a car, he offered to chauffeur them around the city.

As he won Oswald's confidence, he not only drew him out about his experiences in Minsk but also, with flattery, encouraged him to write a detailed memoir for publication in a magazine. He also offered to help edit and select photographs for it— an offer that provided him with a plausible reason for continuing to probe Oswald's past. By October 1962, De Mohrenschildt received Oswald's typed draft of the manuscript, which he told Moore about. Soon afterward De Mohrenschildt suspected that government agents had searched his apartment, and he complained about the break-in to Moore.

During that fall De Mohrenschildt also had introduced Oswald to potential employers in the electronics business. He hoped such meetings might stimulate Oswald to discuss his work in the Minsk factory.

Finally, in mid-March 1963, De Mohrenschildt got the lucrative Haitian government contract for which he had been waiting. He did not know to what extent, if any, he had been helped by his American connections, but he assumed that they had been appreciative. He had, by this time, become a much closer confidant of Oswald than even he realized.

In early April, Marina delivered a memento from Oswald: an inscribed photograph showing Oswald dressed in black, holding, in one hand, the radical newspaper the *Militant* and, in the other, the sniper's rifle with the telescopic sight that he had shown De Mohrenschildt the week before. The photograph was signed "For George, Lee Harvey Oswald" and dated April 5, 1963. Marina had derisively scribbled in Russian "Hunter of Fascists. Ha. Ha"—a comment that became less of a joke on April 10, when De Mohrenschildt heard on the radio that a sniper had fired a shot at General Walker. Only a few weeks before, in the company of three young geologists, De Mohrenschildt recalled that he had heard Oswald single out Walker as a "fascist" who should be dealt with, and, when one of the geologists egged him on by talking of an assassination plot against Hitler, Oswald answered that Hitler should have been shot before he ever achieved power. De Mohrenschildt thus had a "pretty good suspicion who had taken the potshot" at Walker. He immediately rushed over to Oswald's house to find out what had happened and if Oswald had disposed of the rifle. He feared that he could be implicated in the ensuing scandal—as well as those geologists who had egged Oswald on about Walker (and who also might have received the "Hunter of Fascists" photograph). With his Haitian contract at risk, that night was the last time he ever saw Oswald.

I asked him whether he had reported the Walker incident— and the telltale photograph—to Moore. He said, after a long, almost painful, hesitation, "I spoke to the CIA both before and afterward. It was what ruined me."

De Mohrenschildt offered to make the photograph available to me through his lawyer, Pat Russell—who would arrange the transaction.

There was, however, a serious problem with his story. Why had De Mohrenschildt not turned over this evidence to the FBI when he was questioned, or to the Warren Commission when he testified? Concealing such evidence could be a crime, especially since it could have shown that De Mohrenschildt and others had prior knowledge about Oswald's assassination potential.

At this juncture, De Mohrenschildt claimed he had not remembered receiving this photograph when he testified before the Warren Commission. Although Marina must have given him the photograph before the Walker shooting—she would not have written the "Hunter of fascists" joke afterward—he maintained that it got mislaid when he packed to leave for Haiti (the week after the Walker shooting) and that he did not rediscover it until he returned from Haiti in 1967.

Not only did I find this explanation self-serving—his prior failure to tell the FBI about the photograph could be construed as a possible obstruction of justice—but also it turned out to be untrue. Two of De Mohrenschildt's friends told me that he had discussed the photograph, and the problems it raised for him, before he returned from Haiti, and Marina Oswald subsequently testified that she had seen the photograph in De Mohrenschildt's house in 1963 and she recalled being "surprised" that Oswald had given him such an incriminating memento. De Mohrenschildt had promised to provide a fuller explanation for the photograph when he returned that afternoon—but he never would.

After De Mohrenschildt's death, I received the photograph from his lawyer. It was another copy of the celebrated backyard photographs that appeared in the Warren Commission report. Handwriting experts identified both the dating and the inscription as Oswald's writing but were less positive about the printing in Russian on the reverse side, concluding only that it was consistent with but not necessarily Marina's handwriting. Even so, the fact that Oswald gave this photograph to De Mohrenschildt before the Walker shooting—and showed him his rifle—demonstrated that De Mohrenschildt had succeeded in becoming his trusted confidant.

But it did not answer the key question of whether De Mohrenschildt had achieved this proximity, as he claimed in the last interview of his life, at the behest of the CIA. It was also possible that De Mohrenschildt was dragging the CIA into his relation with Oswald as a red herring to divert from his own guilt in not reporting the Walker shooting—or from some more sinister connection he had. I therefore could not accept De Mohrenschildt's story without serious confirmation, which was not to be forthcoming.

To be sure, part of his story fit the established facts. J. Walton Moore was indeed in the CIA's Domestic Contact Service in Dallas, and he had responsibility for debriefing returning visitors from the Soviet Union who had potential intelligence of value. Further, according to a memorandum given to the Warren Commission, after the CIA had been advised that Oswald was returning to the Dallas area in the summer of 1961, it placed a lookout card in his file. At about this time, one CIA staffer suggested that Oswald and his wife be debriefed through the Domestic Contact Service when they returned—but apparently no action was taken on this request.

Moore definitely knew De Mohrenschildt. He had debriefed him in 1958 on his work in Yugoslavia and, according to CIA records, had disseminated the resulting reports to ten government agencies. But there was no indication in these documents that Moore had been in touch with De Mohrenschildt after Oswald had returned to Dallas in 1962. The CIA director at the time, John McCone, testified that no one in the CIA had ever contacted Oswald, interviewed him, talked with him, or "solicited any reports or information from him." The CIA denied, moreover, that it had had any relationship whatsoever with De Mohrenschildt during the time Oswald was in Dallas. Confronted with this apparent stone wall, I sent the CIA the following nine series of questions:

1. George Sergius De Mohrenschildt told me in an interview a few hours before he committed suicide in 1977 that he had been encouraged to maintain his contacts with Lee Harvey Oswald by J. Walton Moore, an employee of the Domestic Contact Service in Dallas in 1962. Did De Mohrenschildt, in fact, discuss Oswald with Moore? If so, was it for the purpose of gaining information for the CIA? Did the CIA's inspector general or other investigative element conduct an investigation into the Dallas office of the Domestic Contact Service to ascertain whether there were any direct or indirect contacts with Oswald?

2. De Mohrenschildt also gave sworn testimony to the Warren Commission that he had talked to Moore about Oswald. Was Moore asked to confirm or deny these charges? If he controverted them, was the Warren Commission (or the Department of Justice) informed of the fact that De Mohrenschildt might be committing perjury?

3. According to CIA document 431-154B, obtained under a Freedom of Information action in 1976, the Office of Security of the CIA was requested by a CIA case officer to perform an "expedite check" on De Mohrenschildt, which

it furnished on April 29, 1963. Is it common for the CIA to request an "expedite check" on a U.S. citizen still residing in the United States? If not, what were the circumstances requiring a check of De Mohrenschildt? Was he an employee at any time of the CIA? Was he suspected of being involved in espionage activities?

4. Was the "expedite check" of De Mohrenschildt requested by another agency? If so, which one? If it originated within the CIA, which division was the case officer who requested it from?

5. Does the fact that it was an "expedite check" mean that some urgency was attached to the request? If so, why was the information needed immediately in April 1963?

6. Oswald left Dallas for New Orleans at about the time the "expedite check" was requested (April 25, 1963). Was the "check" by a case officer in any way connected with the movements or activities of Oswald?

7. In a CIA memorandum written on November 25, 1963, a CIA staff employee reports that he had suggested that Oswald be interviewed on his return from Russia by the Domestic Contact Service or "other suitable channel" so as to provide possible data for the biographic and foreign personality dossiers that the CIA maintains. Was this request ever forwarded to the Domestic Contact Service? If so, which field office? Was Oswald contacted? If not, why not? Was he considered hostile or possibly in the employ of another intelligence service?

8. If Oswald was not contacted because he was considered "hostile," what other "suitable channels" were considered? Were any surreptitious means used? Was any individual asked to speak to Oswald about his experiences in the Soviet Union?

9. In October 1962, De Mohrenschildt claims that he complained to J. Walton Moore about papers in his home being surreptitiously photographed. Is there a record of such a complaint? He suggests that the intrusion took place at a time when he had Oswald's account of his experiences in a factory in Minsk in his home. Did the complaint, if it, in fact, was made, involve Oswald's account?

The CIA response was, "We have reviewed your questions carefully and determined that they do not constitute a request for reasonably described records as prescribed in the Freedom of Information Act." So I published *Legend* in 1977 without giving credence to De Mohrenschildt's story (although I included the CIA's unanswered interrogatives in the appendix).

But, it turned out, I had given up too soon. In early 1978, investigators for the House Select Committee on Assassination managed to gain unprecedented access to the CIA's 144-volume file on Oswald and permission to interview the CIA personnel who had been involved in the CIA's debriefing apparatus in the early 1960s. When the committee published its report in July 1979, it contained three disclosures from the CIA's convoluted archives that, while attracting little interest elsewhere, surprisingly corroborated at least part of De Mohrenschildt's unpublished story. First, although Moore had previously "recalled" meeting De Mohrenschildt only twice in his life—once in 1958 and once in 1961—the documents found in De Mohrenschildt's CIA file showed that there was far "more contact between Moore and De Mohrenschildt than was stated." In fact, they revealed that Moore had interviewed him numerous times over a course of years and prepared reports based on this information. Moore himself testified that he had "periodic" contact with De Mohrenschildt for "debriefing purposes" and, although maintaining he could not recall any discussion about Oswald, acknowledged that these contacts may have extended to 1962.

The second disclosure was an entry in De Mohrenschildt's CIA file showing that he met with CIA staff officer Tony Czaikowski in Washington, D.C., on May 7, 1963. The meeting was arranged by another CIA liaison, Sam Kail, who indicated that De Mohrenschildt's partner Clemard Joseph Charles—a key adviser to Haitian president "Papa Doc" Duvalier—might prove useful in ongoing efforts aimed at overthrowing Castro in Cuba, code-named Operation Mongoose. At Kail's suggestion, Dorothe Matlack, the liaison between U.S. Army intelligence and the CIA, went to the meeting to assess Clemard Charles's potential value. When Charles arrived with De Mohrenschildt, Charles appeared to Matlack to be "dominated" by De Mohrenschildt, she later testified. And although subsequently the CIA became "the prime contact" for Charles, Matlack was concerned enough about De Mohrenschildt's role to request the FBI to look into him. This testimony confirmed that De Mohrenschildt, as he had claimed, had brought his Haitian project—and Haitian partner—to the attention of the CIA, and that indeed he had been in contact with the CIA after as well as before the Walker shooting.

The third disclosure, if accurate, was the smoking gun. It came from a well-respected CIA analyst who, in 1962, had been in the Soviet branch of the Foreign Document Division of the CIA's Directorate of Intelligence, which was the unit in the CIA that pieced together information gleaned from various sources on Soviet economic, technological, and scientific developments. In the summer of 1962 he clearly remembered data coming in from a CIA field office on the operations of the Minsk electronics factory in the form of "contact reports." He recalled that these reports had been based on the experiences of a U.S. ex-Marine who had worked at the Minsk plant after his defection to the Soviet Union. Since there was only one ex-Marine who had worked in this particular Minsk factory, the source of this information had to be Lee Harvey Oswald.

Since Oswald himself had not been openly debriefed by the CIA, as the committee established, the technical details in the "contact reports" that the local field office were relaying to the analyst in the CIA's Foreign Document Division had to be coming from an intermediary. Presumably this "contact" had begun eliciting data from Oswald in the summer of 1962.

This timetable closely dovetailed with De Mohrenschildt's story. De Mohrenschildt not only had access to Oswald and Marina during this period but also had borrowed from Oswald his memoir that described his work in the electronics factory.

The analyst's revelation had, however, far more reaching implications. If his memory was accurate—and Oswald had been debriefed—what had happened to these contact reports and all the routing slips that went with them between Dallas and Washington? Since the committee's investigators found no trace of them, they would have had to have been systematically purged from the files. But why would the CIA, which in those days legally debriefed some twenty-five thousand U.S. citizens a year through its Domestic Contact Service, go to such dangerous lengths to conceal this debriefing?

I was particularly intrigued by the April 25, 1963, request made to the CIA's Office of Security, which is the CIA's internal police force, for an "expedite check" on De Mohrenschildt, which it completed on April 29. Eight days later, the FBI was requested by its liaison with Army intelligence to investigate De Mohrenschildt, but according to Army intelligence, the FBI took "no action." Why had the CIA's Office of Security but not the FBI handled the De Mohrenschildt investigation?

I took this apparent conundrum to an ex-CIA executive who had been part of the CIA's liaison with the FBI in 1963. He said he would talk only about "standard procedures"—not De Mohrenschildt. He then dryly explained, as if he were outlining nothing more than an organizational chart, that investigations in the United States of individuals who were not CIA personnel —and De Mohrenschildt presumably was not a CIA employee— were routinely turned over through the CIA liaison office to the FBI. This procedure was followed in almost all internal security cases because the CIA was prohibited by law from operating in the United States. The only exception occurred when the CIA had an important "proprietary relationship" whose cover would be endangered by a non-CIA inquiry. In this exception to the rule, the Office of Security could investigate an individual involved, even if he was an American.

He suggested that De Mohrenschildt might have had some kind of "proprietary relationship" with the CIA. Such a business arrangement would also explain De Mohrenschildt's motive in spending a considerable amount of his time befriending a penniless returnee from the Soviet Union. But if so, something had happened within this arrangement that brought De Mohrenschildt rushing from Dallas to Washington, D.C., in April 1963 and threatened its security enough to justify the intervention of the CIA's Office of Security.

In early 1981 I went to Port-au-Prince to find out more about De Mohrenschildt's venture, the "Haitian Holding Company" in which, on paper, at least, he and Clemard Charles were partners. Although De Mohrenschildt's company had received a $285,000 contract for a geological survey of potential petroleum reserves in Haiti, he never actually even began the mapping, according to his former associates in Haiti. Nor did he spend any time on the other side of the island managing the derelict sisal plantation that supposedly provided his income during his years in Haiti. He rarely even visited it. Instead, he resided in a lavish home in the same heavily guarded compound as the Haitian dictator and his top generals.

As far as friends of his in Haiti could discern, De Mohrenschildt did not engage in any conventional business activities. At best he appeared to be in a "holding pattern," as one put it. While there were many different theories about his protracted stay in the presidential compound (these included intrigues ranging from smuggling arms to organizing subversion), there was only one observable fact: De Mohrenschildt's tight liaison with Clemard Charles.

CIA interest in Clemard Charles had extended back at least to the early 1960s, when, according to one committee witness, it reportedly "planted" a secretary on him. He was not only the president of the Banque Commerciale d'Haiti—which handled most of the nation's international transactions—but also President Duvalier's principal distributor of largess to American politicians. And President Duvalier had become one of the CIA's secret logistical allies in its clandestine war against Castro—at least until 1964, when these anti-Castro operations were ended.

In any case, De Mohrenschildt's fortunes in Haiti seemed inexorably tied to those of Clemard Charles. Beginning in 1963, sums of money were periodically deposited in De Mohrenschildt's bank account, according to one of De Mohrenschildt's close associates at the Banque Commercial. Most of these deposits were relatively small, came from another Haitian account, and represented "dividends" from the sisal plantation. But there were also several large deposits—one of which exceeded two hundred thousand dollars in late 1963—that came from a Bahamian bank. These deposits stopped shortly before Clemard Charles left Haiti. Soon afterward, in 1967, De Mohrenschildt returned to Dallas (where a teaching position at Bishop College awaited him), and the Haitian Holding Company was dissolved.

Although these posthumous investigations had not filled in all the gaps in the De Mohrenschildt story, the new pieces that emerged from them substantially changed my view of De Mohrenschildt's preassassination activities—and sponsors. I concluded the following:

1. De Mohrenschildt's sole business activity in 1962 was the Haitian venture he was negotiating with Clemard Charles. He had staked everything he had on it. To bring it to fruition, he assumed that he needed help from the U.S. government, and he actively sought it among his contacts in Dallas.

2. Under these circumstances, De Mohrenschildt would not have associated for months with Oswald without sanction from the officials whose favor he desperately needed. He would not have jeopardized the contract he had been working on for two years by openly shepherding around Dallas a malcontented, dishonorably discharged Marine whose claim to fame was betraying his country and who had been deemed "hostile" by the local FBI because he had refused to cooperate by answering its questions—unless, as De Mohrenschildt claimed, this liaison was approved. On the contrary, De Mohrenschildt, who had always been an opportunist, would have only sought out Oswald, and methodically elicited from him the answers he had refused to yield to FBI because he believed it would help him with his government connections.

3. De Mohrenschildt was Oswald's debriefer. He had the language skills and prior intelligence-collection experience, and he had access to Oswald, Marina, and Oswald's typescript. He was the intermediary through which the CIA's Foreign Document Division derived its data about Oswald's work in the Minsk electronics factory. And he continued drawing out Oswald until sometime in April 1963.

4. De Mohrenschildt knew by April 12, 1963—if not before—that Oswald had attempted to assassinate General Walker. He had seen Oswald's sniper rifle. He had heard Oswald make rabid threats against Walker. He had received the signed photograph of Oswald displaying his weapons. He had seen Oswald react when questioned on the subject forty-eight hours after the shooting. Such prior knowledge, which could have enmired him in a police investigation— even made him a suspect—and which, if it became public, could endanger his Haitian venture, caused him to panic. He broke off relations with Oswald and headed for Washington, D.C.

5. De Mohrenschildt took some unexpected action in mid-April, such as disclosing something that the CIA was unprepared to hear and that caused warning bells to go off in the CIA. This disturbance precipitated the Office of Security's "expedite check." It also, in De Mohrenschildt's view, "ruined" him.

6. Whatever De Mohrenschildt might have said that April about Oswald, Walker, Haiti, or other matters, the contact reports that cover that period do not exist in his CIA files. If they ever existed, they were purged after the assassination. De Mohrenschildt was evidently the man who knew too much.

EPILOGUE V

JFK: *The Second Coming of Jim Garrison* (*1992*)

More than a century before the advent of the Hollywood pseudodocumentary, Karl Marx suggested that all great events and personalities in world history happen twice: "the first time as tragedy, the second as farce." Oliver Stone's film *JFK* is a case in point.

In 1969, when Jim Garrison's Conspiracy-to-kill-Kennedy trial collapsed, his entire case that the accused, Clay Shaw, had participated in an assassination plot turned out to be based on nothing more than the hypnotically induced story of a single witness. This witness, Perry Raymond Russo, had testified that he had had no conscious memory of his own conspiracy story before he had been drugged, hypnotized, and fed hypothetical circumstances by the district attorney about the plot he was

supposed to have witnessed. To the dismay of his supporters—
and even three of Garrison's staff resigned—this was the es-
sence of Garrison's show trial: a witness who acknowledged he
could not, after this bizarre treatment, separate fantasy from
reality. After that, Garrison's meretricious prosecution of it was
considered by the press to be, as *The New York Times* noted in an
editorial, "one of the most disgraceful chapters in the history of
American jurisprudence." In this debacle, Garrison himself was
exposed as a man who had recklessly disregarded the truth
when it suited his purposes.

Then, in 1991, a generation later, Garrison reemerges
phoenixlike from the debris as the truth-seeking prosecutor
(played by Kevin Costner) in the film *JFK*—and who brilliantly
solves the mystery of the Kennedy assassination. In this version,
there is no hypnosis: The reborn Garrison resourcefully uncov-
ers cogent evidence that Clay Shaw planned the Dallas ambush
of President Kennedy in New Orleans with two confederates:
David William Ferrie (played by Joe Pesci), a homosexual soldier of fortune, and Lee Harvey Oswald (played by Gary Old-
man). Garrison establishes that this trio, who also participate
together in orgies, all worked for the CIA, and were recruited
into a conspiracy to seize power in Washington.

Filmed in a grainy semidocumentary style, with newsreels as
well as amateur footage incorporated into it, *JFK* purports to
reveal the actual truth about the Kennedy assassination. From
the moment it was released, its director, Oliver Stone, has so
passionately defended its factual accuracy that he became, for
all practical purposes, the new Garrison. What could be more
appropriate in the age of media than a crusading filmmaker
replacing a crusading district attorney as the symbol of the
truth-finder in society? In this capacity, Oliver Stone-Garrison
played out his case on television news programs, talk shows,
magazines, and the op-ed pages of newspapers. He held his own
press conferences, with his attractive researcher at his side, met
with congressional leaders, and he, as the original Garrison had
done a quarter of a century before, used this public platform to
focus attention on the possibility that the government was hiding the truth about the Kennedy assassination. In exploiting this
torment of secrecy, Stone proved far more successful than his

predecessor in rousing interest in releasing the classified files pertaining to the assassination.

But where Jim Garrison failed in building a plausible conspiracy case against Clay Shaw, how did Oliver Stone succeed? The answer is that whereas the original Garrison only attempted to coax, intimidate, and hypnotize witnesses into providing him with incriminating evidence, the new Garrison, Oliver Stone, fabricated for his film the crucial evidence and witnesses that were missing in real life—even when this license required deliberately falsifying reality and depicting events that never happened. Consider, for example, the way he fabricated Ferrie's dramatic confession to Garrison in a hotel room only hours before he died.

In reality, as well as in Jim Garrison's account of the case, David Ferrie steadfastly maintained his innocence, insisting he did not know Lee Harvey Oswald, he was not in the CIA, and that he had no knowledge of any plot to kill Kennedy. The last known person to speak to Ferrie was George Lardner, Jr., of the *Washington Post*, whom Ferrie had met with from midnight to 4:00 A.M. on February 22, 1967. During this interview, Ferrie described Garrison (whom he hadn't seen for weeks) as "a joke." Several hours later, Ferrie died of a cerebral hemorrhage.

In *JFK*, Oliver Stone invents, and falsifies, his own version of Ferrie's last night. Instead of being calmly interviewed by a reporter in his home, *JFK* shows a panicked Ferrie being doggedly interrogated by Jim Garrison in a hotel suite until he finally breaks down and confesses. Ferrie names his CIA controller and, in rapid-fire succession, admits in the film everything he denied in real life. He acknowledges that he taught Oswald "everything." He then explains that not only does he know Clay Shaw but also that he is being blackmailed by him and controlled by him. He also admits that he works for the CIA—along with Oswald, Shaw, and "the Cubans," who were the "shooters" in Dallas. He displays intimate knowledge of the plot by explaining that the "shooters" were recruited without being told whose orders they were carrying out. He tells Garrison that the plot is "too big" to be investigated, implying that powerful figures are behind it, and that, because they know Ferrie is now talking, they have issued a "death warrant" for him.

After Ferrie leaves Garrison and returns to his apartment, he is shown being chased, held down, and murdered by a bald-headed man who forces pills down his throat. The murderer is shown in other fictional scenes as an associate of Shaw, Oswald, and the anti-Castro Cuban shooters. When Garrison arrives at the murder scene and finds the empty bottle of pills, he concludes Ferrie was murdered, which gives Ferrie's earlier revelations to Garrison the force of a deathbed confession. (In reality, the coroner ruled that Ferrie had died from "natural causes"—a verdict that Garrison, as the empowered authority, did not contest.)

Oliver Stone's transformations in this scene, as seen in Table I, involve more than some trivial cinematic contrivances. They provide the critical linkage for the conspiracy. Ferrie's confession connects the team of anonymous Cuban "shooters" in Dallas with Clay Shaw, David Ferrie, and Lee Harvey Oswald in New Orleans and, at a higher level, the CIA "untouchables." It changes the entire story—just as it would change the story about the execution of Julius and Ethel Rosenberg if film fabricated a fictional scene showing the Rosenbergs confessing to J. Edgar Hoover that they were part a Communist conspiracy to steal atomic secrets.

Table I

Ferrie's Last Interview, February 22, 1967

	In Actuality	In *JFK*
Ferrie is:	At home, relaxed.	In Hotel suite, in panic.
With:	Reporter Lardner.	D.A. Garrison.
Ferrie:	1) Denies knowing Oswald.	1) Admits training Oswald.
	2) Never mentions Shaw.	2) Admits Shaw controls him.
	3) Denies he is in CIA.	3) Admits being in CIA.
	4) Denies knowing of plot.	4) Describes plot details.

		Says Oswald, Shaw are CIA.
		Talks of Cuban Shooters.
Death:	Ruled natural	Ferrie shown murdered by Cuban associate of Shaw's.

Ferrie's false confessions are not isolated bits of license. Throughout *JFK*, in dozens of scenes, Oliver Stone substitutes fiction for fact when it advances his case. He even blatantly contradicts the two books he represents as being the bases for *JFK*.* He makes especially effective use of this substitution technique when it comes to witnesses. Here, like all fictionalizers, he has an advantage over fact-finders: He can artfully fashion his replacement witnesses to meet the audience's criteria for what is credible. His substitution of the fictional "Willie O'Keefe" to replace Garrison's flawed witness, Perry Raymond Russo, is a case in point.

Russo, it will be recalled, was Garrison's sole witness to the alleged plot that was planned in Ferrie's apartment. But his credibility suffered from three problems.

First, there was the memory lapse. Russo did not tell his incriminating story until four years after the assassination and then only after he had been rendered semiconscious by sodium pentothal and instructed by a hypnotist to imagine he is watching an important discussion "about assassinating someone."

Second, there were the inconsistent identifications. According to the statement of his first interrogation, Russo, when shown photographs of Shaw, said that he had seen him from afar—but never met the man. Subsequently he changed his story to say he had met him at Ferrie's apartment. One week later he told a homicide officer he was not sure the man he met was Shaw.

Third, there was the misidentification of Oswald. Russo claimed the man introduced to him as "Leon Oswald" had a beard in September 1963 and was Ferrie's roommate. Oswald

---

* Jim Garrison, *On the Trail of the Assassins* (New York: Warner Books, 1988), and James Marrs, *Crossfire: The Plot That Killed Kennedy* (New York: Carroll & Graf, 1990).

was clean-shaven at that time, and Marina's roommate (Ferrie's roommate, at the time, did have a beard).

While Garrison was stuck with this contradictory testimony, Oliver Stone was not. He simply substituted for Russo the fictional character "Willie O'Keefe" (played by Kevin Bacon), who had none of the real witness's deficiencies.

Unlike Russo, a heterosexual with no plausible access to Shaw's secret life, his replacement, O'Keefe is fashioned as a handsome male prostitute who has been Shaw's homosexual lover and drug partner for over a year. Moreover, he is given the political persona of a neo-Nazi and Kennedy-hater—a political stance that more plausibly might allow him to be privy to a discussion as sensitive as the assassination plan. And, unlike Russo, who only popped up after Ferrie's death-seeking publicity on local television, O'Keefe contacts Garrison before Ferrie's death—and before Garrison's investigation has even become public—from state prison. He is serving time for prostitution, and he offers to cooperate with Garrison (whom he also physically admires) because "he has nothing to lose" and presumably because it might lead to a reduced prison sentence.

Unlike the real witness, O'Keefe displays no memory lapses requiring drug or hypnotic "objectification." He voluntarily relates a coherent story: Ferrie first introduced him to Shaw in the summer of 1962; Shaw immediately hired him to participate in elaborate orgies with him and Ferrie. In the course of this relationship, he met Shaw's associates, including Oswald, whom he has no problem identifying as beardless, and the anti-Castro Cuban mercenaries (including one bald one, who murders Ferrie). At one late-night meeting in Ferrie's apartment, after the Cubans depart, Ferrie, Oswald, and Shaw discuss the plan for killing Kennedy, including the "cross fire" and "triangulation of fire."

The fictional O'Keefe's story is supported by Ferrie's fictional confession, which is then given weight by Ferrie's fictional murder by the fictional bald-headed Cuban introduced in O'Keefe's story. Since Oliver Stone's audience is not apprised of the substitutions of fiction for fact, this cross-corroboration makes the New Orleans plot plausible to it.

The New Orleans conspiracy remained a relatively low-level one, involving homosexuals, anti-Castro Cuban killers, Oswald, and CIA employees. To link it to the central coup d'état in Washington, D.C., Oliver Stone resorts to a deus ex machina: a fictional meeting Garrison has with a deep-throat-style anonymous source, who identified himself only as "X."

"X" is a cynical man of military bearing (played by Donald Sutherland). He meets Garrison in late February 1967, just after Ferrie's death, on the steps of the Lincoln Memorial in Washington, D.C. When asked by Garrison whether he is with the CIA, "X" refuses to identify the agency he represents but tells Garrison he is "close, you do not know how close."

After describing the Warren Commission report as "fiction," "X" launches into a remarkable fifteen-minute exposition of the assassination. He discloses that Kennedy was "executed by a device as old as the crucifixion—a military firing squad." It was not some low-level plot but a full-blown "coup d'état," with "Lyndon Johnson waiting in the wings." Its purpose was to prevent Kennedy from withdrawing from Vietnam and ending the Cold War with the Soviet Union. Since the military-industrial complex could not afford to lose this war threat—"one hundred billion dollars" in war contracts was at stake—it ordered the assassination. The secret team of generals and officials who carried out this coup also arranged the "cover story" that framed Oswald as the lone assassin and sabotaged the telephone system in Washington, D.C., after the assassination so no news would leak out. "Nothing was left to chance," X adds.

"X" explains that two weeks before President Kennedy was due to arrive in Dallas, X's superior, "General Y," ordered him to accompany a group of officials on a trip to the South Pole. If he hadn't been sent away, he would have had the "routine duty" of arranging "additional security" for the president in Dallas—which would have made the assassination impossible. When he returned and realized what had happened, he deduced that there could be only one reason for "Y" sending him away at this critical time: to prevent him from interfering with the assassination plan in Dallas. X tells Garrison he cannot publicly reveal these secrets, because, before he could testify, he would be "gagged, arrested, and put in an insane asylum," but he urges him to "make arrests" anyhow. With the New Orleans conspiracy now connected to the Washington conspiracy, Garrison returns to New Orleans and arrests Clay Shaw.

Garrison, in reality, had not met such a source. Rather than going to Washington, D.C., he spent the week between Ferrie's death and Shaw's arrest filling in the lapsed memory of the new witness, Russo (with the help of sodium pentothal). Even though the original Garrison never met "X," Oliver Stone, the new Garrison, not only found "X" but also retained him as his technical adviser for *JFK*. This super source, whose story was anachronistically slipped into the old Garrison's case, is Colonel Leroy Fletcher Prouty. Before his retirement from the Air Force in December 1963, Colonel Prouty had worked in the Pentagon in the Office of Special Operations—which provided planes and other equipment for covert activities. In November 1963, Prouty had been sent to the South Pole at the time of the assassination, but here the similarity between the real and the fictional "X" ends.

Unlike the character in the film, Prouty's duties did not include providing "additional security" for the president's motorcades, according to the Secret Service (which did have that responsibility).*He was not even a liaison with the Secret Service.

Aside from advising Oliver Stone, Prouty is also extremely active with other conspiracy-hunters. He served, for example, as editorial adviser to publications of the futuristic Church of Scientology; as a consultant to the far right Lyndon LaRouche

---

* In his own writings—"The Anatomy of Assassination" in *Uncloaking the CIA*, ed. Howard Frazier (New York: The Free Press, 1978)—Prouty bases this allegation that the president's security was withdrawn not on any personal knowledge (he does not claim here any responsibility for presidential security) but on the failure of the Secret Service to make sure, as is required by its "manual," that all windows on the parade route be sealed, to post countersniper teams on the roofs, and to maintain the speed of the president's car at "44 miles per hour." In fact, however, these procedures were not required by the manual of the Service, the CIA, or the Air Force Military Police. Nor was there anything mysterious about Prouty's November assignment: He had applied for retirement in the summer of 1963 and, while his paperwork was being processed, he had been detached to various temporary duties, including this lark to the antipodes. "X"'s logic that there was a connection between this preretirement trip and the events in Dallas has no apparent basis in reality.

Prouty did demonstrate, however, a penchant for claiming participation in historic events. For example, he puts himself at the Roosevelt-Stalin-Churchill summit in Teheran in 1943 (Churchill at some point revealed to him that the world was ruled by a "high cabal"); at Yale, when George Bush learned "everything he knew" about machinations of the oil cartel; at the surrender of Japan in 1945, where he personally witnessed U.S. intelligence lay the basis of two future wars by covertly shipping "the largest arm cache in history" to North Vietnam and Korea; at the Bay of Pigs in 1961, where he personally procured CIA ships that were renamed after George Bush's wife *Barbara*, George Bush's oil company *Zapata*, and George Bush's residence *Houston*; and in Vietnam, where he reported on "a CIA clandestine operation that got out of hand."

Organization, who also provided its convention with a presentation comparing the U.S. government's prosecution of Lyndon LaRouche (for mail fraud) "to the persecution of Socrates"; a board member of the Populist Action Committee, where he joined Robert Weems, a former leader of the Ku Klux Klan, and John Rarick, the organizer of the White Citizens Council; and as a featured speaker for the anti-civil rights organization called the Liberty Lobby, whose founder, Willis Carto, also set up the Institute for Historic Review, a disseminator of books and videotapes that allege that the Nazi death camps in Europe were fictions devised by Zionist propaganda to justify tax money being donated to Israel. (It also published Prouty's own book, *The Secret Team: The CIA and Its Allies in Control of the United States and the World.)*

Prouty also exposed the machinations of putative global conspiracies. For example, when the Liberty Lobby held its annual Board of Policy Convention in 1991, he presented a special seminar, "Who Is the Enemy?," which blamed the high price of oil on a systematic plot of a cabal to shut down oil pipelines deliberately in the Middle East. "Why?" he asked, and explained to the seminar: "Because of the Israelis. That is their business on behalf of the oil companies. That's why they get $3 billion a year from the U.S. taxpayer." His enemy list also included the CIA, usurers, school textbooks, the media, political parties, international banks, federal crises-planning exercises, and the U.S.-Soviet Trade and Economic Council (which, according to Prouty, had stage-managed, along with David Rockefeller, the liquidation of the Berlin Wall to profit from "the rubles and the gold").

So this is the intellectual provenance of the man Oliver Stone chose as his technical adviser—and the man called "X." In *JFK*, X displays secret knowledge about the ultimate conspiracy behind the Kennedy assassination when he tells Garrison that the "who" and the "how" of the shooting are "just scenery" to hide the "why." The "why," in turn, proceeds from the unbreakable rule of the power elite that "the organizing principle of any society is for war." Because Kennedy violated this precept by taking steps to end the war, he had to die.

Prouty/X's secret knowledge about the elite's organizing principle and the "war system" derives from a very special source— a suppressed Kennedy administration study, which he discussed in the Liberty Lobby's Radio Free America on December 14, 1989. He explained then that this study was so secret that the group of "power brokers" who conducted it met, according to Prouty, "in an underground storage and security area" in the Hudson Valley of New York called "Iron Mountain." The explosive issue they addressed was: Could America survive "if and when a condition of permanent peace should arise"? Their conclusion, which "X" would echo almost word for word in the film *JFK* two years later, was "the organization of society for the possibility of war is its principal political stabilizer"; without a believable war threat "no government could remain in power," and consequently "the elimination of war . . . implies the eventual elimination of national sovereignty." He explains on this radio program and in a subsequent issue of *Spotlight*, the newspaper of the Liberty Lobby, that these conclusions come directly from the report from this Iron Mountain group—which he has obtained a copy of (and that the Institute for Historic Review republished). He concludes the program by relating about the "high cabal . . . calling the shots."

While Prouty quotes accurately from the "Report from Iron Mountain," he fails to realize it was a complete hoax. There was no group in underground storage vaults in Iron Mountain, no study of the elimination of the war threat, no report from power brokers. The "Report from Iron Mountain" was a brilliant spoof by political satirist Leonard Lewin of think tanks in 1967. Victor Navasky, then the editor of the satiric magazine *Monocle*, who thought up the idea, persuaded Dial Press to put Lewin's book on its nonfiction instead of fiction list, which resulted in a front-page news story in *The New York Times* about the "suppressed" report. Subsequently it was revealed by the author for what it was. What neither the author nor Navasky could foresee was that this hoax would reemerge a quarter of a century later, first in radical-right radio broadcasts and Liberty Lobby publications, and then as the connective logic of Oliver Stone's film *JFK*.

Not only did his technical adviser on *JFK* prove unable to distinguish a mirthful hoax from somber reality, but Oliver Stone also himself proved unable to separate the false scenes in *JFK* from the reality of Garrison's case, at a Town Hall meeting in New York in March 1992—a meeting in which he again compared himself to Garrison as one of four people libeled by the media for "representing an unofficial history" of the assassination (the other two in this quarter are, according to Stone, Oswald and President Kennedy). The panel at Town Hall included Norman Mailer, Nora Ephron, and myself, and it was moderated by Victor Navasky, now the editor of *The Nation*. When I pointed out to Stone that his depiction of Ferrie confessing to Garrison was false history, he replied that even though such a meeting never happened, he had "sketched" it into Ferrie's last night because Ferrie had at an earlier point "raved and ranted" to one of Garrison's investigators. Stone saw no problem in his misrepresenting this fiction as fact in his "unofficial history." He also dismissed other challenges to the fictitious evidence he inserted in *JFK*—such as the six scenes depicting someone pasting Oswald's head on a photograph of some other gunman's body to frame him—by responding to the person who had questioned this fiction by meticulously citing the actual photographic evidence, "I don't know where you get your facts." Moreover, he not only vouched for the *bona fides* of Prouty but also presented as pure "truth" X's thesis that the "military-industrial complex" killed Kennedy so he would not end the war in Vietnam.

Oliver Stone, as the new Garrison, demonstrated yet again how easily pierced is the thin membrane that separates the mainstream media from the festering pools of fantasies on its peripheries. What he allowed to ooze into *JFK* from these fringes, with the help of his technical advisers such as Colonel Prouty, is the tormenting concept that "secret teams" and "high cabals" fabricated entire historic events to fool them—a concept that incorporates in its schema even the Iron Mountain hoax. In doing so, Oliver Stone organized a flight from reality. *JFK* thus completes the journey from fact to fantasy that began with the flawed Warren Commission report in 1964. What has been lost en route is the truth.

Afterword
The State of the Evidence,
the Evidence of the State
(1992)

Evidence, by its very nature, can be controverted. If it could not be, it would not be evidence but an act of faith. Any document can be a forgery, any witness can give false testimony, and any object can be either fabricated or misidentified. Nevertheless, some evidence is better than other evidence. And when the best evidence is examined, tested, and placed in the proper context, it provides the best way we have to establish the facts.

In the case of the assassination of President Kennedy, the central facts have been investigated and reinvestigated for nearly three decades. The evidence-testers have included the FBI, the Treasury Department, the Warren Commission, the Rockefeller Commission, the House Select Committee on Assassination, the Department of Justice, independent coroners and forensics experts, and assassination researchers. Consider, for example, the much-disputed autopsy findings of President Kennedy. Although the autopsy examination itself was badly handled by the Navy and insufficiently probed by the Warren Commission, many of the problems were resolved by the reexamination of the X rays and photographs of the president's body by the panel of nine independent pathologists (including one Warren Commission critic) appointed by the House Select Committee on Assassination. These findings, not those of the Warren Commission (or my criticisms of the original process in *Inquest*), constitute the best evidence.

As imperfect as the process has been, it has resulted in filling in much of the reality of what happened on November 22, 1963. I believe that the seven following questions now can be answered—or at least narrowed down to finite possibilities:

1. Where did the bullets come from that hit President Kennedy and Governor Connally?

The best available evidence on the nature of the discernible wounds inflicted on Kennedy is the photographs and X rays of the president taken during the autopsy at Bethesda Naval Hospital. Since a bullet progressively damages a wider swathe of tissue as it passes through a body, its path is unambiguously shown in a series of autopsy photographs. Unlike more tenuous evidence, such as ear witness testimony, which is affected by echoes, such photographs, when competently examined, leave no doubt as to the direction of the bullets.

Although the photographs and X rays were not examined by the Warren Commission or its staff, leading to considerable doubt as to the validity of the commission's conclusions, they were subsequently examined, first by a panel of three pathologists and a radiologist appointed by Attorney General Ramsey Clark in 1968, and then more thoroughly in 1976 by the nineman panel appointed by the House Select Committee on Assassination. The members of this latter panel had among them experience in performing over one hundred thousand autopsies. Moreover, the House Select Committee on Assassination established the authenticity of these photographs by having forensic dentists compare them with Kennedy's premortem dental records and medical X rays.

All these pathologists agreed, without any dissent, that all the detectable wounds in the photographs and X rays of President Kennedy had been caused by bullets fired from behind and above him, confirming the conclusions of the doctors who had performed the autopsy itself as well as those of the FBI and the Warren Commission. They also agreed unanimously from a reconstruction of the medical evidence that Governor Connally's multiple wounds had been caused by a bullet fired from the same direction.

The path of the first bullet to hit the president was further established by the president's shirt and jacket fibers. The FBI analysis as well as the reanalysis showed that they were pushed inward, not outward, by the projectile, which could only have happened if the president was shot from behind.

The path of the bullet that hit Governor Connally was also

confirmed by Governor Connally's testimony that he was certain he was hit from behind.

The panel also unanimously concluded from the X rays that the fatal bullet had entered the rear of the president's head near the cowlick area and exited from the right front. None of the nine pathologists, including Warren Commission critic Dr. Cyril Wecht, was able to find any medical evidence that this massive wound was caused by a bullet fired from in front of or at the side of the president's car. To be sure, a frame-by-frame analysis of the film of the assassination made by Abraham Zapruder shows President Kennedy's head at the time of impact moving backward, not forward, as might be expected. But this is not the evidence it seems to be because, depending on the neurological reactions to such a wound, the head can snap in any direction after being shot. Wound ballistic experts demonstrated this counterintuitive point to the House Select Committee on Assassination through a filmed experiment that clearly showed that, when hit with a rifle bullet from the rear, the head could move either backward or forward. So there is not necessarily a relationship between the direction that the head moves and the direction from which the bullet strikes the head.

By tracing the trajectory of the bullets from the path of the wounds, an analyst from the National Aeronautics and Space Administration was able to plot all three shots to their source— the upper floors of the southeastern face of the Texas Schoolbook Depository. This was the same building from which five witnesses—Howard Brennan, Amos Lee Euins, Carolyn Walther, Arnold Rowland and Barbara Rowland—claimed to have seen a rifle protruding from a southeastern window at about the time of the assassination (Brennan told police he actually saw the rifle being fired and reloaded before the suspect was apprehended).

While it is possible that numerous other shots may have been fired from other locations and directions and missed their target, we know from the best evidence, the autopsy photographs, that the shots that caused all the discernible wounds came from a high window on the southeastern side of the Texas Schoolbook Depository.

2. Did the Mannlicher-Carcano rifle found by police on the sixth floor of the Texas Schoolbook Depository fire these shots?

The best evidence for identifying the assassination weapon is the two bullet fragments found in the president's car and the nearly whole bullet found on a stretcher in Parkland Hospital in Dallas. In 1964, FBI experts ballistically matched this bullet and fragments to the rifle barrel of the Mannlicher-Carcano by microscopically comparing the markings in the barrel with those found on the bullet and fragments. A firearms panel of independent experts appointed by the House Select Committee on Assassination reexamined this evidence in 1977 and reconfirmed that the bullet and fragments had come from that Mannlicher-Carcano rifle.

In addition, the House Select Committee on Assassination employed a very advanced form of neutron activation analysis to match the recovered bullet and fragments to the ammunition used in the Mannlicher-Carcano. In this technique, traces from the ballistics evidence are bombarded by neutrons in a nuclear reactor so that the precise composition of elements—antimony, silver, and copper—can be measured by their emissions on a gamma-ray spectrometer to an accuracy of one-billionth gram. Since different batches of even the same brand name ammunition have different ratios of elements in them, it is possible to determine through this analysis whether or not even minute fragments came from the same or different batches of ammunition. The composition of traces from the bullet and fragments were thus compared to that of the unfired bullet found in the chamber of the Mannlicher-Carcano and found to match exactly. This analysis convincingly showed that all the ballistics material that was recovered, and could be tested, came from two bullets, and both bullets identically matched in their composition the ammunition in the Mannlicher-Carcano rifle.

Although questions can be raised about the general accuracy of the Mannlicher-Carcano rifle found in the depository, there can be no doubt that the particular weapon can be fired with deadly accuracy at a target a hundred yards away—the distance from the depository to the president's car. After the assassination three different FBI agents fired this exact rifle and scored bull's-eyes two of three times.

Although the suspicion has been raised that the Mannlicher-Carcano rifle was "framed" as the murder weapon by a conspirator who planted the nearly intact bullet on a stretcher in Parkland Hospital, it lacks any reasonable persuasiveness because the conspirator would have no certainty that he could recover from the hospital, car, autopsy, and crime scene the "real" bullets that presumably would not match the Mannlicher-Carcano; and it would be pointless to frame the Mannlicher-Carcano, which the conspirators would have had to have in their possession anyway to leave at the murder site, since it was a weapon perfectly capable of hitting its target—so why not use it?

We thus know that the Mannlicher-Carcano found in the depository fired at least two of the shots at the president's motorcade.

3. How many snipers fired at the president's motorcade?

The best evidence of the sequence of events remains the ten-second-long film taken by Zapruder. It fixes the earliest time Kennedy could have been first hit in the back, the latest time Connally was wounded, and the exact moment the president was shot in the head. From an analysis of this film, the Warren Commission staff determined that the interval between the time Kennedy and Connally were first shot was not long enough for a single rifleman to have fired two shots; therefore either both men were hit by the same bullet, or there had to be two riflemen. This conclusion was confirmed by the more sophisticated photographic analysis of the photographic evidence panel of the House Select Committee on Assassination and of independent researchers.

Despite the crucial implications of this photographic evidence, the issue of whether Kennedy and Connally were hit by the same or separate bullets has not been satisfactorily resolved. The FBI concluded it was separate shots, the Warren Commission begged the question as "not relevant," and the House Select Committee on Assassination, which went most thoroughly into this evidence, was unable to reach a definitive conclusion because members of its nine-doctor panel irreconcilably disagreed. Eight doctors believed it was possible, though not necessarily probable, that the bullet recovered had caused both Kennedy's back wound and Connally's multiple wounds; however, one doctor, Cyril Wecht, concluded from the photographic and medical evidence that it was absolutely impossible for those wounds to have been caused by a single bullet. Since Wecht marshals considerable evidence to support his view (as will be recalled from Epilogue I), we are left with two possible scenarios.

The Single-Bullet Single-Gunman Scenario

One rifleman fired three bullets from the Mannlicher-Carcano in the depository. The first bullet missed the motorcade entirely and incidentally wounded a bystander, James Teague. The second bullet hit Kennedy and Connally and was recovered from Connally's stretcher. About three seconds later, the rifleman fired a third bullet, which killed Kennedy; abandoned his rifle; and fled the depository.

The Separate-Shot Two-Gunmen Scenario

From an unidentified rifle, one rifleman fired the first shot, which hit Kennedy in the back. The bullet was not recovered. He then fired a second shot, which went astray and nicked bystander Tague. About one second after the first rifleman fired, a second rifleman, using the Mannlicher-Carcano, hit Connally, and, with his second shot, hit Kennedy in the head. While the first rifleman left the depository with his rifle and shell casings, the second rifleman left his behind.

Both scenarios are consistent with the testimony of eyewitnesses—one of whom saw a second person near the sniper's or snipers' windows—and the fingerprints found on the boxes arranged at the site. So we can conclude that either one or two riflemen participated in the assassination and that the one with the Mannlicher-Carcano killed Kennedy.

4. Whose Mannlicher-Carcano was it?

The best evidence that identifies the ownership of the murder weapon is the handwriting of the person who ordered the rifle under the name "A. Hidell" from a mail order house in Chicago in March 1963 and rented the post office box in Dallas to which it was shipped. FBI and Treasury Department experts determined in 1964 that Lee Harvey Oswald had signed the name "A. Hidell" on both the purchase order for the rifle and the post office box application. A half dozen other documents found in his possession established that Oswald used the alias "Hidell." The House Select Committee on Assassination's panel of questioned document experts, after reexamining the signatures, unequivocally agreed. So Oswald had ordered the murder weapon—and it had been shipped to his post office box from Chicago on March 20, 1963.

Possession

Marina Oswald confirmed that Oswald had received the rifle in late March, and four other witnesses—George De Mohrenschildt, Jeanne De Mohrenschildt, Alexander Taylor, and Gary Taylor—saw that Oswald had a rifle in either late March or early April.

The best evidence of Oswald's actual possession of the Mannlicher-Carcano, however, is the much-disputed photograph of Oswald holding the rifle in his hand that Marina Oswald said she took on Sunday, March 31, 1963, in the backyard of their house in Dallas. Oswald claimed after his arrest that the photograph had been faked by superimposing his head on the rifleman's body, but this theory is contradicted by three pieces of evidence established by the House Select Committee on Assassination. First, De Mohrenschildt produced in 1976 an inscribed copy of the backyard photograph that Oswald had given him in April 1963. The committee's questioned document panel authenticated the signature—which meant that Oswald had signed (and dated) the photograph he later claimed was faked. Second, by examining the negative with enhanced analytic techniques, the committee's panel of photographic experts found a unique random pattern of wear on the rifle in the photograph that corresponded exactly with one on the Mannlicher-Carcano Oswald had purchased. Since the experts agreed that this could not be faked, the rifle in the photograph had to be Oswald's. Third, by microscopically examining the scratch marks that Oswald's Imperial Reflex camera distributed on all negatives pulled through it—which are the equivalent of camera fingerprints—the panel established unequivocally that the backyard photograph could only have been taken by Oswald's camera, just as Marina had testified. Moreover, using digital processing analysis and stereo-optic viewing techniques that did not exist in 1963, the panel concluded there were no signs of having been faked. Even two experts who had previously disputed the authenticity of the photograph (using copies, rather than the original) now agreed that the photograph was genuine. In light of this evidence, there can be no serious doubt that Oswald possessed the murder weapon at the end of March 1963.

Use

Marina Oswald testified to the Warren Commission that when Oswald left their house on April 10, 1963, he left her dramatic instructions in Russian about what she should do if he were arrested, killed, or had to go into hiding, and when he returned late that evening, he explained to her that he had just attempted to kill General Edwin Walker with his rifle. Her testimony is corroborated by three elements of evidence.

First, the Russian handwriting in the note has been unequivocally identified as that of Oswald by the questioned documents experts of both the Warren Commission and the House Select Committee on Assassination. The note, which contains details that date it, confirms that Oswald expected to be killed, arrested, or a fugitive the week of April 10, 1963.

Second, photographs of Walker's house taken from the position where the sniper fired at Walker were found among Oswald's possessions after the Kennedy assassination. Photographic experts established that these photographs were taken with Oswald's Imperial Reflex camera. By referring to construction work in the background, the FBI was able to determine that the photographs were taken on March 9 or 10 (which was just about the date on which Oswald ordered the Mannlicher-Carcano). Such photographs show that Oswald had reconnoitered Walker's house.

Third, the previously discussed neutron activation analysis done in 1977 exactly matched the metallic elements found in the bullet that was recovered in Walker's home to the batch of Mannlicher-Carcano ammunition used in Oswald's rifle in the assassination of Kennedy.

So we know that the murder weapon was purchased, delivered, and shown off in an inscribed photograph, and used in a prior attempted assassination by Oswald.

5. Was Oswald at the sniper's window on the sixth floor of the depository where the murder weapon was found?

The best evidence here is three palmprints (which are as uniquely identifiable as fingerprints) found on the boxes stacked in front of the window to support the rifle and the nearby paper sack, which was long enough to accommodate the Mannlicher-Carcano. FBI experts matched them to Oswald hands. (A fourth palmprint, found on one box, belonged to an unidentified individual.) The House Select Committee on Assassination's palmprint identification panel unanimously confirmed this evidence. Since the "freshness" of palmprints is of limited duration, it was further determined that Oswald had handled those boxes and that paper sack either the day of the assassination or the preceding day. Moreover, two witnesses testified he carried the paper sack into the depository that morning. So we know that Oswald arranged the boxes used by the sniper and handled the paper sack within twenty-four hours of the assassination and, if the witnesses are correct, brought the sack to the sniper's window the morning of the assassination.

6. Was Oswald framed?

Whereas there is no doubt that Oswald's rifle was used to shoot President Kennedy, the possibility exists it was used by another party to frame Oswald. If Oswald was totally innocent, his activities after the assassination would reflect his lack of knowledge of and involvement in the event. Instead, the evidence is persuasive that he fled the building after the assassination; changed his clothing; armed himself with a pistol; fatally shot a policeman; resisted arrest by attempting to shoot another policeman; and, after his arrest, lied repeatedly to his interrogators about owning the rifle, appearing in the backyard photograph with the rifle, and using the alias "Hidell" (with which he purchased both the rifle and the pistol).

The best evidence that he shot the policeman, J. D. Tippit, is that the cartridge cases found at the murder scene matched the firing pin of the revolver taken out of Oswald's hand when he was arrested. The FBI determined that no other weapon could have ejected these cartridges. These conclusions were reaffirmed by the Select Committee on Assassination's firearms panel. Oswald's admission that he had decided only on the spur of the moment to fetch this weapon effectively rules out the possibility he was framed, since no one but Oswald could have known he would be carrying it.

In addition, five witnesses identified Oswald from the police lineup as either the person who shot Tippit or the person who fled from the scene with a gun in hand. The House Select Committee on Assassination produced an additional witness who testified he saw Oswald stand over the downed policeman and fire a bullet into his head.

His postarrest actions, especially his mendacity in consistently denying ownership of the rifle to representatives of the FBI, Secret Service, Post Office Department, and district attorney, further indicate consciousness of guilt about owning the rifle. This would not be consistent with the behavior of a framed and innocent man who believed his rifle was still wrapped in a blanket in a friend's garage.

While none of this evidence is unimpeachable—no evidence is—and none of it proves that Oswald was the only person involved in the shooting of Kennedy, Tippit, or General Walker, it convinces me that he was involved in the Kennedy assassination—and he killed again and lied because he knew it.

7. Was Oswald part of a conspiracy?

One question, perhaps the only one that still matters, cannot be answered by the state's evidence: Was Oswald part of a conspiracy? As we have seen, the reinvestigations of the assassination have left unresolved the issue of whether two shooters were involved, but even if they had definitively established, as the Warren Commission attempted to do, that a lone gunman had fired all the shots on November 22, 1963, it would not logically diminish the possibility that the assassination resulted from a conspiracy.

Conspiracies do not necessarily require more than one rifleman to accomplish their purpose. In many cases, such as the highly sophisticated rightist conspiracy in France to assassinate President Charles De Gaulle, a single "jackal" rifleman was employed. One accurate rifleman might be preferable in a conspiracy when it is expected that the intended victim could be protected by his bodyguard immediately after the first shot is fired, because each additional sniper would increase the chances of detection, both before and after the act, but not necessarily increase the probability of success. Moreover, if multiple gunmen are captured (or killed), it would be difficult to divert the investigation away from the conspiracy, whereas a lone gunman, especially if killed himself, can be dismissed as a lone lunatic.

The larger issue, then, is: Was Oswald, whether firing alone or in tandem, acting at the behest of others?

Oswald was not, to be sure, the sort of well-adjusted individual with whom most people would want to associate. He was wantonly self-destructive (e.g., his suicide attempt in Moscow); militantly hostile toward symbols of authority (e.g., the threat he made to blow up the FBI headquarters in Dallas); contemptuous of legal restraints (e.g., his plan to hijack an airliner to get to Cuba) and homicidal (e.g., his brutal murder of Tippit). As early as 1960, he expressed a cold-blooded willingness to commit political murder in a letter he presciently wrote to his brother from Moscow: "What I say now I do not say lightly or unknowingly . . . I would kill any American who put a uniform on in defense of the American Government, Any American." The one position that such unrestrained aggression would not exclude a person for employment would be as a political assassin.

In this context, the bullet Oswald coolly fired at General Walker was, whether he meant it to be or not, an advertisement of his willingness to kill or be killed for a political cause. Less than a week before he went out to assassinate Walker, he distributed an inscribed photograph of himself to De Mohrenschildt (and perhaps to others). It showed Oswald dressed in black, armed to kill with a rifle and telescopic sight, and holding in his hand the radical newspaper the *Militant*. When he went to Mexico to offer himself to the Cubans, he brought with him the telltale photographs of Walker's house to establish his *bona fides* as a revolutionary. Was his have-gun, will-kill message picked up on any antennae that summer? Just as De Mohrenschildt and Marina learned of his assassination attempt, so may have others in pro-Castro, anti-Castro, and other fringe groups he was active with in the summer of 1963 (not to mention the various intelligence and police agencies monitoring his movements).

There couldn't be that many potential assassins hanging around the militant peripheries of the Cold War with Oswald's perverse virtues: a convenient defector background; military training; complete disregard for human life, including his own; and possession of a rifle he was more than ready to use. Here was an assassin awaiting a mission. Did anyone pick him up as a shooter—or, lacking a sponsor but finding an opportunity, did he act alone?

INQUEST

NOTES

1. Overview: The Ten-Month Investigation

1. *Texas Supplemental Report on the Assassination of President John F. Kennedy and the Serious Wounding of Governor John B. Connally,* pp. 1, 8, 20, Austin, Texas, 1964 (hereinafter *Texas Report).*
2. *Report,* Foreword, p. x (1964), Washington, D.C.
3. *Ibid.,* p. 471 (Executive Order 11130).
4. *Report,* Foreword, p. x.
5. Dulles Interview.
6. *Report,* Foreword, p. x.
7. McCloy Interview.
8. *Ibid.*
9. *Texas Report, op. cit.,* p. 4.
10. *Ibid.,* p. 5.
11. *Ibid.,* p. 6.
12. *Ibid.*
13. Rankin Interview I.
14. *Ibid.*
15. *Ibid.*
16. *Ibid.*
17. Goldberg Interview.
18. *Ibid.*
19. Liebeler Interview.
20. *Report,* Foreword, p. xi. A fifth volume, the Supplemental Report, was submitted on January 13, 1964. See Appendices.
21. Rankin Interview I.
22. McCloy Interview.
23. Rankin Interview II.
24. Dulles Interview.
25. Rankin Interview II.
26. Dulles Interview.
27. *Report,* Foreword, p. xiii.
28. Rankin Interview II.
29. *Report,* Foreword, p. xii.
30. *Ibid.,* p. xiii +.
31. *Ibid.,* p. xii.
32. Willens Interview.
33. *Ibid.*
34. Stern Interview. Also Goldberg Interview.
35. Rankin Interview I.
36. Redlich Interview.
37. Eisenberg Interview I.
38. Rankin Interview I.
39. Redlich Interview.
40. Rankin Interview I. Also Liebeler Interview.
41. Willens Interview.
42. *Report,* p. 476+. Rankin later decided to drop the distinction between "senior" and "junior" lawyers, and all were called "assistant counsel."
43. Liebeler Interview.
44. Rankin Interview I.
45. Rankin Interview I and Willens Interview.
46. Ford Interview.
47. Willens Interview.
48. *Ibid.*
49. Rankin Interview I.
50. Willens Interview.
51. *Ibid.*
52. Liebeler Interview.
53. Adams Interview.
54. Ball Interview.
55. Liebeler Interview.
56. Redlich Interview.
57. *Ibid.*
58. Stern Interview.
59. Willens Interview.
60. *Ibid.*
61. Liebeler Interview.
62. *Ibid.*
63. Rankin Interview I.
64. Liebeler Interview.

65. Dulles Interview.
66. *Report*, Foreword, p. xiii.
67. *Infra*, p. 21.
68. *Report*, Foreword, p. xiii+.
69. *Ibid.*, p. xiv.
70. *Hearings*, Vol. XXIV, p. 445.
71. Rankin Interview I.
72. *Report*, p. 501+.
73. Rankin Interview I.
74. Gerald R. Ford and John R. Stiles, *Portrait of the Assassin*, New York, 1965, p. 13.
75. Rankin Interview II.
76. Ford and Stiles, *op. cit.*, p. 14.
77. *Ibid.*
78. *Ibid.*
79. *Ibid.*, p. 25.
80. U.S. National Archives.
81. *Hearings*, Vol. V., p. 141.
82. Specter Interview.
83. Rankin Interview II and Stern Interview.
84. Rankin Interview II.
85. *Ibid.*
86. *Hearings*, Vol. I, pp. 1*ff.*
87. *Infra*, p. 96.
88. Eisenberg Interview II.
89. Willens Interview.
90. Ball Interview.
91. Liebeler Interview.
92. *Ibid.*
93. Eisenberg Interview I.
94. Rankin Interview I.
95. *Ibid.*
96. *Report*, Foreword, pp. xiv–xv.
97. Liebeler Interview.
98. Willens Interview.
99. Rankin Interview I.
100. Eisenberg Interview I.
101. Ball Interview.
102. Liebeler Interview.
103. Ball Interview.
104. *Hearings*, Vol. III, pp. 140–270, *passim.*
105. *Hearings*, Vol. II, p. 33.
106. *Ibid.*, p. 58.
107. Specter Interview.
108. Liebeler Interview.
109. Eisenberg Interview I.
110. Liebeler Interview. Jenner was to do Oswald's preschool life, Ely his education, and Liebeler his military and work record.
111. Interviews with Goldberg, Willens, Ford, Liebeler, Eisenberg.
112. Ball Interview.
113. Liebeler Interview.
114. Eisenberg Interview I.
115. Willens Interview.
116. Rankin Interviews I and II.
117. Liebeler Interview.
118. Ball Interview.
119. Liebeler Interview.
120. Specter Interview.
121. Goldberg Interview.
122. Liebeler Interview.
123. *Ibid.*
124. Specter Interview.
125. Liebeler Interview.
126. Eisenberg Interview II.
127. Rankin Interview II.
128. *Ibid.*
129. Ball Interview.
130. Liebeler Interview.
131. Goldberg Interview.
132. *N.Y. Times*, June 8, 1964, p. 21:4.
133. *N.Y. Times*, June 19, 1964, p. 13:1.
134. *N.Y. Times*, June 30, 1964, p. 2:5.
135. Liebeler Interview.
136. *Ibid.* Eisenberg came for long weekends, and Stern was available when he was needed.
137. Redlich Interview.
138. Goldberg Interview.
139. Liebeler Interview (and unpublished colloquium).
140. Liebeler Interview.
141. Goldberg Interview.
142. Liebeler Interview.
143. Interviews with Dulles, McCloy, Ford, Boggs, and Cooper.
144. Liebeler Interview.
145. *Ibid.*
146. *Report*, Foreword, p. viii.
147. Liebeler Interview. Also Eisenberg Interview I.
148. *Report*, Foreword, p. xv. All the Commission's documents and working papers were committed to the U.S. National Archives.

2   The Dominant Purpose

1. *Report*, p. 471 (Executive Order No. 11130).
2. *Hearings*, Vol. II, p. 34.
3. *354 U.S. 178*, p. 187.
4. Anthony Lewis, "New Look at the Chief Justice," *N.Y. Times Magazine*, p. 9

(January 19, 1964). The fact that this same story was reprinted in the N.Y. Times on September 28, 1964 (p. 14:6), indicates that it was never denied.

5. Rankin Interview I.
6. Dulles Interview.
7. McCloy Interview.
8. Cooper Interview.
9. Ford Interview.
10. Ford and Stiles, op. cit., p. 19.
11. Ibid., p. 14, and Hearings, Vol. V, p. 242.
12. Ford and Stiles, op. cit., p. 14.
13. Hearings, Vol. V, p. 243.
14. Ibid., pp. 242–43, and Rankin Interview II.
15. Hearings, Vol. V, p. 112.
16. Ibid., p. 242.
17. Ford and Stiles, op. cit., p. 20.
18. Ibid., p. 15.
19. Ibid., p. 22.
20. Ibid., p. 20.
21. Ibid., p. 19.
22. Ibid.
23. Ibid., p. 21.
24. Ibid.
25. Ibid., p. 22.
26. Ibid., p. 24.
27. Ibid., p. 23.
28. Ibid., p. 24.
29. N.Y. Times, February 5, 1964, p. 19:1.
30. Hearings, Vol. XVII, p. 814.
31. Ibid., pp. 815–18.
32. Ibid., p. 741 and Commission Exhibit 825 (ibid.) Warren De Bruey, the FBI agent who allegedly threatened to send an undercover agent to infiltrate the same small New Orleans anti-Castro organization which Oswald later attempted to infil-

trate, did not submit an affidavit. (Vol. X, pp. 33 ff.)
33. Ibid., p. 803.
34. Hearings, Vol. V, p. 112. The Commission was never able to explain fully how Hosty's license plate number found its way into Oswald's address book. The reconstruction showed that Oswald's wife, Marina, could not possibly have seen Hosty's car plates on either of his two visits to the Paine house. Hosty never interviewed Lee Harvey Oswald.
35. Ibid., Vol. V, p. 13.
36. Ibid.
37. Stern Interview.
38. Hearings, Vol. V, pp. 98–119.
39. Rankin Interview II.
40. Ibid.
41. Ibid.
42. National Archives, Commission Document 320.
43. Chronological File, May 21, 1964.
44. Ibid.
45. Liebeler Interview.
46. Ibid. Also, see note 32 supra.
47. Chronological File. Memorandum of May 21, 1964, was returned to Liebeler from Samuel Stern on May 31, with answer "No" to question of whether number was checked in FBI files.
48. Referred to in Hoover testimony, Wade testimony, and Commission Exhibit 833, but never given.
49. Commission Document 320, National Archives (Control Number 767 is withheld).
50. Eisenberg Interview II. Also Hearings, Vol. V, p. 12.

3. The Vulnerability of Facts

1. Redlich Interview. Said while maintaining that both men were hit by the same bullet.
2. Report, pp. 98–105. The established trajectory, still photographs, and preponderance of eyewitnesses proved Kennedy was not hit before the oak tree.
3. Hearings, Vol. IV, pp. 114, 128.
4. Hearings, Vol. V, p. 153.
5. Report, pp. 193–94, and Hearings, Vol. III, p. 407.
6. Hearings, Vol. XVII, p. 48.
7. Report, Appendix IX, pp. 538–543.
8. Ibid., p. 543.

9. Report, p. 88.
10. Nate Haseltine, "Kennedy Autopsy Report," Washington Post, p. A-3, December 18, 1963. Haseltine told me in an interview that his source was authoritative, and had medical knowledge, and he inferred it came from the White House.
11. E.g., the New York Herald Tribune, December 19, 1963, p. 8, stated that the pathologist who performed the autopsy reported "that the first bullet lodged in Kennedy's lung." The Journal of the A.M.A. (January 4, 1964, Vol. 187, No. 1, p. 15), said that the first bullet "did not go

through the shoulder and was recovered during the autopsy." *Newsweek* (December 30, 1963, p. 55) reported: "This bullet, the Navy doctors believe, probably dropped out of the President's body and was the one reportedly found on his stretcher at Parkland."

12. *N.Y. Times,* December 18, 1963, p. 27.
13. *Ibid.,* January 26, 1964, p. 68. "Twelve Unanswered Questions," Jack Langguth.
14. *Hearings,* Vol. V, p. 98.
15. *Ibid.,* p. 98.
16. *Report,* Foreword, p. xi.
17. *Investigation of Assassination of President John F. Kennedy,* p. 18. (Hereinafter FBI Summary Report.) See Appendix A of this book, p. 184.
18. *Ibid.*
19. *Ibid., Supplemental Report, January 13, 1964,* p. 2 (Hereinafter FBI Supplemental Report.) See Appendix B of this book, p. 198.
20. *Report,* p. 88+.
21. *Hearings,* Vol. II, pp. 99, 131.
22. Adams Interview. Adams stated that the FBI had color photographs of the autopsy as well.
23. Specter Interview.
24. *Hearings,* Vol. II, p. 131.
25. *Supra.*
26. The December 9 FBI Summary Report includes an interview with Marina Oswald conducted on December 3, 1963. See p. 186.
27. *Report,* p. 88.
28. *Ibid.*
29. FBI Summary Report, p. 18. See Appendix A, p. 184.
30. *Report,* p. 88.

31. *Hearings,* Vol. II, p. 350.
32. *Ibid.,* p. 368.
33. According to Francis W. H. Adams, these photographs were in the custody of Attorney General Robert F. Kennedy. Rankin said that they were not introduced into evidence for "reasons of taste."
34. *Ibid.,* Vol. XVII, p. 45.
35. *Ibid.,* Vol. II, p. 143.
36. *Report,* p. 111.
37. *Ibid.,* p. 81 (Kellerman), *Ibid.,* p. 127 (Greer).
38. Photographs were included in Commission Exhibits 393, 394, and 395, but they do not show the bullet holes.
39. *Hearings,* Vol. V, p.
40. *Ibid.,* p. 60.
41. Interview with Dr. Milton Helpern in Ithaca, N.Y., October 27, 1965 (hereinafter Helpern Interview).
42. *Ibid.*
43. *Ibid.*
44. *Hearings,* Vol. II, p. 93.
45. Helpern Interview.
46. *Hearings,* Vol. II, p. 127.
47. *Ibid.*
48. *Ibid.,* p. 361.
49. *Ibid.,* p. 368.
50. FBI Supplemental Report, pp. 2*ff.* See Appendix B, p. 198.
51. *Report,* p. 88*ff.*
52. *Hearings,* Vol. III, p. 372.
53. *Ibid.,* Vol. VI, p. 5.
54. *Report,* p. 88.
55. *Hearings,* Vol. VI, p. 55.
56. *Report,* p. 50.
57. Helpern Interview.
58. *Hearings,* Vol. V, p. 2+ and Vol. XVIII. Commission Exhibit 833.

4. The Limits of the Investigation

1. Rankin Interview I.
2. Interview with Dr. James Rhodes, Civil Archivist of the National Archives, as well as a limited examination and "spot check" of the investigative reports.
3. *Report,* Foreword, p. xii.
4. Rankin Interview I.
5. *Hearings,* Vol. V, pp. 73–74. Also Vol. II, p. 383.
6. *Report,* p. 249.
7. One witness, James R. Worrell, Jr., testified that he saw an unidentified man run out of the Depository immediately after the shots. *Hearings,* Volume II, p. 196.

Also, Amos Lee Euins said in his testimony that another unidentified witness reported seeing a man run from the building. *Ibid.,* p. 205.
8. *Report,* p. 22.
9. *Ibid.*
10. *Hearings,* Vol. XXIV, p. 522.
11. *Ibid.*
12. *Ibid.*
13. National Archives, *Index of Commission Documents.*
14. *Hearings,* Vol. XV, index, as well as working papers in Liebeler's files, index of material in *National Archives,* and Specter Interview.

15. For example, two witnesses, Robert E. Edwards and Ronald B. Fisher, among those to see a man in window prior to the assassination, believed originally it was fifth-floor window. *Hearings*, Vol. XIX, pp. 473, 475.
16. *Hearings*, Vol. VI, p. 313 (Harkness).
17. *Hearings*, Vol. VI, pp. 197*ff.* (Fisher), pp. 203*ff.* (Edwards), Vol. XIX, p. 470 (Brennan), Vol. II, p. 171 (Rowland). These were four other witnesses who saw the assassin prior to assassination.
18. *Ibid.*, Vol. II, p. 175.
19. *Report*, p. 252.
20. *Ibid.*, p. 250.
21. Chronological File. Rankin Interviews I and II.
22. Interviews with Willens, Rankin (I and II), Liebeler, and Redlich.
23. *Life*, October 2, 1964, pp. 41*ff. N.Y. Times*, September 28, 1964, p. 28 (editorial: "The facts, exhaustively gathered, independently checked and cogently set forth . . . destroy the basis for the conspiracy theories that have grown weedlike in this country and abroad"). *Washington Post*, September 28, 1964, p. A-12 (editorial: ". . . the whole truth and nothing but the truth").
24. The 26 volumes of supporting evidence were not released until November 1964.
25. Goldberg Interview.
26. Rankin Interview I.
27. *Ibid.*
28. *Ibid.*
29. Adams Interview.
30. Willens Interview.
31. *Ibid.*
32. Specter Interview.
33. *Ibid.*
34. *Ibid.*
35. *Ibid.*
36. *Hearings*, Vol. VI, pp. 1–148.
37. The exception is Jean Hill, a witness identified by Mark Lane in his testimony. After his investigation was completed, Specter returned to Dallas to interview Jack Ruby on two occasions.
38. *Report*, p. 90+.
39. *Hearings*, Vol. II, p. 93.
40. *Ibid.*, Vol. II, p. 368.
41. *National Archives*, Commission Documents 5 and 7. Also, Commission Document 3 (the Secret Service Summary Report).
42. *Hearings*, Vol. II, p. 368.
43. *Ibid.*, pp. 368*ff.*
44. *Ibid.*, p. 368.
45. *Hearings*, Vol. VI, p. 130.
46. *Ibid.*, p. 131. *"Specter:* And at the time we started our discussion, it was your recollection at that point that the bullet came off stretcher A [Connally's], was it not? *Tomlinson:* B [the other stretcher]. *Specter:* Pardon me, stretcher B, but it was stretcher A you took off the elevator."
47. *Ibid.*, pp. 131*ff.*
48. Specter Interview.
49. *Report*, p. 81.
50. *Hearings*, Vol. VI, pp. 138, 142.
51. *Ibid.*
52. *Ibid.*, Vol. II, p. 382.
53. *Report*, p. 19 (conclusion e-2).
54. *Hearings*, Vol. II, pp. 375–76 (Humes), Vol. IV, p. 113 (Shaw), Vol. IV, p. 127 (Gregory).
55. *Ibid.*, Vol. XXIV, p. 412.
56. *Ibid.*, Vol. VI, pp. 138–43.
57. Specter was in Dallas March 17, 25, also on May 21, 24 during the period from March 14 to June 1 (investigation).
58. Specter Interview.
59. *Report*, p. 116.
60. *Hearings*, Vol. XXIII, p. 915. (Radio Log: "Patrolman L. L. Hill: 'I have one guy who was possibly hit by a ricochet from the bullet off the concrete.' ")
61. Specter Interview, Willens Interview.
62. *Hearings*, Vol. XXIV, p. 540.
63. Ball Interview.
64. Specter Interview.
65. *Hearings*, Vol. XXI, p. 472.
66. Liebeler Interview.
67. *Hearings*, Vol. VII, pp. 553*ff.*
68. *Ibid.*, pp. 544*ff.*
69. *Ibid.*, Vol. XXI, p. 476 (August 12, 1965).
70. *Ibid.*, Vol. XXI, pp. 472*ff.*
71. Liebeler Interview.
72. *Report*, p. 117.
73. Liebeler Interview.
74. Ball Interview.
75. *Ibid.*
76. *Ibid.*
77. *Ibid.*
78. *Ibid.*
79. *Ibid.*
80. *Ibid.*
81. *Report*, pp. 84–85, 118*ff.*
82. Ball Interview, Liebeler Interview.
83. *Report*, p. 249.
84. Liebeler Interview Chronological File.
85. Ball Interview.

86. *Hearings*, Vol. XXII, p. 833 (Simmons), Vol. VI, p. 225 (Miller), Vol. VI, p. 244 (Holland), Vol. XXII, p. 835 (Murphy), Vol. VI, p. 230 (Reilly), and Vol. VI, p. 251 (Foster).

87. *Hearings*, Vol. XXII, p. 833 (Simmons), Vol. VI, p. 225 (Miller), Vol. XXII, p. 836 (Johnson), and Vol. VI, p. 244 (Holland).

88. *Hearings*, Vol. VI, p. 244.

89. *Hearings*, Vol. XX, p. 843 (J. Newman), Vol. XX, p. 843 (W. Newman), Vol. VII, p. 571 (A. Zapruder), Vol. XIX, p. 486 (A. Millican), Vol. XXIV, p. 525 (J. Chism),

Vol. XIX, p. 472 (M. Chism), Vol. XXII, p. 841 (C. Hester), Vol. XXII, p. 841 (M. Hester), Vol. XXIV, p. 520 (M. Woodward).

90. Liebeler Interview.

91. *Hearings*, Vol. XIX, p. 479 (J. Hill), Vol. XIX, p. 467 (H. Betzner), Vol. VII, p. 517 (J. Altgens), Vol. VII, p. 563 (J. Tague), Vol. XXII, p. 846 (J. Franzen), Vol. XIX, p. 487 (M. Moorman), Vol. XXIV, p. 525 (Mrs. Franzen), Vol. XXII, p. 837 (C. F. Brehm).

92. *Hearings*, Vol. II, p. 43, Vol. VI, pp. 205*ff*.

93. *Ibid.*, Vol. VII, pp. 552*ff*.

5. The Limits of the Investigators

1. *Report*, Foreword, p. xiii.

2. *Ibid.*, p. x.

3. Rankin Interview I.

4. *Report*, pp. 479–82 (Staff Biographies).

5. Alfredda Scobey, "A Lawyer's Notes on the Warren Commission Report," *A.B.A. Journal*, Vol. 51, January 1965, p. 39.

6. Ball Interview.

7. Rankin Interview I.

8. Eisenberg Interview I.

9. Ball Interview.

10. Liebeler Interview.

11. *Hearings*, Vol. II, p. 183.

12. *Ibid.*, p. 184+.

13. *Report*, p. 251.

14. *Ibid.*

15. Liebeler Interview.

16. *Ibid.*

17. Chronological File (September 1, 1964, Memorandum to Willens).

18. Ball Interview.

19. *Hearings*, Vol. V, p. 99.

20. National Archives, Commission Document 1107.

21. E.g., 29 lengthy FBI reports concerned the acquaintances of George Lyman Paine, the father of Michael Paine, with whose wife, Ruth, Marina Oswald was living at the time of the assassination (Commission Documents 600–628).

22. Liebeler Interview.

23. National Archives Index of Investigative Report.

24. Ball Interview, Liebeler Interview. Also, National Archives Index, and all available Secret Service Reports in the National Archives.

25. Rankin Interview I.

26. *Ibid.*

27. *Ibid.*

28. *Ibid.*

29. Liebeler Interview.

30. Ball Interview.

31. Liebeler Interview.

32. *Ibid.*

33. *Ibid.*

34. Chronological File. February 28, 1964. Memorandum: Redlich-Rankin.

35. Liebeler Interview.

36. *Hearings*, Vol. V, p. 607 (and pp. 588*ff*. for other contradictions revealed at this late date).

37. Liebeler Interview.

38. *Hearings*, Vol. V, pp. 255–56.

39. *Ibid.*

40. *Ibid.*, p. 256.

41. *Ibid.*, p. 258.

42. Liebeler Interview.

43. Rankin Interview II.

44. *Report*, p. 813.

45. *Ibid.*, pp. 815–16.

46. Liebeler Interview.

47. *Report*, p. 315.

48. *Ibid.*

49. *Ibid.*, pp. 316–17. Also *Hearings*, Vol. XI, pp. 275*ff*.

50. *Ibid.*, Vol. XI, pp. 275*ff*.

51. Liebeler Interview.

52. *Ibid.*

53. Chronological File. April 3, 1964, Memorandum from Willens.

54. Eisenberg Interview II.

55. Although Congress had given the Commission power to compel testimony from witnesses who claimed the Fifth Amendment (by granting the witnesses immunity), the Commission declined to use this power on several occasions (e.g.,

Surrey). The reason given by Rankin was that the question of "double jeopardy" (resulting from immunity) was before the courts, and Warren did not want to prejudice his position.

56. Rankin Interview I.
57. McCloy Interview, Dulles Interview.
58. Boggs Interview, Ford Interview, and Cooper Interview.
59. Goldberg Interview.
60. *Report*, pp. 216–21.
61. *Ibid.*, p. 221+.

62. Liebeler Interview.
63. *Report*, p. 219.
64. *Ibid.*, p. 322.
65. Liebeler Interview.
66. *Ibid.*
67. *Ibid.*
68. *Report*, p. 124 "While the FBI had not yet completed its investigation into this matter at the time the report went to press, the Commission had concluded that Lee Harvey Oswald was not at Mrs. Odio's apartment in September of 1963."

6. The Commission Hearings

1. Of the 552 witnesses, 395 were examined by staff lawyers, 61 submitted affidavits, and two witnesses (President and Mrs. Lyndon B. Johnson) submitted unsworn statements.
2. *Hearings*, Vol. I–V.
3. *Hearings*, Vol. II, p. 32, and Vol. V, p. 546 (Mark Lane).
4. *Hearings*, Vol. V, p. 181 (Jack Ruby), and Vol. V, p. 588 (Marina Oswald).
5. Gerald R. Ford, "Piecing Together the Evidence," *Life* magazine, p. 42 (October 2, 1964).
6. *Hearings*, Vol. V, pp. 1–47, 97–129, 213–307, 348–87, 567–88, etc.
7. Eisenberg Interview II.
8. *Hearings*, Vol. II, p. 361 and *passim*.
9. Helpern Interview.
10. *Hearings*, Vol. II, p. 191.
11. Ford Interview.
12. *Hearings*, Vol. II, p. 195+.
13. *Report*, p. 252.

14. *Supra*, Chapter 5.
15. Ball Interview, Liebeler Interview.
16. Liebeler Interview.
17. Ball Interview.
18. Rankin Interview I.
19. Some of the Commissioners had assistants. Senator Russell requested that Alfredda Scobey, a Georgia lawyer, be appointed to the staff. Gerald Ford had three assistants (John R. Stiles, former Congressman John H. Ray, and Francis X. Fallon, Jr.) to help him in reading and analyzing the record. John J. McCloy had assistance from Patrick Burns, a young lawyer in his office. Senator Cooper, Congressman Boggs, and Allen Dulles stated that they did not have assistants.
20. Rankin Interview II.
21. McCloy Interview.
22. *Ibid.*
23. Rankin Interview II.
24. *Ibid.*

7. The Hypothesis

1. *Report*, Foreword, p. xi.
2. *Ibid.*, pp. 18–20.
3. Redlich Interview.
4. *Ibid.*
5. FBI Summary Report, p. 1. See Appendix A, p. 167.
6. Eisenberg Interview II.
7. *Ibid.*
8. *Hearings*, Vol. V, p. 141.
9. Eisenberg Interview II.
10. Report, p. 98.
11. *Hearings*, Vol. XVII, p. 882.
12. *Ibid.*, Vol. III, p. 407.
13. Eisenberg Interview I.
14. *Hearings*, Vol. V, p. 138.

15. Specter Interview.
16. *Hearings*, Vol. IV, pp. 114, 128.
17. Specter Interview.
18. FBI Summary Report, p. 18. See Appendix A, p. 184.
19. *Hearings*, Vol. II, p. 373, and Vol. XVII, p. 48.
20. *Ibid.*, Vol. XVII, p. 48.
21. FBI Supplemental Report, p. 2. See Appendix B, p. 198.
22. *Hearings*, Vol. II, p. 368.
23. *Ibid.*, p. 377.
24. *Ibid.*, p. 368.
25. *Ibid.*, p. 375.
26. Eisenberg Interview I.

27. *Hearings*, Vol. II, p. 368.
28. *Ibid.*
29. *Supra*, Chapter 4.
30. *Hearings*, Vol. II, p. 382.
31. *Supra*, Chapter 4.
32. *Report*, p. 19.
33. *Hearings*, Vol. IV, pp. 135–36.
34. *Ibid.*
35. *Hearings*, Vol. XVIII, p. 724 (Kellerman), Vol. VI, p. 294 (Hargis), *Ibid.*, p. 291 (B. J. Martin), Vol. XVIII, p. 742 (Clinton Hill), Vol. VII, p. 493 (Willis), Vol. VII, pp. 448*ff.* (O'Donnell), *Ibid.*, p. 473 (Powers), Vol. XVIII, p. 762 (Hickey).
36. *Hearings*, Vol. IV, p. 147.
37. *Ibid.*, p. 116.
38. *Ibid.*, pp. 114, 128.
39. Specter Interview.
40. *Hearings*, Vol. II, p. 381.
41. Specter Interview.
42. *Report*, pp. 580–585.
43. *Hearings*, Vol. V, pp. 86–87.
44. *Ibid.*, p. 86.
45. *Ibid.*, pp. 86–87.
46. *Ibid.*, p. 95.
47. *Ibid.*, p. 96.
48. Specter Interview.
49. *Ibid.*
50. Rankin Interview II.
51. *Report*, p. 97.
52. *Hearings*, Vol. V, p. 171.
53. *Ibid.*
54. *Ibid.*, p. 172.
55. *Ibid.*, pp. 172–73.
56. *Ibid.*
57. Specter Interview.
58. *Ibid.*
59. Liebeler Interview.
60. *Report*, p. 105.
61. *Ibid.* (footnote 292).
62. *Hearings*, Vol. V, p. 174.
63. *Ibid.*
64. *Report*, p. 107.
65. Redlich Interview.
66. *Infra*, Chapter 10.

8. Writing the Report

1. Rankin Interview I.
2. Goldberg Interview.
3. Rankin Interview II.
4. Goldberg Interview.
5. Redlich Interview.
6. *Ibid.*
7. *Ibid.*
8. *Ibid.*
9. Willens Interview.
10. Redlich Interview.
11. Liebeler Interview.
12. Goldberg Interview.
13. *Ibid.*
14. Ball Interview.
15. Liebeler Interview.
16. *Ibid.*
17. Rankin Interview II.
18. *Ibid.*
19. Eisenberg Interview II.
20. *Ibid.*
21. Redlich Interview.
22. *Ibid.*
23. Chronological File, September 8, 1964. The lawyer who wrote it told me that the memorandum was never officially submitted because the deadline was extended from September 11 to September 20.
24. Goldberg Interview.
25. *Ibid.*
26. The first six appendices (33 pages) are procedural documents and information (biographies of Commissioners, List of Witnesses, etc.). Appendix VII, "A Brief History of Presidential Protection," was prepared by Alfred Goldberg and his assistant, Arthur K. Marmor. Appendices VIII and IX are medical documents. Appendix X pertains to expert testimony, and was prepared by Specter, Eisenberg, and Redlich. Appendix XI consists of reports of Oswald's interrogation. Appendix XII deals with "Speculations and Rumors," and was written by Goldberg. Appendix XIII, the longest appendix (72 pages), is a biography of Lee Harvey Oswald, and was written by Lloyd L. Weinreb, then a Department of Justice lawyer temporarily working with the commission. Appendix XIV is an analysis of Oswald's finances prepared by three Internal Revenue Service agents, Philip Barson, Edward A. Conroy, and John J. O'Brien. Appendix XV consists of information concerning Marina Oswald. Appendix XVI is a biography of Jack Ruby written in part by Laulicht. Appendix XVII is Ruby's polygraph examination written up by Specter. Appendix XVIII consists of reference notes.

9. The Selection Process

1. "A Critique of the Warren Report," *Esquire*, March 1965, p. 61.
2. Redlich Interview.
3. Colloquium (unpublished), July 1964.
4. Willens Interview.
5. Ball Interview.
6. *Ibid.*
7. *Ibid.*
8. *Ibid.*
9. *Ibid.*
10. *Ibid.*
11. Liebeler Interview.
12. *Ibid.*
13. *Ibid.*
14. Chronological File, September 6, 1964.
15. *Report*, p. 168.
16. Ball Interview.
17. *Report*, p. 145.
18. *Ibid.*
19. *Ibid.*
20. Ball Interview.
21. *Report*, p. 144.
22. Ball Interview.
23. *Ibid.*
24. *Report*, p. 143.
25. *Ibid.*, p. 145.
26. Ball Interview.
27. *Ibid.*
28. Chronological File, February 28, 1964. See Chapter 5, note 34.
29. Ball Interview.
30. *Ibid.*
31. Redlich Interview.
32. *Ibid.*
33. Liebeler Interview.
34. *Ibid.*
35. Chronological File, September 6, 1964.
36. Liebeler Interview.
37. Chronological File, September 6, 1964.
38. *Report*, p. 128.
39. *Ibid.*, p. 131.
40. Chronological File, September 6, 1964.
41. *Report*, p. 133.
42. *Ibid.*, p. 134.
43. *Ibid.*
44. *Ibid.*
45. Chronological File, September 6, 1964.
46. *Ibid.*
47. *Report*, p. 136.

48. Chronological File, September 6, 1964.
49. *Hearings*, Vol. IV, p. 81.
50. *Ibid.*
51. Chronological File, September 6, 1964.
52. *Hearings*, Vol. IV, p. 87. Eisenberg said, "Now, is it inconsistent with that answer that no fibers were found on the gun which matched the fibers in the blanket?"
53. Chronological File, September 6, 1964.
54. *Ibid.*
55. *Report*, p. 98. The assassin would have had more time if one bullet had hit both the President and Governor Connally, but, as the Commission was unable to decide on whether this happened, the chapter had to show that the assassin had time to fire three separate shots (Redlich Interview).
56. *Hearings*, Vol. III, pp. 403–405.
57. *Ibid.*, p. 404.
58. *Ibid.*
59. *Ibid.*, p. 407.
60. *Ibid.*, p. 405.
61. *Ibid.*, p. 406.
62. *Ibid.*, pp. 441*ff.*
63. *Ibid.*, pp. 446–47.
64. *Ibid.*, p. 444.
65. *Ibid.*, p. 407.
66. *Ibid.*
67. *Ibid.*, p. 444.
68. Chronological File, September 6, 1964.
69. *Ibid.*
70. *Hearings*, Vol. XI, pp. 306*ff*, pp. 301*ff.*
71. *Ibid.*
72. *Ibid.*
73. Chronological File, September 6, 1964.
74. *Ibid.*
75. *Ibid.*
76. *Ibid.*
77. *Report*, p. 191.
78. *Report*, p. 192.
79. Chronological File, September 6, 1964. Also Liebeler Interview.
80. Liebeler Interview.
81. *Hearings*, Vol. VIII, p. 235.
82. *Ibid.*
83. Chronological File, September 6, 1964.
84. *Ibid.*

85. *Ibid.*, March 9, 1964 (Commission Document 434, 451).
86. *Ibid.*
87. Liebeler Interview.
88. *Ibid.*
89. *Ibid.*
90. *Ibid.*

91. *Ibid.*
92. *Ibid.*
93. Rankin Interview II.
94. *Report*, p. 194.
95. *Ibid.*, p. 141, p. 137.
96. *Ibid.*, p. 130.

10.   The Commission's Conclusions

1. Ford Interview.
2. *Report*, pp. 18–19.
3. Redlich Interview, Eisenberg Interview II, Specter Interview, Liebeler Interview.
4. *Supra*, Chapter 4. Also, *supra*, Chapters 3 and 7.
5. Ford Interview.
6. Goldberg Interview.
7. Cooper Interview.
8. Boggs Interview.
9. Dulles Interview, McCloy Interview.
10. McCloy Interview.
11. *Ibid.*
12. *Ibid.*
13. *Ibid.*
14. *Report*, p. 19.

15. *Ibid.*, pp. 19–20.
16. *Supra*, Chapter 9.
17. *Ibid.*
18. *Report*, p. 22+.
19. *Ibid.*, p. 23.
20. Liebeler Interview.
21. *Ibid.*
22. Ford Interview.
23. *Hearings*, Vol. V, pp. 607*ff.*
24. Ball Interview.
25. Ford Interview.
26. McCloy Interview.
27. *Report*, p. 22.
28. *Supra*, Chapter 4.
29. *Infra*, Appendices A and B.
30. *Supra*, Chapter 3.

COUNTERPLOT

NOTES

Prologue: Oswald in New Orleans

1. *Hearings before the President's Commission on the Assassination of President Kennedy*, Washington, D.C., 1964 (hereinafter *Hearings*), Vol. I, p. 18.
2. *Hearings*, Vol. III, pp. 59–60.
3. *Report of the President's Commission on the Assassination of President Kennedy*, Washington, D.C., 1964 (hereinafter *Report*), p. 726.
4. *Hearings*, Vol. II, pp. 468–71.
5. *Report*, p. 727, and *Hearings*, Vol. II, p. 517, also Commission Exhibit 1117, and *Hearings*, Vol. X, p. 271.
6. Commission Exhibit 408.
7. *Hearings*, Vol. I, pp. 68, 85.
8. *Hearings*, Vol. XI, p. 331, pp. 326–39 *passim.*
9. Commission Exhibit 93. Oswald's erratic spelling has been corrected and the punctuation regularized.
10. *Hearings*, Vol. XX, pp. 512–21.
11. Commission Document 75, U.S. National Archives, and Commission Exhibits 1413, 1414, 3119.
12. Commission Document 75.
13. *Hearings*, Vol. XX, pp. 512–21.
14. *Hearings*, Vol. X, p. 90.
15. *Hearings*, Vol. V, p. 401.
16. *Hearings*, Vol. I, p. 25.
17. *Hearings*, Vol. XXVI, p. 771.
18. *Hearings*, Vol. I, p. 64.
19. *Hearings*, Vol. XX, p. 525.
20. *Hearings*, Vol. XX, p. 524.
21. *Report*, p. 533.
22. *Hearings*, Vol. X, pp. 33–34, 82–83.
23. *Hearings*, Vol. X, p. 35.
24. *Hearings*, Vol. X, pp. 35–38.
25. *Hearings*, Vol. X, p. 54.
26. *Hearings*, Vol. IV, pp. 436*ff.*
27. *Hearings*, Vol. XX, p. 529.
28. *Hearings*, Vol. XXI, p. 621.
29. *Hearings*, Vol. XXI, pp. 634*ff.*
30. *Hearings*, Vol. XI, p. 171.
31. *Hearings*, Vol. XX, pp. 529–30.
32. *Hearings*, Vol. XX, pp. 263–64.
33. *Report*, p. 412.
34. *Hearings*, Vol. I, p. 24.

35. *Hearings*, Vol. I, p. 22.
36. *Hearings*, Vol. I, p. 22.
37. *Hearings*, Vol. XI, p. 372.
38. *Report*, p. 413*ff.*, and *Hearings*, Vol. XXIV, p. 590, also *Report*, p. 731.
39. *Hearings*, Vol. I, p. 50.

I. The Prosecutor

1. *New Orleans Times-Picayune*, February 25, 1967.
2. Edward Jay Epstein, *Inquest: The Warren Commission and the Establishment of Truth*, New York, The Viking Press, 1966.
3. *Ibid.*, p. 103.
4. *Hearings*, Vol. XXII, pp. 826–27.
5. *Hearings*, Vol. XXVI, p. 771.
6. *Hearings*, Vol. XXII, p. 826.
7. For an example of this conflict, see Epstein, *op. cit.*, pp. 31–42.
8. Fred Powledge, "Is Garrison Faking?" *New Republic*, June 17, 1967, p. 16, and James R. Phelan, "The Vice Man Cometh," *Saturday Evening Post*, June 8, 1963, pp. 67–71.
9. A. J. Liebling, *The Earl of Louisiana*, New York, Simon and Schuster, 1961, pp. 83–84.
10. Allan P. Sindler, *Huey Long's Louisiana*, Baltimore, Johns Hopkins Press, 1968, pp. 94–116, and V. O. Key, Jr., *Southern Politics*, New York, Vintage, 1949, pp. 156*ff.*
11. Phelan, *op. cit.*, pp. 67–71.
12. Garrison *v.* Louisiana, 379 U.S. 64 (1964).
13. *Times-Picayune*, April 13, 1967.
14. *Ibid.*, March 3, 1967, and Edward Weggman (counsel for Clay Shaw), interview with author (hereinafter Weggman Interview).
15. *Ibid.*, April 4, 1967.
16. *Ibid.*, May 13, 1967.
17. *Ibid.*
18. "The JFK Conspiracy: The Case of Jim Garrison," NBC-TV, June 19, 1967 (hereinafter "JFK Conspiracy," NBC-TV). The original interview with Garrison took place on WDSU-TV, New Orleans, an NBC affiliate.
19. *Times-Picayune*, May 18, 1967.
20. "JFK Conspiracy," NBC-TV.
21. "JFK Conspiracy," NBC-TV.
22. Jim Garrison, interview with author (hereinafter Garrison Interview).
23. *Los Angeles Free Press*, November 17, 1967. A similar statement was also made by Garrison on "Page One," WABC-TV, New York, September 24, 1967.

II. The Suspect

1. James A. Autry, "The Garrison Investigation: How and Why It Began," *New Orleans*, April 1967, p. 8.
2. Garrison Interview.
3. William W. Turner, "The Garrison Commission on the Assassination of President Kennedy," *Ramparts*, January 1968, p. 52.
4. Fred Powledge, *op. cit.*, p. 14.
5. Harold Weisberg, *Oswald in New Orleans: A Case of Conspiracy with the CIA*, Canyon Books, 1967, p. 395.
6. Richard H. Popkin, "Garrison's Case," *New York Review of Books*, September 14, 1967, p. 28.
7. Rosemary James and Jack Wardlaw, *Plot or Politics*, New Orleans, Pelican, 1967, p. 72.

8. *Hearings*, Vol. VIII, p. 14, Vol. XXII, pp. 826–27.
9. Popkin, *op. cit.*
10. James and Wardlaw, *op. cit.*, pp. 42–43.
11. *Ibid.*, p. 45.
12. *Ibid.*
13. *Ibid.*, p. 46.
14. *Ibid.*
15. Garrison Interview.
16. James and Wardlaw, *op. cit.*, p. 45.
17. *Times-Picayune*, February 27, 1967. Also quoted in Secret Service Report (Control No. 620), National Archives.
18. Thomas Bethell, interview with author (hereinafter Bethell Interview).
19. Secret Service Report quoted in Weisberg, *op. cit.*, p. 180.
20. Garrison Interview, and *New York World Journal Tribune*, March 5, 1967.
21. James and Wardlaw, *op. cit.*, p. 49.
22. Garrison Interview.
23. *Ibid.*
24. *Hearings*, Vol. XI, pp. 334, 337.
25. Andrew J. Sciambra, interview with author (hereinafter Sciambra Interview).
26. Garrison Interview.
27. David L. Chandler, interview with author (hereinafter Chandler Interview).
28. Richard N. Billings, "Garrison and the JFK Plot," *Long Island Press*, May 15, 1968.
29. Chandler Interview, and *Times-Picayune*, June 28, 1967.
30. Garrison Interview.
31. *Times-Picayune*, April 25, 1967.
32. Letter from Gordon Novel.
33. James and Wardlaw, *op. cit.*, p. 34.
34. *Ibid.*, pp. 38–39.
35. Richard N. Billings, "Garrison Convinced of Plot," *Miami Herald*, May 22, 1968, and interview with author (hereinafter Billings Interview).
36. *Times-Picayune*, February 26, 1967, and James and Wardlaw, *op. cit.*, p. 41.
37. *Ibid.*, February 23, 1967.
38. *Ibid.*, February 26, 1967.
39. Billings Interview.
40. *Times-Picayune*, June 28, 1967.
41. Transcript of Preliminary Hearing, Russo Testimony, p. 188.
42. *Ibid.*, pp. 182–83, 206.
43. Sciambra Memorandum. (Author's files.)
44. Billings Interview.
45. *Ibid.*
46. James R. Phelan, interview with author (hereinafter Phelan Interview).
47. Billings Interview, and Sciambra Interview.
48. *New York Times*, March 14, 1967.

III. The Witnesses

1. *"Playboy* Interview: Jim Garrison," *Playboy*, October 1967 (hereinafter *Playboy*), p. 62.
2. *Ibid.*
3. *Times-Picayune*, March 15, 1967.
4. *Ibid.*
5. Transcript of proceedings in connection with Preliminary Hearing, Clay L. Shaw, Arrestee (hereinafter *Transcript*), pp. 227ff., 212–14.
6. *Transcript*, p. 208.
7. *Transcript*, p. 279–80.
8. *Transcript*, p. 192.

9. *Transcript*, pp. 231–32.
10. *Transcript*, p. 203.
11. *Transcript*, p. 204.
12. *Transcript*, p. 246.
13. *Transcript*, p. 114.
14. William H. Gurvich, interview with author (hereinafter Gurvich Interview).
15. *Times-Picayune*, March 18, 1967.
16. *Ibid.*, March 23, 1967.
17. James R. Phelan, "Rush to Judgment in New Orleans," *Saturday Evening Post*, May 6, 1967, pp. 21–25.
18. *Ibid.*
19. Sciambra Memorandum.
20. Billings Interview, and *supra*, Chapter III.
21. *Report*, pp. 726–30.
22. "JFK Conspiracy," NBC-TV (statements of Ruth Paine and Mrs. Jesse Garner).
23. *Report*, pp. 730–38.
24. "JFK Conspiracy," NBC-TV.
25. Boston *Globe*, March 28, 1967.
26. Phelan, "Rush to Judgment in New Orleans," *op. cit.*
27. Sciambra Memorandum.
28. *Ibid.*
29. *Ibid.*
30. "JFK Conspiracy," NBC-TV.
31. *Playboy*, p. 62.
32. "JFK Conspiracy," NBC-TV.
33. Phelan Interview.
34. *Times-Picayune*, June 21, 1967.
35. "JFK Conspiracy," NBC-TV, and *New York Times*, June 12, 1967.
36. *New York Times*, August 14, 1967, and *Times-Picayune*, April 13, 1967.
37. *Times-Picayune*, August 13, 1967.
38. *Los Angeles Free Press*, November 17, 1967 (transcript of speech by Garrison).
39. *Times-Picayune*, August 13, 1967.
40. Bethell Interview.
41. Official Clerk's Records for the Criminal District Court for the Parish of Orleans, "State of Louisiana *v.* Clay L. Shaw," and Supplemental Memorandum.
43. *New York Times*, February 14, 1968.
44. *New York Times*, May 29, 1968, and U.S. District Court, Eastern District of Louisiana, "Clay L. Shaw *v.* Jim Garrison," Civil Action 68 1063, Section B.
45. *New York Times*, August 14, 1968.
46. Weggman Interview, and Garrison in *Los Angeles Free Press*, August 23, 1968.
47. *New York Times*, December 10 and 12, 1968.

IV. The Search

1. Bethell Interview.
2. Garrison Interview.
3. Letter from Bethell to author.
4. Bethell Interview.
5. *New York Times*, December 11, 1967.
6. Garrison Interview, and *New York World Journal Tribune*, March 5, 1967.
7. Garrison Interview, and *Times-Picayune*, July 12, 1968.
8. *Times-Picayune*, May 24, 1967, also Part III, CBS-TV News, June 27, 1967, and Garrison interviewed by Boy Jones, WWL-TV, New Orleans, May 21, 1967.
9. *Playboy*, p. 165.
10. James D. Squires, "Cuban Guerrilla Team Killed JFK, Garrison Thinks," *Nashville Tennesseean*, June 22, 1967.

11. *Playboy*, p. 170.
12. Bethell Interview.
13. "Page One," WABC-TV, New York, September 24, 1967 (hereinafter "Page One").
14. *Times-Picayune*, April 8, 1967.
15. "Page One."
16. *Ibid.*, and *Playboy, passim.*
17. "Page One."
18. *Ibid.*
19. *Playboy*, p. 159.
20. "Page One."
21. "Tonight" Show, NBC-TV, January 31, 1968.
22. *Playboy*, p. 162, and *Times-Picayune*, September 22, 1967.
23. "Joe Dolan Talk Back" Program, KNEW, Oakland, California, September 15, 1967.
24. "Face to Face with Murphy Martin," WFAA-TV, Dallas, Texas, December 9, 1967.
25. Bethell Interview.
26. "Face to Face with Murphy Martin," *op. cit.*
27. *Ibid.*
28. *Times-Picayune*, July 13, 1968.
29. *Playboy*, p. 166.
30. *Ibid.*, and *Berkeley Barb*, September 15–21, 1967.
31. FBI Report, June 11, 1964, Commission *Report* 1245; also, letter from Bethell.
32. Bethell Interview.
33. *Playboy*, p. 166.
34. "Tonight" Show, *op. cit.*
35. Bethell Interview, and Turner, *Ramparts, op. cit.*
36. *Playboy*, p. 160.
37. Letter from Bethell.
38. Garrison Interview, and Turner, *Ramparts, op. cit.*
39. *Playboy*, p. 163, and Bethell Interview.
40. Letter from Bethell.
41. Eric Norden, interview with author.
42. "Gordon Novel, Plaintiff, *v.* Jim Garrison and HMH Publishing Co., Inc., a Delaware Corporation, Defendants." Case No. 67 C 1895, in the United States District Court for the Northern District of Illinois, Eastern Division (hereinafter *Playboy File*). Exhibit B.
43. Bethell Interview.
44. James D. Squires, *op. cit.*
45. Bethell Interview. (Also, Garrison allowed author to read Johnson's statement.)
46. Bethell Interview. Also, Statement of Cedric Younger Von Rolleston, Oneda P. Von Rolleston, July 17, 1967. Author's files.
47. Affidavit of Oneda P. Von Rolleston and Cedric Younger Von Rolleston, March 16, 1968. Author's files.
48. *Times-Picayune*, June 28, 1967.
49. *Playboy*, pp. 167–68.
50. Bethell Interview.
51. *New York Times*, November 9, 1968.
52. *Chicago Tribune*, December 30, 1967.

V. The Thousand-Pound Canary

1. Ramond Moley, *Politics and Criminal Prosecution*, Minton, Balch & Co., 1929, p. 50, and *passim.*
2. *New York Times*, June 12, 1967.
3. *Ibid.*
4. "JFK Conspiracy," NBC-TV.
5. "JFK Conspiracy," NBC-TV.

6. Hugh Aynesworth, "The JFK Conspiracy," *Newsweek,* May 15, 1967.
7. *Playboy,* p. 64.
8. *Ibid.*
9. Gurvich Interview.
10. *Ibid.*
11. Dean Andrews, interview, June 1967, and Interviews taped for NBC News with Andrews, October 1967 (hereinafter Andrews Interviews).
12. Andrews Interviews.
13. *Ibid.*
14. *Ibid.*
15. *Ibid.*
16. *Ibid.*
17. *Ibid.*
18. *Times-Picayune,* April 13, 1967.
19. Andrews Interviews.
20. *Ibid.*
21. *Supra,* Chapter III.
22. Memorandum by David Lifton concerning Kerry Thornley (hereinafter Lifton Memorandum).
23. *Ibid.*
24. *Ibid.*
25. *Ibid.,* and *Miami Herald,* February 1, 1968.
26. Bethell Interview, and Letter from Harold Weisberg to Fred Newcomb.
27. Lifton Memorandum.

VI. The Tangled Web

1. Richard H. Rovere, *Senator Joe McCarthy,* New York, Meridian, 1964, p. 140.
2. The speech is reprinted in its entirety in *The Los Angeles Free Press,* December 22–28, 1967.
3. Edward A. Shils, *The Torment of Secrecy,* New York, The Free Press, 1956, pp. 24–25, and *passim.*
4. *Saturday Evening Post,* May 6, 1967, pp. 22–25.
5. *New Orleans States-Item,* April 25, 1967, and Rosemary James, interview with author.
6. *Newsweek,* May 15, 1967, pp. 36–40.
7. Martin Waldron, "Some Say It's Garrison Who's in Wonderland," *New York Times,* May 14, 1967, and Jack Wardlaw, interview with author.
8. *Times-Picayune,* May 9, 1967.
9. *New York Times,* May 10, 1967.
10. *Times-Picayune,* May 10, 1967.
11. *Infra,* Chapter VII.
12. *Chicago Tribune,* December 30, 1967, and Stephen White, *Should We Now Believe the Warren Report?,* New York, Macmillan, 1968, p. 276.
13. *Times-Picayune,* May 22, 1967. (The interview was carried on WWL-TV, New Orleans, May 21, 1967.)
14. "JFK Conspiracy," NBC-TV.
15. Epstein, *op. cit.,* pp. 98–100.
16. *Times-Picayune,* June 20, 1967.
17. *Times-Picayune,* June 21, 1967, and unpublished portion of transcript of *Playboy* interview.
18. "Statement by Jim Garrison," NBC-TV, July 15, 1967.
19. *Playboy,* p. 108.
20. *New York Times,* July 17, 1967.
21. *Times-Picayune,* July 19, 1967.
22. *New Orleans States-Item,* June 23, 1967.

23. White, *op. cit.,* pp. 274–75 (see note 12).
24. *Times-Picayune,* June 27, 1967.
25. *Times-Picayune,* June 24, 1967.
26. *Playboy,* p. 68.
27. "Page One."
28. "Warren Foresees Trial News Curbs," *New York Times,* September 5, 1967.
29. "Garrison Assails Tokyo Words of Chief Justice," *Times-Picayune,* September 5, 1967.
30. *Ibid.*
31. Billings Interview.
32. "Witness in Assassination Plot Hints at Cuban Link," *New York Times,* April 4, 1967.
33. "Novel Will Be Returned—Ohio," *Times-Picayune,* May 10, 1967.
34. Bethell Interview.
35. "Ohio Frees 'Witness' Sought by Garrison," *New York Times,* July 4, 1967.
36. *Playboy,* p. 172.
37. *Los Angeles Free Press,* November 17, 1967.
38. *Times-Picayune,* July 12, 1968.
39. *Time,* August 2, 1968, p. 56.
40. *Times-Picayune,* July 12, 1968.
41. *Ibid.*

VII. The CIA

1. Richard Hofstadter, *The Paranoid Style in American Politics and Other Essays,* New York, Vintage, 1967, p. 4.
2. "Issues and Answers," ABC-TV, May 28, 1967.
3. Martin Waldron, "Garrison Charges CIA and FBI Conceal Evidence on Oswald," *New York Times,* May 10, 1967.
4. *Times-Picayune,* May 18, 1967.
5. "Garrison Says CIA Knows the Slayers," *New York Times,* May 23, 1967, and *Times-Picayune,* May 22, 1967.
6. *Times-Picayune,* May 24, 1967, and Associated Press Interview with Garrison by Laura Foreman, May 23, 1967.
7. *Los Angeles Free Press,* November 17, 1967.
8. "Tonight" Show, *op. cit.*
9. Transcript of Interview with Dutch television, Reel 1, p. 2.
10. *Playboy,* pp. 70, 72, 74, 160.
11. *Times-Picayune,* May 7, 1967, and *Playboy,* p. 70.
12. Epstein, *op. cit.,* pp. 93–94.
13. Garrison Interview.
14. *Playboy,* p. 74.
15. Interview with James B. Rhodes, Deputy Archivist, U.S. National Archives (hereinafter Rhodes Interview).
16. Wesley J. Liebeler, interview with author.
17. *Playboy,* p. 74.
18. *Los Angeles Free Press,* December 22, 1967.
19. *Playboy,* pp. 167–68.
20. Josiah Thompson, *Six Seconds in Dallas,* New York, Bernard Geis Associates, 1967, p. 217, and Billings Interview.
21. *Playboy,* p. 72.
22. *Los Angeles Free Press,* November 17, 1967.
23. *Hearings,* Vol. XVIII, p. 188.
24. *Los Angeles Free Press,* November 17, 1967.
25. *Playboy,* p. 70, and Garrison Interview.
26. Commission Document 75, FBI File 89–69.
27. Garrison Interview.

28. *Report*, pp. 697–98.
29. *Supra*, Chapter IV.
30. *Playboy*, p. 70.
31. *Ibid.*
32. Interview with Fred Freed, producer of "JFK Conspiracy," NBC-TV.

VIII. The Media

1. Jim Garrison, "With Liberty and Justice for All," foreword to Harold Weisberg, *op. cit.*, p. 13.
2. "Statement by Jim Garrison," NBC-TV, July 15, 1967.
3. *Hearings*, Vol. IV, p. 22.
4. *Hearings*, Vol. IV, p. 24.
5. *Report*, p. 123, and Commission Exhibit 2637.
6. *Report*, pp. 560–62.
7. *Hearings*, Vol. III, p. 494.
8. *Report*, p. 152.
9. Josiah Thompson, *op. cit.*, pp. 254–70.
10. Stephen White, *op. cit.*, p. 248, and Transcript of CBS-TV News "Inquiry," Part II, June 26, 1967.

IX. The Federal Establishment

1. *Los Angeles Free Press*, November 17, 1967 (text of speech by Garrison).
2. "Face to Face with Murphy Martin," WFAA-TV, Dallas, Texas, December 9, 1967, and *supra*, Chapter IV.
3. "Garrison Says Oswald Gave FBI a Tip Before Assassination," *New York Times*, December 27, 1967.
4. *Ibid.*
5. *Ibid.*
6. "Tonight" Show, NBC-TV, January 31, 1968.
7. "Face to Face with Murphy Martin," *op. cit.*
8. Rhodes Interview.
9. *Ibid.*, and letter from McGeorge Bundy. Author's files.
10. *Ibid.*
11. *Playboy*, p. 72.
12. Richard H. Rovere, *op. cit.*, pp. 148–50.
13. *Ibid.*, pp. 47–48, and "McCarthy: A Documented Record," *The Progressive*, April 1954, pp. 59–63 and *passim*.
14. Richard Hofstadter, *op. cit.*
15. *Los Angeles Free Press*, November 17, 1967.
16. The indictment reads, "Clay L. Shaw . . . did willfully and unlawfully conspire with David W. Ferrie, herein named but not charged, *and Lee Harvey Oswald*, herein named but not charged, and others, not herein named, to murder John F. Kennedy" (italics mine), *Times-Picayune*, March 23, 1967.
17. *Playboy*, p. 178.
18. *Ibid.*

X. The Torment of Secrecy

1. Garrison Interview, WWL-TV, New Orleans, May 21, 1967.
2. "Face to Face with Murphy Martin," *op. cit.*
3. Garrison on Dutch television, reel 2.
4. "Tonight" Show, NBC-TV, January 31, 1968.

5. Garrison on Dutch television.
6. Edward A. Shils, *op. cit.*, pp. 234, 37–47 and *passim.*
7. See p. 138, *supra.*
8. "Tonight" Show, *op. cit.*
9. Bethell Interview.
10. *Ibid.*
11. Synopsis of letters received by *Playboy* (author's file).
12. *Washington Post*, March 6, 1967.
13. *Washington Post*, May 29, 1967.
14. *News and Observer*, Raleigh, N.C., September 20, 1967.
15. *Washington Post*, October 19, 1964.
16. *Washington Post*, October 19, 1964.
17. *Supra*, Chapter VIII.
18. "Tonight" Show, *op. cit.*
19. *Report*, pp. 123–24.
20. "Tonight" Show, *op. cit.*
21. *Playboy*, p. 66.
22. Bethell Interview.
23. *Ibid.*
24. Hannah Arendt, *Between Past and Future*, New York, Viking Compass Edition, 1968, pp. 250–51.
25. *Playboy*, pp. 74, 157.

XI.   The Making of a Demagogue

1. "A Matter of Reasonable Doubt," *Life*, November 25, 1966, pp. 38–53.
2. Chandler Interview.
3. *Ibid.*, and Billings Interview.
4. Billings Interview.
5. Garrison Interview.
6. Billings Interview.
7. Chandler Interview.
8. *Ibid.*
9. Billings Interview, and *infra*, Chapters II, III.
10. Billings Interview.
11. *Playboy* File, Exhibit H-1.
12. *Playboy*, p. 62.
13. *Playboy* File, July 20, 1967, Memorandum, Exhibit E.
14. *Playboy* File, July 19, 1967, Memorandum, Exhibit D.
15. *Playboy* File, Exhibit C-1.
16. *Playboy*, p. 162 Cf. *Hearings*, Vol. XIX, p. 534.
17. *Playboy* File, Exhibit H-1.
18. "Page One."
19. *Ramparts*, January 1968, front cover.
20. *The Councilor*, Shreveport, Louisiana, June 1, 1967.
21. William Turner, "The Press Versus Garrison," *Ramparts*, August 1968, p. 12.
22. *The Councilor*, May 12, 1967. Cf. *Ramparts*, January 1968, p. 2.
23. *The Councilor*, "Russo Says: David W. Ferrie Was a Marxist," June 15, 1967.
24. Richard H. Popkin, "Garrison's Case," *New York Review of Books*, September 14, 1967, p. 20.
25. *Ibid.*, p. 25.
26. *Infra*, Chapter I. Cf. *Playboy*, p. 174, and cf. Garrison Interview, "Issues and Answers," ABC-TV, May 28, 1967.
27. Jerrold D. Footlick, "Jim, Do You Really Believe All This Stuff?" *National Observer*, January 22, 1968, p. 1.
28. *Playboy*, p. 162.

29. Popkin, *op. cit.*, p. 21.
30. *New York Times*, June 12, 1967.
31. The witnesses were John Cancler, Miguel Torres, Sandra Moffit, Fred Lemanns, Alvin Beauboeuf, Dean Andrews.
32. Gurvich Interview.
33. Popkin, *op. cit.*, p. 23.
34. Fred Powledge, *op. cit.*, p. 18.
35. Hannah Arendt, *op. cit.*, p. 243.

LEGEND

NOTES

Prologue: Message from Moscow

SOURCE NOTES

The prologue is based on personal interviews I did with Nosenko and CIA officers who had direct knowledge of the following aspects of his case: (1) his original contact with the CIA in 1962 in Geneva; (2) his debriefing in Geneva in 1964; (3) his defection to the United States; (4) his residence in Washington and his trip to Hawaii; (5) his original interrogation in Washington; (6) his hostile interrogation (1964–1967); (7) the Soviet Russia Division's critique of Nosenko; (8) the counterintelligence staff's critique of the Nosenko reports; (9) the Office of Security's report on Nosenko; and (10) the rebuttal in 1967 of the Office of Security's report. I have also interviewed James J. Angleton and members of his counterintelligence staff who were involved with the Nosenko case, and Sam Papich, the FBI liaison to the CIA during this period. William Sullivan, then assistant director of the FBI, and other FBI officers have also discussed the case with me.

The case is further supported by documents obtained under the Freedom of Information Act, including (1) a synopsis of sections of the 900-page Soviet Russia Division report on Nosenko; (2) the forty-four questions; (3) the FBI report of the interview with Nosenko; (4) the counterintelligence report on Nosenko's debriefing in Geneva in January 1964 by James Angleton; and (5) Warren Commission documents summarizing its knowledge of the Nosenko case.

The section about J. Edgar Hoover and the FBI's internal security case on Oswald comes from the Final Report of the Senate Select Committee to Study Governmental Operations with Respect to Intelligence Activities (hereafter known as the Schweiker Report). The quotes are taken from a memorandum written by J. H. Gale, assistant director of the FBI's Inspection Division, to Clyde Tolson on December 10, 1963, and from Hoover's handwritten notes on that memorandum.

The material about the State Department derives from documents obtained under the Freedom of Information Act.

The section on the Warren Commission is based on interviews with the commission's members and staff which were originally conducted in 1965 and on more recent interviews with W. David Slawson, Wesley J. Liebeler and Leon Hubert.

The executive minutes of the Warren Commission meeting on January 27, which were obtained under the Freedom of Information Act, are the source for all the material regarding the commission's questioning of Marina Oswald. The staff memorandum on Marina was examined in the National Archives and first quoted in *Inquest*.

The quote from Slawson's handwritten notes was likewise obtained from the National Archives.

The so-called Coleman-Slawson report was a document prepared for the Warren Commission and obtained under the Freedom of Information Act.

The information on Stone comes from discussions with Thomas Fox, then chief of counterintelligence of the Defense Intelligence Agency, who participated in the debriefing of Stone, William Sullivan, James Angleton and members of Angleton's counter-intelligence staff.

The portions on the executive decisions of the CIA come from personal interviews with Richard M. Helms, then deputy director of Plans, and Walter Elder, then executive assistant to John McCone, the Director of Central Intelligence. The meeting between Chief Justice Warren and Helms was described to me by Helms.

The material on Fedora comes from interviews with officers of the FBI and CIA.

Everything concerning Marina's testimony on Oswald's visit to Mexico derives from a comparison of the pertinent FBI reports with the Warren Report.

FOOTNOTES

1. The Soviet Committee for State Security, best known by its Russian initials, KGB, is descended from CHEKA of the revolutionary period and has passed through several name changes. At the present time the KGB handles all counterintelligence operations and, in addition, is responsible for the internal security of the Soviet state and the safety of its leaders. It shares responsibility for foreign espionage activities with the GRU, which is the intelligence component of the Ministry of Defense.

2. See footnote 8 for Chapter XV, page 327.

3. The first mention that Nosenko had provided information on the Oswald case came from documents given to the author in 1965 by a lawyer on the Warren Commission's staff. This brief mention was subsequently published in *Inquest*, and the lawyer, Wesley J. Liebeler, later heard that he had committed a serious security breach in allowing Nosenko's name to come out. The next public mention of Nosenko's connection to the Oswald case was in John Barron's *KGB* in 1974. Nosenko had walked into the *Reader's Digest* office in Washington and volunteered information. In 1975 the Rockefeller Commission reviewed the CIA's treatment of Nosenko from the point of view of his public rights, and his name was again reported in the press.

4. In another extraordinary development, a Soviet journalist approached the French magazine *Paris Match* with an offer to provide photographs of "Colonel" Nosenko's deserted family. The research chief of CIA's counterintelligence later commented that there was no precedent for the Soviets providing photographs of defectors, and he considered the offer a suspicious attempt to establish Nosenko publicly as a defector.

5. See Appendix C for the full text of the forty-four questions.

6. For a fuller discussion, see Edward Jay Epstein, *Inquest* (New York: Viking Press, 1966), pp. 95–97.

7. Angleton had no doubt that the Soviets had the capacity for mounting disinformation operations and looked upon the "Trust" of the 1920s as the model for such deceptions. In the "Trust," Soviet intelligence deliberately created an anti-Soviet underground that it could control. As the group inside Russia which could carry out spying and sabotage missions for anti-Soviet groups outside Russia, it could also coordinate the flow of information from the Soviet Union to the Western intelligence agencies cooperating with the anti-Soviet émigrés. The Soviet idea of creating its own "enemy" is similar to that of creating biological analogues for insect control: The insects, unable to differentiate between the man-made simulacrum and the real larvae, attempt to breed with the artifice, which is, of course, sterile. In this case Soviet intelligence arranged a series of initial successes for the anti-Soviet underground to prove the efficacy of the "Trust" inside Russia. Once the "Trust" was established as the mainstay of the Soviet resistance movement, the Soviet agents operating it spoon-fed to Western intelligence agencies information supposedly obtained from defectors in place at the highest levels of the Soviet government. The fabricated reports from the "Trust" were then confirmed by other fake anti-Soviet groups set up by Soviet intelligence. This well-coordinated campaign of disinformation channeled through intelligence agencies helped Moscow persuade Western governments that it was abandoning its plans for world revolution and was moving more toward nationalism than communism. (Payments by twelve Western intelligence agencies to the "Trust" for these false reports financed not only the

"Trust" but also provided almost the entire budget for Soviet espionage activities abroad.)

8. In the case of British intelligence, Kim Philby, a Soviet agent who was recruited at his university, rose to be head of the counterintelligence division of MI 5 and then had the responsibility as liaison with the CIA. For a complete account of this case, see Bruce Page, *The Philby Conspiracy*. In the case of West German intelligence, the Soviets managed to promote their own agent, Heinz Felfer, to the head of counterintelligence through an intricate series of maneuvers in which they sacrificed their own agents like pawns in a chess game.

9. The chief of operations wrote out, following an interview with the author, what he considered to be the mode in which the Soviets would handle a defector such as Oswald. He pointed out that even if Oswald had not had information about radar, the Soviets would still have been interested in him as a former Marine: "Marines have been prime KGB (and GRU) targets since they started guarding American embassies. The First Chief Directorate would have had an interest even after he was discharged. . . . in fact, it is known that the KGB visa screening process for tourists called special attention to ex-servicemen."

10. Popov himself had provided one "answer" to the question in his last meeting with the CIA in Moscow in 1959. At that time he had already been caught by the KGB and had been imprisoned, but in an apparent attempt to compromise his CIA case officers, the KGB allowed him to attend this prearranged rendezvous. After indicating with hand gestures that he had been wired for sound with a hidden microphone and was under KGB control, he handed the American a six-page note written on scraps of toilet paper.

The note explained that he had been detected by Soviet surveillance. If this explanation was accepted at face value, it meant no betrayal was involved in the case. But since Popov was known to be a prisoner at the time he handed this extraordinary message to the CIA and since the American diplomat involved in posting the letter insisted that he had not been followed, there was some suspicion that Popov's "answer" was a KGB fabrication.

11. The only other confirmation of Cherepanov came from Yuri Loginov, a KGB agent who posed as a CIA double agent until 1967. After his capture in South Africa, he redefected to the Soviet Union in 1968. While supplying the CIA with information about Cherepanov, he was presumably a controlled channel of the KGB.

12. *The Penkovskiy Papers*, a best-seller in 1965, detailed much of the data Penkovskiy revealed.

13. Between 1962, when Nosenko first contacted the CIA, and 1964 he was seen in activities of the Second Chief Directorate. Prior to 1962, however, there seems to have been only one independent identification of such activities.

14. For a fuller description of the purpose behind the commission see Edward Jay Epstein, *Inquest*, Chapter II. Also see Executive Minutes, Warren Commission.

Chapter I, "Race Car"

SOURCE NOTES

The information about Oswald and the U-2 comes from personal interviews with the Marines who served with him at Atsugi and in the Philippines. (See footnotes below for details.)

The material about Oswald's early history comes from testimony before the Warren Commission given by Marguerite Oswald, Robert Oswald, John Pic and Lillian Murret. It is also drawn from the probation reports included in the Warren Commission exhibits of John Carro, Dr. Renatus Hartogs, Evelyn Strickman and others who dealt with Oswald. Other sources were FBI reports on some of Oswald's young friends, including Palmer McBride, William E. Wulf and Edward Voebel, and two published books, *A Mother in History* by Jean Stafford and *Lee* by Robert Oswald.

FOOTNOTES

1. With varying descriptions, more than 35 of the men stationed with Oswald in the Far East recall details of the U-2. Some, like Dale Dooley, didn't know it by name, but simply remembered it as "a gigantic glider . . . It had little wheels on its wing tips."

James R. Persons, who is now a bank president in Mississippi, recalls a landing of the U-2: "It made very little noise, and it came in very slowly—only at 60 or 70 miles per hour—and it would drift in and come down the runway to a standstill and then tip over on one wing, sort of like a glider." He recalls that the plane had "tremendous lift" on takeoff and would soon be out of sight. He remembers little wheels under the wing tips that would fly off when the plane was airborne.

Persons believes that he knew the craft as a U-2 at that time and thought it was a weather plane.

Joseph Macedo, who was on Oswald's radar crew and is now a railroad engineer working out of Chicago, saw the U-2 many times. "Everyone called it the U-2," Macedo recalls. "I don't know how we knew, but we all knew." Macedo also states that Oswald was as familiar with the U-2 as the rest of the crew: "Everyone in radar center could listen on any channel at any time. . . . He was on the same radar crew, and it was his job as much as anyone else's."

Miguel Rodriguez, a career Marine who now is a postal worker in San Antonio, remembers the U-2: "It was like a glider . . . it had a long wingspan. It was an odd-looking skinny plane. It looked too simple, and it had little wheels under the wing tips that dropped off on takeoff." He recalls that the plane took off very quickly, using only one-half to three-quarters of the runway. He believed that it was a test plane of some description and thinks that photographing it would have been simple, although he believes there was a base regulation against taking pictures of any of the planes.

George Wilkins, an Oswald friend who now is a partner in an auto garage in Brooklyn, New York, recalls once that the U-2 belly-flopped short of the runway and the Marines were chased off by Air Force guards.

Jerry E. Pitts, today the sheriff of Hamilton County, Tennessee, recalls: "The most amazing thing about the plane was how fast it gained altitude on takeoff—almost straight up and out of sight." He describes the plane as others do, but he doesn't remember its being called a U-2, only that it was a test plane, adding that anyone could have taken a picture of it.

Pete F. Connor was aware of the U-2, while walking guard duty at Atsugi, because of the high whine like an electrical generator, which was different from the muffled explosive noise of a jet. "It was almost scary the way the whining noise increased as the plane rushed down the runway and lifted into the air. . . . It was gone before you could see it. Unbelievable."

Richard Cyr, now a police lieutenant in Needham, Massachusetts, states that on the basis of the amount of time the U-2 would be aloft, the men deduced that it had to be a glider that used its engines only to take off and to gain sufficient altitude for its missions, which Cyr could only guess at. He also remembers that it would have been easy to photograph the U-2: "You could have gotten a shot from different parts of the base, especially with a telephoto lens. The end of the runway, where we were located, would have been a good location, especially when it came in so slowly."

Peter Cassisi, today a police sergeant in Ossining, New York, was in the motor pool when he knew Oswald at Atsugi. Despite security regulations, Cassisi and his friends never had difficulty getting into the radar bubble to watch the blips and listen on the radio signals, which they enjoyed doing. Cassisi was present once when a request for "winds aloft at ninety thousand feet" came in—a request that could have come only from the U-2, indicating that any special security measures which were established when the secret aircraft was taking off or while it was aloft were not strictly enforced.

Cassisi, who always heard the aircraft called a U-2, understood that it was a spy plane and believed that it was usually out twelve to sixteen hours. "When it would return, it would circle very low and slowly over the town, and it always caused a big commotion with the townspeople. Anyone could have photographed it. The plane made a high, shrill whistle that was unique, and this would cause people to rush outside to watch."

2. The officer who recalls Oswald's interest in the U-2 is John E. Donovan, a former lieutenant in the Marine Corps. Donovan remembers clearly that Oswald called his attention to radar images of the U-2, and that this incident took place at Cubi Point. However, other officers and enlisted men from Oswald's unit remember that their unit did not set up radar operations at Cubi Point at that time. One possible explanation for this discrepancy is that a number of different Marine squadrons were temporarily camped in the same vicinity, and Oswald may have come into contact with Donovan while their individual units were together at Cubi Point.

Donovan was also Oswald's officer at the Marine Air Station at El Toro, California in 1959, where he worked constantly with Oswald in the radar bubble. It is conceivable that after nearly twenty years, Donovan is recalling an incident that took place there. In any case, since there are no other witnesses, it cannot be resolved where, and if, this incident took place.

3. None of the people who knew him during his childhood and adolescence remember Lee's being traumatized by the lack of a father. Edward Voebel, his closest friend in junior high school, does not recall his ever mentioning his father, nor do Marguerite, Robert, John Pic or Lillian Murret (Lee's aunt) remember his being curious about the parent he never knew. Only in 1963, when he was twenty-three years old, did Lee make an effort to locate members of his father's family in New Orleans.

4. In 1965 Marguerite Oswald told author Jean Stafford for her book *A Mother in History* that Lee once told her excitedly that he'd spent the entire day riding the subway rather than attending classes. "Now I want to say this in defense of my son," she said. "How many boys at age thirteen that play hookey from school would come home . . . and tell his mother that he did so?"

5. Oswald wrote most of his letters by hand, and they contain numerous spelling and grammatical errors. Since many of these involve the transposition of letters, some observers have suggested that he might have suffered from dyslexia. However, none of the social workers or clinical psychologists who examined him while he was alive ever noted such a learning disability. In many of the letters Oswald later wrote from New Orleans such errors do not occur. It is therefore possible that his poor spelling resulted from his being largely self-educated.

6. Despite a treaty with the Japanese that banned the presence of nuclear weapons on U.S. military bases, at least six of the witnesses who served with Oswald at Atsugi reported a belief that such armaments were available. One officer provides what conceivably is an eyewitness report.

The five enlisted men's comments ranged from a belief that atom bombs were housed at Atsugi because it was "a striking base for anywhere in that area" to general comments that "we all had the impression that nuclear weapons were kept there."

Lieutenant Charles Rhodes reports, however, that one afternoon he was playing golf with one of the senior colonels on the base. In the middle of the golf game the colonel said he had some business to attend to, and he invited Rhodes to come along with him. No one told Rhodes what he saw that afternoon, and he never asked about it, sensing that it was none of his business. Rhodes knows nothing about nuclear weaponry, so even today he does not claim to know what he saw. However, here is what he recalls:

He and the colonel went down into a heavily guarded area that was at least three stories below ground. He remembers that the cave seemed to have full facilities for living and, he specifically recalls, running water and toilets. The main feature of the cave was a long, wide concourse with railroad tracks running down the middle. Lining each side of the concourse were large bays—or indentations that appeared to be about 20 feet long and about 18 feet high. In each bay was a large, "fat-looking" armament that, Rhodes assumed, was a bomb of some description. He recalls that each bomb was about 18 feet long and 15 feet wide. He recalls that there were a "good number" of them, but he declined to guess how many. "It was one of the most amazing things I've ever seen," says Rhodes.

Rhodes was there for several minutes while the colonel spoke to someone, and then they left.

Chapter II, The Queen Bee

SOURCE NOTES

With one exception, all the quotes and descriptions in this chapter come from Marines who were interviewed for this book. The exception is the assertion that Oswald had met Communists in Japan. This comes from the testimony of George De Mohrenschildt (Volume IX, page 242). De Mohrenschildt later repeated this to me in an interview in March 1977.

FOOTNOTES

1. Jerry E. Pitts lived in the same barracks with Oswald at Atsugi, and he recalls that every new man coming into the unit was put through an initiation of sorts: "In Oswald's case, the guys found out he didn't like being called Harvey or Harve, so that's what a lot of the guys called him." He explained that savvy Marines could breeze right through such treatment, laughing off the insults and swapping them back. But Oswald was the exception. He seemed to take each insult seriously and responded with a quiet fury that he was incapable of converting into physical violence. "We all had to go through the same thing," Pitts recalls, "but Oswald never understood that. . . . He just never knew how to read the system. If he could have just taken the initial insults, he would have become one of the boys."

Pitts, who says he was never friendly with Oswald but never harassed him either, remembers that there were certain areas—such as indecent references to his mother—that really set Oswald off, and these were the areas the antagonists concentrated on. Pitts believes that Oswald felt the men were picking on him strictly because he was Oswald, never seeming to realize that he was bringing the trouble on himself by reacting as he did.

2. The unit even had a medium-sized mongrel, named Macs, as the mascot of the MACS-1 unit. Marines would even give him bowls of precious vodka to lap up—a libation that Macs reputedly relished. And on paydays they would take him along with them to the bars and brothels, where they would pay the girls to cavort with Macs.

3. Several witnesses recall a wild place in Yamato pronounced "Negashaya," where men wore dresses and lipstick. One witness described the place as a "queer bar" and reported that he and Oswald once went there—at Oswald's suggestion—and took out two deaf-mute girls. "Oswald seemed to know his way around in the place," the witness, who prefers not to be identified by name, recalls. "I don't remember that he knew anyone by name, but he was comfortable there."

4. Two lawyers for the Warren Commission, W. David Slawson and William T. Coleman, Jr., suggested in a report which was released under the Freedom of Information Act: that ". . . there is the possibility that Oswald came into contact with Communist agents at that time, i.e., during his tour of duty in the Philippines, Japan, and possibly Formosa. Japan, especially because the Communist Party was open and active there, would seem a likely spot for a contact to have been made. . . . Whether such contacts, if they occurred, amounted to anything more than some older Communist advising Oswald, who was then eighteen or nineteen years old, to go to Russia and see the Communist world is unclear." The Warren Commission did not, however, pursue this in its final report.

5. Pete Connor remembers one occasion distinctly when Oswald was with a girl because it was the night Conner won $40 playing bingo at the enlisted men's club: "She was a good-looking Japanese girl wearing nice clothes. . . . Half the guys on the base would have gone for her. Oswald never deserved her. . . . I don't know what she was

doing with Oswald, unless he had a few extra bucks." Connor recalls that Oswald and the girl sat apart from the rest of the crowd, who were watching a floor show, and he doesn't recall that they danced or showed any affection toward each other. They sat and talked. Marina Oswald later told her biographer that, in 1963 in Dallas, Oswald had vaguely described a number of women he had been involved with in Japan. The first was nearly twice his age; the second was thin and extremely promiscuous, and the third was fat and used to cook for him.

6. Lieutenant Charles Rhodes recalls an incident at Atsugi when a girl he was friendly with informed him that she was sorry to hear that he was going on maneuvers to Formosa. Rhodes, an officer assigned to MACS-1 as an air controller, told her that she was misinformed—that there were no plans for the unit to go to Formosa. Ten days later Rhodes was officially informed of the maneuver.

7. Descriptions of the same incident by different men seem to vary remarkably.

Three of the witnesses—Pete Connor, Jerry Pitts and John Radtke—think the incident occurred in the daytime. Thomas Bagshaw believes that the discharged bullet hit the ceiling—not Oswald. Connor insists that the derringer, which Oswald was playing with as he sat on a bunk, discharged and sent a bullet seven inches above Connor's head to slam into a wall locker. Connor concedes that he and some others had been tormenting Oswald and that the initial suspicion was that the shot could have been on purpose, although today Connor believes the pistol went off by mistake. Connor is adamant in his account, although he notes that he "vaguely remembers" another incident in which Oswald wounded himself. Connor reports that after the incident in which he was almost hit, Oswald was removed from the barracks for a few days and then returned. By that time Connor and some of his friends had been moved to a different part of the barracks.

Pitts recalls hearing about the incident the way Connor reports it, while conceding that he did not witness it firsthand. Radtke is certain the incident happened in the early afternoon, although he believes Oswald sustained a minor injury.

Three other witnesses recall the incident—all agreeing that Oswald sustained a minor injury—but none of these three is able to place a time for the occurrence.

Unfortunately this incident is not remembered by the medical personnel involved. Reached two decades later in Ukiah, California, where he now has a practice, Dr. Guthrie was not able to recall treating Oswald. The chief of surgery when Oswald was treated was Dr. Haskell M. Wertheimer, who states that there were simply too many injured Marines in his career for him to remember Oswald. Dr. H. W. Russell, now in Honolulu, could not recall signing the report of the shooting incident to Oswald's commanding officer.

Given such lapses and conflicts of memory after twenty years, one is compelled to resolve the conflicts on the basis of the contemporaneously written medical reports.

8. A photograph taken by an officer shows Oswald and a group of friends waiting to board the USS *Terrell County*. (See photograph section.) Lee Oswald is in the front center of the scene. On the far left is a local Filipino selling knives to the troops. Other Marines in the immediate group are, from the left: Godfrey Jerome Daniels, George A. Wilkins, Jr., Zack Stout (face obscured by Oswald), Bobby J. Warren and James R. Persons. None of these men was ever questioned by either the Warren Commission or the FBI.

9. According to my Marine sources, the rates of exchange in the local economy—which fluctuated with supply and demand—broke down to one U.S. military blanket being worth 12 pints of rum.

10. James R. Persons, the first man to reach Schrand, believes the weapon was "right beside the body," not a matter of feet away. However, Persons also recalls picking up the gun at one point and being told to put it back where he had found it, thus raising the possibility that the gun was moved after the shooting.

11. A number of Marines asserted that Oswald was on guard duty that night and was possibly involved in the Schrand incident. After questioning nine officers and enlisted men who were at Cubi Point that night, I was unable to find any corroborating evidence indicating that Oswald was even a witness to Schrand's death.

12. Lieutenant Charles Rhodes witnessed the incident: "I walked in right after it

happened—before the MPs got there—and there were three or four guys standing around ready to let Oswald have it. . . . Rodriguez was about to let him have it, but some of his friends convinced him it wasn't worth getting into a fight over." Rhodes says that he later told Rodriguez that he believed a sound thrashing would have been just what Oswald needed. Rhodes recalls that Oswald had been complaining to him that Rodriguez had been picking on him. Rhodes, who knew Rodriguez and remembers him as a well-respected sergeant who treated the men evenhandedly, went to Rodriguez to discuss the matter. Rodriguez told him that Oswald was wrong—that he was not being picked on and that Rodriguez was beginning to get tired of his constant carping about it. Rhodes then told Oswald that he was being unreasonable—that he was imagining things if he thought he was being singled out for undesirable assignments.

Rodriguez, who today does not claim to understand the incident, recalls a meeting of NCOs shortly before his trouble with Oswald at which they were told there was going to be a crackdown on Marines who persisted in getting into fights in town bars. The NCOs were told that the best place to start was among themselves. Rodriguez believes that he possibly would have been demoted if he had got into a fight with Oswald at the Bluebird.

13. The doctors who treated Oswald were not able to recall their specific contact with him, citing the routine nature of his ailments. Dr. Paul Deranian, for example, who was the senior medical officer, noted that complaints about heavy lifting were extremely common and that one of his jobs was to assess whether it seemed the man was gold-bricking and then to decide whether to give him a note stating that he should not lift anything that weighed more than a certain number of pounds.

Chapter III, The Defector

SOURCE NOTES

This chapter is based on personal interviews with Marines.

The section about Nelson Delgado is also based on FBI and Secret Service reports on him, as well as a personal interview I had with him in Germany.

The parts on Oswald's relatives are based either on their Warren Commission testimony or on Robert Oswald's book *Lee*.

The section on Oswald's date with Rosaleen Quinn derives from a personal interview I had with her.

The material on Oswald's travel from the United States to the Soviet Union is based on FBI reports from the National Archives and CIA documents obtained under the Freedom of Information Act. Other sources were a personal interview with Colonel and Mrs. Church and the affidavit Billy Joe Lord submitted to the Warren Commission.

Oswald's activities at the American Embassy in Moscow were described to me by Richard Snyder and John McVickar. I also consulted their Warren Commission testimony and FBI reports for a more contemporaneous account of their contact with Oswald.

All of Oswald's letters which are quoted can be found in the exhibits of the Warren Commission.

Of the journalists Oswald saw in Moscow, the material about Robert Korengold and Aline Mosby comes from personal interviews, while the part about Priscilla Johnson derives from the interview notes which she submitted to the Warren Commission investigators.

The section at the end of the chapter dealing with the CIA's subsequent interpretation of Oswald derives from interviews with James J. Angleton and his staff.

FOOTNOTES

1. Oswald objected to nonclassical music to the extent that he once broke a Johnny Cash record owned by a corporal.

2. William Alexander Morgan, formerly of Toledo, Ohio, had served with the Army's 82nd Airborne Division in Japan. He appeared in the Escambray Hills of central Cuba in 1957 to fight beside Cubans in a second front against the Batista regime. After capturing a large part of Las Villas Province, the ill-equipped guerrilla band joined with Castro's 26th of July Movement. When Castro took power in January 1959, Morgan was given command of the southern port city of Cienfuegos and acquired the title Major.

In August 1959 Morgan received extensive publicity in the American press when Castro credited him with the suppression of a counterrevolutionary plot. Apparently he had duped Generalissimo Rafael Leonidas Trujillo Molina of the Dominican Republic into believing that he, Morgan, was leading a counterrevolutionary band in Las Villas. He asked that Trujillo send a plane with supplies and extra men. When Morgan's guerrillas ambushed the plane, taking as prisoners the ten armed men Trujillo had sent, fighting broke out between Morgan's forces and the true anti-Castro forces in Las Villas. The counterrevolutionary group was crushed, and Morgan became a heroic figure in Castro's Cuba.

3. In May 1975, the former CIA liaison with the Warren Commission, prepared a memorandum for the Commission on CIA Activities Within the United States (headed by Nelson A. Rockefeller) on his assessment of what areas involving possible foreign conspiracies in the assassination of President Kennedy the Warren Commission had failed to explore. He noted that "such evidence could exist in Moscow and/or Havana, whose voluntary inputs to the Warren Commission were minimal in quantity and quality, designed to cover up any admissions of knowledge of, or connection with, Oswald. . . . Therefore, the belief that there was Soviet and/or Cuban (KGB and/or DGI) connection with Oswald will persist and grow until there has been a full disclosure by these governments of all elements of Oswald's handling and stay in the Soviet Union and his contacts in Mexico City. The Warren Commission report should have left a wider 'window' for this contingency."

As an example of a possibly significant but unpursued lead, he cited the testimony of Nelson Delgado: "Actually Delgado's testimony says a lot more of possible *operational* significance than is reflected by the language of the Warren report, and its implications do not appear to have been run down or developed by investigation."

The analysis concluded that "Delgado's testimony has the cast of credibility. Granting that, it is of basic importance to focus attention on the male visitor who contacted Oswald at El Toro Camp. . . . Delgado's presumption is that he was from the Cuban consulate in Los Angeles. Assuming that, the questions are: Who was it, and was there reporting from Los Angeles to Washington and Havana that could, in effect represent the opening of a Cuban file on Oswald?"

4. In 1964 Delgado was sharply and hostilely cross-examined about his knowledge of Spanish, even though it was the language spoken in his home. This led to considerable confusion in his testimony, and today Delgado, a cook with the U.S. Army in Germany, is unable to recall what led him to the conclusion that the stranger who visited Oswald was connected with Cuba.

5. Another Marine, James Botelho, also vaguely remembers Oswald having these spotter photographs. Delgado did not mention these photographs to the Warren Commission, and his memory, eighteen years after the event, is vague. In my first interview with him in Germany, he mentioned the photographs to me, but indicated that he had shipped them to an address in Brooklyn. In subsequent interviews, however, he recalled that he had merely left the photographs in a locker. In any case, there is no record of these photographs or what happened to them.

6. On June 19 Oswald sent in his $25 deposit and a covering letter, stating, "I am very glad to have been accepted for the third term of your college next year. . . . Any new information on the school or even the students who will attend next year would be appreciated." The letter was apparently designed to further the impression that he actually planned to attend the college.

7. It was a fortuitous coincidence for Oswald that his mother had recently written him of an injury she had sustained while working at a candy store at the time that he was trying to secure an early discharge from the Marines. In fact, when Lee wrote her in

June, Marguerite had already spent six months attempting to collect on an insurance claim against the Fort Worth Ridglea Fair store, where she had hurt her nose when a large jar of candy fell off a shelf. Marguerite claimed that she was disabled and could no longer work. The three or four doctors she saw in the weeks after the accident could find nothing wrong with her, as she complained to Robert, but she was apparently still pressing the suit six months later.

8. He had deposited this when on leave in December 1958, after his return from Japan. Assuming that this $203 was the total amount he saved in Japan, his total savings as of September 1959 *could* have amounted to the following:

Oswald made $1,076.92 between December 1958 and September 11, 1959. The sum includes his basic pay (less withholding and Social Security), his mileage on discharge, unused leave settlement as of September 11, 1958, less the difference between an August 1959 allotment to Marguerite and the adjustment for this payment given to Oswald (a net loss of some $40).

In addition, Oswald incurred the following expenses:

$91.56 For transportation from El Toro to Fort Worth
$25.00 Registration fee, Albert Schweitzer College
$10.00 About what Rosaleen Quinn says he spent on their two dates
         Trip to Tijuana with Delgado
         Several trips to Los Angeles
         Trip to San Juan de Batista, to which Oswald contributed for gas
         Subscriptions
         Film and processing
         Beers

Assuming Oswald spent $20 a month on these unknown expenses, he would have saved $950.36 ($1,076.92 minus $126.56, the sum of his major known expenses), minus $200 ($20 per month times 10 months), which is about $750. With the $203 he withdrew from his Fort Worth savings account, Oswald would have had about $950 when he left Fort Worth on September 14, 1959.

9. The CIA checked all available timetables without finding any flight between London and Helsinki that would fit Oswald's schedule. The gap led some investigators to speculate that he might have flown in a private aircraft.

10. Because Sweden and Finland are in the same customs union, Oswald could have entered and left Sweden from Finland without having had his passport stamped.

11. In addition to this $300, Oswald had given his mother $100; paid $15 fare from Fort Worth to New Orleans; an estimated $5 for a night at the Liberty Hotel; $220.75 for a ticket to Le Havre; $20 for the journey from Le Havre to Southhampton; $111.90 plane fare to Helsinki; an estimated $20 for lodging in Helsinki; and $44 for train fare to Moscow. Thus he spent $836. Since he could have saved no more than $950, this would have left him with a little over $100, taking no additional expenses into account. In England he declared to Customs officials that he had $700, suggesting that he had been supplied with additional funds by an unidentified source, or he had lied to the customs officials.

12. The State Department was later concerned that Oswald had received his visa in Helsinki in a shorter period of time than usual, which would indicate that there might have been some preparation for his defection. The Warren Commission's analysts of this problem, William Coleman and W. David Slawson, assumed that Oswald received his visa on October 14 after arriving in Helsinki on the tenth, though he may have applied for it as late as the twelfth, leading to the conclusion that "Oswald probably received his visa four days after he applied for it, but he may have received it only two days later."

They recognized that the speed with which Oswald received his visa could lend credence to the CIA theory they quoted as suggesting that "Soviet authorities had advance warning of Oswald's arrival and had been ready and waiting to handle him rapidly once he arrived." A second scenario they considered was that Soviet authorities were entirely ignorant of Oswald's pending arrival, but when he did arrive and immediately made known his "strong sympathy with the Communist cause, his intention to defect and possibly even the fact that he had been a radar operator in the United States Marine Corps and the 'fact' (doubtful) that he possessed secret information related to this job which he was ready to disclose," the Soviets processed his application as rapidly as they could.

Since there was no way of exploring either of these intriguing scenarios, the Warren Commission concluded, simply, that the time it took Oswald to receive his visa was "shorter than usual but not beyond the range of possible variation. . . . Prompt issuance . . . may have been . . . due in part to the fact that the summer rush had ended . . . that Oswald was unusually urgent in his demands that his visa be issued promptly . . ." (WC Report, page 258).

13. Without access to full Soviet records, it is impossible to determine whether Oswald ever actually applied for Soviet citizenship. In the sheaf of documents sent by the Soviet government to the Warren Commission, there is no application for citizenship, nor is there any indication that Oswald was ever interviewed regarding obtaining Soviet citizenship. However, on December 11, 1963, Soviet Ambassador Anatoly F. Dobrynin informed the U.S. government on the question of Oswald's citizenship: "The competent Soviet authorities that considered Oswald's application did not find convincing grounds which would allow to draw a conclusion that he complied with the requirements provided for Soviet citizens in the Constitution and legislations of the U.S.S.R. The motives which made Oswald file his application were also not clear. The fact that Oswald made critical remarks about the State the citizen of which he was, could not, of course, be decisive in considering his application. In view of the above-mentioned considerations Oswald's application for Soviet citizenship was rejected." The fact that he mentioned the word "application" four times makes it unlikely that he said it erroneously. If Oswald indeed filed an application for citizenship, as this statement indicates, it would also show that the Soviets carefully selected the material for their "Oswald file."

14. Oswald later wrote his own version of this interview with Snyder (reprinted here verbatim):

EMBASSY MEETING
Oct. 31, 1959

12.30 Arrive in "Bolga" type taxi. Two Russian policemen stand at the embassy. One salutes as I approach entrance of the embassy and says "passport." I smile and show my passport. He motions me to pass inside as I wish. There can be little doubt I'm sure in his mind that I'm a American. Light overcoat, no hat or scarf and non-Russian button down shirt & tie. Entering I find the office of "Consular" aide. Opening the door I go in. A secretary busy typing looks up. "Yes"? she says. "I'd like to see the consular" I say. "Will you sign the tourist registar please" she says dryly, going back to her typing. "Yes, but before I'll do that, I'd like to see the consular," laying my passport on her desk, as she looks up puzzled, I'm here to dissolve my American citizenship". She rises, and taking my passport goes into the open inner office, where she lays the passport on a man's desk, saying "There is a Mr. Oswald outside, who says he's here to dissolve his U.S. citizenship. "O.K." the man says, "Thanks." He says this to the girl without looking up from his typing. She, as she comes out, invites me into the inner office to sit down. I do so, selecting an armchair to the front left side of Snyder's desk (it was Snyder whom I talked to, Head Consular). I wait, crossing my legs and laying my gloves in my lap. He finishes typing. Removes the letter from his typewriter and adjusting his glasses looks at me. "What can I do for you," he asks, leafing through my passport. "I'm here to dissolve my U.S. citizenship and would like to sign the legal papers to that effect." Have you applyed for Russian citizenship? Yes. He taking out a piece of paper says "Before we get to that I'd like some personal infor." He asks name, personal information to which I answer, than: "Your reasons for coming." I say I have experienced life in the U.S., American military life, "American Imperialism, I am a Marxist, and I've waited two years for this I don't want to live in the U.S. or be burtained by American citizenship." He says O.K. Thats all. Unless you want to profound your "Marxist beliefs," you can go. I said "I've requested that I be allowed to sign legal papers devasting myself of U.S. citizenship. Do you refuse me that right?" He says Ugh. No, but the papers will take some time to get ready. In the meantime where are you staying. "Room 212 at the Metropole." I state, angry at being refused a right. I started to leave "You'll tell us what the Russ. do next." I turn very mad, "of course," I say and leave.

15. Snyder explained that he wanted to delay action in the Oswald case because he thought the Soviets might expel Oswald shortly. This reasoning was based on the embassy's recent experience with would-be defector Nicholas Petrulli. The embassy's November 2 dispatch to the State Department regarding Oswald's October 31 visit noted that the Soviet government, "after allowing Petrulli to languish 'illegally' [i.e., his visa had run out] in a local hotel for a month, [had concluded] that he was no asset as a Soviet citizen . . . and suddenly invited him to depart, pointing out that he had 'overstayed' his visa."

In fact, Petrulli, who had mailed the embassy a statement of renunciation on September 3, 1959, and had been "invited to depart" on September 22, was only one of several American civilians seeking Soviet residence in 1959. In October 1960 the Office of Security and the Office of Intelligence Resources and Collection, Bureau of Intelligence Research, both of the State Department, undertook to identify Americans who had defected to the Soviet bloc and to Communist China in the past eighteen months. They used the following criteria to define "defectors": "Those persons . . . who have either been capable of providing useful intelligence to the Bloc or those whose desire to resettle in Bloc countries has been significantly exploited for Communist propaganda purposes." (As cited in an October 25, 1960, letter to Richard Bissell from Hugh S. Cumming, Jr.)

With the help of Richard Bissell, the CIA's deputy director of Plans, and of the FBI, they were able to identify fourteen such defectors. Of these, five were servicemen stationed in Germany who had crossed into East Germany; two—Bernon Mitchell and William Martin—were mathematicians from the National Security Agency; and one couple defected to China. In addition, there were four civilian defections to the Soviet Union excluding Oswald. All these civilian cases presented complications for the embassy, since after varying periods of residence in the Soviet Union, they all decided to return to the United States.

At the time Oswald appeared at the American embassy in October, the embassy was uninformed of the whereabouts of another American couple who had arrived in the Soviet Union in July. This couple was next heard from in December, when a propaganda piece attributed to one of them appeared in *Pravda-Ukraini*. The article stated that the husband was living in Odessa and working as a metalworker in a ship-repair yard. The following July the wife, apparently separated from her husband, appeared at the embassy to request that her American passport be renewed. She was told that it would be renewed when she made final her plans to return to the United States. She next appeared at the embassy in March 1962, when she sought passport facilities for herself and her husband, with whom she was reunited. She stated that she would not travel without her husband. Several weeks later he applied for a passport, admitting that he and his wife had been members of the Communist Party of America prior to their trip to the Soviet Union. The State Department considered their case and determined that neither had committed any expatriative act. It made receipt of their passports, however, contingent on each signing sworn statements regarding membership in the Communist Party. In January 1963 the wife signed such an affidavit, but the husband refused to do so at the time. The embassy was authorized to issue her a passport and her husband an Emergency Certificate of Identification for return to the United States. It took the Soviet Union until May 1964—well over a year after the United States has agreed to readmit them—to issue them exit visas. They arrived in the United States in June 1964.

16. This telegram also included a request for information about Robert Edward Webster, a former Navy officer who had renounced his citizenship barely two weeks before

Oswald arrived at the embassy. Webster's case closely parallels Oswald's. A plastics technician of about thirty, Webster had visited Moscow twice during 1959 to represent his employer, the Rand Development Corporation of Cleveland, at the American National Exhibition. According to later statements to the FBI, it was during his third visit, in July, that Webster discussed with Alexander Shiskin, a Russian official at the exhibition, the possibility of remaining in the Soviet Union. Shiskin arranged an interview with a Mr. Popof, who had Webster fill out a questionnaire on his background and his reasons for wishing to remain in the Soviet Union. His initial reason—that he wished to better himself in the plastics industry—was not accepted, and Webster changed it to state that he wanted to remain in the USSR because he objected to the fact that the government controlled all business in the United States. Webster later told the FBI that he had been interviewed four times by Popof and others to determine his certainty that he wanted to defect and to determine his technical qualifications and experience.

Meanwhile, Webster continued to work at the American exhibition, even remaining to help pack up his company's exhibit. He disappeared on September 10, 1959. Upon returning to the United States, Dr. Rand, Webster's employer, reported his disappearance to the State Department, and the U.S. Embassy in Moscow wrote a note to the Soviet Foreign Ministry requesting information on Webster. When he had received no reply regarding his former employee by October 14, Rand returned to Moscow. On October 17 he and Richard L. Snyder of the American Embassy obtained an interview with Webster at the Police Department's section for the registration of foreigners. Webster, who had been brought to Moscow from an undisclosed address in Leningrad, then handed Snyder a signed statement renouncing his United States citizenship and declaring that he chose to remain in the Soviet Union. He told Snyder and Rand that the Soviets, after questioning him thoroughly about his personal history and motives for defecting, had promised him Soviet citizenship. He told Snyder that he would send him his American passport as soon as he returned to Leningrad. (According to the CIA defector list, Webster handed Snyder his passport on October 19, 1959.)

According to official documents, Webster worked as a plastics technician at the Plastics Institute of Leningrad. (Coincidentally, Marina Oswald's address book contained an entry for a Lev Grizentsev, whose address—Apartment 7, Kondratyevskiy Prospect 63, Leningrad—was in the same building where Webster occupied Apartment 18. Marina claimed in her 1963 interviews with the FBI that Grizentsev was someone she had met at a rest home near Leningrad in 1960.)

In a March 3, 1960, letter to his father, Webster stated that he wished to return to the United States. Webster went to the American Embassy in Moscow on May 4, 1960, and applied to the Soviet government for an exit visa on August 5, 1960. On October 24, 1960, he was told that his request had been denied and that he should reapply in one year. He did so and received a Soviet exit visa on March 9, 1962. On May 8 he filled out the final papers at the American Embassy in Moscow, and he left for the United States on May 15, 1962, two weeks ahead of Lee Harvey Oswald.

The close coincidence between the movements of Oswald and Webster, as well as their not dissimilar physical appearance, possibly accounts for a number of mistaken identifications. Fritz Dieter Jaeger of the German Merchant Marine told the FBI in 1963 that he had met Oswald in Leningrad in 1961 and gone to the movies with him. It turned out that he had met Webster. Secondly, a psychologist working on assignment for the CIA might have confused Webster with Oswald. (See Chapter IX, Note 14.) Thirdly, after the assassination a number of people who had come across a Russian-speaking defector had assumed it was Oswald when, in fact, it was Webster.

17. The communications between the agencies indicate a possible effort to conceal the extent of Oswald's activities in the Marine Corps from the Soviets. For example, a November 2, 1959, memorandum from the Office of Naval Intelligence to the FBI omits from its summary of Oswald's Marine record the fact that he had been stationed in Japan, Formosa, the Philippines or any base outside the United States.

18. As a UPI correspondent Mosby had had the opportunity to observe other Western defectors to the USSR. In 1962 she wrote a book entitled *The View from Number 13 People's Street* on her experiences in Moscow. In a short section on American defectors

to the Soviet Union she discusses (without mentioning names) the cases of Webster and one other defector but omits mention of Oswald. At the time her encounter with Oswald did not leave a strong enough impression for her to include it.

In a report of her interview with Oswald prepared for the Warren Commission, she notes that he did not fit into either of the two main categories of defector. He was neither a "high-level official who had played an important role in his country and decided to transfer his knowledge to the Soviet side" nor "of the romantic variety who flees behind the Iron Curtain in the hopes of escaping personal problems." Of the several American defectors to the USSR in 1959, only Oswald claimed to be motivated solely by his ideological beliefs. In fact, perhaps because Oswald knew that other defectors were presumed to be merely escaping unbearable family lives, he insisted to Priscilla Johnson, the American correspondent who interviewed him, "My decision was unemotional and not set off by any fight with my wife, since I have no wife."

19. Oswald, apparently embarrassed by Mosby's attempts to belittle his motives for defecting, later wrote his own version of his interview with Mosby (reprinted here verbatim):

INTERVIEW   Nov. 15, 1959
Nov. 15 with Miss Mosby

Miss Mosby enters. Greets me and sits down. I start by saying. I wish it understood that I wish to see the story before it is sent. "All Right" she says "It's all the same to me what you do in regards to your life, I'm just taking down your words." O.K. I say, First the reasons for my coming. She asks about military service I answer questions about my military service and then she asks why did you apply for Soviet citizenship? What are your reasons for coming here? I have waited for two years in order to dissolve my American citizenship I have seen too much hate and injustice in the U.S. I have served in the occupation forces in Japan and occupation of a country of imperialistic, what the Russians would call "imperialism". I have chosen a Socialist country since their are only two main systems in the world, "Why the USSR," she asks, "why not checkovia, where the housing problem is not so bad". "I have chosen the USSR since it is the leader of the Socialist camp, and the symbolic champion of the cause of communism." What other reasons lead you to change your loyalty. "In the U.S., as all know, their are many shortcomings, racial segregation and the suppression of the under dog, U.S. communist party". How long have you been studying Marxism. "I first started studying "Marxism" when I was 15. "I always had to dig for my books in the back, dusty, shelfes of libarys and old outdated books were the back bone of my reading, books on phlosiphy, political ecomy ect." "In any libary the most obvious places their are the prominint anti-communist books we know so well but as I say I allways had to dig for my book. "What were some impresstions you observed in the occupation forces." I saw the American military hauling cannon up mountain side, the tools of war and oppristion I learned to hate the U.S. imperialistic military". Thank you she says.

20. The official record of this investigation remains missing or at least unavailable. The FBI inquired about it after the assassination but apparently never received it or, in any event, never turned it over to the Warren Commission. In the course of my research, the Marine Corps, which was otherwise extremely cooperative, searched its files but found no trace of the investigation. The Office of Naval Intelligence and the Naval Investigative Services replied to my Freedom of Information request by stating that the report of the investigation was not in their files. The CIA has also denied to me that it conducted such an investigation. Finally, the Air Force Office of Special Investigations, which was responsible for base security at Atsugi, also denied partaking in any such investigation.

21. The practice of doing net damage reports also persisted immediately after Oswald defected: An Army sergeant defected in July 1960, and an Army private defected in August 1960. Army counterintelligence suspected both had had prior contact with the KGB while serving in the Army, and both were under military investigation at the time

of their defection. The two defectors from the National Security Agency in June 1960 were also suspected of having had prior KGB connections. Indeed, in all military cases where defectors had access to classified information—except for the Oswald case—there was some indication of a predefection relation with the KGB, though since Soviet records are never available, such contact is never positively established.

Chapter IV, A Missing Year

SOURCE NOTES

Oswald's diary and the other documents that have been quoted come from the materials found in his possession after his arrest. These are all included in the Warren Commission exhibits. The traces on individuals inside the Soviet Union were done by the CIA and have become available under the Freedom of Information Act.

There are no witnesses to this period of Oswald's life.

FOOTNOTES

1. After the assassination Chief Justice Warren asked the Soviet Union for statements from Soviet citizens who might have met Oswald during his residence in that country, but they were never provided. In 1977 I requested permission from the Soviet Foreign Ministry to interview some alleged witnesses to Oswald's life. After a wait of nearly six months, the request was turned down by Andrei Gromyko on the grounds that none of the witnesses I requested to see desired to be interviewed. The Soviet press attaché to the Washington embassy, Igor Agou, suggested to me at an informal meeting that I might speak to Nosenko, who had defected from the Soviet Union to the United States in 1964. I had already interviewed Nosenko, but I found this an extraordinary suggestion coming from a Soviet official.

2. According to William Coleman and David Slawson's report to the Warren Commission on "Oswald's Foreign Activities . . ." "virtually all such guides are KGB agents and we can assume that in all her actions Shirokova was guided by KGB orders or at least by her training in KGB methods."

3. Another, more sanitized version of the interview, also in Oswald's handwriting, was found in Oswald's belongings: "I made a recording for the Moscow Tourist Radio travel log, in which I spoke about sight-seeing and what I had seen in Moscow tourist circles. I expressed delight in all the interesting places, I mentioned in this respect the University, Museum of Art, Red Square, the Kremlin. I remember I closed this two minute recording by saying I hoped our peoples would live in peace and friendship." To the question "Did you make statements against the U.S. there?" Oswald replied, "No." The CIA, however, has assumed that Setyayev was probably "one more person sent by the KGB to sound [Oswald] out."

4. Oswald's account of his attempted suicide does not accord with Moscow hospital records. His file at the USSR Ministry of Health states that Oswald was admitted to the hospital at 4 P.M. rather than 8 P.M. and that he was brought by ambulance, though there is no record of who summoned the ambulance. Oswald stayed a day on the "admissions ward," where his injury was described as "light, without functional disturbance." He told the examining physician there that he had no intention of returning to the United States. He was moved to the psychiatric ward for observation a day or two later. He told the psychiatrist that he regretted his action and intended to return to the United States after his release from the hospital. On October 23 Oswald was transferred to the somatic department. "The patient is not dangerous for other people," the psychiatric department noted. The stitches were removed on October 27, and he was released on October 28. "The interpreter who was with him every day was informed ahead of time," according to the assessment on official records supplied by the Soviets.

According to Nosenko's recollection, Oswald slashed both wrists and had a male interpreter, which again is inconsistent with hospital records.

The CIA, according to the officer who was liaison with the Warren Commission, subsequently considered the possibility that Oswald's suicide attempt was an entire fabrication. Under this hypothesis, the period from October 16 to October 31 (the first time Oswald appeared at the embassy and the embassy's first awareness that he was even in Moscow) could have been used by the KGB to subject Oswald to the "most intensive kind of political and psychological analysis to determine whether he was 'good agent material.' " Oswald would thus have been conveniently removed from contact with the Western world and subjected to whatever analysis or training the Soviets felt was appropriate.

This theory received some support from the fact that another defector was also hospitalized shortly after his arrival in Moscow. According to his statement to the FBI in 1964, he spent twenty-one days in a Soviet hospital.

To determine whether or not Oswald was ever actually in the hospital, the CIA asked the FBI to search for the elderly American Oswald had identified in his diary as having been in his hospital ward. After an intensive search the FBI located Waldemar Boris Kara-Patnitsky, a seventy-five-year-old Russian-born New York businessman who had been hospitalized for a prostate condition during a business trip to the Soviet Union. Mr. Kara-Patnitsky, however, insisted that he had never seen or met Oswald or any other American when he was in the hospital.

The scar on Oswald's inside left wrist found upon autopsy could confirm the attempted suicide. Marina Oswald testified that she asked Oswald about this scar shortly after they were married, but that he did not answer. He never told any of his friends or relatives about the suicide attempt. Although the doctors who performed the autopsy found such a scar consistent with a suicide attempt, they couldn't exclude the possibility that it had occurred from any number of other injuries. Thus, the presence of the scar does little to confirm or dispute the suicide. In any case, the wound was not very deep.

5. For Oswald's own extensive version of this interview, see Note No. 14, Chapter III, page 625.

6. During the time Oswald lived in the Soviet Union he carried an "identity document for stateless persons," No. 311479, which he first received on January 5, 1960. Each identity card was valid for up to a year, so that in January 1960, 1961 and 1962, Oswald signed a statement acknowledging that the residence and travel regulations for persons without citizenship and the responsibility for violating such regulations had been explained to him.

7. Oswald went on to claim: "As soon as I became completely disgusted with the Soviet Union and started negotiations with the American Embassy in Moscow for my return to the U.S. my 'Red Cross' allotment was cut off. This was not difficult to understand since all correspondence in and out of the Embassy is censored as is common knowledge in the Embassy itself."

Oswald refers to the "Red Cross" in a note to Marina written in the spring of 1963. Before he set out, purportedly to shoot General Edwin A. Walker, he left Marina a list of things to do in the event that he did not return. All his advice was written in Russian with the exception of the words "Red Cross"; "We have friends here [*i.e.*, the United States]. The Red Cross will help you." Marina was unable to tell the Warren Commission whether Oswald might have had the MVD, the "Red Cross" that had helped him in the Soviet Union, in mind.

8. The Ministry of Internal Affairs, or MVD, was for many years the designation of the organization responsible for civil law enforcement and administration of prisons and internal controls in the Soviet Union. During part of its history it also directed vast economic combines and forced labor camps on behalf of the Soviet state. In January 1960 the central or all-union MVD was abolished, and its powers were transferred to the MVDs of the several Soviet republics. A further change took place in the summer of 1962, when the republic MVDs were renamed Ministries for the Preservation of Public Order and Safety.

9. The two Intourist guides were named Rosa and Stellina. Oswald later wrote about

a Rosa at his twenty-first birthday party, and there is a Rosa Kuznetsova listed in his address book. A CIA memo to the Warren Commission notes that Oswald's friend may be identical with Rosa Kuznetsova, the first wife of Augustin Trueba (Calvo).

10. Of the plant itself Oswald wrote:

The Minsk Radio and Television plant is known throughout the Union as a major producer of electronic parts and sets. In this vast enterprise created in the early '50's . . . the party secretary . . . controls the activities of the 1,000 communist party members here and otherwise supervises the activities of the other 5,000 people employed at this major enterprise. . . .

This factory manufactures 87,000 large and powerful radio and 60,000 television sets in various sizes and ranges. . . . It is this plant which manufactured several console model combination radiophonograph television sets which were shown as mass produced items of commerce before several hundreds of thousands of Americans at the Soviet Exposition in New York in 1959. After the Exhibition these sets were duly shipped back to Minsk and are now stored in a special storage room on the first floor of the Administrative building—at this factory, ready for the next International Exhibit.

. . . The plant covers an area of 25 acres in a district one block north of the main thoroughfare and only two miles from the center of the City with all facilities and systems for the mass production of radios and televisions; It employs 5,000 full-time and 300 part-time workers, 58% women and girls.

Oswald went on to describe the various shops within the plant, the "huge stamp and pressing machines" on which 500 people work during the day shift; the shop for "cutting and finishing of rough wood into fine polished cabinets," which also employs 500 workers; the stamp-making plant, in which 150 people work; the electric shop; the plastics department, where "the workers suffer the worst condition of work in the plant, an otherwise model factory. . . . These workers are awarded thirty days vacation a year, the maximum for workers. Automation is now employed at a fairly large number of factories, especially the war industry. However for civilian use, their number is still small.

". . . the Kollective, or intershop group . . . with the shop or section party chiefs and foremen, are the worlds in which the Russian workers live. All activities and conduct of members is dependent upon the will of the Kollective."

11. It seems inconsistent with American travelers' reports of Russian fear of contact with Westerners that Oswald's fellow workers would have received him so enthusiastically. A 1968 defector to the United States I interviewed, who knew several people employed at the Byelorussian radio and TV plant during the time Oswald worked there, says that as far as he knew, the workers went out of their way to avoid being seen with Oswald, sometimes going so far as to lie to him about where they were meeting for an outing so that he could not find them.

12. When he returned from the Soviet Union, Oswald told Dennis Hyman Ofstein, a fellow employee at the Dallas photographic plant Jaggars-Chiles-Stovall, that he had been in Moscow for a May Day parade and that "the Soviets made a big show of power of their latest tanks and planes." If true, this could only have been May 1960. See: Chapter V, p. 406.

In a manuscript written late in 1961, he wrote:

At the Minsk radio factory, holiday demonstrations . . . May Day, and Revolution Day, are arranged in the following manner. Directives are passed down the communist party line until they reach the factory shop and mill "Kollectives." Here they are implemented by the Communist party secretary who issues instructions as to what time the demonstrators are to arrive. At the arrival point, names are taken well in advance of the march so that late comers and absentees may be duly noted, neither one is allowed. At the collection point, signs, drums, and flags are distributed and marchers formed in ranks. In the city of Minsk on such days, all roads are closed by driving trucks across them, except the prescribed route. This, as well as meticulous attention to attendance, insures a 90% turnout of the entire population.

13. Alexander Romanovich Ziger and his family remained close to Oswald throughout his stay in Minsk and continued to correspond until at least September 1962. Ziger was a Polish Jew who had emigrated to Argentina in 1939. He returned to his homeland (by then part of the USSR) in 1956 with his wife and two Argentina-born daughters. He is described by Oswald as a "qualified engineer and department head . . . in his late 40's, mild-mannered and likeable." He reportedly spoke English with an American accent, having worked for an American company in Argentina.

14. In the 1961 manuscript, Oswald describes the party secretary as follows:

The key person in the shop, as everyone appreciates, is Comrade Liebezen, 45 years old, the party-secretary. His background is that after serving his alloted time in the Young Communist League before the war, he became a member in good standing in the Communist Party of the Soviet Union (CPSU). During the war, he was for a short time a tankest [?], but his talents seemed to have been too good for that job so he was made a military policeman after the war, starting at this newly built factory. He was appointed by the factory Communist Party Chief as shop secretary, responsible for shop discipline, party meetings, distribution of propaganda, and any other odd job that might come up, including seeing to it that there are always enough red and white signs and slogans hanging on the walls. Liebezen holds the title (besides Communist) of "shock worker of Communist labor." This movement was started under Stalin a decade ago in order to get the most out of the extreme patriotism driven into Soviet children at an early age. Indeed, Liebezen is a skilled mechanic and metal worker and for his work he receives 130–140 rubles/month minus deductions.

15. The provenance of the thirty-page manuscript on Soviet life that Oswald brought back to the United States with him in June 1962 is not clear. He had parts of it typed later that month. It was most likely written in October 1961, because it focuses on the 22nd Party Congress, which took place from October 17 to October 27 of that year, and provides film and TV schedules for that month in Minsk.

16. The analysis of Oswald's handwriting here and elsewhere was done for me by Thea Stein Lewinson, a psychologist who specializes in using handwriting as a diagnostic tool for determining states of mind. She generally does this diagnosis for other psychologists and psychiatrists who send her samples of their patients' handwriting. I asked her to determine, if possible, whether Oswald had written these documents at separate sittings or in one continuous session, and whether he was ever writing from dictation or copying from other documents.

17. The downing of the U-2 on May Day, 1960, and of the RB-47 in July of that year provided the Soviet press with evidence for its anti-American stands on a number of matters. The repercussions of the incidents were made to extend far beyond the issue of espionage into indictments of capitalism's inherent immorality, cruelty and warmongering.

As the furor over the espionage flights finally died down in early 1961, the Berlin crisis began to occupy the headlines. By the spring of 1961 Berlin had become a "hotbed of war danger." As summer approached, Soviet news was full of reports that "aggressive German militarism" was on the rise in West Germany. The United States' refusal to reach an agreement on the Germany question was described as tantamount to "steps . . . toward a premeditated aggravation of international tension." In August the borders of West Berlin were sealed. The gravity of the situation was manifested in Khrushchev's late August call to "enhance vigilance and combat readiness in every way." To the reader of the Soviet press during this period, war with the Western nations, including the United States, was all but imminent.

Oswald could not have avoided the virulent anti-Americanism in the Soviet press in 1960 and 1961, and he must have been moved by it one way or another. Yet these major world events find no mention in Oswald's diary, either as examples of Soviet propaganda or as indictments of American capitalism.

18. Nosenko asserted that Oswald's hunting club membership was reported in KGB records and commented that some of the reports in Oswald's file were from fellow huntsmen, who observed that Oswald was such a poor shot that they often had to give him some of their game so that he would not return empty-handed.

Oswald's membership in a hunting club might also have been an effective means of covering the fact that he was receiving some kind of instructions or training from Soviet authorities.

Lawyer W. David Slawson of the Warren Commission noted in a memorandum on February 10, 1964, that the Soviet government should be asked about Oswald's hunting activities "to find out whether the gun club and these activities were some sort of cover-up for sabotage or espionage training." The question was never asked in that form.

In 1972 an admitted KGB spy, whom John Barron in his book *KGB* calls Sabotka, told Canadian officials that his training in Russia had been partly done under the cover of a "sporting club" (where he practiced shooting at a target which consisted of a silhouette of the upper half of a man's body).

19. The information concerning Oswald's association with this group comes from a conversation among leaders of the Fair Play for Cuba Committee held on a Cuban plane in 1964 which was electronically intercepted by the CIA.

20. This particular training school, well known to citizens of Minsk because of its one-way windows and the high stone wall surrounding it, was identified to me by a former engineer from Minsk who defected to the United States in 1968. In 1964 the CIA informed the Warren Commission that it had no firm evidence that such a training facility existed in Minsk. The engineer is sure he pointed it out to his CIA debriefing officer in 1968.

21. This was quite a departure for Oswald. On arriving in Japan in 1957, he told fellow Marines that he had never had sex with a woman. Although he subsequently apparently had a girlfriend in Japan, when he returned to California in 1959, he remained celibate so far as is known.

Chapter V, Wreck of "Race Car"

SOURCE NOTES

The section about Francis Gary Powers is based on personal interviews with Powers and on his book, *Operation Overflight*. The importance of the U-2 to intelligence was confirmed to me by Richard Bissell, Richard Helms and Kelly Johnson, the designer of the U-2.

The section about Nosenko comes from interviews with him and from material on his 1964 debriefing which was obtained under the Freedom of Information Act.

The letters from Oswald to his brother Robert are all reproduced in the Warren Commission exhibits.

The assessment of the Soviet press coverage of the U-2 was done through an examination of *Pravda* and its Byelorussian edition during the relevant period.

FOOTNOTES

1. Khrushchev and the Soviet press made a major propaganda point of this poisoned needle. In a May 7 speech—in which it was first revealed that Powers was alive and well and in the Soviets' hands—Khrushchev commented on the needle: "What barbarism!" It was cited as an example of capitalist inhumanity that those in power would expect their hirelings to commit suicide simply to protect their employers. A photograph of the poison pin was included in the May exhibit of U-2 memorabilia in Moscow.

2. Lieutenant Robert Gulyassi, who had commanded Oswald's radar crew at Atsugi,

stated in an interview in 1977 that he remembered Powers from Atsugi in 1958–59 and heard him calling in over the radio.

3. According to Marina, it had to have been 1960, since in 1961 he was supposedly honeymooning with her in Minsk, and in 1962 he was frantically preparing his return to the United States.

Chapter VI, The Double Turncoat

SOURCE NOTES

Much of the material about the FBI's administrative response to Oswald's defection is taken from Alan H. Belmont's testimony before the Warren Commission (see Volume V, page 1) and from a lengthy memorandum prepared by the FBI for the Warren Commission on the subject of its investigation of Oswald (see Exhibit 833, Volume XVII). There were, however, significant gaps in the FBI's account of its handling of the case, including any mention of the fact that Oswald had been asked—and refused—to take a polygraph test upon his return from the Soviet Union. This fact did not become known until the Schweiker Committee published its final report in 1976.

Copies of FBI Agent John W. Fain's report on his interviews with Robert and Marguerite Oswald were obtained from the National Archives.

The bulk of the State Department file on Oswald, including the internal memoranda between Washington and the embassy in Moscow which is quoted in this chapter, was freely available at the National Archives. This material was supplemented by additional State Department documents obtained under the Freedom of Information Act.

The account of Marguerite Oswald's trip to Washington was taken primarily from her testimony before the Warren Commission (see Volume I).

Richard Snyder described for me in a personal interview his reaction to getting a letter from Oswald in February 1961. The text of this letter (and all the other correspondence between Oswald and the embassy in Moscow) can be found among the Warren Commission exhibits. For a more contemporaneous account of Snyder's handling of Oswald's repatriation, I also consulted his Warren Commission testimony (see Volume V, page 260) and his many State Department reports.

The section on Oswald's interaction with Katherine Mallory comes from a personal interview with Miss Mallory.

FOOTNOTES

1. In 1960 not only did Soviet intelligence have 134 electronic eavesdropping devices operating in key sections of the embassy, but the consular section, where Oswald's case was handled, employed a number of Soviet nationals, who it was assumed were reporting back to the Second Chief Directorate of the KGB.

2. See Note 13, Chapter III, page 288.

3. Soviet authorities would frequently intercept letters they suspected might be detrimental or harmful, according to KGB defector Anatoli Golitsin. For example, another letter Oswald claimed to have sent to the U.S. Embassy in December 1960 never arrived, suggesting that Soviet authorities did not want Oswald to begin the process of repatriation at that time.

4. Actually, to this day, Katherine Mallory cannot swear it was Oswald that she met in Minsk. After the assassination it was her mother who suggested that the American Katherine had written home about might be Oswald, but Miss Mallory herself said she couldn't be absolutely positive. When the FBI contacted her in January 1964, they showed her many pictures of Oswald, and finally, because of some resemblance around the mouth to the man she had met and because the investigators pointed out that of all American defectors to the Soviet Union, only Oswald could have been in Minsk in March 1961, she agreed that the man she had met was Oswald.

5. On August 10, 1961, an American tourist, Monica Kramer, accidentally photographed Oswald in Minsk while taking a picture of the Palace of Culture there, thus providing another bit of evidence that Oswald was actually in Minsk during this period.

6. At the time he was first given permission to stay in the Soviet Union, Oswald signed a statement indicating that the travel regulations and the penalties for violating them had been explained to him. It appears that he was correct in assuming that a person in his position would require permission to travel within the Soviet Union. In 1964 the CIA advised the Warren Commission that bearers of a Soviet "passport for foreigners" were required to obtain travel authorization from the Visa and Registration Department (OVIR) (or Passport Registration Department) [PRO] in smaller towns) if they desired to leave the city (or oblast) where they were domiciled. This same requirement was believed to apply to persons, such as Oswald, holding Soviet "stateless passports." In the FBI's interrogation of Nosenko, he was asked whether an individual could travel between cities in the Soviet Union without official permission, and he answered, "Certainly," which was technically correct. The CIA instantly pointed out that Nosenko's answer referred to Soviet citizens—not to a person like Oswald who carried a stateless passport—and was therefore irrelevant to the issue at hand.

Chapter VII, Marina's Story

SOURCE NOTES

The story of Marina's family background and early life was gleaned from her testimony before the Warren Commission (see Volume I) and from the reports of her many interviews with the FBI and Secret Service. Her description of her marriage to Oswald and their life in Russia comes from a short manuscript she prepared in 1964, which was included in the Warren Commission exhibits (see Volume XVIII, page 596).

Oswald's version of his courtship and marriage is taken from his "Historic Diary" (see Volume XVI of the Warren Commission Exhibits).

The section on the CIA's concerns regarding Marina's identity derives from documents obtained under the Freedom of Information Act. They include a set of probing questions which the CIA's Soviet specialists prepared as a guide for the Warren Commission to use in questioning Marina.

The only other source of information about Marina's life is the new biography *Marina and Lee* (New York: Harper & Row, 1977), which was written by Priscilla Johnson McMillan after years of interviews with Marina.

FOOTNOTES

1. Marina's family tree. (See opposite page.)
2. The Soviets have strictly retained the Russian custom of the patronymic whereby every person's middle name consists of a form of the father's first name, which indicates the person's paternity. Since Marina did not offer any explanation to the Warren Commission for the use of the patronymic Nikolaevna and since her surname, Prusakova, is her mother's maiden name, the commission assumed that she was born out of wedlock. Later Marina told her biographer that her father's name was Nicolai Didenko, but offered no explanation of why she withheld this from the Warren Commission.
3. There is some confusion over exactly how many children Marina's mother actually had. There are at least two children which she had by Medvedev: a boy, Peter, and a girl, Tatiana. It is possible that a third child was born of this marriage sometime after 1949. This is implied in a letter to Marina from one of her former girlfriends who had visited the Medvedevs and found Tanya (presumably Tatiana) and Vera (whom she called Marina's favorite) at home. In one interview after the assassination, Marina implied that she had two half sisters, but she later told the Warren Commission that the pension paid upon her mother's death was split three ways: among herself, Peter and Tatiana.

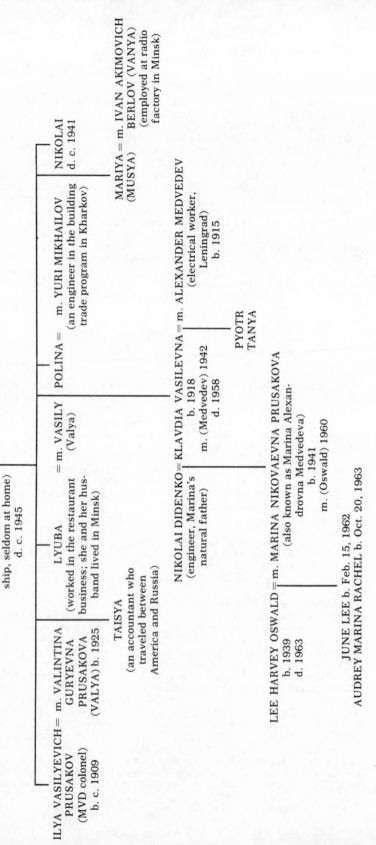

MARINA OSWALD'S FAMILY TREE

VASILY PRUSAKOV = TATYANA YAKOVLEVNA
(Marina's grandfather,
captain of commercial
ship, seldom at home)
d. c. 1945
(Marina's grandmother)
d. c. 1958

ILYA VASILYEVICH = m. VALINTINA
PRUSAKOV   GURYEVNA
(MVD colonel)   PRUSAKOVA
b. c. 1909   (VALYA) b. 1925

LYUBA
(worked in the restaurant
business; she and her husband lived in Minsk)

TAISYA
(an accountant who
traveled between
America and Russia)

POLINA = m. YURI MIKHAILOV
(an engineer in the building
trade program in Kharkov)

NIKOLAI
d. c. 1941

MARIYA = m. IVAN AKIMOVICH
(MUSYA)   BERLOV (VANYA)
          (employed at radio
          factory in Minsk)

= m. VASILY
(Valya)

NIKOLAI DIDENKO = KLAVDIA VASILEVNA = m. ALEXANDER MEDVEDEV
(engineer, Marina's   b. 1918   (electrical worker,
natural father)   m. (Medvedev) 1942   Leningrad)
                       d. 1958   b. 1915

PYOTR
TANYA

LEE HARVEY OSWALD = m. MARINA NIKOVAEVNA PRUSAKOVA
b. 1939   (also known as Marina Alexan-
d. 1963   drovna Medvedeva)
                    b. 1941
                    m. (Oswald) 1960

JUNE LEE b. Feb. 15, 1962
AUDREY MARINA RACHEL b. Oct. 20, 1963

4. The CIA was interested in the seeming ease of Medvedev's move from Zguritsa to Leningrad. In its set of questions for Marina, the comment is made: "If he was transferred to Leningrad as a move within the same organization, he must have had a very good position and reputation. Also, according to the interview record, he was a skilled electrical worker, yet judging by letters (postcards) which Marina received from her family—if her stepfather signed these, he is nearly illiterate."

5. Counterintelligence analysts at the CIA were amazed that Marina had quit her first job after only one day. Her explanation that graduates had a three-day trial period in which to decide whether or not to retain a professional job was not altogether satisfying: "It is one thing—not common, but not unheard of—to fail to appear for work at the place to which a graduate may be assigned; but it is another thing to go to work and then quit after one day. Whether or not there exists a right to a three-day trial period such as Mrs. Oswald has mentioned, it is almost impossible for her to have quit and gone on vacation so easily. . . . She would have been in trouble immediately with the Komsomol and her trade union."

6. Marina provided the FBI and the Warren Commission with few details about her work at the hospital. Apparently because she was afraid of retribution against the people with whom she had worked, she declined to give the names of her supervisor and co-workers. Concerning her salary, Marina has said that her aunt and uncle refused to accept any contribution toward the cost of her living expenses.

7. There is a photograph of Marina taken at the dacha of Mikhail Smolskiy, a prominent engineer, whose father, B. M. Smolskiy, a well-known professor at the Institute of Energetics in Minsk, had acted as the Soviet principal in an exchange of professors and students between the Institute of Energetics and the University of Minnesota.

8. After the assassination Marina wrote: "One of his friends introduced me to Lee, calling him Alik (all his friends and the people with whom he worked called him Alik, in that way rebaptizing him with a Russian name since the name Lee sounds too unusual in Russian)." The CIA found this explanation unconvincing: "Had their acquaintances really experienced some difficulty with the name Lee, the obvious next choice would have been Lev. . . ." It is possible, however, that Oswald shunned the nickname Lev because it is considered primarily a Jewish name. In any case, we know that he himself used the nickname Alik because of all the letters he signed that way.

9. Marina later told the FBI that she had first noticed the building where Oswald's apartment was located on a vacation trip to Minsk more than two years before she met her future husband. At that time she had admired the balconies with their lovely river views, never imagining that she would ever live in one of them.

10. The coincidental similarity between Marina's description of herself—"red brocade dress, hair a la Brigitte Bardot"—and Oswald's description—"red dress, French hairdo"—suggests that one diary was prepared from the other rather than being two independent statements.

11. Marina's other uncle in Kharkov, Yuri Mikhailov, was a high-ranking official in the building trades program and a member of the Communist Party. Marina never mentioned whether her marriage was discussed with him.

12. It has not yet been determined exactly when Marina Oswald first learned of her husband's plan to return to the United States. In her testimony before the Warren Commission she claimed not to have known about Oswald's plan to repatriate until a month after their marriage. She said that this discovery came as a surprise in light of a conversation they had had before the marriage in which Oswald had told her that it was impossible for him ever to return since he had given up his documents at the American Embassy and stated publicly his intention of becoming a Soviet citizen. However, this version is different from that expressed in a letter from Oswald which the embassy received on May 25, advising them: "My wife is Russian, born in Leningrad, she has no parents living and is quite willing to leave the Soviet Union with me and live in the United States."

13. James Allen Mintkenbaugh, who confessed to being a Soviet spy in 1965, states that he was brought to the Soviet Union for training in espionage techniques in September 1959—the month before Oswald arrived in Moscow—and once there was asked to

marry a Soviet agent whom Soviet intelligence wanted to establish in the Washington, D.C., area.

14. When Marguerite Oswald testified before the commission, she wondered aloud why her daughter-in-law had both the names Nikolaevna and Prusakova. Congressman Gerald Ford then confusedly replied, "Isn't one her maiden name and the other by her mother and the other from her stepfather?" Rankin then interjected patronizingly (but incorrectly) that "the explanation was that Prusakova was the identification of the father."

15. The CIA also became concerned with this July birth certificate. In 1964 it suggested Marina be questioned on: "How did she obtain this copy? Did she travel to Arkhangelsk [her home province] and apply in person for it? Did she write for it, was it sent through the mail to her? Did she pick it up at Minsk Militia headquarters? What reason did she give [the] militia for requesting the copy?" Satisfactory answers were never received.

Chapter VIII, The Russian Gambit—Accepted

SOURCE NOTES

The material in this chapter derives largely from personal interviews with American Embassy and State Department personnel, including Richard Snyder, John McVickar, Boris Klosson, Joseph P. Norbury, and Dr. Alex Davison, as well as the testimony some of these witnesses gave to the Warren Commission.

Another important source was the State Department file on Oswald which was obtained from the National Archives. This included information on the procedures involved in Oswald's repatriation, Marina's immigration, and the granting of a State Department loan to assist them with travel expenses. Records turned over to the Warren Commission by the Soviet government (which are reproduced in Volume XVIII) were also consulted.

The information regarding the CIA's mail cover of correspondence between the United States and the Soviet Union is described in the Hearings Before the Senate Select Committee to Study Governmental Operations with Respect to Intelligence Activities, Volume 4, Mail Openings. Letters Oswald wrote to Senator Tower, John Connally, and the Naval Discharge Review Board can be found in Volume XXII of the Warren Commission. Other of Oswald's writings, including the notes he wrote on Holland American line stationery, can be found in Volume XVI of the Warren Commission.

The description of the Oswalds' trip to America is taken from Marina Oswald's testimony and from a short manuscript she wrote in 1964 (see Volume XVIII of the Warren Commission).

The analysis of Oswald's handwriting was done for me by Thea Stein Lewinson.

The reference to Pieter Didenko, the Russian speaking waiter on the S.S. *Maasdam*, is taken from Priscilla Johnson McMillan's *Marina and Lee* (Harper and Row, 1977).

FOOTNOTES

1. The State Department never resolved the issue of whether Oswald could have traveled from Minsk to Moscow without permission. On the one hand, the department reasoned: "We believe that if Oswald went to Moscow without permission, and this was known to the Soviet authorities, he would have been fined or reprimanded." This was based on the case of another American defector who was fined for not getting permission to go from Odessa to Moscow. However, the department went on to say: "We know that at least one 'stateless' person often traveled without permission of the authorities and stated that police stationed at railroad stations usually spotchecked the identification papers of every tenth traveler, but that it was an easy matter to avoid such checks." In a further shift of position, the department concluded: "The Soviet authorities proba-

bly knew about Oswald's trip even if he did not obtain advance permission, since in most instances the Soviet militia guards at the Embassy ask for the documents of unidentified persons entering the Embassy grounds." The Soviets must, in fact, have known of Oswald's trip since all of Marina's co-workers were informed of her visit to the American Embassy before she returned to Minsk, according to her testimony.

2. According to the version that Marina told her biographer, Priscilla Johnson McMillan, Oswald had brought with him to Moscow, a letter from Alexander Ziger to the Embassy of Argentina. Since Soviet citizens are prohibited from contacting foreign embassies, Oswald had agreed to mail this letter from the American Embassy. Marina does not explain why Oswald, who himself was in Moscow illegally, would undertake such a mission.

3. Oswald later referred in his 1961 manuscript to the film festival then going on in Moscow, noting that the anti-Stalinist film *Clear Sky* had won first prize in the competition.

4. The Hotel Berlin is one of the two main hotels used by the KGB (the Metropole being the other) to keep foreigners under surveillance.

5. Oswald's inquiry about Webster was reported in Priscilla Johnson McMillan's biography *Marina and Lee*. Webster himself denied to the State Department that he had ever met or spoken with Oswald. His case, however, had certain parallels to that of Oswald. (For a discussion of the Webster case see Note 16, Chapter III).

6. In 1964 the CIA advised the Warren Commission that as far as it was able to determine, there is technically no Soviet law which would prevent a Soviet citizen married to a foreign national from accompanying his or her spouse from the USSR. "In practice, however, permission for a Soviet wife to accompany her foreign national husband abroad is rarely given. In almost every case available for our review, the foreign national was obliged to depart the USSR alone and either return to escort his wife out, or arrange for her exit while he was still abroad. In some cases, the wife was never granted permission to leave." However, the CIA pointed out later in the same report that the majority of the cases reviewed bore little similarity to the Oswalds, in that none involved a defector who married prior to repatriating.

7. This uncle, Yuri Mikhailov, was married to Polina Vasilyevna Mikhailova, who was Marina's mother's sister. According to Marina, he held a "very responsible and influential position" in the building trades program. One of the perquisites of his job was a large, comfortable three-room apartment, where Marina stayed when she visited. Marina was already four months pregnant when she made the trip to Kharkov and consequently spent most of her time there resting and relaxing.

8. There is some conflict in the exact date of Marina's return. Marina later told the FBI that her Kharkov trip was of three weeks' duration and that she had returned five days after Oswald's birthday, which would be October 23. In a letter to his mother Oswald said Marina was expected back on the twenty-ninth, while in his diary he says she returned on November 2.

9. The handwriting analysis of this letter to Connally indicates that it was spontaneously written. Oswald apparently was under great pressure to do something about his discharge and felt himself in a difficult predicament. Further, stresses in the handwriting suggest that he was venting considerable anger toward Connally.

10. Compared to the letter to Connally on the same subject, this letter is almost tranquil.

11. A handwriting analysis of the document indicates that it was prepared under active tutelage by a second party. In writing it, Oswald seemed to be put under great pressure to succeed—*i.e.*, to reverse his discharge.

12. Oswald accepted this name for his daughter only with reluctance. In a diary entry dated February 28, he wrote: "I go to register (as prescribed by law) the baby. I want her name to be June Marina Oswald but those bureaucrats say her middle name must be the same as my first. A Russian custom supported by law. I refuse to have her name written as 'June Lee.' They promise to call the City Ministry (city hall) and find out in this case since I do have a U.S. passport." February 29: "I am told that nobody knows

what to do exactly but everyone agrees go ahead and do it 'po-Russki.' Name: June Lee."

13. The handwriting analysis leaves little doubt that this "diary" was prepared at one time rather than reflected separate entries on different dates.

14. Erich Titovets was apparently Oswald's earliest and possibly his closest friend in the USSR. They met when Titovets was in his fourth year at the Medical Institute and could speak English very well. He remained in contact with Oswald until at least September 13, 1963, the date of his last known letter.

15. According to the account furnished the CIA by Yuri Nosenko, Prusakov had only advised Oswald and his wife not to speak critically of the United States. If they were given any further briefing in Minsk, Nosenko omitted to mention it.

16. The Oswalds were seen off by Pavel Golovachev and probably by Mr. and Mrs. Ziger and their daughter Anita. Pavel, in a letter to the Oswalds addressed to Davenport Street, Fort Worth, and dated July 4, 1962, states that he is enclosing the photos he took when the Oswalds were leaving Minsk. (See photographic section.) He also refers to Erich Titovets, who regretted missing seeing the Oswalds off. He was not at home the day they left, Pavel writes, and did not know they were leaving. Recall that Oswald had written in his diary in March that he intended to wait until the last minute to tell Titovets that he was leaving the Soviet Union. Apparently he never did get around to telling him.

17. Some ten months later, Dr. Davison was expelled by Soviet authorities from Moscow because he was alleged to have acted as the contact for the CIA with Colonel Oleg Penkovskiy, who was arrested by the Soviets in March 1963 for spying and was subsequently executed.

18. The Oswalds' total savings amounted to $64.29 at this point, or approximately 90 rubles (the equivalent of 900 old rubles), which supposedly included the money they received for their furniture and personal effects in Minsk.

In Moscow, in January 1960, the "Red Cross" gave Oswald 5,000 rubles. Of this 2,200 rubles paid his hotel bill; 150 went for his train ticket to Minsk. Thus, Oswald arrived in Minsk with 2,650 rubles. He worked twenty-eight months and was paid between 700 and 900 rubles a month. At an average of 800 rubles a month, he earned 22,400 rubles at the factory.

In addition, his "Red Cross" subsidy was 700 rubles per month. It was cut off after his communication with the American Embassy in February 1961. He thus received an extra 700 a month for approximately thirteen months, for a total of 9,100.

Marina earned 450 rubles a month. They were married ten months while she was salaried—May 1961 through March 1962—for a total of 4,500.

The Oswalds earned a grand total of 38,650 rubles in Minsk. Their major expenses included the following:

Rent, 60 rubles per month, 29 months	= 1,740 rubles
Two round-trip (July 1961) tickets to Moscow (approximately)	= 1,100 rubles
Hotels in Moscow, July 8–July 14, 1961, May 24–June 3, 1962 (approximately)	= 60 rubles

If Oswald had been as frugal as he supposedly was in the Marines, he might have saved a large part of the remaining 35,750 rubles ($3,575). The fact that he had only 900 rubles left after selling his furniture indicates either that he had found ways of spending his money in the Soviet Union or that he had been saving money in the USSR for his return.

19. Marina said they were first registered at the Hotel Ostankino but later moved to the Hotel Berlin.

20. Oswald never gave his name to the couple but was identified by them in 1964 from photographs.

21. The train from Moscow passed through Minsk at 3 A.M. No one met the Oswalds there. In his letter (cited in Note 16, above) Pavel Golovachev expressed regrets at

missing them—he'd received their card informing him that they would be passing through Minsk too late, because it had been addressed wrong.

Marina's aunt, Mrs. Prusakova, also referred to their trip through Minsk in a letter to Marina. She explained that her husband had been away on a business trip and that she hadn't wanted to go to the station alone at that hour.

22. Other foreign travelers have complained about having had written material confiscated at the border. In this case, the Second Chief Directorate of the KGB presumably knew Oswald would be carrying this manuscript out since he wrote about it to his mother on March 27, 1962. He had "about fifty pages of longhand notes" about his trip to Russia that he would consider turning into a "story" on his return. Even Oswald stated that international mail was read by Soviet authorities.

23. The handwriting of this document suggests that Oswald wrote these answers in an upset frame of mind. He apparently did not like the job and showed impatience and carelessness in writing down the answers. Near the end, according to this analysis, he became particularly rebellious toward the task.

24. Handwriting analysis shows that both documents were written under conditions where wave and motor vibration existed.

25. The Warren Commission was not able to locate any witness, other than Marina, who saw him aboard the SS *Maasdam*.

Chapter IX, The Homecoming

SOURCE NOTES

Information on the Oswalds' arrival in Hoboken and their processing through customs, immigration, and the New York Department of Welfare was drawn from a personal interview with Spas Raikin, and FBI reports on the other people involved. Also consulted were the Department of Welfare file (see Isaacs Exhibit, Volume XX of the Warren Commission), the Traveler's Aid Society file (see Volume XXVI), and Spas Raikin's testimony.

The section on the Oswald's arrival in Ft. Worth and their relations with Oswald's family derives from the testimony of Marguerite, Marina, and Robert Oswald and from Robert Oswald's book *Lee*. Oswald's efforts to have his manuscript typed were described for me by his typist, Miss Pauline Bates. I learned about his contacts with the Russian community in Dallas and Ft. Worth through interviews with Paul Gregory, Elena Hall, Max Clark, Ilya Mamantov, Bishop Dimitri, and Lydia Dymitruk, as well as from the testimony these and other witnesses gave to the Warren Commission.

The portions on the FBI's interest in Oswald come from a memorandum prepared by the FBI for the Warren Commission (see Volume XVII) and from the Schweiker report. I also reviewed the notes of Special Agents John Fain and Tom Carter of the FBI on their interview with Oswald.

The speculation that Oswald may have been given a mission by the Soviets was discussed with me by Thomas Fox of the Defense Intelligence Agency.

The portions on the Oswalds' correspondence with the Soviet Embassy in Washington comes from a document prepared by the CIA entitled "Contacts between the Oswalds and Soviet Citizens June 1962 through November 1963," which was obtained under the Freedom of Information Act.

The information on Oswald's dealings with the Texas Employment Commission is taken from FBI interviews and from the testimony of Mrs. Helen Cunningham (see Volume X).

FOOTNOTES

1. The information about Oswald's being taken to Pennsylvania Station comes from an interview F'N Pierre gave to Jones Harris, a New York-based investigator of the

Kennedy assassination. F'N Pierre told Harris that he left the Oswalds at the railroad station, assuming that they would soon be departing by train. These details were not included in FBI Agent Hopkin's report of this interview. It is possible that Oswald took a train to Washington, D.C., that evening. A psychologist code-named Cato on assignment for the CIA claimed to have interviewed a Russian defector at the Roger Smith Hotel who resembled Oswald. Oswald could then have returned in time to visit the Welfare Department the following morning. This, of course, would be inconsistent with Marina's testimony that she and Oswald spent the evening in New York.

2. Although Oswald himself blamed the hair loss on the severe Russian winters, his brother later speculated that it might have been caused by medical or shock treatments.

3. It is not clear whether the manuscript that Robert read is the one Oswald had typed that week or the one found in 1963 (see Note 4 below). Robert was not questioned extensively about the manuscript he read, nor was his typewriter ever analyzed to see if it corresponded with the typing Oswald had done.

4. There is nowhere any indication that Oswald had an English-language typewriter, or any typewriter for that matter, while in the Soviet Union. All his correspondence from the Soviet Union was written in longhand.

5. A typewriting analysis done for me by Joseph P. McNally indicates that only ten pages of the forty-page manuscript found after Oswald's death were typed by Mrs. Bates' Royal typewriter. The remaining thirty pages were typed on a standard Smith-Corona with a defective "w". This machine was never located or identified by the FBI or Warren Commission.

6. Peter Paul Gregory was born in Chita, Siberia, and came to the United States in 1923 after a two-year residence in Japan. In 1929 Gregory was graduated from the University of California at Berkeley with a degree in petroleum engineering. A resident of Fort Worth for more than twenty years, Gregory was a consulting geologist for several oil companies and was chairman of a group of engineers supervising activities at a Pecos County, Texas, oilfield. For several years he also taught Russian at the Fort Worth Public Library.

7. In mid-July John Tackett, a reporter for the Fort Worth *Press*, heard that Oswald had brought some notes out of Russia with him and attempted to contact him through his brother and Peter Paul Gregory. Oswald did not respond to the offer of an interview. Finally, on June 22, he wrote Oswald a long letter asking him to contact him, but it went unanswered.

8. The fact that Oswald was asked and refused to take a lie-detector test was not acknowledged by the FBI until 1975, when it was published in the report of the Senate Select Committee to Study Governmental Operations with Respect to Intelligence Activities, headed by Senator Richard Schweiker. However, during the Warren Commission investigation, Marguerite Oswald stated in her testimony that Lee told her, "[Fain] wanted me to take a lie-detector test, which I refused." Although the commission promised to "check out" her allegations, it never did.

9. Marguerite Oswald was convinced that Marina could speak and understand a considerable amount of English at the time of her arrival in the United States. Speaking of the summer of 1962, Marguerite later testified to the Warren Commission: "She spoke English . . . she was in the process of learning . . . she understood more than she could speak." Oswald, however, insisted that his wife knew no English and spoke to her only in Russian. When questioned by Peter Gregory on why he was not helping Marina learn English, Oswald said that he had no objection to Marina's learning it, but he would not help her because he was afraid of losing his fluency in Russian. He also mentioned wanting his daughter to learn Russian.

10. There is some dispute about how content the various participants were with this living arrangement. Marguerite has said of the time her son and his wife lived with her, ". . . that was a very happy month . . . Marina was very happy and I was very happy to have the children . . . we had no quarrels." Robert, however, testified that Lee told him that they quarreled constantly "because he felt that Mother was trying to run their lives." Marina agreed with Robert and told the commission, "There were quite a few scenes when he would return from work and he didn't want to talk to her."

11. The assassin of Trotsky, Ramón Mercador, had spent almost five years creating a legend for himself as Jacques Mornard, a Belgian. As part of the long-range plan, he met, seduced and became the companion of Trotsky's secretary in Paris, Sylvia Ageloff, and then insinuated his way into Trotsky's compound for more than a year before he murdered him. "Mornard" remained silent in a Mexican prison for twenty years, never revealing his true nationality or name. After his release in 1960 he disappeared in Prague without a trace. For a detailed examination of the case and a tracing of the assassin through the phases of the legend building, see Isaac Don Levine's *The Mind of an Assassin.*

12. In 1975 the FBI explained to the Schweiker Committee that it had decided against a separate investigation of Marina because they felt that her activities would be adequately surveyed in the ongoing investigation of her husband, even though the Oswald investigation was about to be terminated.

13. Richard Helms testified to the Warren Commission: ". . . there is no material in the Central Intelligence Agency, either in the records or in the mind of any of the individuals, that there was any contact had or even contemplated with [Oswald]."

In 1976 William Colby was interviewed by Dan Rather and Les Midgely of CBS News.

"Did anyone with the CIA debrief Oswald when he returned to the country?" he was asked.

"No, the CIA did not debrief him," Colby replied. He went on to insist: "We had no contact with Oswald before he went to the Soviet Union, and no contact after he returned from the Soviet Union, and no contact with him while he was in the Soviet Union."

14. Thomas Fox, the former chief of counterintelligence for the Defense Intelligence Agency, said in 1977 that he found it inconceivable that the CIA and other friendly intelligence services would not have an operational interest in ascertaining details about the levels of interrogation to which Oswald was subjected. Such information would be necessary if any of these agencies had decided to "plant" a fake defector on the Russians.

One Washington-based psychologist who specialized in indirect examination for the CIA and other governmental agencies recalls that in the summer of 1962 he was asked by a CIA case officer to examine an American who had recently returned from the Soviet Union. He met the American at the roof garden of the Roger Smith Hotel and heard a story of defecting to the Soviet Union several years before, marrying a Russian woman and then deciding to return to the United States. He noted that this defector was extremely self-centered, almost to the point of being a megalomaniac, and was unpleasant in the way he asserted himself.

In November 1963, when he saw Oswald's photos in the newspapers, the psychologist recognized him as the individual whom he had indirectly examined at the behest of the CIA. However, when I discussed this debriefing with him and told him that another American, Robert Edward Webster, had defected and returned at almost the same time as Oswald, he became uncertain whether the person he examined was Oswald or Webster.

The psychologist was then shown photographs of both Webster and Oswald, but since there was a marked similarity in their appearances, he was unable to distinguish between them.

Even if it was Webster who was examined by the CIA upon his return, this raises the question of why Oswald was not examined. If the CIA had enough interest to debrief one American who had redefected, it would seem logical that it would want to examine the second American who redefected less than one month later so that it could corroborate the details of their experiences.

15. Anna Meller was born in Bolgorod, Russia, in 1917. She left the Soviet Union in 1934 with the German Army and traveled to Germany by way of Poland. The Mellers met and married in Germany in 1946. Her husband, Teofil, had been born in Poland and attended two universities, where he qualified as a professor of philosophy and a teacher of physical education.

The Mellers came to the United States in 1952 as refugees and moved to Dallas shortly after. Mrs. Meller worked as a draftsman for Dallas Power and Light. Her husband pursued neither of his two vocations and instead worked for twelve years for a Dallas department store.

16. Until 1963 George Bouhe was personal accountant to Lewis W. MacNaughton of DeGolyer-MacNaughton, a Dallas oil-consulting firm, whom Bouhe described as "a very prominent Dallas geologist." Bouhe was born in 1904 in Saint Petersburg (now Leningrad). In the early 1920s he was an office boy for the American Relief Commission in that city. When the office closed in 1923, Bouhe's supervisors arranged for him to emigrate to the United States. He lived in Dallas from 1939 and had for years been active in aiding immigrants from what he called "the former Russian Empire."

17. Elena A. Hall was born in 1926 in Teheran, Iran, of Russian parents, who had fled there in 1920 to escape the Communists. She came to the United States in 1957 to attend a school of dental technology in New York. There she met her future husband, John Hall, who in 1959 convinced her to marry him and go to Texas rather than Iran. She and Hall were subsequently divorced and then remarried in New York City in November 1962.

Chapter X, The Handler

SOURCE NOTES

Because of De Mohrenschildt's history of relations with intelligence agencies and his close relationship with Oswald, I conducted an extensive investigation into his life. In the course of this research, I interviewed dozens of De Mohrenschildt's friends, business associates, and relatives, including his wife Jeanne, his daughter Alexandra, and his former son-in-law Gary Taylor. I also read the hundreds of pages of material on De Mohrenschildt compiled by the various intelligence agencies and released under the Freedom of Information Act. On two separate occasions, I met with De Mohrenschildt, the first in Dallas in the spring of 1976, and then in Palm Beach in March 1977.

The sections in this chapter on De Mohrenschildt's and Oswald's association with Admiral and Mrs. Bruton derive from extensive interviews with the Brutons, and Philip Weinert, none of whom had been interviewed by the FBI or the Warren Commission.

FOOTNOTES

1. De Mohrenschildt told the FBI in one of his original interviews in Haiti that he had met Oswald through George Bouhe or Max Clark, but both Bouhe and Clark have stated that they were not present at the original meeting between Oswald and De Mohrenschildt. Bouhe did say that he might have been the one to give De Mohrenschildt Oswald's address. In his interview with the author, De Mohrenschildt was vague, again suggesting that he had met the Oswalds in Orlov's company.

2. Colonel David L. Schurger, a Czech-born engineer who had designed part of the glider program in World War II and served in Air Force intelligence, had owned the house in Farmers Branch between 1954 and 1958. He did not build it, however, or add the swimming pool (though he did construct the barbecue). De Mohrenschildt was acquainted with Schurger during this period, and a frequent guest, but he did not, according to Schurger, contribute to the design of the pool or landscaping—as he claimed—though he might have helped with the barbecue.

3. In the proceedings there was some consideration of using De Mohrenschildt as a witness against Maydell, but for undisclosed reasons he was never officially involved in the case. Maydell was released in 1946 and deported.

4. De Mohrenschildt explained to me that he was using Matsukata only as a channel for communicating with his father, who he claimed was then living in Germany.

5. The intelligence war in Mexico during this period is discussed in William Stevenson's A Man Called Intrepid.

6. De Mohrenschildt attributed the expulsion to the fact that he was having an affair with the mistress of the President of Mexico, rather than to any subversive activity on his part.

7. Although the ONI investigation is listed in CIA summary records on De Mohrenschildt, the Navy denies it has any record of this.

8. He married Dorothy Romagne Pierson, an heiress, in Palm Beach in 1944, had a daughter, Alexandra, on Christmas Day of that year and was divorced by his wife in 1945.

9. This version comes mainly from Jim Savage, who met De Mohrenschildt at the Rangely field and remained close friends with him until the day of De Mohrenschildt's death in 1977.

10. The Warren Commission had access to the extensive files both the CIA and FBI had on De Mohrenschildt, including the ones quoted in this chapter. Having chosen to keep these files secret, the Commission concluded disingenuously in its final report: "The Commission's investigation has developed no signs of subversive or disloyal conduct on the part of either of the De Mohrenschildts. Neither the FBI, CIA, or any witnesses contacted by the Commission has provided any information linking the De Mohrenschildts to subversive or extremist organizations."

11. De Mohrenschildt later explained that the encounter with Mikoyan was merely the result of a "joke." He knew the Mexican pilot who was flying Mikoyan through Mexico, and as a lark, he arranged through the pilot for his wife, Jeanne, to speak with Mikoyan. According to De Mohrenschildt, Mikoyan was shocked that a Russian-speaking person had somehow got through his security and quickly drew away from her.

12. The period of time in Guatemala could be dated only from November 1960, when he left Mexico and turned in his six-month tourist card.

13. Bruton has no recollection of discussing Oswald with De Mohrenschildt, though he states that it is certainly possible that he did. De Mohrenschildt claimed to vividly recall once even bringing Oswald over to meet Admiral Bruton and Bruton saying something to the effect of "Get this man away from me." Following the assassination, neither Admiral nor Mrs. Bruton were questioned by the FBI, Secret Service, Warren Commission, or any other investigation agency.

14. At one point, Admiral Bruton was taken aback when De Mohrenschildt showed knowledge of the Navy crosses that Bruton had won as a submarine commander in the Pacific in World War II. Jeanne De Mohrenschildt later told the author that she had come across these crosses while searching through bureau drawers in the Bruton home and later told her husband about them. (She never explained what she had been looking for in the Brutons' drawers.)

15. De Mohrenschildt's assertions about his meeting with J. Walter Moore have not been confirmed, denied or commented on by Moore. When asked about the matter, he replied that CIA policy prohibits agents from commenting to journalists. When the CIA was asked about the allegations of De Mohrenschildt, it replied, coining a new verb, "We're no commenting it."

16. De Mohrenschildt's claim that he would not have continued associating with Oswald, without Moore's assurance that he was "harmless," was made in his last interview with me on March 29, 1977, about three hours before he committed suicide.

17. De Mohrenschildt suspected that there were other break-ins in the years that followed. When he lived in Haiti in 1964, he was certain that his home was searched because of his relations with a Kuwaiti sheikh named Mohammed Fayad. Also, when I asked him about his relations with Lundberg Aerial Explorations, a company involved in aerial surveillance, he insisted that the FBI could have known about that company only by "breaking into his apartment."

Chapter XI, The Underground Man

SOURCE NOTES

The material on Oswald's life in Dallas in the fall of 1962 is based on interviews with many of Oswald's acquaintances there, including Gary and Alexandra Taylor, George and Jeanne De Mohrenschildt, Alex Kleinlerer, Elena Hall, and Max Clark.

The section on Oswald's employment at Jaggars-Chiles-Stovall grew out of interviews with Louise Latham of the Texas Employment Commission and Oswald's fellow employees, including Jack Bowen, Dennis Ofstein, and Leonard Calverley. Additional material was taken from the testimony of John Graef and Robert Stovall (Volume X of the Warren Commission).

FOOTNOTES

1. This letter was to the Central Committee of the Communist Party, USA, dated August 28, 1963. He asked, "Whether in your opinion, I can compete with anti-progressive forces above ground, or whether I should always remain in the background, i.e. underground."

2. The exact chain that led Oswald to his job is not clear. Jeanne De Mohrenschildt insists that her husband helped him get his job, and Alexandra De Mohrenschildt Taylor remembers that her father was involved in arranging Oswald's job in Dallas. Anna Meller, however, who prevailed on her husband to call Mrs. Cunningham, recalls that Oswald asked her for help.

3. The lack of security is corroborated by other former employees, including Dennis Ofstein and Jack Bowen. Robert Stovall, the president of the company, testified before the Warren Commission that the security procedures were enforced, and implied that Oswald would not have had access to the classified materials. However, all the employees who were interviewed insisted that the security procedures were not enforced. Calverley further claims that the employees were instructed after the assassination not to discuss with anyone Oswald's access to classified material, presumably because it could endanger the firm's contracts with the government.

4. "Jack Bowen," as he was known at Jaggars-Chiles-Stovall, was actually an alias. Bowen's real name was John Caesar Grossi, but since he had been convicted of bank robbery and served time in prison, he frequently changed his name.

5. Oswald seemed purposely to use the term "White Russian" ambiguously. Most commonly, it refers to an anti-Communist Russian (as opposed to a "Red" Russian). Also, however, Minsk is in the Republic of Byelorussia, which means literally "White Russia." Marina, strictly speaking, was from Arkhangelsk and Leningrad, neither of which is in Byelorussia.

6. Leonard Calverley, who was questioned by the FBI about the leather pouch and asked never to discuss the interview with anyone, recalls finding, shortly after Oswald had left Jaggars-Chiles-Stovall, some false identification papers that Oswald had apparently reproduced.

7. During the month of October Gary Taylor presumed that Oswald was living at the YMCA since he often dropped him off there. However, Oswald was registered at the YMCA on only four days—October 15–18, leaving his residency during the rest of the month an unsolved mystery.

8. The October 27 meeting between De Mohrenschildt and Oswald took place after De Mohrenschildt had dinner with Dabney Austin and his wife. Mr. and Mrs. Austin met Oswald, then went with him and De Mohrenschildt to see the film that De Mohrenschildt had made of his travels the year before in Mexico and Central America.

Chapter XII, Out of Control

SOURCE NOTES

The Christmas party at Declan Ford's house was described for me by Lev Aronson, Yaeko Okui, and the De Mohrenschildts. Additional details were taken from the testimony of George Bouhe and Katya and Declan Ford.

Oswald's political activities in early 1963, including his correspondence and reading material, is documented in numerous Warren Commission exhibits.

The gatherings at De Mohrenschildt's and Everett Glover's were described for me by those present, including Betty MacDonald, Norman and Elke Fredricksen, Volkmar Schmidt, Richard Pierce, and Ruth Paine.

Information on the backgrounds of Ruth and Michael Paine comes from FBI reports obtained from the National Archives.

The photograph of Oswald with his rifle gained wide publicity in 1963. It was not known at the time, however, that Oswald and Marina had made copies or had written on any of them. This fact was revealed to me by George De Mohrenschildt in 1977. De Mohrenschildt gave me permission to see his copy of the picture with the inscriptions that Oswald and Marina had written on it.

Oswald's attempt to assassinate General Walker is well documented in the Warren Commission's Report.

FOOTNOTES

1. When interviewed in Tokyo in 1976, Okui said that she did not remember the subject of her conversation with Oswald, but that the one brief contact with him had "ruined her life." She would not elaborate further.

2. One of these books, *The Shark and the Sardine,* is a long tendentious and unrelenting attack on U.S. policy toward Cuba, accusing the Kennedy administration of everything from political assassination to economic sabotage.

3. From June 1, 1962, until January 28, 1963, Oswald earned a total net salary of $1,403 and received gifts of $10 from his mother, $5 from George Bouhe and $35 from Paul Gregory (for Russian lessons). Added to the $63 he had brought back with him from Russia, this makes a total of $1,516 for this period. Out of this amount, he paid $377.13 toward rent, utilities and a post office box; $226.21 for his transportation from New York to Fort Worth (and hotel accommodation in New York); $22.47 for magazine subscriptions; $10 for typing; $9.60 for travel between Fort Worth and Dallas; and $9 on the typing course. This makes a total of $654.41 in known expenses, which left him with $861.59. Out of this amount, he repaid the State Department $435, leaving only $476.59 for all other expenses during this eight-month period, or about $53.32 a month for the support of his family (not including rent on his unknown rooms in October and November). Out of $53.32 a month then, Oswald would have had to have bought food, clothing, bus fares, postage, drugs and incidental supplies for a family of three.

4. The opinions that Oswald voiced to Schmidt seemed to echo what he was reading in the *Militant,* to which he subscribed. The January 21 *Militant,* for example, reprinted portions of a speech by Fidel Castro in which he denounced President Kennedy as a "vulgar pirate chieftain" guilty of murder and sabotage. The January 7 *Militant* headline was KENNEDY FLAUNTS ANTI-CUBA CRIME.

5. Kuetemeyer had been experimenting, according to Schmidt, on a group of schizoids during World War II. The experiments had been interrupted in 1944, when Kuetemeyer had become involved in the plot to assassinate Hitler and had been forced into hiding from the Nazis.

6. This party apparently took place in late January or early February. The other guests included Chaim Richmond, a Dallas nuclear physicist, and Samuel Ballen, the man from whom Oswald had earlier sought employment. Glover also suggests, though his

memory is admittedly hazy, that Schmidt was present at that gathering, but Schmidt categorically denies it.

7. The Oswalds' moves are as follows: (1) On October 8, they both moved from Mercedes Street in Fort Worth, Marina to the Taylors and (2) Oswald to an unknown address, (3) Marina then moved to Elena Hall's in Fort Worth, (4) George De Mohrenschildt's in Dallas, (5) Anna Meller's, (6) Declan Ford's, and (7) Anna Ray's—all in October and November 1962. (8) Oswald then moved to the YMCA between October 15 and 19 and (9) to another unknown residence from October 20 to November 4. (10) Both Oswald and Marina moved to Elsbeth Street on November 4, though Marina left again almost immediately, not to return until November 18.

8. Taylor's conversation with Marina in the spring of 1963 raises a question about Marina's proficiency in English. Marguerite Oswald claimed that Marina had some understanding of English at the time she arrived from the Soviet Union, but all of Marina's friends in the Russian community in Dallas insisted that she understood only Russian.

Lydia Dymitruk, a Russian-speaking emigree, once drove the Oswalds to a hospital in November 1962 when their daughter June was ill. According to Dymitruk, Oswald told a nurse (in English) a false story about being unemployed, and Marina instantly called him a liar in Russian, which indicates that she understood at least that one exchange.

In the spring of 1963, after Marina's conversation with Gary Taylor, she and Oswald dined at the home of Oswald's aunt, Lillian Murret. Again, Murret's impression was that Marina was able to understand what her husband was saying, yet Ruth Paine, with whom Marina had lived just prior to this, says that she and Marina could communicate only in Russian.

9. The FBI was later able to determine precisely the date of the photographs taken by Oswald's camera by dating the construction work shown in the background.

10. Before he testified before the Warren Commission in 1964, George De Mohrenschildt told a friend in Houston, Jim Savage, that he had inadvertently given Marina the money Oswald used to buy the rifle. Marina said to him that spring, "Remember the twenty-five dollars you gave me? Well, that fool husband of mine used it to buy a rifle."

11. When Ballen testified before the Warren Commission he was unsure of the exact date of his meeting with Oswald, and said only that it might be late 1962 or early 1963. In an earlier FBI report, however, he had stated that he had seen Oswald only a few days after he had been at De Mohrenschildt's house with Regnar Kearton and his wife Chris, who was De Mohrenschildt's stepdaughter. (According to Ballen, he also saw a young foreigner at De Mohrenschildt's house that day, and assumed he was Oswald. This person was subsequently identified by Kearton as Rudy Bukovsky, a refugee from East Germany.) In 1977, Kearton reviewed his records and found that he could only have been in Dallas during the last two weeks of March or early in April 1963. The meeting between Ballen and Oswald must have occurred during the last week in March (when Oswald found out he was to be dismissed from Jaggars-Chiles-Stovall) or the first two weeks in April. This would explain why he did not tell Ballen about his previous job and lied about where he had acquired the photographic skills he claimed to have.

12. This, at least, was what he told Marina. The *Militant* was not able to find a copy of the photograph in its files after the assassination.

13. Marina never mentioned the existence of this photograph to the FBI, Secret Service, Dallas police, Warren Commission or any other investigative agency. Both Jeanne and George De Mohrenschildt confirm, however, that it was Marina who wrote on it, and a handwriting analysis supports that conclusion.

George De Mohrenschildt brought up the subject of this photograph in an interview with me only a few hours before he committed suicide. At that time he claimed that he had found the photograph after the assassination. However, it seems unlikely that Marina would have sent such an incriminating photograph to De Mohrenschildt *after* her husband had shot at General Walker on April 10, 1963. At that point it was no longer a joke and could not be circulated.

14. Oswald wrote this note on the "Red Cross" on the ship coming back from Russia in June 1962. See Note 7, Chapter IV.

15. When questioned about that statement by the Warren Commission staff in April 1964, De Mohrenschildt said that he recollected saying jokingly, "Did you take the potshot at Walker?" In discussing the matter with me in March 1977, he said that he knew Oswald had taken the shot through some sort of ESP (extrasensory perception) which he had with Oswald.

16. It is not clear, however, how he knew that the rifle had telescopic sights. In his testimony he said he never actually saw the rifle, but his wife had told him about it. His wife, however, testified that she knew little about rifles and could not have discerned telescopic sights.

Another way De Mohrenschildt could have known about the rifle, its sights and the assassination attempt is if the photograph Marina took of Oswald holding the rifle had been given to De Mohrenschildt before the Walker shooting, as the date on the photograph suggests.

Chapter XIII, Oswald's Game

SOURCE NOTES

The section on Oswald's trip to New Orleans and first few weeks there is drawn from the testimony of Oswald's relatives, the personnel from the Louisiana Department of Labor, and his coworkers at the Reily Coffee Company.

The material on Marina's arrival derives from a personal interview with Ruth Paine.

Oswald's personal and political activities during this period were described for me by Adrian Alba, Carlos Bringuier, Orest Pena, William Kirk Stuckey, Edward Butler, John Corporon, Bill Slatter and Lt. Francis Martello. The tape of William Stuckey's interview with Oswald was made available to me by Mr. Stuckey.

For additional information on activities and events relating to Cuba, I relied on FBI reports obtained from the National Archives, and transcripts of speeches made by Fidel Castro and President Kennedy during this period. I also did a survey of the *Militant*'s coverage of Cuban-American relations, since Oswald was known to be an avid reader of that publication.

FOOTNOTES

1. Marina also claimed that Oswald had attempted to assassinate Nixon a week or so after his attempt on Walker but that she had thwarted him by locking him in the bathroom. This story, which she told in 1964, while discussing the sale of her memoirs to *Life* magazine, contradicted earlier statements. The Warren Commission found the story difficult to accept in light of the facts that: (1) the bathroom had no lock on it and (2) Nixon was not in Dallas at the time, nor was it announced that he was coming.

2. From January 28, 1963, when he repaid the State Department loan (see Note 3, Chapter XII), to April 25, 1963, Oswald earned a total of $693.34. He paid out $217.81 for rent, utilities and post office box rental; $10.82 for magazine subscriptions; $42.67 for his rifle and pistol; and $13.85 bus fare for the trip to New Orleans—a total of $285.15 in known expenses. This left him $408.19 from which he had to pay his family's food and living expenses for twelve weeks. On April 2, he gave Marina $60, which she may later have returned to him.

3. Later that summer Oswald told the same story to William Stuckey, a New Orleans radio interviewer. He said then that Marina's father, his "father-in-law," was a "Russian colonel." Marina, it will be recalled, insisted to investigators that she never knew her real father or even his name, and her stepfather was not in the military.

4. Oswald also went to other employment agencies. On his application with the A-1 Employment Agency, he claimed to have left Jaggars-Chiles-Stovall because of a "cut in the night shift" and listed his supervisor as "John Grieves" instead of John Graef. He

also went to the Commercial Employment Agency, where he was interviewed on May 7 by Don Pecot.

5. His readings included *The Huey Long Murder Case* by Herman B. Deutch, *Mao Tsetung: Portrait of a Revolutionary* by Robert Payne, *Soviet Potentials* by George B. Cressey, *Portrait of a President* by William Manchester, *Russia Under Khrushchev* by Alexander Werth and *Profiles in Courage* by John F. Kennedy. He also read books about communism and, at the end of June, turned increasingly toward science fiction, James Bond novels and historical novels.

6. According to Marina, at one point Oswald even contemplated hijacking an airliner with her assistance.

7. Oswald had had previous contacts with the Fair Play for Cuba Committee. In the summer of 1962, while still living in Fort Worth, he had written asking for pamphlets. And in the spring of 1963 he actually staged a one-man demonstration in Dallas, wearing a "Hands Off Castro" placard around his neck.

8. Samuel Newman, the owner of the building at 544 Camp Street, recalls renting the office but then evicting his tenant shortly thereafter when he discovered that he represented a pro-Castro organization.

9. This seemed to be a repeat of his one-man demonstration in Dallas (see above, Note 7). A New Orleans patrolman, Girod Ray, expelled Oswald after he said he had not obtained permission from the Dock Board to "issue these papers."

10. Oswald's note was dated July 1, 1963. Subsequently, on July 8, Marina again wrote the Soviet Embassy, asking them to expedite her requests.

11. Since he had been a defector, the FBI should have had a lookout card in Oswald's State Department files which would have alerted the bureau if he applied for a new passport. For reasons that were never satisfactorily explained, such a lookout card was never placed in Oswald's file.

12. Andrews subsequently testified that Oswald was accompanied to his office on at least two occasions by a well-built Mexican, whom he was unable to identify further. He also claimed that Oswald was referred to him by a young blond homosexual named Clay Bertrand.

Although the FBI was never able to find a trace of this person, Jim Garrison, the New Orleans district attorney, erroneously identified him as Clay Shaw, who was neither young nor blond, and indicted him on conspiracy charges. Shaw was subsequently found not guilty. For a fuller discussion of this bizarre incident, see my book *Counterplot*.

13. The FBI was not able to find any trace of a job application at the Michoud facility under Oswald's name. It is not, however, unlikely that he considered trying to get employment there since two of his fellow employees at the Reily coffee company, Alfred A. Claude and John D. Branyon, both got jobs during this period at Michoud.

14. The Jesuits were very impressed with Oswald's speaking ability, though not with his politics. Father John F. Moore said that he had the impression that "Oswald had at least a college education." Father Malcolm P. Mullen, professor of philosophy, said, "Oswald spoke very well." He too thought he was a college graduate. One seminarian, Robert J. Fitzpatrick, later compiled a five-page summary of Oswald's talk.

15. While there is no evidence that any student or professor ever joined Oswald's chapter, there are a few unmistakable traces of his activity. One graduate student at Tulane, Harold Gordon Alderman, who had been involved in Fair Play activities elsewhere, had one of Oswald's handbills tacked on his door. He denied, however, ever meeting Oswald. Similarly, one of Oswald's handbills was reported by the New Orleans police intelligence unit to have been found in the car of a professor there, Leonard Reissman. Another student, Vereen Alexander, believes she attended a party with Oswald and other pro-Castro students in the summer of 1963. Oswald himself told Carlos Quiroga (see Chapter XIII, page 227) that he was taking a language course at Tulane and told his aunt that he visited a language professor there.

16. Above the list in his address book is the name of a New Orleans reporter, David Crawford, and a city editor, Cowan, which suggests that the list came from one of these newsmen.

17. Only a week before, the camp had been closed down because of FBI pressure, and Bringuier was helping the exiles return to Miami.

18. His suspicions were not without some basis. Earlier that week Fernando Fernandez, who was part of the group under training, came into his shop to make arrangements for his return trip to Miami. He was subsequently identified by the FBI as an Cuban intelligence agent, and Bringuier was informed.

The FBI had also been attempting to find out the movements and plans of anti-Castro organizations that summer and, just the week before, had raided and closed down a major exile arms depot on Lake Pontchartrain.

19. After first looking for the demonstration at another location, Bringuier went to Canal Street, accompanied by two other anti-Castro Cubans, Celso Hernandes, who had originally spotted Oswald protesting, and Miguel Cruz.

20. A number of other Marines in his unit during that period recall both Oswald's pro-Castro sympathies and his unexplained trips to Los Angeles. Nelson Delgado recalls Oswald having pro-Castro material in the barracks. From the mail Oswald received, Delgado assumed that he was in contact with a pro-Castro group; he assumed it was the Cuban Consulate. (See Chapter III, p. 375-76).

21. The pamphlet was by Corliss Lamont and entitled *The Crime Against Cuba*.

22. Oswald also told Quigley similar lies about his personal history, claiming he had married "Marina Prossa" in Fort Worth and omitting any mention of his residence in the Soviet Union or Dallas.

23. One assistant was Charles Hall Steele, Jr., a nineteen-year-old student, who was given $2 for a few minutes' work; he had no knowledge of the political content of the pamphlets. The other assistant, although photographed, has never been identified.

24. According to Marina, Oswald was certain that Quiroga was an "infiltrator" from the start but played along with him.

25. Stuckey had heard about Oswald from Carlos Bringuier the day before. Bringuier had wanted him to "expose Oswald," however, not to give him air time to present his views.

26. The only other bar that Oswald was reported to have been in was the Habana Bar, which is located a few doors away from Bringuier's shop on Decatur Street. Both the bartender, Everisto Rodriguez, and the owner, Orest Pena, claim to have seen him there. Rodriguez described him as having been there with a Mexican, not dissimilar to the unidentified Mexican with whom Dean Andrews saw Oswald in his law office (see Note 12, above).

27. His known expenses for Fair Play activities were $37.73 for printing, $5 for a rubber stamp set, a $10 fine, and $2 for distribution expenses, making a total of $54.73. He also rented an office (and may have given the landlord rent of $30 or $40), hired an unknown assistant and had telephone and transportation expenses.

Oswald's total income for this period (April 26 to September 1) including wages, income tax refund for 1962 and unemployment insurance, was $803.81. His rent and post office box rental was $296.64. Thus, he was left with $452.44 for twenty-one weeks' living expenses for his family, as well as the balance of his political expenses.

28. The FBI still had a pending security case on Oswald. Agent Hosty had visited his Neely Street address in Dallas but found that Oswald had moved and left no forwarding address. The New York office had informed the Dallas office of his correspondence with the FPCC on June 27, and on July 17 the New Orleans office advised Dallas that Oswald was in New Orleans. On August 22 the FBI obtained a transcript of Oswald's interview with WDSU, and on August 23 the New Orleans office was asked to submit to the Dallas office a report on its investigation of Oswald.

Chapter XIV, The Cuban Connection

SOURCE NOTES

The story of the CIA's involvement with Cubella is taken almost entirely from the Schweiker Report. I also interviewed Senator Richard Schweiker in relation to the hearings his committee held.

Sylvia Odio's contact with the three unidentified men was described for me in a lengthy personal interview with Miss Odio. I also consulted her testimony and then reports of interviews she gave the FBI.

Oswald's trip to Mexico and his visits to the Soviet and Cuban embassies were investigated in depth by the CIA, FBI, and local officials, and I consulted all these agencies' extensive files, including some of which were released under the Freedom of Information Act. I also went to Mexico City and interviewed personnel at the hotels where Oswald had stayed.

FOOTNOTES

1. There is some dispute among the CIA officials involved in overseeing this operation about whether it necessarily included "assassination" or simply sought to get rid of Castro in a coup d'état. The CIA case officer who dealt with Cubella is certain, however, that Cubella believed it was an assassination operation.

2. The warning was carried in New Orleans in its entirety; in New York, however, the *Times* deleted the portion of the story in which Castro warned that American leaders would be in "danger"—presumably because it was considered too provocative.

3. The members of the Special Group, in addition to Kennedy and Taylor, were CIA director John McCone; General Lyman Lemnitzer of the Joint Chiefs of Staff; Alexis Johnson of the State Department; McGeorge Bundy, the National Security Adviser to the President; and Undersecretary of Defense Roswell Gilpatric.

4. The memorandum of this meeting was furnished to the Select Committee to Study Government Operations of the United States Senate, which published parts of it in its final report (1976).

5. Sylvia Odio is not sure if this occurred on Wednesday, September 25 or the next day. However, since Oswald was in Mexico the next day—and she is sure that the man she spoke to was he—it must have occurred on the twenty-fifth.

Part of the confusion stems from Miss Odio's perception of what the Warren Commission was attempting to establish. The Warren Commission lawyer who interviewed her, J. Wesley Liebler, according to Miss Odio, took her to dinner with Marina Oswald's lawyer. During the conversation, the question came up of what Warren would do if he found evidence of a conspiracy. "He wouldn't use it," Liebler said. While Liebler may well have been joking or venting his personal annoyance with the Chief Justice, Miss Odio interpreted his chance remark to mean that the Commission did not want evidence that Oswald was involved with others.

6. Her sister, Annie Odio, was staying at her house that evening and witnessed the arrival of the three men. After seeing pictures of Oswald on television two months later, she recognized him as one of the three.

7. Oswald apparently boarded the bus at 2:35 A.M. the night before in Houston. Before boarding, he called Estelle Twiford, whose husband was a member of the Socialist Workers Party (though he denies knowing Oswald). When he was told Twiford was not in Texas, he stated that he was "flying" to Mexico.

8. The two Australian girls were Patricia C. R. Winston and Pamela L. Mumford. Oswald had struck up a conversation by offering to help them with their baggage and ended up discussing his trip to Russia, claiming that he had gone there to study. He recommended the Hotel Cuba to them, saying that he had stayed there himself. Neither the FBI nor the Warren Commission was able to find any record of a prior visit of Oswald to Mexico. In 1976, I interviewed employees of the Hotel Cuba and found a

chambermaid, Maria Segura, who was certain that Oswald had stayed there. She said confirmation of this could be gotten from a former employee, Guadalupe Ramerez. Unfortunately, Ramerez had emigrated from Mexico by that time and I was unable to locate her.

9. Nosenko claims to have been consulted when the telegram arrived in Moscow since the First Chief Directorate had no prior record of Oswald. He advised that Oswald not be given a visa. However, his story contains two discrepancies. First, the First Chief Directorate would have had a record of Oswald's contact with the Soviet Embassy in Washington, and secondly, Nosenko himself insisted that the Oswald file was kept in Minsk without copies in Moscow. Therefore, he would have had to have rendered an opinion without having read the file.

10. One student leader claimed to have seen Oswald at the School of Philosophy at the University of Mexico speaking with pro-Castro students but is unsure of the date.

11. The only car resembling the one described by Guitterrez was a Renault which the FBI traced to the household of Silvia Duran.

12. As of 1968, the CIA stated categorically that "Kostikov was an identified officer of the Thirteenth Department of the KGB." In 1963, when Oswald referred to him, neither the CIA nor the FBI was certain of his activities in the Thirteenth Department.

13. The erroneous substitution of "Henry" for Harvey was apparently a transcription error. See David Phillips' book, *The Night Watch*, for a fuller description of the processing of this report.

14. The Navy, for unexplained reasons, never forwarded the photograph of Oswald to the CIA.

15. The FBI report was forwarded to the Warren Commission in 1964 and released under the Freedom of Information Act in 1976. However, the content of Castro's remarks was deleted. Daniel Schorr, writing in the *New York Review of Books* (October 13, 1977), managed to acquire these deleted portions from his own sources. (Schorr also quotes from an interview which Comer Clark, a British journalist, claims to have had with Castro under impromptu circumstances in Havana in July 1967. In this interview, which seems to have taken place under dubious conditions as far as I can ascertain, Castro was again reported as saying that Oswald had spoken of assassination on his visit to the embassy.)

If Oswald did, in fact, discuss assassinating President Kennedy at the Cuban Embassy, as both Castro and the FBI source suggest, then it tends partially to confirm information provided by Gilberto Alvarado, a Nicaraguan agent who had been infiltrated into the Communist underground.

Alvarado had contacted the CIA in Mexico City on November 26, 1963, and stated that while he had been in the inner chambers of the Cuban Embassy in Mexico City on September 18, 1963, he had seen Oswald receive $6,500 from a dark-skinned Cuban with red hair, after he suggested that he was "man enough" to kill Kennedy.

Although Alvarado was to establish that he had indeed been in the Cuban Embassy during this time period (through his identification of Cuban Embassy personnel), the CIA doubted his story since Oswald was not in Mexico on September 18, 1963, and it seemed highly implausible he would be openly given money. Moreover, Alvarado failed a polygraph examination and then, after being turned over to the Mexican police for interrogation, admitted his story was a fabrication.

Despite this disavowal, the story received some unexpected support from a CIA source who claimed that at a "twist party" at Silvia Duran's home in September she saw Oswald with two Cubans whose description closely matched the descriptions of the Cubans provided by Alvarado.

One possible explanation of this confusion is that Alvarado heard the story from someone else who was in the embassy the day Oswald had his argument with the consul and then embellished it with untrue details, such as the $6, 500.

In any case, his story was disbelieved by both the CIA and the Warren Commission (and undoubtedly was untrue in many important aspects).

16. On November 1, 1963, Oswald wrote Arnold Johnson, the information director of the Communist Party, outlining these activities in Dallas in the preceding week:

"Through a friend, I have been introduced into the American Civil Liberties Union local chapter. . . . The first meeting I attended was on October 25th. . . . On October 23rd, I had attended an ultra-right meeting headed by General Edwin A. Walker." He suggested that the local Communist Party should contact him and asked advice on whether he should attempt to heighten the ACLU's "progressive tendencies."

Chapter XV, Day of the Assassin

SOURCE NOTES

The book that I found most reliable in giving a general view of Oswald and President Kennedy's movements during the day of November 22nd was Jim Bishop's *The Day Kennedy Was Shot*. For details of the funeral, I relied on William Manchester's *The Death of a President*.

The Schweiker committee report was used to determine Desmond Fitzgerald's movements.

I have drawn from personal interviews with Ruth and Michael Paine, Marguerite Oswald, Chief Jesse Curry, Lt. Jack Revill, and Detective V.J. Brian to describe Oswald's interrogation. I also spoke several times with Ilya Mamantov, who translated for Marina on the day of the assassination. Isaac Don Levine's book, *Eyewitness to History*, also provided useful insights.

FOOTNOTES

1. This and all other times given in this chapter are Central Standard Time, except where noted.
2. The receptionists later testified that Oswald's note threatened to bomb FBI headquarters; Hosty, on the other hand, claimed that it threatened only to "take appropriate action."
3. Hosty denies that he ever told Revill that he had information that Oswald had the "capacity" to do the assassination. The credibility of this denial is seriously undercut by the fact that he had received a threatening note from Oswald and had deliberately withheld this information from the Warren Commission even when he testified under oath. In fact, he testified that he had no reason to believe that Oswald had a potential for violence. If the note did contain a threat, as both receptionists assert, then Hosty seriously misinformed the commission.
4. The twelve hours of interrogation of Oswald were not tape-recorded since Captain Fritz had not been given the recording equipment he had previously requested. FBI, Secret Service, postal authorities, homicide detectives and a U.S. marshal witnessed various parts of the interrogation, but stenographic notes were not taken. The questions and answers are thus based on the recollections of Fritz and the other participants.
5. The physical evidence is reviewed in greater detail in Appendix A.
6. Marina's denials about the rifle were on November 28, her denials about the alias on November 29, her concealment of the Walker shooting continued until the first week in December; and her false statements about Oswald's trip to Mexico were not corrected until her testimony before the Warren Commission in February 1964. Oswald himself lied about the same points in the interrogation—denying that he owned a rifle, or used an alias, or went to Mexico, and omitting to mention the Walker shooting.
7. The heavyset man photographed by the CIA camera was not identified by the CIA. According to the available records, no investigation was ever instigated to determine either his identity or his business at the Embassy during this period.
8. The CIA had cameras fixed on both the Soviet and Cuban embassies. Later, in testimony before the Rockefeller Commission in 1975, CIA officials explained that the Cuban camera was broken during part of Oswald's visit (September 27 to October 4, 1963)—accounting for his unobserved entrances and exits—and the Soviet camera was

not used on weekends—accounting for the absence of photographs on September 28. However, the camera was operating on October 1, when Oswald again visited the Soviet Embassy, and on September 27 as well. No explanation was provided for why he wasn't photographed on these dates.

9. The report of Kostikov's intended travels on November 22 was contradicted by information the CIA later received.

10. The remaining seven questions dealt with Oswald's travels and residences in the Soviet Union and with whom he saw at the Cuban Embassy.

11. Mexico was one of the few countries in Latin America to have relations with Cuba, and the government was under pressure by right-wing factions to sever them and by left-wing factions to maintain them. Ambassador Mann himself believed, according to a telex sent by an FBI representative in Mexico to FBI headquarters on November 24, 1963, that: "Soviets much too sophisticated to participate in direction of assassination of President by Oswald but . . . Cubans stupid enough to have participated in such direction even to the extent of hiring subject. If this should be the case, it would appear likely that the contract would have been made with subject in U.S., and the purpose of his trip to Mexico was to set up get away route."

12. Senora Duran was rearrested on November 28, when it was suspected that she might flee to Cuba. According to information which staff lawyers said was available to the Warren Commission, she was subjected to torture by the Mexican police during the second interrogation.

13. Hosty's supervisor confirmed in an affidavit in 1975 that he had found the note and memorandum in Hosty's workbox and had brought them to Shanklin. Shanklin refused to admit that he had any memory of the incident; however, William Sullivan, then assistant director of the FBI, stated that when he discussed the Oswald case with Shanklin, Shanklin admitted that "he had an internal problem involving one of his agents who had received a threatening message from Oswald. . . ."

14. This is a normal CIA procedure designed to protect agents from those who do not have a need to know about operations they are not involved in. Counterintelligence records include only biographical data; divisions maintain the operational data. When a trace is ordered in the records, the case officers in the division are automatically notified of who is requesting the information.

15. In the context of intelligence operations, "provocation" is the term used to describe any act of an adversary designed to provoke a specific reaction.

Epilogue: Inside Out

SOURCE NOTES

The epilogue is based on information provided by sources and documents specified in the notes to the prologue.

Details of Nosenko's detention and final establishment in American society come from conversations with Stanley Pottinger. Supplementary information concerning the final resolution of the case derives from interviews with Gordon Stewart, John Hart, Admiral Rufus Taylor and Victor Marchetti.

I also consulted documents obtained under the Freedom of Information Act concerning the CIA investigation of Oswald in Mexico; the Schweiker Report for material on Hoover; and Seymour Hersh's series of articles on the CIA in the New York *Times* in December 1974.

FOOTNOTES

1. The CIA officer who accused his superior was at that time the case officer of a Soviet double agent, Yuri Loginov. Since Loginov returned to the Soviet Union and was

presumably under KGB control the whole time he pretended to be a CIA double agent, the information he fed his case officer must be regarded as extremely suspect.

2. Most of the "cases" that Nosenko provided involved American tourists, business-men, or correspondents in Moscow, who had been compromised in one way or another by the KGB. None had had access to classified information or were actually recruited as agents. And some of the cases were very questionable. For example, Nosenko named Sam Jaffe, a correspondent for ABC, as one of those approached by the KGB. Jaffe later lost his job and found himself unemployable, but he was not allowed to confront his accuser. Eventually, when he pressed the FBI for the basis of the charges against him, he was referred to the CIA, where William Colby said that there was no evidence against him.

3. For other reasons, senior officials in the FBI believed that there might have been a Soviet penetration in the bureau's counterespionage section during this period. In March 1976, a former senior FBI official told the *New York Times* that "the conclusion that an agent assigned to the bureau's Washington field office had become a paid Soviet spy was virtually inescapable." In the early 1960's, three top secret documents were reported missing from the Washington field office and later turned up in the possession of the Soviets. Subsequently, these documents were traced to an FBI agent who, it was learned, habitually made contact with his Soviet "control" from a certain telephone booth in suburban Maryland. The FBI had the booth put under surveillance and the agent was observed receiving a call, but since the polygraph test to which the agent was subjected proved inconclusive, he was permitted to resign from the bureau without publicity.

4. At one point, counterintelligence had even raised some questions about Colby's own contacts with a French citizen in Saigon who was suspected of being a Soviet agent. All CIA personnel were supposed to report contacts they had with foreign nation-als in Vietnam and Colby failed to report meeting this person. When questioned about it, it appeared to have been merely an oversight on his part.

APPENDIX A

THE CONTACTS OF LEE HARVEY OSWALD (1958–1963)

Oswald's Marine Service—
Japan and the Philippines (1957–1958)

Marines in Oswald's unit:

Donald Athey
Robert Augg
Thomas Bagshaw
A. J. Baldeschwieler
Lonnie C. Bates
Sam Berry
Frederick Burnett
Floyd Raymond Burt
Mark E. Campbell
Raymond Cantu
Robert Raymond Demers
Joseph L. Dilla
Thomas Driscoll
Billy Gabriel
Francis Gajewsky
Robert N. Gulyassi (Gary)
John Rene Heindell
John Kane

Peter Cassisi
Hugh Cherrie
Laurel Clauston
James Colburn
Peter F. Connor
Sherman Cooley
Ronald Crawley
Richard Allen Cyr
Jerome Daniels
Owen Dejanovich
Paul Edward Murphy
Keigo Obata
James Russell Persons
Richard Peschka
Jerry E. Pitts
Daniel P. Powers*
John C. Radtke
Charles R. Rhodes

KEY: The underlined names are people who were interviewed for this project. Those marked with an asterisk* gave testimony before the Warren Commission. Those witnesses who gave signed affidavits or FBI reports but did not testify before the commission have not been marked with an asterisk.

Thomas Kline
Anthony Kukosky
Edward Littler
Joseph Macedo
John Marckx
John P. Meibaum
Charles L. Moon
Lyle E. Moss

Sidney Robinson
Miguel Rodriguez
Ronald Rowe
Zack Stout
Bobby J. Warren
George Wilkins
Norman C. Wiley

Doctors who treated Oswald:

P. Deranian
R. S. Guthrie
H. M. Wertheimer

Oswald's Marine Service—
El Toro, California (1959)

Marines in Oswald's unit:

Robert E. Block
James A. Botelho
Camilous Brown
Richard Dennis Call
Anthony Calore
Donald Peter Camarate
Sherman Cooley
Owen Dejanovich
John Donovan*

Nelson Delgado*
W. B. Funk
David Christie Murray
Paul Edward Murphy
Mack Osborne
Henry Roussel
Buddy Allen Simco
William Steinkoff
Kerry Wendell Thornley*

Marine medical officer:

J. T. Vincent

Oswald's relatives:

Marguerite Oswald* (mother)
Robert Oswald* (brother)
Vada Oswald (sister-in-law)

Civilians:

Rosaleen Quinn (airline stewardess with whom LHO had a date)

Unidentified man (seen with LHO at Santa Ana by Nelson Delgado)

Unidentified Japanese man (seen with LHO at Santa Ana by John Donovan)

Oswald's Defection to Moscow:
September 14, 1959–January 7, 1960

Oswald's relatives:

Marguerite,* Robert* and Vada Oswald (LHO visited them in Forth Worth in September)

Personnel of Travel Consultants, Inc:

Unknown booking agent for the <u>Marion Lykes</u> line (from whom LHO obtained his ticket)

Oswald's fellow passengers:

<u>Billy Joe Lord</u> (LHO's roommate)
<u>Lieutenant Colonel George B. Church, Mrs. George Church</u>

Soviet consular officer, Helsinki:

G. Golub (?)

Intourist guides and translators, Moscow:

Rima Shirokova

Rosa Agafonova

Ludmilla Dimitrova (LHO wrote about these women in his "Historic Diary")

MVD officials:

Unidentified (LHO claimed to have been interviewed by four officials)

Note: Nosenko claimed the KGB handled LHO's interviews

American Embassy personnel, Moscow:

<u>Richard E. Snyder*</u> (stationed in Moscow 1959–61)

John A. McVickar* (stationed in Moscow 1959–61)

Verna Dean Brown (secretary, U.S. Embassy, Moscow)

Journalists:

A. I. Goldberg (U.S. journalist, met LHO in Moscow)

Priscilla Johnson* (U.S. journalist, obtained extensive interview with LHO in Moscow)

R. J. Korengold (U.S. journalist, Moscow, 1959)

Aline Mosby (U.S. journalist, obtained extensive interview with LHO in Moscow)

Lev Setyayev (LHO claimed in his diary to have been interviewed by a person of this name from Radio Moscow)

Oswald's Time in Minsk: January 8, 1960–June 1, 1962

Oswald's friends in Minsk:

Ella German (mentioned in LHO's diary as a girlfriend)

Pavel P. Golovachev (the son of General Golovachev, a co-worker and close friend of LHO)

Yuri Merezhinski (a medical student friend of LHO)

Erich Titovets (medical student and LHO's best friend)

Alfred (LNU) (identified in a letter as a Cuban sent to Minsk to study, an acquaintance of LHO)

Nell Korobko (student in Minsk Foreign Language Institute and a girlfriend of LHO)

Enna Tachina (student in Minsk and girlfriend of LHO)

Rosa Kutnetsova and

Stellina (LNU) (Intourist guides in Minsk who befriended LHO)

Alexander R. Ziger (Polish engineer and close friend of LHO)

Anna Ziger (Alexander's wife)

Anita and Leonora Ziger (Alexander's daughters)

M. Tishkevich (personnel manager in factory where LHO worked)

Minsk officials:

V. I. Sharapov (the mayor of Minsk, who greeted LHO on his arrival in January 1960)

Colonel Nikolai Aksenov (MVD official who assisted LHO in obtaining an exit permit)

Oswald's wife and her family:

Marina Prusakova Oswald* (pharmacist, Minsk; met LHO in March 1961 and married him one month later)

Note: Marina Prusakova Oswald was also known as Marina Alexandrovna Medvedeva

Colonel Ilya Prusakov (MVD offical and Marina's uncle)

Valetina Prusakova (Ilya's wife and Marina's aunt. Both she and her husband befriended LHO)

Americans in Minsk:

Katherine Mallory (tourist in Russia, 1961)

Monica Kramer (tourist in Russia, 1961)

Embassy personnel who handled Oswald's repatriation:

Richard Snyder*

John McVickar*

Joseph Norbury, Jr.

Jack Matlock

Dr. Alexander Davison

Mr. G. J. Van Hattum

Oswald's Return to Fort Worth:
June 2–October 7, 1962

The voyage to America:

Pieter Didenko (?) (a Russian-speaking individual identified by Marina as someone who talked with LHO and her)

Officials in New York:

Spas T. Raikin (caseworker with Travelers Aid; met LHO in Hoboken when his ship arrived)

Frederick Weidersheim (Immigration and Naturalization Service; processed the Oswalds at the dock)

Cleary F'N Pierre (Travelers Aid caseworker)

Janet F. Ruscoll (Department of Welfare, New York)

Mrs. Edna Norman (Travelers Aid supervisor)

Filemon Villereal (Department of Welfare, New York)

Marvin Lehrman (Department of Welfare, New York)

Martin Isaacs (Department of Welfare, New York)

Oswald's relatives:

Robert Oswald* (with whom LHO and Marina stayed when they first arrived in Fort Worth)

Vada Oswald (Robert's wife)

Marguerite Oswald* (LHO and Marina lived with LHO's mother for several weeks in Fort Worth before getting their own apartment)

Employment counselor, Fort Worth:

Annie Laurie Smith (Texas Employment Commission)

Journalist:

Johnny Tackett (Fort Worth reporter who tried unsuccessfully to get an interview with LHO in June 1962)

Typist employed by Oswald:

Pauline Virginia Bates* (typed a manuscript for LHO on his experiences in Russia, June 1962)

Oswald's co-worker:

Tommy Bargas* (LHO's foreman at Leslie Welding Company)

Members of the Fort Worth-Dallas Russian émigré community:

Peter Paul Gregory* (consulting engineer and Russian teacher; certified LHO's Russian-language ability)

Paul Gregory* (Peter's son; took Russian lessons from Marina in summer, 1962)

George Bouhe* (accountant; assisted LHO and Marina in 1962)

Anna Meller* (assisted LHO and Marina from June–December 1962)

Gali Clark (assisted LHO and Marina)

Elena Hall* (dental technician; assisted LHO and Marina in various ways, including arranging free dental care for Marina and putting her up in her home)

George De Mohrenschildt* (friend of LHO; contacted him at unknown point in summer of 1962)

People Oswald met through George De Mohrenschildt:

Admiral C. H. Bruton (De Mohrenschildt claims to have introduced LHO to Bruton, but Bruton does not recall meeting him)

Frances Bruton (wife of Admiral Bruton; met LHO and Marina on October 1, 1962, at her home)

Philip Weinert (met LHO and Marina at the Bruton's home)

Oswald's contact with the FBI:

John W. Fain* and

B. T. Carter (these FBI agents interviewed LHO in Fort Worth in the summer of 1962)

Arnold J. Brown (another FBI agent who interviewed LHO)

Miscellaneous people with whom Oswald came into contact:

Colin Barnhost* (desk clerk, YMCA, Dallas, where LHO stayed)

Chester A. Riggs (LHO's landlord in Fort Worth)

People with whom Oswald corresponded:

Eric Titovets and

A. Ziger and

Pavel Golovachev and

E. I. Sobeleva (all Russian friends of LHO and Marina)

N. Reznichenko, Soviet consul, Washington

Oswald's Five Months in Dallas: October 7, 1962–April 24, 1963

Members of the Dallas-Fort Worth Russian émigré community:

Elena Hall* (LHO and Marina stayed in contact with Elena Hall and her husband, John, after they moved to Dallas)

Alexander Kleinlerer (friend of Elena Hall's; met the Oswalds through her)

Anna Meller*

Teofil Meller

Max E. Clark* (Fort Worth lawyer; met LHO at Elena Hall's home)

Gali Clark (Max's wife; assisted Marina)

George Bouhe*

Declan Ford* (consulting geologist; put Marina up in his home)

Katya Ford* (Declan's wife; assisted Marina)

Lydia Dymitruk* (assisted LHO and Marina in November 1962)

Frank Henry Ray* (put Marina up at his home)

Valentina Ray* (Frank's wife; assisted Marina)

Jancheri Upcheshaw

George De Mohrenschildt*

People Oswald met through George De Mohrenschildt:

Jeanne De Mohrenschildt* (George's wife)

Alexandra Taylor* (George's daughter; spent time with the Oswalds between October 7, 1962 and November 13, 1962)

Gary Taylor* (De Mohrenschildt's son-in-law; knew LHO from October 1962 to January 1963)

Samuel Ballen* (president of oil data company in Dallas)

Chaim Richmond (nuclear physicist; he and his wife met LHO at De Mohrenschildt's home)

Dabney Austin (oil entrepreneur; both he and his wife met LHO)

Everett D. Glover* (chemical engineer, Magnolia Laboratories)

Volkmar Schmidt (geologist, Magnolia Laboratories had long political discussion with LHO)

Thomas Attridge (insurance agent)

Colonel Lawrence Orlov (oil entrepreneur)

Other friends and acquaintances of Oswald:

Yaeko Okui (met LHO at a party at Declan Ford's house in December 1962)

Lev Aronso (met LHO at the Fords' party)

Thomas Ray* and

Natalie Ray* (met LHO at the Fords' party)

Mr. and Mrs. Alan Jackson (met LHO at the Fords' party)

Mr. and Mrs. Charles E. Harris (met LHO at the Fords' party)

Richard Pierce (geologist, Magnolia Laboratories; met LHO through Volkmar Schmidt, February 1963)

Norman Fredricksen (geologist, Magnolia Laboratories; met LHO through Volkmar Schmidt, February 1963)

Elke Fredricksen (with her husband attended discussion group at which LHO spoke)

Betty MacDonald (librarian, Magnolia Laboratories; attended discussion group at which LHO spoke)

Ruth Paine* (met LHO and Marina in February 1963; Marina later came to live at her house, and LHO spent considerable time there, too)

Michael Paine* (Ruth's husband; first met LHO in April 1963)

Oswald's co-workers:

Ray Hawkins (employee, Jaggars-Chiles-Stovall, Dallas)

Wallace A. Pope (employee, JCS)

John Graef* (supervisor, JCS; hired LHO)

Robert L. Stovall* (president, JCS)

Dennis Hyman Ofstein* (employee, JCS)

John Bowen (also known as Caesar Grossi, fellow employee at JCS)

Leonard Calverley (employee, JCS)

People Oswald met while job hunting:

Helen P. Cunningham* (employment counselor, Texas Employment Commission)

R. L. Adams* (placement counselor, Texas Employment Commission)

Louise Lathma (job interviewer for Texas Employment Commission)

L. L. Stewart (manager, radio station in Alice, Texas; claimed LHO came to see him about a job)

H. G. Joiner (Dallas roofing contractor; says LHO applied to him for a job)

Oswald's relatives:

Robert Oswald*

Vada Oswald

John Pic, Jr. (LHO's half brother)

Mrs. John Pic (LHO and Marina went to Robert Oswald's house for Thanksgiving dinner, 1962)

Miscellaneous people with whom Oswald came into contact:

Robert Adrian Taylor (gas station employee, Irving, Texas; claims LHO sold him a gun in March or April 1963)

Gladys Yoakum (typing teacher, Crozier Technical High School; LHO took a course from her)

Mr. and Mrs. M. F. Tobias* (LHO's landlords at Elsbeth Street)

M. W. George (LHO's landlord, Neely Street)

People with whom Oswald corresponded:

Farrell Dobbs* (national secretary, Socialist Workers Party)

Bob Chester (Socialist Workers Party)

Horace Twiford (Socialist Labor Party)

James J. Tormey* (executive secretary, Gus Hall-Benjamin Davis Defense Committee)

Louis Weinstock (general manager, the *Daily Worker*)

V. Gerasimov (officer, Soviet Embassy, Washington)

Joseph Task (Socialist Workers Party)

The New Orleans Interlude: April 25–September 25, 1963

Oswald's relatives:

Lillian Murret* (LHO's aunt, with whom he stayed when he first came to New Orleans)

Charles "Dutz" Murret* (LHO's uncle)

John,* Eugene, Joyce and Marilyn Murret (LHO's cousins)

Hazel Oswald (LHO's aunt, whom he once visited in New Orleans)

People Oswald met while job hunting:

John R. Rachal and

Don Pecot, Commercial Employment Agency, and

John DeRoche, A-1 Employment Agency, and

Teddy Guichard (all employment interviewers)

Philip A. Blappert (manager, Rosen Photography; interviewed LHO for a job)

Ralph C. Hirdes (Cosmo shipping; interviewed LHO for a job)

Oswald's co-workers:

Emmett Barbe (LHO's supervisor, Reily coffee company)

Charles J. LeBlanc (employee, Reily coffee company)

John D. Branyon (employee, Reily coffee company)

A. A. Claude (employee, Reily coffee company)

Arturo Mendez Rodriguez (employee, Reily coffee company)

People Oswald met in connection with Fair Play for Cuba activities:

Samuel Newman (rented office to FPCC)

Personnel of Jones Printing Company (printed forms for LHO)

Brian Ampolsk (student; witnessed LHO demonstrating)

Girod Ray (New Orleans policeman; evicted LHO from picketing on a wharf)

Charles Hall Steele, Jr.* (LHO hired Steele and another, as yet unidentified youth to distribute FPCC leaflets)

Carlos Bringuier* (delegate for anti-Castro group, DRE)

Vance Blalock* and

Philip Geraci III* and

Celso Hernandez and

Miguel Cruz and

A. Guitar and

Carlos Quiroga (all anti-Castro Cubans; supporters of Carlos Bringuier)

Law enforcement officers involved in Oswald's arrest in August 1963:

William Gallot and

Frank Hayward and

Frank Wilson and

Horace A. Austin and

Captain James Arnold and

Warren Roberts (all New Orleans policemen)

Lieutenant Francis Martello* (interrogated LHO during detention on his political views)

John L. Quigley (FBI agent; interviewed LHO during his detention)

Journalists:

William Kirk Stuckey* (radio reporter; interviewed LHO on his FPCC activities)

John Corporon (TV executive)

Bill Slatter (interviewed LHO for radio)

Miscellaneous people Oswald came into contact with:

Adrian Thomas Alba* (owner of Crescent Street garage, next door to Reily coffee company)

Dean Andrews, Jr.* (New Orleans attorney; LHO asked him for legal advice on his Navy discharge)

Emile Bruneau (friend of Murret family; helped LHO obtain bail)

Robert J. Fitzpatrick and

Malcolm Mullen and

John F. Moore and

Paul Piazza (all Jesuits who attended a seminar given by LHO at Spring Hill College, Mobile, Alabama)

Orest Pena* (owner, Habana Bar, New Orleans)

Evaristo Rodriguez* (bartender, Habana Bar; claimed to have seen LHO)

Edward S. Butler (debated LHO on Stuckey's radio program)

Myrtle Evans* (friend of LHO's mother in New Orleans)

Ruth Paine* (friend of Marina's; brought Marina to New Orleans and took her back to Dallas in September)

Ruth Kloepfer (a Quaker woman who contacted the Oswalds at Ruth Paine's request); her two daughters, names unknown, also visited at LHO's house)

Vereen Alexander (claims to have seen LHO at a party for young socialists)

Unidentified man (seen with LHO by Evaristo Rodriguez)

Unidentified Latin (seen with LHO by Dean Andrews)

Jacob Leichner (library assistant, New Orleans Public Library, from which LHO checked out books)

Oswald's neighbors:

Mr. and Mrs. J. J. Garner* (LHO's landlords)

Mr. and Mrs. Alexander Eames (LHO's next-door neighbors)

Mrs. Louise N. Rico

E. Rogers

Gladys Rogers

Catherine Schmidt

Person with whom Oswald corresponded:

V. T. Lee (national director, Fair Play for Cuba Committee)

Oswald's Trip to Mexico:
September 25–October 3, 1963

People who saw Oswald before he reached Mexico:

Mrs. Horace Twiford (wife of a member of the Socialist Labor Party residing in Houston)

Sylvia Odio* (member of JURE, an anti-Castro Cuban group; resided in Dallas)

Annie Odio* (Sylvia's sister)

Leopoldo (?) and

Angelo (?) (Unidentified Latin Americans seen with LHO by the Odio sisters)

Dr. and Mrs. John MacFarland and

Patricia C. R. Winston and

Pamela L. Mumford* and

Albert Osborne (also known as Bowen) and

Hector Francis Cosarrano (all passengers on the same bus bound for Mexico City as LHO)

People who saw Oswald in Mexico City:

Silvia Tirado de Duran (employee, Cuban Consulate, Mexico City)

Eusebio Azque (Cuban consul, Mexico City)

Valery Vladimirovich Kostikov (KGB officer and attaché, Soviet Embassy, Mexico City)

Ivan Obyedkov (guard, Soviet Embassy, Mexico City)

Sebastian Pérez Hernández (desk clerk, Hotel Comercio)

Pedro Rodríguez Ledesma (night clerk, Hotel Comercio)

Dolores R. de Barreiro (proprietress, café adjacent to Hotel Comercio)

Guillermo Garcia Luna (manager, Hotel Comercio)

Maria Segura (chamber maid, Hotel de Cuba)

Ernesto Lima Juárez (guest)

Unidentified Cubans (seen in company of LHO by Juárez)

Contacts on the trip home:

Enlalis Rodríguez (only witness to LHO's return on a bus, October 2, 1963, to Texas)

The Dallas Ending:
October 3–November 24, 1963

Personal friends of Oswald:

Ruth Paine* (host to Marina, September 26 to November 24)

Michael Paine* (husband of Ruth)

People Oswald met job hunting:

Ted Gangl (employment interviewer, Dadgett Printing Company)

Helen Cunningham* (Texas Employment Agency)

Samuel Weiner (employment interviewer, Weiner Lumber Company)

J. E. Hunter (Solid State Electronics; interviewed LHO)

Linnie Mae Randle* (neighbor of Ruth Paine; told Paine to tell LHO of opening at Texas School Book Depository)

Fellow employees at the Texas School Book Depository:

Roy Truly* (Manager)	Junior Jarman*
Victoria Adams*	Billy Nolan Lovelady*
Danny G. Arce*	Joe R. Molina*
Warren Caster*	Harold Norman*
J. E. Dougherty*	William H. Shelley*
Charles Given*	

Miscellaneous people Oswald met before November 22:

Joe McCree (clerk at YMCA)

Mary E. Bledsoe* (LHO's landlady at 603 North Marsalis Street, Dallas)

A. C. Johnson* (LHO's landlady, 1026 North Beckley Street, Dallas)

Earlene Roberts* (housekeeper, 1026 North Beckley Street)

Raymond Frank Kristinik* (met LHO at an ACLU meeting)

Mrs. R. F. Kristinik (met LHO at ACLU meeting)

Byrd Helligas (Unitarian minister, ACLU meeting)

Albert Guy Bogard* (claims to have given LHO a test drive in car at Lincoln Mercury dealer where he works)

Robert McKeown (?) (a gun runner in Houston who claims to have spoken to LHO in November 1963 about high-powered rifles)

Edward A. Brand (insurance agent whom LHO contacted about auto insurance, November 1963)

Garland Slack* and

Malcolm Price* (both claim to have seen LHO target shooting at the Sports Drome Rifle Range)

FBI receptionists (LHO left a note with them for Agent Hosty)

Person Oswald corresponded with:

Arnold Johnson* (director of information, Communist Party USA)

People in contact with Oswald after the assassination:

Officer M. L. Baker* (encounters LHO in book depository immediately after shooting)

William Whaley* (taxi driver)

Cecil McWatters* (bus driver)

Johnny Brewer* (shoe salesman; spotted LHO after assassination)

Officer J. D. Tippit (encounters LHO in Oakcliff)

Officer M. N. McDonald* and

Detective Bob K. Carroll and

Deputy Sheriff E. R. Walthers and

Officer Ray Hawkins (all arresting officers of LHO, Texas Theater, November 22)

David L. Johnston* (judge; arraigns LHO, November 22, 23)

Marguerite Oswald* and

Robert Oswald* (both visit LHO in jail)

People present at Oswald's interrogation:

Captain Will Fritz*

Inspector Thomas J. Kelly* (Secret Service)

James Hosty* (FBI)

James Bookhout* (FBI)

Manning Clements* (FBI)

Forrest Sorrels* (Secret Service)

David Grant (Secret Service)

H. D. Holmes* (postal inspector)

Robert Nash (U.S. marshal)

Fay M. Turner* (Dallas police)

Elmer Boyd* (Dallas police

APPENDIX B

FORTY-FOUR
QUESTIONS
FOR NOSENKO
—FOR THE KGB ARCHIVES

KNOWLEDGEABILITY

1. Did you handle the OSWALD case yourself? If not, to what extent were you involved in it? Did you ever see or talk to OSWALD? During what period were you in close touch with the case? How did you keep up with it after it was no longer in your field of responsibility?

INITIAL KGB INVOLVEMENT

2. When and how did OSWALD first come to KGB attention? Was his visa application in Helsinki processed by the KGB in Helsinki? In Moscow? Describe routine handling procedure of U.S. tourists to the Soviet Union. Was OSWALD's trip handled any differently?

OSWALD's CITIZENSHIP REQUEST

3. When and how did the KGB hear of OSWALD's request for Soviet citizenship? Did OSWALD make a written request? Did you examine this written request? Can you describe its contents in full? (To whom addressed, how dated, text as closely to verbatim as possible—what asked, what offered, what reasons given). How long had OSWALD been in Moscow before he made his request? Was it sent immediately to the KGB? Was it ever sent to the Supreme Soviet?

PRELIMINARY KGB ASSESSMENT

4. What steps did the KGB take to investigate the request? At whose direction? How was OSWALD's bona fides established? How was the sincerity of his request tested? How was his operational potential investigated and evaluated? Did the KGB ever think that OSWALD might be an agent of American

intelligence? If so, how did it go about investigating this possibility? Describe as fully as possible the KGB elements involved, the KGB personnel involved, the progressive steps taken, the time required.

5. When and by whom was it decided that the KGB had no interest in OSWALD? Was this the decision of the Second Chief Directorate alone, or was the First Chief Directorate consulted? Which element of the Second Chief Directorate was responsible for OSWALD after the decision had been made to grant him a residence permit?

CITIZENSHIP DENIED

6. When, how, and by whom was OSWALD apprised of the decision that he must go home and request citizenship from there? At what level of the government or Party was this decision reached? How much influence did the KGB have in this decision?

SUICIDE ATTEMPT

7. Who found OSWALD bleeding to death in his room? Police, hotel employees, Intourist personnel?

8. To what hospital was OSWALD taken? Approximately what was the date of the attempted suicide? How long did he remain in the hospital? Was he visited by KGB personnel while there? What kind of treatment was he given there? Why was the American Embassy not informed?

9. What action did the KGB take on discovering that OSWALD had tried to commit suicide? What recommendations did it make, if any? Did the KGB consider it wise for the Soviet Union to allow OSWALD to stay after this? Why was OSWALD not turned over to the American Embassy? Did OSWALD's attempt tend to confirm the KGB's opinion that asking OSWALD to leave had been a wise move, or did it raise the possibility of reconsideration of his case?

CONTROLS

10. Was OSWALD's room at the Berlin Hotel bugged? At the Metropole Hotel? If so, was it a routine bug, or was it installed especially for OSWALD? What "take" was there, if any? Did you personally review it?

11. Was OSWALD's American passport held at the Metropole Hotel? If so, when and how did he get it back in order to take it to the American Embassy and turn it in?

PSYCHOLOGICAL ASSESSMENT

12. Did the KGB make a psychological assessment of OSWALD—describe the methods used in as much detail as possible? What were the professional qualifications of those making this assessment? Were they professional psychologists, psychiatrists, intelligence officers, or what? Were nonprofessional

observers employed to report on the activities of OSWALD and the results evaluated by psychologists, for example?

13. What was the Soviets' opinion of OSWALD's personality?

EXPLOITATION

14. Was the KGB interested in OSWALD's positive intelligence potential, and was he interrogated or debriefed on his knowledgeability or on substantive military or other matters? Did OSWALD ever offer to give information on the U.S. Marine Corps or other matters to the Soviets? If the KGB did not try to get such information from him, why not?

15. Was any attempt made to exploit OSWALD for propaganda purposes (Radio Moscow broadcasts, or material for them; TV interviews; lectures; public appearances)?

RESIDENCE PERMIT

16. How long was it before OSWALD was given permission to reside in the USSR? When and by whom was he notified that permission had been granted? What did he do while awaiting the decision?

17. What level of the government decided that OSWALD should be sent to Minsk?

KGB CONTROL IN MINSK

18. Did OSWALD receive any money from the Soviet government at any time, other than his salary at the factory where he worked in Minsk? How much? Why? By whose decision? Is this a standard practice? From the budget of what organization would these funds be allotted?

19. Did the KGB actually have no further interest in OSWALD after he moved to Minsk, or did it continue to monitor his activities and to assess his potential from time to time?

20. Describe controls the KGB exercised over OSWALD. Was he physically surveilled? His apartment bugged? His mail monitored, etc? Other? Compare this with controls exercised over other defectors.

INITIAL EFFORTS TO RETURN TO U.S.

21. When and how did the Soviets first learn that OSWALD was interested in returning to the U.S.? Was the KGB aware of OSWALD's letter to the American Embassy in February 1961 in which he indicated this wish?

22. In a letter written in February 1961, OSWALD referred to a previous letter which he claimed he had sent in December 1960. Was such a letter ever observed by the KGB? Would such letters to a foreign embassy, in particular the American Embassy, be withdrawn from mail channels?

Marina PRUSAKOVA

23. How did OSWALD meet Marina PRUSAKOVA? Was the KGB involved in any way?

24. Your statement indicated that the KGB was familiar with Marina's background and character. Was this information available before she met OSWALD? If not, when was she investigated? How extensively? What were the sources of information on Marina, in particular the information that she was "stupid and not educated." She was, after all, a graduate pharmacist.

25. Did the KGB consider recruiting Marina as an informer on OSWALD? As an agent after her arrival in the U.S.? If she was not recruited, what was the basis of this decision? Would you have been aware of a recruitment of Marina?

26. Can you provide any biographic information on Marina and her relatives? As much detail as possible.

27. Can you explain the fact that Marina claims not to know who her father was and bears her mother's surname, thus indicating that she was born out of wedlock, yet she also bears the patronymic "Nikolayevna," indicating that her father was known?

28. To what extent was Marina surveilled, or otherwise observed before and after her marriage to OSWALD?

29. On what grounds did the KGB consider Marina "anti-Soviet" at the time she wished to leave the USSR with OSWALD? She appears to have been promoted in her job after her marriage. Why was this allowed?

30. What was the name of Marina's uncle whom you mentioned? What was his relationship to the KGB? What details can you provide on his background, employment, etc.? When, by whom, and under what circumstances was he briefed on what he should say to OSWALD regarding OSWALD's comments on the USSR after his return to the U.S.? What was the substance of the briefing given to the uncle?

31. How did it happen that there were so few difficulties in the way of Marina's marriage to a foreigner and departure from the country with him? Have not similar situations in the past usually resulted in prolonged and often unsuccessful negotiations with the Soviet government? What level of the government or Party would make the final decision regarding Marina's marriage to OSWALD and their departure from the country? What official briefings would Marina have received prior to her departure? OSWALD?

32. If the Soviets were glad to be rid of OSWALD and Marina, why did it take so long for action on their exit visas (July–December 1961)?

KGB PRESENCE AND ACTIVITIES

33. Was there any direct contact between OSWALD and KGB officials at any time while OSWALD was in the Soviet Union? Give specifics where possible, including names, reasons. Was OSWALD witting that any individuals he talked to were KGB representatives? Would any KGB officials have identified themselves to OSWALD as representatives of some other organ, such as TASS, MVD, etc.? Can you supply the names of any KGB officials who worked on any aspect of the OSWALD case?

34. Did the KGB consider that OSWALD had retained his American citizenship while he was in the USSR? During the period in which the KGB was assessing OSWALD would the KGB have considered it important that he retain U.S. citizenship until such time as the KGB had decided whether to use him? Would the KGB have taken any steps to ensure this, such as intercepting and confiscating OSWALD's mail from the Embassy? Did the KGB intercept the U.S. Embassy letter of 6 November 1959 to OSWALD inviting him in to formalize the renunciation of his U.S. citizenship?

OSWALD'S CONTACTS

35. Can you give any information on OSWALD's personal contacts in the Soviet Union? Were any of these people "planted" on OSWALD, i.e., were they KGB employees, informants or agents?

36. Were all of the Intourist personnel with whom OSWALD came in contact KGB agents (or employees)?

KGB PROCEDURE

37. In what ways, if any, was the OSWALD case handled differently from other American defector cases?

38. Was the First Chief Directorate given any information regarding OSWALD? If so, through what channel and at what stage? Was any interest shown in OSWALD or Marina by the First Chief Directorate? Would such interest have been known to the Second Chief Directorate?

OSWALD IN THE U.S.

39. Were you aware of any efforts by OSWALD or his wife to return to the USSR in 1962 or 1963?

40. If so, what did the KGB do with regard to these requests?

41. Do you have any information on OSWALD's trip to Mexico in September 1963? Whom he saw and what he said at the Soviet Embassy?

42. Did the KGB have any information on OSWALD's contacts with Cubans in the Soviet Union? Any information regarding his contacts with Cubans or the Cuban government after his return to the U.S.?

43. What was the reaction in the KGB when it was learned that OSWALD had killed President Kennedy? Did the KGB undertake any further investigation of OSWALD's activities in the Soviet Union after the assassination? Was there a review of his file, was there an additional field investigation? Was any additional information developed?

44. The Soviet Embassy in Washington turned over to the U.S. government certain documents which it said were its consular file on OSWALD. What other files did the Soviet government have on OSWALD—especially KGB files? Describe them. What was the KGB's role in this release of files?

APPENDIX C

NINETEEN QUESTIONS FOR U.S. INTELLIGENCE AGENCIES ARCHIVES (WHEN, AND IF, CLASSIFIED FILES ARE RELEASED)

Questions for the CIA, Director of Central Intelligence

1. Did the CIA maintain any electronic surveillance device, other than on the telephone, in the Cuban embassy? If so, did it produce any conversations between Oswald and the embassy staff?

2. In a report subsequent to the assassination the CIA identifies Kostikov as a KGB officer of the Thirteenth Department, which is the division responsible for assassinations, sabotage and kidnapping, according to another CIA report. When did the CIA learn of information associating Kostikov with the Thirteenth Department? Was it before or after his contacts with Oswald?

3. On October 1, 1963, Oswald apparently managed to enter and leave the Soviet Embassy in Mexico City without his movements being recorded by a CIA surveillance camera. Does this indicate that he used a private entrance or other clandestine route to avoid surveillance?

4. When Yuri Ivanovich Nosenko contacted the CIA in Geneva in the spring of 1962, he claimed to have been the deputy head of the Tourist Department of the Second Chief Directorate of the KGB. To evaluate his bona fides, were any Americans processed by the Tourist Department during Nosenko's putative tenure there questioned? If so, was there any consideration of questioning Oswald in this context?

5. In 1964 the CIA informed the Warren Commission that it had no information to indicate that the KGB had a training facility in Minsk from 1960 to 1962, when Oswald was a resident there. Since 1964 has the CIA received any information from defectors, immigrants or Soviet citizens to indicate that there was, in fact, a training center in Minsk during this period? If so, how does the CIA evaluate this information? Does it still maintain there was no training facility in Minsk?

6. Was the CIA informed that Marina Oswald had been known in official records as Marina Alexandrovna Medvedeva? If so, when?

7. Did the CIA mail cover between 1959 and 1963 intercept any letters written by Lee Harvey Oswald? If so, which letters? Specifically, was the 1959 letter in which he threatened he would "kill *any* American" intercepted? How was it interpreted?

8. Did the CIA cause any psychological assessments to be done of defectors between 1959 and 1963? If so, which element of the CIA supervised the assessments? Was Oswald used as a component in any such assessment? If so, was he given any pseudonym?

9. Oswald took part in a discussion group in 1963 with Norman Frederickson, Everett Glover, Richard Pierce and Volkmar Schmidt which was the subject of a report to the CIA after the assassination. Were any of the above-named individuals ever employees or informants of the CIA?

Questions for the FBI

10. Did the FBI know by mail intercept or other means about Oswald's contacts with Vitaliy A. Gerasimov in the Soviet Embassy in Washington, D.C., and Valery Vladimirovich Kostikov in the Soviet Embassy before the assassination of President Kennedy?

11. Did it know through either surveillance or other means that Kostikov was in contact with illegal agents operating in the United States? Did it have information that he was a KGB officer? Did it know that he was suspected of being in the Thirteenth Department of the KGB? If so, what precautions did it take after the CIA reported Oswald had met with Kostikov on November 9, 1963?

12. Did the FBI know through surveillance or other means that Gerasimov was a Soviet intelligence agent? Did it have information or reports that he was handling illegal agents within the United States? Did it have information that he served as a "paymaster" for an espionage network? If so, did these reports have any bearing on the security case against Oswald?

13. In CIA document 487-195a, which was released in a Freedom of Information action in 1976, it was stated by J. Lee Rankin, general counsel to the Warren Commission, that FBI Agent James Hosty had suggested "Oswald had

contacted two known subversive agents about 15 days before the assassination." Was the Dallas office aware of any contacts Oswald had with subversive agents? Was Agent Hosty referring to Oswald's trip to Mexico? Or was he referring to contacts with personnel in the Cuban and Soviet embassies?

14. Was Oswald's letter dated "November 9" (1963) to the Soviet Embassy intercepted by the FBI? If so, was any attempt made to identify the Soviet he referred to as "Kostin"? Was his statement that he had "business" with the Soviet Embassy in Havana interpreted to mean that he was engaged in some sort of clandestine activity? Was his statement that he was traveling under a false name interpreted to mean he was engaged in clandestine activities? If so, what measures were taken to investigate these activities?

15. After the assassination, was the Soviet Embassy informed through either official or unofficial channels that the FBI had intercepted this letter?

16. In the FBI interrogation of Oswald in 1962 after his return from Russia did the FBI receive suggestions of what questions to ask from the CIA? Department of State? Office of Navy Intelligence? If so, what were the interests of these agencies?

17. Did the FBI attempt to acquire information about Oswald's activities in the Soviet Union through any means other than the two informal interrogations in June and August 1962? Were any informants requested to provide data on Oswald? If so, who?

18. James Allen Mintkenbaugh, who admitted spying for the Soviet Union, stated that he was brought to the Soviet Union for the purposes of training in espionage techniques in September 1959 and, once there, was asked to marry an agent whom the Soviets wished to establish as his wife in the Washington, D.C., area. Since Mintkenbaugh was in Moscow at the same time that Oswald arrived, was Mintkenbaugh asked about Oswald? Was he shown any photographs of the women Oswald knew to see if he could identify them as contacts he had known during his period in the Soviet Union? If so, did he identify any individuals?

19. Did the FBI conduct any investigation into the attempted assassination of General Edwin A. Walker on April 10, 1963? Was this done prior to the assassination of Kennedy? If so, what were the results of this investigation? Specifically, did it suggest it was the work of a single sniper or more than one person?

Index

About the Author

Edward Jay Epstein graduated Cornell University in 1965 and
received his Ph.D. in government from Harvard University in
1973. He has taught at Harvard, M.I.T. and U.C.L.A. and served
as a fellow of the Drug Abuse Council. He resides in New York
City.

DATE DUE	
OCT 2 0 1993	
OCT 2 5 1993	
DEC 1 4 1993	
FEB 2 3 1995	
APR 1 5 1995	
OCT 1 8 1995	
MAY 0 3 1997	
DEC 0 3 1998	
NOV 1 6 1999	
MAY 0 4 2000	
NOV 1 4 2000	
MAR 1 1 2002	
DEC 0 8 2003	
APR 0 7 2009	
APR 3 0 2013	

GAYLORD

PRINTED IN U.S.A.